Environmental Law in Serbia

Environmental Law in Serbia

Second Edition

Vid Vukasović†
Dragoljub Todić

This book was originally published as a monograph in the International Encyclopaedia of Laws/Environmental Law.

Founding Editor: Roger Blanpain
General Editor: Frank Hendrickx
Volume Editor: Kurt Deketelaere

Wolters Kluwer

Published by:
Kluwer Law International B.V.
PO Box 316
2400 AH Alphen aan den Rijn
The Netherlands
Website: lrus.wolterskluwer.com

Sold and distributed in North, Central and South America by:
Wolters Kluwer Legal & Regulatory U.S.
7201 McKinney Circle
Frederick, MD 21704
United States of America
Email: customer.service@wolterskluwer.com

Sold and distributed in all other countries by:
Air Business Subscriptions
Rockwood House
Haywards Heath
West Sussex
RH16 3DH
United Kingdom
Email: international-customerservice@wolterskluwer.com

Printed on acid-free paper

ISBN 978-90-411-9471-8

e-Book: ISBN 978-90-411-9493-0
web-PDF: ISBN 978-90-411-9514-2

Printed in the United Kingdom.

The Authors

Dr Vid Vukasović completed studies at the Faculty of Law of the Belgrade University; he received his Masters and his Doctorate at the same University. He received his Diploma in Air and Space Law from McGill University (1968, Montreal, Canada). From 1968 to 2006, he was Research Fellow at the Institute of International Politics and Economics (Senior Research Staff from 1974), Belgrade. He was the Head of the International Law Department (1984–1987) and Chairman of the Scientific Council of the Institute (1984–1995 and 2000–2005).

He is member of International Council of Environmental Law (ICEL), the International Law Association (ILA), the Serbian International Law Association and the Serbian Association of Lawyers. He is also member of other Yugoslav and international organizations and other bodies dealing with international law, environmental protection and air and space law.

He has participated in a number of important international conferences and projects, for example, in the work of the Intergovernmental Working Group of experts on natural resources shared by two or more States which drafted the principles concerning the shared natural resources (Geneva 1976, Nairobi 1977); the Ad Hoc Meeting of Senior Government Officials Expert in Environmental Law (Geneva 1981 and Montevideo 1981) on which the System Wide Medium Term Environment Programme (SWMTEP) was drafted; the Mediterranean Action Plan (MAP) project 'Blue Book'; Project concerning the interrelation between human rights and the development of science and technology commissioned by the United Nations University (Tokyo) in 1988–1990; various UNEP's working groups, sessions of the UNEP's Governing Council, a number of conferences dealing with the protection of the Mediterranean Sea, etc.

Dr Vukasović is member of editing boards of various publications, including the main Yugoslav International Law Journal (*The Yugoslav International Law Review*) and International Problems. Books: *International Law and the Development of Science and Technology* (in Serbian, with summaries in English and Russian), Belgrade 1978; *Protection and Improvement of the Environment-International Legal Regulation* (in

Serbian with a summary in English), Belgrade, 1980; *Environmental Protection and the United Nations* (in Serbian, with a summary in English), Belgrade, 1985; (with D. Todić) *International Organizations in the Field of Environmental Protection* (in Serbian) 'Prometej', Novi Sad, 1999; Edited (with D. Todić) 'Pravo na adekvatnu zivotnu sredinu – pravo na informisanje i ucesce u odlucivanju prema Arhuskoj konvenciji' (*The Right to Adequate Environment – Right to Environmental Information and to Public Participation according to the Aarhus Convention and to Yugoslav legislation*), Regional Environmental Centre for Central and Eastern Europe, Belgrade Office, Belgrade, 2001; Edited (with D. Todić), 'Zaštita životne sredine u međunarodnom i unutrašnjem pravu' (*Protection of the Environment in International and National Law*), Uprava za zaštitu životne sredine Ministarstva zdravlja i životne sredine Republike Srbije, Belgrade, 2001; Monograph (with D. Todić), *Serbia and Montenegro, Environmental Law, International Encyclopedia of Laws*, Supplement 37, Kluwer Law International, The Hague, London, New York, 2002; (with D. Todić) 'Ekološka kriza u svetu i odgovor međunarodne zajednice (izbor najznacajnijih međunarodnih dokumenata i jugoslovenskih propisa)', Savezni sekretarijat za rad, zdravstvo i socijalno staranje, Sektor za životnu sredinu i Institut za međunarodnu politiku i privredu, Belgrade, 2002; (One of the authors) 'Enciklopedija – Životna sredina – Održivi razvoj', Published by: ECOLIBRI, Beograd, Zavod za udžbenike i sredstva, Srpsko Sarajevo, 2003; (with D. Todić), Zbirka propisa u oblasti životne sredine, Megatrend univerzitet, Belgrade 2007.
Besides the mentioned books, he has published more than 300 articles and other shorter works in various periodicals. He has lectured in Serbia and abroad. For example, he lectures at the Specialized Course in High Administration and Comparative Governance 2003–2004, University of Bari and the Institute of International Politics and Economics, Bari and Belgrade and lectures at the Specialized Course 'The Law of Energetic', Faculty of Law, Belgrade 2005 and 2006, etc.

Dr Dragoljub Todić earned his Masters and PhD at the Faculty of Law, University of Belgrade and Bachelors at the Faculty of Political Science, University of Belgrade. He is presently employed at the Institute of International Politics and Economics (Belgrade). He served as a Professor at Megatrend University from 2001 to 2012. His fields of interest include legal regulation of environmental protection, human rights protection, the EU environmental policy and law, sustainable development migration, etc. He is member of the International Law Association (ILA), the Serbian International Law Association (JUMP), the Serbian Association of Lawyers, and several environmental NGOs. Dr Todić has participated in a number of conferences in Serbia and abroad. Published books: (with V. Vukasović) 'Međunarodne organizacije i međunarodna saradnja u oblasti zaštite životne sredine' (International organizations and International cooperation in the field of the environment), published by 'Prometej', Novi Sad, 1999; Editor-in-Chief of 'Zakonodavstvo Evropske unije o životnoj sredini i zemlje u tranziciji' (The EU Environmental Legislation and Countries in Transition), published by the Federal Ministry for Development, Science and the Environment, Belgrade, 2000; Coordinator of the project (and one of the Editors) 'Pravo na adekvatnu životnu sredinu – pravo na informisanje i ucesce u odlucivanju prema Arhuskoj konvenciji' (*The Right to Adequate Environment – Right to Environmental Information and to Public Participation According to the Aarhus Convention and to Yugoslav Legislation*) Regional Environmental Centre for Central and Eastern Europe, Belgrade Office, Belgrade, 2001; Edited (with V. Vukasović) Zastita životne sredine u međunarodnom i unutrašnjem pravu (*Protection of the Environment in International and National Law*), Uprava za zaštitu životne sredine Ministarstva zdravlja i životne sredine Republike Srbije, Beograd, 2001; Monograph (with V. Vukasović), Serbia and Montenegro, Environmental Law, International Encyclopaedia of Laws, Supplement 37, Kluwer Law International, The Hague, London, New York, 2002; (with V. Vukasović) 'Ekološka kriza u svetu i odgovor međunarodne zajednice (izbor najznačajnijih međunarodnih dokumenata i jugoslovenskih propisa)', Savezni sekretarijat za rad, zdravstvo i socijalno staranje, Institut za međunarodnu politiku i privredu, Belgrade, 2002; (One of the authors) 'Enciklopedija – Životna sredina – Održivi razvoj', Published by: Ecolibri, Beograd, Zavod za udžbenike i sredstva, Srpsko Sarajevo, 2003; (with V. Vukasović) Zbirka propisa u oblasti životne sredine, Megatrend univerzitet, Belgrade 2007. Ekoloski menadžment u uslovima globalizacije (*Environmental Management in Circumstances of Globalization*), Megatrend, Belgrade, 2008; Savremena politika i pravo životne sredine (*Contemporary Environmental Policy and Law*), Megatrend Univerzitet, Beograd, 2008;Todić D., Nikolić, M. (Eds). *Strateški pravci razvoja i utvrđivanja položaja Srbije u savremenim međunarodnim odnosima* (The strategic directions of development and determining the position of Serbia in contemporary international relations), Institut za međunarodnu politiku i privredu, Beograd, 2013; Grbić, V., Antevski M., Todić, D. *Finansiranje i zajedničke politike Evropske unije* (Financing and Common Policies of the European Union), Institut za međunarodnu politiku i privredu, Beograd. 2013; Todić, D. 'Montenegro' in *International Encyclopaedia of Laws: Environmental Law*, Ed. Kurt Deketelaere, Alphen aan den Rijin, NL: Kluwer Law International, 2013; Todić, D. *Klimatske promene u pravu i reforma sistema upravljanja* (Climate change in law and reform of the governance system), Institut za međunarodnu politiku i privredu, Beograd, 2014; Grečić V., Vekarić, V., Todić, D. *Migration Law in Serbia,* Wolters Kluwer, Law & Business, Alphen aan den Rijn, The Netherland, 2014; Todić, D., Grbić, V., Antevski M. *Pridruživanje Evropskoj uniji i održivi razvoj* (EU accession and sustainable development), Institut za međunarodnu politiku i privredu, Beograd, 2014; Todić D., Ignjatić M., Vukasović V. *Environmental Law – Bosnia and Hrezegovina,* International Encyclopaedia of Laws: Environmental

Law, (Ed). Kurt Deketelaere. Kluwer Law International, Alphen aan den Rijn, NL: Kluwer Law International, 2014; Grbić, V., Todić, D., Brnjas, Z. *Savremene tendencije u poljoprivredi Evropske unije i problem navodnjavanja*, (Contemporary tendencies in the agriculture of the European Union and the problem of irrigation), Institut za ekonomiku poljoprivrede, Beograd, 2015.
Besides that he published more than two hundred articles and other shorter works.

Table of Contents

Table of Contents

List of Abbreviations

ABS	Accreditation Board of Serbia
AECQ	Ch. 27 Answers to the European Commission's Questionnaire, Chapter 27 (Environment), Government of the Republic of Serbia, Belgrade, 2011.
AERS	Energy Agency of the Republic of Serbia
AP	Autonomous Province
APV	Autonomous Province Vojvodina
BAT	Best Available Techniques
BPEO	Best Practical Environmental Options
CARDS	EU Community Assistance for Reconstruction, Development and Stabilization
CC	Constitutional Court
CDM	Clean Development Mechanism of the Kyoto Protocol
CEHAP	Children's Environment and Health Action Plan
CITES	Convention on International Trade in Endangered Species of Wild Flora and Fauna
CLRTAP	UNECE Convention on Long-Range Transboundary Air Pollution
CR, 2016	Commission Report – European Commission, Serbia 2016 Report, Brussels, 9.11.2016 SWD(2016) 361 final
CO, 2011	Commission Opinion on Serbia's application for membership of the European Union, Communication from the Commission to the European Parliament and the Council, {COM (2011) 668}, SEC (2011) 1208, European Commission, Brussels, 12 October 2011.
DU	Depleted Uranium
EC	European Commission
EEA	European Environmental Agency
EIA	Environmental Impact Assessment
EIONET	European Environment Information and Observation Network
ELVs	Emission Limit Values
EMEP	Protocol to the Convention on Long-Range Transboundary Air Pollution on Financing of the Cooperative Programme for Monitoring and Evaluation of the Long-Range Transmission of Air Pollutants in Europe
EMS	Environmental Management System

List of Abbreviations

EMAS	Eco-Management and Audit Scheme
EPA	Environmental Protection Agency
EPL	Environmental Protection Law (Law on Environmental Protection)
EPR (2003)	Environmental Performance Reviews, Yugoslavia, 2003
EPR (2007)	Environmental Performance Reviews, Republic of Serbia, 2007
EPR (2015)	Environmental Performance Reviews, Serbia, 2015
EU	European Union
FAO	Food and Agriculture Organization
FRY	Federal Republic of Yugoslavia
GMO	Genetically Modified Organisms
IAEA	International Atomic Energy Agency
ICAO	International Civil Aviation Organization
ICPDR	International Commission for the Protection of the Danube River
IDPs	Internally Displaced Persons
ICP Forest	International Co-operative Programme on Assessment and Monitoring of Air Pollution Effects on Forests
IPA	Instrument for Pre-accession Assistance
IPPC	Integrated Pollution Prevention and Control
IRENA	International Renewable Energy Agency
LSG	Local Self-Government
LMO	Living Modified Organism
MAEP	Ministry of Agriculture and Environmental Protection
MATFW	Ministry of Agriculture, Trade, Forestry and Water Management
MCPFE	Ministerial Conference on the Protection of Forests in Europe
MEA	Multilateral Environmental Agreement
MEMSP	Ministry of Environment, Mining and Spatial Planning
MESP	Ministry of Environment and Spatial Planning
MOU	Memorandum of Understanding
MP	Member of Parliament
NAMAs	National Appropriate Mitigation Actions
NATO	North Atlantic Treaty Organization
NEPP	National Environmental Protection Programme

List of Abbreviations

NGO	Non-governmental Organization
NPAA	National Programme for the Adoption of the EU Acquis, European Integration Office, July 2014
NPAA, II revision	National Programme for the Adoption of the EU Acquis, European Integration Office, November 2016
NREAP	National Renewable Energy Action Plan
NPI	National Programme for Integration with European Union
NSDS	National Sustainable Development Strategy
OECD	Organisation for Economic Co-operation and Development
OJ	Official Journal
OJ – IT	Official Journal – International Treaties
OSCE	Organization for Security and Co-operation in Europe
PEBLD	Pan-European Biological and Landscape Diversity Strategy
PBB	PolibromovaneBiphenyls
PBDE	PolibromovaneDiphenylethers
PCBs	Polychlorinated Biphenyls
PRTR	Pollution Release and Transfer Register
POPs	Persistent Organic Pollutants
REACH	EC Regulation on Registration, Evaluation, Authorization and Restriction of Chemicals
REC	Regional Environmental Centre
RES	Renewable Energy Sources
RHMS	Republic Hydro Meteorological Service
RM	Republic of Montenegro
RS	Republic of Serbia
SAA	Stabilization and Association Agreement
SAB	Serbian Accreditation Body
SAICM	Strategic Approach to International Chemicals Management
SAP	Stabilization and Association Process
SAPK	Socialist Autonomous Province of Kosovo-Metohija
SAPV	Socialist Autonomous Province of Vojvodina
SEA	Strategic Environmental Assessment
S&M	Serbia and Montenegro
SEPA	Serbian Environmental Protection Agency
SFRY	Socialist Federal Republic of Yugoslavia

SRM	Socialist Republic of Montenegro
SRPNA	Serbian Radiation Protection and Nuclear Safety Agency
SRS	Socialist Republic of Serbia
SRS, Ch 27	Screening report Serbia, Chapter 27 – Environment, WP Enlargement + Countries Negotiating Accession to EU MD 114/16, 08.06.16.
UN	United Nations
UNECE	United Nations Economic Commission for Europe
UNEP	United Nations Environment Programme
	United Nations Educational, Scientific and Cultural Organization
UNHCR	Office of the United Nations High Commissioner for Refugees
UNMIK	The UN Interim Administration Mission in Kosovo
UNSC	United Nations Security Council
US	United States
WEEE	Waste Electrical and Electronic Equipment
WFD	Water Framework Directive
WMO	World Meteorological Organization
WHO	World Health Organization

Acknowledgements

The author would like to thank Sean Bawden, Molly Grindley, John Lindsay, Carolyn Eliott Magwood and Anna Poliszot for research assistance in connection with the preparation of this volume.

The authors wish to thank Ms Mladenka Ignjatić (independent consultant, Belgrade) for her suggestions and contributions.

General Introduction

Chapter 1. General Information

§1. Geography and Population

1. The Republic of Serbia is located in south-eastern Europe. Its total territory is 88.499 km².[1] The country lies between 41° 11' and 46°11' northern geographical latitude and 18° 49' and 23°00' eastern geographical longitude. Border countries are Albania, Bosnia and Herzegovina, Bulgaria, Croatia, Hungary, the Macedonia, Montenegro and Romania. The total boundary is 2,361.7 km (total land boundary is 1,567.3 km; river boundary is 751.1 km and lake boundary is 43.3 km).[2] It is important to add that some parts of the borders have not finally been demarcated yet.

2. The terrain varies extremely. There are rich fertile plains in the north (Vojvodina and Macva) and some river valleys (the Sava Valley, the Morava Valley, etc.), while most of the other parts consist of mountains (the highest being Đeravica in the Prokletija range – 2,656 m), high lands and hills. There is 55% of arable land and 27% is forested. The main water resources are rivers. They belong to the basins of the Black, Adriatic and Aegean Seas. The Danube, Sava and Tisa are navigable. The longest river is the Danube, which flows through Serbia for 588 km along its 2,857 km long course.

3. The climate is moderately continental (cold winters and usually hot and humid summers). The most rainy period is late spring and early summer. The annual precipitation during the 1961–1990 period, averaged for whole country is 896 mm. It varied depending on the altitude and other characteristics of the different parts of the country.[3]

---

1. *Statistical Yearbook of the Republic of Serbia 1016*. Belgrade: Statistical Office of the Republic of Serbia, 2016, 18.
2. *Ibid.*, 18. Data on established state borders have been taken over from the border documentation available in the Borders Service of the Ministry of Foreign Affairs of the Republic of Serbia.
3. 'Dry areas with precipitation below 600 mm are situated in the north-eastern parts of the country, in the South Morava valley and part of Kosovo. Average annual precipitation at the Pester plateau and Mt. Kopaonik was much higher (up to 1,000 mm), and some mountainous summits in the south-west of Serbia had even heavier precipitation of over 1,000 mm'. B. Karadžic (ed.),*Environment in Serbia – An Indicator-Based Review*49 (Ministry of Science and Environmental Protection 2007).

4. The latest 2011 census puts the population of Serbia (excluding Kosovo-Metohija) at 7,120,666.[4] Serbs make up 82.86% of the population. National minorities are: Hungarians 3.91%, Bosniaks 1.81%, Roma 1.44%, Yugoslavs 1.08%, Croats 0.94%, Montenegrins 0.92%, Albanians 0.82%, Slovaks 0.79%, Vlachs 0.53%, Romanians 0.46%, Macedonians 0.34%, Bulgarians and Vojvodina Croats 0.27% each, Muslims 0.26%, Ruthenians 0.21%, Slovaks and Ukrainians 0.7% each, Gorans 0.06%, Germans 0.05%, and Russians and Czechs 0.03% each.[5]

There is a very low population growth rate, except in Kosovo-Metohija. (The year 1999s estimation was 0.02%).

5. Thousands of Serbs and members of other ethnic groups moved during the war and crisis of 1990s, because of military actions and ethnic conflicts, to Serbia from other parts of the former Yugoslavia (estimated number of refugees is more than half a million). At the same time, thousands, in most cases young and highly educated people, emigrated because of economic and political reasons mainly to the Western Europe and overseas countries. The impact of these migrations is still felt.

According to the registration of refugees in Serbia, carried out from 27 November 2004 to 25 January 2005, there are 139,483 persons with the refugee status, which is 50% less in relation to the registration from 2001. According to a June 2010 Office of the United Nations High Commissioner for Refugees (UNHCR) report, with 86,000 refugees and 21,000 internally displaced persons (IDPs), Serbia is still at the top of the list of countries in Europe in terms of forced migration, as well as one of the five countries in the world facing a prolonged refugee crisis.[6] A priority of the Republic of Serbia is organized repatriation, in cooperation with the UNHCR, of refugees to the countries from which they fled, under condition that they are accepted into their communities of return 'and provided conditions to live in security and dignity'. The other two ways of solving the problem are integration into the communities in Serbia to which the refugees have already settled and/or emigration to a third country.[7] Another

4. The AP of Kosovo-Metohija is, according to Resolution 1244 of the UN Security Council (1999), under the United Nations Interim Administration Mission (UNMIK), and is not covered in this Monograph. For text of the Resolution, *see* , S/RES/1244 (1999, 10 Jun. 1999; https://documents-dds-ny.un.org/doc/UNDOC/GEN/N99/172/89/PDF/N9917289.pdf?OpenElement; *See also*http://www.srbija.gov.rs/kosovo-metohija/. *See2011 Census of Population, Households and Dwellings in the Republic of Serbia*, First Results, Statistical Office of the Republic of Serbia, Belgrade 2011, 15.
5. *Statistical Yearbook of the Republic of Serbia – 2007* (Belgrade: Statistical Office of the Republic of Serbia, 2007), 76. (However, the data on nationality or ethnicity, gender and age, religion and other characteristics will be successively made public from mid-2012 until the end of 2013.) *See* , The Official Website of the Government of Serbia, http://www.srbija.gov.rs/pages/article.php?id=36.
6. The Official Website of the Government of Serbia, http://www.srbija.gov.rs/pages/article.php?id=61.
7. *Ibid.*, for more details, *see* , http://www.kirs.gov.rs/articles/onama.php?lang=ENG.

category is IDPs from Kosovo-Metohija. By July 2001, there were more than 200,000 IDPs registered in Serbia.[8]

6. In 2015 RS has become significantly more frequent transit country for many migrants from Syria, Afghanistan, Iraq, Iran and Pakistan who want to go to the EU. The number of migrants who declared intention for asylum is in a significant increase. In 2015, there were 579,518 expressed intentions for asylum in the RS (313,335 men and 92,188 women). The largest number of asylum seekers coming from Syria (52.1%) and Afghanistan (27.82%), then from Iraq (13.13%), Iran (1.99%) and Pakistan (1.57%), all due to the increased influx of migrants from the Middle East and Africa. As of May 2015, suddenly began to grow the number of people who expressed their intention to seek asylum in the Republic of Serbia. It rapidly increased and reached a number that is almost thirty-five times higher than in 2014.[9]

7. The state of health of the population in Serbia was far from satisfactory at the end of the crisis in 1990s. Certainly one of the reasons was environmental pollution, but the more serious reason was overall poverty.[10] During the decade 1990–2000 of grave economic and political crisis, hundreds of thousands of refugees, and wrong economic policy of the former regime, caused further fall of living standards what was, among other things, reflected on health. After the normalization in 2000, both standard of living and state of health have steadily improved due to economic development and donations and investments from abroad.[11]

---

8. *Ibid.*; *See also*, Report of the Secretary-General on the United Nations Interim Administration Mission in Kosovo S/2004/348, 30 Apr. 2004, paras 2–17; 'Failure to Protect: Anti-Minority Violence in Kosovo, March 2004', *Human Right Watch*, 16, no. 6(D), July 2004. *See also*, National Strategy for Refugees and Internally Displaced Persons from Kosovo and Metohija (April 2002), Republic of Serbia – Commissariat for refugees http://www.zavodsz.gov.rs/PDF/Nacionalna%20strategija%20za%20resavanje%20pitanja%20izbeglih%20i%20interno%20raseljenih%20lica.pdf. In 2011 Serbia still has 60 refugee centres with more than 4,700 refugees and IDPs. *See* http://www.srbija.gov.rs/pages/article.php?id=61. *See also*, National Strategy For Resolving Problems Of Refugees And Internally Displaced Persons For the Period From 2011 To 2014, 3 Mar. 2011.http://www.kirs.gov.rs//docs/National%20Strategy%20For%20Resolving%20Problems%20Of%20Refugees%20And%20Internally%20Displaced%20Persons%20For%20the%20Period%20From%202011%20To%202014.pdf.
9. *Migration Profile of the Republic of Serbia for 2015*. Belgrade: Government of the Republic of Serbia, 64, and 41. http: //vvv.kirs.gov.rs/docs/migracije/migracioni%20profil%202015.pdf. (15 Jun. 2017).
10. The Poverty Reduction Strategy paper (PRSp) for Serbia has been adopted in 2003, as a medium-term development framework directed at reducing key forms of poverty. *See also*, *Second Progress Report on the Implementation of the Poverty Reduction Strategy in Serbia* (Belgrade: Government of Serbia, 2007).
11. For more details *see* , S. Šolak, Pravo na zdravlje i ekonomska osnova njegovog ostvarenja [*Right to Health and Economic Bases of Its Realization*], *Pravni život*, godina LVI, br. 9/2007, 277–308.

§2. Political History and Structure

8. Serbia was in the medieval centuries a kingdom and even for a while an empire (in fourteenth century). The Ottoman Empire occupied it in fifteenth century and it was liberated in nineteenth century, gaining full independence from Ottoman Empire in 1878. Serbia was a principality until 1885 when it became a kingdom.[12] In 1918 it became a part of the Kingdom of Yugoslavia, and after the Second World War a constituent Republic of the Socialist Federal Republic of Yugoslavia.[13]

It must be added, however, that, some parts of present Serbia were until 1918 a part of Austro-Hungarian Empire (Vojvodina province). Some other territories also belonged, until 1912, to the Ottoman Empire (Kosovo-Metohija and some other parts of southern and south-western Serbia).

9. One of the main characteristics of Socialist Federal Republic of Yugoslavia, from its establishment after the Second World War till its end in 1990s, was the specific socialist model combined of self-management system in internal affairs and of non-aligned policy on the international scene. After the disintegration of the Former Socialist Federal Republic of Yugoslavia, which consisted of six republics (Slovenia, Croatia, Serbia, Bosnia and Herzegovina, Montenegro and Macedonia) five new States appeared on the political map of South-Eastern Europe. While other constituent republics proclaimed independence, Serbia and Montenegro remained, for a while, a federation (Federal Republic of Yugoslavia, proclaimed in 1992) sometimes called the Third Yugoslavia. It was transformed in 2003 into loose semi-confederal State Union of Serbia and Montenegro which lasted till 2006 when Serbia and Montenegro became independent States:

> It is important here to stress that the former Yugoslavia was different in many ways from the members of the Soviet Block. It was a non-aligned country that had a rather intensive international cooperation and important role not only in the region but in world politics (for instance, the former President of Socialist Federal Republic of Yugoslavia (SFRY) Tito was one of the founders of the non-aligned movement). Among other things, the country was more active than other socialist countries in environmental protection, taking active part on important international conferences (for instance, the 1972 Stockholm Conference), environmental action plans (for instance, the Mediterranean Action Plan – MAP) and actively participating in the work of international organizations and other bodies (United Nations Environment Programme (UNEP), United Nations Economic Commission for Europe (UNECE), World Health Organization (WHO) etc.).

10. One of the Serbian autonomous provinces (APs) Kosovo-Metohija has, after 1999 North Atlantic Treaty Organization (NATO) intervention (24 March–10 June),

---

12. On this part of Serbian history, *see* , S.K. Pavlović, Srbija: istorija iza imena [*Serbia: The History behind the Name*] (Beograd: Clio, 2004), 1–138.
13. About Serbian history in Yugoslavia, *see* , Lj. Dimić, Istorija srpske drzavnosti, knjiga III, Srbija u Jugoslaviji 1918–1990 [*History of the Serbian Statehood, Book III, Serbia in Yugoslavia*] (Beseda, Novi Sad: SANU, 2001).

a special status according to the United Nations Security Council (UNSC) resolution 1244. Under the UNMIK governance, the whole new legal system has been formed with some UNMIK regulations concerning the environmental protection as well.[14] Among other things, the Administrative Department of Environmental Protection was established.[15]

11. After the elections in September and December and the mass demonstration on 5 October 2000, the Serbia has become a State of pluralistic and parliamentary democracy devoted to the promotion of the rule of law, market economy, social justice, human rights, equality and welfare of all citizens. Its position in the international community was improved considerably, after the United Nations (UN), European Union (EU) and United States (US) sanctions were lifted and after its position in the UN and other international key organizations were normalized. In spite of that, it had many unresolved political, economic and other problems. Two main political problems were future of the Federation and the status of Kosovo-Metohija. The first one was resolved when the Federation was first transformed to the State Union of Serbia and Montenegro and finally when the bond between two republics was cut and they became two independent States. The other problem (Kosovo-Metohija) is still one of the main political problems of Serbia.[16]'Negotiations between Belgrade and Prishtina on issues of importance to the life of Serbs and other non-Albanian population in Kosovo-Metohija began in March 2011 in Brussels, with the mediation of the European Union.'[17]In the meantime the 'Republic of Kosovo' is recognized by some countries, although five EU states refuse to recognize it.

12. In 2006 the new Serbian Constitution was adopted. Serbia is a republic with an elected President. The Prime Minister is elected by the Parliament. The Parliament has one house with 250 members. The new convocation of the National Assembly was established on 3 June 2016, during which the Speaker and the Deputy Speakers were elected, Secretary General appointed and members of the working bodies of the National Assembly and members of Parliamentary delegations in international institutions designated. Sixteen delegation groups were formed and three delegates were not members of any delegation group.[18]

13. The territorial organization of Serbia includes five regions (Belgrade region, Vojvodina region, Sumadija and western Serbia region, eastern and southern Serbia region and Kosovo-Metohija region). They include the City of Belgrade as a separate territorial unit established by the Constitution and law, and twenty-nine administrative

14. UNMIK Regulations, http://www.unmikonline.org/regulations/index.htm.
15. UNMIK Regulation 032/2000.
16. This especially after 17 Feb. 2008, when the Assembly of Kosovo adopted 'Declaration of Independence'. *See also*, Decision on the annulment of the illegitimate acts of the provisional institutions of self-government in Kosovo and Metohija on their declaration of unilateral independence, adopted by the Government of the Republic of Serbia http://www.srbija.gov.rs/kosovo-metohija/index.php?id=43159. 'Kosovo's declaration of independence from Serbia in 2008 triggered the possibility of renewed instability in the Balkans after a decade-long peace maintained by the UN Interim Administration Mission in Kosovo (UNMIK) and the NATO-led Kosovo Force (KFOR).' *See* : http://www.un.org/en/events/tenstories/08/kosovo.shtml.
17. *See* : http://www.srbija.gov.rs/kosovo-metohija/index.php?id=43376.
18. For details, *see* : NPAA, II revision, 7, 8.

areas, twenty-three cities, twenty-eight urban municipalities, 150 municipalities, 6,158 villages and 195 urban settlements.[19]

14. The Republic of Serbia made a formal application to join the EU on 22 December 2009. The Stabilization and Association Process started in 2001. On 14 October 2004, the Serbian National Assembly adopted the Resolution on EU Accession. The most crucial step on the path of accession so far was the signing of the Stabilization and Association Agreement (SAA) on 29 April 2008.[20]In March 2012, the country was granted EU candidate status. The European Council decided to open accession negotiations with Serbia in June 2013. The EU-Serbia SSA entered into force in September 2013. Accession negotiations were launched in January 2014. The first negotiating chapters were opened including Chapter 35 dealing with normalization of relations between Serbia and Kosovo,[21] and the rule of law (Chapter 23 on judiciary and fundamental rights, and Chapter 24 on justice, freedom and security).[22]

§3. Economic Characteristics

15. Serbia is an agricultural-industrial country.[23] The economy was, generally speaking, after almost a decade of civil wars, UN, EU and US sanctions, NATO 1999 air raids and internal political crisis, in bad condition. Lifting of the sanctions and the improvement of the international position of the country gave hope that the economy, with investments and donations from abroad and well-conceived economic policies, could be improved, after the shocks of the first phase of transition which has begun later than in any other former socialist country.

16. In comparison with other countries in transition, Serbia was late in starting reforms, because of the situation in the nineties of the previous century: internal conflicts in former Yugoslavia, international isolation, the 1999 NATO intervention, etc.

National Strategy of Economic Development of the Republic of Serbia for the period 2006–2012 represents first developmental document that defines, in a consistent and complete way, basic developmental priorities of the country and methods of their implementation in coming years.

17. The 2001–2006 period was characterized by numerous reforms, establishment of macroeconomic stability and sustainable and stable economic development,

19. Law on Territorial Organizations of the Republic of Serbia (OJ RS, Nos 129/07 and 18/16).

20. At http://www.seio.gov.rs.

21. 'This designation is without prejudice to positions on status, and is in line with UNSCR 1244/1999 and the ICJ Opinion on the Kosovo declaration of independence.'

22. The decision on the opening of negotiating Chs 5 (Public procurement) and 25 (Science and Research) was made at the Fourth Intergovernmental Conference in Brussels (13 Dec. 2016). The decision on the opening of negotiating Chs 20 (Enterprise and Industrial Policy) and 26 (Education and Culture) was made at the Fifth Intergovernmental Conference in Brussels (27 Feb. 2017). For more information, *see* : http://www.seio.gov.rs/eng/serbia-and-eu/history/ (13 May 2017).

23. About socio-historical aspects of the industrial development of Serbia from 1815 to 1941, *see* , M.Z. Calić, Socijalna istorija Srbije 1815–1941: usporeni napredak u industrijalizaciji [*Social History of Serbia 1815–1941: Slow Progress in Industrialization*] (Belgrade: Clio, 2004).

restructuring of big systems, privatization of companies, and initiating the process of accession to the EU, the process which includes adoption of numerous legal regulations in all domains of economy and society. After the changes in 2000, Serbian economy had *continued accelerated growth*. The average annual growth rate in the period 2000–2006 was 5.2% 'what ranks it among European countries with fastest economic growth'.[24] Macroeconomic trends in 2013 were 'more favorable than in the prior period – economic activity increased thanks to the recovery of agricultural and industrial production'. Inflation was on the decline throughout the year, measuring 2.2% in December. Positive trends were also observed in the labour market. The greatest progress made was in reducing external imbalances. 'In 2013, economic activity increased by 2.5%, primarily thanks to the recovery of agricultural and industrial production…'.[25]

18. In 2003, significant foreign direct investment (FDI) started and foreign investment totalled EUR 1,200 million by means of privatization of large industrial complexes. In 2003 and 2004 there was a slowdown of FDI (EUR 770 million in 2004 and EUR 1,250 million in 2005), but 2006 was a record year for FDI influx amounted to EUR 4.08 billion or 16.1% of GDP.

In 2006 the foreign debt of Serbia reached a level of 58.9% of GDP. It represented maintenance in the relative level of overall foreign indebtedness, in comparison with previous two years. The main reason for the rise in foreign debt in the mentioned year was rise in private debt, which reached 33.5% in comparison of 25.4% in 2005. At the same time, the public foreign debt was reduced from 36.6% in 2005 to 25.4% of GDP in 2006.[26]

19. Unemployment in Serbia keeps continuous growth in line with progress of reforms and restructuring. The first National Employment Strategy for the Republic of Serbia, which covers the period from 2005 throughout the end of the first decade of twenty-first century, has been adopted. 'The rate of unemployment according to ATS is 14.6% in 2003 (unemployment rate according NES data is even 29.83% in 2003) and is still at the level of the average in the countries in transition…'.[27] However, according to the Statistical Yearbook (2015) 'the unemployment rate, i.e., the share of unemployed persons in the total economically active population is 22.4%. The unemployment rate in women (23.6%) is somewhat higher than in men (21.6%)'.[28]

---

24. Nacionalna strategija privrednog razvoja Republike Srbije od 2006. do 2012. godine (National Economic Development Strategy of the Republic of Serbia 2006–2012), 5. (http://www.gs.gov.rs/lat/strategije-vs.html); *see also*, *National Sustainable Development Strategy*, Draft (Belgrade: The Government of the Republic of Serbia, 2008), 48; *Millennium Development Goals* (Belgrade: Government of the Republic of Serbia, 2006).
25. For details, *see* , NPAA, 69–72.
26. *See* , Second Progress Report on the Implementation of the Poverty Reduction Strategy in Serbia (Belgrade: Government of the Republic of Serbia, August 2007), 25–31. However, in the meantime foreign debt increased, and 2013 it was 88% GDP. NPAA, 68 (*See* table: 'Basic Macroeconomic Indicators').
27. National Employment Strategy (Belgrade: Government of the Republic of Serbia, 2005), 18–19.
28. *Statistical Yearbook of the Republic of Serbia 2015*, 32. After three years of growth, the unemployment rate was reduced by 1.8 pp in 2013 relative to the previous year. According to the Labour Force Survey, it amounted to 22.1%.NPAA, 70.

20. One of the characteristics of economic development of Serbia is unbalanced development and great differences between regions. To solve this problem, the Government of Serbia adopted (2007) a special Strategy of Regional Development of the Republic of Serbia for the period 2007–2012.[29]

§4. Social and Cultural Characteristics

21. According to Article 1 of the Constitution, Republic of Serbia is a State 'based on the rule of law and social justice, principles of civil democracy, human and minority rights and freedoms, and commitment to European principles and values'. One of the main strategic objectives in achieving social welfare in Serbia is, according to National sustainable development Strategy (NSDS), promotion and development of sustainable lifestyles and promotion of 'values based on political liberalism and civic participation'.[30]

22. The official language in Serbia is Serbian (in former Yugoslavia it was called Serbo-Croatian) and the script in official use is Cyrillic, while Latin script is also used. In areas where ethnic minorities live, their languages and scripts are in official use. The Constitution of the Republic of Serbia guarantees rights to minorities, in accordance with international standards.

23. The main religion of Serbia is Christian Orthodox. Besides the Christian Orthodox, there are also other religious communities in Serbia: Islamic, Roman Catholic, Protestant, Jewish and others.

24. Western European, Mediterranean, Oriental, Eastern European and other cultural influences mixed with each other on the territory of Serbia were producing in some cases original contributions (e.g., fresco paintings in Serbian medieval monasteries) to the European and world culture.

25. Cultural policy in the former Yugoslavia was more liberal than in other countries dominated by communists, although some intellectuals were persecuted from political reasons and, generally speaking, educational and cultural budgets were low and far from sufficient. During the crisis on the territory of former Yugoslavia, and especially due to the sanctions imposed by the UN, EU and US, the situation became even worse because culture was not regarded as one of the priority issues. After the introduction of the democratic regime in 2000, the situation is still not very satisfactory. Culture and education are still not a priority issue, but the country is now open for exchange, Non-governmental Organization (NGO) activities and the inflow of various donations and/or internationally funded projects, some of which are even commercial in character.

26. Article 71 of the Constitution prescribes that everyone shall have the right to education. All citizens shall have access under equal conditions to higher education. The Republic of Serbia shall provide for free tertiary education to successful and

29. At http://www.gs.gov.rs/english/strategije-vs.html.
30. NSDS, 48.

talented students of lower property status in accordance with the law. Primary education is mandatory and free, while secondary education is free, but not mandatory.[31]

The 2011 Census results indicate that 1.96% of the population in the Republic of Serbia are illiterate (aged 10 and over). Illiteracy is most common in women (82.1%) and in the age group 65 and over (70.5%).[32]

§5. Main Environmental Problems

27. It could be said that the main environmental issues in Serbia are inadequate management of domestic, industrial and hazardous waste,[33] air pollution in Belgrade[34] and other industrial cities, inefficient use of energy and air pollution from thermoelectric plants, water pollution from industrial wastes dumped into riversand chemical pollution from chemicals used in agriculture (pesticides, herbicides, fertilizers, etc.). A significant part of the problem originates from obsolete technological processes in industries as well as from inadequate legal regulation and weaknesses in public administration. There is also imported pollution, especially by inflow rivers. Most of inflow rivers are already polluted and sometimes heavily (as for instance, the pollution of Tisza River in 2000 caused by the discharge of dangerous substances from the Romanian gold mine, Baia Mare).[35]

28. A serious source of pollution was caused by the 1999 NATO intervention.[36] In some 35,000 air strikes, refineries and chemical plants were destroyed; also depleted uranium (DU) ammunition, as well as other legally problematic weapons like cluster bombs and graphite bombs, were used. The bombing of Serbia had certainly, especially in some cases, characteristics of an ecological war, damaging not only man-made objects but also natural environment, including some areas of natural heritage (four national parks were bombed). Many animals and plants were destroyed or disturbed in their natural habitats and some animals were forced to seek shelter in the areas outside Serbia. Several thousands of persons were killed and many wounded and the

31. In this field Government adopted two strategic documents: Adult Development Education Strategy (2006) and Vocational Education Development Strategy (2006), http://www.gs.gov.rs/english/strategije-vs.html.
32. *Statistical Yearbook of the Republic of Serbia 2015*, 32.
33. For more information, *see* , B. Karadžic (ed.), *Environment in Serbia – An Indicator-Based Review* (Ministry of Science and Environmental Protection 2007); *Environmental Performance Reviews – Republic of Serbia*, Second Review, UN, New York and Geneva, 2007; Izvestaj o stanju životne sredine u Republici Srbiji za 2007. godinu [*Report on State of Environment in Serbia for 2007*], Ministarstvo životne sredine i prostornog planiranja (Beograd, 2008).
34. *See* , Kvalitet životne sredine grada Beograda u 2007. godini [*Quality of the Environment in Belgrade*], Beograd, Sekretarijat za zaštitu životne sredine, Gradski zavod za javno zdravlje, Regionalni centar za životnu sredinu za Centralnu i Istočnu Evropu, 2007.
35. *See* , International Law and the Baia Mare Cyanide Spill, Regional Environmental Centre for Central and Eastern Europe, with the support of the Government of the United Kingdom September 2001; Rapid Environmental Assessment of Tisza River Basin (UNEP, 2002).
36. For general international law aspects, *see* , D. Todić, Međunarodnopravna zaštita životne sredine za vreme oružanih sukoba [*International-Law Protection of the Environment in Time of Armed Conflicts*] (Belgrade, Vojno delo, No. 2/98), 40–55.

environment was endangered not only locally but to a certain extent in surrounding countries. The survey of the economic facilities destroyed or damaged in the NATO bombing of Serbia, shows that, among other civilian objects, were destroyed or badly damaged: 78 industrial plants, 43 installations for energy production, 115 objects in the field of transport, including most of the bridges and airports and, among many other objects even six installations for water management.[37]

The whole damage done by the bombing has not been precisely estimated, but it is certainly enormous and it certainly has had a negative impact on the environment in Serbia and, to a certain extent on a wider area. One of the main tasks after the change of regime in 2000, was cleaning so-called hotspots caused by the NATO bombing, cleaning debris from the Danube river and building new bridges and other infrastructure (especially in Novi Sad where all bridges were destroyed) with financial and other help of the EU and other international factors.[38]

29. The main natural hazards are destructive earthquakes, especially in some seismically more active areas (like, for instance, southern Serbia),[39] floods[40] and storms. 'Serbia in general has a very high risk of flooding. Among the 10 worst natural disasters (with respect to the number of affected people) in Serbia from 2006 to 2013 there have been six floods (in 2007, 2009, and twice in 2010 and in 2013) with 23,150 people affected.'[41]

30. It is a fact nowadays that the state of environment is closely linked to practically all human activities and due to that all phenomena in the society have their environmental aspect. In a society with so many problems, as is the case with Serbia,

37. Posledice NATO bombardovanja na životnu sredinu SR Jugoslavije – Izvestaj SRJ [*Consequences of NATO Bombing for Environment in FR Yugoslavija – Report of the FR Yugoslavia*] (Beograd: Savezno ministarstvo za razvoj, nauku i životnu sredinu, 2000), 65–70.
38. *See* generally, *The Kosovo Conflict. Consequences for the Environment & Human Settlements* (Switzerland: UNEP, 1999); *From Conflict to Sustainable Development – Assessment of Environmental Hot Spots – Serbia and Montenegro* (UNEP, Ministry of Science and Environmental Protection of the Republic of Serbia, Ministry of Environmental Protection and Physical Planning of the Republic of Montenegro, 2004).
39. Provisions in the field of civil protection field are contained in following regulations: Law on Protection from elementary and major disasters (OJ SRS, Nos 24/85, 27/85, 6/89 and 52/89, and OJ RS, Nos 53/93, 67/93, 48/94 and 101/2005), Fire Protection Law (OJ RS, No. 37/88), National Defence Law of the RS (OJ RS, No. 116/07), etc. although some of them are not fully in agreement with the relevant EU legislature.
40. S. Bogdanović, Pravni i institucionalni aspekti upravljanja poplavama [*Translation of the WMO Publication Legal and Institutional Aspects of Integrated Flood Management*] (Novi Sad: Jugoslovensko udruženje za vodno pravo, 2006). *See also*: General Plan for Flood Protection for the period 2012–2018 (OJ RS, 23/12).
41. EPR (2015), 117. A severe storm event hit the Balkans region strongly in May 2014, affecting Serbia mainly in the catchments of the Sava River and its tributaries. 'As a result of the flooding, 34 persons died – 13 by drowning – and over 30,000 were evacuated from their homes. Serious damage was also caused to coal mines, chemical plants, power plants and road infrastructure, which were entirely flooded, shut down or subject to landslides.' *Ibid*, 140. For more detail *see* : Izveštaj o stanju životne sredine u Republici Srbiji za 2014. godinu, [*Report on the state of the environment in Serbia for 2014*]. Ministarstvo poljoprivrede i zaštite životne sredine, Agencija za zaštitu životne sredine [Ministry of Agriculture and Environmental Protection, Environmental Protection Agency]. Beograd, 2015, 153–163.

two issues deserve special attention: environmental aspect of the development and the environmental aspect of human rights. The really higher standard of living of the population can be achieved only if based on the adequate environment, that is, if the economic development is based on sustainability.[42]

31. One of the key institutional challenges is the remaining overlaps in policy and implementation responsibilities and lack of coordination, which hampers effectiveness. Water quality monitoring is a prime example.[43]

32. Monitoring has been improved but needs further strengthening.[44] The legal basis for an integrated environmental monitoring system was established by the 2004 *Law on Environmental Protection* (EPL), while EPL (Official Journal (OJ) RS, 14/2016) prescribes that:

> Monitoring is carried out by systematic monitoring of indicator values, i.e. by monitoring of adverse impacts on the environment, the state of the environment, measures and activities to be taken in order to reduce negative impacts and increase the quality of the environment. The government sets the criteria for determining the number and distribution of measuring points, the network of measuring the points, extent and frequency of measurements, classification of occurrances that are monitored, work methodology and indicators of environmental pollution and their monitoring, deadlines and the way of delivering the data on the basis of special Laws(Article 70, paragraph 1 and 2).

The Law also provides for the establishment of an environmental information system (Article 74)[45] and a National and Local Register of polluters (Article 75).[46] This system is to be more specifically regulated by sectoral laws (Law on Water, Law on Waste Management, Law on Nature Protection, Law on Air Protection, Law on Statistical Research, etc.) which are also expected to be harmonized with relevant EU directives.

33. The state of the environment in the RS can be assessed in different ways depending on the segment of the environment (water, air, land, nature, etc.). Serbia produces its 'state of the environment report' annually. The last report was published in 2015 (for 2014).[47] It is difficult to give a general assessment. In a country in transition

42. For general aspects *see National Sustainable Development Strategy*, 19–32, 73–110.
43. Environmental Protection in Serbia, Progress since Kiev 2003 and Challenges Ahead, World Bank, October 2007, 5.
44. CR, 76, 77. For more details, *see* , EPR (2015), 81–89.
45. The information system shall be run by the environmental agency and the government shall prescribe more closely the contents and the manner of maintenance of information system, methodology, structure, common bases, categories and levels of data compilation, as well as the contents of information regulatory and obligatory released to public.
46. *See* , Rulebook on the methodology of the national and local register of pollution sources, as well as the methodology related to types, methods and deadlines of data collection (OJ RS, No. 91/10).
47. *See* http://www.sepa.gov.rs/download/Izvestaj2014.pdf (16 Jun. 2017). However, 'this frequency can be questioned, in particular because in such a short period of time it is impossible to observe visible changes in trends and impacts for the majority of thematic areas assessed in the report. Furthermore, this period of time may be insufficient to implement some of the actions recommended in the previous report'. EPR (2015), xxvi.

(like Serbia), there are many systemic issues which have to be solved as a precondition to solve environmental problems. However it can be said that in the process of harmonization of national legislation with EU legislation the elements of the system of environmental management and monitoring have been establishing. The adoption of the relevant EU legislation, in particular their implementation, requires considerable investment in infrastructure during the long period of time. The total cost of the approximation was estimated at EUR 10.6 billion.[48]

34. According to the Screening Report (Chapter 27), 'overall, Serbia's legislation has a satisfactory level of alignment with the *acquis* ..., but implementation and enforcement are at an early stage. There is a substantial amount of work to be undertaken as regards the implementation of legislation and the establishment of the necessary administrative and enforcement and control capacities required by the *acquis*'.[49] The latest annual report of the European Commission (EC) notes that the Serbia has achieved 'some level of preparation in this area. Some progress has been made in further aligning policies and legislation with the *acquis*, including in waste, nature protection and climate change'.[50] In addition, Serbia improved its strategic planning and set up a Green Fund.

48. *Nacionalna strategija za aproksimaciju u oblasti životne sredine (National Environmental Approximation Strategy for the Republic of Serbia)*, Vlada Republike Srbije (Government of the Republic of Serbia) 2011, 12.
49. SRS, Chs 27, 17.
50. CR, 2016, 75.

Chapter 2. Basic Principles of Environmental Law

§1. Definitions and Notions

35. Although all basic laws contain provisions with definitions, the most important definitions in the field of environmental protection can be found in Article 3 of the EPL. Following definitions, out of total of thirty-three definitions included in the article, deserve special attention:[51]

- *Environment*: a set of natural and man-made values whose complex mutual relations make up the environment, that is, area and conditions for life.
- *Environmental quality*: a state of environment in terms of physical, chemical, biological, aesthetic and other indicators.
- *Natural value*: natural wealth which comprises air, water, soil, forests, geological resources, plants and animal life.
- *Protected natural good*: a preserved part of nature with special values and characteristics (geodiversity, biodiversity, scenery, landscape, etc.), due to which they have permanent ecological, scientific, cultural, educational, health recreational, tourist and other significance and therefore as a public good it enjoys special protection.
- *Public natural good*: a cultivated or uncultivated part of natural wealth, that is, air, water goods, water-fronts, underground goods, forests, sceneries or landscapes equally accessible to all.
- *Activity affecting the environment ('activity')*: any action (permanent or temporary) which changes or may change the status and conditions in the environment and relates to utilization of resources and natural goods; production and circulation processes; distribution and use of materials; emissions of pollution into water, air, or soil; waste and wastewater management; chemicals and harmful matters management; noise and vibrations; ionizing and no ionizing radiation; and accidents.
- *Polluter*: a legal or natural entity who by its activity or inactivity pollutes the environment.
- *Pollutants*: substances whose outflow into the environment affects or may affect its natural composition, properties and integrity.
- *Environmental pollution*: introduction of polluting matters or energy into the environment, caused either by human activities or natural processes, which has or may have adverse effects towards quality of the environment and human health.
- *Environmental capacity*: the ability of environment to accept certain quantity of pollutants per unit of time and space so as to avoid irreparable damage towards the environment.
- *Load to the environmental*: individual or cumulative effect of activities to environment, which may be expressed as aggregate (several similar components),

51. Other relevant definitions, if needed, are given in following text of this monograph.

common (several heterogeneous components), permitted (within the permitted limit values), excessive (exceeding limit values) load.

- *Accident:* sudden and uncontrolled event that occurs with release, leakage or dispersion of dangerous substances, in the course of performing activities of production, utilization, processing, storage, disposal or long-term inadequate keeping (hereinafter, the chemical accident).[52]
- *Degradation of environment*: a process of degradation of environment quality caused either by natural or human activity or it occurs as a consequence of non-performance of measures for elimination of causes of degradation of quality or damage towards the environment, natural or any man-made values.
- *Environment pollution sources:* location-wise specified and spatially limited point, line and area sources of pollutants and energy into the environment.
- *Responsible authority*: an authority responsible for implementing obligations within competences determined by this Law, in particular Ministry responsible for environment; provincial authority responsible for environment; responsible authority of the Local Self-Governments (LSG) unit.
- *Operator:* any natural or legal person that, in accordance with regulations, manages the installation or an establishment or controls it or is authorized for making economic decisions in the field of technical functioning of an installation.
- *Seveso installation*, that is, installation where activities are performed in which dangerous substance is present or may be present in equal or higher quantities than prescribed (hereinafter, the Seveso installation): a technical unit within the establishment where dangerous substances are produced, utilized, stored or handled. Installation shall include all equipment, buildings, pipelines, machines, tools, internal tracks and warehouses, wharfs, unloading ports for installations, piers, storehouses or similar structures, on water or land, which are necessary for the operation of installations.
- *Establishment:* the spatial unit under control of an operator where dangerous substances are present in one or several installations, including individual or common infrastructure or individual or common activities.
- *Requirements related to environmental quality:* a set of conditions and requirements that must be met at the specified time and on the specified area or in certain environmental media, in accordance with special regulations.

36. 'Public' has been defined in the same way in Law on Strategic Environmental Assessment (SEA), Law on Environmental Impact Assessment (EIA) and Law on Integrated Pollution Prevention and Control (IPPC), as one or several private or legal entities, their associations, organizations or groups.

The 'public concerned' is defined similarly in all three laws and it includes:

52. Article 1 of the Law on Amendment of the Environment Protection Law (EPL) (OJ RS, 36/09). By this amendment several new definitions have been introduced. For example: operator, Seveso installation, requirements related to the environmental quality, etc. In addition, by the Art. 1 of the Amendment on the EPL (OJ RS, 14/16) several new definitions have been introduced. For example: dangerous substance, waste, sludge, public authorities, environmental information, etc.

- 'public affected or likely to be affected by the operation of the installation[53] and execution of activities, including non-governmental organizations dealing with environmental protection and being registered with the competent authority' (IPPC);
- 'public affected or public likely to be affected by the plan or programme and/or having interest in decisions related to environmental protection, including non-government organizations involved in environmental protection and registered with the competent authority' (SEA);
- 'public affected by or likely to be affected by the project, including non-governmental organizations that promote environmental protection and are registered with the competent authority' (EIA).[54]

§2. Constitutional Provisions

37. The Constitution of the Republic of Serbia (2006) contains following six provisions dealing with the environment, stricto sensu: Article 74 (right to healthy environment), Article 83 (freedom of entrepreneurship), Article 88 (use of land), Article 97, point 9 (competences of the Republic of Serbia), Article 183, point 2 (competences of the APs) and Article 190, point 6 (competences of LSG).[55]

I. Right to Healthy Environment

38. From the point of view of human rights protection,[56] most important is provision of Article 74 of the Constitution. According to the first part of this Article, 'everyone shall have the right to healthy environment and the right to timely and full information about the state of environment'. But, it is also prescribed that 'everyone, especially the Republic of Serbia and autonomous provinces, shall be accountable for

53. 'Installation' is defined as a stationary technical unit where one or more activities are performed, for which special regulations have been determined and permit has been issued, as well as any other activity where there is a technical connection to the activities that are performed at the place and which, as a result, may cause emission and pollution (Art. 3, point10 of the EPL).
54. Amendment of the EPL in Art. 1, para. 2 have introduced definitions of the 'public concerned': 'public which is affected or may be affected by decision-making of the responsible authority or which has an interest therein, including citizen associations and social organizations engaged in the environmental protection, that are recorded with the responsible authority'.
55. OJ RS, No. 98/06.
56. On this subject *see* , A. Jerosimic (ed.), *Human Rights in Serbia 2007: Legal Provisions and Practice Compared to International Human Rights Standards*292–293(The Belgrade Centre for Human Rights 2008).

the protection of environment' and 'everyone shall be obliged to preserve and improve the environment'.[57]

39. EPL proclaims that one of the basic principles of the system of environmental protection is the 'principle of protection of right to healthy environment and access to justice'.[58]

II. Constitutional Competencies

40. The issue of competence for undertaking activities in the environmental field the Constitution regulates in a general way by defining competences of the Republic, APs and municipalities.[59]

A. Competencies of the Republic

41. It is prescribed by Article 97 that the Republic of Serbia organizes and provides for, *inter alia*:

(1) sovereignty, independence, territorial integrity and security of the Republic of Serbia, its international status and relations with other countries and international organizations;
(2) single market; legal status of business entities; system of performing particular economic and other activities; commodity reserves; monetary, banking, foreign exchange and customs system; international economic relations; system of foreign credit relations; fiscal system;
(3) sustainable development; system of protection and improvement of environment; protection and improvement of flora and fauna; production, trade and transport of arms, poisonous, inflammable, explosive, radioactive and other hazardous substances;
(4) system in areas of health care, social security, protection of war veterans and the disabled, protection of children, education, culture and protection of cultural goods, sport, public information, system of public services;

57. It is interesting to compare provisions of the Article with Art. 1 of the 1998 Convention on Access to Environmental Information, Public Participation in Decision-making and Access to Justice in Environmental Matters (Aarhus Convention). It is clear that there is a difference between the contents of the human right formulated in the Serbian Constitution and the Aarhus Convention. The difference is obvious at least in two elements. First, the Aarhus Convention stresses that the right belongs to both individuals of present and future generations. Second, the manner in which the right to sound environment is formulated in the Convention is more subtle. The right does not deal only with human health but with human wellbeing in wider sense. Because of these important differences, it could be concluded that the formulations in the Serbian Constitution is narrower than in the Convention. It could be a problem when it comes to the implementation of the Convention, and especially its third column-access to justice.
58. According to Art. 9, point 11, 'a citizen or groups of citizens, their associations, professional and other organizations shall be entitled to exercise their right to healthy environment before the competent authority or the court in accordance with the law'.
59. This issue is regulated in detail by various laws.

(5) development of the Republic of Serbia, policy and measures for spurring balanced development of particular areas of the Republic of Serbia, including the development of underdeveloped areas; organization and utilization of space; scientific and technological development;
(6) regime and security in all areas of transport.

B. Competencies of the APs

42. APs shall, according to Article 183, 'in accordance with the Constitution and their Statutes, regulate the competences, election, organization and work of bodies and services they establish'.

APs shall, in accordance with the Law, regulate the matters of provincial interest in the following fields:

- urban planning and development;
- agriculture, water economy, forestry, hunting, fishery, tourism, catering;
- spas and health resorts, environmental protection, industry;
- craftsmanship, road, river and railway transport and road repairs;
- organizing fairs and other economic events;
- education, sport, culture, health care and social welfare and public;
- informing at the provincial level.[60]

C. Competencies of the Municipality

43. The municipality shall, as prescribed by Article 190:

(1) regulate and provide for the performing and development of municipal activities;
(2) regulate and provide for the use of urban construction sites and business premises;
(3) be responsible for construction, reconstruction, maintenance and use of local network of roads and streets and other public facilities of municipal interest; regulate and provide for the local transport;
(4) be responsible for meeting the needs of citizens in the field of education, culture, health care and social welfare, child welfare, sport and physical culture;
(5) be responsible for development and improvement of tourism, craftsmanship, catering and commerce;
(6) be responsible for environmental protection, protection against natural and other disasters; protection of cultural heritage of the municipal interest;
(7) protection, improvement and use of agricultural land;
(8) perform other duties specified by the Law.[61]

60. *See also*, Law on Establishing Competencies of the APV (OJ RS, Nos 99/09 and 99/12 CC), and The Statute of The APV (OJ APV, No. 20/14). http://www.skupstinavojvodine.gov.rs/Strana.aspx?s=statut&j=EN (13 Jun. 2017).
61. *See also*, Law on Self-Government (OJ RS, Nos 129/2007, 83/14 and 101/16).

D. Other Relevant Constitutional Provisions

44. According to Article 83, 'entrepreneurship is permitted' but it can be restricted by the Law, 'for the purpose of protection of people's health, environment and natural goods and security of the Republic of Serbia'.

45. In accordance with Article 87 natural resources, goods which are stipulated by the Law as goods of public interest and assets used by the bodies of the Republic of Serbia shall be State assets. Natural and legal entities may obtain particular rights on particular goods in public use, under the terms and in a manner stipulated by the Law.[62] Natural resources shall be utilized under the terms and in a manner stipulated by the Law.

According to Article 88, 'utilization and management of agricultural land, forestland and municipal building land on private assets shall be permitted'. The Law may restrict the models of utilization and management in order to eliminate the danger of causing damage to environment or prevent violation of rights and legal interests of other persons.

§3. Strategic Framework of National Environmental Policy and Environmental Law

46. The strategic framework of national environmental policy and environmental law has been defined in a number of strategic documents. The importance of these documents stems from their strategic character, from the point of view of general framework, goals, instruments, etc. They are guidelines for implementation of different activities. The mentioned activities include identification of the most important problems as well as projection of further development, drafting, adoption and implementation of relevant legal regulations.

47. Strategic planning in the environmental field is prescribed by the *EPL (2004)*. According to Article 12 of the Law:

> Sustainable usage and protection of natural values shall be provided for within the Strategy for spatial development of the Republic and within the National strategy of sustainable use of natural resources and goods. National strategy of sustainable utilization of natural resources and goods (hereinafter, National strategy) shall be enacted by the Government for the period of minimum ten years.

48. The Action Plan is a short-term instrument for the implementation of the National Programme. The Action Plan elaborates on regulatory and institutional activities, monitoring activities, studies, preparation of project documentation, economic and financial instruments, information, education, management and capital investment (Article 65).

62. Foreigners may obtain a concession right for natural resources and goods, as well as other rights stipulated by the Law (Art. 85, para. 2).

49. Serbia has adopted a number of basic strategic documents relevant to the environment, as for example Biodiversity Strategy of the Republic of Serbia for the period 2011–2018 (2011), National Environmental Approximation Strategy for the Republic of Serbia (2011), National Strategy for Incorporation of the Republic of Serbia into Clean Development Mechanism (CDM)–Waste Management, Agriculture and Forestry Sector (2010), National implementation plan for implementation of the Stockholm convention (2010), Strategy on safety and health at work in the Republic of Serbia for the period 2009–2012 (2009), Strategy of introducing cleaner production in the Republic of Serbia (2009), National Strategy on Sustainable Development (2008), Spatial Plan (2011), National Waste Management Strategy for period 2010–2019 (2010), Water Management Strategy on the territory of the Republic of Serbia until 2034 (2016), Agriculture and Rural Development Strategy of the Republic of Serbia for the period 2014–2024 (2014), Energy Development Strategy of the Republic of Serbia until 2025, with projection until 2030 (2015), Mineral Resources Management Strategy until 2030 (2015), Strategy of Safety and Health at Work for the period 2013–2017 (2013), Nuclear Safety and Security Programme (2014), Strategy for Development of Forestry (2006), Poverty Reduction Strategy (2003), Strategy for Development of Tourism (2006), Strategy for Official Statistics (2006), Public Administration Reform Strategy (2014), Strategy on Science and Technology Development for the period 2016–2020 (2016), etc.[63]

50. It should be added that the National Environmental Protection Programme (NEPP) has also been adopted (OJ RS No. 12/2010).[64] The adoption of a number of other environmental strategic documents is planned in the short term (by the end of 2012). These are:

- Sustainable Use of Natural Assets and Resources Strategy based on the provisions of the EU Framework Strategy on Sustainable Use of Natural Resources (by the end of 2010);
- the National Children's Environment and Health Action Plan (CEHAP);
- the First Framework Action Plan related to Environmental Education for Sustainable Development.

63. For the full list of strategies adopted by the Serbian Government, *see* , http://www.srbija.gov.rs/vesti/dokumenti_sekcija.php?id=45678.

64. At http://www.ekoplan.gov.rs/en/upload-centar/dokumenti/zakoni-i-nacrti-zakona/english/1.1%20National%20Environment%20Protection%20Programme.pdf. NEPP defines fundamental principles of environmental protection and sustainable development, as well as priorities for the institutional framework. One of the goals is development of a comprehensive legal environmental system, by adoption of and by improvement of law enforcement monitoring and of the judiciary system.

§4. Principles of the Environmental Protection in Serbia

51. Although it is not quite clear what concrete practical implications it should (or could) have,[65] the basic principles of the environmental protection in Serbia have been formulated in several basic legal Acts and strategic documents. The principles are, for example, mentioned in the EPL, SEA, IPPC, Law on Waste Management, Water Law, Law on Nature Protection, as well as in the National Environmental Strategy, in the NSDS, in the National Waste Management Strategy,[66] in the Water Management Strategy of the territory of the Republic of Serbia until 2034, in the Mineral Resources Management Strategy of the Republic of Serbia until 2030, in the Energy Development Strategy of the Republic of Serbia until 2025, with projection until 2030, etc.

52. It could be said that basic meanings have the principles defined in the EPL. In its Article 9 of the Law the following eleven principles are mentioned:

(1) Integration principle.
(2) Principle of prevention and cautiousness.
(3) Principle of natural value preservation.
(4) Principle of sustainable development.
(5) Principle of polluters' and legal successors' liability.
(6) Principle 'polluter pays'.
(7) Principle 'user pays'.
(8) Principle of subsidiary liability.
(9) Principle of incentives.
(10) Principle of public information and participation.
(11) Principle of protection of right to healthy environment and access to justice.

53. The development and implementation of the NEPP is based on the following policy principles:

- Principle of sustainable development.
- Principle of preservation of natural values.
- Principle of cross-sectoral integration.
- Polluter-pays principle.
- User-pays principle.
- Incentives principle.
- Principle of shared responsibility.

65. On this subject *see* , P.W. Birnie & A.E. Boyle, *International Law and Environment*24–27(Oxford University Press 2002).

66. National Waste Management Strategy, differs 'critical principles of waste management' and 'other principles'. Critical principles, which have to be considered during the definition and implementation of, waste management planning are Principle of sustainable development, Principle of closeness, and regional approach to waste management, Principle of precaution, Principle 'the polluter pays', Principle of waste management hierarchy, Principle of implementation of the most practical environmental options, Principle of producer's liability. *National Waste Management Strategy* (Belgrade: Government of the Republic of Serbia, 2003), 9–11.

- Subsidiarity principle.
- Prevention and precautionary principle.
- Awareness-raising principle.
- Access to information and public participation principle.
- Principle of liability of polluter or his/her legal successor.
- Principle of the right to a healthy environment and access to justice.
- Principle of the approximation with the EU environmental acquis.[67]

54. The NSDS is based on the following principles:

- Inter- and intra-generations solidarity.
- Open and democratic society-public participation in decision-making.
- Knowledge as a factor of development.
- Inclusion in social processes.
- Integration of environmental issues in other sectoral policies.
- The precautionary principle.
- The polluter/user-pays principle, full inclusion of environmental costs in the product price.
- Sustainable production and consumption.[68]

55. The principle of the sustainable development has become, under the influence of contemporary tendencies in environmental law, a leading principle included in all new legal regulation. In addition the principle is often mentioned in various strategic documents, but it is not quite clear whether the content and the meaning of this principle are properly interpreted. The way in which principle of sustainable development is applied in practice can be discussed in various ways.

It is formulated in the EPL in following way:

> the sustainable development is harmonized system of technical/technological, economic and social activities in the overall development, where the natural and acquired values of the republic are used in a cost efficient and reasonable manner, in order to preserve and enhance the quality of the environment for the present and future generations. The system of environmental protection shall be implemented through promulgation and implementation of decisions producing balance between the environmental protection and the interest of economic development (Article 9, paragraph 4).[69]

56. Development of the new environmental legal regulation in Serbia is based on several principles of environmental protection with common economic incentives idea. *EPL* contains the 'polluter pays' principle, 'user pays' principle, principle of

67. NEPP, 8–12.
68. NSDS, 16–17.
69. *See* , D. Todic, Održivi razvoj i principi politike i prava životne sredine [*Sustainable Development and Principles of Environmental Policy and Law*] *Pravni život*, br. 9/2007, 429–443.

incentives, principle of polluters' and legal successors' liability, etc. The whole Part VI of the Law (Articles 83–101) is dedicated to economic instruments.[70]

A more radical novelty is also provisions concerning the formation of Environmental Protection Fund (Articles 90–100).[71]

70. Besides that, several other charges and taxes, relevant for environmental protection, have been prescribed by other legal regulations (in the fields of water, forestry, fishing, building, transport, etc.). In the framework of the Law on IPPC, it is planned that pollution charges for the 250 potential IPPC industrial installations will be progressively increased from 20% to 100% as of 2016.

71. Law on Amendment of the EPL (2009) have introduced new provisions related to the Fund. Besides that, it should be kept in mind that *EPL* Fund has been adopted (OJ RS, No. 72/09). This Law was repealed (25 Sep. 2012) by the Law on Repealing the Law on the Fund for Environmental Protection (OJ RS, No. 93/12). However, Green Fund of the Republic of Serbia is established as a budgetary fund for recording the funds intended for financing the preparation, implementation and development of programs, projects and other activities in the field of conservation, sustainable use, protection and improvement of the environment – Law on Amendment of the EPL (19 Feb. 2016, OJ RS, No. 14/16). Green Fund is established for an indefinite period of time (Art. 90,Paras 1 and 2).

Chapter 3. Historical Background of Environmental Law

57. In a broader sense, some provisions regulating the environmental protection, or at least elements of it, could be found in Serbia already in middle ages. There were, for instance, some such provisions in the Emperor Dushan's Code from fourteenth century, as well as in legal Acts of some coastal cities (in the Middle Ages Serbia was a maritime State).[72]

58. Research on biodiversity has a long tradition in Serbia. In a series of articles and monographs, a known Serbian scientist Josip Pancic (1860, 1867, 1869, 1874 and 1883) initially described Serbian flora and fauna. His classical work '*Flora Principatus Serbiae*', initiated intensive floristic investigations. As a result of accumulated knowledge, the ten volume edition of '(vascular) Flora of SR Serbia' was published (Josifovic, 1970–1977; Saric, 1986).[73]

59. The first legal Acts with some provisions concerning the environment (although the term 'environment' was, of course, not used in that time) were enacted in Serbia in the nineteenth century. These earlier regulations were actually linked with the management of public hygiene. For example, there is a provision in one decree from the year 1841 dealing with obligations to keep cleanliness in Belgrade.

60. Modernization of Belgrade was one of the main issues in this period of Serbian history. The first Serbian urbanist Emilijan Josimovic gave special contribution to this process (regulation of streets, connecting Kalemegdan fortress with city centre, choosing new site for the botanical garden, etc.). In this period the first legal regulations, which according to modern methodology could be regarded as environmental regulations, were adopted. So, as examples, could be mentioned following by-laws:

- Regulation No. N. 561, C. 1098, from 22 July 1839 regarding inspection over timber cutting.
- Decision of the Council from 1 April 1840 concerning the above-mentioned regulation, signed by Serbian duke M.M. Obrenovic, by which fine was prescribed for those who cut timber without permit.
- Order of M.M. Obrenovic, Duke of Serbia, No. 640 of 25 May 1840, concerning hunting regime of specific species of game: deer and does, rabbits, wild goats and certain species of birds.
- Regulation No. 1640 of 17 September 1840 on ban of use of poisons for fishing and punishment of offenders.
- The Law on Waters and Their Use from 26 December 1878.
- The Law on Fruit Growing of 3 July 1878.
- The Law on Hunting of 16 July 1898.
- Regulation of Ministry of Interior Affairs No. 12.625 of 1 June 1901, on punishment of illegal hunters.

72. *See* , Strategija razvoja sumarstva Republike Srbije (Forestry Development Strategy of the Republic of Serbia). http://www.srbija.gov.rs/vesti/dokumenti_sekcija.php?id=45678, 4.

73. B. Karadžic (ed.), *Environment in Serbia – An Indicator-Based Review* 135(Ministry of Science and Environmental Protection, 2007). On this subject *see also* M.M. Janković, Razvoj ekološke misli u Srbiji [*Development of Ecological Thought in Serbia*] (Beograd: Ekocentar, 1996).

- The Law on Forestry of 23 March 1904.
- Rules on cutting and trading with timber No. S 23.638 – 30 September 1901.
- Regulation of the Ministry of Economy No. S 7107 from 4 April 1904 on supervision over forests and prosecution of offenders.
- Regulation of Ministry of Interior Affairs No. P 18630 from 13 July 1904 banning cutting monastery wood without permission.

61. Legal regulations of the environment were already developed to a certain extent in the new Kingdom of Serbs, Croat and Slovenes created in 1918 (which later became the Kingdom of Yugoslavia). The Kingdom of Yugoslavia had a number of legal sources concerning environment and related fields, as the following for example:

- Regulations on supervision of drinking water (OJ of the Kingdom of Yugoslavia, No. 17-VI, 24 January 1931).
- The Law on Use of Hydro-energy (OJ of the Kingdom of Yugoslavia, No. 154-LI, 10 July 1931).
- The Law on Convention Regulating Definitive Status of the Danube River (OJ of the Kingdom of Yugoslavia, No. 180-LXI, 20 August 1931).
- The Law on Hunting (OJ of the Kingdom of Yugoslavia, No. 285-XCIII, 5 December 1931).
- The Law on Maritime Fishing (OJ of the Kingdom of Serbs, Croats and Slovenes, No. 243-XXXIII, 31 October 1922).
- The Law on Forestry (OJ of the Kingdom of Yugoslavia, No. 307-CXXXI, 31 December 1929).
- Regulations on forestation of deforested land therein and quick send (OJ of the Kingdom of Yugoslavia, No. 208-LXXII, 12 September 1930).
- Law on Control on Seeds of Cultivated Plants in Import and Internal Marketing (OJ of the Kingdom of Serbs, Croats and Slovenes, No. 125, 10 June 1922).
- The Law on the Protocol on the Ban of Use in War of Suffocating, Poisons and Similar Gases and Bacteriological Means, etc. (OJ of the Kingdom of Serbs, Croats and Slovenes, No. 117-L, 21 May 1929).
- Regulation on development of regulatory plans (OJ of the Kingdom of Yugoslavia, No. 152-LXIX, 16 July 1932).

62. It must be added, however, that the Northern part of Serbia (APV) was until 1918 a part of Austro-Hungarian Empire, so the legislation concerning the environmental protection (and closely related fields) which was until 1918 in force in the Empire was at that time in force in Vojvodina as well. Some other territories also belonged until 1912 to the Ottoman Empire and had special legal regulation in matters of the environmental protection and related issues.

63. After the Second World War the Federal Peoples Republic of Yugoslavia was formed (the name which was later changed to Socialist Federal Republic of Yugoslavia). Its whole legal system was in the beginning, more or less, based on the Soviet Marxist model, but later (from 1950) it evolved with the introduction of self-government and steadily rising autonomy of the Republics. The 1974 Constitution introduced practically elements of State sovereignty for all republics and transferred most of the Federal competencies, including those relevant to environmental protection, to the Republics, which had their own ministries or other bodies competent for the environmental protection.

The same Constitution was, it should be added, one of first Constitutions in the world introducing provisions regarding the environment (for instance, Articles 87, 192, 193, etc.). The Federation had only certain competencies in the field of the environment (coordinated by the Committee of the Federal Government for the environment and spatial regulation). The Socialist Federal Republic of Yugoslavia (FRY) had relatively developed environmental regulation on both federal and republican levels; was a contracting party to many international treaties; and was active in the UNEP and other organizations in the environmental field.

64. The FRY (Serbia and Montenegro) was proclaimed in 1992, after the disintegration of the former Yugoslavia. The competences in the field of the environment were divided between the Federation in which a Ministry for the environment was formed (later merged with some other institutions into the Ministry for development, science and the environment and later into the Ministry for Health and Social Politics), and the Republics.

The Serbian APs Kosovo-Metohija has, after 1999 NATO intervention, a special status according to the UNSC Resolution 1244. There are many open issues and such a situation has an impact on the various environmental related issues in Serbia and Kosovo*.

65. The first Serbian Ministry for environmental protection was formed in accordance of the Law on Ministries (Article 22a, OJ RS, No. 44/91, 25 July 1991). The first specific law regulating environmental protection in contemporary sense of the word was adopted in 1991. That was the EPL (OJ of RS, Nos 66/91, 83/92, 67/93, 48/94 and 53/95). The new EPL (OJ RS, Nos 135/04, 36/09 – other law and 72/09 – other law) was adopted on 21 December 2004 and significantly amended on 19 May 2009 (OJ of RS, No. 36/09), and on 19 February 2014 (OJ of RS, No. 14/16).

66. In 2003, the FRY was transformed in to a semi-confederal State Union of Serbia and Montenegro which lasted until 2006 when Serbia and Montenegro became independent States.

Chapter 4. The Role of Governmental Institutions in the Shaping and Administration of Environmental Law and Policy

§1. The Governmental Institutions and Their Competences

67. A number of different institutions are involved in the shaping and administration of environmental law and policy in Serbia and one of the most serious problems is their cooperation and coordination. Depending on the issue and relevant legal regulations different institutions are competent in different cases.

Competence in the field of environment is divided vertically and horizontally among several different authorities (Assembly, Government, Ministries and other Institutions). Provisions concerning the competence have been prescribed by the Constitution of the Republic of Serbia[74] and by the following legal Acts:

- Law on Ministries (OJ RS, Nos 44/14, 14/15, 54/15 and 96/15).
- Law on State Administration (OJ RS, Nos 79/05, 101/07, 95/10 and 99/14).
- Law on State Servants (OJ RS, Nos 79/05, 81/05, and corr. 83/05, 64/07, 67/07, 116/08, 104/09 and 99/14).
- Law on Government (OJ RS, No. 55/05 and corr. 71/05, 101/07, 65/08, 16/11, 68/12 – CC, 72/12, 74/12 – corr. CC, 7/14 – CC and 44/14).
- Rules of Procedure of the Government (OJ RS, Nos 100/05, 61/06, 69/08, 88/09, 33/10, 69/10, 20/11, 37/11, 30/13 and 76/14).
- Law on Certain Competences of the AP (OJ RS, Nos 99/09 and 67/12CC).
- Law on Local Self-Government (OJ RS, Nos 129/2007, 83/14 and 101/16).
- Law on General Administrative Procedure (OJ FRY, Nos 33/97 and 31/01 and OJ RS, No. 30/10), etc.

68. The highest legislative body in the Republic of Serbia is the National Assembly.[75] It consists of 250 Members of Parliament (MPs), who are elected by free and secret ballot to a four-year term of office. The National Assembly adopts legal Acts proposed by the Government[76] in different areas, including the environment. It has nineteen standing committees, including the Committee for Environmental Protection.[77]

---

74. *See* , the part devoted to 'constitutional provisions'.
75. *See* , Art. 98 of the Constitution of the RS. For more information *see* http://www.parlament.gov.rs/national-assembly.467.html*See also*, Law on National Assembly (OJ RS, No. 9/10).
76. *See* , http://www.srbija.gov.rs/?change_lang=en.
77. *See* , Art. 46 of the Assembly's Rules of Procedure, OJ RS, No. 20/12 http://www.parlament.gov.rs/national-assembly/important-documents/rules-of-procedure/working-bodies-of-the-national-assembly.1355.html.

69. The President of the Republic[78] proposes to the National Assembly the candidate for Prime Minister Elect, having heard the opinion of representatives of elected party lists.

70. According to the Constitution, the Government's competences are required to do the following:

(1) Define and pursue policies.
(2) Enforce laws and other general acts of the National Assembly.
(3) Adopt decrees and other general acts in order to enforce laws.
(4) Propose laws and other general acts to the National Assembly and provide opinion on them when other proponent submits them.
(5) Direct and harmonize the work of ministries and other bodies of public administration and supervise their work.
(6) Perform other duties set forth by the Constitution and law. The Government[79] is accountable to the Parliament for the Republic of Serbia's policies, for law enforcement and for the work of public administration bodies.

71. The Government's term of office lasts until the end of term of the Parliament that elected it, and starts from the day of taking oath before the Parliament. That means that the Government's term always ceases along with that of MPs who elected it – be it with the expiry of their term, that is, after four years or with the disbanding of the National Assembly. Besides the above-mentioned, the Government's term can also cease before the end of the Parliament's term in cases of a no-confidence vote, Prime Minister's resignation and failure to vote confidence. Non-confidence vote for the Government or an individual member can be requested by a minimum of sixty MPs. The National Assembly accepts the proposal of non-confidence vote if more than half of the MPs vote for it.[80]

The Government with the ceased term, until a new Government is elected, can perform only current and urgent duties set forth by law.[81]

72. The Prime Minister leads and guides the Government, takes care of unity of its political actions, harmonizes the work of its members, represents it and calls for and chairs its sessions. The Prime Minister can give mandatory directives and special

78. *See* , http://www.predsednik.rs/default.asp?lng=eng.
79. The Government consists of the Prime Minister, one or more deputies and ministers. The Prime Minister leads and guides the Government's work, takes care of its even political activities, harmonizes the work of Government members and represents the Government. The ministers are accountable to the Prime Minister, Government and Parliament for their work and situation in the scope of their ministries' competences.
80. The government can request vote on its confidence. The National Assembly accepts proposal of confidence vote if more than half of all MPs vote for it. If the National Assembly does not vote for confidence to the government, the government's term ceases. The Prime Minister can offer his/her resignation to the National Assembly. The government's term ceases on the day of noting the Prime Minister's resignation.
81. A government member's term of office can cease before the time of its duration with noting of their resignation, no-confidence vote in the Parliament and relieving from office by the Parliament, at the Prime Minister's proposal.

assignments to other Government members, in accordance with the Government's programmes and policies. The Prime Minister takes decisions[82] and provides solutions.

73. A minister can submit to the Government proposals to regulate issues under the Government's and Parliament's jurisdiction and demand that the Government take a stand on an issue from his/her competences. The minister is obliged to inform the Government of everything of consequence for the Government's policy and decision-making. The minister is responsible for implementation of the Government's programme and policy, for decisions and actions that he/she has taken or failed to take and for the execution of mandatory directives and special assignments the Prime Minister allotted to him.

74. A Government member cannot perform any other public function in a State body, or any authority of AP, local council, city, the city of Belgrade, nor can he/she deal with any activity unmatchable with the duty of Government member, nor create a possibility of conflict between public and private interest.

75. According to the Law on Ministries (OJ RS, Nos 44/14, 14/15, 54/15 and 96/15),[83] the main ministry for the environmental protection is the Ministry of Agriculture and Environmental Protection (MAEP) (Article 5). It has, besides activities concerning spatial planning and mining, the following responsibilities:

- Management of the system for environmental protection and sustainable use of natural resources (air, water, land, minerals, forests, fish, and wild plant and animal species).
- Preparation of strategic documents, plans and programmes or research work.
- Environmental protection measures in spatial planning and building.
- EIA and environmental permitting.
- Monitoring of the state of the environment, management of the information system for environmental protection.
- Inspection for environmental protection and sustainable use of resources.
- Nature protection: identification of potential nature conservation areas.
- Establishment and management of natural areas remarkable for the Republic.
- Climate change and ozone layer protection.
- Protection against noise and vibrations.

82. Decisions taken by the Prime Minister are published in the 'Official Journal of the Republic of Serbia'.

83. By the 2016 EPL Amendment definition of the 'organ of public authority' has been introduced. 'The organ of public authority is the authority responsible for the implementation of the obligations under authorizations under this Law, as follows: – the ministry responsible for the environment; – provincial authority responsible for environmental protection; – the competent authority of the local government; – other state body, territorial autonomy, local authorities and organizations entrusted with public authority;–natural or legal persons performing public functions and exercising public powers, including specific duties, activities or services in relation to the environment, as well as any other natural or legal persons performing public functions, or providing public services relating to the environment, and are under their control; – a legal entity established by the state authorities, territorial autonomy, local authorities and organizations entrusted with public authority, or which is funded in its entirety, or predominantly from the budget.' (Art. 3, point 29a). It seems that the inspiration for this definition is found in the provisions of the Aarhus Convention.

- Protection against ionizing and non-ionizing radiation, chemicals, waste and harmful materials in production, trade, transportation, storage and disposal.
- Preparation of geological research for sustainable use of resources and ground waters.
- Transboundary movement of wastes and endangered species of wild flora and fauna.
- Transboundary air and water pollution.
- International cooperation in the field of environment.

76. Another important body is the Environmental Protection Agency (EPA),[84] established by Article 4 of the Law on Changes and Additions of the Law on Ministries (OJ RS, No. 19/04). It is competent for following: coordination and management of the national environmental information system; collection of environmental data and their systematization, data processing, reporting on the state of the environment, participation in the implementation of national environmental policy; development of methods of environmental data processing and of their assessment; collection of data related to the 'Best Available Techniques'(BAT) and their practical application; cooperation with the European Environmental Agency (EEA) and with the European Environment Information and Observation Network (EIONET), etc.

77. The following ministries and institutions have also certain competencies in the field of environment:

- Ministry of Mining and Energy.[85]
- Ministry of Public Administration and LSG.[86]
- Ministry of Health.[87]
- Ministry of Economy.[88]
- Ministry of Labour, Employment, Veteran and Social Policy.[89]
- Ministry of Interior.[90]
- Ministry of Culture, and Information.[91]
- Ministry of Education, Science and Technological Development.[92]
- Customs Administration.[93]
- Republic Hydro-Meteorological Service.[94]
- Institute for Nature Conservation.[95]
- Agency for Protection against Ionizing radiation and Nuclear Safety of Serbia.[96]

---

84. At http://www.sepa.gov.rs/index.php.
85. At http://www.mre.gov.rs/latinica/index.php.
86. At http://www.mduls.gov.rs/english/index.php.
87. At http://www.zdravlje.gov.rs/index.php?.
88. At http://www.privreda.gov.rs/?lang=lat.
89. At http://www.minrzs.gov.rs/cms/en/home.
90. At http://www.mup.gov.rs/wps/portal/en/ministry.
91. At http://www.kultura.gov.rs/en/.
92. At http://www.mpn.gov.rs/?lng=lat.
93. At http://www.carina.rs/en/Pages/default.aspx.
94. At http://www.hidmet.gov.rs/index_eng.php.
95. At http://www.zzps.rs/novo/index.php?jezik=en&strana=naslovna.
96. At http://www.srbatom.gov.rs/srbatom/#.

- Institute of Public Health of Serbia.[97]
- Statistical Office of the Republic of Serbia.[98]
- Republic Agency for Spatial Planning.[99]
- Institute of Soil, Belgrade.[100]
- Institute of Field and Vegetable Crops, Novi Sad.[101]
- Institute of Forestry.[102]
- Institute of Nuclear Sciences, Vinca.[103]
- Serbian Institute of Occupational Health,[104] etc.

78. The Directorate for Water deserves special attention. It is a part of the MAEP, and it is responsible for the development of water management policy, use of water resources, provision of water supply, flood protection, protection and rational consumption of water, monitoring and maintenance of national and transboundary water courses, as well as other tasks defined by law.

The public water management enterprise 'Srbijavode' manages water resources in Serbia, and public water management enterprise 'Vode Vojvodine' has similar role in the APV.

79. An important role is also played by the Institute for Nature Protection, which is responsible for protection of nature and protected areas (parks, nature reserves, wild flora and fauna habitats, etc.) and for supervision of these natural values.

80. The Chemicals Agency was founded in accordance with Article 5 of the Law on Chemicals (OJ RS, No. 36/09) as an independent, developmental, specialized and regulatory organization that performs public authorizations with the aim to provide administrative capacities for quality, efficient and safe management of chemicals and biocidal products.[105]

81. Pursuant to Article 5 of the Law on Ionizing Radiation Protection and Nuclear Safety (www.sepa.gov.rs/index.php RS, Nos 36/09 and 93/12), the Serbian Agency for Ionizing Radiation Protection and Nuclear Safety was established as an independent regulatory body in compliance with the Law on Public Agencies (OJ RS, Nos 18/05 and 81/05 – corr.).

82. The Environment Protection Fund has been established in accordance with Article 90 of the EPL (OJ RS, Nos 135/2004, 36/09 and 72/09) for the purposes of

97. At http://www.batut.org.rs/index.php?lang=2.
98. At http://webrzs.stat.gov.rs/WebSite/.
99. At http://www.rapp.gov.rs/.
100. At http://www.soilinst.rs/.
101. At http://www.nsseme.com/en/.
102. At http://www.forest.org.rs/?sLang=en.
103. At http://www.vin.bg.ac.rs/index.php/en/.
104. At http://www.imrs.rs/.
105. The Chemicals Agency ceased to exist by the adoption of the Law amending the Law on chemicals, 25 Sep. 2012 (OJ RS, No. 93/12).

securing financial resources for encouragement of protection and improvement of environment in the Republic of Serbia.[106]

83. Several other institutions responsible for environmental monitoring also deserve to be mentioned. They are as follows:

- The Hydro-Meteorological Institute performs the functions of a hydro-meteorological service in the territory of the Republic of Serbia, including monitoring quality of the environment.
- The Public Health Institute monitors local air quality in urban areas, surface water quality in urban areas, drinking water quality and noise.
- The Public Forest Enterprises are responsible for the improvement and utilization of State-owned forests. The public management enterprise 'Serbia forest' manages forests in Serbia, and public water management enterprise 'Vojvodina forest' has similar role in the APV.
- The Directorate for Plant Protection controls production, import, trade, storage and application of plant protection agents.
- Statistical Office collects and process data relevant for the state of the environment (water, waste, air pollution, etc.).

I. Autonomous Provinces

84. One of the key aspects of system of environmental policy in Serbia is the role of the AP and local authorities in environmental management. The role is prescribed by the Law on Definition of Competencies of the Autonomous Province and by the Law on Local Self-Government. The competencies of the autonomous province, according to the Law on Definition of Competencies of the Autonomous Province (Article 25)[107] are as follows:

(1) to regulate, improve and ensure the environmental protection for the territory of APV;[108]

(2) to pass the Act of putting under protection the natural goods, in accordance with the Law regulating the nature protection;

106. '1,916,593,000 dinars (19.964.510 EUR) were invested for the purposes of protection and improvement of environment during the last three years through the activities of the Environment Protection Fund'. Answers to the European Commission's Questionnaire (AECQ), Chs 27 and 12. However, the Fund ceased to exist on 25 Sep. 2012 (OJ RS, No. 93/12). Later, on 19 Feb. 2016, the Green Fund of the Republic of Serbia as a budgetary fund was established – Amendments to EPL (OJ RS, No. 14/16).

107. Besides Art. 29 of the Law, a number of other Articles contain provisions concerning legal framework for competencies in different issues. For example, Art. 30 (Urban Planning), Art. 31 (Construction), Arts 36–40 (Mining and Power), Arts 41–49 (Agriculture), etc.

108. *See also* Art. 13 of the Statute of APV ('The AP of Vojvodina shall provide conditions for environmental protection and improvement and undertake measures for prevention and elimination of detrimental effects which endanger environment and represent a threat to human life and health').

(3) to enact the programme of environmental protection in its territory in compliance with the National Programme, the action and remediation plans and its interests and specificities;
(4) to enact plans and programmes for management of natural resources and goods, in accordance with the strategic documents;
(5) to control the use and protection of natural resources and goods in the territory of APV;
(6) to ensure continuous control and monitoring of the environmental situation and enact the monitoring programme for its territory which shall comply with the monitoring programme enacted by the Government for the period of two years;
(7) to ensure conditions for provision of measures and conditions of environmental protection, at the request of the body responsible for preparation and enactment of spatial and urban plans, based on the requirements and opinion of competent professional organizations;
(8) to participate in the process of preparation and enactment of spatial and urban plans and other plans;
(9) to enact the external plan for protection against accidents, the plan being an integral part of the response plan for emergency situations based on the competences under the regulation governing the field of protection and rescue;
(10) in case of an accident, declare the situation of environmental endangerment in the territory of APV, in accordance with the Law governing environmental protection;
(11) to establish the budget fund pursuant to the regulation governing the budget system, which shall be financed from the revenues collected in the territory of APV.[109]

109. According to the Art. 28 of the Law, APV, through its agencies shall perform the following tasks: (1) perform inspections in the field of environmental protection and take measures to prevent irregularities in the area, except for inspection control: in case of accident, in the field of ionizing radiation, in cross-border movement of goods, subject to jurisdiction of the Republican Inspectorate for Environmental Protection, and filled the conditions of the operator for permission to cross-border movement of goods (radioactivity, waste, poisons, substances that damage the ozone layer, protected plant and animal species), of certain facilities in the territory of Vojvodina, which will be defined by special Act; (2) Give consent to the study on the assessment of environmental impacts for projects for which approval for the building issued by the competent provincial authority for urban affairs; (3) Approves the report on strategic assessment of environmental impact for the territory of the APV; (4) issue of integrated permits for installations and activities for which permission and approval for the construction and start work, or the performance or the conduct of activities, issued by other competent provincial authority; (5) gives preliminary approval in the process of making foundation, plans and programs to protect and improve protected natural goods, flora and fauna, forests and water in the territory of the APV; (6) establish an information system for the protection and improvement of the environment as part of a unified information system of the Republic of Serbia; (7) Consider complaints against the municipal or city government in the territory of the APV; (8) Carried out inspection of the use and protection of natural assets and resources. Jobs in para. 1 of this Article shall be as committed.

85. APV, through its agencies, shall establish the Provincial Institute for Nature Conservation of Vojvodina Province, to perform the tasks of nature protection and protection of natural resources that is entirely in the territory of Vojvodina (Article 26).[110]

86. According to Article 19 of the Statute of APV (OJ APV, No. 20/14), the APV through its bodies shall enact the following legal and other Acts: the Statute as the supreme legal Act of the APV Provincial Assembly decisions for issues which, under the Constitution, fall directly within the scope of competences of the APV, or are defined under the law as issues relevant to the Province; provincial decrees, decisions, declarations, resolutions, rules of procedure, books of regulations, directives, orders, rulings, recommendations, conclusions and other Acts.[111]

II. Local Self-Government

87. The Constitution of the Republic of Serbia establishes the right to LSG. Citizens exercise this right directly, or through their freely elected representatives (Article 176, paragraph 1).

88. The Public Administration Reform Strategy in the Republic of Serbia (2014) proclaims, *inter alia*, that the key principles that the Government policy in this field are the same as the principles of the European Administrative Space, and include: (1) reliability and predictability and/or legal certainty, (2) openness and transparency of the administrative system and promotion of the participation of citizens and social entities in the work of the public administration, (3) accountability of public administration bodies, and (4) efficiency and effectiveness. In addition to the specified European principles, any further public administration reform (PAR) process in Serbia will rely on the principles that had already been promoted by the PAR Strategy, and these are: decentralization, depolitization, professionalization, rationalization and modernization.[112]

In accordance with this principle, following laws have recently been adopted:

- Law on Local Self-Government (OJ RS, Nos 129/07, 83/14 and 101/16).
- Law on Financing Local Self-Government (OJ RS, Nos 62/2006, 47/2011, 93/12, 99/13, 125/14, 95/15, 83/16, 91/16 and 104/16).
- Law on Local Elections (OJ RS, Nos 129/07, 34/10 CC and 54/2011).
- Law on Capital City (OJ RS, Nos 129/07, 83/14 and 101/16).
- Law on Territorial Organization of the Republic of Serbia (OJ RS, Nos 129/07 and 18/16).
- Law on Definition of Competencies of the Autonomous Province of Vojvodina (OJ RS, Nos 99/2009 and 67/12 CC).

89. The Law on Local Self-Government (OJ RS, Nos 129/07, 83/14 and 101/16) prescribes responsibilities of municipalities as follows: to enact development programmes,

110. At http://www.pzzp.rs/rs/en/ (13 Jun. 2017).
111. At http://www.skupstinavojvodine.gov.rs/Strana.aspx?s=statut&j=EN (13 Jun. 2017).
112. Public Administration Reform Strategy in the Republic of Serbia (OJ RS, Nos 9/14 and 42/14 – corr.), 11. *See* : http://www.mduls.gov.rs/english/reforma-javne-uprave.php (13 Jun. 2017).

city plans, budget and an annual financial report; to organize and ensure performance and development of public services (urban sanitation, maintenance of deposit sites, etc.) as well as to ensure organizational, financial and other conditions for their realization; to take care of environmental protection, to adopt programmes for utilization and protection of natural values and environmental protection programmes, that is, local actions and sensitization plans in accordance with strategic documents and interests, define tax for environmental protection and improvement, etc. (Article 20).

III. Competencies of the AP and LSG According to the Environmental Laws

90. Different environmental laws transfer certain jurisdiction to the AP and LSG.[113] By adoption of the second set of environmental laws in May 2009, decentralization of competences was continued through competence shifts to provincial and local levels.

The AP and LSG units are entrusted with the activities based on environmental laws which pertain to several aspects including following: EIA, SEA, IPPC, air protection (local network of measurement stations, air quality plans and short-term action plans), water management, waste management (inert and non-hazardous one), nature protection, chemicals management, protection from non-ionizing radiation, protection and sustainable management of fish resources, protection against noise (acoustic zoning, development of strategic noise maps and action plans), spatial planning and building and so on.

A. *Law on Environmental Protection*

91. On the basis of Article 5 of EPL (OJ RS, Nos 135/04, 36/09, 72/09, 43/11CC and 14/16), for the implementation of environmental protection system, among other subjects, the LSG is responsible for any activity that changes or can change the state of and conditions in the environment, that is, for not taking environmental protection measures, in accordance with the Law.[114]

92. According to Article 13, the AP and LSG, within the competencies prescribed in the present and specific law, shall issue their respective plans and programmes of

113. In accordance with the Arts 4, 21 and 22 of the *Law on Local Self-governments* (OJ RS', Nos 129/07, 83/14 and 101/16), the Republic of Serbia may entrust by a law to LSG particular matters within its competency, such as enforcement of laws and regulations, and LSGs are obliged and responsible to carry out these tasks as entrusted in a quality and efficient manner. Also, based on Art. 78, para. 2 bodies of the Republic supervise the legality of the work and acts of LSG bodies, in accordance with the Constitution and the law. *See also* Arts 4, 5, 45, 46, 48, 51–56, 59, 73, 75, 86 and 90 of the Law on State Administration (OJ RS, Nos 79/05, 101/07, 95/10 and 99/14); as well as Arts 4, para. 3; 12, para. 11; 44, para. 2, point 16; 50, para. 3; and 54, para. 1 of the Law on Inspection (OJ RS, No. 32/15).

114. On the basis of Art. 9, Item 1 of EPL, bodies of LSG provide integration of protection and improvement of environment in all sectoral policies by implementation of mutually agreed plans and programs and implementation of regulations through a system of permits, technical and other standards and regulations, by funding, stimulation and other measures of environmental protection.

natural resources and property management in accordance with the strategic documents referred to in Article 12 of this Law and their specific requirements.[115]

93. The conditions for measures and conditions of environmental protection shall be issued by the Ministry, the AP body or LSG on the request of the authority in charge of plan preparation and passing, on the basis of conditions and measures of competent authorities (Article 34). The LSG shall be obliged to obtain the prior consent of the Ministry for the proposal for an Act to determine the status of endangered environment and priorities for rehabilitation and remediation for areas of local significance, and for areas of local significance in the territory of the AP, the consent of the responsible authority of the AP (Article 43).

94. In the case of accident, depending on its scope, within or outside the plant and estimated consequences, which may cause direct or deferred threat towards human health and environment, the state of endangerment of environment shall be proclaimed, and the public shall be informed of the measures taken. The state of endangerment referred to in paragraph 1 of this Article shall be proclaimed by the Ministry, namely the authority of the AP and LSG (Article 62).

95. The AP and LSG shall promulgate the programme for environmental protection in their territory, namely local action and rehabilitation plans, in accordance with the national programme and plans referred to in Articles 65 and 66 of this Law and their interest and specificities (Article 68). The AP, namely LSG shall adopt the programme of monitoring on its territory that must be in accordance with the programme referred to in paragraph 3 of this Article (Article 69).[116]

96. The AP and LSG shall be obliged to establish the budget fund in accordance with the law governing budget system (Article 100) and shall perform inspection, supervision of the implementation of tasks delegated by this Law and regulations adopted based on this Law (Article 109).[117]

B. Law on Environmental Impact Assessment

97. According to Article 2 of the Law on EIA (OJ RS, Nos 135/04 and 36/09) 'competent authority' means the authority responsible for carrying out the EIA procedure within the functions set forth by this Law, that is, the Ministry responsible for environmental protection matters (the Ministry) – for those projects for which the permit for project implementation is under the responsibility of the Republic authority; the provincial authority responsible for environmental protection matters – for those projects for which the permit for project implementation is under the responsibility of the authority of the AP; the LSG authority responsible for environmental protection

115. Article 12 of the Law refers to the Strategy of spatial development of the Republic of Serbia and the National Strategy of sustainable use of natural resources and goods.

116. The responsible authority of the AP and/or the responsible authority of the LSG shall submit data for preparation of the report, quarterly, to the EPA, in particular for the first, second and third quarter no later than two months after the elapse of the quarter, and for the last quarter by January 31 (Art. 76).

117. The responsible authority of the AP shall decide on the appeal against first instance decision of the responsible municipal, namely city authority from the territory of the AP, adopted in the course of performing delegated tasks (Art. 114).

matters – for those projects for which the permit for project implementation is under the responsibility of the LSG authority.

C. *Law on Strategic Environmental Assessment*

98. Article 3 of the Law on SEA (OJ RS, Nos 135/04 and 88/10) prescribes that 'authorities and organizations concerned' are the authorities and organizations of the Republic, AP and LSG authorities having interest, in accordance with their responsibilities, in the decision-making process related to environmental protection (point 4).

D. *Law on Integrated Pollution Prevention and Control*

99. Pursuant to the Law on Integrated Pollution Prevention and Control (OJ RS, Nos 135/04 and 25/15), the provincial authority responsible for environmental protection shall grant the permit in accordance with this Law for installations or activities for which permit or consent for construction and commencement of operation, or execution of activities were issued by other competent provincial authorities.[118]

100. The LSG authority responsible for environmental protection shall grant the permit in accordance with this Law for installations or activities for which permit or consent for construction and commencement of operation, or execution of activities were issued by other competent LSG authorities.[119]

E. *Law on Waste Management*

101. According to Article 20 of the Law on Waste Management (OJ RS, Nos 36/09, 88/10 and 14/16), the LSG must perform the following tasks, *inter alia*: (1) adopt local plan for waste management (in accordance with Articles 13 and 14), provide conditions and care of its implementation; (2) regulate, provide, organize and implement municipal waste management (Article 43, paragraphs 5 and 7 and Article 55, paragraph 6 – waste vehicles), and non-hazardous or inert waste on its territory, in accordance with the Law; (3) regulate the procedure of services payment in the area of municipal, non-hazardous and inert waste management in accordance with the Law; (4) issue permits in accordance with Article 60, paragraph 4 (for the city) and paragraph 5 (for the municipality); (5) give approvals and other documents pursuant to this Law; (6) keep records and submit data to the ministry; (7) at the request of the ministry or the competent body of the AP, provide opinion in the process of issuing permits in

---

118. The AP is entrusted with the task of inspection supervision over the installations and activities for which the permit is granted by the competent provincial authority in accordance with this Law.

119. The LSG unit is entrusted with the task of inspection supervision over the installations and activities for which the permit is granted by the competent LSG authority in accordance with this Law.

accordance with this Law; and (8) supervise and control measures of dealing with waste in accordance with this Law.[120]

102. The AP: (1) shall participate in the preparation of the Strategy and individual national waste management plans; (2) shall coordinate and perform waste management relevant to the AP, and shall monitor performance;[121] (3) shall grant approval on regional waste management plans on its territory; (4) shall issue permits, approvals, certificates and other acts in accordance with this Law;[122] (5) shall supervise and control waste handling measures on its territory in accordance with this Law;[123] and (6) shall perform other activities prescribed by the Law (Article 19).[124]

103. The AP shall adopt the Waste Management Plan for certain waste types relevant to the AP in accordance with the Strategy and national plan referred to in paragraph 3 of this Article (Article 11).[125]

F. Law on Packaging and Packaging Waste

104. In accordance with the Law on Packaging and Packaging Waste (OJ RS, No. 36/09), packaging waste from the Republic of Serbia is collected, transported, stored and treated under the terms and in the manner, prescribed by the Law which

120. Also, the LSG is obliged to determine by an Act the departments and bodies responsible for carrying out these tasks. Furthermore, based on Art. 97 Law on Waste Management, LSGs are obliged to draw up until May 2010 a list of unregulated landfills in their area which do not fulfil the requirements of this Law (Art. 97, item 1), i.e., until May 2011 to develop projects of remediation and recultivation of unregulated landfills, which is approved by the Ministry or AP (Art. 97, item 2).
121. In case of disagreement among LSG regarding the location of the waste management facility, the location decision, on the proposal of the Ministry, that is, the competent authority of the AP shall be brought by the Government. In case of construction of the facility for treatment and hazardous waste disposal, the Ministry shall decide on the location, in accordance with the law and upon obtaining the opinion of the LSG as well as of the AP regarding facilities constructed on its territory (Art. 34).
122. The AP shall be entrusted with issuance of permits for the collection, transportation, storage, treatment and disposal of waste for all activities performed on the territory of the AP and for all facilities for which the construction permit is issued by the competent authority of the AP (Art. 60).
123. The AP shall be entrusted with performance of inspection supervision over waste management activities completely carried out on the territory of the AP and over the operation of the waste management facility for which the competent authority of the AP issues a permit on the basis of this Law (Art. 84).
124. Once in two years the assembly of the AP shall consider the report on the implementation of regional and local plans on its territory (Art. 74).
125. The regional waste management plan may also be adopted in case of municipalities with less than 200,000 inhabitants in accordance with the previously drafted feasibility study on the adoption of the regional plan, for which the Ministry, that is, the competent authority of the AP, shall issue an approval (Art. 12).

regulates waste management, by the law which regulates public utilities and by this Law.[126]

G. Law on Air Protection

105. The Law on Air Protection (OJ RS, Nos 36/09and 10/13) entrusts the following tasks to the AP or LSG: within its competence established by law, provide monitoring of air quality (Article 9); for air quality monitoring the AP or LSG should establish a local network of measuring stations and/or measuring points; monitoring of air quality in the local network shall be conducted in accordance with the programme adopted by the competent authority of the AP or LSG for the respective territory, which must be in conformity with the programme referred to in Article 11, paragraph 3 of this Law (Article 15); perform monitoring of air quality through an authorized legal entity (Article 15); publicly announce and submit data on the results of air quality monitoring to the Agency by the fifteenth day in the month for the previous month, and annual report within sixty days after the end of the year for the previous year (Article 17); inform public, when concentration exceeds those established by law or exceed the concentration of certain pollutants hazardous to human health; provide air quality plan (Article 31); provide short-term action plans (Article 33); issue licenses for work of stationary sources of pollution (Article 39); perform inspection over the implementation of measures for protection of air pollution in buildings for which the competent body of the AP or LSG issues approval for the construction or uses permit (Article 56); the AP shall be entrusted inspection and supervision of activities over the implementation of measures related to air protection against pollution in objects for which the AP competent authority has issued construction and occupancy permits (Article 74); and the first-degree appeal to be filed against a ruling issued by competent authority of municipality, that is, city in the territory of the AP, shall be decided upon by competent authority of AP (Article 78).

H. Law on Nature Protection

106. Law on Nature Protection (OJ RS, Nos 36/09, 88/10, 91/10-corr. and 14/16) entrusts to the LSG the following tasks: initiate proclamation and proclaim protected areas, such as nature parks, nature monuments, as well as a region with exceptional features which are not of great cultural importance, and where the whole protected area is in the territory of the LSG; provide nature protection programme; submit report

126. The AP shall be in charge of controlling the supervision of the activities of packaging waste management on its territory. The inspection supervision shall be carried out by inspectors in charge of environmental protection in compliance with the Law on Waste Management and this Law (Art. 47).

on the state of nature in its area; and perform inspections of the implementation of this Law in protected areas proclaimed by the competent body of the LSG.[127]

I. Law on Chemicals

107. Law on Chemicals (OJ RS, Nos 36/09, 88/2010, 92/2011, 93/2012 and 25/2015) entrusts to the LSG with the following tasks: issue licenses for conducting of turnover activities, particularly for hazardous chemicals to dealer who is not an importer, manufacturer or future user, as well as grant permission for the use of particularly hazardous chemicals; and perform inspection of tasks entrusted by this Law (Article 67, paragraph 2).

J. Law on the Protection from Non-ionizing Radiation

108. According to the Law on the Protection from Non-ionizing Radiation (OJ RS, Nos 36/09 and 93/12) the programme of systematic testing of non-ionizing radiation levels is prepared by the Ministry in collaboration with the AP competent authority.

127. The habitat and landscape of exceptional characteristics inside of which there is no cultural good of exceptional significance, if the entire area is located within the territory of the AP; as well as a natural park with its entire area located in the territory of two or more LSG in the territory of the AP, is declared as protected area by the competent authority of the AP, according to the previously acquired consent by the Ministry and the previously acquired opinions of the competent ministries (Art. 41). The competent authority of environment protection in the AP, and/or LSG, give consent to the plan for managing the protected area, and the annual programme for the previous year and the annual management programme for the following year that has to be delivered before Dec. 15 of the current year (Art. 54). The competent authority of environment protection in the AP, and/or LSG gives consent to the rulebook on interior order and stewardship (Art. 56). The AP or LSG are obliged to pay the compensation for prohibition or restriction of usage rights (Art. 63). The competent authority of the AP and/or the competent authority of the LSG, shall establish fulfilment of the conditions for manager's performance of operations of protection, improvement, promotion and sustainable development of protected natural asset in the manager selection procedure. The selection of the manager shall be carried out on the basis of a vacancy announcement, and if such selection is not possible, the manager shall be determined or appointed by the decision on the declaration (Art. 67). Financing of the protected area (Art. 69) and activities of the Provincial Institute for Nature Protection (Art. 103) are under competencies of the AP. The medium-term programme for protection of natural goods is to be approved by the Government, and the annual programme for protection of natural goods is to be approved by the Ministry, i.e., by the competent authority of AP (Art. 104). Nature protection organizations shall submit the report on implementation of medium-term and annual programmes for protection of natural goods to the Ministry, i.e., to the competent authority of AP (Art. 104). The competent authority of AP and LSG, in accordance with the Government Strategy on Nature and Natural Values Protection, should adopt the programmes on nature protection, for the period of ten years (Arts 111 and 113). The AP i.e., LSG shall prepare nature performance reports for their territories, which shall be submitted to the Ministry (Art. 114). Competent authority of the AP supervises over legality of Provincial Nature Conservation Institute's work (Art. 118). The AP shall be entrusted with performance of inspection supervision over the application of provisions contained in this Law in protected areas which are located on the AP territory (Art. 119).

The Republic or AP are obliged to provide funding for the implementation of the programme (Article 5).[128]

109. The AP competent authority, by decision, determines fulfilment of conditions for persons who may utilize the non-ionizing radiation sources of special interest (Article 6); the AP competent authority, by decision, determines fulfilment of conditions for persons who can perform testing of non-ionizing radiation sources of special interest, and may also revoke the authorization (Article 10); the industrial company, the company, legal entity or entrepreneur, or the operator, are obliged to inform the competent authority of the Republic, AP or LSG about the special event immediately, and within twenty-four hours (Article 12); the testing of non-ionizing radiation exposure, on the request of the AP competent authority, shall be performed a special testing financed by the same authority, except in cases where determination is by measuring irregularities in the work or where the prescribed limits of broadcasting are exceeded, in which case the costs are paid by the owner of the radiation emitter (Article 13); provincial inspection for inspecting the non-ionizing radiation sources in the territory of AP, except for those for which approval for the construction and starting is issued by the competent authority of LSG, in which case LSG inspection is competent (Article 14).[129]

K. Law on Noise Protection

110. According to the Law on Noise Protection (OJ RS, Nos 36/09 and 88/10) the Republic of Serbia entrusts to the AP and/or LSG the following tasks: to establish measures and conditions of protection against noise, that is, sound protection in plans, programmes and projects, including those for which approval is in the process of strategic impact assessment, EIA, that is, in procedure for issuing integrated permits for installations and activities; to perform acoustic zoning in their area, determine restriction measures and limitations in accordance with this Law; to provide the development of strategic maps for noise within the competence of AP/LSG; to adopt an action plan for agglomerations in the territory of the AP/LSG as well as for facilities and activities for which integrated permit is issued by the competent authority of the AP/LSG for protection against noise in the environment, and provide conditions and take care of its implementation; to provide and finance noise monitoring in the environment in the territory of the AP/LSG; the AP and LSG are obliged to provide to the SEPA strategic noise maps within one month from the date of their creation; and to supervise and control the implementation of measures for noise protection in the environment.

128. Persons who carry out systematic testing, in the territory of the AP, are obliged to deliver to the AP competent authority an annual report on the results of testing, not later than 31 Mar. of the current year for the previous year, and in case of extraordinary events, immediately (Art. 5).

129. On the basis of the Art. 14, para. 4 of the Law on the Protection of Non-ionizing Radiation to the AP or LSG are entrusted inspection tasks on the sources of radiation for which approval for the construction and beginning of work issue competent body of AP or LSG.

L. Law on the Protection and Sustainable Use of Fish Reserves

111. According to the Law on the Protection and Sustainable Use of Fish Reserves (OJ RS, No. 128/14) AP carries out the tasks referred to in Articles 5, 6, 7, 8, 9, 17, 21, 31, 38, 44, 47, 49 and 52 of this Law as entrusted tasks.[130] The Ministry shall supervise the work of the competent authority of AP in the performance of the entrusted affairs (Article 53).

M. Law on Spatial Planning and Building

112. According to the Law on Spatial Planning and Building (OJ RS, Nos 72/09, 81/09-corr, 64/10 CC, 24/11, 121/12, 42/13CC, 50/13CC, 98/13/CC, 132/14 and 145/14) APs are authorized, *inter alia*, for granting building permits for facilities specified in Article 133 of this Law which are built in whole on the community's territory (Article 134, paragraph 1). LSG units are authorized for granting building permits for the facilities which are not specified in Article 133 of this Law (Article 134, paragraph 2).

130. The fees for use of fishing areas in the territory of AP, is income for the AP's budget (Art. 7, para. 3).

Chapter 5. Sources of Environmental Law

§1. International Sources of Environmental Law

113. One of the main characteristics of the position of Serbia in environmental international treaties is that it is still lagging behind other countries of the region. This is usually explained as a result of legacy of the past, the crisis in the nineties, international sanctions, etc. Besides the formal participation in international treaties, more important is the question of their interpretation and implementation.[131]

114. International environmental cooperation of Serbia has been significantly improved after political changes in 2000 in all relevant fields. Besides the mentioned political changes, important factors which contributed to the process were strategic approaches of the Serbian Government and other relevant subjects, present improved geopolitical position of Serbia in the region, economic interests and the transboundary character of pollution.[132]

The most important part of international cooperation relates to the ratification and implementation of a significant number of international conventions and agreements in the field of environmental protection.

115. The Serbian Constitution contains several provisions concerning international sources of environmental law and relevant for international cooperation in the field of environment in general. The term 'cooperation' is also defined in National Strategy of Environmental Protection as a priority.

Article 16 of the Constitution prescribes that 'generally accepted rules of international law and ratified international treaties shall be an integral part of the legal system in the Republic of Serbia and applied directly'. The same Article states that foreign policy of Serbia is based on generally accepted principles and rules of international law.

116. Two general rules are prescribed by the Constitution, when relationship between international and national sources of law are defined:

- laws and other general acts must be in compliance with the Constitution, generally accepted rules of the international law and ratified international treaties; and
- ratified international treaties must be in accordance with the Constitution (Article 16, paragraph 3).

131. *See* , review of the state of implementation of the multilateral environmental agreements (MEAs) by the FR Yugoslavia in D. Todić, Međunarodne konvencije u oblasti životne sredine i SR Jugoslavija [*International Conventions in the Field of Environment and FR Yugoslavia*] (Belgrade, REC, 2002); For other States of the region, *see* , the analysis in http://www.rec.org/REC/Programs/REReP/AIMS/outpust.html.

132. Especially important event was The Sixth Ministerial Conference 'Environment for Europe' held in Belgrade in October 2007 titled 'Building Bridges to the Future', *See* , http://www.unece.org/env/efe/Belgrade/welcome.html.

117. It should be added that, Article 194 of the Constitution prescribes that:

> Ratified international treaties and generally accepted rules of the international law shall be part of the legal system of the Republic of Serbia. Ratified international treaties may not be in non compliance with the Constitution. Laws and other general acts enacted in the Republic of Serbia may not be in non-compliance with the ratified international treaties and generally accepted rules of the International Law.[133]

118. Procedure of ratification of international treaties is regulated by provisions of several legal Acts, from the Constitution to the Law on Government, the Law on Ministries, Law on State Administration, Rules of Proceedings of Work of the Government and National Assembly, etc.[134]

119. Serbia is the contracting party in a number of MEAs and other agreements regulating the field of environment. This is partly due to succession from the former Yugoslavia and partly when it became a contacting party after FR Yugoslavia (Serbia and Montenegro) was proclaimed an independent State in 1992, and finally after Serbia became an independent State.[135] By 2007 Serbia became a member of the following MEAs:

- Convention Concerning the Use of the White Lead in Painting (1921).
- Agreement for the Establishment of a General Fisheries Council for the Mediterranean (1949).
- International Convention for the Protection of Birds (1950).
- Convention for the Establishment of the European and Mediterranean Plant Protection Organization (1951).
- International Plant Protection Convention (1952).
- International Convention for the Prevention of Pollution of the Sea by Oil (1954).
- Convention on Protection of Cultural Goods in Case of Armed Disputes (1954).
- European Agreement Concerning the International Carriage of Dangerous Goods by Road (ADR) (1957).
- Treaty on Fishery in the Danube River Waters between Government of FNRJ, Peoples Republic of Bulgaria, Romanian Peoples Republic and USSR (1958).
- Convention on the High Seas (1958).

---

133. In case when an interpretation is needed, the Constitutional Court (CC) decides (Art. 167 of the Constitution).

134. Formally speaking, the basic regulation relevant for concluding and implementation of international treaties, including those in the environmental field, is the Law on Conclusion and Implementation of International Agreements (OJ RS, No. 32/2013), and the Rules of Procedure of the Government (OJ RS, Nos 61/2006 – consolidated text, 69/2008, 88/2009, 33/2010, 69/2010, 20/2011, 37/2011, 30/2013 and 76/14). However, the lack of obligation to perform analysis of the effects resulting from the ratification law, and the absence of the public debate in the process of preparation of the Law on Ratification of International Treaties could be considered as a major deficiency.

135. On this subject, *see* , D. Todić & V. Vukasović, Ekološka kriza u svetu i odgovor međunarodne zajednice [*Environmental Crises in World and Response of International Community*] (Belgrade: Institut za međunarodnu politiku i privredu, 2003).

- Convention on Fishing and Conservation of the Living Resources of the High Seas (1958).
- Convention on the Territorial Sea and Contiguous Zone (1958).
- Convention on the Continental Shelf (1958).
- International Convention for the Safety of Life at Sea (1960).
- Vienna Convention on Civil Liability for Nuclear Damage (1963).
- Treaty Banning Nuclear Weapon Tests in the Atmosphere, in Outer Space and Under Water (1963).
- European Agreement Concerning the International Carriage of Dangerous Goods by Road (ADR); Annex A – Provisions Concerning Dangerous Substances and Articles; Annex B – Provisions Concerning Transport Equipment and Transport Operations (1967).
- European Convention for the Protection of Animals during International Transport (1968).
- European Convention on the Protection of Archaeological Heritage (1969).
- International Convention on Civil Liability for Oil Pollution Damage (1969).
- International Convention Relating to Intervention on the High Seas in Case of Oil Pollution Casualties (1969).
- Convention on Measures for Banning and Preventing Illegal Import, Export and Transfer of Properties of Cultural Goods (1970).
- Convention on Wetlands of International Importance Especially as Water Flow Habitat (1971).
- Treaty on the Prohibition of the Emplacement of Nuclear Weapons and other Weapons of Mass Destruction on the Sea-Bed and Ocean Floor and in the Subsoil Thereof (1971).
- Convention Concerning Protection Against Hazards of Poisoning Arising from Benzene (1971).
- International Convention for Compensation for Oil Pollution Damage (1971).
- Convention on Prohibition and Stockpiling of Bacteriological (Biological) and Toxin Weapons, and on Their Destruction (1972).
- International Convention on the International Regulations for Preventing Collision at Sea (1972).
- Convention Concerning the Protection of the World Cultural and Natural Heritage (1972).
- Convention on the Prevention of Marine Pollution by Dumping of Wastes and Other Matter (1972).
- International Convention for the Prevention of Pollution from Ships (1973).
- Protocol Relating to Intervention on the High Seas Cases of Marine Pollution by Substances other than Oil (1973).
- Yugoslav-Italian Treaty on Cooperation on Pollution Protection of the Adriatic Sea Waters and Coastal Areas (1974).
- Convention Concerning Prevention and Control of Occupational Hazards Caused by Carcinogenic Substances and Agents (1974).
- European Convention for the Protection of Animals Kept for Farming Purposes (1976).
- Convention for the Protection of the Mediterranean Sea against Pollution (1976).

- Protocol for the Prevention of Pollution of the Mediterranean Sea by Dumping from Ships and Aircraft (1976).
- Protocol Concerning Cooperation in Combating Pollution of Mediterranean Sea by Oil and Other Harmful Substances in Cases of Emergency (1976).
- Convention Concerning the Protection of Workers Against Occupational Hazards in the Working Environment due to Air Pollution, Noise and Vibration (1977).
- Protocol of 1978 Relating to the International Convention for the Prevention of Pollution from Ships (1978).
- European Convention for the Protection of Animals for Slaughter (1979).
- Convention on Long-Range Transboundary Air Pollution (CLRTAP) (1979).
- Convention on the Physical Protection of Nuclear Material (1979).
- Protocol for the Protection of the Mediterranean Sea against Pollution from Land-Based Sources (1980).
- Convention Concerning Occupational Safety and Health and the Working Environment (1981).
- Protocol Concerning Mediterranean Specially Protected Areas (1982).
- United Nations Convention on the Law of the Sea (1982).
- Protocol to the 1979 Convention on Long-Range Transboundary Air Pollution on Financing of the Cooperative Programme for Monitoring and Evaluation of the Long-Range Transmission of Air Pollutants in Europe (EMER) (1984).
- Vienna Convention for the Protection of the Ozone Layer (1985).
- Convention Concerning Occupational Health Services (1985).
- Convention for the Protection of the Architectural Heritage of Europe (1985).
- Treaty on Pollution Protection of the Tisza River Waters and Its Tributaries (1986).
- Convention Concerning Safety in Use of Asbestos (1986).
- Convention on Early Notification of a Nuclear Accident (1986).
- Convention on Assistance in the Case of a Nuclear Accident or Radiological Emergency (1986).
- Montreal Protocol on Substances that Deplete the Ozone Layer (1987).
- Basel Convention on the Control of Transboundary Movements of Hazardous Wastes and Their Disposal (1989).
- UN Framework Convention on Climate Change (1992).
- Convention on the Prohibition of the Development, Production, Stockpiling and Use of Chemical Weapons and on Their Destruction (1993).
- Treaty between the Federal Government of FRY and Government of the Russian Federation on Cooperation on Environmental Protection (1996).
- Treaty between the Federal Government of FRY and Government of the Russian Federation on Cooperation on Preventing Industrial Hazards, Natural Disasters and Remediation of their Consequences (1996).
- Convention on Biological Diversity (1992).
- Convention on International Trade in Endangered Species of Wild Flora and Fauna (CITES-1973).
- Convention on Cooperation for the Protection and Sustainable Use of the Danube River (Danube River Protection Convention).
- Amendments to the Montreal Protocol on Substances Depleting Ozone Layer.

- Framework Agreement on the Sava River Basin, Protocol on the Navigation Regime Additional to the Framework Agreement on the Sava River Basin and the Agreement Amending the Framework Agreement on the Sava River Basin and the Protocol on the Navigation Regime Additional to the Framework Agreement on the Sava River Basin.
- Treaty Establishing the Energy Community between the European Community and the Republic of Albania, Republic of Bulgaria, Bosnia & Herzegovina, Republic of Croatia, Former Yugoslav Republic of Macedonia, Republic of Montenegro, Romania, Republic of Serbia and the United Nations Interim Administration Mission in Kosovo Pursuant to the United Nations Security Council Resolution 1244.

120. In 2007 Serbia ratified the following multilateral environmental treaties:

- Kyoto protocol to the United Nations Framework Convention on Climate Change (1997).
- Framework Convention on the Protection and sustainable Development of the Carpathians (2003).
- Convention on the Conservation of European Wildlife and Natural Habitats (1979).
- Convention on the Conservation on Migratory Species of Wild Animals (1979).
- United Nations Convention to Combat Desertification in Countries Experiencing Serious Drought and/or Desertification, Particularly in Africa (1994).
- Convention on Environmental Impact Assessment in Transboundary Context (1991).

121. During the last phase, Serbia ratified the following international treaties:

- Convention on the Transboundary Effects of Industrial Accidents (1992).
- Convention on the Protection and Use of Transboundary Watercourses and International Lakes (1992).
- Convention on Access to Environmental Information, Public Participation in Decision-Making and Access to Justice in Environmental Matters (1998).
- Convention on the Prohibition of the Development, Production, Stockpiling and Use of Chemical Weapons and on their Destruction (1993).
- Stockholm Convention on Persistent Organic Pollutants (2001).
- Rotterdam Convention on the Prior Informed Consent Procedure for Certain Hazardous Chemicals and Pesticides in International Trade (1998).
- Protocol on Strategic Environmental Assessment to the Convention on Environmental Impact Assessment in a Transboundary Context (2003).
- Amendment to Annex B to the Kyoto Protocol (2006).
- Statute of the International Renewable Energy Agency (IRENA) (2009).
- Agreement Between Republic of Serbia and Regional Environmental Centre for Central and Eastern Europe on Legal Status of the Regional Environmental Centre in Republic of Serbia (2008).
- European Landscape Convention (2000).

122. Following multilateral environmental treaties were in the process of preparation for ratification:

- Basel Protocol on Liability and Compensation for Damage Resulting from Transboundary Movements of Hazardous Wastes and their Disposal (1999).
- Convention on Civil Liability for Damage Resulting from Activities Dangerous to the Environment, Lugano (1993).
- Protocol on Pollutant Release and Transfer Registers-PRTR, Kiev(2003).
- Helsinki Protocol on the Reduction of Sulphur Emissions or their Transboundary Fluxes by at least 30% (1985).
- Sofia Protocol concerning the Control of Emissions of Nitrogen Oxides or their Transboundary Fluxes (1998).
- Geneva Protocol concerning the Control of Emissions of Volatile Organic Compounds or their Transboundary Fluxes (1991).
- The 1994 Oslo Protocol on Further Reduction of Sulphur Emissions.
- Protocol on Heavy Metal, Arhus (1998).
- Protocol on Persistent Organic Pollutants (POPs), Arhus (1998).
- Protocol to Abate Acidification, Eutrophication and Ground-level Ozone, Gothenburg (1999).
- Convention on the Law of the Non-navigational Uses of International Water Courses, New York (1997).[136]

123. Serbia is participating in bilateral cooperation in environmental protection with a number of countries, with an emphasis on cooperation with neighbouring countries and receiving technical and other assistance from donor countries. In most cases, the effectiveness of cooperation depends less on the existence of formal agreements than on the availability of funds for joint programmes and projects, primarily in the context of regional cooperation. However, Serbia gives importance to the signing of such agreements and/or memorandums of understanding (MOUs). The following bilateral agreements on environmental cooperation have been ratified: with Azerbaijan (OJ RS – International Treaties (IT), No. 10/11); with Turkey (OJ RS – IT, No. 8/11); with Russian Federation (OJ FRY – IT, No. 6/96). MOUs have been concluded with several countries including: Italy (2002), Bulgaria (2007), Spain (2009), Austria (2010), Portugal (2011) and Republic of Srpska (2011).

136. AECQ, Chs 27, 83. Meanwhile, the following treaties have been ratified: Protocol on Pollutant Release and Transfer Registers to the Convention on Access to Information, Public Participation in Decision-making and Access to Justice in Environmental Matters, Protocol on Heavy Metals to 1979 CLRTAP, Protocol on Persistent Organic Pollutants to 1979 CLRTAP, Amendment to the Espoo Convention on Impact Assessment in Transboundary Context, Amendment to the Convention on the Physical Protection of Nuclear Material, Protocol on Water and Health to the Convention on the Protection and Use of Transboundary Watercourses and International Lakes and amendments to the Arts 25 and 26 of the Convention on the Protection and Use of Transboundary Watercourses and International Lakes, Protocol on Flood Protection to the Framework Agreement on the Sava River Basin, Protocol on the prevention of water pollution caused by navigation to the Framework Agreement on the Sava River Basin, Protocol on sediment management to the Framework Agreement on the Sava River Basin, etc.

124. Several bilateral infrastructural environmental projects have been implemented or will be implemented in the Republic of Serbia.[137]

§2. National Sources of Environmental Law

125. According to Article 99 of the Constitution, the National Assembly, as the highest legislative body in the Republic, *inter alia*, adopts 'laws and other general acts within the competence of the Republic of Serbia' (point 7). Laws and other general acts must be in compliance with the Constitution and with the ratified international treaties and generally accepted rules of the International Law (Article 195). It is also prescribed by the Constitution that 'laws and all other general acts shall be published prior to coming into force'.[138]

126. A right to propose laws, other regulations and general Acts belongs to every deputy, the Government, assemblies of APs or at least 30,000 voters (Article 107). Procedure of adoption is defined, besides the constitutional provisions, also by the Law on State Administration, by Proceedings for the work of the Government and National Assembly, etc.

127. In accordance with the Law on State Administration (OJ RS, Nos 79/05, 101/07, 95/2010 and 99/14), State administration authorities (ministries and special organizations) may pass following legislation:

- Regulations, orders and directives.
- A Regulation prescribes in detail specific provisions of law and legislation of the Government.
- An Order – order or prohibit action in one situation that is of general importance.
- A Directive regulates ways in which State administration authorities and holders of public powers enforce certain provisions of law and other legislation.
- All these sources of law must be published in the OJ RS (Article 15).[139]

128. Article 185 of the Law on State Administration regulates the right of APs to pass regulations, as following:

- The Statute shall be the supreme legal Act of the AP.
- The Statute of the APV shall be adopted by its Assembly, subject to prior approval of the National Assembly.
- The AP shall enact other decisions and general Acts pertaining to matters within its competences.

137. *See* , AECQ, Ch. 27, 14–21.
138. Article 196 of the Constitution prescribes the obligation to publish laws and by-laws. They have to be published in the OJ of the Republic, i.e., of the AP (statutes, decisions and other general Acts of Aps).
139. According to the Art. 16, Ministries and special organizations may only pass legislation when they are explicitly authorized by law or by the Government. Ministries and special organizations cannot by their legislation determine their or foreign competences, or rights and obligations of natural and legal persons that are not already prescribed by law.

Statutes, decisions and other general Acts of APs[140] and LSG units[141] must be in compliance with the Law. All general Acts of APs and LSG units must be in compliance with their statutes.

129. Municipal authorities are also authorized to pass legal Acts. The Statute of municipal authorities is the supreme legal Act of the municipality. The Statute has to be adopted by the Municipal Assembly. The Municipal Assembly shall pass general Acts within its competences, adopt the budget and annual balance sheet, adopt the development plan and the municipal spatial plan, schedule the municipal referendum and perform other duties specified by the Law and the Statute (Article 191).

130. Belgrade has a special position, as the capital city, including certain competences in the environmental field.[142] The basic legal Act of the City of Belgrade is a Statute (Article 2). The Assembly of the City, in accordance with the Law, adopts Statute and Rule of Procedure, adopts development programmes, adopts urban plans and regulates utilization of the construction lands, adopts regulations and other general Acts, etc. (Article 12). In accordance with Article 33, city administration, *inter alia*, is to prepare drafts of the regulations and other Acts which have to be adopted by the Assembly of the City, Mayor or City Council.

131. The list of environmental legal regulation in Serbia is too voluminous to be cited here. Different criteria could be used for classification of numerous legal and sub-legal Acts regulating this field and/or closely related domains.[143] Relevant legal regulation will be mentioned in the proceeding text.

The framework for environmental protection consists, in Serbia, of following four basic laws adopted in 2004 and later amended:

(1) *EPL* (OJ RS, Nos 135/2004, 36/2009 and 36/09 – other law, 72/2009 – other law, 43/11CC and 14/16).
(2) Law on Environmental Impact Assessment (OJ RS, Nos 135/2004 and 36/2009).
(3) Law on Strategic Environmental Impact Assessment (OJ RS, Nos 135/2004 and 88/2010).
(4) Law on Integrated Pollution Prevention and Control (OJ RS, Nos 135/2004 and 25/2015).

132. 'Since 2007, the legal framework has evolved in two main directions: (i) further extending the scope of environmental regulation; and (ii) improving instruments

140. According to Art. 185 of the Constitution, 'the autonomous province shall enact other decisions and general acts pertaining to matters within its competences'.
141. According to Art. 191 of the Constitution, 'the Municipal Assembly shall pass general Acts within its competences, adopt the budget and annual balance sheet, and adopt the development plan and the municipal spatial plan …'.
142. Special position of Belgrade has been regulated by the Law on the Capitol City (OJ RS, Nos 129/2007 and 83/14 –other law, and 101/16 – other law).
143. *See* , D. Todić & V. Vukasović, Zbirka propisa u oblasti životne sredine [*Collection of the Environmental Regulations*] (Belgrade: Megatrend univerzitet, 2007); D. Milenković, Zbirka propisa u oblasti zaštite životne sredine [*Collection of the Environmental Protection Regulations*] (Beograd: Službeni glasnik, 2006).

and procedures of compliance assurance.'[144] Group of new environmental laws adopted in National Assembly on 12 May 2009 includes the following:

- Law on Air Protection (OJ RS, Nos 36/09 and 10/13).
- Law on Nature Protection (OJ RS, Nos 36/09, 88/10, 91/10 – corr and 14/16).
- Law on Noise Protection (OJ RS, Nos 36/09 and 88/10).
- Law on Non-ionizing Radiation Protection (OJ RS, No. 36/09).
- Law on Ionizing Radiation Protection and Nuclear Safety (OJ RS, Nos36/09 and 93/12).
- Law on Waste Management (OJ RS, Nos 36/09, 88/10 and 14/16).
- Law on Packaging and Packaging Waste (OJ RS, No. 36/09).
- Law on Chemicals (OJ RS, Nos 36/09, 88/10, 92/11, 93/12 and 25/15).
- Law on Prohibition of Development, Production, Storage and Use of Chemical Weapons and their Destruction (OJ RS, No. 36/09).
- Law on Biocidal Products (OJ RS, Nos 36/09, 88/10, 92/11 and 25/15).
- Law on Protection and Sustainable Use of Fish Resources (OJ RS, No. 128/14).

Although there are still some open questions, where these laws are concerned, the goal of their adoption was harmonization with EU regulations. Different level of compliance is achieved. In addition, there are some problems in implementation (capacity, coordination, financial resources, public awareness, etc.).

144. EPR (2015), 42.

Part I. Pollution Control

Chapter 1. General Law

§1. Legislation

133. Pollution control is subject of regulation in many legal Acts of general as well as of specific character. Some of them primarily and directly regulate protection of the environment, while others regulate other issues that are important for protection of the environment and in some way related to it. During several recent years, a considerable number of systemic laws and other legal Acts have been adopted and/or drafted for adoption. It could be said that Serbia has, generally speaking, made significant progress in developing environmental legislation, although the implementation practice needs careful analysis of the progress made in different sub-fields.[145]

134. As mentioned above, most important general legal Acts that regulate directly the environmental protection are as follows:

- *EPL* (OJ RS, Nos 135/04, 36/09 and 36/09 – other law, 72/09 –other law, 43/11CC and 14/16).
- Law on Environmental Impact Assessment (OJ RS, Nos 135/04 and 36/09).
- Law on Strategic Environmental Impact Assessment (OJ RS, Nos 135/04 and 88/10).
- Law on Integrated Prevention and Control of Environmental Pollution (OJ RS, Nos 135/04 and 25/15).

I. Environmental Protection Law

135. The basic framework legal Act which regulates environmental issues in Serbia is the EPL adopted in 2004. Judging from a number of criteria and reasons, the EPL is a complex legal Act, which is even more obvious if we view it within the

145. For more details concerning these issues, *see* , S. Bogdanović (ed.), Zastita životne sredine Republike Srbije – između politike i prakse približavanja EU [*Protection of the Environment of the Republic of Serbia – Between Policy and Practice of Association with the EU*] (Novi Sad: Jugoslovensko udruženje za vodno pravo, Yugoslav Association for Water Law, 2008).

context of political, economic, institutional, legal, international and other circumstances.[146] It is the basic legal Act regulating almost all important issues in the field, and having functional relation with legal and sub-legal Acts in other fields, more or less, related to the environment. Another reason for its complexity is the attempt of its creators to introduce novel solutions (in relation to the previous Law),[147] taken from contemporary European and widerworld legal regulation.

136. According to Article 122, legal and private persons were obliged to harmonize their activities with the Law within a year from the day when this Law entered into force. This period has expired.

137. The EPL regulates 'the integral system[148] of environmental protection which shall ensure the human right to live and develop in healthy environment as well as balanced economy growth and protection of the environment in the Republic' (Article 1). Provisions of the Law are divided into following chapters:

(1) *General provisions*: subject of the environmental protection system, definitions, subject's liability, awareness raising, civil societies, cooperation, principles of environmental protection and special laws[149] (Articles 1–10).
(2) *Management of natural values*: planning and utilization of natural values – management of natural values, strategic documents, plans and programmes of the AP and LSG units (Articles 11–32).

146. For more information, *see* , G. Petković, 'New Legislation on Environmental Management,' *Pravni život*, Belgrade, Nos 9/2005, 551–572. D. Todić, 'Novi zakoni Republike Srbije u oblasti životne sredine i univerzalne vrednosti' [New Environmental Laws of the Republic of Serbia and Universal Values], *Pravni život*, No. 9/2005, 573–586.

147. The EPL contains some radically new solutions, in comparison with the previous one, establishing a modern environmental management framework in line with the EU legislation, and introducing following novelties: introduction of development of strategies, establishment of the EPA, introduction of EMAS, the Environmental Protection Fund, introduction of economic instruments, introduction of higher level of decentralization, introduction of public participation in environmental procedure, establishment of legal basis and framework for Strategic Environmental Assessment and IPPC, eco label, etc. On the basis of this Law, many new by-laws and amendments of the existing ones have been adopted, as for example, rulebook on type of equipment, content and mark/badge of inspector for environment protection (OR RS, Nos 35/05, 23/06, 7/07, 64/07 and 94/08), rulebook on the form of legal identification card of inspector for environment protection (OJ RS, Nos 5/14 and 81/15 – other rulebook), regulation on criteria for determining charges for protection and improvement of the environment, and maximum charge amount (OJ RS, No. 11/09), regulation on criteria for determining the status of endangered environment and priorities for rehabilitation and remediation (OJ RS, No. 22/10), etc.

148. System of environmental protection in Serbia comprises the following elements: (1) sustainable management, preservation of nature balance, integrity, diversity and quality of natural values and conditions for survival of all living beings; and (2) prevention, control, reduction and rehabilitation of all kinds of environmental pollution (Art. 2).

149. Special laws and other regulations (sub-legal Acts and programme documents) include: (1) EIA of plans, programmes and projects; (2) integrated prevention and pollution control; (3) protection of nature; (4) protection of air, water, soil, forests, geological resources; (5) chemicals management; (6) waste management; (7) ionizing and non-ionizing radiation; and (8) protection against noise and vibrations, (8a) control of the major risks of accidents involving dangerous substances; (8b) transboundary movement and trade in wild species (Art. 10).

(3) *Measures and conditions for environmental protection*: preventive measures, conditions for environmental protection, environmental quality standards and emission standards, environmental protection management system, products, processes and services standards, measures of protection from dangerous substances, production and placement on the market, handling dangerous substances, programmes and plans (Articles 33–68).
(4) *Environmental monitoring*: contents and mode of monitoring, authorized organization, polluter self-monitoring, data submission, information system, Integrated Polluter Cadastre, Environmental State Report (Articles 69–77).
(5) *Information and public participation*: access to information, data supply at request and rejecting request for data supply, participation of public in decision-making, limited participation of public in decision-making (Articles 78–84).
(6) *Economic instruments*: financing environmental protection, types of economic instruments, charges for use of natural resources, environmental pollution charges, types of incentives, etc. (Articles 83–90 and 100–101).
(7) *Liability for environmental pollution*: liability of legal and private entities, liability for pollution, liability for damage, insurance, reimbursement of damage (Articles 102–108).
(8) *Supervision*: administrative supervision, rights and duties of the inspector, powers of inspectors (Articles 109–115).
(9) *Penalty provisions*: commercial offences, offences (Articles 116–121).
(10) *Transitional and final provisions* (Articles 122–130).[150]

A. Subjects of the Environmental Protection System

138. Subjects of the environmental protection system in Serbia are as follows: (1) Republic; (2) AP; (3) municipality, that is, the city (hereinafter, 'local self-governance body'); (4) companies, other domestic and foreign legal entities and entrepreneurs who use natural values in their economic and other activities, to endanger or pollute the environment (hereinafter, 'legal and natural entities'); (5) scientific and expert organizations and other public services; (6) citizens, groups of citizens, their associations, professional and other organizations[151] (Article 4).

150. When this Law entered into force, the following ceased to be in force: (1) Law on Bases of Environmental Protection (OJ FRY, Nos 24/98, 24/99 and 44/99); (2) *EPL* (OJ RS, Nos 66/91, 83/92, 53/93, 67/93, 48/94 and 53/95), apart from the provisions referring to protection of air, nature protection and protection from noise (Art. 129). Until the promulgation of regulations on the basis of authorizations from this Law, the regulations promulgated on the basis of the following shall be applied: (1) Law on Bases of Environmental Protection (OJ FRY, Nos 24/98, 24/99 and 44/99); (2) *EPL* (OJ RS, Nos 66/91, 83/92, 53/93, 67/93, 48/94 and 53/95) (Art. 128).

151. Article 7 of the EPL prescribes a general framework for activities of civil societies, established in the field of environmental protection as a subject of system of environmental protection. They are expected to prepare, promote and realize their protection programmes, protect their rights and interests concerning the environment, propose activities and measures conducive to protection, participate in the decision-making process in compliance with the law and help or directly disseminate information about the environment.

Besides the obligation 'to preserve and develop the environment' (Article 4, paragraph 2) all subjects have the general obligation to cooperate, provide for coordination and harmonization in decision-making and decision implementation. The Republic cooperates with other States and international organizations in the environmental field (Article 8).

139. When the liability is concerned, Article 5 of the EPL prescribes that the Republic, AP, local self-governance body, legal and natural persons are responsible for every activity with which they change or may change environmental status and conditions, that is, by which they fail to implement environmental protection measures as regulated by the Law. In performing their activities, legal and natural persons are obliged to provide rational use of natural resources, calculation of environmental protection expenditures in their investment and running costs, implementation of regulations, all according to the Law.

140. Article 6 imposes general obligation, where 'raising awareness' is concerned, on State authorities, scientific institutions, educational, information, cultural and other institutions, as well as other types of societies, that they should be, in the field of their work, inspired to ensure better awareness concerning the importance of environmental protection.[152]

B. Management of Natural Values

141. 'Management of natural values' is one of the central parts of the EPL. It has been prescribed in general that natural values[153] management shall be carried out by planning sustainable utilization and preservation of their quality and versatility, in accordance with the conditions and measures of environmental protection set out in this and in special laws (Article 11). Strategic framework for the activities in the field of natural values management has been established by the Strategy for spatial development of the Republic and by the National Strategy of Sustainable Use of Natural Resources and Goods[154] (Article 12). The AP and local self-governance unit shall, besides that, issue their respective plans and programmes of natural resources and property management in accordance with the National Strategy.

142. Article 14 of the EPL prescribes that control over utilization and protection of natural resources and property is ensured by competent institutions of the Republic, AP and unit of self-governance, in accordance with the EPL and special laws, and in particular by the following:

152. Environmental awareness is imparted through education and upbringing system, scientific research and technological development, public information and popularization of environmental protection (Art. 6, para. 2).
153. Article 3, point 3 defines natural value as 'natural wealth which comprises air, water, soil, forests, geological resources, plants and animal life'. Article 11 prescribes that 'natural value' means (1) natural resources as renewable or non-renewable geologic and biologic values, which are, directly or indirectly, usable or exploitable, and which have real or potential economic value; (2) protected natural goods; and (3) public natural goods.
154. Serbian National Assembly shall enact the National Strategy of Sustainable Utilization of Natural Resources and Goods for the period of minimum ten years. It shall be implemented through plans, programmes and principles on every individual resource or good enacted by the Government of the Republic of Serbia (Art. 12, paras 2 and 4).

(1) implementation of the National Strategy, plans, programmes and principles;
(2) application of standards, norms and regulations on utilization and protection of natural resources and good;
(3) strategic impact assessment of plans, programmes, principles and other documents governing the utilization of natural values and environmental protection;
(4) EIA of projects at all levels of research and exploitation;
(5) integrated prevention and pollution control;
(6) harmonized system of licenses, approvals and consents;
(7) maintenance of cadastre of utilization of natural resources and goods;
(8) organized monitoring of utilization of natural resources and goods and monitoring of the status of environment by means of compilation, integration and analysis of data and quantification of trends.

1. Consents

143. Articles 15 and 16 establish the basis for activities of the Ministry competent for the environment with regard to management of natural resources. According to Article 15, a competent authority may not issue an approval for the use of natural resources without a given consent[155] to an environmental protection and rehabilitation project during and after the use of the natural resource (paragraph 1).[156]

144. Apart from that, a legal or natural person degrading the environment shall perform rehabilitation and remediation of the degraded environment, in accordance with a rehabilitation and remediation project (Article 16, paragraph 1).[157] When the person referred to in paragraph 1 of this Article does not perform rehabilitation and/or remediation of the degraded area, the Ministry shall, at the expense of the person referred to in paragraph 1 of this Article, perform the required actions in order to rehabilitate and/or remediate the degraded area (paragraph 6).[158] The minister shall prescribe in more detail the content of the rehabilitation and remediation project, procedure and conditions for provision of consent to the project, and the documentation that should be submitted with the application for provision of consent referred to in paragraph 2 of this Article (paragraph 9).

155. The consent to the project referred to in para. 1 of this Article is issued by the Ministry (para. 3). However, the consent referred to in para. 1 of this Article shall not be obtained for works and activities on the use of natural resources which are, in accordance with special law, subject to the EIA procedure and for which the environmental protection and rehabilitation measures during and after the use of the resources are laid down in the framework of the impact assessment procedure (para. 2).

156. The Minister responsible for environmental protection shall prescribe in more detail the content of the project referred to in para. 1 of this Article, as well as the procedure and conditions for the issuance of the consent to the project (para. 4).

157. The Ministry shall give consent to the rehabilitation and remediation project referred to in para. 1 of this Article, except for rehabilitation and remediation projects for mining facilities (para. 2).

158. In case of an initiated procedure of winding up or bankruptcy of the person referred to in para. 1 of this Article, the rehabilitation and remediation costs shall be covered from the bankruptcy estate (para. 7).

2. Protected Natural Goods

145. Where 'protected natural goods' are concerned, the EPL stipulates that they shall be used and developed in a manner that enables their permanent preservation and advancement in accordance with the Law on Nature Protection.[159] Activities threatening environmental capacity, natural balance, biodiversity, hydro-graphic, geomorphologic, geological, cultural and landscape values or which in any way degrade the quality and properties of the natural goods shall not be allowed within a protected natural good (Article 17).[160]

146. Regarding 'public green areas in settlements and other places covered by spatial and urban plans', Article 20 stipulates that they shall be made and maintained in a way which shall enable preservation and development of natural and man-made values.[161] Assembly of the LSG unit shall adopt a special decision to regulate the general conditions of protection, the manner of establishment and maintenance, rehabilitation of degraded public green areas as well as keeping records concerning public green areas (paragraph 3).

147. Protection of natural values (land and soil, water, air, forest, biodiversity, flora and fauna, waste, etc.)[162] is ensured by application of measures for their quality, quantity and reserves preservation, as well as their natural processes, interrelation and overall natural balance (Article 21).

C. Measures and Conditions for Environmental Protection

148. 'Measures and conditions for environmental protection' are prescribed in the third chapter of the EPL. The Chapter consists of four sub-chapters. The first group of measures are preventive; the second group relates to 'conditions for environmental protection'; the third group relates to 'measures of protection from dangerous substances' and the fourth group of measures relates to the 'plans and programmes'.

149. Preventive measures include measures regarding planning and construction (Article 33), spatial and urban planning (Article 34), SEA (Article 35), EIA (Article 36), IPPC (Article 37) and chemical accident protection (Article 38).

150. The Ministry, AP authority or local self-governance unit participates in preparation and planning of spatial planning, use of natural resources and goods established by spatial and urban plans and other plans – plans of spatial arranging and agricultural land basis, forests, water-system, hunting basis and programmes of enhancement of fishery in fishing areas as well as other plans – in a way established by law (Article 33, paragraph 2).

159. Only the general obligations of the competent subjects are mentioned here, and 'protected natural goods' will be later elaborated in more detail.

160. Article 18 prescribes generally that public natural goods and goods of general interest shall be used in a way and under conditions that shall enable development and permanency of their natural, physical, health or aesthetic values in accordance with the regulations.

161. If a public green area has been destroyed, partially or totally, due to facility construction, it will be restored in a way determined by local self-governance unit.

162. Articles 22–32 have been devoted to these issues. This will be elaborated in the next chapters.

151. Article 34 prescribes that spatial and urban plans shall ensure measures and conditions of environmental protection[163] and that conditions for measures shall be issued by the Ministry, AP body or self-governance units, at request of the authority competent for plan preparation and adoption.

152. Conditions for environmental protection relate to: (1) environmental quality standards and emission standards (Limit Values (Article 39)),[164] Conditions for Facilities' Work and Activities (Article 40),[165] Limits to Enable Standards (Article 41),[166] Public Alerts (Article 42), Status of Endangered Environment (Article 43);[167] (2) Environmental Protection Management System (Articles 44–50); (3) Products, Processes and Services Standards (Technology, Process, Finished and Semi-products, Raw Materials (Article 51), Warning in the Declaration (Article 52), Ecological Label (Article 53), Awarding and Withdrawal of Ecological label (Article 54) and Appreciations and Awards (Article 55)).

153. Article 51 prescribes that domestic or imported technologies or processes can be applied, or products produced or offered on the market on the territory of Serbia, if they meet the requirements related to the environment and/or product quality requirements, or if technology, process, product, semi-finished product or raw material

---

163. In particular: (1) to determine special regimes for preservation and use of the areas of protected natural goods, water springs, thermal and mineral springs, forests, agricultural land, public green areas, recreation areas and spas; (2) to determine areas of threatened parts of the environment (polluted areas, areas endangered with erosion and torrents, exploitation of mineral raw materials, flooded areas, etc.) and determination of measures for these areas rehabilitation; (2a) to determine measures of integrated protection and planning of landscape, aimed at regulating long-term conception, purpose and organization of landscape and harmonizing multipurpose utilization of space that threatens the landscape (agriculture, forestry, water management, mining, energy, transportation, habitation, recreation and other); (2b) to determine areas in which appropriate distances shall be maintained in long-term between facilities where one or more dangerous substances are present or may be present in quantities higher than prescribed and residential areas, public areas, as well as areas of special interest, for the purpose of protecting human life and health and the environment; and (3) to determine measures and conditions of environmental protection according to which space intended to be exploited for minerals shall be utilized, or according to which industrial and energetic plants shall be constructed, as well as facilities for waste storage, preparation for reuse, treatment and/or recovery and disposal, infrastructure and other facilities whose construction or utilization may threaten the environment.
164. The Government determines limit values of the emissions for pollutants at the place of their outflow into the environment and the levels of imissions for pollutants in the environment (Art. 39, para. 3).
165. Construction and other activities may proceed only if the set standards for emission and imission and equipment that reduce or prevent emission of pollutants or energy and provide for its conservation are fulfilled.
166. With the view to progressive implementation of standards for emission and imission and conservation of natural values, The Government may, for a period of time, limit the operations of installations and activities in certain area.
167. The Government determines criteria for the status of specially endangered environment, i.e., the status of endangered environment and for prioritization for rehabilitation and remediation (Art. 43, para. 3).

is not prohibited in the exporting country.[168] Producer or distributor is obliged to warn, of possible environmental pollution and damage to human health, which the product or its packaging causes or may cause, in the declaration of raw material, semi-finished or finished products.

154. Article 53 prescribes that the ecological label shall be established for products intended for general consumption, except foodstuffs, agricultural and other products obtained in accordance with regulations governing organic production, production of beverages, production of pharmaceutical products and medical equipment, if their production, marketing, consumption and disposal cause less environmental pollution compared with similar products, or if they are produced by waste recycling.

155. The Law also contains measures of protection from dangerous substances in following Articles: Import, Export and Transit of Waste (Article 57); Chemical accident protection– Obligations of Legal and Natural Entities (Article 58); Content of the Policy for Accident Prevention (Article 58a); Obligation to Submit Notification (Article 59); Content of the Report on Safety and Plan on Protection from Accident (Article 60); Submitting the Report on Safety and Plan on Protection from Accident (Article 60a); Submitting Information from the Plan on Protection from Accident (Article 60b); Public Availability, Presentation and Public Debate on the Report on Safety (Article 60c); Evidence in the Report on Safety (Article 60d); Evidence in the Plan on Protection from Accident (Article 60e); Consent on the Report on Safety and the Plan on Protection from Accident (Article 60f); Decision Prohibiting Operation or Start-Up of Seveso Installation (Article 60g); Appointment of the Special Working Group (Article 60h); Obligation of Keeping Records (Article 60i); Register of Installations and Register of Reported Accidents (Article 60j); Informing of the Accident (Article 60k); Obligations of Competent Authority (Article 61); Notification on Operators or Seveso Installations or Establishments of activities which may cause Chemical Accident with Transboundary Effects (Article 61a); Obligation to Submit Notification of the Responsible Authority of Other Country (Article 61b); Exceptions (Article 61c); Proclamation of the State of Endangerment (Article 62) and Rehabilitation Measures and Subsidiary Liability (Article 63).

156. The Fourth group of measures and conditions for environmental protection relate to 'programmes and plans' and include National Programme (Article 64);[169] Action Plan (Article 65); Rehabilitation Plan (Articles 66 and 67); Programmes and Plans of AP and Local Self-governance Unit (Article 68).[170]

---

168. The Ministry may, in case of any doubts, request the evaluation of damaging effects of the technology, process, finished or semi-finished product or raw material, even if duly accompanied by regulated documents (Art. 51, para. 2). Production and trade of certain products and performance of certain activities may be prohibited for a specific period of time, or on a part of Republic territory, also by AP or local self-governance unit, in order to prevent danger for environment and human health (Art. 51, para. 4).

169. *See* , Introduction – Ch. 2. Basic Principles of Environmental Law, 'Strategic Framework of National Environmental Policy and Environmental Law'.

170. The AP and/or local government units shall adopt environmental protection programmes, action and/or rehabilitation plans referred to in Art. 68 of the *EPL* within a year from the date of entry into force of this Law (Art. 33 of the EPL Amendment, 2016).

D. Monitoring

157. Provisions concerning the environmental monitoring are divided into three parts: Monitoring (Articles 69–73); Information System and Manner of Data Submission (Articles 74 and 75) and Environmental State Report (Articles 76 and 77).

EPL distinguishes between State monitoring carried out by the State authorities, AP, LSGs and monitoring performed by polluters. State authorities have a duty to monitor the state of the environment, for example, air, water, and soil, climate, ozone layer, etc. while the operator is obliged to monitor emissions.

158. The authorized organization may include monitoring, provided that it meets conditions concerning human resources, equipment and space, accreditation for the measurement of given parameter and SRPS standards in the domain of sampling, measurement, analysis and reliability of data in compliance with law (Article 71).

159. Article 72 of the EPL establishes legal basis for regulation of self-monitoring.[171] The operator of the installation or establishment that represents source of emissions and environmental pollution shall be obliged to, in accordance with law, through the responsible authority, authorized organization or independently, if it meets the conditions prescribed by law, perform monitoring, that is, to: (1) monitor the emission indicators and/or indicators of effect of its activities on the environment, indicators of efficiency of applied measures for prevention of occurrence or reduction of the level of pollution; (2) ensure meteorological measurements for big industrial establishments or facilities of special interest for the Republic of Serbia, AP or LSG unit (paragraph 1). The polluter shall prepare plan for monitoring performance, duly keep records on monitoring and submit reports, in accordance with this Law (paragraph 2).[172]

The Government shall determine types of activities and other occurrences which are subject to monitoring, work methodology, indicators, manner of recording data, deadlines for submission and keeping data, based on special laws (paragraph 3).

160. Article 74 of the EPL prescribes that an information system for environmental protection shall be established, for more efficient identification, classification, processing, monitoring and record keeping of natural values and environmental management. The

171. Another legal Act relevant for self-monitoring is the Law on IPPC. It prescribes obligation for operators of installations being subject-matter of this Law. The operator applying for the integrated permit must submit, among other documents, the monitoring plan (Art. 9, para. 1.3). The decision of the competent authority concerning application must contain requirements relating to the monitoring of emissions, specifying the following: monitoring methodology, time-scale for measurements, rules for interpreting measurement results and obligation for submitting data to the competent authority. The operator is obliged to carry out monitoring in accordance with the monitoring plan and requirements specified in the permit (Art. 16, para. 2.8). He/she is also obliged to send results of monitoring to the competent authority (Art. 17, paras 1.2 and 2).

172. The polluter shall plan and provide the financial resources for performing monitoring, as well as for other measurements and monitoring the effect of its activity on the environment (para. 4).

information system shall be run by the EPA (paragraph 3).[173] National and local registers of sources of environmental pollution shall be maintained in accordance with this Law for the purpose of monitoring qualitative and quantitative changes in the environment and undertaking measures for the protection of the environment (Article 75, paragraph 1). National register of sources of environmental pollution shall be maintained by the EPA, and local register of sources of environmental pollution shall be maintained by the responsible authority of the LSG unit (paragraphs 2 and 3).[174]

161. The Government is obliged to report annually to the National assembly on state of the environment in the Republic (Article 76, paragraph 1).[175] The report shall contain following data: (1) state and changes of the state of environment based on data and information obtained through monitoring of relevant indicators; (2) implementation of strategy, National Programme and action plans; (3) rehabilitation plans and other measures undertaken; (4) financing the system of environment protection; and (5) other data which are relevant for management of natural values and environmental protection (Article 77).

E. Economic Instruments

162. Provisions concerning economic instruments could be divided into following groups: Charges for Use of Natural Resources (Article 84), Environmental Pollution Charges (Articles 85–88), Budgetary and International Financial Assistance Funds – Funds for Financing Environmental Protection (Article 89),Green Fund of the Republic of Serbia(Articles 90–90g) and Economic Incentives (Article 101). Environmental funds can also be provided through donations, loans, international assistance funds, foreign investment funds intended for environmental protection, funds from instruments,

173. EPA shall establish and maintain the National Metaregister for Environmental Information (hereinafter, referred to as the National Metaregister), which is a constituent part of the Information System (para. 5). In addition EPA shall establish and maintain the means for processing environmental information (para. 8).
174. EPA shall, on its own or in collaboration with a competent inspection, monitor data submission for the National Register of Pollution Sources and the accuracy of submitted data. The Agency shall initiate misdemeanour proceedings charges against persons who are obliged to report to the National Register of Pollution Sources and who have not submitted the required data or data were not submitted in the prescribed manner and within the statutory deadline and/or who have submitted inaccurate data (Art. 75a).
175. EPA shall draft the report referred to in para. 1 of this Article on the basis of collected and available data and information no later than 31 May of the current year (para. 2).

programmes and funds of the EU, UN and international organizations (Article 83, paragraph 2).[176]

163. The following environmental taxes and charges are prescribed by the Law: pollution charges (emission taxes, industrial waste charges and product charges),[177] natural resource use charges, deposit refund schemes, subsidies, tax incentives and exemptions from charge payments and fine for non-compliance with environmental standards. Where ozone-depleting substances are concerned, their import is subject to an environmental tax.

164. Charges for the use of natural goods are prescribed by Article 84. The user of the natural values shall pay a charge for the utilization of natural values. He/she will also bear the cost of rehabilitation and recultivation of degraded area, in compliance with special law.[178]

165. In accordance with relevant regulation, and depending on the kind of natural resource it refers to, the user of a natural resource is obliged to pay the charge for its use and bear expenses of restoration and recultivation of degraded area. The Regulation on Control of Use and Trade of Wild Flora and Fauna (OJ RS, Nos 31/2005, 45/2005, 22/2007, 38/2008, 09/2010 and 69/2011) specifies details concerning the charge for commercial use of collected wild flora and fauna.

166. Article 85 prescribes 'charges for environmental pollution'. Paragraph 1 of Article 85 prescribes in a general way the duty 'of the polluter to pay charges for environmental pollution' and paragraph 2 defines the following criteria for assessment of the amount of charge:

(1) kind, quantity or characteristics of emissions from specific sources;
(2) kind, quantity or characteristics of emissions of produced or dumped waste; and
(3) contents of environmentally harmful substances in raw materials, semi-products and products.

167. The environmental charge payer is, according to the Law, 'every person who causes environmental pollution by emissions, waste or products, or who uses or puts on the market raw materials, semi-products and products containing environmentally

176. Total cumulative disbursements of development assistance for the sector 'environment protection' amounted to EUR 106 million during the period 2007–2013. Annual disbursements corresponded to some 0.05% of GDP. Some 95% of funds were provided in the form of grants; the remainder (some EUR 6 million) was concessional loans. EPR (2015), xxvi. For some information on the IPA program results, *see* : Ignjatić, M., Todić, D. Rezultati i problemi u sprovođenju IPA programa prekogranične saradnje od značaja za oblast životne sredine i Poglavlje 27. [Results and Problems in the Implementation of the IPA Cross Border Cooperation Program relevant for Environmental field and Ch. 27],Collection of Papers, A.Mihajlov (ur).*Poglavlje 27- Životna sredina i klimatske promene*, Beograd: Ambasadori održivog razvoja i životne sredine, 2014, str. 16–21.

177. The Regulation on types of pollution, criteria for calculation of cost recovery for environmental pollution, and amount and calculation methods for fees (OJ RS, Nos 113/2005, 6/2007, 8/10, 102/10, 15/12 and 91/12) prescribes pollution charge rates and their calculation.

178. Funds collected from the charge referred to in para. 1 of this Article shall be revenue of the Republic budget and budget of the AP and/or LSG unit, in accordance with special law (para. 2).

harmful substances' (Article 85, paragraph 3).[179] According to paragraph 5 of this Article, 60% of the financial means obtained from the charges are allocated to the Republic budget and 40% to the budget of the local self-governance unit.

168. Pursuant to Article 85A the Government shall determine areas of special State interest in the environmental protection area (upon proposal of the Ministry responsible for environment issues) (paragraph 1). The amount and manner of payment of the charge for environment pollution in areas referred to in paragraph 1 of this Article shall be specified by the Government (paragraph 3).[180]

169. According to Article 87 the LSG unit may, within the scope of its rights and duties, prescribe the charge for protection and enhancement of the environment.[181]

170. The charge referred to in paragraph 1 of Article 87 shall be prescribed on the grounds of the following: (1) use of residential and commercial buildings, flats and business premises for residence or performing business activity, as well as for the use of land for performing the regular activity (hereinafter, referred to as 'the real estate');[182] (2) performance of certain activities affecting the environment, which are specified by the Government;[183] (3) transport of oil and oil derivatives, as well as raw material, products and semi-finished products of chemical and other dangerous substances from the industry or for the industry on the territory of LSG unit with the status of endangered environment on the area of importance for the Republic of Serbia (paragraph 3).[184]

179. The Government 'prescribe in more details' the following elements necessary for environmental charge payment: (1) kind of pollution, (2) criteria for charge assessment, (3) environmental charge payers and (4) the amount of environmental charge and assessment procedure.

180. From the funds collected as the charge referred to in para. 3 of this Article, 80% shall be revenue of the budget of the Republic of Serbia, and 20% shall be revenue of the LSG unit and they shall be used for the protection and enhancement of the environment in accordance with programs, namely action and rehabilitation plans that are adopted in accordance with this Law and special laws (Art. 85A, para. 4).

181. The charge shall be prescribed in the Act of the assembly of LSG unit (para. 2). The responsible authority of the LSG unit shall be obliged to obtain opinion of the Ministry on the proposal of Act (para. 9). The Government shall prescribe criteria for determining charge as well as the highest amount of such charge (para. 7). The LSG unit shall determine in Act referred to in para. 2 of this Article the amount, deadlines, payers, manner of payment of the charge and relief for certain categories of payers, in accordance with the defined criteria referred to in para. 7 of this Article (para. 8).

182. Payers of the charge on the grounds referred to in para. 3 item 1 of this Article shall be holders of the property right for real estate, or lessees if the real estate is used based on the lease right, and the amount of charge shall be determined according to the area of the real estate and it shall be paid monthly up to the amount that may not exceed the amount prescribed in accordance with this Law (para. 4).

183. Payers of the charge on the grounds referred to in para. 3 item 2 of this Article shall be legal persons and entrepreneurs which perform certain activities (para. 5).

184. Payers of the charge on the grounds referred to in para. 3 item 3 of this Article shall be the owners of trucks, and/or legal and natural persons engaged in transportation of oil and oil derivatives, as well as raw material, products and semi-finished products of chemical and other dangerous substances from industry or for the industry on the territory of the LSG unit with status of the endangered environment on the area of importance for the Republic of Serbia (para. 6).

171. The funds collected from the charge referred to in paragraph 1 of Article 87 shall be used, through the budget fund, for the protection and enhancement of the environment according to adopted programmes of budget fund use and/or local action and rehabilitation plans, in accordance with the strategic documents that are adopted based on this Law and special laws (paragraph 10).[185]

172. When incentive measures are concerned the EPL in Article 101 stipulates that:

> for the legal and natural entities applying technologies, produce and place on the market the products environmentally more friendly than others, namely use renewable energy sources (energy of the Sun, wind parks, biogas, etc.) plant and equipment directly protecting the environment, may have taxation, customs and other relief or exemption provided under the terms and conditions of special law.[186]

173. According to Article 90 of the EPL (2016),[187] the Green Fund of the Republic of Serbia shall be established as budgetary fund designed to track the allocation of assets earmarked for financing the preparation, implementation and development of programmes, projects and other activities related to the protection, sustainable use and improvement of environment.[188]

174. Using the resources of the Green Fund of the Republic of Serbia shall be done in accordance with the law, the NEPP and strategic documents, as well as a list of priority infrastructure projects in the field of environment, for the following: (1) protect, preserve and improve the quality of air, water, land and forests, as well as reducing the impact of climate change and to take adaptation measures, including protection of the ozone layer; (2) remediation of landfills, waste reduction, reuse, treatment, and recovery and disposal of waste; (3) the programmes, projects and other investment and operational activities in the field of waste management, in accordance with the Law governing waste management; (4) the introduction of cleaner production

185. The LSG unit may not prescribe charges that are prescribed based on Arts 84, 85 and 85a of this Law (para. 11).
186. For consumers who, in an organized manner, return used and non used devices or parts thereof, products or their packaging, the producers of plastic carrier bags, operators of the facilities for reuse and/or recovery, collectors and other subjects in the waste management system, special incentives such as subsidies, deposits and their refund may be determined, under the terms and in the manner stipulated in this Law and special law (Art. 101, para 2). For the purpose of assigning incentive payments, the Government shall determine the amount, criteria, conditions and manner of awarding the incentives as well as the classification of beneficiaries enjoying the incentives referred to in para. 2 of this Article, taking into account the classification of operators and other waste management entities stated in the law governing waste management (para. 3).
187. Fund for Environmental Protection ceased to work by adopting the law (OJ RS, No. 93/12 – 25. Sep. 2012).
188. Budgetary fund shall be established for an indefinite period of time in accordance with law governing budgetary system. Budgetary fund will be managed by the Ministry (Art. 90, paras 2 and 3). *See also* Decision on the establishment of the Green Fund of the Republic of Serbia (OJ RS, No. 91/2016).

for the operation of facilities and activities, as well as to fulfil the requirements of environmental protection; (5) technologies and products that reduce stress and pollution of the environment; (6) protection and conservation of biodiversity, waste of injured, sick, seized or confiscated specimens of wild flora and fauna, including active protection measures such as reintroduction, repopulation and maintenance of habitats; (7) Promoting the use of renewable resources; (8) promoting environmentally friendly mode of transport; (9) promoting sustainable development, in addition to projects to improve energy efficiency, etc. The Ministry is obliged to keep records of taxpayers for paying all fees in the field of environmental protection (Article 90g).

175. The AP and LSG shall be obliged to establish the budget fund in accordance with the law governing budget system (Article 100). Charges collected based on Articles 85, 85a and 87 of this Law (Article 100 paragraph 2). Budget fund resources shall be used for financing of environmental protection and improvement, for financing action and rehabilitation plans in accordance with the National Programme and/or for financing programmes and plans of AP and LSG unit referred to in Article 68 of this Law (Article 100 paragraph 3).[189]

176. When the results of implementation of this Law are assessed, it should be kept in mind that it is a framework legal Act.[190] Also, implementation of such a complex and systemic legal Act is influenced by many factors. There is no doubt that by adoption of such framework legal Act Serbia has acquired an Act which covers almost all important issues concerning the environment, as well as the fact that the Law has been adopted simultaneously with other systemic laws which regulate EIA, SEA and IPPC. Some issues are, however, still to be elaborated, as for example, the following:

- relationship between EPL and other relevant laws;
- overlaps in policy and implementation responsibilities;
- coordination between different subjects;
- capacities of various Government agencies (inspection, EPA, etc.) and other subjects;
- efficiency of use of the means of the Environment Protection Fund;
- state of environmental consciousness of public in general, professionals, scientific community, NGOs, etc.

189. Budget fund resources shall be used based on the defined programme of use of budget fund resources that is adopted by the responsible authority of the AP and the LSG unit. The responsible authority of the LSG unit shall obtain consent of the Ministry on the proposal of the programme of use of budget fund resources referred to in para. 1 of this Article (Art. 100, para 3). The AP and local self-government unit shall submit to the Ministry a report on the use of the budgetary funds no later than 31 March of the current year for the previous year and/or at the request of the Ministry (para. 4).

190. The 2004 EPL outlines principles of environmental protection and sets the framework for the system of environmental protection. For most areas covered by the Law, detailed special laws and regulations have been adopted. For more information *see* EPR (2015), 13, 25, 42, 52, 56, 59, 65, 93.

II. Environmental Impact Assessment

A. International Law

177. Serbia is a contracting party of the Convention on EIA in a Transboundary Context, Espoo, 1991 (OJ RS, No. 102/07), and Sofia (2001) and Cavtat (2004) amendments (OJ RS, No. 4/16). Besides that, Serbia has signed a multilateral agreement among the countries of South-Eastern Europe for implementation of the Convention on EIA in a Transboundary Context, in at the fourth meeting of the Parties (Bucharest, May 2008).[191] The Agreement contains detailed provisions concerning consultations, detailing appropriate means for providing information to authorities and to the public.[192]

B. National Law

178. EPL in Article 36, paragraph 3 stipulates that EIA shall be an integral part of the technical documents; without it no project execution may start and it shall be realized in accordance with the procedure stipulated by special law.[193]

179. The Law on Environmental Impact Assessment was adopted in 2004 (OJ RS, Nos 135/2004 and 36/09). It contains forty-seven Articles divided into five chapters: Basic Provisions (Articles 1–5); Impact Assessment Procedure (Articles 6–34a); Supervision (Articles 35–39); Penalty Provisions (Articles 40–43); and Transitional and Final Provisions (Articles 44–47).

180. According to Article 1 of this Law it:

> regulates the impact assessment procedure for projects that may have significant effects on the environment, the contents of the Environmental Impact Assessment (EIA) Study, the participation of authorities and organizations concerned, the public participation, transboundary exchange of information for projects that may have significant impact on the environment of another state, supervision and other issues of relevance to impact assessment.[194]

---

191. Participating countries are Albania, Bosnia and Herzegovina, Bulgaria, Croatia, Greece, Montenegro, Romania, Serbia and the former Yugoslav Republic of Macedonia.
192. *See* , http://www.unece.org/env/eia/documents/bucharest/SEE_miltilateral_agreement_final.pdf.
193. EIA has been introduced in legal system of Serbia by the previous EPL (1991) and by relevant by-laws.
194. The provisions of this Law do not apply to projects designated for national defence purposes (Art. 1).

181. EIA[195] is based on the elaboration of EIA study,[196] public consultation and participation and analyses of alternative measures, with the aim of collecting data, of foreseeing the harmful effects of certain projects on the environment and human health, flora and fauna, soil, water, air, climate and landscape, material and cultural resources and the interactive effects of these elements, and of determining and proposing measures that may be implemented in order to prevent, reduce or eliminate such harmful effects, having in mind the feasibility of these projects (Article 2, paragraph 5).

182. The impact assessment is applied to planned projects, to projects which are being implemented, changes in technology, reconstruction, extension of capacity, termination of operations and termination of projects that may have significant negative impact on the environment. Impact assessments is obligatory for projects in mining, energy production, transport, tourism, agriculture, forestry, water management, waste management and utility services, and all other projects in areas with protected natural resources of special value and in protected zones of cultural resources. It should be added that the law introduces screening, scoping and public participation in accordance with the EU Directive on EIA.

183. The project developer[197] has, according to Article 5, an obligation to obtain the impact assessment approval. Developer of a project for which impact assessment is mandatory and of a project for which need for impact assessment has been established, shall not start implementation and/or construction and realization of the project without the approval of the EIA Study from the competent authority (Article 5). In accordance with Article 18 of the Law on EIA, the EIA Study and approval of the EIA Study, that is, the decision that states that EIA shall not be needed, shall be an inseparable part of documentation that is submitted along with the application for construction permit or with the notification of the commencement of the project implementation (construction, workmanship, technology change, change in business activity and other activities).

184. The main stakeholders in the EIA procedure are as follows:

195. EIA is a preventive measure of environmental protection, based on the elaboration of a Study, public consultation and participation and analyses of alternative measures, with the aim of collecting data, of foreseeing the harmful effects of certain projects on the environment and human health, flora and fauna, soil, water, air, climate and landscape, material and cultural resources and the interactive effects of these elements, and of determining and proposing measures that may be implemented in order to prevent, reduce or eliminate such harmful effects, having in mind the feasibility of these projects (Art. 2, point 5).
196. 'Environmental impact assessment study' is defined as the document analysing and evaluating the qualitative elements of the environment and their sensitivity within certain areas, the interactive effects of the existing and planned activities, foreseeing the direct and indirect harmful effects of projects on elements of the environment, as well as measures and conditions for prevention, reduction and elimination of harmful effects on the environment and human health (EIA Study) (Art. 2, para. 6).
197. 'Project developer' means the applicant for a permit or an approval for construction or reconstruction of structures or for other interventions in nature and the environment (Art. 2, para. 3). The project developer shall cover the costs of the EIA Study elaboration, its modifying, amending and updating, the costs of elaboration of the Study of the current status, and the costs related to the information and public participation proceedings in the impact assessment procedure and the work of the Technical Commission (Art. 33).

- Competent authorities (ministries, autonomous region and local authorities).[198]
- Project developer (investor).
- Authorities and organizations concerned.[199]
- General public and public concerned.

1. EIA Procedure

185. Articles 6–34 of the Law on EIA prescribe environmental impact assessment. According to Article 6, the procedure in Serbia comprises the following steps:

(1) the decision on the need for an impact assessment of projects referred to in Article 4, paragraph 1, point 2 of this Law (Articles 8–11);
(2) the definition of the content and scope of an impact assessment (Articles 12–15); and
(3) the decision on the approval for an EIA Study (Articles 16–28).

186. Article 10 prescribes that the competent authority is obliged to inform the authorities, organizations and public concerned about the submitted application for a decision, concerning the need for an impact assessment, within ten days from the date of receipt of the complete application. The competent authority shall decide on the application within ten days, taking into account the opinions of the authorities, organizations and the public concerned (Article 14, paragraph 4).[200] The competent authority may determine scope and contents of the EIA Study through the decision establishing the need for EIA of a project. The decision establishing that EIA shall not be needed may contain minimal environmental protection requirements, as decided by competent authority, in compliance with specific regulations. The competent authority shall submit the decision referred to in paragraph 4 of this Article to the project developer, and shall inform stakeholders and organizations and public about it within three days from making such decision (Article 10, paragraphs 5–7).

198. According to Art. 2 of the EIA Law 'competent authority' means the authority responsible for carrying out the EIA procedure within the functions set forth by this Law, i.e., the Ministry responsible for environmental protection – for those projects for which the permit for project implementation is under the responsibility of the Republic authority; the provincial authority responsible for environmental protection matters – for those projects for which the permit for project implementation is under the responsibility of the authority of the AP; the LSG authority responsible for environmental protection matters – for those projects for which the permit for project implementation is under the responsibility of the LSG authority.

199. 'Authorities and organizations concerned' means the authorities and organizations of the Republic, the AP, LSG and companies granted the authority to set conditions and issue permits, authorizations and approvals for the construction of structures, for planning and spatial regulation, for environmental status monitoring, and for the execution of activities for protection and use of natural and man-made resources (Art. 2, para. 8).

200. The project developer and the public concerned are entitled to file a complaint against the decision of the competent authority concerning the application for a decision on the need for an impact assessment (Art. 11, paras 1 and 2). The competent authority of the second instance shall decide on the complaint within thirty days from the date of receipt of the complaint (Art. 11, para. 3).

187. The second phase starts with the application for a decision on the scope and content of the EIA Study (Article 12). The developer of a project that is subject to a mandatory impact assessment, and of a project for which the competent authority has determined that an impact assessment is required, shall submit the application. The competent authority shall inform the authorities, organizations, and the public concerned about the application within ten days from the date of receipt of the application for a decision on the scope and content of the EIA Study (Article 14 paragraph 1).[201]

188. The competent authority is obliged, within ten days from the expiry of the period anticipated for collection of opinions, to deliver the decision on the scope and content of the EIA Study, taking into account the opinions of the authorities, organizations and the public concerned (Article 14, paragraph 3). The competent authority is obliged to deliver this decision to the developer and inform the authorities, organizations and the public concerned about such decision, within three days from the date on which the decision was made (Article 14, paragraph 4).[202]

189. In the third phase, the project developer is obliged to submit to the competent authority the application for the EIA Study approval ('approval application') together with the EIA Study (Article 16). If the competent authority has decided on the scope and content of the EIA Study,[203] the project developer shall submit the application for an approval within one year from the date of receipt of the final decision on the scope and content of the EIA Study.[204]

190. One of the obligations of competent authority is to make the EIA Study available to public and to arrange a public presentation and debate on the Study (Article 20). Within seven days from the date of receipt of the application for the EIA Study approval, the competent authority is obliged to inform the project developer, the authorities, organizations and the public concerned about the time and venue for public consultation, presentation and debate on the EIA Study. Public debate may not be held sooner than twenty days from the date when the public was informed. The project developer is obliged to participate in the public presentation and debate on the EIA Study.

191. Technical Commission for the purpose of the EIA Study evaluation has to be established by the competent authority within at most ten days from the reception

201. The authorities, organizations and the public concerned may submit their opinions on the application with regards to the application within twenty days from the date of receipt of notice referred to in Art. 14, para. 1.
202. The project developer and public concerned are entitled to file a complaint against the decision of the competent authority on the application for a decision on the scope and content of the EIA Study (Art. 15). The competent authority of the second instance shall decide on the complaint within thirty days from the date of receipt of the complaint (Art. 15, para. 3).
203. Article 17 prescribes obligatory elements of content of the EIA Study.
204. If the project developer submits the application for an approval after the expiry of the prescribed period, the competent authority shall decide on the application depending upon the circumstances of the individual case.

of the approval application as prescribed by Article 22.[205] The competent authority shall submit the EIA Study to the Technical Commission within three days upon the establishment thereof. Upon the finalized public checking, that is, public presentation and consultations, the competent authority shall submit to the Technical Commission a report containing opinions from stakeholders and interested organizations and public (Article 22a). The commission has the task to evaluate the EIA Study, together with the systematized report on the consultations of the authorities, organizations and the public concerned and the report on the completed impact assessment procedure, and evaluate the suitability of the measures envisaged to prevent, reduce or eliminate the likely harmful effects of the project on the environment at the specific site and its vicinity during the construction and operation of the project, in cases of accidents, and upon the termination of the project operation (Article 23, paragraph 1). The competent authority as proposed by the Technical Commission may demand that the project developer make certain modifications and amendments to the submitted EIA Study within a certain time limit (Article 23, paragraph 3). If the project developer fails to act in full compliance with paragraph 3 of this Article, the competent authority may, as proposed by the Technical Commission, approve maximally one additional deadline for amendment of the EIA Study.[206]

192. The competent authority has the duty to adopt the decision granting the approval of the EIA Study, or to refuse the application for approval of the EIA Study, based on the completed EIA procedure and the report of the Technical Commission (Article 24).[207] Decision shall be submitted to the competent environmental inspector by the competent authority (Article 24, paragraph 3).

193. The competent authority is obliged, within ten days from the date of adoption of the decision, to inform the authorities, organizations and the public concerned about its decision to grant the approval for the EIA Study or to refuse the application for approval for the EIA Study (Article 25).[208]

205. Members of the Technical Commission are persons with university education corresponding to the field and appointed by the following: (1) the employees or appointed persons of the competent authority; (2) the employees or appointed persons of the authorities and organizations concerned; (3) independent experts. Members of the Technical Commission shall not be the persons who: (1) have participated in the EIA Study elaboration that is the subject of evaluation; (2) are founders of a juridical person or entrepreneurs who carried out the EIA Study or employees of such persons; (3) are founders or employees of the project developer; (4) are spouses, blood relatives up to the fourth level of kinship and relatives of spouses up to the second level of kinship of persons listed in points (1) to (3) (Art. 22, paras 3 and 4).

206. The Commission is obliged to submit the report with the evaluation of the EIA Study and the proposed decision to the competent authority, within thirty days from the date of receipt of the EIA Study from the competent authority. This period shall not be in effect during the period granted to the project developer to make modifications and amendments to the EIA Study (Art. 23, paras 5 and 6).

207. The decision granting the approval of the EIA Study shall contain conditions and measures, that should be undertaken to prevent, reduce or eliminate adverse impacts on the environment.

208. It is prescribed that the notice must contain: (1) the content of the decision; (2) the main reasons for the decision and (3) the most important measures that the project developer shall undertake in order to prevent, reduce or eliminate adverse effects.

194. The decision of the competent authority mentioned above is final, but the applicant and the public concerned are entitled to initiate the Administrative Court proceeding against the decision (Article 26).

2. Consultation in Transboundary Context

195. If the planned project could cause a significant impact on the environment of another State, or when another State in which the environment could be significantly threatened requests the information, the Ministry shall, within the shortest possible period, at the latest simultaneously with notifying its own public, submit to the State concerned with all relevant information.[209]

196. Basic provisions of the EIA Law have been further elaborated by adoption of the following sub-legal Acts:

(a) Regulation on the list of projects for which EIA is obligatory (List I) and the list of projects for which EIA may be required (List II) (OJ RS, No. 114/2008).
(b) Rulebook on the procedures of public access, presentation and public debate on study of the EIA (OJ RS, No. 69/2005).
(c) Rulebook on work of technical commission for assessment of the study of the EIA (OJ RS, No. 69/2005).
(d) Rulebook on contents of the study on EIA (OJ RS, No. 69/2005).
(e) Rulebook on contents, forms and method of keeping of public book on executed procedures and adopted decisions regarding EIA (OJ RS, No. 69/2005).
(f) Rulebook on contents of the application on needs for the impact assessment and contents of application for determination of size and contents of the study of the EIA (OJ RS, No. 69/2005).

197. The EIA Directive 2011/92/EU is partially transposed by the Law on EIA, EPL and by other implementing legislation. The amendments introduced by the Directive 2014/52/EU have not been transposed. Full transposition of EIA Directive 2011/92/EU as amended by Directive 2014/52/EU will be achieved in 2017.[210] According to the last EC report, 'the environmental impact assessment process has improved but needs further strengthening especially for projects in the hydropower and mining sectors, partly through capacity-building at all levels'.[211]

III. Strategic Environmental Assessment

198. Article 35 of the EPL is devoted to the SEA. It is stipulated, *inter alia*, that 'strategic environmental impact assessment must be harmonized with other environmental

209. Article 32 defines types of information that have to be submitted to another State in the process of transboundary consultation.
210. SRS, Chs 27, 3.
211. CR, 2016, 76.

impact assessments, as well as with the plans and programmes for the protection of environment and shall be made in keeping with the procedure set out in special law'.[212]

199. The Law on SEA has introduced strategic assessment of effects on the environment into the legal system of Serbia (OJ RS, Nos 135/2004 and 88/2010). The Law contains twenty-seven Articles divided into four chapters: Basic Provisions (Articles 1–4); Strategic Assessment Procedure (Articles 5–24); Penalty Provisions (Article 25) and Transitional and Final Provisions (Articles 26 and 27).

200. The Law on SEA prescribes that:

> the conditions, methods and procedure according to which the assessment of impact of certain plans and programmes on the environment shall be carried out in order to provide for the environmental protection and improvement of sustainable development through integration of basic principles of environmental protection into the procedure of preparation and adoption of plans and programmes (Article 1).

A. Subjects of the SEA

201. Article 5 of the Law prescribes that subjects of strategic assessment are plans, programmes, grounds and strategies[213] in the field of spatial and urban planning or land use, agriculture, forestry, fishing, hunting, energy, industry, transport, waste management, water management, telecommunication, tourism, protection of natural habitats and wild flora and fauna, by which the framework for obtaining a permit for future developmental projects is prescribed by regulations regarding EIA.[214]

202. The decision on the strategic impact assessment, in cases of plans and programmes which determine the use of smaller areas at the local level, or in cases of minor modifications to plans and programmes that do not require the formal adoption procedure, as well as of plans and programmes that are not listed in paragraph 1 of Article 5, is made by the competent planning authority if, according to the criteria[215]

---

212. AP or local self-governance units, within their rights and responsibilities, shall stipulate the types of plans and programmes subject to the strategic impact assessment.

213. '"Plans and programmes" are all development and other plans and programmes, bases, strategies, including their amendments, which are prepared and/or adopted by the authority at the Republic, provincialor local level, or which are prepared by the competent authority for the purpose of adoption in the appropriate procedure by the National Assembly or Government of the Republic of Serbia, or the assembly or the executive authority of the autonomous province or self-government units, as well as plans and programmes adopted pursuant to legislation' (Art. 3, point 1).

214. Exempted are 'plans and programmes designated to the national defence purposes, plans of mitigation and elimination of consequences of natural disasters and financial and budget plans' (Art. 2).

215. Criteria for determining the possibilities of significant impact of plans and programmes on the environment and passing of the decision on elaboration of strategic assessment are listed in Annex I to this Law (Art. 6).

prescribed by this Law, it determines that there is a possibility of significant impact on the environment (Article 5, paragraph 2).[216]

203. The strategic EIA shall be carried out based on the plan or programme level, type, objectives and contents and scope (Article 7).[217]

B. Procedure

204. Articles 5–24 prescribe strategic assessment procedure, which is, in accordance with Article 8, composed of following three stages:

(1) The preparation stage includes:

- the decision on the strategic assessment elaboration;
- the selection of the strategic assessment developer;
- the participation of authorities and organizations concerned.

(2) The strategic assessment report.

(3) The decision-making procedure includes:

- the participation of authorities and organizations concerned;
- the participation of the public concerned;
- the report on the results of participation of authorities and organizations and public concerned;
- the evaluation of the strategic assessment report;
- the approval of the strategic assessment report.

1. Preparation Stage

205. Competent planning authority, in accordance with the previously obtained opinion of the competent environmental protection authority and other authorities and organizations concerned, makes the decision on the strategic assessment elaboration (Article 9).[218] In accordance with the procedure set forth by the Law, the competent planning authority decides on selection of the strategic assessment report developer.[219]

206. The competent planning authority has obligation to request, in preparation of the decision on strategic assessment elaboration, or the decision on non-elaboration

216. The Minister responsible for environmental protection shall closely determine the list of plans and programmes for which strategic EIA shall be mandatory and the list of plans and programmes for which strategic EIA may be required (Art. 5, para. 3).
217. If the plan or programme makes an inseparable part of certain hierarchy structure, the strategic EIA shall be carried out in compliance with guidelines for strategic EIA for plan or programme of higher hierarchy level (Art. 7, para. 2).
218. However, the competent planning authority may decide not to elaborate the strategic assessment based on the previously obtained opinion of the competent environmental protection authority and other authorities and organizations concerned.
219. The strategic assessment report developer can be legal or natural person, inscribed in the corresponding Register as entitled to execute activities related to spatial planning and elaboration of plan documents, or town planning and elaboration of town plans (Art. 10, para. 2).

of the strategic assessment, the competent environmental protection authority and other authorities and organizations concerned, to submit their opinions (Article 11).[220]

2. Strategic Assessment Report

207. The strategic assessment report describes, evaluates and assesses the potential significant impact on the environment, which could result from implementation of plans and programmes.[221] It also defines measures for reduction of adverse effects on the environment (Article 12).

208. A strategic assessment report should include particularly the following: (1) the bases of the strategic assessment;[222] (2) the general and specific objectives of the strategic assessment and selection of indicators; (3) the evaluation of likely impact with the description of measures planned for reduction of adverse effects on the environment; (4) the guidelines for elaboration of lower-level strategic assessments and assessments of environmental impact of projects; (5) the programme of monitoring of environmental status during the execution of plans and programmes (monitoring); (6) the outline of methodology applied and difficulties encountered during the strategic assessment elaboration; (7) the outline of decision-making methods, description of reasons vital for selection of the given plan and programme from the aspect of alternative solutions considered and the outline of methods in which the environmental issues have been included in plans and programmes; (8) the conclusions reached in the process of strategic assessment report elaboration presented in the way understandable for public; and (9) other data of relevance for the strategic assessment.[223]

---

220. The submission deadline for opinions is fifteen days from the receipt of the request for opinion submission. If it is not submitted within this period, it shall be considered that no comments to the proposed content of the decision on strategic assessment elaboration, or the draft decision on non-elaboration of the strategic assessment, were submitted.
221. Article 3, point 3 defines 'Strategic assessment report' as a part of documentation that is attached to plans or programmes and that includes the identification, description and assessment of potential significant effects on the environment caused by implementation of plans and programmes, as well as alternatives considered and adopted based on the objectives and area occupied by plans and programmes.
222. According to Art. 13, the background information in the strategic assessment shall include: (1) the short outline of the content and objectives of plans and programmes and relationship with other plans and programmes; (2) the outline of the current status and quality of the environment in the area that the report refers to; (3) the characteristics of the environment in areas likely to be exposed to significant impact; (4) the environmental protection issues and problems that have been considered in plans and programmes and the outline of reasons for omission of certain issues and problems out of the assessment procedure; (5) the outline of the prepared alternative solutions relating to the environmental protection in plans and programmes, including the zero alternative solution for plans and programmes and the most favourable solution from the aspect of environmental protection; and (6) the results of previous consultations with authorities and organizations concerned that are relevant from the aspect of objectives and evaluation of potential impact of the strategic assessment.
223. Obligation of the competent planning authority is to provide for participation of authorities and organizations and the public concerned in the procedure of granting the approval for the strategic assessment report in the way set forth by the Law (Art. 12, para. 3).

209. Both general and specific objectives of the strategic assessment are defined on the basis of requests and objectives related to environmental protection in other plans and programmes, environmental protection objectives set at national and international levels, data collected on the status of environment and significant questions, problems and proposals related to environmental protection in plans or programmes (Article 14).[224]

210. The strategic assessment report includes the developed guidelines for plans and programmes at lower hierarchy levels that include the determination of the need for the strategic assessment elaboration and elaboration of assessment of impact of projects on the environment. They also define the environmental protection aspects and other questions of relevance for assessment of impact of lower hierarchy level plans and programmes on the environment.

211. The elements of assessment of possible impacts of plans and programmes on the environment are defined by Article 15. Among these elements are the data on air, water, soil, climate, ionizing and non-ionizing radiation, noise and vibrations, plant and animal life, etc.[225]

3. The Decision-Making Procedure

212. First obligation of the competent planning authority, in the decision-making procedure, is submission of the strategic assessment report (referred to in Article 12) to the authorities and organizations concerned, and requesting their opinion.

The competent planning authority must, prior to submission of application for granting the approval for the strategic assessment report, provide participation of the public.[226]

213. The competent planning authority is obliged to compile the report on participation of authorities and organizations and the public concerned (Article 20). The report shall include all opinions referred to in Article 18, paragraph 2, as well as the opinions submitted during the public insight and public debate on plans and programmes, and the strategic assessment report referred to in Article 19.[227]

214. The competent planning authority must, after that, submit the strategic assessment report to the competent environmental protection authority for evaluation, with the report on participation of authorities and organizations and the public concerned (Article 21). The competent environmental protection authority shall evaluate the report, based on the criteria contained in Annex II. In accordance with that the competent

224. The appropriate indicators that shall be used in the strategic assessment are selected on the basis of defined objectives.
225. Criteria for assessment of possible characteristics of important impacts are defined in Annex I of the Law and criteria for the assessment of the strategic assessment report are given in Annex II.
226. The public shall consider the report, within the procedure of making the plans and programmes available for public insight and during the public debate, if it has not been otherwise provided for by the Law.
227. The report must be compiled within thirty days from the date of the public debate completion and it shall include the rationale for all the accepted or rejected opinions.

environmental protection authority shall approve or refuse the application (Article 22).

4. Exchange of Information on Transboundary Impacts

215. The Ministry responsible for environmental protection has obligation to conduct the exchange of information on transboundary impact of plans and programmes on the environment (Article 23).[228] Besides that, the Ministry has also obligations:

(1) to inform the authorities and organizations and public concerned about the received information relating to transboundary impact of the proposed plans and programmes of another State in the way set forth in Article 19, paragraph 3 of this Law; and
(2) to take into account the results of consultations and obtained opinions of the authorities and organizations and public concerned when submitting the opinion to the competent authority of another State (Article 24).

216. It is important to add that the Law on SEA is almost completely in compliance with the Directive 2001/42/EC. The only provision of the Directive that has not been transposed yet is Article 11.1 related to the carrying out of environmental assessment 'without prejudice to any of Directive 85/337/EEC requirements & to any other EU law requirements'.[229] Serbia has ratified the Espoo Convention on EIA in a Transboundary Context and the Protocol on the Strategic Environmental Assessment to the Convention on the EIA in a Transboundary Context. Serbia plans to achieve full transposition of the SEA Directive in 2017 by adopting amendments to the existing laws and to the implementing legislation.[230]

IV. Integrated Pollution Prevention and Control and Risk Management

217. EPL prescribes only general obligations. According to Article 37 of the EPL, 'the operation of new and existent installations that may have negative impact on human health and environment shall require an integrated permit which shall secure the prevention and control on the environmental pollution. Types of activities and

228. In the period 2010–2012, Serbia participated in three transboundary SEAs (the National Energy Programme of Slovenia, the River Basin Management Plan of Croatia, and for the Energy Development Strategy of Montenegro). The only case where Serbia, as a party of origin, notified neighbouring states was in relation to the SEA for the new Energy Sector Development Strategy for the period until 2025 with projections to 2030 (2013). EPR (2015), 28.
229. On this subject, *see also*, D. Todić, Strateška procena uticaja na životnu sredinu u pravu Evropske unije [Strategic Environmental Assessment in the EU law], *Evropsko zakonodavstvo* [*EU Legislation*] (Belgrade: Institut za međunarodnu politiku i privredu) (Institute for International Policy and Economy), No. 7/2004), 57–60. However, according to the last EC report 'strategic environmental assessments need to be expanded to cover all relevant plans and programmes'. CR, 2016, 76.
230. SRS, Chs 27, 3.

installations, conditions and procedure of granting of integrated permit, control and other issues relevant for IPPC shall be governed by special law.

218. The rules for issuance integrated permits are prescribed by the Law on Integrated Pollution Prevention and Control (OJ RS, Nos 135/2004 and 25/2015) which contains thirty-five Articles divided in six chapters: Basic Provisions (Articles 1–3); Integrated Permit (Articles 4–9); Permit Granting Procedure (Articles 10–25); Supervision (Articles 26–28); Penalty Provisions (Articles 29–32); and Transitional and Final Provisions (Articles 33–35).[231]

A. *Types of Activities and Installations*

219. Article 4 of the Law prescribes that:

> types of activities and installations, for which the integrated permit shall be granted, shall be sorted according to the level of pollution and risk that such activities may have to human health and the environment, including other technically similar activities that can cause emissions and environmental pollution.

The types of activities and installations relate to both new and existing installations.[232]

B. *Competent Authorities*

220. The following authorities are competent for granting the permit:

(1) the Ministry responsible for environmental protection (for installations or activities for which the permit or consent for construction and commencement of operation or execution of activities were issued by other competent Ministry);
(2) the provincial authority responsible for environmental protection (for installations or activities for which permit or consent for construction and commencement of operation or execution of activities were issued by other competent provincial authority); and
(3) the LSG authority responsible for environmental protection (for installations or activities for which permit or consent for construction and commencement of operation, or execution of activities were issued by other competent LSG authority).

231. The Law on IPPC regulates 'the conditions and procedure of granting of integrated permits for installations and activities that may have adverse effects on human health, environment or material resources, types of activities and installations, supervision and other issues that are of relevance for environmental pollution prevention and control' (Art. 1).
232. *See* , the regulation on kinds of activities and installations for which the integrated permit is issued (OJ RS, No. 84/2005).

C. IPPC Permit[233]

221. The IPPC permit is the key element of the system established by the Law.[234] The operators[235] have obligation to obtain the permit for the operation of installation and execution of activities from the competent authority (Article 7). They must submit relevant documents together with the permit granting application. The deadline for issuing permits for existing plants and activities has been extended until 31 December 2020 at the latest (Article 34).

222. Article 2, point 10 of the Law on IPPC describes 'integrated permit' as the decision of the competent authority adopted in the written form, approving the start-up of the whole or of a part of installation, or the execution of the activity, the integral part of which is the documentation containing the prescribed conditions which guarantee that such installation or activity is in compliance with the requirements prescribed by this Law. The competent authority keeps the register of the permits granted, as a part of environmental information system and which is available to public (Article 25). The Law regulating the general administrative procedure shall accordingly be applied in the case of the elements of the procedure not regulated by Law on IPPC (Article 25a).

223. The application for permit issuance, which the operator submits to the competent authority, should contain data on emission sources, and the nature and quantity of foreseen emissions to water, air or soil, originating from installations (Article 8 of the Law on IPPC).

224. Participation of organizations and the public regarding the process of permit issuance is regulated by Article 8 of the Law.[236] Competent authorities are obliged to inform authorities and organizations in various domains (agriculture, water management, forests, planning, building, transport, energy, mining, etc.), as well as authorities of local governments, on whose territory the activities are planned or the installations

233. 'Up to now IPPC permits have not been issued. Sixteen applications were submitted in 2010 and two in 2011. All requests are incomplete except one which has entered into the procedure. There are significant problems in the capacity of the operators who have to prepare application documents for a permit. The prescribed deadlines for issuing permits (120 or 240 days) are not realistic for complex systems. There is a need for additional harmonization of legislation'. D. Todic, Review of Serbian Implementation and Enforcement Procedures in the Environment Sector, Country External Assessment Report – Serbia, Regional Environmental Network for Accession, Working Group 4, Activity 4.2. (July 2011), http://www.renanetwork.org/index.php?view=wgroup&groups=wgroups&id_group=4, 34.

234. Besides the IPPC permit, there are several other permits related to the environment: land-use permits, construction permits (accompanied by the EIA procedure), operation permits, water use permits and permits for the use of other natural resources (fish, medicinal herbs, timber, game, etc.). There is no emission permits for air pollution. Authorities competent for issuing permits are the respective ministries, APs, municipalities or appointed institutions.

235. Operator is defined as 'any natural or legal person which operates or controls the installation in accordance with the regulations, or to whom decisive economic power over the technical functioning of the installation has been delegated and onto the name of which the integrated permit is granted' (Art. 2, point 15).

236. More precise provisions are prescribed by Art. 23, regarding the ways of informing other authorities, organizations and public which is explicitly related to the Arts 11, 12 and 15.

are situated. They are allowed to submit their opinions which have to be taken into account in the decision-making process.[237]

225. In the next phase, the competent authority is obliged to prepare the draft permit within forty-five days from the date of receipt of the complete permit granting application. During the drafting, the competent authority shall consider the opinions of other authorities and organizations and of the public concerned. Besides that the competent authority is obliged to inform other authorities and organizations and the public concerned about the draft permit and possibilities of their insight into the enclosed documentation; and to submit the draft permit to the above-mentioned parties, on their request, within five days from the date of receipt of such request (Article 12).

D. The Role of the Technical Commission

226. The Technical Commission, established by the decision of the competent authority, has to make assessment of conditions prescribed in the draft permit.[238] It includes obligation to consider the operator's application and the attached documentation, draft permit, opinions of other authorities and organizations and of the public concerned, as well as the opinions obtained in the procedure of exchange of information and consultations on transboundary impact (Article 14).

227. The competent authority makes a decision on permit granting on the basis of the operator's application, the attached documentation, reports and evaluation of the Technical Commission, as well as on the basis of the obtained opinions of other authorities and organizations and the public concerned within 120 days from the date of receipt of complete permit granting application.[239] According to the provision of Article 15, paragraph 5, the competent authority shall refuse the permit granting application in cases where:

(1) the installation for execution of activities for which the permit is required does not satisfy the prescribed permit conditions;
(2) based on the data and documentation contained in the application, it concludes that conditions for implementation of the set environmental quality standards are not fulfilled; and when
(3) the application contains incorrect data that are of relevance for permit granting.

E. Conditions Determined by Permit

228. In accordance with Article 16, the permit shall prescribe conditions for operation of installations and execution of activities and operator's obligations,

237. Other authorities and organizations and representatives of public concerned may submit their opinions to the competent authority within fifteen days from the date of receipt of information.
238. The document on establishment of the Technical Commission defines its composition, tasks and other issues of relevance for the work of Technical Commission (Art. 13, para. 2).
239. In exceptional cases, based on the operator's request or on the initiative of the competent authority, the period set in para. 1 of this Article may be extended, but not for more than 240 days from the date of receipt of the complete application (Art. 15, para. 2).

depending on the nature of activities and their impact on the environment.[240] The conditions include the following:

(1) implementation of the BAT[241] or other technical requirements and measures;
(2) measures contained in the EIA study or study of the current status;
(3) emission limit values (ELVs) for pollutants determined for the relevant installation;
(4) measures necessary for air, water and soil protection;[242]
(5) measures relating to management of waste generated during the operation of the installation;
(6) measures relating to reduction of noise and vibrations;
(7) measures relating to the efficient energy consumption;
(8) requirements relating to monitoring of emission;[243]
(9) measures for prevention of accidents and elimination of their consequences;
(10) reduction of pollution including the transboundary pollution of the environment;
(11) measures planned for commencement of operation, for momentary stoppages in cases of disruption in functioning of the installations as well as for the termination of operations;
(12) undertaking of measures of protection of the environment after the final termination of activities aimed at avoiding the risk of pollution and returning of the site into the satisfactory status;
(13) method and frequency of reporting and scope of data contained in the report that shall be submitted to the competent authority in accordance with the regulations;
(14) results of the review of conditions and obligations set by the permit;

---

240. When environmental quality standards require stricter conditions than those achievable by the use of the BAT, the permit shall contain additional measures for implementation of these standards. At the same time, the Law prescribes that the permit may contain the temporary exemption from compliance with the prescribed conditions in case that the adopted programme of rehabilitation provides for implementation of measures leading to reduction of pollution and fulfilment of conditions (Art. 16, paras 3 and 5).
241. The notion BAT means the most effective and advanced stage in the development of activities and their methods of operation which enable more suitable implementation of particular techniques for compliance with the ELVs prescribed to prevent and, where that is not practicable, generally to reduce emissions and impact on the environment as a whole. Certain elements of the term BAT shall have the following meanings: technique means the way in which the installation is designed, built, maintained, operated and decommissioned or closed, including the technology used; available means techniques that have been developed on a scale which allows the implementation in the relevant industry sector, under economically and technically acceptable conditions, including costs and benefits, as long as they are reasonably accessible to the operator; the best means the most effective in achieving a high general level of protection of the environment as a whole (Art. 2, point 14).
242. According to the provisions of Art. 33, the Government should define, in the period of six months after the IPPC comes in force, the thresholds values of emissions into air and water for the first five years, of adaptation of certain branches of the economy to the provisions of this Law. Determination of ELVs still remains to be done and is in connection with adoption of new laws concerning air and water protection which are being drafted.
243. With the specified methodology, the defined frequency of measuring, the defined rules for interpretation of results, the set obligation to submit the data to the competent authority.

(15) other specific requirements.[244]

229. The validity period of the permit may be extended on the request of the operator, according to the provision in Article 21, but the issued permit is subject to reconsideration at least twice during its validity (Article 18).[245] The competent authority may amend the conditions set by the permit in cases of permit review by duty and in cases of the planned changes of installation or its operation that do not mean substantial changes in the sense of this Law (Article 20).[246]

F. Exchange of Information on Transboundary Impacts

230. In accordance with Article 24, the Ministry exchanges information on transboundary impact of operation of installations and activities on the environment. Consultations on transboundary impact shall be organized in the way and within periods set by arrangements between the competent State authorities based on the principles of reciprocity and equality.

231. There are two elements concerning the information exchange on transboundary impact:

- first, when the operation of certain installation is likely to have significant adverse effects on the environment in another State, or when the State likely to be significantly affected so requests, the Ministry shall submit the information to another State, requesting its opinion; and
- second, the Ministry is obliged to inform another State, which has been consulted in the decision-making procedure, about the decision on the permit granting or the decision on refusal of application for its granting.[247]

---

244. When defined conditions are concerned, operator has obligations prescribed in Art. 17 of the Law on IPPC, including the following: (1) to act in compliance with conditions set by the permit; (2) to submit the results of monitoring to the competent authority; (3) to inform the competent authority about all changes in operation, namely functioning of the installation or on accident, with possible visible effects on the environment or human health; (4) to submit to the competent authority the annual report on execution of activities that the permit was issued for; (5) to inform the competent authority on the planned change of operator; and (6) to undertake all measures that the competent authority set upon expiry of the permit validity.
245. The competent authority starts the review procedure officially or at the request of the operator (Art. 18, para. 2). In case that the competent authority initiates the permit reconsideration procedure, it shall inform the operator about the reasons for such action and request him to submit the data (Art. 18, para. 4).
246. The competent authority may request the operator to submit new application for permit granting, if too many changes aggravate the efficient control of activities (Art. 20, para. 2).
247. By means of submitting the information on the following: (1) the content of the decision on permit granting or decision to refuse the permit granting application and (2) the reasons that the decision has been based on, including the information on the public participation procedure (Art. 24, para. 3).

232. Apart from the above-mentioned, two additional obligations of the Ministry have been established concerning the exchange of information on transboundary impact:

(1) to inform the public concerned on the received information on transboundary impact of installations and activities in another State in the way set forth in Article 23, paragraph 1 of this Law;[248]
(2) to take into consideration the results of consultations and the obtained opinions of the public concerned in giving its opinions to the competent authority of another State.

G. *Sub-legal Acts*

233. It should be added that, based on the IPPC, the following important sub-legal Acts have been adopted:

- Regulation on kinds of activities and installations for which the integrated permit is issued (OJ RS, No. 84/2005).
- Regulation on criteria for defining of the BAT, for application of quality standards, as well as for defining of thresholds values of emissions in the integrated permit (OJ RS, No. 84/2005).
- Regulations on contents of programme of measures of adaptation of work of existing installation or activities according to the prescribed conditions (OJ RS, No. 84/2005).
- Regulation on determining the Programme on the timetable of filing applications for the issuance of integrated permits (OJ RS, No. 108/2008).
- Rulebook on content and method of keeping the Register of the issued permits (OJ RS, No. 69/2005).
- Rulebook on the content, appearance, and the manner of submitting a request and issuing an integrated permit (OJ RS, Nos 30/06 and 32/16).
- Rulebook on the integrated permit content and presentation (OJ RS, No. 30/06).

V. Risk Management

234. Besides the Law on IPPC, several other regulations in the field of risk[249] management are relevant. First of all, the EPL contain provisions that are directly

248. According to Art. 23, para. 1: 'The competent authority shall inform other authorities and organizations and public in cases referred to in Arts 11, 12 and 15 of this Law through the public media, publishing the information about them in at least one local newspaper published in the territory that will be affected by the impact of activities and installations and on the Internet'.
249. Risk is defined as 'a certain level of probability that certain activity, directly or indirectly, shall cause danger towards the environment, life and human health' (Art. 3, point 23 of the EPL).

relevant for protection from chemical accidents (Articles 58–63).[250] According to Article 60j of the Law, the operator shall inform without delay the Ministry, LSG unit and authorities responsible for acting in emergency situations of the chemical accident,[251] in accordance with regulations governing protection and recovery, in particular of the following: the circumstances in connection with the chemical accident, present dangerous substances, available data for the assessment of consequences of the chemical accident for humans and the environment and of the undertaken urgent measures.[252] A part from that, operator shall inform the responsible authorities of the subsequently collected data that affect the previously found facts and conclusions and shall inform the responsible authorities within a reasonable period of the planned measures for removing mid-term and long-term consequences of a chemical accident and for the prevention of reoccurrence of an accident (Article 60j, paragraphs 2 and 3).[253]

235. In the case of accident, depending upon its scope, within or outside the plant and estimated consequences, which may cause direct or deferred threat towards human health and environment, the site of endangerment of environment shall be proclaimed, and the public shall be informed of the measures taken.[254]

236. In order to prevent further spread of pollution caused by an accident, legal and natural person is obliged to immediately take, at its own cost, rehabilitation measures planned for protection. If the polluter, who is responsible for the accident,

250. However, provisions of Arts 58–61b (and Art. 38) of this Law shall not apply to the following: military installations; accidents caused by ionizing radiation; transportation of dangerous substances in road, rail, water, air and sea traffic, and transportation outside the establishments encompassed by this Law, including loading and unloading or transportation to and from other means of transportation on wharfs, piers or marshalling yards; transportation of dangerous substances by pipelines including pumping stations, outside the Seveso installation or establishment encompassed by this Law; accidents in the course of research and exploitation of mineral raw materials, except if raw materials are chemically or thermally processed or stored, and they contain dangerous substances in the prescribed quantities; locations of waste materials landfills, except active waste barren soil including artificial lakes and dams, which contain dangerous substances and in particular those that derive from chemical and thermal mineral processing (Art. 61v).

251. 'Accident' is a sudden and uncontrolled event or series of events which occur with uncontrolled release, leakage or dispersion of dangerous substances in the process of production, circulation, utilization, transport, processing, storage, disposal or long-term inadequate storage. This term shall not cover: military facilities; nuclear accidents; GMOs; transport of dangerous substances through pipe systems, including pump stations; accidents during the research and exploitation of mineral raw materials; damages to dams, with an exception of consequences from industrial accidents caused by such damages (Art. 3, point 24).

252. The Ministry shall conduct supervision and control of the fulfilment of obligations of operators (Art. 60j, para. 5).

253. The operator shall be obliged to implement urgent mid-term and long-term measures for removing the consequences of the chemical accident, as well as to provide, following the analysis of all aspects of the chemical accident, recommendations for the future prevention measures (Art. 60j, para. 4).

254. State of endangerment shall be proclaimed by the Ministry, the authority of AP, or unit of local self-governance. For the accidents with transboundary effects, the state of the endangerment shall be proclaimed by the Government (Art. 62, paras 2 and 3).

is determined subsequently, the authority that paid the cost of elimination of the consequences of environmental pollution shall claim the reimbursement (Article 63).

237. Pursuant to the EPL, Article 58, an operator of Seveso installation, that is, the complex where activities are performed that might include one or more dangerous matters, in quantities higher or equal to the prescribed, is obligated to submit to the Ministry of Environment, Mining and Spatial Planning a notification and to create accident prevention policy or safety report and accident prevention plan, depending on the quantities of dangerous substances used for performance of the activities and to take measures for prevention of chemical accident and limiting of impact of the accident to human lives and health and environment.[255]

238. The operator that is obliged to prepare the Policy for Accident Prevention shall, prior to preparing the Policy for Accident Prevention, submit to the Ministry the notification on: (1) new Seveso installation or establishment at least three months before commencing operation; (2) existing Seveso installation or establishment six months from the day this Law comes into force at the latest; (3) existing Seveso installation or establishment the activities of which were such that the dangerous substances were present in quantities lower than prescribed, in case of increase in quantities of dangerous substances up to the quantities prescribed in Article 58 of this Law, within three months from the day of change at the latest; (4) the permanent termination of operation of Seveso installation or establishment, as well as in case of modification of Seveso installation or establishment, or any change that may affect the possibility of chemical accident occurrence (Article 59, paragraph 1).[256]

239. According to Article 60a, the operator referred to in Article 58 of this Law shall be obliged to prepare and submit to the Ministry the Report on Safety[257] and the Plan on Protection from Accident:[258] (1) for new Seveso installation or establishment at least three months before commencing operation; (2) for existing Seveso installation or establishment at the latest within eighteen months from the day this Law comes into force; (3) for existing Seveso installation or establishment the activities of which were such that the dangerous substances were present in quantities lower than prescribed, in case of increase of quantities of dangerous substances up to the quantities prescribed in Article 58 of this Law, within six months from the day of change at the latest.

240. The operator shall periodically review the Report on Safety and as needed update it: (1) at least every five years; (2) on its own initiative or upon request of the

255. The Minister shall prescribe list of dangerous substances and their quantities and criteria for determining types of documents prepared by the operator (Art. 58, para. 2) and content of the Policy for Accident Prevention (Art. 58a, para. 4).

256. The Minister shall prescribe content of the Notification referred to in para. 1 of this Article (Art. 59, para. 2).

257. Report on Safety shall contain, in particular, the following: information on the system of management and organization of operator for the purpose of preventing chemical accident; description of location of Seveso installation or establishment; description of Seveso installation or establishment; analysis of risk from chemical accident and manner of its prevention; protective measures and intervention measures for limiting consequences of chemical accident; listing of dangerous substances and other (Art. 60, para. 1).

258. The Plan on Protection from Accident shall contain in particular measures that are undertaken within the Seveso installation or establishment in case of chemical accident or in case circumstances arise which may cause chemical accident (Art. 60, para. 2).

Ministry due to the new facts obtained based on the analysis of other chemical accidents or evaded accidents (Article 60a, paragraph 4).[259]

241. The operator referred to in Article 58 of this Law shall ensure that the information on safety measures and procedures in case of chemical accident from the Plan on Protection from Accident is submitted to all legal persons and public institutions (schools, hospitals, etc.), as well as to natural persons, that may be affected by the consequences of a chemical accident (Article 60b).[260]

242. The operator shall ensure that the Report on Safety and the list of dangerous substances that are present in the Seveso installation or establishment are publicly available.[261] The responsible authority shall ensure public availability, organize presentation and administer public debate regarding the Report on Safety in the procedure of deciding on providing consent on the Report on Safety (Article 60c, paragraphs 1 and 2). The responsible authority shall inform the person submitting the report, interested bodies and organizations and the public on the time and place for the public insight, public presentation and the public debate on the Report on Safety within seven days from the date of the receipt of the Report on Safety (paragraph 4).[262]

243. Apart from the above-mentioned EPL regulates following issues: Evidence in the Report on Safety (Article 60d); Evidence in the Plan on Protection from Accident (Article 60e); Consent on the Report on Safety and the Plan on Protection from Accident (Article 60f); Decision Prohibiting Operation or Start-Up of Seveso Installation (Article 60g); Appointment of the Special Working Group (Article 60h); Obligation of Keeping Records (Article 60i); Register of Installations and Register of Reported Accidents (Article 60k); Obligations of Responsible Authorities (Article 61); Notification on Operators or Seveso Installations or Establishments the Activities of Which May Cause Chemical Accident with Transboundary Effects (Article 61a); and Obligation to Submit Notification of the Responsible Authority of Other Country (Article 61b).

244. Following legal and sub-legal Acts also deserve mentioning:

---

259. In the event of modification of the work process, change of nature or quantity of dangerous substance or other changes that may affect the danger of occurrence of chemical accident, the operator must immediately enter changes in the Report on Safety and the Plan on Protection from Accident and submit them to the Ministry, and in the event the changes refer to the modification of installations or storehouses, prior to introducing such modifications. The operator shall be obliged to review, test and, if needed, update the Plan on Protection from Accident at least every three years (Art. 60a, paras 5 and 6).
260. Information referred to in para. 1 of this Article shall be updated every three years, and especially in case circumstances referred to in Art. 60a, para. 5 of this Law arise. Updated information referred to in para. 1 of this Article must be publicly available. The period between two regular submissions of information to the public may not be longer than five years (Art. 60b, paras 2–4).
261. The person submitting the Report on Safety may be allowed, upon approval of the responsible authority, not to provide for public availability and presentation of certain parts of the report due to protecting industrial, commercial and personal secret, public safety or defence of the country (Art. 60c, para. 3).
262. The regulation on the procedure of public availability, presentation and public debate regarding the study on EIA shall apply *mutatis mutandis* on the procedure of public availability, presentation and public debate concerning the Report on Safety (Art. 60c, para. 7).

- Law on Emergency Situations (OJ RS, Nos 111/09, 92/11 and 93/12).
- Law on Protection from Fire (OJ RS, Nos 111/2009 and 20/15).
- Rulebook on the content of the notice about new Seveso facility or complex, existing Seveso facility or complex and about permanent cessation of Seveso facility or complex (OJ RS, No. 41/10).
- Rulebook on the content of accident prevention policy and the content and methodology of the Report on the safety and accident protection plan (OJ RS, No. 41/10).
- Rulebook on the list of hazardous substances and their amounts and criteria for determining the type of documents produced by the operator of Seveso facility or complex (OJ RS, Nos 41/10 and 51/15).
- Rulebook on the manner of notice, i.e., exchange of data on SEVESO installation, i.e., establishment, whose activities may cause chemical accidents with cross-border effects (OJ RS, No. 26/13).

245. Serbia has ratified UNECE Convention on the Transboundary Effects of Industrial Accidents on 31 July 2009.[263]

246. According to the EC report (2016) regarding the industrial pollution and risk management, 'alignment with most EU directives and regulations is at an early stage'. 'Serbia needs to address the acquis requirement for either a fully integrated permitting process covering all areas or formal consultation between permitting authorities.'[264]Full legislative alignment with the Directive 2010/75/EU (IED) will be achieved by 2018, by adopting amendments to the existing laws, adopting new laws and new by-laws.[265] The Seveso III Directive (Directive 2012/18/EU on the control of major accident hazards involving dangerous substances) is at an initial stage of transposition. Full legislative alignment is planned by 2018 by the adoption of a Law on the control of major accident hazards involving dangerous substances and several rulebooks transposing the relevant annexes.[266]

247. When implementation of the Law on IPPC is concerned, there are some difficulties mainly due to lack of specific knowledge and experience of all participants in the process of issuing integrated permits. The Law on Integrated Pollution Prevention and Control requires all newly built industrial plants to obtain the integrated permit for operation before commencing with activities. Existing plants must apply for, and obtain an integrated permit until 2020. The project for Strengthening Environmental Capacities for 2003, financed by the European Agency for Reconstruction, lays down a foundation for an IPPC Pilot Project – 'Simulated issuance of the cement factory Holcim Concern integrated operation permit, in Popovac, Serbia'. Another case is a simulated issuance of an integrated operation permit for the Pancevo Oil Refinery, which was conducted as a part of the ISLA project – Institutional support in regulation implementation in the field of industrial pollution, funded by the Government of Norway, geared towards building and strengthening capacities for IPPS related laws

263. *See* , http://www.unece.org/env/teia/parties.html.
264. CR, 2016, 77.
265. SRS, Chs 27, 11.
266. *Ibid.*

and their implementation.[267] Capacity problems at the municipal level are significant, notably for IPPC. Short-time training delivered to representatives of LSGs cannot compensate for the lack of staff and financing.[268]

§2. ACCESS TO INFORMATION AND PUBLIC PARTICIPATION IN THE FIELD OF THE ENVIRONMENT

I. International Law

248. A key issue, when environmental protection is concerned, is the right of the public to participate in decision-making in the field of the environment as well as the right to be informed.[269] These rights have been regulated at the international level by the 1998 Convention on Access to Environmental Information, Public Participation in Decision-making and Access to Justice in Environmental Matters (also known as Aarhus Convention). Serbia has ratified the Aarhus Convention on 31 July 2009.[270]

Besides that, Serbia ratified the Convention's Protocol on Pollutant Release and Transfer Registers – in force from 23 November 2011. Almaty amendment (2005) Serbia has not ratified.

II. National Law

249. The public participation as well as access to information has been regulated on national level. A number of legal and sub-legal Acts deserve mentioning. In the first place, it is the Constitution of Serbia (2006) which declares that citizens have the right to be informed about the state of the environment apart from the right to a healthy environment.

250. Publicity of work of State authorities[271] is one of the basic principles of the work of State administration, according to the Law on State Administration (OJ RS, Nos 79/05, 101/07, 95/10 and 99/14). Article 11 of the Law prescribes that 'The

267. NPI, 661.

268. 'Besides the issue of technical capacity, most of the 32 municipalities with competences on IPPC installations on their territory have serious problems with financing the permitting procedure, while the IPPC fee is entirely paid to the national budget.' EPR (2015), 41.

269. EPR (2007), 33.

270. For the Second Serbian National Implementation Report (2014), *See* https://www.unece.org/env/pp/reports_trc_implementation_2014.html (3 May 2017).

271. On this subject, *see* , J. Ignjatović & S. Đorđević, Priručnik za predstavnike javne vlasti o pristupu informacijama od javnog značaja u oblasti voda i životne sredine [*Guide of Public Authorities on Access to Information of Public Importance in the Field of Water and Environment*] (Belgrade: Reginalni centrar za životnu sredinu za centralnu i istočnu Evropu, Jugoslovenski forum za zastitu životne sredine dunavskog sliva, 2006), http://archive.rec.org/REC/Programs/PublicParticipation/DanubeRiverBasin/project_products/serbia_manual_for_officials.pdf. D. Todic & Durac, *Demokratizacija politike životne sredine* [*Democratization of the Environmental Policy*] (Belgrade: REC, 2003).

work of state administration authorities shall be public. State administration authorities shall be obliged to enable the public to have access to their work in accordance with the law regulating free access to information of public importance'.[272] Public debate is subject of regulation of Article 77 of the Law. 'A ministry and a special organization shall be obliged to undertake public debate in the procedure of preparation of a law which essentially changes the legal regime in one field or which regulates issues of particular relevance for public'.

251. Article 8 of the Law on Civil Servants (OJ RS, Nos 79/05, 81/05, 83/05, 64/07, 67/07, 116/08, 104/09 and 99/14) prescribes that 'Information on work of civil servants shall be accessible to the public in accordance with the law that regulates the free access to information of public interest'.

252. Several other documents deserve mentioning: The 2004 Law on Free Access to Information of Public Interest (OJ. RS, Nos 120/2004, 54/2007, 104/2009 and 36/2010) and Instruction for the creation and publication of the Information Booklet on Public Authority Work (OJ RS, No.68/2010). Both documents entitle citizens to enquire about the work of government bodies in general, including those in environmental field. They can require such bodies to report to the public about their responsibilities, organizational structure, budget, services, public procedures, procedure for requesting information, and so on. Citizens are also given the possibility to voice their opinions about the Government's work and procedures.

253. In accordance with Article 5, 'everyone shall have the right to be informed whether a public authority holds specific information of public importance and/or whether such is otherwise accessible to him/her (paragraph 1)'.[273]

254. Information of public importance, within the meaning of this Law, is information held by a public authority body, created during or relating to the operation of a public authority body, which is contained in a document and concerns anything the public has a justified interest to know (Article 2, paragraph 1).[274] For information to be considered information of public importance, it shall be irrelevant whether the source of information is a public authority or another person, which medium carries the document containing the information (paper, tape, film, electronic media, etc.), on which date the information was created or in which way the information was obtained, nor shall any other similar properties of such information bear any relevance for this purpose (Article 2, paragraph 2).

272. Similar provision is also provided in Art. 76, by which it is prescribed that 'State administration authorities shall be obliged to inform the public about their work through means of public information or through other relevant means. Employees who are authorized to prepare information and data connected to informing the public shall be responsible for their accuracy and punctuality'.

273. Everyone shall have the right to access information of public importance by being allowed to examine a document containing information of public importance, by being entitled to make a copy of that document, and by being entitled to receive a copy of such document on request, by mail, fax, electronic mail or otherwise (Art. 5, para. 2).

274. Justified public interest to know within the meaning of Art. 2 of this Law shall be deemed to exist whenever information held by a public authority concerns a threat to, or protection of, *public health and the environment*, while with regard to other information held by a public authority, it shall be deemed that justified public interest to know within the meaning of Art. 2 of this Law exists unless the public authority concerned proves otherwise (Art. 4).

255. A public authority shall, without delay, and within fifteen days of receipt of a request at the latest, inform an applicant whether it holds the requested information, grant him/her access to the document containing the requested information or issue or send to the applicant a copy of the document, as the case may be. A copy of a document shall be deemed to be sent to an applicant sent on the day it leaves the office of the public authority from which the information was requested (Article 16, paragraph 1).[275]

256. For the purpose of exercising the right of access to information of public importance held by public authorities, this Law shall provide for the establishment of the institution of the Commissioner for Information of Public Importance (Commissioner)[276] as an autonomous Government body independent in the exercise of its powers (Article 1, paragraph 2).[277]

257. The basic law governing the protection of personal data is the Law on Personal Data Protection (OJ RS, Nos 97/2008, 104/2009, 68/12 CC and 107/12) which entered into force on 4 November 2008. Article 1 paragraph 3 of the Law prescribes that the affairs related to the personal data protection are performed by the Commissioner for the Information of Public Importance and Personal Data Protection (the Commissioner) as an autonomous State authority, independent in the performance of their duty. Every natural person shall be entitled to personal data protection regardless of their nationality and residence, race, age, gender, language, religion, political and

275. However, if a request relates to information which can reasonably be assumed to bear on the protection of a person's life or freedom and/or the protection of public health and *the environment*, a public authority must inform the applicant it holds such information, grant access to the document containing the requested information or issue a copy of the document to the applicant, as the case may be, within forty-eight hours of receipt of the request (Art. 16, para. 2).

276. For more information *see* http://www.poverenik.org.rs/en/pravni-okvir-pi.html (2 May 2017). *See also*, Part V Juridical Actions of Individuals, Ch. 3 Other Forms of Juridical Actions of Individuals.

277. In 2009 the Office of the Commissioner for Information of Public Importance and Personal Data Protection processed a total of 2,689 cases in the field of freedom of information, 1,865 of which were received in the course of 2009, while further 824 remained from earlier periods. Since the establishment of the Office only thirty-seven complaints relating to access to information about the environment have been submitted. The percentage of these compared to the total number of complaints that reached 7,274 by September is quite small. (The complaints submitted to the Commissioner are about withholding information as to whether EIA studies has been conducted in industrial zones that are being set up in some local areas, the information about the amount of funds spent to ensure the functioning public authorities and organizations of the Republic of Serbia responsible for environmental protection, as well as the data about pollution of the environment caused by the activities carried out by some large industrial facilities. A total of thirty-seven complaints related to the environment refers only to those that have to do with the environment in the narrowest sense of the term. This number should be added to numerous complaints (295 resolved cases of complaints) about the protection of animals, public procurement, the construction of facilities requiring investments such as oil refineries, roads, etc. which may be significant from the point of view of environmental protection). However, the commissioner does not possess exact data regarding the number of requests submitted to public authorities, because a number of public authority bodies have not submitted the reports thereof. *See* , Aarhus Convention Implementation Report, Republic of Serbia, 2010. http://www.unece.org/fileadmin/DAM/env/pp/reporting/NIRs%202011/Serbia_NIR_2011_e.pdf, 24–25.

other affiliations, ethnicity, social background and status, wealth, birth, education, social position or any other personal characteristic (Article 1, paragraph 2).[278]

258. Pursuant to Article 14 data shall be collected from data subjects and from public authorities authorized under the Law to collect such data. Data may also be collected from third parties if, *inter alia*, data are collected for the purpose of achieving or protecting vital interests of a data subject, in particular his/her life, health and physical integrity (paragraph 2, point 5).[279]

259. Data Secrecy Law (OJ RS, No. 104/2009) regulate a single system of the classification and protection of secret data which are of interest for the national security and public safety, defence, internal and foreign affairs of the Republic of Serbia; protection of foreign classified data; access to classified data and their declassification; competence of authorities and oversight of the implementation of this Law, as well as accountability for non-implementation of obligations arising from this Law, and other issues of importance for data secrecy protection (Article 1).[280]

A. The 2004 EPL

260. The 2004 EPL contains a number of provisions of systemic character relevant for access to environmental information and public participation (Articles 78, 80, 81, 81a and 82). First of all, Amendments to the EPL (2016) introduced the

278. 'Personal data' means any information relating to a natural person, regardless of the form of its presentation or the medium used (paper, tape, film, electronic media, etc.), regardless on whose order, on whose behalf or for whose account such information is stored, regardless of the date of its creation or the place of its storage, regardless of the way in which such information is learned (directly, by listening, watching, etc. or indirectly, by accessing a document containing the information, etc.) and regardless of any other characteristic of such information (data) (Art. 3, point 1).
279. The right to notification, access and copy may be restricted in the following cases, *inter alia*, if the provision of such information would seriously prejudice privacy or a vital interest of the data subject, in particular his/her life, health and physical integrity; (Art. 23, para. 1, point 8).
280. 'Classified data' means any data of interest for the Republic of Serbia, which have been classified and for which a level of secrecy has been determined by law, other regulations or decisions of a competent authority brought under law (Art. 2, point 2); 'Data of interest for the Republic of Serbia' means any data or documents in possession of a public authority, related to territorial integrity and sovereignty, protection of the constitutional order, human and minority rights and freedoms, national security and public safety, defence, internal affairs and foreign affairs (Art. 2, point 1); 'Foreign classified data' means any data delivered to the Republic of Serbia by another country or an international organization, committing the Republic of Serbia to keep them as classified data; as well as classified data arising from cooperation between the Republic of Serbia and other countries, international organizations and other international entities, under an international agreement concluded by the Republic of Serbia with another country, international organization or other international entity (Art. 2, point 3).

definitions of the following notions: 'environmental information',[281] 'information held for a public authority', 'applicant for environmental information', and 'information concerning environmental threats or environmental protection' (Article 3 points 33a, 33b, 33d and 33e).

Generally speaking, state authorities, authorities of the AP, authorities of LSG units and authorized and other organizations shall be obliged to regularly, timely, fully and objectively inform the public on the state of the environment, namely occurrences that are observed within the monitoring of the pollutant level and emission, as well as warning measures or development of the pollution which may pose threat to human life and health, in accordance with this Law and other regulations (Article 78, paragraph 1). However, access to environmental information shall be exercised in accordance with the Law on Free Access to Information of Public Importance (paragraph 2).[282]

261. Article 81 of the Law prescribes that:

In accordance with law, public and the public concerned have the right to participate in the process of decision-making on: (1) Strategic EIA of plans and programmes; (2) Impact assessment of projects whose implementation may lead to the pollution of the environment or may present a risk for the environment and human health; (3) Approval of operations of new and/or existing installations; (4) Developing, amending, reviewing and adopting air quality plans, regional and local waste management plans, i.e., hazardous waste management plans, national waste management plan, waste prevention programmes, action plans for environmental noise prevention, and water pollution protection plan (paragraph 1):

281. Similarly as it makes the Aarhus Convention, the EPL defines the notion of environmental information as follows: all information in written, visual, aural, electronic or other material form, held by or for a public authority, on: (1) the state of environmental factors such as air and atmosphere, water, land, soil, regions and natural areas, including swamp, inshore, river and lake areas, biodiversity and its components, geodiversity and geological inheritance, GMOs, and interaction of these factors; (2) factors such as substances, energy, noise, radiation or waste, including radioactive waste, emissions, discharges and other releases into the environment affecting or likely to affect the elements of the environment referred to in subpoint 1 of this point; (3) measures (including administrative measures) such as public policies, strategies, legislation, plans, programmes, environmental agreements, and activities affecting or likely to affect the elements and factors referred to in subpoints 1 and 2 of this point, and established measures or activities for the protection of these factors; (4) reports on the implementation of environmental legislation; (5) cost-benefit analysis, economic analysis and assumptions used within the framework of the measures and activities referred to in subpoint 3 of this point; (6) the state of human health and safety, including the threatened food webs, and, if necessary, conditions of human life, immovable cultural property and their protected environment, and construction facilities, in as much as they are or might be affected by the state of environmental factors referred to in subpoint 1 of this point, through such factors, the state of any factors referred to in subpoints 2 and 3 of this point (Art. 3, point 33a).

282. When application is related to information referred to in Art. 3, para. 1 point 33a subpoint 2 of this Law relating to measurement procedures, including analysis, sampling and sample pretreatment, that were used for information gathering, public authority, with a notification about web page with available information, shall deliver to the applicant a notification on standard procedure used as well (para. 3).

> Public participation regarding strategic impact assessment shall be ensured within the framework of the public presentation of a spatial and urban plan and/or other plan or programme referred to in Article 35 of this Law. Public participation in decision-making on environmental impact assessment of projects shall be enforced in the framework of public presentation of projects and public debate (paras 2, and 3).[283]

B. The Law on Environmental Impact Assessment

262. The 2004 Law on Environmental Impact Assessment defines public participation, prescribing that the public should be informed at three different stages of the process and has the right to voice its opinion at each of these stages. The authorities must, if requested to do so, at all stages provide complete documentation, related to an EIA procedure. Specified confidential business or state information is exception. According to Article 20 of the Law on EIA, the competent authority shall make the EIA Study available to public and arrange for a public presentation and debate on the Study. Within seven days from the date of receipt of the application for the EIA Study approval, the competent authority shall inform the project developer, the authorities, organizations and the public concerned about the time and venue for public consultation, presentation and debate on the EIA Study. Public debate may not be held sooner than twenty days from the date when the public was informed. 'The project developer shall participate in the public presentation and debate on the EIA Study.'[284]

C. The Law on Strategic Environmental Assessment

263. The 2004 Law on Strategic Environmental Assessment prescribes that the public has the right to be informed about programmes in preparation and their impact on the environment. The authorities must inform and consult the public, before granting approval, about the content of the report. The Law also defines the procedure for public participation in the development and adoption of programmes and plans.

264. Article 19 of the Law on SEA prescribes that:

---

283. Public participation in decision-making on commissioning new and/or existing facilities shall be enforced during the issue of new permits for IPPC (para. 4). The Government shall establish the public participation procedure in decision-making on developing, amending, reviewing and adopting plans and programmes referred to in para. 1 point 4 of this Article (para. 5). The interested public, in the process of exercising right to healthy environment, shall have the right, as a party, to initiate the decision-review procedure before the responsible authority or court, in accordance with the law (Art. 81a). In order to protect the interests of national security and defence, Serbian Government may 'limit participation of public in decision-making from Art. 81 of this Law' (Art. 82).

284. For more details, *see* , S. Bogdanović, S. Nojković & A. Vesić, *Vodič kroz postupak procene uticaja na životnu sredinu* [*Guide through the Legislation on Environmenal Impact Assessment*] (Espoo: Ramboll – Finnconsult; Stockholm: Ramboll – Natura; Beograd: REC; Novi Sad: Ministarstvo za nauku i zaštitu životne sredine Republike Srbije [Ministry for Science and Environmental Protection of the Republic of Serbia], 2005).

> the competent planning authority shall provide for public participation in the strategic assessment report consideration prior to submission of application for granting the approval for the strategic assessment report. The public referred to in paragraph 1 of this article shall consider the report within the procedure of making the plans and programmes available for public insight and during the public debate, if it has not been otherwise provided for by the Law. The competent planning authority shall inform the public referred to in paragraph 1 of this article about the method and deadlines for insight into the content of the report and submission of opinions, as well as about the time and venue of public debate organized in accordance with the Law regulating the procedure of adoption of plans and programmes.

In accordance with this, the Law on Planning and Building (OJ RS, Nos 72/09, 81/09, 64/10CC, 24/11, 121/12, 42/13CC, 50/13CC, 98/13CC, 132/14 and 145/14) defines procedure for adoption of relevant urban and spatial plans.[285]

D. *The Law on Integrated Pollution Prevention*

265. The Law on IPPC prescribes public consultation in all phases, from preparation to adoption of integrated permits. The Register of permits is available to the public.

Article 11 prescribes that the competent authority 'shall inform competent authorities and organizations and public concerned on submission of application within five days from the date of receipt of a complete permit granting application'.

266. The competent authority is also obliged to inform, in cases referred to in Articles 11, 12 and 15, other authorities and organizations and public, through the public media (including the Internet), publishing the information about them in at least one local newspapers published in the territory that will be affected by the impact of activities and installations (Article 23).

267. The Law on meteorological and hydrological activity (OJ RS, No. 88/10) also prescribes that the data and information on the weather, climate, water and quality of air and water, obtained by performing meteorological and hydrological operations of interest to the Republic of Serbia, are public, except those that represent an official or military secret (Article 30).

268. Certain issues concerning the access to environmental information and public participation are regulated by sectoral regulations (e.g., water, GMOs, statistical research, ombudsman, consumer protection, etc.).

E. *Role of NGO*

269. Due to the fact that the basic direct beneficiary of rights from the Aarhus Convention is the citizen, and/or organizations of citizens, for implementation of the Convention is relevant a vast number of Acts regulating position of citizens and their organizations. As of March 2014, there were over 2,000 environmental NGOs registered

285. Presentation of the plan to the public is conducted, according to the Arts 41–45, 45a, 50–51.

in Serbia, of which 466 were registered in 2013.[286] The Constitution of Serbia contains several provision of importance for the work of NGO and their relation towards the public. It guarantees freedom of association (Article 55) and the CC is competent to pass judgment on 'whether are in accordance with Constitution and law general acts of organizations entrusted with public authorities, political parties, trade unions, associations of citizens, and collective contracts' (Article 167, paragraphs 1, 5).

270. The EPL in Article 7 defines role of NGO on general way.[287] Article 7 prescribes that:

> civil societies, founded for the environmental protection shall prepare, promote and realize their protection programme, protect their rights and interest in the environmental protection, propose activities and measures conducive to protection, participate in the decision-making process in compliance with the law, help or directly disseminate information about the environment.

271. Article 81a of EPL envisages that the public concerned, in the process of exercising right to the healthy environment, shall, as a party, have the right to initiate the decision-review procedure before the responsible authority or court, in accordance with the Law. LEP, in Article 3, point 28, defines the term public concerned so that it presents the public affected or the one that can be affected by the decision made by the competent authority or which has some interest in it, including citizens' associations and community organizations engaged in environment protection and that are registered at the competent authority.[288]

272. The Law on Associations (OJ RS, Nos 51/2009 and 92/11) regulates the establishment and legal status of associations, their entry and deletion from the Register, membership and bodies, associations' status changes and termination as well as any other issues of importance to their activities. The Law also regulates the status and operations of foreign associations.

F. Institutional Aspect

273. Collection of information related to the environment, and the obligation to make it public, are in competence of a number of authorities and other institutions.

The EPA of Serbia has the task of publishing reports about the environment. The websites of the EPA and the MAEP provide some information about the state of the

286. EPR (2015), 34.
287. *See* , part of the monograph devoted to the EPL (subject of the environmental protection system).
288. Similar provisions are provided in Art. 2, items 1 and 7 of the Law on EIA (OJ RS, No. 135/04) which provides for that the public concerned includes the public which is or can be affected by the plan or programme and/or which has interest in making decisions concerning environmental protection, including NGOs for environmental protection and which are registered with the competent authority, in Art. 2, points 16 and 17 of the Law on IPPC. (OJ RS, Nos 135/04 and 25/15) which provides for that public concerned includes the public affected by the work of installations and performing of activities or is likely to be affected by it, including NGOs for environmental protection registered within the competent authority.

environment.[289] The MAEP organizes, for example, regular meetings with NGOs and consults them when programmes and regulations are in the process of being adopted. The Institute for Nature Protection also informs various stakeholders (schools, news media, etc.).[290] In the framework of Office for Cooperation with Civil Society activities during 2013 the Guidelines for participation of civil society in law-making procedures were elaborated (OJ RS, No. 90/14), although the real significance of this document in practice can be challenged.

274. The Commissioner for information of public importance has been established, as an independent State official, by the Law on the Free Access to Information of Public Importance (OJ RS, Nos 120/04, 54/07, 104/09 and 36/10). He/she is autonomous in performing his/her duties, in order to provide realization of the right to free access to information of public importance.

There are significant results in the exercise and enforcement of the right of free access to information of public importance, but there is no doubt that the effects of implementation of the Law on Free Access to Information could be much better. The average of three to four thousand formally lodged complaints a year (in the past four years) is proof that information is still difficult to obtain from public authorities in many cases without the Commissioner's intervention and shows that citizens trust this independent state body when seeking protection of their rights.[291]

275. The Office for Serbia of the Regional Environmental Centre (REC) also deserves mentioning. It plays an important role in facilitating cooperation between NGOs, donors and the MEMSP. It implemented a number of projects, at the regional and local levels, to support implementation of provisions of the Aarhus Convention (Guidelines for Aarhus Convention implementation exist in two versions, one aimed

289. *See* , for example, *Izvestaj o stanju životne sredine u Republici Srbiji za 2014.* godinu [*Report on State of the Environment in the Republic of Serbia for 2014*] (Beograd: Ministry of Agriculture and Environmental Protection, 2015); http://www.sepa.gov.rs/download/Izvestaj2014.pdf. The national PRTR register is published online and included, in 2013, 277 facilities which were the most significant sources of pollution in Serbia. Serbia also reports to E-PRTR on voluntary basis from 2011. EPR (2015), 3.

290. Other competent institutions in the field are the regional and local authorities, the five Aarhus Centres (Kragujevac, Subotica, Novi Sad, Nis and Belgrade) as well as the Administrative Court of Serbia, etc. *Ibid.*

291. *See* , Summary of the Report on implementation of the Law on Free Access to Information of Public Importance and The Law on Personal Data Protection for 2016, http://www.poverenik.org.rs/en/commissioners-report/2568-izvestaj-poverenika-za-2016-godinu.html (4 May 2017).

at experts and the other at the general public), including its 'Second column' (participation of the public).[292]

276. Regarding the availability of environmental information, the vast array of environmental information and data in Serbia is available to the public and other stakeholders through Ecoregister (sub-domain on the website of SEPA).[293]Directive 2003/4/EC on public access to environmental information and Directive 2003/35/EC on public participation and access to justice are partly transposed. Full transposition had to be done by 2016 and implementation will be done by 2018.[294]According to the EC report, 'further progress has been made in transposing EU directives on public access to environmental information and public participation in environmental decision-making. Amongst others, Serbia has opened a fifth Aarhus centre in December 2015 in Belgrade. Additional efforts are required to further increase the effectiveness of public consultations'.[295]

§3. Environmental Management System (EMS) and Eco-Management and Audit Scheme (EMAS) in Serbia

277. Different legal and sub-legal Acts contain legal framework for introduction and application of standards of the environmental management system (EMS)[296] and eco-management and audit scheme (EMAS).[297] Most important are the legal Acts by which issues of competences for certain activities in connection with standardization and the environment have been regulated as well as sub-legal Acts by which these two issues have been regulated in more details.

292. *See* , for example, D. Todić & V. Vukasović (ed.), *Pravo na dostupnost informacija, učešće javnosti u donošenju odluka i dostupnost pravosuđa prema Arhuskoj konvenciji i jugoslovenskim propisima* (Beograd: Reginalni centar za životnu sredinu za centralnu i istočnu Evropu) [REC – Regional Environmental Centre for Central and East Europe], 2006; http://www.rec.rs/images/stories/knjige/2001/pravo-na.pdf; S. Bogdanović & M. Gucić, Arhuska Konvencija u Republici Srbiji – vodič kroz propise o učešću javnosti u donošenju odluka i pravu na zaštitu u pitanjima zaštite životne sredine [*Arhus Convention in the Republic of Serbia – Guide Through Legislation on Public Participation and Access to Justice in the Environmental Maters*] (Beograd: Reginalni centar za životnu sredinu za centralnu i istočnu Evropu [REC – Regional Environmental Centre for Central and East Europe], 2006).

293. EPR (2015), 88.

294. SRS, Chs 27, 11.

295. CR, 76.

296. According to the ISO Survey at the end of 2006, companies from Serbia have eighty-four certifications for ISO 1401:2004. ISO Survey – 2006, 24.

297. On this subject, *see* , D. Todić, 'Sistem upravljanja i kontrole zaštite životne sredine (EMAS) u pravu Evropske unije' ['Environmental Management System – EMAS – in EU Law'], *Evropsko zakonodavstvo* [*EU Legislation*], Belgrade: Institut za međunarodnu politiku i privredu [Institute for International Policy and Economy], No. 11/05), 44–47.

I. Overview of the EMS/EMAS Legislation Competencies

278. The Serbian Constitution does not contain explicit provisions regarding standardization but contains several provisions dealing with the environment.[298] Article 97, point 6, of the Constitution prescribes that the Republic of Serbia regulates and guaranties 'Common market; legal position of the business subjects; system of the undertaking of certain business and other activities…'. Besides that the Republic regulates the following:

- other economic and social relations of general interests (point 8);
- scientific and technological development (point 12);
- financing of implementation of the rights and duties of the Republic of Serbia, as prescribed by the Constitution and law (point 15);
- organization, competencies and work of the organs of the Republic (point 16); and
- other relations of the interests of the Republic of Serbia, in accordance of the Constitution (point 17).

279. According to Article 4 of the Law on Ministries (OJ RS, Nos 44/14, 14/15, 54/15 and 96/15 – other law), the Ministry of Economy is competent for standardization issues. Standardization is also in competence of the Serbian Institute for Standardization.[299] The rights, obligations and responsibilities of the Institute have been stipulated by the Law on Standardization.

280. Serbian Accreditation Body (SAB)[300] is responsible for accreditation of conformity assessment organizations. SAB, as an independent non-profit organization, has been established by the Government's decree (OJ RS, Nos 96/2006, 14/11 and 95/16), based on the Law on Accreditation (OJ RS, No. 73/10), for the purposes of establishing the competency of organizations for performing the conformity assessment activities.

II. General Regulations in the Field of Standardization

281. Following are general legal Acts by which the field of standardization and EMS is regulated in Serbia:

- Law on Standardization (OJ RS, Nos 36/2009 and 46/15).
- Law on Accreditation (OJ RS, No. 73/2010).
- Law on Technical Conditions for Products and for Testing of Products with Prescribed Requirements (OJRS, No. 36/2009).

298. *See* chapter devoted to the 'constitutional provisions'.

299. *See* http://www.iss.rs/en.

300. The SAB is a legal successor of the Accreditation body of the former Serbia and Montenegro, or prior to that, of the Yugoslav Accreditation Body (YUAT), which was established in 1987 by the Federal Government (FRY) for the purposes of implementation of the then Law on Standardization, namely in order to perform accreditation activities. *See* http://www.ats.rs/en.

- Law on Metrology (OJ RS, No. 15/16).

282. Of importance are also following sub-legal Acts:

- Decision on establishment of the Institute for Standardization of Serbia (OJ RS, Nos 88/2009, 93/15 and 27/16).
- Decision on the Establishment of the Serbian Accreditation Body (OJ RS, Nos 96/2006, 14/11 and 95/16).
- Regulation on the manner of recognition of foreign documents and marks of conformity (OJ RS, Nos 98/09 and 110/16).
- Regulation on manner of performing conformity assessment, content of the document of conformity, and shape, appearance and content of mark of conformity (OJ RS, Nos 98/09 and 23/17).
- Regulation on the manner of designation and authorization of conformity assessment bodies (OJ RS, No. 98/09).
- Regulation on legal units of measurement (OJ RS, No. 43/11).
- Regulation on manner of providing information and notification of technical regulations, conformity assessment and standards (OJ RS, No. 45/10).
- Rulebook on manner of affixing marks of conformity on products and use of marks of conformity (OJ RS, No. 25/10).
- Rulebook on the establishment of a list of Serbian standards in the area of general product safety (OJ RS, No. 48/16).
- Rulebook on content and manner of keeping registers referring to technical regulations (OJ RS, No. 33/10).
- Rulebook on the noise emitted by equipment used in open space (OJ RS, No. 1/13), etc.[301]

III. Law on Standardization

283. The Law on Standardization governs the principles and objectives of standardization[302] in the Republic of Serbia, organization and activity of the national

301. For more information on legislation *see* : http://www.tehnis.privreda.gov.rs/en/Download.html (13 Jun. 2017).
302. 'Standardization' shall mean a set of coordinated activities aimed at adoption of standards and related documents (Art. 3, point 1).

standardization body, and the adoption, publication and application of Serbian standards[303] and related documents (Article 1).[304]

284. Pursuant to Article 5 of the Law, the objectives of standardization in the Republic of Serbia shall include: (1) improvement of the protection of life, health and safety of humans, animals and plants, as well as the environment protection; (2) raising the quality of products, processes and services, their typification, compatibility and substitutability; (3) ensuring a unique technical basis; (4) developing and improving the production and circulation of products, construction works, namely provision of services through the development of internationally harmonized standards with the aim of efficient use of labour, material and energy; and (5) improvement of international trade, through the prevention and elimination of unnecessary technical barriers.[305]

The Law also regulates establishment, activities, organs, membership and financing of Institute of Standardization (Articles 6–11).

285. Article 7 (paragraph 1) of the Law prescribes that the Institute shall perform following tasks:

(1) adopt, publish, review and withdraw Serbian standards, in accordance with the rules of the Institute;
(2) provide the interpretation of Serbian standards, as well as interpretation of the application of Serbian standards, at the request of the interested parties;
(3) ensure the compliance of Serbian standards with international and European standards;
(4) keep the Register of adopted and withdrawn Serbian standards, in accordance with the rules of the Institute;
(5) participate in the preparation and review of international and European standards in the areas of interest for the Republic of Serbia;

303. 'Standard' shall mean a publicly available document, defined by a consensus and adopted by a recognized body, which determines, for general and multiple use, the rules, requirements, characteristics, instructions, recommendations or guidelines for the activities or their results with the aim of achieving the optimal level of regulation in a specific area in relation to the current or potential problems (Art. 3, para. 1, point 2).

304. This Law shall apply to standards and related documents that are adopted and published by the national standardization body in the Republic of Serbia, as well as to international standards and related documents of the recognized international and European organizations for standardization referred to in Art. 3 items 12 and 13 of this Law which constitute the basis for adoption of Serbian standards (Art. 2).

305. Standardization in the Republic of Serbia shall be based on the following principles: (1) the right of all interested parties to voluntarily take part in adoption of Serbian standards; (2) consensus of interested parties; (3) prevention of the precedence of individual interests over the common interest of the interested parties; (4) transparency of the standardization procedure and public availability of Serbian standards and related documents; (5) mutual consistency of Serbian standards and related documents; (6) taking into account development of technology and rules of international and European organizations for standardization and relevant international agreements; and (7) non-discriminatory treatment of foreign products or services and same or similar domestic products or services, in accordance with ratified international agreements to which the Republic of Serbia is a signatory (Art. 4).

(6) cooperate with the international and European organizations for standardization and national bodies for standardization of countries signatory of relevant agreements in the area of standardization;
(7) perform the standardization related tasks, in accordance with the obligations arising from ratified international agreements to which the Republic of Serbia is a signatory;
(8) ensure the public availability of adopted and withdrawn Serbian standards, publications, as well as standards and publications of relevant international, European and national bodies for standardization, and carries out their sale;
(9) at the request of the State administration authority, provide the information whether a relevant Serbian standard has been adopted in the area that is being regulated by a technical regulation, or its adoption is pending, namely whether relevant international or European standard exists;
(10) act as an enquiry point for standards, for providing information and notifications related to standards, in accordance with the requirements provided for in the relevant international agreements and the obligations arising from the membership in relevant international and European organizations for standardization;[306]
(11) represent and act in the interest of the Republic of Serbia in the area of standardization in the international and European organizations for standardization;
(12) approve the use of national mark of conformity with the Serbian standards, in accordance with the rules of the Institute;
(13) issue the rules based on which Serbian standards are adopted, published, reviewed and withdrawn;
(14) delegate to the interested parties, in accordance with its rules, preparation of proposals of Serbian standards in specific areas;
(15) promote the application of Serbian standards; and
(16) perform other tasks in the area of standardization, in accordance with the law and articles of association.[307]

286. The Law regulates by its III and IV Chapters issues of adoption, publication and application of standards and related documents (Articles 12–19). So Article 12 prescribes following:

> Serbian standards shall be adopted and published in accordance with this Law and the rules of the Institute, which are harmonized with the rules of international and European organizations for standardization and the Code of Good Practice

306. The manner of providing information and notifications referred to in para. 1 item 10 of this Article shall be governed by a regulation adopted by the Government (para. 4).
307. The Institute shall not perform tasks referred to in para. 1 of this Article with the aim of acquiring profit (para. 3).

for the Preparation, Adoption and Application of Standards from the Agreement on Technical Barriers to Trade of the World Trade Organization (paragraph 1).[308]

IV. Law on Accreditation

287. The Law on Accreditation (OJ RS, No. 73/10) regulates accreditation, status and operation of the national accreditation body in the Republic of Serbia and other issues relevant to the accreditation (Article 1).[309]

288. Article 3 prescribes that accreditation shall be used to determine the competence of conformity assessment bodies to carry out the following activities: (1) testing; (2) calibration; (3) inspection;(4) certification of products; (5) certification of management systems; and (6) certification of persons.[310]

289. In accordance with Article 5, the Accreditation Board of Serbia (ABS) is the sole accreditation body in the Republic of Serbia that is hereby entrusted to perform accreditation activities referred to in Articles 3 and 8[311] of this Law.[312] ABS shall be independent from the conformity assessment bodies it assesses. ABS must not: (1) provide consultancy services to conformity assessment bodies; (2) perform activities or provide services provided by conformity assessment bodies; and (3) have proprietary and/or managerial rights or any other financial interests in conformity assessment bodies (Article 10).

308. As a rule, international standards and related documents shall be used as the basis for adoption of Serbian standards. In the event that international standard does not exist in particular area or the existing international standard is unsuitable, European or national standards and related documents of other countries may be used as a basis. The Institute shall publish in its OJ the notice on the instigation of procedure for adoption of a Serbian standard and, when it is necessary, for related document, as well as the notice on the placement of a standard or related document in the public discussion process (Art. 12, paras 2 and 3).

309. 'Accreditation' is an act of verification performed by the national accreditation body in order to confirm whether the conformity assessment bodies fulfil requirements of relevant Serbian and/or international and European standards and, where applicable, any additional requirements defined for specific fields, to carry out specific conformity assessment activities (Art. 2, point 1).

310. In addition to the competence to perform these activities accreditation shall be used to determine competence to perform other conformity assessment activities, in accordance with the specific law (para. 2). Accreditation is compulsory only if regulated by a specific law (Art. 4, para. 2).

311. It includes following activities: (1) set forth and publish the Rules of Accreditation based on the relevant Serbian, international and European standards, and on documents of international and European organizations for accreditation; (2) keep a public Register of Accredited Conformity Assessment Bodies; (3) participate in the work of international and European organizations for accreditation; and (4) perform other activities in accordance with the law, Establishment Act and Statute.

312. Founder of ABS is the Republic of Serbia, whereas the Government of the Republic of Serbia shall, under legal powers, exercise the rights of the Founder. ABS shall use Government property as means for performing its tasks and activities and ABS shall not operate on a profit-making basis (Art. 5, paras 2–4).

V. Other Relevant Regulations

290. Law on Technical Requirements for Products and Conformity Assessment (OJ RS, No. 36/09) governs the manner of prescribing technical requirements for products and adoption of technical regulations, assessment of conformity of products with prescribed technical requirements (conformity assessment),[313] obligations of suppliers of products and owners of products in use, validity of foreign documents of conformity and conformity markings, notification of technical regulations and conformity assessment procedures and supervision of the implementation of this Law and regulations adopted based on this Law (Article 1).[314] Technical requirements for individual products or groups of products (technical requirements) shall be prescribed in a technical regulation directly, by specifying such requirements in the text of the regulation, or indirectly, by the reference in the technical regulation to the Serbian standard or technical specification (Article 4).[315]

291. Technical regulation shall mean any regulation which, for individual product or groups of products (the product)[316] governs at least one of the following elements: (1) technical requirements that must be met by a product being made available on the market; (2) conformity assessment procedures; (3) safety requirements for product throughout its lifecycle; (4) regular and extraordinary inspection of product throughout its lifecycle; (5) documents that accompany product when placed on the market or put to use; (6) marking and manner of marking the product; (7) requirements that must be met by the conformity assessment body; and (8) requirements with regard to packaging and labelling (Article 5, paragraph 1).[317]

292. The Law on Metrology (OJ RS, No. 30/10) regulates organization of metrology activities, legal units of measurement and standards of Republic of Serbia, placing on the market and use of measuring instruments, conformity assessment of measuring instruments with prescribed requirements, pre-packaged products, the

---

313. 'Conformity assessment' shall mean any activity whereby it is determined whether a product or production process is in compliance with the prescribed technical requirements (Art. 3, point 9).

314. If specific laws and regulations referred to in para. 1 of this Article do not govern matters related to the appointment and/or authorization of conformity assessment bodies and validity of foreign documents of conformity and conformity markings, the provisions of this Law shall apply to such matters. The provisions of this Law governing notification of appointed and authorized conformity assessment body, keeping of registers and notification of technical regulations shall also apply to the products for which technical requirements are governed by specific laws and regulations adopted based on such laws (Art. 1, paras 2 and 3).

315. In respect of ensuring market regulation in regard to safety of products for which there are no specific technical regulations, the Law on General Product Safety was adopted (OJ RS, No. 41/09).

316. 'Product' shall mean any product which is, as the result of certain process, made or in any other manner obtained, regardless of the level of processing, if it is intended for placement on the market or making available on the market (Art. 3, point 1).

317. Technical regulations and technical requirements contained therein shall be adopted for the purpose of protecting the safety, life and health of humans, protecting animals and plants, environment protection, protection of consumers and other users and protection of property (Art. 5, para. 2).

validity of documents and marks of conformity of foreign origin, supervision, as well as other matters regarding metrology (Article 1). The purpose of this Law is to ensure unified measurements and the use of accurate measuring instruments in the Republic of Serbia as well as compatibility of the national units of measurement with the International System of Units and traceability of standards of Republic of Serbia to the international standards or national standards of other countries (Article 2).

293. In accordance to Article 6, paragraph 2, technical and their related executive activities in the field of metrology shall be performed by the Directorate for Measures and Precious metals, an administrative authority responsible for metrology activities (the Directorate).[318] Directorate shall in particular: (1) be responsible of the system of legal units of measurement in Republic of Serbia; (2) develop, realize, keep, proclaim, maintain and continuously improve measurement standards of Republic of Serbia; (3) provide metrological traceability; (4) conduct activities of metrological expertise; (5) conduct testing of pre-packaged products in order to check the fulfilment of metrological requirements; (6) represent the Republic of Serbia in the international metrological organizations and establish collaboration in the field of metrology; (7) perform metrological supervision; (8) perform conformity assessment of measuring instruments; (9) make decision in administrative proceedings in the field of metrology; (10) take part in preparation of regulations in the field of metrology; (11) keep registers of measuring instruments that are subject to legal control; (12) provide metrological information and publish OJ; (13) perform activities of distribution of time; and (14) conduct other activities in the field of metrology in accordance with the law.[319]

VI. Environmental Regulations Relevant for EMS/EMAS

294. The four systemic laws adopted at the end of 2004 are most important when regulations concerning the environment are regarded. They are as follows:

- Environmental Protection Law.
- Law on Environmental Impact Assessment (EIA).
- Law on Strategic Environmental Assessment (SEA) and
- Law on Integrated Pollution Prevention and Control (IPPC.[320]

---

318. Activities of verifying measuring instruments are performed by economic operators and/or other legal persons that are in accordance with this Law authorized to perform such activities (authorized bodies). Activities of conformity assessment of measuring instruments are performed by economic operators and/or other legal persons that are in accordance with this Law designated to perform such activities (Designated bodies) (Art. 6, paras 3 and 4).
319. Apart from activities referred to in para. 1 points 1–13 of this Article the Directorate shall perform the activities of verification of measuring instruments for whose verification there are no authorized bodies, in a manner which ensures impartiality of performing these activities (Art. 7, para. 2).
320. All of them have been adopted on 21 Dec. 2004 (OJ RS, No. 135/2004).

A. Law on Environmental Protection

295. EPL contains provisions directly related to the EMS and EMAS. The other three systematic laws are important primarily because they are systematic regulations by which certain environmental policy instruments, important for the functioning of the system as a whole, have been introduced.

296. The legal basis for the system of EMAS has been formed by EPL. The Law contains a special section 2.2 devoted to Environmental Protection Management System (Article 44).

297. Legal and natural person may certify the environmental protection management system according to SRPS-ISO 14001, in accordance with law. Legal and natural person may register the certified environmental protection management system for the purpose of integration into the system of environmental protection management and control of the EU (the EMAS system), in accordance with this Law.[321]

298. Some other provisions of the EPL should also be mentioned and especially in provisions concerning the following:

- Rights and Duties of the Inspector (Article 110).
- Powers of Inspectors (Article 111).
- Offences (Articles 117, 120 and 121).[322]

299. 'Voluntary initiatives, such as adoption of certified environmental management systems, continued to develop steadily but remained at a comparatively modest level.'[323] There are no enterprises certified according to the EU EMAS. Government action on promoting compliance has apparently focused on providing financial support to the regulated community.'

Serbia indicated its intention to align its legislation by the end of 2015 with Regulation (EC) No. 1221/2009 on EMAS and Regulation (EC) No. 66/2010 on the EU Ecolabel. 'The implementation of the two Regulations is at an early stage ...'. Serbia plans to fully implement those Regulations by 2020.[324]

§4. Enforcement and Control

300. The environmental inspection is performed according to the Law on Inspection (OJ RS, No. 36/2015). The National Assembly of the Republic of Serbia adopted (on 15 April 2015), the Law on Inspection (OJ RS, No. 36/2015) which entered into force on 29 April 2015, and is applicable in twelve months upon entering into

321. The registration into the EMAS system shall be carried out on the basis of the request from legal and natural person submitted to the Ministry.
322. 'For the offence from Arts 117 and 118 of this Law, along with the penalty, a protective measure may be imposed by confiscating objects which have been used or intended to be used for an offence, or which have occurred or have been obtained in an offensive action.'
323. EPR (2015), 51.
324. SRS, Chs 27, 11.

force, i.e., as of 30April 2016 (Article 70).[325] Previously, the matter of inspection was regulated by the provisions of the Law on State Administration (OJ RS, Nos 20/92, 6/93 – CC, 48/93, 53/93, 67/93, 48/94 and 49/99 – other law, 79/05 – other law, 101/05 – other law, and 87/11 – other law).

301. This Law shall govern the contents, types and forms, as well as the procedure of the inspection supervision, powers and obligations of the participants in the inspection supervision and other issues significant for the inspection supervision (Article 1).[326]

302. According to Article 2 of the Law the inspection supervision shall be the task of the state administration, the contents of which as well as the term have been specified by this Law, which governs the operation of the state administration, carried out by the state administration authorities, as well as the authorities of the AP and authorities of the local self-government units, with the aim of taking preventive actions or imposing measures that secure legality and safety of operation and actions of the supervised entities, and thus prevent or remove the damaging consequences incurred to the goods, rights and interests protected by the law and other regulation.[327]

303. The intended purpose of the changes is to enhance coordination between the bodies charged with conducting inspection, determination of the inspector's competences, increase transparency in the operation of inspection, etc. The Law, *inter alia,* introduced a new term – 'unregistered entity'. An unregistered entity shall mean a supervised entity, which operates or performs activities, and which is not registered with a relevant register maintained by the Business Registers Agency, or other body or organization competent for the registration of incorporation of a legal entity and other entity (hereinafter, referred to as the basic register), when registration with this register has been specified as a requirement for operation or performance of activities (Article 3, point 4).[328]

304. Environmental inspection control is performed by the Ministry through its environmental inspectors.[329] Articles 109–115 of the EPL define position of

325. Except for the provisions governing non-registered entities and the treatment of non-registered entities which became applicable as of 30July 2015, or as of 30 Sep.2015.
326. The inspection shall mean an authority within, an internal organizational unit or inspectors of the state administration authorities, i.e., authorities of the AP or local self-government unit or other entity holding public powers, which perform the inspection supervision (Art. 3, point 1).
327. Other forms of supervision and control shall comply with the inspection supervision, the performance of which shall examine the application of the law and other regulations, by direct insight into the operation and actions of the supervised entity, which shall be carried out by the authorities referred to in para. 1 of this Article as well as other entities holding public powers, in line with a special law (Art. 2, para. 2).
328. Inspection over 'unregistered entities' can be performed even when this was not anticipated in the inspection plan (Art. 33). In addition, such entities can be inspected without any prior notice or issuance of the inspection order, within the scope determined by the inspector. Immediately when it discovers an unregistered entity, the inspector will render a decision containing measures for elimination of irregularities and prohibiting the entity's further activities.
329. During 2007, totally 4,234 inspections were made in the fields of nature protection, nature resources and fishery; 7,068 in the field of industry and 10,271 border checkups, *Godisnji izvestaj sektora za kontrolu i nadzor za 2007.* godinu [*Annual Report of the Sector for Control and Supervision*], Data for 2010 *see* Annual Report 2010. Sector for Control and Survelliance, Ministry of Environment and Spatial Planning.

environmental inspection (rights and duties of inspectors, competencies of inspectors, etc.).

I. Rights and Duties of Inspectors

305. Rights and duties of inspectors, in performing inspection control, are prescribed by the several provisions of the Law on inspection (Articles 21, 24, 25, 26, 27, 28, 29, etc.) and by provisions of Article 110 of the EPL.

306. According to Article 110 of the EPL, the inspector has the right and duty to determine, *inter alia*, the following: (1) whether the management, namely sustainable use and protection of natural resources and goods are carried out in line with strategic documents and conditions and measures; (2) whether collecting and placement on the market of wild flora and fauna and their developing forms and parts are carried out in accordance with prescribed conditions; (3) whether import, export and transit of endangered and protected species of wild flora and fauna and their developing forms and parts are carried out in compliance with prescribed conditions; (4) whether the measures and conditions of environmental protection in planning and constructing are being implemented; (5) whether the standards of environmental quality and emission are being applied; (6) whether the conditions for operation and activation of the installation have been fulfilled; (7) whether domestic or imported technologies or processes are being applied in compliance with prescribed norms of environmental protection; (8) whether prescribed prohibitions on production and trade with certain products and performance of certain activities are being implemented; (9) whether ecological label for products, processes or services is being used in a prescribed manner; (10) whether import and export of substances depleting ozone layer (and import, export and transit of waste) are being carried out in compliance with this Law; (11) whether dangerous substances in production, use, transport, trade, processing, storage and disposal are treated in accordance with prescribed measures; (12) whether monitoring of environmental state is being performed; (13) whether information system and integrated cadastre of polluters are being kept; (14) whether the Fund's finances are being earmarked; and (15) whether the obligations from ratified international agreements from the area of environmental protection are being implemented.

307. In accordance with Directive on Planning and Reporting on Environmental Inspections (republic level) No. 353-03-2196/2006-01, entered into force on 31 January 2007 and compliant to the Council of Europe and the European Parliament Recommendation from 4 April 2001. (2001/331/EC) on Introduction of Minimum Criteria for Environmental

Inspections (RMCEI), the planning method, reporting and record keeping on inspections have been unified for all republic inspectors.[330]

II. Authorization of the Inspector

308. Authorization of the inspector is prescribed by Article 26 of the Law on State (generally) and by Article 111 of the EPL more precisely. According to Article 111 of the EPL inspector is authorized, to:

(1) order the correction of irregularities in implementation of the measures of protection, reclamation and rehabilitation of the environment in the process of utilization of natural resources and goods, within a specified period;
(2) prohibit the use or utilization of natural resources and goods without approval or contrary to the approval and to instruct rehabilitation and/or undertaking of other appropriate protective measures;
(3) prohibit the introduction and growing of flora and fauna of foreign origin for the purpose of free habitation in nature, which could threaten autochthonic species and their spreading;
(4) prohibit destroying or damaging of wild flora and fauna and their habitats;
(5) prohibit collecting or placing on the market wild flora and fauna, their developing forms and parts without license;
(6) prohibit importation and exportation of endangered and protected species of wild flora and fauna, their developing forms and parts whose circulation is prohibited by international agreements;
(7) prohibit importation and exportation of endangered and protected species of wild flora and fauna, their developing forms and parts whose circulation is permitted if it is carried out without a license;
(8) prohibit construction and use of installations or establishments and performance of activities if the prescribed requirements and norms regarding emissions and pollutant levels are not met, if they do not have appropriate and functioning equipment and devices which reduce or prevent the emission of pollutants or energy or if other measures and conditions of environmental protection have not been undertaken;
(9) prohibit production and circulation of means of transportation that do not meet the conditions regarding emission for mobile sources of pollution;

---

330. This means that all inspectors within their proscribed duties have to perform at least fifteen environmental inspections in one month and draft a monthly report and plan for the next month, delivered to his/her immediate manager at the beginning of the month (first day of the month). All the reports are grouped by divisions, for six-month period and annually and at the end of the year they are published on the website of the Ministry. The inspector's plan for the next month must be compliant to the annual work plan of the department. Furthermore, planned inspection visits may or may not be announced to operators. D. Todić, *Review of Serbian Implementation and Enforcement Procedures in the Environment Sector*, *supra* 41. For the number of inspections in 2010, *see* , *ibid.*, 3.

(10) prohibit release of polluting and dangerous substances, wastewaters or energy into air, water and soil in a manner and in quantities, namely concentrations or levels exceeding the prescribed ones;
(11) prohibit operation, use or utilization of technology, technological process that are not allowed according to the provisions of this Law;
(12) prohibit use or utilization of products, semi-finished products or raw material that are not allowed according to the provisions of this Law;
(13) instruct that, in case of doubt, certain technology, storing, technological process product, semi-finished product or raw material be examined with respect to potential harmful effect on the environment and to temporarily prohibit their use or utilization until the results of examination are presented;
(14) suspend operation of devices until the efficiency of devices for elimination or treatment of pollutants for which there are no prescribed limit values has been examined;
(15) prohibit placing on the market raw materials, semi-finished products or products which do not have visible mark on the potential threat to the environment;
(16) prohibit use of ecological label contrary to the provisions of this Law;
(17) prohibit importation of hazardous waste of foreign origin;
(18) prohibit importation, exportation and transit of waste contrary to the provisions of this Law and to order their return to the sender;
(19) prohibit operation of the Seveso installation or establishment when measures prescribed in the Policy on Accident Prevention or the Report on Safety or the Plan on Protection from Accident are not implemented or are insufficiently implemented;
(20) order preparation of the Policy on Accident Prevention or the Report on Safety or the Plan on Protection from Accident and undertaking of appropriate preventive and other measures for protection of the environment from dangerous substances, in accordance with this Law;
(21) prohibit operation of the Seveso installation or establishment if the Notification, Policy on Accident Prevention or the Report on Safety or the Plan on Protection from Accident have not been submitted within the specified period;
(22) in case of an accident, order undertaking of intervention measures and procedures for response to accidents, implementation of measures in accordance with the Plan on Protection from Accident, engaging of people, resources and undertaking of measures for rehabilitation and prevention of spread of pollution caused by the chemical accident;
(23) order the performance of monitoring in the prescribed manner;
(24) order implementation of measures of environmental protection, in accordance with this Law;
(25) prohibit use of funds from the account of a legal person, entrepreneur and natural person on the basis of an executive conclusion;
(26) take samples of soil, waters, waste, and air through the authorized organization;
(27) in the procedure of enforced execution of a decision, carry out sealing of premises, installations or establishments, equipment or areas that have caused or might have caused polluting or damage to the environment, in accordance with law;
(28) carry out an order of other prescribed obligations within the specified period.

III. Cooperation Between Inspectors

309. Cooperation between inspectors from different domains is regulated by the Law on State Administration, and by provisions of specific laws which regulate certain domains. Especially important is provision of Article 27 of Law of State Administration by which it is prescribed that, inspector while performing his/her duties cooperates with other inspectors, judicial organs, magistrates and other interested organs and organizations.[331]

IV. Transferring Competence of Inspection

310. Certain activities concerning inspection control could be, by law, transferred to organs of counties, city of Belgrade, other cities and APs (Article 22 of the Law on State Administration).

Chapter VII of the Law on State Administration regulates conflict of competencies between: ministries, ministries and special organizations, between special organizations, organs of State administration and organs to whom duties of State administration were transferred, organs of State organizations and enterprises, institutions and other organizations, organs to whom are transferred duties of administration from the competencies of the Republic, between enterprises, institutions and other organizations when in performing administrative competencies make decision concerning specific rights and duties from the domain of rights and duties of Republic, etc. (Articles 72–74).

311. Article 109,paragraphs 3 and 4 of the EPL prescribes that the AP shall perform inspection supervision over the implementation of the activities given by this Law and regulations made on its basis. Local self-governance unit shall perform inspection supervision over the implementation of the activities given by this Law and regulations made on its basis.[332]

V. Other Legal Regulations Relevant for Environmental Inspection

312. Duties of environmental inspectors are also performed according to following environmental regulations:

---

331. Article 113 of the EPL prescribes general rules of cooperation of environmental inspectors with inspectors competent in other domains. It is prescribed by the Article that inspector is obliged 'to inform other competent authority aside from taking measures under his authorization', and that 'the other competent inspection authority shall inform the inspector of the measures taken'. In cases when inspector determines that a violation of law is also in the competence of other inspection authorities, he/she 'is obliged to inform the Minister thereof, without further delay, so that they could jointly perform inspection and take adequate measures'.
332. The Ministry shall supervise work of the EPA, authorities responsible for environmental protection in the AP and responsible authorities of the local self-governance unit, as well as authorized legal persons, in the performance of delegated tasks (Art. 109a).

- Law on National Parks (OJ RS, No. 84/15), Article 25 regulates supervision.
- Law on Nature Protection (OJ RS, Nos 36/09 and 88/10), Articles 118–124.
- Law on Protection and Sustainable Use of Fish Reserves (OJ RS, No. 128/14), Articles 53–57.
- Law on the Protection from Non-ionizing Radiation (OJ RS, No. 36/09), Articles 14–16.
- Law on Ionizing Radiation Protection and Nuclear Safety (OJ RS, Nos 36/09 and 93/12), Articles 76–83.
- Law on Air Protection (OJ RS, Nos 36/09 and 10/13), Articles 73–77.
- Law on Waters (OJ RS, Nos 36/09, 93/12 and 101/16), Articles 196–208.
- Law on Environmental Impact Assessment (OJ RS, Nos 135/04 and 36/09), Articles 35–39.
- Law on Integrated Pollution Prevention and Control (OJ RS, Nos 135/04 and 25/15), Articles 26–28.
- Law on Chemicals (OJ RS, Nos 36/09, 88/10, 92/11, 93/12 and 25/15), Articles 86–96.
- Law on Biocidal Products (OJ RS, Nos 36/09, 88/10, 92/11 and 25/15), Articles 50–58.
- Law on Noise Protection (OJ RS, Nos 36/09 and 88/10), Articles 29–32.
- Law on Waste Management (OJ RS, Nos 36/09, 88/10 and 14/16), Articles 83–86.
- Law on Packaging Waste (OJ RS, No. 36/09), Articles 46–49.
- Law on Genetically Modified Organisms (OJ RS, No. 41/09), Articles 37–44, etc.

313. Besides that, there are a number of legal Acts regulating inspection, and especially the following:

- Law on Ministries (OJ RS, Nos 44/14, 14/15, 54/15 and 96/15– other law).
- Law on Determining the Jurisdiction of the Autonomous Province of Vojvodina (OJ RS, Nos 99/2009 and 67/12 CC).
- Law on Local Self-Government (OJ RS, Nos 129/07 and 83/14 – other law and 101/16 – other law).
- Law on the Capital (OJ RS, Nos 120/2007 and 83/14 – other law and 101/16 – other law).
- Law on Communal Activities (OJ RS, Nos 88/11 and 104/16).
- Law on General Administrative Procedure (OJ SRJ, Nos 33/97 and 31/01, and OJ RS, No. 30/10).
- Criminal Code (OJ RS, Nos 85/2005 and 88/2005 – corr, 107/2005 – corr, 72/09, 111/09, 121/12, 104/1, 108/14 and 94/16).
- Law on Economic Offences (OJ SFRY, Nos 4/1977, 36/1977, 14/1985, 74/1987, 57/1989 and 3/1990, OJ FRY, Nos 27/1992, 24/1994,28/1996 and 64/2001, and OJ RS, No. 101/05 – other law).
- Law on Offences (OJ RS, Nos 65/13, 13/16 and 98/16 CC), etc.

VI. Other Relevant Inspections

314. There are several other inspections, besides environmental ones, relevant for environmental issues, as for example health inspection, sanitary inspection, forestry inspection, hunting inspection, agricultural inspection, phytosanitary inspection, veterinary inspection, water inspection, tourist inspection, market inspection, labour inspection, mining inspection, spatial planning inspection, building inspection, geodesic inspection, electro-energetic inspection, inspection for equipment under pressure, fire protection inspection, public roads inspection, administration inspection, communal inspection, etc.

315. Republic environmental protection inspection is faced with problems that can be grouped into following areas: state of legislation, cooperation with ministries, state bodies and organizations, provincial and local governments, justice, cooperation with other sectors in the Ministry, professional competences of inspectors, technical equipment of inspection, relation with the media, entrusted activities, and employment new staff.[333] In its overall design, the system of inspection largely follows Recommendation 2001/331/EC providing for minimum criteria for environmental inspections in the Member States.[334]

316. The Environmental Inspection 'remain issues of concern, especially in relation to the overall capacity of these institutions to ensure effective implementation and enforcement of the acquis'.[335] According to the EC, in the coming period, Serbia should in particular, *inter alia*, 'intensify efforts regarding implementation and enforcement including closing noncompliant landfills, investing in waste separation and recycling, reinforcing air quality monitoring and advancing on river basin management'.[336]

§5. Legal Harmonization

317. To a certain extent, harmonization of the Serbian environmental law with the EU environmental *acquis* has begun already in mid-nineties. A commission for harmonization of the Yugoslav law with the EU law and the Council of Europe law had been established in 1995, on the federal level, but due to the overall crisis and isolation of the country it did not fulfil its task. After the political changes in 2000, the new federal Government formed an interdepartmental group with the assignment to coordinate activities concerning law harmonization. In Serbia, several expert groups

333. The Report of the Environmental protection inspection for 2016, MAEP, Belgrade, 2017, 37–39.

334. EPR (2015), 52.

335. SRS, Chs 27, 18. A more effective coordination between MAEP, MoI and other relevant ministries, institutions, bodies and the local authorities is required. Efforts under way to strengthen inspection and enforcement need to be accompanied by the removal of inconsistencies and gaps in legislation that prevent effective enforcement. *Ibid.* On inspection in the field of air quality, nature protection, industrial pollution and risk management, chemicals, *see also*, pages 19, 23, 24, 25.

336. CR, 2016, 75.

were established and given the task of producing drafts of new legislation and/or amendments of the existing environmental legislation that should be harmonized with the relevant *acquis communautaire*. In November 2000, Serbia, as one of the two Republics of former FR Yugoslavia, became a part of the Stabilization and Association Process (SAP).

318. Serbian National Assembly adopted in 2004 a resolution on Serbia's European future,[337] and Serbian Government adopted in 2005 the National Strategy for Accession to the EU.[338] The document outlines, *inter alia*, activities which Serbia should undertake in harmonizing its legal system (including the environmental field), as to be able to become a member of the EU by 2012.

However, due to political reasons, the decision to start negotiations concerning conclusion of the SAA was not made until April 2005. By the decision of the EC, negotiations on SAP were resumed in June 2007 and successfully concluded by initialling the SAA on 7 November 2007.

It means that, in practice, all new draft legislation, including environmental legislation, is submitted to the European Integration Office of the Government of Serbia. The Office is responsible for coordination of Government activities in the framework of the EU SAP, including analysis of compatibility of draft legislation with *acquis communautaire*. It should be stressed that Serbia is, since 2006, also eligible for EU pre-accession financial assistance under the EU Community Assistance for Reconstruction, Development and Stabilization (CARDS) programme, and since 2007 under the Instrument for Pre-Accession Assistance (IPA).

319. The SAA was finally signed on 29 April 2008 and ratified by Serbia in September 2008 (OJ RS, No. 83/2008).[339] The Stabilization and Association Agreement between Serbia and the EU entered into force in September 2013.

Signing of the SAA obliged Serbia to gradually harmonize its environmental legislation with environmental *acquis* and to implement it consistently. According to Article 72 of the SAA, it is under obligation, in agreement with the EC, to prepare a programme for the implementation of obligations arising from the SAA, which will be monitored by the EU.[340]

The European Council granted Serbia the status of candidate country in 2012. Accession negotiations were launched in January 2014. The first four negotiating

---

337. *See* http://www.parlament.gov.rs/activities/european-integration/documents.611.html.

338. The key goal of the Strategy is to provide an expert foundation for the decision-making in the European integration process, and to prepare a coordinated set of measures, policies and institutions necessary for the EU association, including the plan for the approximation of the domestic legislation with the *acquis communautaire*. 16 Sep. 2008, http://www.seio.gov.rs/upload/documents/nacionalna_dokumenta/national_strategy-pdf.pdf.

339. *See also*, Council Decision (2008/213/EC) of 18 Feb. 2008 on the principles, priorities and conditions contained in the European Partnership with Serbia including Kosovo as defined by United Nations Security Council Resolution 1244 of 10 Jun. 1999 and repealing Decision 2006/56/EC, OJ L 080, 19 Mar. 2008 P. 0046-0070.

340. The Art. 72 prescribes that 'The Parties recognise the importance of the approximation of the existing legislation in Serbia to that of the Community and of its effective implementation. Serbia shall endeavour to ensure that its existing laws and future legislation will be gradually made compatible with the Community acquis. Serbia shall ensure that existing and future legislation will be properly implemented and enforced.'

chapters are opened including Chapter 35 dealing with normalization of relations between Serbia and Kosovo□[341] and the rule of law Chapters 23 and 24.

320. The Government of Serbia adopted, in June 2008, the National Programme for integration with EU that contains assessment of the state of harmonization of legal regulations and which sets short- and long-term priorities in relevant domains.[342]

While 'environment' is mentioned in several Articles of the SAA, Article 111 is completely devoted to it:

> The parties shall, in particular, establish cooperation with the aim of strengthening administrative structures and procedures to ensure strategic planning of environment issues and coordination between relevant actors and shall focus on the alignment of Serbia's legislation to the Community acquis. Cooperation could also centre on the development of strategies to significantly reduce local, regional and transboundary air and water pollution, to establish a framework for efficient, clean, sustainable and renewable production and consumption of energy, and to execute environmental impact assessment and strategic environmental assessment. Special attention shall be paid to the implementation of the Kyoto Protocol.

The National Plan for the Adoption of Acquis (NPAA) (2014–2018) has been adopted. The NPAA defines development and strategic goals on the one hand and policies, reforms and measures required for the realization of these goals on the other. It also establishes a detailed plan, time frame and priorities for the adoption of legislation and appoints bodies responsible for their implementation.[343] In the meantime, the second revision of the NPAA was adopted in November 2016.[344]

341. This designation is without prejudice to positions on status, and is in line with UNSCR 1244/1999 and the ICJ Opinion on the Kosovo declaration of independence.

342. *Short-term priorities* are determined to accelerate harmonization of Serbian legislature with the *acquis communitaire*; implement existing laws, in particular in the area of environmental protection; commence with the Kyoto Protocol implementation; adopt and implement the National Environmental Protection Strategy; strengthen administrative capacities of bodies in charge of planning, licensing, controlling, monitoring and project managing; strengthen local-level capacities and ensure operational coordination between local and central levels; continue further development of and commence with the implementation of waste management plans, and begin the construction of hazardous waste recycling and safe disposal facilities. *Mid-term priorities* are full implementation of legislation that has been harmonized with the *acquis communitaire*; implement relevant international conventions and the Kyoto Protocol; adopt and commence with the implementation of Air Pollution, Waste Management and Environmental Protection Strategy; fully implement the National Environmental Protection Strategy and Water Strategy; continue strengthening national- and local-level administrative capacities in charge of environmental issues; implement years-long environmental policy financing plan, including the investment plan for this area; complete the construction of facilities for hazardous waste disposal' NPI, 619.

343. Full realization of the goals set in NPAA is envisaged to be completed by 31 Dec. 2018, with the exception of those obligations for which interim timeframes for adapting will be set during the course of the negotiations, after acquiring the EU membership. NPAA, 3.

344. NPAA, II revision, European Integration Office, Government of the Republic of Serbia, November 2016.

321. Explanatory and bilateral screenings on Chapter 27 – Environment and Climate Change were held from September to November 2014. 'Following the bilateral screening, the Negotiating Group 27 was required to prepare a Post-Screening Document which contains a detailed description of the transposition and implementation: the strategic framework for full transposition and implementation of directives, preliminary deadlines for full implementation of EU legislation regarding this chapter, particularly for heavy investment directives, as well as financial sources to fund the implementation, with the aim to demonstrate Serbia's preparedness in the accession process.'[345]

322. According to the last Report of the EC:

> Serbia has achieved some level of preparation in this area. Some progress has been made in further aligning policies and legislation with the acquis, including in waste, nature protection and climate change. Serbia improved its strategic planning and set up a Green Fund, both key recommendations in 2015.[346]

§6. Critical Evaluation of the Efficiency of the Existing Serbian Environmental Law

323. A much more voluminous text would be needed for a detailed analysis of the evaluation of the efficiency of the Serbian legal provisions concerning the environmental protection. The extent and the result of the analysis would also depend upon the chosen evaluation criteria and irregular and extremely difficult conditions under which the Serbian legal system in general and the environmental law in particular, has been functioning. One of the most important facts is, without doubt, the fact that former FR Yugoslavia (Serbia and Montenegro) had been, between 1992 and 2000, practically excluded from all, or almost all, forms of international environmental relations. The crisis had grave consequences upon the functioning of the legal system in general, as well as the legal regulation of environmental protection, including malfunctioning of the judiciary. A very important problem has been the corruption of the system,[347] including in some cases even corruption of judges. Generally gloomy circumstances in Serbian society, including the pauperization of most of the population,

345. NPAA, II revision, 1148. The Post-Screening Document entitled 'Transposition and Implementation of Environmental and Climate Change Acquis (Chapter 27): Status and Plans' was adopted on 4 Sep. 2015 and submitted to the EC. For more information on the activities of the negotiating group (Ch. 27), *see* http://www.pregovarackagrupa27.gov.rs/dokumenti/?lang=en (18 Jun. 2017).

346. CR, 75. In the coming period, Serbia should in particular, *inter alia*, enhance administrative and financial capacity by strengthening the EPA's monitoring and reporting, adequately resourcing the new environmental finance facility (Green Fund) and improving inter-institutional coordination at both central and local level; intensify efforts regarding implementation and enforcement including closing non-compliant landfills, reinforcing air quality monitoring and advancing on river basin management; ratify the Paris Agreement and start implementing it, including by developing a comprehensive strategy for climate change. *Ibid.*, 75–76.

347. On this subject *see* , Nacionalna strategija za borbu protiv korupcije [*National Anti-corruption Strategy*] adopted by the Government (2004), http://www.srbija.gov.rs/vesti/dokumenti_sekcija.php?id=45678.

and rising role of the crime, caused in that time degradation of the legal system in general, including of course the environmental law, which is still felt to a certain extent today.

324. The state of environmental legislation is almost entirely determined by the process of EU integration. During the last several years, legislation of the RS is in the process of continuous monitoring and assessment of conformity with EU legislation. There is a detailed assessment of the level of compliance of all environmental regulations. However, generally speaking it can be concluded that there are significant problems in the implementation of regulations in almost all areas (industrial pollution, waste management, water management, air protection, environmental protection, etc.). The capacity of the competent authorities is not satisfactory. The issue of coordination between different bodies (horizontal and vertical) can be significantly improved.[348] Financing in certain sectors is a serious problem, etc.

325. During the past several years, a considerable improvement has been achieved, especially since 2004. For instance EIA has been the most efficient regulatory instrument since it was implemented in Serbia,[349] numerous international treaties have been ratified or are planned to be ratified soon, much has been done in upgrading institutional structure, new laws and other legal Acts have been adopted and serious effort made in the process of harmonization of Serbian environmental legislation with the EU standards. It should also take into account the elements of the positive impact of the EU integration process on international cooperation and the achievement of national goals in the environmental policy.[350]

326. When it comes to the degree of harmonization with the environmental *acquis*, the intensive legislative activity of the relevant institutions 'led to a significantly raised level of transposition of the relevant EU regulations'. According to the Progress Monitoring Report 2013, 'the major part of EU directives relating to the so-called horizontal sector, environment protection, chemicals management, noise protection, is completely or almost completely transposed into the national legislation'. 'Most of the EU regulations' in the field of air quality, waste management, water protection and industrial pollution control are transposed into the national legislation 'to a large degree.'[351]

327. The issue of stakeholder participation in the process of harmonizing national regulations with EU regulations is not at a level that ensures the creation of quality regulations. In the state administration rules governing this issue, there are gaps which

348. The mechanisms of horizontal coordination and integration of environmental policy initiated in the short-term will need to be further expanded and institutionalized in the medium-term (waste management, river basin management, etc.). NEPP, 145.

349. EPR (2007), 91.

350. On details, *see* : Todić, D., Dimitrijević, D., Priority goals in international co-operation of the Republic of Serbia in the field of environment and sustainable development, *International Environmental Agreements: Politics, Law and Economics*: 14, 2/2014, 163–179.

351. NPAA, 735.

create conditions for the adoption of regulations without the efficient participation of the public concerned. Public participation at local level is much more specific.[352]

328. Regulatory impact assessment was introduced in the law preparation system (not by by-laws and international treaties) in 2005. There are certain results. However, the existing methodology of regulatory impact assessment – assessing costs of laws adoption and implementation that would affect the budget, citizens, the economy and other factors, cannot be taken as reliable. As a whole, it can be recognized that there is some unevenness present including the problems in providing necessary indicators for the assessment of state, anticipation of possible consequences and selection of alternative solutions.[353]The legal framework relevant for assessment of opportunities of the economy and the society for implementation of the national legislation harmonized with EU legislation has not been established in a satisfactory manner. The issue of administration capacities to assess the needs for transitional periods deserves more attention.[354]

329. A part of problems, concerning the state of environmental legislation in Serbia, could be linked to general situation in Serbian judiciary which is still not efficient enough. This causes difficulties to citizens, enterprises and NGOs when they are subject of court procedure. It usually takes time for a court proceeding to result in a court order and an adequate sanction, which often are not imposed or are largely symbolic. Judges are not adequately trained in environmental law, nor are State prosecutors and police bodies. 'There is a perception that the judiciary is ineffective when it comes to imposing sanctions for environmental offences. It can take some time for a court proceeding to result in a court order and an eventual sanction; then, in many cases, sanctions are not imposed or are largely symbolic.'[355]

330. According to the NEPP, the medium-term phase (2015–2019) should focus 'on implementation and expanding of the various regulatory instruments introduced or reformed in the short-term phase. Emphasis should be put on introducing permitting to all significant polluters'.[356] Regarding the monitoring and information systems, the following reforms are envisaged for medium-term period: strengthening of quality

352. For details, *see* Bobić M., Todić, D. Harmonisation of national regulations of the Republic of Serbia with EU regulations and public participation, in G.Marković (Ed). Collection of Papers, *Relationship between the EU Law and the Law in the Region*, Istočno Sarajevo: Pravni fakultet, 2015, 458–472.

353. Presentations D. Todić, 'Europeanisation' of law of the Republic of Serbia: Between (un)clear goals and (in)appropriate indicators, International Conference, *Law and Transition,* University of Belgrade – Faculty of Law,in cooperation with German Foundation for International Legal Cooperation (IRZ), Belgrade, 23 and 24 Mar. 2017. *See also,*Todić, D. Harmonization of legislation of the Republic of Serbia with EU law: open issues and dilemmas, *Review of international affairs,* 1-2/2014, 96–109.

354. For some observations, *see* Todić, D., Dragišić, N., EU i Srbija: od obaveze usaglašavanja nacionalnih propisa sa propisima EU i njihove primene do prelaznih rokova [EU, and Serbia: from the obligation to harmonize national regulations with EU regulations and their application to the transitional periods]. *Evropsko zakonodavstvo*, 47–48/2014, 30–39. Todić, D. Evropske integracije i nacionalni interesi [European integration and the 'national interests'], *Politička revija,* 44, 2/2015, 1–18.

355. EPR, (2015), 56.

356. NEPP, 116.

assurance and quality control in the certified monitoring institutions and laboratories, further expansion of self-monitoring and compliance monitoring, introduction of continuous ambient air (and noise) monitoring in smaller agglomerations, broadening the network for monitoring of wastewater discharges, introduction of regular monitoring of heavy metal content in sewage sludge, and heavy metal and pesticide concentration in soil, etc.[357]

331. 330. In the field of environmental financing system, the medium-term 'reforms will require further strengthening of the environmental revenue collection, expanding the revenue base, fiscal decentralization, privatization and further increase of tariffs to achieve full cost recovery'.[358] 'Substantial extension and modernization of environmental infrastructure will take place in the medium term when efficient environmental financing system is put in place and investment priorities are established.'[359] Substantial extension and modernization of environmental infrastructure will take place in the medium term 'when efficient environmental financing system is put in place and investment priorities are established'.[360]

357. NEPP, 125.
358. NEPP, 140.
359. NEPP, 154.
360. NEPP, 154.

Chapter 2. Air Pollution

332. The main sources of air pollution in Serbia include the energy sector (thermo-power plants and district heating plants), oil refineries, chemical industry, metal processing industry, individual heating boiler plants, traffic, inadequate storage, waste dump sites including flotation tailing ponds, etc. The old vehicle fleet still uses leaded fuel and low-quality motor fuels (diesel fuel with high sulphur content).[361]

§1. The Monitoring System

333. The national network for monitoring air quality is in competence of the Agency for Environmental Protection in accordance with the Law on Air Protection (OJ RS, Nos 36/09 and 10/13).[362]First Bi-annual Programme for Air Monitoring in Serbia dates from 1993 (OJ RS, No. 70/93). Air pollution monitoring is presently regulated by Articles 9–17 of the Law on air protection[363] and by the EPL (OJ RS, Nos 135/04, 36/09, 72/2009, 43/2011 and 14/2016). By Article 24 of the EPL, it is prescribed that 'measures of systematic air quality monitoring' should be undertaken, while Article 69 prescribes that 'The Republic, AP, and local self-governance unit, within their respective competencies under the law, shall provide for continual control and monitoring of the state of the environment'.

334. According to Article 70 of EPL monitoring is carried out by systematic monitoring of indicator values, and monitoring of negative impacts on the environment, the state of environment, measures and actions to be taken in order to reduce negative impacts and improving the quality of the environment. Government establishes the criteria for determining the number and distribution of measuring points, the network of measuring points, extent and frequency of measurements, classification of phenomena that are monitored, methodology and indicators of environmental pollution and its monitoring, deadlines and manner of submitting data.

335. Pursuant to Article 12 of the Law on Air Protection, the national network consists of stations for air quality monitoring in various areas and for different purposes: (1) regional and transboundary atmospheric transmission of polluting substances in air and aerosols within international obligations; (2) air quality in settlements, industrial and non-living areas; (3) air quality in protected natural areas and protected environment

361. NEPP, 29–30.
362. For more information *see* : http://www.sepa.gov.rs/index.php?menu=300&id=20028&akcija=showAll (2 Jun. 2017).
363. Its provisions are specific with the following by-laws: Regulation for air quality monitoring and air quality requirements (OJ of RS, Nos 11/10, 75/10 and 63/13), Regulation on the establishment of programs for air quality control in national network (OJ of RS, No. 58/11), and Regulation on the establishment of zones and agglomerations (OJ of RS, Nos 58/11 and 98/12).

of immovable cultural goods; (4) air quality in areas under the influence of certain sources of pollution, including mobile sources; and (5) allergenic pollen.[364]

336. The state network covering mainly the zone of Serbia with only a few stations in the zone of Vojvodina, consisting of forty automatic stations altogether; the regional network in the zone of Vojvodina consisting of seven stations; local networks consisting of Belgrade with five stations, Pančevo with four and Bor with one.[365]

337. National network of automatic stations for air quality monitoring includes forty-eight stations.[366] SEPA set the first stations for automatic air quality monitoring at the end of 2006 in Smederevo and Bor. The EU project (CARDS project 'Supply of equipment for air quality monitoring') has donated equipment for twenty-eight measuring stations, calibration laboratory, analytical laboratory, a mobile station and one vehicle. Preparatory activities and much of the project was implemented in the period 2008–2010, and it was completed in 2011. Besides Agency, crucial support for project activities gave the Fund for Environmental Protection.

§2. State of Air Pollution

338. According to the data for 2015, in the zone Serbia, except for the city of Valjevo and Kragujevac, in 2015 the air quality was of the category I, i.e., clean to slightly polluted air. In the agglomerations Beograd, Bor, Uzice and Pancevo during 2015 air was of the category III, over-polluted air. In Bor because of sulphur dioxide, and in Beograd, Uzice and Pancevo because of suspended particles PM10.[367] In the cities Valjevo, Kragujevac and Sremska Mitrovica during 2015 air was of the category III, over-polluted air, due to concentrations that exceeded tolerant value of suspended particles PM10. In the zone Vojvodina in 2015, the air was of the category I, i.e., clean to slightly polluted air, except in Sremska Mitrovica. In the agglomeration Novi Sad, during 2015 air was of the category II, i.e., moderately polluted air due to the presence of suspended particles PM10. [368]

364. The territory of Serbia is divided into three zones for monitoring the air quality. There are also eight agglomerations selected to be closely monitored on air quality: Belgrade, Bor, Kosjerić, Niš, Novi Sad, Pančevo, Smederevo and Užice. EPR (2015), 81.
365. *Ibid.*
366. *See* http://www.amskv.sepa.gov.rs/stanicepodaci.php?lng=en (4 May 2017).
367. In the agglomerations Smederevo, Nis and Kosjeric during 2015, it was not possible to determine the category of air quality due to the lack of data.
368. Godišnji izveštaj o stanju kvaliteta vazduha u Republici Srbiji 2015. godine [Annual Report on the Condition of Air Quality in the Republic of Serbia 2015], MAP, EPA, Beograd, 2016, 10.

§3. Legislation

I. International Treaties

339. Serbia has ratified following international treaties regulating air protection and air quality control:

- United Nations Framework Convention on Climate Change (OJ FRY – IT, No. 2/97).
- Kyoto Protocol to the United Nations Framework Convention on Climate Change (OJ RS IT, No. 88/07).
- Amendment to Annex B to the Kyoto Protocol to the United Nations framework Convention on Climate Change (OJ RS – IT, No. 38/09).
- Vienna Convention for the Protection of the Ozone Layer (OJ FRY – IT, No. 1/90).
- Montreal Protocol on Substances that Deplete the Ozone Layer (OJ FRY – IT, No. 16/90).
- Amendments to the Montreal Protocol: 1990 London Amendment, 1992 Copenhagen Amendment, 1997 Montreal Amendment and 1999 Beijing Amendment (OJ SM – IT, No. 24/04) – CLRTAP (OJ SFRY – IT, No. 11/86).
- Protocol to the 1979 CLRTAP on Long-term Financing of the Cooperative Programme for Monitoring and Evaluation of the Long-Range Transmission of Air Pollutants in Europe, EMEP (OJ SFRY – IT, No. 2/87).[369]

II. National Legislation

A. *Environmental Protection Law*

340. Provisions concerning air protection are contained in all four systemic environmental laws (EPL, Law on SEA, Law on EIA and Law on IPPC). They differ depending on the basic subjects of their regulations. However, the basic legal instrument is Law on Air Protection adopted in 2009 (OJ RS, Nos 36/2009 and 10/2013).

341. Certain provisions of the EPL (OJ RS, Nos 135/04, 36/09, 72/09, 43/11 CC and 14/16) are relevant for air protection having in mind character of the air and possibilities for pollution. 'Air' is defined as element of the 'natural value'[370] and 'public natural goods'.[371] Key issues concerning general air protection have been regulated by Article 24 which prescribes that 'measures of air protection[372] shall ensure

369. Serbia has ratified Protocol on Heavy Metals to 1979 CLRTAP (OJ RS – IT, No. 1/12) and Protocol on Persistent Organic Pollutants to 1979 CLRTAP (OJ RS – IT, No. 1/12).
370. Besides the water, soil, forests, geological resources, plants and animal life (Art. 3, point 3).
371. Besides the 'water goods, water-fronts, underground goods, forests, sceneries or landscapes' (Art. 3, point 5).
372. These are 'measures of systematic air quality monitoring, technical-technological and other necessary measures ...'.

overall atmosphere preservation with all the processes and climate characteristics thereof', aiming at 'Reducing air pollution to regulated limit values and below'.

342. According to Article 39, the Government is in charge to determine limit values of the emissions for pollutants at the place of their outflow into the environment and the levels of emissions for pollutants in the environment.[373] The Government is also obliged to determine criteria for the number and layout of measurement points, measurement point's network, scope and frequency of measurement, classification of phenomena monitored, methodology and indicators about the pollution of the environment and their monitoring, deadlines and manner of data submission has been stipulated according to Article 70, paragraph 2.

343. Action Plan for protection of air and atmosphere is anticipated to be prepared in accordance with Article 65 of the EPL.

344. The use of funds of the Green Fund of the Republic of Serbia shall be carried out in accordance with the law, the national environmental protection programme and the strategic documents as well as the list of priority infrastructure projects in the field of environment, for, *inter alia,* the protection, preservation and improvement of air, water, soil and forest quality, as well as the mitigation of climate change impacts and the adoption of adaptation measures, including the protection of the ozone layer (Article 90v, paragraph 1).

B. Law on Air Protection

345. The Law comprises the following chapters: I Basic provisions (Articles 1–4), II Controlling the air quality (Articles 5–17), III Air quality requirements (Articles 18–25), IV Strategy, plans and programmes (Articles 26–39), V Measures for air quality improvement (Articles 40–58), VI Measurement the emissions and level of the pollutants in the air (Articles 59–64), VII Informing and reporting (Articles 65–67), VIII Information system (Articles 68–70), IX Funding the protection and improvement of air quality (Articles 71–72), X Supervision (Articles 73–77), XI Competence for resolving upon the complaint (Article 78), XII Penal provisions (Articles 79–83), and Transitional and final provisions (Articles 84–90).

346. This Law regulates the air quality management and establishes the measures, manners of organization and control of the protection implementation and improvement of the air quality as a natural value of a general interest that is especially protected.[374] (Article 1) The regulations of this Law are not to be implemented to the pollutions caused by radioactive matters, industrial accidents and natural disasters.

347. Pursuant to Article 4 of the Law, the protection and improvement of the air quality shall be performed by the Republic of Serbia, AP, LSG unit, business

373. Article 40 prescribes that pollutants and dangerous substances, wastewater or energy shall be released into air, water and soil in the manner prescribed and in the quantities, namely concentrations or levels not exceeding the prescribed limit values. The means of transportation made and placed on the market must comply with the conditions for emission from mobile pollution sources.

374. Air is the air in troposphere in the open space that does not include air in the closed space(Art. 3, part 1).

associations, entrepreneurs, as well as other legal and physical entities.[375] Monitoring both the air quality and emissions into the air are done by competent bodies of State administration and legal entities provided with the license to perform these activities.

1. Controlling the Air Quality

348. The air quality is assessed in the Republic of Serbia regarding the level of the pollutants, depending on upper and lower assessment threshold, as follows: (1) in all the zone and agglomerations where the level of the pollutants exceeds the upper assessment threshold for that matter, for assessing the air quality there are used the data obtained by fixed measurements, to which the data obtained by technical modelling and/or indicative measurements can be added; (2) in all the zones and agglomerations where the level of the pollutants is below the established upper assessment threshold for these pollutants, for assessing the air quality there can be used the combination of fixed measurements and technical modelling and/or indicative measurements; (3) in all the zones and agglomerations where the level of the pollutants is below the established lower threshold for these pollutants, for assessing the air quality there are used technical modelling and/or assessment techniques (Article 7).

349. Assessing the air quality is done mandatorily in terms of concentrations of sulphur dioxide, nitride dioxide and oxide nitrates, particulate matters (PM10, PM2.5), lead, benzene and carbon monoxide, ground ozone, arsenic, cadmium, nickel and benzo(a)pyrene (further on: pollutants), and can also be done for other pollutants, identified as such by relevant international regulations (Article 8).

350. With the aim of controlling, maintaining the state and/or improving the quality of the air, the Government identifies zones[376] and agglomerations in the Republic of Serbia territory.[377]

375. Business associations, other legal entities and entrepreneurs while performing their activities affect or could affect the air quality must do the following: provide technical measures for preventing or decreasing the emission into the air; plan the costs of protecting the air against pollution within investment and manufacturing costs; monitor the effect of their activities to the air quality; provide other protection measures, in accordance with this Law and laws regarding environment protection (Art. 4, para. 2).

376. The zone is the part of the Republic of Serbia territory with defined borders, specified with the aim of assessing and managing the air quality, being a characteristic functional whole from the point of controlling, maintaining and/or improving the state of the air quality. Agglomeration is the zone with more than 2,50,000 inhabitants. Agglomeration can also be a zone with fewer inhabitants, if the population density in that zone is higher than prescribed, so that justifies the need to assess and manage the air quality. The Government prescribes the population density for identifying agglomeration in event of number of inhabitants in the zone being fewer than 2,50,000 (Art. 5).

377. Zones and agglomerations are identified based on the air quality assessment, depending upon the identified upper and lower assessment limit (Art. 6, para. 1).

2. License for Measurement of the Emissions and Level of the Pollutants in the Air

351. Pursuant to Article 60 authorized legal entities can exercise the measurement after being issued a license by the Ministry, if they meet the conditions in terms of staff, equipment and space, as well as if they are technically enabled according to the requirements of the standard SRPS ISO 17025.[378]

352. The operator exercising the air quality and/or emission measurement independently must obtain the agreement from the Ministry, provided that, within their registered activity, they independently exercise the tasks of measurement of the air quality and/or emission and that they are professionally and technically able according to the requirements of the standard SRPS ISO 17025 (Article 61).

3. Strategy, Plans and Programmes

353. Air Protection Policy and Planning instruments are as follows: (1) Air Protection Strategy; (2) air quality plans; (3) short-term action plans; (4) National Programme for gradual decrease of annual national emission ceilings of the pollutants; and (5) operator's plans for decreasing emissions from stationary installations (Article 26, paragraph 1).

4. Air Protection Strategy

354. Air Protection Strategy (Strategy) is the basic document based on which the plans of air quality, short-term action plans and programmes for decreasing emissions of pollutants into the air are brought into action and need to be in consolidation with it.[379]

Strategy implementation is achieved through bringing the action plan for protecting the air, atmosphere and stopping climate changes, which is its integral part and contains the following: (1) concrete measures taken in order to implement the Strategy's aims; (2) timelines for Strategy's aims achievement; and (3) activities' implementers. Ministry, in cooperation with other competent bodies, has the obligation to develop plan(Article 29).

5. Air Quality Plans

355. In zones and agglomerations where the air quality category is 3, that is, when the air pollution exceeds the effects of the measures implemented, that is, when the environment capacity is endangered or there is permanent air pollution in the specific area, the competent body of AP and competent body of an LSG unit must bring the Air Quality Plan with the aim to reach appropriate limit values or target values identified by the Act from Article 18, paragraph 1 of this Law (Article 31).

---

378. A complaint cannot be made upon the resolution by which the license from para. 1 of this Article is issued or cancelled, but an administrative dispute can be initiated (Art. 60, para. 4).
379. The Ministry prepares draft Strategy that is brought into action by the Government for a six-year period (Art. 27).

6. Short-Term Action Plans

356. In accordance with Article 33, the competent body of AP, that is, the competent body of a LSG unit is due to bring in short-term action plans in the zone or agglomeration in their territory in events as follows: (1) if there is a danger that the levels of the pollutants in the air exceed one or more alert thresholds, determined by the act from Article 18, paragraph 1 of this Law; (2) if there is a danger to exceed the alert threshold of the ground ozone, identified by an act from Article 18, paragraph 1 of this Law, if the competent body makes an assessment, considering geographical, meteorological and economic conditions, that there is a significant potential to decrease the risk, duration and seriousness of such an exceedance. Short-term action plans can be, with the aim to protect people's health and/or environment as required, brought also in the case of a danger of exceeding one or more limits or target values for individual pollutants that are established by the act from Article 18, paragraph 1 of this Law.

7. National Programme for Gradual Decrease of Annual National Pollutant Emission

357. National Programme for gradual decrease of annual national pollutant emission ceilings (henceforth, National Programme) is brought by the Government for a four-year period. National Programme contains the following: (1) data on the adopted instruments of air protection policy and measures for decreasing the pollutants emission from Article 26, paragraph 3 of this Law; (2) quantified assessment of policies and measures from point 1 of this paragraph regarding the pollutants emissions from year 2000, which is taken as a reference; (3) approximate assessment of possible significant changes in geographical distribution of national emission ceilings; and (4) other data and documentation. National Programme needs to be available to the public and interested public (Article 37).[380]

8. Operator's Plan for Decreasing the Emissions from Stationary Installations

358. In the area which air is assessed as the air quality category 3, the body competent for the environment matters orders the operator to develop a plan for decreasing emissions from stationary sources of air pollution and establishes the timeline for this plan's realization.[381] Operator is obliged to develop a plan for decreasing

380. National plan for decreasing the emissions from the existing combustion installations is the part of the National Programme from Art. 37 of this Law. National plan for decreasing the emissions from the existing combustion installations specifically contains the following: (1) aims and defined target values in accordance with them; (2) measures and timelines for achieving the aims and target values; (3) procedure of monitoring this plan's implementation (Art. 38).

381. S*tationery pollution source* is a stationery technical unit, including the combustion installation, where one or more activities that can lead to the air pollution are performed, as well as any other activity technically connected with the activities performed at the location and that can produce emissions and pollution (Art. 3, para. 34).

emissions from stationary air pollution sources in a timeline specified in paragraph 1 of this Article (Article 39).[382]

9. Air Quality Requirements

359. With the aim of monitoring the air quality, the Government, upon the Ministry's proposal, prescribes the air quality requirements.[383] The air quality requirements are numeric values of limit values of the pollutants level in the air, upper and lower threshold of air quality assessment, critical levels, margins of tolerance and tolerant values, target values and (national) long-term aims of the pollutants in the air, concentrations dangerous to human health and the concentrations to be reported to the public (Article 18).[384]

360. According to the pollution level, starting from the prescribed and limit and tolerant values and based on the measurement results, the following air quality categories are established: (1) Category 1 – pure or slightly polluted air where the limit values of none of the pollutants are exceeded; (2) Category 2 – moderately polluted air where limit values of one or more pollutants are exceeded, but tolerant values of none of the pollutants are not exceeded; and (3) Category 3 – too polluted air where tolerant values for one or more pollutants are exceeded (Article 21).[385] Special types of pollution are pollutions from natural sources and exceedances because of sanding or salting of roads (Articles 24 and 25).

10. Measures for Air Quality Improvements

361. Pursuant to Article 40 measures for preventing and decreasing the air pollution and improving the air quality include the following: (1) prescribing the limit

382. Operator's plan for decreasing emissions from stationery sources of pollution contains the following: (1) description of an exceeded air pollution implications; (2) the zone where the operator is; (3) measures for achieving the air quality improvement; (4) description of selected technological and other solutions; (5) cost assessment; (6) order of the planned activities' implementation; (7) timeline for the planned activities implementation; (8) resources for the plan's implementation; and (9) other data and documentation.

383. When the information threshold, in line with the act from Art. 18 para. 1 from this Law, or the specific alert threshold, is exceeded, the Ministry, competent body of the AP and a competent body of an LSG unit is due to inform the public through radio, TV, daily newspapers, Internet and/or other appropriate manner (Art. 23).

384. The act from para. 1 of this Article also prescribes timelines for reaching limit and/or target values, in events when they are exceeded.

385. In event of a pollutant not having a prescribed tolerance limit, its limit value shall be taken as the tolerant one. Air quality categories are established once a year for the previous calendar year. The list of air quality categories by zones and agglomerations at the Republic of Serbia territory is brought by the Government and published in 'The Official Journal of the Republic of Serbia', electronic media, as well as the websites of the Government and the Ministry (Art. 21, paras 2–3).

values of the pollutants emissions from the stationary pollution sources;[386] (2) prescribing the limit values of the pollutants emissions from the mobile pollution sources;[387] (3) consolidation with national emission ceilings after their establishment for individual pollutants;[388] (4) prescribing the allowed amounts of individual pollutants in specific products;[389] (5) decreasing the emission of greenhouse gases; (6) gradual decrease of the use of substances that deplete the ozone layer; and (7) other measures for pollution preventing and decreasing.

11. License for Work

362. A newly built or reconstructed stationary pollution source that has the obligation of issuing an integrated license, that is, developing a study on the impact on the environment, and is not prescribed for can start working after obtaining the license for work (Article 56).[390] The work of a newly built or reconstructed stationary air pollution source, as well as performance of other activities in an open space that

386. The Government prescribes the following: (1) limit values of the pollutants emissions into the air; (2) manner, procedure, frequency and methodology of measurement the pollutants emission; (3) criteria for establishing the measurement locations for measurement the emission; (4) procedure of evaluating the results of emission measurement and consolidation with the prescribed normatives; (5) content of the report on the taken emission measurement and emission result; and (6) manner of submitting the data on emissions for the needs of the information system and timelines for the data submission (Art. 41). A part from that, the Government prescribes the ELVs of the pollutants from the existing combustion installations having in mind the type, capacity, age, planned working use of the installation and fuel used in it, as well as the methods, manner of measurement of the pollutants emission, criteria for selecting the measurement locations, manner of verifying the measurement accuracy (control measurement and calibration), manners of analysing the measurement results, manners and timelines for data submission and procedure of establishing total annual emission from the combustion installation (Art. 42).
387. Mobile pollution sources can be used and marketed if the pollutants in exhaust emissions from those sources do not exceed limit emission values established by technical provisions, in accordance with the Law. Mobile pollution sources emissions are controlled during regular, irregular and control technical examination, in accordance with an appropriate technical provision and the law regarding the traffic safety (Art. 46).
388. National emission ceilings are established for acidifying and eutrofying pollutants and ozone precursors, for the following: sulphur dioxides (SO_2), nitrate oxides (NO_x), volatile organic compounds and ammonia (NH_3), with the aim of improving and protecting the environment and people's health from the harm of acidification, eutrofication and ground ozone, and in order of achieving long-term aims including the maintenance of critical levels and population protection (Art. 47).
389. For fossil fuel (Art. 48), Paints and polishes (Art. 49), Emissions of greenhouse gases (Art. 50), and Use of substances that deplete the ozone layer (Arts 51–54).
390. The license from para. 1 of this Article is issued by the body competent for the matters of the environment protection in the form of resolution. A complaint can be stated upon the first instance resolution of the competent body of the AP and the competent body of an LSG unit from para. 2 of this Article. Ministry's first instance resolution from para. 2 of this Article is final in the administrative procedure and an administrative dispute can be initiated against it (Art. 56, paras 2–4).

can lead to the uncontrolled release of the pollutants, is banned, until the license for work from Article 56 paragraph 1 of this Law is obtained (Article 57).

363. The operator[391] must do the following: (1) submit the data on the stationary pollution source and its every change (reconstruction) to the Ministry, that is, Agency, competent AP body and competent LSG unit body; (2) enable regular emission monitoring and keep records on that; (3) enable permanent measurement of the emission when prescribed for specific pollutants and/or pollution sources, independently, through automatic machines for permanent measurement, with the Ministry agreement; (4) enable control measurements of the emission through an authorized legal entity, if performing the measurement independently; (5) enable prescribed occasional emission measurements, through an authorized legal entity, twice a year, if not exercising a permanent measurement; (6) provide air quality monitoring upon the order of a competent inspection body, independently or through an authorized legal entity; (7) keep records on the exercised measurements with the data on measurement locations, results and frequency of measurements and submit the data in the prescribed written report form to the Ministry, that is, Agency, competent AP body and competent LSG body, for the following measurements: from paragraph 1 points 2 and 3 of this Article, once in three months within fifteen days after the trimester finishes, from paragraph 1 point 5 of this Article, within thirty days after the exercised measurement, for annual measurements in the form of annual report at the latest by January 31 of the running year for the previous calendar year; (8) keep records on type and quality of raw materials, fuel and waste in the combustion process; and (9) keep records on the work of installations for preventing or decreasing the pollutants emission, as well as measurement installations for emission measurement (Article 58).[392]

12. Public Information and Information System

364. According to Article 65 of the Law, competent body must inform the other bodies and organizations and public through electronic and printed media at least in one local magazine in each official language, as well as through Internet about the following: (1) air quality; (2) plans of air quality and postponing the reaching of limit value for nitrate dioxide, benzene and particulate matter ten for a certain period of time; (3) plans for reaching limit values in zones and agglomerations with the exceedance of limit values; and (4) annual report on all pollutants included in this Law.[393]

---

391. *Operator* is a business association, other legal entity or entrepreneur that manages the installation in accordance with the provisions, controls it or is authorized to make economic decisions in the field of installation's technical functioning (Art. 3, para. 24).
392. The operator must implement the measures for decreasing the pollutants decreasing, determined by the plan for its own stationery air pollution sources, at their own cost.
393. The competent body informs the public about the following: (1) air quality, in the form of annual report on the air quality condition, until July 31 of the current year for the previous one, and after 2012 until February 28 of the current for the previous year; (2) plans of air quality and postponing the reaching of limit value for nitrite dioxide, benzene and particulate matter ten for the certain period of time, within eight days after the adoption; and (3) plans for reaching limit values in zones and agglomerations with the exceedance of limit values, within eight days after the adoption (Art. 67).

365. Air quality information system for the Republic of Serbia is managed by the Agency (Article 68, paragraph 3).[394]

366. The Ministry mediates and exchanges the data on air quality and emissions with international organizations and other countries in accordance with he/she confirmed international contracts (Article 70).[395]

C. Substances Depleting the Ozone Layer

367. Serbian legislation covering ozone-depleting substances is based on the provisions of the Montreal Protocol and the EC Regulation 2037/2000 of the European Parliament and of the Council on substances that deplete the ozone layer.[396] There is a ban on production of ozone-depleting substances in Serbia, pursuant to Article 53 paragraph 1 of the Law on Air Protection (OJ RS No. 36/09) (below: the Law). There is a ban on consumption of substances listed in Annex A (Groups I and II), Annex B (Groups I, II and III) and Annex C (Groups II and III) in Serbia.[397]

368. With a view to implementing the Montreal Protocol, Articles 51–54 of the Law on Air Protection prescribe the management of ozone-depleting substances (phase-out of ozone-depleting substances, handling of these substances, handling of products and equipment that contain or have been manufactured using these substances, handling of ozone-depleting substances after the products and equipment containing them are no longer in use, ways of recovery, recycling and reclamation, consumption and final disposal of substances, placing on the market and calculation of costs for ozone-depleting substances reuse, and ways of labelling products and equipment containing ozone-depleting substances); handling of certain fluorinated greenhouse gases and products and equipment containing these gases; bans on and records of ozone-depleting substances and fluorinated greenhouse gases.[398]

394. State bodies and organizations, operators and authorized legal entities must timely and without charges submit the data from their competence, as well as the other data required for managing the air quality information system, to the Agency, with the aim of developing plans and reports, in accordance with this Law (Art. 68 para. 4).
395. The Agency mediates and exchanges the data with the European Agency for Environment Protection and European Network for Information and Monitoring (Art. 70 para. 2).
396. Republic of Serbia is an Art. 5 party of the Montreal Protocol (as developing country) with a delayed phase-out schedule until total elimination of consumption of controlled substances, considering that its annual calculated level of consumption of the controlled substances from Annex A is less than 0.3 kg per capita and of the controlled substances from Annex B is less than 0.2 kg per capita on the date of the entry into force of the Protocol following ratification, or at any time thereafter until 1 Jan. 1999. All activities relating to implementation of the Montreal Protocol in the Ministry are carried out and coordinated by the National Ozone Unit, established in December 2008 within the Sector for Protection of Natural Resources, Air Protection Unit. AECQ, Chs 27, 246.
397. Consumption of substances listed in Annex C, Group I (hydrochlorofluorocarbons) is allowed without limitations. Consumption of substances listed in Annex E, Group I (methyl bromide) is allowed, with the total annual quota of maximum 6.64 metric tonnes.
398. Pursuant to Art. 51 of the Law, the Ministry prepared the Regulation on ozone-depleting substances management as well as on conditions for license issuance for import and export of such substances (OJ RS No. 22/10).

369. According to Article 53 of the Law at the Republic of Serbia territory, the following actions are prohibited: (1) manufacturing the substances that deplete the ozone layer; (2) import and/or export of the substances that deplete the ozone layer that are assessed by the verified international contract, that is, products and equipment containing these substances, imported and/or exported from the countries into countries that are not the signing parties of that contract; (3) import and/or export and marketing without the permission of the substances that deplete the ozone layer and fluorinated greenhouse gases; (4) import and/or export and marketing of the new products and equipment containing the substances that are controlled, but that deplete the ozone layer, apart from chlorofluorohydrocarbons; (5) emission of the substances that deplete the ozone layer and fluorinated greenhouse gases; (6) loading the products and equipment containing fluorinated greenhouse gases with the substances that deplete the ozone layer; (7) washing out by substances that deplete the ozone layer; (8) retail marketing of the substances damaging ozone layer and fluorinated greenhouse gases; and (9) import and/or export and marketing the used products and equipment containing substances that deplete the ozone layer.

D. Climate Change: Policy and Legislation

370. The Republic of Serbia has been a member of the United Nations Framework Convention on Climate Change – UNFCCC since 10 June 2001. Kyoto Protocol entered into force in the Republic of Serbia on 17 January 2008. The Republic of Serbia, as a non-Annex I country (developing country), is not obligated to implement quantified GHG emission reduction in the first commitment period (2008–2012).[399]

371. Adoption of the Kyoto Protocol created the opportunity for the Republic of Serbia to contribute to global reduction of GHG emissions through reduction of 'local' environmental pollution through implementation of CDM of the Kyoto Protocol projects.[400] The National Strategy for incorporation of the Republic of Serbia into CDM for waste management, agriculture and forestry sectors was adopted on 11 February 2010 (OJ RS No. 8/2010). The Ministry of Mining and Energy has developed Strategy for the implementation of CDM in energy sector in 2009.

372. The MAEP, is responsible for climate change issues. MAEP is the national focal point for the implementation of the United Nations Framework Convention of United Nations on Climate Change and its Kyoto Protocol. The SEPA established in 2004 within the MESP, is responsible, among other things, for data collection, processing

399. Serbia, also, ratified Doha amendment to the Kyoto Protocol (OJ RS – IT, No. 2/17), and Paris Agreement (OJ RS – IT, No. 4/17). For more information, *see* : Todić, D. Pariski sporazum o klimi u sistemu međunarodnih ugovora od značaja za EU integracije Republike Srbije [Paris Agreement on Climate in the System of International Agreements relevant for the EU Integration of the Republic of Serbia], *Evropsko zakonodavstvo*, 58/2016, 111–129.

400. Designated National Authority (DNA) for the implementation of CDM projects, a prerequisite for participation in this set of projects, has been fully operational since 21 Nov. 2008. So far, Serbia has been realized seven CDP project. *See* : http://www.klimatskepromene.rs/cdm-projekti (3 May 2017).

and reporting on greenhouse gases.[401] The Law on Meteorological and Hydrological Activity (OJ RS, No. 88/10) defines the competences of the Republic Hydro Meteorological Service (RHMS) as a specific organization within the Governmental system of the Republic of Serbia regarding the adoption and carrying out of multi-annual programmes of monitoring, research and forecasting climate changes, creating scenarios of regional and local climate change and participation in the programmes of multidisciplinary research of the impacts, vulnerability and adaptation options of certain economic sectors to climate change.

373. Initial National communication defines mitigation and adaptation related programmes as well as plans for capacity building and awareness raising, scientific research and climatic observation.[402]The Second National Communication has also been prepared. Serbia submitted First Biennial Update Report,[403] and Intended Nationally Determined Contribution.[404]The government aimed at providing emission reduction of 9.8% by 2030 compared to 1990 levels. Serbia elaborated the Nationally Appropriate Mitigation Actions (NAMAs) Development Guideline and submitted NAMAs to the registry.[405] However, Serbia has no national strategy on climate change. Certain national strategic documents consider the climate change issue as one of the key development issues. The NSDS and Action Plan for the Implementation of the NSDS for the period 2009–2017 put climate change issue as a key environmental risk factor and defines certain actions related to adaptation and mitigation.

374. Serbia has achieved some level of preparation but implementation is at a very early stage. A national strategy on climate change, remains to be developed. During 2016 Legislation on greenhouse gas emissions monitoring, reporting and verification for aligning with the EU emissions trading system has been drafted.[406] 'Overall, Serbia has achieved a limited level of legislative alignment with the EU climate *acquis*. Implementation is at a very early stage.'[407]

401. Besides the MAEP and SEPA, ministries that have certain competences related to the climate change are: Ministry of Mining and Energy; Ministry of Economy; Ministry of Construction, Traffic and Infrastructure; Ministry of Finance and Ministry of Public Administration and LSG; Research is done by several universities and the Institute of Field and Vegetable Crops in Novi Sad.
402. *See* http://unfccc.int/essential_background/library/items/3599.php?such=j&symbol=%20SRB/COM/1%20E#beg.
403. At http://unfccc.int/essential_background/library/items/3599.php?rec=j&priref=7838#beg.
404. At http://www4.unfccc.int/Submissions/INDC/Published%20Documents/Serbia/1/Republic_of_Serbia.pdf.
405. At https://unfccc.int/files/cooperation_support/nama/application/pdf/nama_development_guideline_en.pdf.
406. EC, 2016, 77. Serbia advanced on implementing a number of acquis provisions on ozone-depleting substances, fluorinated greenhouse gases and fuel quality. Considerable strengthening of administrative capacity is needed, together with awareness-raising activities.
407. SRS, Ch. 27, p. 27. There is some progress with Regulations on Fluorinated Gases and Ozone Depleting Substances and limited progress towards legislative alignment with the EU ETS. Priority needs to be given to monitoring, reporting and verification.

E. *Other Relevant Legislation*

375. Besides the above-mentioned laws, following legal Acts also regulate air protection in Serbia:

- Law on Meteorological and Hydrological Activities (OJ RS, No. 88/2010).[408]
- Law on Protection of Population from Exposure to Tobacco Smoke (OJ RS No. 30/2010).[409]
- Law on Transport of Dangerous Goods (OJ RS, Nos 88/2010 and 104/16).[410]
- Air Transport Law (OJ RS, Nos 73/2010, 57/2011, 93/2012, 45/2015 and 66/2015).
- Regulation on limit values of air pollutant emissions from stationary sources of pollution, except from combustion installations (OJ RS, No. 111/15).
- Regulation on limit values of air pollutant emissions from combustion installations (OJ RS, No. 06/16).
- Regulation on the methodology for the development of air pollutant emissions and projections inventory (OJ RS, No. 3/16).
- Regulation on measurement of air pollutant emissions from stationary sources of pollution (OJ RS, No. 5/16).
- Regulation on determining the list of air quality categories by zones and agglomerations in the territory of the Republic of Serbia for 2014 (OJ RS, No. 105/15).
- Regulation on handling fluorinated greenhouse gases and conditions for issuing import and export permits for these gases (OJ RS, No. 120/13).
- Regulation on the list of installations and activities, in which volatile organic compound (VOC) emissions shall be controlled, on VOC emission values at certain consumption of solvents and total allowed emissions, and schemes to reduce VOC emission (OJ RS, No. 100/11).
- Regulation on methodology of collection of data for national greenhouse gas emissions inventory (OJ RS, No. 81/2010).
- Regulation on the methodology for data collection for the national inventory of unintentional emission of persistent organic pollutants (OJ RS, No. 76/2010).
- Regulation on determining the air quality control programme within the state network (OJ RS, No. 58/11).

---

408. The Law regulates meteorological and hydrological activities, organization and manner of performing meteorological and hydrological activities of interest for the Republic of Serbia and other meteorological and hydrological activities, meteorological and hydrological disasters early warning system, meteorological and hydrological data information fund, protection of Hydrological Information System, international cooperation, as well as other issues of importance for meteorological and hydrological activities.
409. New law completely bans smoking in health and social care facilities, educational, cultural, sport facilities, at meetings, in all public administration buildings, in facilities where drugs and food are prepared or stored, shopping centres, etc. Regarding restaurants and bars, completely smoke-free are only those which belong to buildings in which smoking is completely banned. Significant fines are imposed on owners and managers of buildings in which smoking is banned.
410. Out of forty-two accidents in 2008, fourteen occurred during the transport of dangerous substances (33%). NEPP, 55.

- Regulation on handling ozone-depleting substances, as well as on conditions for the issuance of permits for import and export of such substances (OJ RS, No. 114/13).
- Regulation on work method, criteria and timeframe for assessing and approving potential project on CDM by National body for implementing CDM Projects under Kyoto Protocol (OJ RS, No. 44/2010).
- Regulation on conditions for monitoring and requirements for air quality (OJ RS, Nos 11/2010, 75/10 and 63/13).
- Rulebook on the content of short-term action plans (OJ RS, No. 65/2010).
- Rulebook on the methods for exchanging information concerning measuring points within the State and local networks, on measuring techniques, as well as on the methods of exchanging data obtained by air quality monitoring in the State and local network (OJ RS, No. 84/2010).
- Rulebook on content of the plan for air quality (OJ RS, No. 21/2010).
- Rulebook on requirements of approvals for operators to measure air quality and/ or emission from stationary pollution sources (OJ RS, No. 16/12).
- Rulebook on conditions for issuing air quality measurement permits and the permits for measurement of emission from stationary pollution sources (OJ RS, No. 1/12).
- Rulebook on technical measures and requirements relating to the allowed volatile organic compound emissions resulting from storage and transport of petrol (OJ RS, Nos 1/12 and 48/12).

376. Serbia has a good level of alignment with the *acquis*. Serbia needs to adopt a national air protection strategy. The national air quality monitoring network requires considerable reinforcement. Further work is needed to finish transposing and to implement EU directive on volatile organic compound emissions and to comply with EU requirements on sulphur content in liquid fuels.[411] During the period 2018, the activity of transposition of remaining provisions of the Directive 2008/50/EC, Directive 2004/107/EC and other relevant directives that set obligations of the EU Member States towards the EC, will be undertaken.[412]

---

411. CR, 76. 'Serbia has two air quality plans, one for Bor (2013) and one for Belgrade (2016). Air quality plans for other areas where the level of pollutants exceeds limit values remain to be adopted.'
412. NPAA, II revision, 1173.

Chapter 3. Water Pollution

§1. Water Availability and Use

377. Serbia is not too rich in water, especially not in its own water sources. Less than 8% (about 500 m^3/s) of all available water resources originates within the territory of Serbia. Remaining 92% are transit waters entering the country from neighbouring States. The annual precipitation varies in different regions. While in the plains it ranges from 550 to 650 mm, in the mountainous regions it is 800–1,200 mm.[413]

378. Most important international water course in Serbia is the Danube river that, with its vast basin and huge potentials (both for navigational and non-navigational uses), deserves special attention and international cooperation concerning its protection and use in navigational and non-navigational purpose. Besides the Danube, there are many other rivers, some of which are international (for instance, Sava, Tisza and Drina). The ten longest rivers are: Danube 588 km (total 2,783 km), Zapadna Morava 308 km (308 km), Juzna Morava 295 km (295 km), Ibar 272 km (272 km), Drina 220 km (346 km), Sava 206 km (945 km), Timok 202 km (202 km), Velika Morava 185 km (185 km), Tisa 168 km (966 km) and Nisava 151 km (218 km).[414]

There are also a number of lakes and some wetlands of international importance (for instance, Ludosko Lake and Obed Swamp). There are also some artificial lakes, the biggest and most important of which is the Iron Gate Lake. Ground water sources should also be mentioned with, among other things, more than 500 registered mineral water sources.

Of great importance for Serbia are groundwater resources. Their potential is estimated to be 60,000 l/s–90,000 l/s. About 21,000 l/s of it is used for drinking water supply.

379. The use of water resources varies on a regional level. In some of the regions with low level of available freshwater, the exploitation index reaches 100%. At the national level the average exploitation index for drinking water resources has steadily increased during last twenty years. It has reached around 80% which can be seen as an alarming value.[415]

380. The intake from ground water sources, for public water supply systems, has volume of about 500 million m^3/year. The intake from surface water sources is about 200 million m^3/year, of which the population uses about 55%, while the industry and public consumption make up for about 20%, and other uses (consumption within the treatment process, network losses, etc.) make up for 25%. Per capita water consumption in Serbia averages about 350 l/capita per day (for cities about 400, and

413. *Statistical Yearbook of Serbia* (2007), 31.
414. *Ibid.*, 20.
415. One must have in mind the fact that, according to the EEA methodology, the threshold value for extreme pressure on water resources is defined as 40%. B. Karadžic (ed.), *Environment in Serbia – An Indicator-Based Review*, *supra* , 91.

for rural areas about 80 l/capita per day). Industrial enterprises are supplied mostly through their own systems.[416]

§2. Water Pollution Sources

381. Most important causes of water pollution in Serbia are industrial waste water discharges, water pollution caused by agricultural production, communal waste water discharges, sanitary wastewater discharges. Most of the water pollution is generated in cities and other settlements (both from industrial and non-industrial zones) apart from mining and agriculture.[417] It should be stressed that only 13% of municipal waste water is treated prior to discharge.[418]

382. International water courses that enter Serbia are already polluted. The quality of water in most of Serbian rivers is, according to the official water classification, between class II and class IV (class III prevails). So, for instance, the quality of the Danube water is usually class II or class III, and in Tisza River the quality is often class III and IV. Sometimes heavy accidental pollution occurs in the upstream countries. One of the most serious cases was heavy pollution (by cyanide and heavy metals) of the Tisza River in 2000 caused by a serious accident in a golden mine in Romania.

There are 153 public water supply systems in Serbia covering about 60% of population. Additional 15% of population possess some other sort of water supply. Although the coverage with water supply systems is very high, many systems are still not well maintained what results in losses of water in the distribution networks and temporary interruptions of water supply.[419] Drinking water is supplied to a large part of Northern Serbia (Vojvodina) by abstraction of the groundwater from basic aquifers. Serbia is rich with mineral and thermal springs.[420]

383. During 2009, in the territory of the Republic of Serbia, 156 of central water supply systems were controlled (113 in central Serbia and 43 in APV). The central water supply systems are water supply systems of city and municipal centres and rural settlements managed by public communal enterprise. Approximately, one-half of the population of Serbia is supplied with drinking water from controlled water supply systems. It has been found that during 2009, out of the total number of controlled water supply systems, (1) Eighty-two water supply systems (53%) had less than 5% of microbiologically contaminated and less than 20% of physically-chemically contaminated water samples, seventy-seven in Central Serbia (49%) and five in Vojvodina (3%); (2)

416. NSDS, 77.
417. On this subject, *see* , S. Bogdanović, 'Korišćenje voda u poljoprivredi Srbije-Propisi i institucije, stanje i trendovi' ('Use of Water in Agriculture of Serbia – Legislation and Institutions, Current State and Trends'), in *Agrarna i ruralna politika Srbije – reforme u periodu tranzicije i predlog mera za 2008* [*Agrar and Rural policy of Serbia – Reforms in Transitions Time and Proposal of Measures for 2008*] (Belgrade: Proceedings of the of Society of Agrar Economists, 2007), 79–87.
418. EPR (2007), 13.
419. A UNICEF report reveals that 48% of surveyed households reported regular or temporary interruptions of water supply. EPR (2007), 13.
420. There are over 350 registered natural springs and sites where groundwater is abstracted. NES, 15.

60,019 drinking water samples were tested, of which 8,296 (14%) were contaminated in regard to physical-chemical composition, where 100% of samples in mid-Banat district, 98% in North-Banat district and 53% of samples in Srem district, while in Kolubara district there was 0.3% of contaminated samples; and (3) 63,803 drinking water samples were tested, of which 3,128 (5%) were contaminated due to presence of microorganisms, where 25% of samples in North-Backa district, while in Podunavlje District there were no contaminated samples.[421]

384. Regular measurement of water quality is done by the competent hydro-meteorological (hydrological, chemical, physical, biological and bacteriological characteristics) and health protection institutions (the quality of drinking water). The main institutions to be mentioned here are the Republic Hydro-Meteorological Institute, the Institute of Public Health and other specialized organizations and institutes.

It is important to add that Serbia is active in international cooperation in the field of water protection. A good example of such cooperation is its membership in the International Commission for the Protection of the Danube River (ICPDR) established according to the 1994 Convention on Cooperation for the Protection and Sustainable Use of the Danube River.

385. Water sector in Serbia is mostly under the competence of the MAEP (i.e., under its Directorate for Water and two public water companies). The Directorate for Water is, according to the Law on Ministries, responsible for water resources management policy, multipurpose water usage, water regime, protection from water, water protection measures maintenance and other activities, as prescribed by the Law on Water.

The following ministries are also involved in the management and protection of water: Ministry of Construction, Transport and Infrastructure, Ministry of Health, Ministry of Mining and Energy, Ministry of Public Administration and Local Self-Government, etc. Water sector is also managed by the Secretariat for Agriculture, Water Management, and Forestry of Vojvodina AP. Urban water and sanitation services are decentralized and delegated to the municipalities.

386. Responsibilities for the enforcement of the Law on Waters are divided among three inspectorates: water, sanitary and environment. The water inspectorate (twenty people), which is part of the Water Directorate, checks compliance and enforces requirements related to the water use regime and quality of surface waters and groundwater, as well as to any activities that could affect water quality.[422]

---

421. Data on rural water supply systems, not managed by public communal enterprise, and on water supply systems of the food manufacturers, are not entered into the mentioned annual report. The exact number of water supply systems used for public water supply in the Republic of Serbia is not known. AECQ, Chs 27, 171. For more information on the quality of surface water and of groundwater *see* : *Rezultati ispitivanja kvaliteta površinskih i podzemnih voda 2015* [Results of testing the quality of surface and groundwater 2015], MAEP, EPA, 2017. http://www.sepa.gov.rs/download/KvalitetVoda2015.pdf (19 Jun. 2017).

422. EPR (2015), 39. 'Responsibilities between water and environmental inspectorates are not entirely delineated and there are overlaps in the area of water quality, but, in practice, they find ways to overcome them and cooperation on the ground is good.' *Ibid.*, 40.

§3. Legislation

I. International Treaties

387. Serbia has ratified following international treaties relevant to use, management and protection of water resources:

- Convention on Cooperation for Protection and Sustainable Use of the Danube River (OJ S&M – IT, No. 2-2/2003).
- Framework Agreement on the Sava River Basin and Protocol on the Navigation Regime Additional to the Framework Agreement on the Sava River Basin (OJ S&M – IT, No. 12/2004).[423]
- Convention Regarding the Regime of Navigation on the Danube (1948) (OJ FPRY, No. 8/49; OJ FRY – IT, No. 6/98).
- Framework Convention on the Protection and Sustainable Development of the Carpathians (OJ RS – IT, No. 102/07).[424]

Serbia ratified the Helsinki Convention on the Protection and Use of Transboundary Watercourses and International Lakes, the treaty of key importance. (OJ RS – IT, No. 1/10).

388. Besides the above-mentioned multilateral treaties, Serbia is a contracting party of a number of bilateral agreements with neighbouring States which regulate cooperation in the field of waters. They are as follows: Agreement between the Government of FPRY and PR of Hungary on water management issues (1955), Agreement between the Government of FPRY and PR of Hungary on fishery in boundary waters (1957), Agreement between the Government of FPRY and PR of Hungary on water transport on River Tisza (1959), Agreement between the Government of FPRY and PR of Bulgaria on water management issues (1958), Agreement between the Government of FPRY and PR of Bulgaria on fishery in boundary waters (1962), Agreement between the Government of FPRY and PR of Romania on hydroelectric questions on hydroelectric systems and water courses along the boundary or cut by boundary (1955), Agreement between the Government of FPRY and PR of Romania on fishery in boundary waters (1961), Agreement between the Government of FPRY

423. And Protocol on Flood Protection to the Framework Agreement on the Sava River Basin (OJ RS – IT No. 16/14), Protocol on the prevention of water pollution caused by navigation to the Framework Agreement on the Sava River Basin (OJ RS – IT No. 19/15), Protocol on sediment management to the Framework Agreement on the Sava River Basin (OJ RS – IT No. 20/15). For more details, *see* , S. Bogdanović, *The Sava River Basin – New Legal Frameworks for Shared Water Resources* (YUAWL – Yugoslav Association for Water Law 2004).

424. And Protocol on Conservation and Sustainable Use of Biological and Landscape Diversity to the Framework Convention on the Protection and Sustainable Development of the Carpathians (OJ RS – IT No.1/13), Protocol on Sustainable Forest Management to the Framework Convention on the Protection and Sustainable Development of the Carpathians (OJ RS – IT No. 5/15), Protocol on Sustainable Tourism to the Framework Convention on the Protection and Sustainable Development of the Carpathians (OJ RS – IT No. 5/15).

and PR of Romania on building an exploitation of the hydroelectric and navigation system Dzerdap (1963, 1964, 1967, 1976, 1977, 1987 and 1998).

Presently several bilateral agreements, concerning water use and protection with neighbouring countries (Croatia, Bulgaria, Romania, Bosnia and Herzegovina, etc.), are in the process of being prepared.

II. National Legislation

A. Strategic Documents

389. Water Management Strategy in the Republic of Serbia for the period up to 2034 (OJ RS, No. 3/17) is basic document adopted after preparations during several years.[425] It is 'a master planning document that will serve as a blueprint for the implementation of water sector reforms through the year 2034, aimed at achieving needed water management standards at the national, regional and local levels, and at fulfilling water management objectives. The Strategy also proposes the structural and nonstructural measures required to achieve set objectives and outlines the needed funding, the implementation timetable, and the functions whose proper performance will govern the effective achievement of objectives. Additionally, the Strategy sets forth priority projects'.[426]

B. Water Law

390. The water domain is regulated by numerous laws and regulations. The basic legal Act is the Water Law (OJRS, Nos 30/10, 93/12 and 101/16).[427]*The Law on Waters* has entered into force on 15 May 2010. It has the following twelve parts: Part I – General Provisions (Articles 1–3), Part II – Water resources (Articles 4–12), Part III – Water facilities (Articles 13–23), Part IV – Integrated Water Management (Articles 24–112), Part V – Water Acts and water documentation (Articles 113–132), Part VI – Prohibitions, limitation of rights and obligations of owners and users of water land and water facilities (Articles 133–139), Part VII – Other water management subjects (Articles 140–146), Part VIII – Information and water information system (Articles 147–149), Part IX – Financing of water management (Articles 150–195), Part X – Supervision (Articles 196–208), XI – Penalties (Articles 209–215), XII – Transitional and final provisions (Articles 216–228). Independent Articles of the Amendments of the Water Law (2016) are Articles 106 (s2)–116 (s2).

425. *See* : http://www.rdvode.gov.rs/doc/Strategija_FINAL.pdf (16 Jun. 2017).Furthermore, the River Basin Management Plan for the Danube River Basin in Serbia has been adopted.
426. Executive Summary for the Water Management Strategy of the territory of the Republic of Serbia, MAEP, Belgrade. http://www.rdvode.gov.rs/doc/dokumenta/javne-rasprave/strategija/Strategija%20SUMMARY.pdf (16 Jun. 2017).
427. The basic general goal of the amendments which were introduced in 2016 is to achieve full compliance with EU legislation.

According to Article 1, Water Law regulates the legal status of waters,[428] integrated water management, the management of water constructions and water land, sources of funding, supervision of the implementation of this Law, and other matters of importance to water management.

391. The provisions of this Law apply to all surface waters and groundwaters[429] within the territory of the Republic of Serbia, including thermal and mineral waters, but excluding groundwater's from which useful mineral raw materials or geothermal energy can be extracted (Article 2, paragraph 1). Provisions of this Law also apply to watercourses that define or intersect the State border of the Republic of Serbia, as well as associated groundwater's thereof, unless otherwise regulated by a specific Law (Article 2, paragraph 2). It also applies to the extraction of river deposits which do not contain admixtures of any other useful mineral raw materials (Article 2, paragraph 3).

1. Water Management Principles

392. Water management is founded on following principles: (1) *The principle of sustainable development* – water management must be conducted in a manner whereby satisfying the demands of the present generations does not compromise the ability of future generations to satisfy their own demands, that is, water use based on long-term protection of the quantity and quality of available water resources[430] must be ensured. (2) *The principle of holism* – natural processes of which water is a significant component, as well as the association and interdependency of aquatic ecosystems and riparian ecosystems, must be respected. (3) *The principle of water-system*[431] *unity* – water management within a single water space must be conducted in harmony with the development of the Republic of Serbia, in order to maximize economic and social benefits equitably, and at the same time international agreements must be respected. (4) *The principle of ensuring protection against the adverse effects of water* – the population and its property must be protected against water, while at the same time laws governing natural processes and the protection of natural treasures, as well as the economic viability of such protection must be respected. (5) *The 'user pays' principle* – anyone who uses a water asset, water construction or water system, as an asset of general interest, shall pay a realistic price for such use. (6) *The 'polluter pays' principle* – anyone whose activities result in water pollution shall pay the costs of any measures required for the elimination of such pollution. (7) *The principle of public participation* – the public has a right to information regarding the status of waters and the performance of competent authorities in the water sector, as well as to be involved in water management plan preparation, delivery and implementation supervision processes. (8) *The principle of recognizing best-available techniques* – best known

428. *Waters* means all flowing and standing waters on the ground surface, and all groundwaters (Art. 3, point 8).
429. *Groundwaters* means all water below the surface of the ground in the saturation zone and in direct contact with the ground or subsoil (Art. 3, point 44).
430. *Water resources* means all surface waters and groundwaters, in terms of quantity and quality (Art. 3, point 11).
431. *Water system* means all waters, water lands and water constructions in a particular area (Art. 3, point 12).

and best-available techniques, which represent the most advanced achievements in respective fields, shall be applied in water management (Article 25, paragraph 1).

2. Integrated Water Management and Water Management Planning Documents

393. Integrated water management (water management), as contemplated herein, is a set of measures and activities aimed at preserving and improving the water regime,[432] providing the necessary amounts of water of required quality for different uses, protecting waters against pollution and ensuring protection against the adverse effects of water (Article 24, paragraph 1). Water management is under the jurisdiction of the Republic of Serbia (Article 24, paragraph 2). The Republic of Serbia shall realize water management via the Ministry and other competent ministries, the competent authority of the AP, the competent authority of the local self-governing unit and the public water management enterprise (Article 24, paragraph 3).

394. Article 29 of the Law defines strategic documents for water management, particularly: (1) Water Management Strategy for the territory of the Republic of Serbia; (2) Water Management Plan; (3) Annual Water Management Programme; (4) Plans Regulating Protection from adverse effects of water, particularly: flood risk management plan, general and operative plans for protection against floods and plans regulating water protection (plan for protection of water against pollution and monitoring programme). The Law also prescribes programme of measures for achievement of objectives of previously mentioned documents and active participation of public in passing of planning documents.

395. Water Management Strategy is a planning document which establishes long-term directions for water management (Article 30, paragraph 1). The Strategy shall be proposed by the Ministry and delivered by the Government for a period of at least ten years (Article 31, paragraph 1). The strategy is implemented through an action plan. Action plan is made by the Government (at the proposal of the Ministry) for a period of five years (Article 31a).

396. Water management plan of waters within a water district[433] shall be delivered, pursuant to the Strategy, for the Danube River Basin and for the water districts (Article 33, paragraph 1). According to Article 34, paragraph 1, the Water Management Plan for the Danube River Basin is to be prepared by the Ministry, which is to be updated every six years (Article 35, paragraph 1).

397. The annual water management programme (hereinafter, the annual programme) is a planning document which identifies water constructions, types and scope of any works and/or actions funded during the time period for which the annual programme is delivered, the cost of such works and/or actions, the level of participation, and other matters pertaining to the construction, reconstruction, repair, rehabilitation

432. *Water regime* means the qualitative and/or quantitative status of groundwater's and surface waters, resulting from natural or human activity, in a particular area and at a particular time (Art. 3, point 10).

433. *Water district* means the area made up of one or more neighbouring river basins and sub-basins or parts thereof within the territory of the Republic of Serbia, together with associated groundwaters, which is identified as the main unit for water management (Art. 3, point 13).

and/or maintenance of water constructions, and for the undertaking of any actions which, as contemplated herein, are deemed to be actions of general interest (Article 42, paragraph 1). The annual programme is to be consistent with the Strategy and the Water Management Plan (Article 42, paragraph 2).[434]

398. Plans which address protection against the adverse effects of water, include the Flood Risk Management Plan, the general Flood Defence Plan and the Operational Flood Defence Action Plan, as well as plans which address water protection (the water pollution protection plan and the monitoring programme) (Article 29, paragraph 1, point 4).[435]

3. Development of Watercourses and Protection Against the Adverse Effects of Water

399. Watercourse development, as contemplated herein, includes: (1) the erection and maintenance of water constructions for watercourse development; and (2) the undertaking of works in connection with the maintenance of bank stability or a watercourse channel, and with the increase and/or maintenance of the water, ice and/ or sediment conveyance capacity thereof (Article 44, paragraph 1). *Protection against the adverse effects of water* includes measures and works for river flood and internal flood protection, ice protection, protection from erosion and torrential streams and the elimination of resulting consequences (Article 45, paragraph 1).

400. The management of risks from the adverse effects of water shall include the preparation of a preliminary flood risk assessment;[436] the preparation and

434. The government, and on the territory of the AP authority of the AP, makes an annual program (Art. 42, para. 3).

435. *See also* Arts 54 and 55.

436. A preliminary flood risk assessment shall be prepared by the Ministry for the territory of the Republic of Serbia and shall include, but not be limited to: (1) maps of water districts of suitable scale, identifying the boundaries of sub-basins and showing topography and land uses; (2) a description of past flood events which have resulted in significant harmful consequences to human health, the environment, cultural heritage and/or economic activity, and an indication of the likelihood of comparable events, which might have similar consequences, occurring in the future; and (3) an assessment of potential harmful consequences of future flood events to human health, the environment, cultural heritage and/or economic activity, considering the topographic, hydrologic and geological characteristics and the location of the watercourse, including flood-prone areas, the effectiveness of existing flood defences, the locations of populated areas and industrial zones, long-term development plans and climate change as relevant to flood events (Art. 47, para. 1).

implementation of flood risk management plans;[437] the general flood defence plan;[438] and flood defence action plans;[439] the undertaking of ordinary and extraordinary flood defence; and protection from erosion and torrential streams (Article 45, paragraph 3).

4. Water Development and Water Use

401. Water development, as contemplated herein, is a set of measures and works aimed at conserving and/or controlling water quantity in order to: (1) ensure the quantitative, spatial, and temporal distribution of waters for the provision of water supply to the population, industry, and other users; (2) ensure good status of aquatic and riparian ecosystems; (3) watercourses increase during periods of low flow; and (4) ensure conditions for special water use (Article 66).[440]

Any use of water which does not fall within the scope of general water use constitutes a special use of water (Article 68, paragraph 1). The right to special use of water shall be acquired on the basis of a water permit or, if special water use is exercised based on a concession agreement, pursuant to such agreement (Article 68, paragraph 2).

5. Protection of Water from Pollution

402. Protection of water, as contemplated herein, is a set of measures and activities by which surface water and groundwater quality is protected and improved, as well as protected from any impact of transboundary pollution, in order to: (1) preserve human life and health; (2) reduce pollution and prevent any deterioration of water status; (3) ensure harmless and unhindered use of water for different purposes; and (4) protect aquatic and riparian ecosystems, and achieve environmental quality

437. The flood risk management plan shall ensure risk management through the reduction of potential harmful consequences of floods to human health, the environment, cultural heritage, and/or economic activity (Art. 49, para. 1). The flood risk management plan shall be delivered for the territory of the Republic of Serbia and for its water districts (Art. 49, para. 2). It shall be based on the flood hazard map and flood risk map (Art. 49, para. 3) and is to be delivered in the same manner and following the same procedure as for the water management plan (Art. 50). A flood hazard map and a flood risk map shall be prepared for flood-prone areas, where are presented or where might occur significant risks of flooding (Art. 48, para. 1). The flood risk map shall include information about any potential harmful consequences of floods to human health, the environment, cultural heritage, and/or economic activity, and other information relevant to flood risk management (Art. 48, para. 1).
438. A general flood defence plan (hereinafter, the general plan) shall be delivered for first and second order waters and internal waters (Art. 54, para. 1). It should be prepared by the Ministry and delivered by the Government for a period of six years (Art. 54, para. 2).
439. A flood defence action plan (hereinafter, the action plan) shall be delivered for (Art. 55, para. 1): (1) First order waters and internal waters; and (2) Second order waters. The action plan referred to in para. 5 of this Article shall include, but not be limited to information required for operational flood defence, criteria for the declaration of flood defence, names of flood defence managers and entities, and warning and information dissemination methods (Art. 55, para. 6).
440. General use of water is the use without any prior treatment, or without the use of special devices (pumps, vacuum units, etc.) or the erection of water constructions (Art. 67, para. 1).

standards pursuant to the regulation which addresses environmental protection and environmental objectives (Article 92, paragraph 1).

403. With the goal of preventing any deterioration of the quality of water and the environment, ELVs, as well as methods and conditions for the discharge of pollutants and the application of the ELVs shall be specified for: (1) process wastewater prior to the discharge thereof into a public sewerage system; (2) process wastewater or other wastewater discharged directly into a recipient; (3) water discharged upon treatment from a public sewerage system into a recipient; and (4) wastewater discharged into a recipient from a septic or collection pit (Article 93, paragraph 1).

Government, at the recommendation of the Minister and the minister responsible for environmental protection, determines the physical-chemical parameters and limit values for emissions of pollutants, methods and conditions of the discharge of pollutants, as well as the terms and conditions of application of the ELVs referred to in paragraph 1 of this Article, and deadlines to achieve them (Article 93, paragraph 2).[441]

404. Water protection shall be implemented pursuant to a water pollution protection plan[442] (Article 94, paragraph 1).

405. Any legal entity, entrepreneur or individual who discharges or disposes of any substance(s) which may pollute water, unless the natural person who uses water for drinking and sanitary needs of their own, shall, prior to the release thereof into a public sewerage system or recipient, partially or completely remove such substances and to purify wastewater pursuant to this Law and special laws which regulate environmental protection and/or regulations delivered based on these laws (Article 98, paragraph 1).[443]

6. Monitoring

406. Article 107 of the Law prescribes monitoring of surface and ground water for achievement of harmonized and comprehensive State overview. Monitoring is performed pursuant to annual monitoring programme that prescribes number and position of measuring points, manner and number of quantity and level measuring, for surface and ground water, manner and procedure of water quality testing, number and conditions of testing and contents of reports on determined water quality (108). The authority responsible for conducting state-level water quality monitoring in cooperation with the republic organization responsible for hydro-meteorological affairs performs monitoring, and submits quarterly and annual reports to the competent institutions. Legal persons accredited by the A and with relevant references can perform

441. A new Art. (93a) has been introduced – relating to the standards of environmental quality and limit values for polluting substances.

442. The Ministry shall propose and the Government shall deliver the water pollution protection plan for a period of six years (Art. 95, para. 1).

443. Wastewater treatment referred to in para. 1 of this article is carried out to a level that corresponds to the ELVs or to a level that does not impair the quality standards of the environment of the recipient, in accordance with regulations governing the limits of pollutants into surface waters and groundwater, limit values priority, and other hazardous pollutants and regulation governing the limit values for emissions of pollutants into the water, taking more stringent criteria of these two (Art. 98, para. 2).

water quality testing as well. These legal persons are obliged to submit data of the testing results to organization of the authority responsible for conducting state-level water quality monitoring (Article 109).

7. Classification of Surface Water and Groundwater Bodies

407. With the goal of protecting and improving the quality of surface and ground waters, bodies of surface and groundwater shall be classified depending on their quantitative and chemical status (Article 111, paragraphs 1 and 2). Classified bodies of surface water and classified bodies of groundwater shall be identified in the water management plan (Article 111, paragraph 4).[444]

Article 133 prescribes activities which are to be prohibited in order to conserve and maintain bodies of surface water, bodies of groundwater, protective water constructions, and other water constructions, to prevent any deterioration of the water regime, to ensure the conveyance of high flows and the implementation of flood defence and to protect the environment.

8. Water Enactment, Water Documentation and Information Dissemination

408. Water enactments and water documentation are regulated in Chapter V of the Law. In order to ensure a single water regime and water management, in accordance with the Strategy, Water Management Plan and the relevant technical documentation, Water Acts are issued. The water acts are the following: (1) water conditions; (2) Water Consent; and (3) Water Permit. Water Act from paragraph 2 Items(2) and (3) of this Article are administrative acts, which are adopted in accordance with the regulation governing the general administrative procedure (Article 113). The competence for issuing of mentioned water enactments is divided between the MAEP – Republic Water Directorates, competent bodies of AP, and local self- government and a public water management company, depending on the type of structures and works (Article 114, paragraph 1).

409. The water permit is issued by an authority, or a public water company, responsible for issuing water conditions (Article 122, paragraph 3). The water permit is issued for a definite period of time, not longer than fifteen years (Article 122, paragraph 5).[445]

444. The Regulation on water classification (OJ SRS, No. 5/68), that regulates general classification of water into four classes according to the pollution level and purpose, prescribes water of the class II as suitable for bathing, recreation and water sports. The Regulation contains indicators and their limit values for each of the classes. The Regulation is not complied with the Council Directive 2006/7 of 15 Feb. 2006 on water quality intended for recreation purposes.

445. The right granted on the basis of water permit cannot be transferred to other user without consent of the body that issued the water permit (Art. 125, para. 1).

410. Water documentation shall include: (1) Water book[446] and (2) Water Register[447] (Article 129, paragraph 1).

411. The Ministry and the public water management enterprise shall ensure the transparency of their activities through information dissemination via public media outlets and formal releases (Article 147). A water information system shall be set up for purposes of water classification, water regime monitoring and improvement, water-system development planning, and water management in the Republic of Serbia (Article 148, paragraph 1).

9. Funding of Water Management

412. Financing of water management is regulated in Chapter IX of the Law. The activities financed in line with this Law are given in Article 150. Issues related to basis for paying of fees and defining of fee payers and criteria for paying of fees, in some cases exceptions to paying, etc. are regulated by Articles 153–177đ, 183 and 184.

413. Activities of general interest funded pursuant to this Law shall include: (1) watercourse development and protection against the adverse effects of water; (2) water development and water use; (3) water protection from pollution; (4) the construction, maintenance and management of reclamation systems – public ownership; (5) the construction, maintenance, and management of regional and multipurpose water systems; and (6) other activities of general interest (Article 150, paragraph 1). Funding for these activities shall be provided from: (1) the budget of the Republic of Serbia; (2) the budget of the AP; (3) water fees;[448] (4) concession fees; and (5) other sources (Article 151, paragraph 1).

414. A budgetary water fund of the Republic of Serbia (the National Fund) shall be established to earmark funds for activities of general interest which shall be financed pursuant to this Law within the territory of the Republic of Serbia, excluding the territory of the AP (Article 185, paragraph 1).[449] In addition, a budgetary water fund of the AP (hereinafter, the Provincial Fund) shall be established to earmark funds for activities of general interest which shall be financed pursuant to this Law within the territory of the AP (Article 188, paragraph 1).

446. A water book is a Register of water enactments which has been delivered (Art. 130, para. 1).

447. Water registers shall be maintained in order to ensure the availability of information required for water management, or water use, water protection and protection against the adverse effects of water (Art. 131, para. 1). Water registers include the following: (1) water asset Register; (2) Register of water constructions; (3) Register of water uses; and (4) Register of polluters (Art. 131, para. 2).

448. Water fees include the following: (1) water use fee; (2) water discharge fee; (3) water pollution fee; (4) drainage fee; (5) water constructions and systems fee; and (6) fee for extracted river sediment (Art. 153).

449. *See also*, Decision on the Water Budget Fund of the Republic of Serbia (OJ RS, No. 9/11).

10. Inspection Supervision

415. The issue of inspection surveillance in the field of water is prescribed in Chapter X of the Law on Waters. Surveillance of implementation of this Law and regulations passed on the basis of it, other regulations and general acts is performed by the inspector competent for water management activities (water management inspector), sanitary inspector and inspector for environmental protection, pursuant to competences prescribed by Law (Articles 196–208), by the Law on Determining the Jurisdiction of the Autonomous Province of Vojvodina (OJ RS, Nos 99/2009 and 67/2012 CC) and the Law on the Capital (OJ RS Nos 129/2007 and 83/14 – other law, 101/16 – other law) and other relevant laws.

416. Penalty system is laid down by Chapter XI of the Law on Waters.

C. Law on Environmental Protection

417. According to Article 23 of the EPL, waters may be used and burdened, and wastewaters discharged into waters with the application of adequate treatment, in the manner and up to the level that shall not represent threat to natural processes or to renewal of quality and quantity of water and which shall not reduce the possibility of their multipurpose utilization (paragraph 1).[450] Legal entity and/or entrepreneur who has a plant for wastewater treatment or need to be built and which discharges its effluent into the recipient or the public sewerage system (except installations subject to integrated permitting), should adopt an action plan for the gradual establishment of ELVs pollutants in water, set deadlines for their gradual achievement, and to act in accordance with the action plan (paragraph 3). Protection of waters shall be achieved through undertaking of systematic and control-monitoring measures of water quality, reducing pollution of waters with pollutants below the prescribed limit values and undertaking technical-technological and other measures necessary for their treatment, in order to avoid introduction of dangerous, waste and other harmful substances in waters, as well as through monitoring the effect of polluted waters on the health of humans, animals and plants and the environment. Protection of waters shall include protection of waters from the impact of transboundary pollution, in a manner to ensure the overall preservation of waters (paragraph 7).

D. Other Regulations

418. Until adoption of by-laws on the basis of the Law on Waters (OJ RS, Nos 30/10, 93/12 and 101/16), by-laws in force are, particularly:

- Regulation on categorization of watercourses (OJ RS, No.5/68).

450. Protection and utilization of waters shall be realized within the integral water management through undertaking and implementation of measures for preservation of surface and underground waters and their reserves, quality and quantity, as well as through protection in accordance with special law (para. 2). For the purpose of protection and preservation of quantities and quality of underground water reserves, detailed research work shall be conducted, as well as preparation of balance of reserves of underground waters (para. 6).

- Regulation on classification of water (OJ RS, No. 5/68).
- Rulebook on dangerous matters in water (OJ RS, No. 31/82).

419. In addition, the following by-laws, *inter alia*, are applied:

Regulation on water management programme for 2017 (OJ RS, No. 17/17).

Regulation on water charges for 2017 (OJ RS, No. 36/17).

Order on determining of Operational Plan for flood defence for 2017 (OJ RS, No 05/2017)

Operational Flood Defense Plan for 2017.[451]

Regulation on monitoring water status in 2016 (OJ RS, No. 36/16).

Regulation on limits of polluting substances emission in water and deadlines for implementation (OJ RS, Nos 67/2011 and 48/2012).

Regulation on limits of polluting substances in surface and subsurface waters and sediments and deadlines for implementation (OJ RS, No. 50/2012).

Regulation on limits of priority and priority hazardous substances polluting surface waters and deadlines for implementation (OJ RS, No. 35/2011).

Rulebook on the manner and conditions for measuring the quantities and examining the quality of waste water and the content of reports on performed measurements (OJ RS, No. 33/16).

Rulebook on the contents and form of water acts application and contents of the opinion in the procedure of issuing water requirements (OJ RS, Nos 74/2010, 116/2012 and 59/14).

Rulebook on land reclamation areas and their boundaries (OJ RS, No. 38/2011).

451. *See* http://www.rdvode.gov.rs/doc/dokumenta/podzak/operativni%20plan%202017.pdf (3 Apr. 2017).

Rulebook on sub-basin boundaries (OJ RS, No. 54/2011).

Rulebook on the contents, keeping and form of water ledger (OJ RS, No. 86/2010).

Rulebook on the contents and keeping of the cadastre of water facilities (OJ RS, No. 34/2011).

Rulebook on the contents and keeping of the water information system, methodology, structure, categories and levels of data collection as well as the contents of data public is being informed about (OJ RS, No. 54/2011).

Rulebook on reference requirements for surface water types (OJ RS, No. 67/11).

Rulebook on requirements related to technical-technological equipment and organizational and personnel capacities for exercising activities of general interest in the sphere of water management and the method of keeping record of issued and revoked licenses (OJ RS, No. 23/12 and 57/13).

Rulebook on requirements and criteria of financing and the method of financing activities of general interest in the sphere of water management (OJ RS, No. 27/05 and 31/05).

Rulebook on the parameters of ecological and chemical status of surface waters and parameters of chemical and quantitative status of subsurface waters (OJ RS, No. 74/2011).

Decision on the Water Budget Fund of the Republic of Serbia (OJ RS, No. 9/11).

Decision on water area boundaries (OJ RS, No. 75/10).

Decision on establishment of the National Water Conference (OJ RS, No. 55/11), etc.

420. Besides mentioned, following legal Acts also deserve mentioning:

- Law on Meteorological and Hydrological Activities (OJ RS, No. 88/2010).

- Law on Local Self-Government (OJ RS, No. 97/16).
- Law on Communal Utilities (OJ RS, Nos 88/11 and 104/16).
- Law on Public-Private Partnership and Concession (OJ RS, Nos 88/11, 15/16 and 104/16).
- Law on Planning and Building (OJ RS, Nos 72/09 and 81/09 – corr, 64/10 CC, 24/11, 121/12, 42/13 CC, 50/13 CC, 98/13 CC, 132/14 and 145/14).
- Law on the Transport of Dangerous Goods (OJ RS, No. 88/10, 104/16).

421. According to the NSDS, problems in water sector relate to following: the lack of plan for implementation of the EU Water Framework Directive, insufficient institutional and other capacities, inadequate funding of water management, low price for water and services and lack of economic incentives, lack of harmonization in sectoral policies with other sectors, insufficient percentage of connection to public systems of water supply, lack of rational use of water and bad quality of water in certain areas, and bad quality of water in certain water courses and insufficient protection of water quality.[452]

422. Adoption of the new Law of Water which will transpose the remaining provisions of Directive 2000/60/EC on establishing a framework for Community action in the field of water policy is planned for 2017, and adoption of relevant by-laws for the full transposition of the Directive, by the end of 2018.[453]Based on the water quality, the level of alignment is moderate. Serbia needs to make significant efforts to further align its legislation with the *acquis*, to implement it and to strengthen administrative capacity, in particular for enforcement and inter-institutional coordination.[454]

452. NSDS, 66.
453. NPAA, II revision, 1204.
454. 'Preparatory work on river basin management plans is ongoing. Some progress has been made towards adopting a water management strategy and a water management plan for the Danube river basin.' CR, 76.

Chapter 4. Waste

423. Poor waste management is still one of the major environmental problems in Serbia, and those problems mainly originate from the so far social attitude to waste. High costs, irrational organization, low service quality and insufficient care for the environment are results of this smashing situation in waste management organization. Local land filling was virtually the only way of waste management in Serbia until recently, whereas these local landfills did not satisfy even basic hygiene and technical-technological conditions, except for a very few of them; in addition, some of the existing disposal sites are practically filled up.[455]

§1. Industrial Waste

424. There are a number of factors causing problems with industrial waste, as for example, use of polluting technologies, inadequate organization, insufficient waste recycling, too slow introduction of sustainable industrial production, etc. The economic and financial crisis in which Serbia was for almost a decade in the nineties, has also contributed to, among other things, problems with the industrial waste. Most of the waste is generated by chemical industry and metallurgy, mining and energy production. Heavy industry in the Republic of Serbia is mostly connected to mining, and it includes processing industry, metallurgical and chemical industry, etc. Other industrial production includes cement and other construction materials, fertilizers, electrical equipment, wood processing, paper, leather and fur products, rubber, textile, food products.[456]

It is estimated that safe deposition of ash is one of the biggest problems. Disposal sites cover an area of about 1,800 ha and contain about 170 million tonnes of ash, which is considered hazardous waste. It is often stored improperly and local water sources are at risk of contamination.[457]

455. NEPP, 47. For more information on the packaging and packaging waste management, and products which after the use become special waste streams during 2016, *see* : *Izveštaj o upravljanju ambalažnom i ambalažnim otpadom u 2016. godini* [Report on the Management of Packaging and Packaging Waste in 2016], MAEP, EPA, Beograd, 2017. http://www.sepa.gov.rs/download/NRIZ_podaci/Ambalaza_2016.pdf (19 Jun. 2017); *Proizvodi koji posle upotrebe postaju posebni tokovi otpada u Republici Srbiji u 2016. godini* [Products which after use become special waste streams in the Republic of Serbia in 2016], MAEP, EPA, Beograd, 2017. http://www.sepa.gov.rs/download/NRIZ_podaci/PTO_2016.pdf. (19 Jun. 2017). *Plastične kese u Republici Srbiji u 2016. godini* [Plastic bags in the Republic of Serbia], MAEP, EPA, Beograd, 2017. http://www.sepa.gov.rs/download/NRIZ_podaci/PlasticneKese_2016.pdf. (17 Jun. 2017.

456. The National Waste management strategy for the period 2010–2019 (OJ RS, No. 29/201023.

457. EPR (2007), 99. *See also*, EPR (2015), 150 (Energy generation waste), 157, 176 (Recommendation 7.6).

§2. Municipal Waste

425. Municipal solid waste in Serbia includes household waste, waste produced by commercial enterprises and institutions, bio-medical waste, street sweepings and demolition.

Averagely, for per person is generated approximately 290 kg of waste per year. About 63% is generated by households and 20% by businesses. There are 163 official disposal sites of communal waste in Serbia and a large number of illegal waste dumps in rural areas.[458] Municipal waste grew at the lowest rate of all waste categories, by 26.57%, from 2007 to 2012. Such a large increase was probably due to the increase in scale and quality of local government reporting on municipal waste. After 2008 and up to 2012, the growth rate was only 2.75%. The amount of municipal waste collected in 2007 was 2,070 thousand tons and in 2012, 2,620 thousand tons.[459]

§3. Dangerous Waste

426. Most of the dangerous waste consists of oils and emulsions, but there are also various wastes from metal, plastic, paper, paint, etc. The mining industry is the biggest generating sector. Other major sources are chemical, petrochemical, metallurgical, paper, leather and textile industries.

In the first half of 2008, a database was formed containing dangerous substances located at the operators. The database was developed on the basis of collected data from 400 operators that deal with dangerous substances. According to the data provided by the Ministry/EPA, about 5,200,000 tonnes of hazardous waste was generated in 2007, and about 5,700,000 tonnes in 2008. Out of that quantity, fly ash generated in thermal power plants makes up more than 5,000,000 tonnes. Hazardous waste is generated by non-IPPC operators as well. There are facilities for treatment of certain waste streams (batteries, electronic and electric waste, waste oils, old cars). There are no facilities for permanent storage of hazardous waste, and temporary disposal is usually carried out within the establishment in which such waste had been generated, quite commonly in inadequate manner.[460] In such circumstances, hazardous waste generators store hazardous waste temporarily in their own locations in temporary storages, although waste has been stored for twenty or more years in some of them. The circulation of waste is subject to the permit system, in conformity with the Law on Ratification of the Basel Convention on the Control of Transboundary Movements of Hazardous Wastes and their Disposal as well as the EPL. Hazardous waste import is prohibited. Exceptionally, certain types of hazardous waste which are needed as secondary raw materials in the processing industry in the Republic of Serbia, in

---

458. *Statistical Yearbook of Serbia 2007*, 45. According to the Screening Report, the country has seven regional operational landfills for non-hazardous waste that are in line with the requirements of the Landfill Directive; it has164 non-compliant landfills. SRS, Ch. 27. 6.

459. EPR (2015), 8.

460. NEPP, 48.

compliance with the national goals of that waste type processing, may be imported according to the permit.[461]

§4. Legislation

427. The three basic legal Acts concerning waste are the *EPL* (OJ RS, Nos 135/04, 36/09 and 36/09 – other law, 72/09 – other law, 43/11 CC and 14/16),[462] the Law on Waste Management (OJ RS, Nos 36/09, 88/10 and 14/16) and the Law on Packaging and Packaging Waste (OJ RS, No. 36/09).

428. The Law on Waste Management (OJ RS, Nos 36/2009, 88/2010 and 14/16) determines the entities competent for waste management, along with their defined obligations and responsibilities. The entities competent for waste management are: (1) Republic of Serbia; (2) AP; (3) LSG Unit; (4) EPA; (5) professional organizations for waste analysis; (6) NGOs, including consumer organizations; and (7) other bodies and organizations, pursuant to the Law (Article 17).

429. The Republic of Serbia oversees waste management on its territory through the competent bodies and organizations. The EPA keeps and updates the waste management database in the environmental protection information system regulating environmental protection. Professional organizations and/or accredited laboratories perform testing of waste for transboundary shipment, treatment of waste and disposal of waste in accordance with their authority for testing waste. In the Republic of Serbia there are six authorized laboratories for testing of waste. NGOs, including organizations for the protection of consumers and other authorities and organizations (urban planning, nature protection, municipal services and internal affairs) submit their opinions to the LSG units in the process for issuing waste management permits.

I. National Waste Management Strategy

430. The basic framework document providing conditions for the rational and sustainable waste management is the National Waste Management Strategy for the period 2010–2019 (adopted in 2010) (OJ RS, No. 29/2010). According to it, the main principles of the waste management are sustainable development, regional approach to waste management, precaution, 'the polluter pays', waste management hierarchy, implementation of the best practical environmental options (BPEO), and producer's responsibility. Specific short-term (2010–2014) objectives are as follows:

- Harmonize national regulations in the sphere of waste management with the EU legislation.
- Adopt national plans for certain waste streams.
- Develop regional and local waste management plans up to 2014.

461. The National Waste management strategy for the period 2010–2019, 26.
462. Apart from the EPL, several provisions of the Law on SEA (2004), Law on EIA (2004) and Law on IPPC (2004) are also relevant for waste management.

- Increase number of citizens included in the system for waste collection to 75%by 2014.
- Develop the system of primary selection of waste in LSG units.
- Construct twelve regional centres for waste management by 2014 (regional landfills, plants for the selection of recyclable waste, plants for separation of recyclable waste, plants for a biological treatment of waste and transfer stations in every region).
- Establish the system of hazardous waste management (establish central regional storages for hazardous waste and start the construction of the plant for physical-chemical treatment of hazardous waste by 2014).
- Establish the system for the management of specific waste streams (waste tyres, used batteries and accumulators, waste oils, end-of-life vehicles, Waste Electrical and Electronic Equipment (WEEE)).
- Establish the system for the management of medical and pharmaceutical waste.
- Establish the system for the management of waste of animal origin and adopt are levant regulation.
- Encourage the use of waste as an alternative fuel in cement plants, steelworks plant and thermal plants, in accordance with the principle of waste hierarchy.
- Improve the sanitary conditions of current landfills that represent the highest risk for environment and of sites called 'hot spots' from historical pollution with hazardous waste.[463]

II. Law on Environmental Protection

431. A number of Articles of the EPL are related to waste management. Article 30 prescribes that:

> Waste[464] management shall be enforced according to regulated conditions and measures of waste treatment through system of collecting, transport, preparation for reuse, i.e. reuse of waste treatment and disposal, including supervision over those activities and concern for the facilities for waste treatment after their closure. The owner of the waste is obliged to undertake measures of waste management in order to prevent or reduce waste generation, reuse and recycle; separation of secondary raw materials and use of waste as energents, that is. waste disposal.

463. The National Waste management strategy for the period 2010–2019, 44–45.
464. According to Art. 3, point 20 of the EPL, 'waste' is defined as any object or substance defined by the waste management law.

III. Law on Waste Management

432. It has following fifteen parts: Part I – General Provisions (Articles 1–6), Part II – Types and Classification of Waste[465] (Articles 7 and 8), Part III – Waste Management Planning (Articles 9–16), Part IV – Waste Management Authorities (Articles 17–24), Part V – Responsibilities and Obligations in Waste Management (Articles 25–31), Part VI – Organization of Waste Management (Articles 32–46), Part VII – Specific Waste Streams Management (Articles 47–58), Part VIII – Waste Management Permits (Articles 59–70), Part IX – Transboundary Waste Movement (Articles 71–73), Part X – Reporting on Waste and Database (Articles 74–76), XI – Waste Management Financing (Articles 77–82), Part XII – Supervision (Articles 83–86), Part XIII – Competence for Settlement of Appeals (Article 87), Part XIV – Penalty Provisions (Articles 88–92), Part XV – Transitional and Final Provisions (Articles 93–105), as well as independent Articles of the Law Amending the Law on Waste Management (OJ RS, No. 88/2010, Articles 23–26).[466]

433. According to Article 1, the Law on Waste regulates types and classifications of waste,[467] waste management planning, waste management entities, responsibilities and obligations in waste management,[468] waste management organization, managing of special waste flows, conditions and procedures for issuing of permits; transboundary movement of waste, reporting on waste and databases; financing of waste management; and supervision, as well as other issues relevant to waste management.

---

465. *Waste* is each substance or object to be rejected, intend to be reject or which is necessary to be rejected by holder (Art. 5, point 17) (Art. 5, point 17). 'Construction and demolition waste' means waste generated in the execution of construction works on construction sites or construction site preparation works, as well as waste generated as a result of the demolition or reconstruction of buildings, and this includes non-hazardous and hazardous construction and demolition waste, namely: – Non-hazardous construction and demolition waste not containing hazardous materials, the composition of which is similar to that of municipal waste (recyclable, inert, etc.), – Hazardous construction and demolition waste requiring specific handling and/or having one or more hazardous characteristics making it hazardous waste (wastes containing asbestos, wastes with high heavy metal content, etc.) to which specific regulations apply (Art. 17a).
466. The provisions of this Law shall not apply to: (1) gases that are emitted into the atmosphere; (2) land (in situ) land (in situ) including unexcavated contaminated land and buildings permanently connected with land; (3) uncontaminated soil and other materials from nature, excavated during construction activities where it is certain that the material will be used in construction purposes in its natural form on the site where it was excavated; (4) radioactive waste; (5) deactivated explosives; (6) faeces, if they are not covered by para. 2, item 2) of this Article; (7) Straw and other natural non-hazardous agricultural or forest materials used in farming, forestry or for the production of energy from such biomass through processes or methods which do not threaten the environment or endanger human health; and (8) sludge from sewerage systems and septic tanks contents, other than plants from waste water treatment. (Art. 4, para. 1).
467. *Classification of waste* is the process of classifying of waste disposal to one or more waste lists which are regulated by special regulation, and according to its origin, composition and further purpose (Art. 5, point 10).
468. *Waste management* is the implementation of the prescribed measures for waste management including collection, transport, storage, treatment, i.e., reuse and waste disposal, including supervision of these activities and taking care of waste management facilities after the closure of the activities undertaken by the trader and agent (Art. 5, point 36).

434. Article 2 prescribes that aim of this Law is to provide and ensure conditions for: (1) waste management in a way that does not endanger human health and the environment;[469] (2) prevention of waste, particularly through development of cleaner technologies and rational use of natural resources, as well as eliminating the risk of its harmful effects on human health and the environment; (3) reuse and recycling of waste, separation of secondary raw material from the waste and using waste as fuel; (4) development of procedures and methods for waste disposal;[470] (5) rehabilitation of unarranged landfills;[471] (6) monitoring of existing and newly created landfill; and (7) developing-raising awareness of waste management.

A. Principles of Waste Management

435. There are five generally accepted principles on which waste management is based (Article 6, paragraph 1):(1) *selection of the most optimal option for the environment* – application of the most optimal options for the environment establishes for the given objectives and circumstances, the option or combination of options that gives the greatest benefit or minimum damage to the environment as a whole, at an acceptable cost and profitability, in the long term, as well as in short term; (1a) *principle of self-sufficiency*–application of the principle of self-sufficiency means the establishment of integrated and adequate network of facilities for reuse and disposal of mixed municipal waste collected from households, including the collection of this type of waste generated by other waste producers, taking into account the BAT in accordance with this Law;(2) *proximity and regional approach to waste management* – the waste is treated or disposed as close as possible to their place of generation, that is, in the region of generation, with the aim to avoid negative effects to the environment during the transport. Regional waste management is provided by development and implementation

469. Waste management is performed in a way that provides the least risk to human life and health and to the environment, control and mitigation of (Art. 3, para. 1): (1) water, air and soil pollution; (2) threats to flora and fauna; (3) the threat of the emergence of an accident, explosion or fire; (4) negative impact on landscapes and natural goods of exceptional value; (5) the level of noise and unpleasant odour.

470. *Waste disposal* is any operation which is not reuse of waste, even when the operation has a secondary effect of the formation of substances or energy (D list is non-exhaustive list of disposal operations) (Art. 5, point 16).

471. *Landfill* is a place for the final disposal of sanitary waste surface or below the surface of the earth including: internal disposal sites (landfill where the manufacturer is disposed their own waste at the source); permanent locations (more than one year) used for temporary storage of waste, but excluding warehouses where waste is unloaded for the purpose of preparation for further transport to the place for treatment, i.e., reutilization or disposal on other locations, and waste storage prior of treatment, i.e., reuse up to three years or waste storage before disposal up to one year) (Art. 5, point 5).

of regional strategic plans based on European legislation and national policy;[472] (3) *the principle of hierarchy of waste management* – the hierarchy of waste management is the order of priorities in waste management practices; (4) *the principle of responsibility* – producers, importers, distributors and retailers of products affecting the growth of the waste are responsible for waste generated as a result of their activities. The producer is obliged to strive to reduce waste, developing products that are recyclable, as well as developing markets for reuse and recycling of their products; and (5) *polluter pays principle* – the polluter has to bear the full cost of expenses of their activities. Costs for waste generation, treatment and disposal must be included in the price of the product.

B. *Types and Classification of Waste*

436. According to Article 7, paragraph 1, types of waste are the following: (1) communal waste[473] (home waste);[474] (2) commercial waste;[475] and (3) industrial waste.[476]

437. Waste is classified according to the catalogue of waste (Article 8, paragraph 1). Catalogue of waste is a summary list of non-hazardous[477] and hazardous waste[478] according to the place of generation, and composition (Article 8, paragraph 2). Hazardous waste is classified when necessary, according to limited values of dangerous substances

472. In terms of the implementation of the waste hierarchy to which the waste management hierarchy refers, actions shall be taken to initiate solutions to achieve the best overall result in terms of the environment, which in case of specific waste streams, may require deviations from the hierarchy where this shall be justified with the life cycle, taking into consideration total effects on such waste generation and management (para. 3). Development of the waste management legislation and policy shall be a fully transparent process, in accordance with applicable regulations on consultations and involvement of the citizens and all stakeholders (para. 4). In the implementation of the hierarchy principle, account shall be taken in to general principles of environmental protection, precaution and sustainability, technical feasibility and economic value, and protection of resources as well as of the overall effect on the environment, human health, and economic and social effects (para. 5).
473. *Communal waste* is waste from households (household waste), as well as other waste which is, because of its nature or composition, similar to waste from households (Art. 5, point 13).
474. Depending upon hazardous charasteristics that influence human health and the environment, communal waste can be (Art. 7, para. 2): (1) inert; (2) non-hazardous; and (3) hazardous.
475. *Commercial waste* is waste generated in enterprises and other institutions that are wholly or partly engaged in trade, services, office affairs, sport, recreation or entertainment, except household waste and industrial waste (Art. 5, point 11).
476. *Industrial waste* is waste from any industry or from the location of industry, except mullock and supporting mineral raw materials from mines and quarries (Art. 5, point 7).
477. *Non-hazardous waste* is waste that does not have characteristics of hazardous waste (Art. 5, point 15).
478. *Hazardous waste* is a waste which by its origin, composition or concentration of hazardous substances can cause danger to the environment and human health and has at least one of the hazardous characteristics defined by special regulations, including packaging in which hazardous waste was or is packed.

concentration (Article 8, paragraph 3). The owner of the waste, that is, the operator[479] is obliged to classify the waste in the prescribed manner, in accordance with this Law[480] (Article 8, paragraph 4).

438. The Minister in charge for environmental protection prescribes: (1) waste catalogue; (2) a list of categories of waste (Q list); (3) a list of categories of hazardous waste by the origin and composition (Y list); (4) a list of hazardous waste characteristics (H list); (5) a list of waste components for which it is considered hazardous waste (C list); (6) concentration limits of harmful components in the waste, on which characteristics of waste are determined; (7) a list of procedures and methods of disposal and reutilization of waste (listD & Rlist); (8) type, content and form of report on testing of waste; (9) types of parameters to determine the physical and chemical characteristics of hazardous waste to be used for physical-chemical treatment; (10) types of parameters for waste testing for thermal treatment purpose; (11) types of parameters for waste testing and testing of eluate intended for disposal; and (12) manner and procedure for classification of waste (Article 8, paragraph 6).[481]

C. Planning, Responsibilities and Organizing of Waste Management

439. For planning of waste management, the following planning documents are adopted in the Republic of Serbia (Article 9, paragraph 1): (1) Waste Management Strategy (hereinafter, Strategy); (2) national plans for individual waste streams; (3) regional waste management plan; (4) local waste management plan; (5) waste management plan in the facility of which integrated permit is issued; and (6) work plan for waste management facilities.

440. Entities responsible for waste management are (Article 17, paragraph 1): (1) the Republic of Serbia; (2) AP; (3) LSG unit; (4) EPA; (5) professional organizations for the examination of waste; (6) NGOs, including consumer organizations; and (7) other agencies and organizations, in accordance with the Law.

---

479. *Operator* is any physical person or legal entity who, in accordance with the regulations, manages the installation or controls it or is authorized to make economic decisions in the area of technical functioning of the facility and on whose name is issued a permit for waste management (Art. 5, point 19).

480. In order to determine the composition and characteristics of hazardous waste, the owner of the waste, i.e., operator is obliged to perform testing of hazardous waste, as well as waste which by the origin, composition and characteristics might be a hazardous waste (Art. 8, para. 5).

481. In the regulation referred to in para. 6 points 2, 3 and 5 of this Law, the Minister shall make a list of Serbian standards which shall contain technical requirements for waste categories and elements (para. 7). The inclusion of a substance or an object in the list referred to in para. 7 of this Article shall not mean that this shall be waste in all cases, but will be deemed waste only in so far it complies with the requirements in accordance with this Law (para. 8). The reclassification of hazardous waste as non-hazardous waste shall not be achieved by waste diluting or mixing so as to reduce the initial concentration of hazardous materials to the level below the limit values for the definition of hazardous waste (para. 9). Waste may be deemed non-hazardous waste in accordance with the waste catalogue referred to in para. 2 of this Article (para. 10). Amendments to the Law (2016) introduced also, *inter alia*, new provisions concerning the following issues: by-product, proving compliance with by-product related requirements and end of waste status (Art. 8a–8d).

441. The producer of products is obliged to use technologies and develop production ensuring rational use of natural resources, materials and energy, and also encourage reuse and recycling[482] of products and packaging and promote ecologically sustainable management of natural resources (Article 25, paragraph 1).

442. A producer or an importer whose product becomes hazardous waste is obliged, after use of such product, to take over that waste, without compensation costs and treat it in accordance with this Law and other regulations (Article 25, paragraph 2) or to authorize other legal entity to take over the products after use on his/her behalf (Article 25, paragraph 3).

443. The owner of waste shall bear all waste management costs (Article 27, paragraph 1). Disposal costs shall be borne by the holder (owner) and/or previous holder (owner) or the product producer who has produced the waste (Article 27, paragraph 3). The responsibilities and obligations of waste holder as a person is like one who participates in turnover of waste as an indirect holder of waste, but actually does not own waste (Article 27, paragraph 4).[483]

444. Waste management is organized in a way that does not pose threat to human health and the environment in accordance to the Law (Article 32, paragraph 1). The Minister may order additional measures for managing of certain types of waste in case that: (1) the waste handling endangers or may endanger human health and the environment; (2) there are additional requirements for the implementation of provisions of international treaties binding on the Republic of Serbia (Article 32, paragraph 2).

445. A person[484] who collects or transports waste, collects waste from producers or owners and transport it to the waste management facilities, or to the collection centre, storage centre, transfer station or to the facility for treatment or disposal (Article 35, paragraph 1) is obliged to separate different kinds of waste during the transportation (Article 35, paragraph 4). If pollution occurs during waste transportation, carrier is responsible for cleaning and removal of pollution (Article 35, paragraph 6). Hazardous waste is to be separately collected and transported (Article 35, paragraph 9).

446. The waste is stored in places that are technically equipped for temporary waste storage at the site of the manufacturer or of the owner and/or other waste holder in collection centres, in transfer stations and other locations in accordance to this Law (Article 36, paragraph 1). Hazardous waste cannot be temporarily stored at the site of the manufacturer, owner and/or other waste holder for more than twelve months, unless the process of obtaining permits is ongoing, a maximum of 120 days from expiring of deadline from this paragraph (Article 36, paragraph 4).

---

482. *Recycling* means any operations of reuse processing waste into a product, materials or substances, regardless of whether are used for the original or other purposes, including reprocessing of organic materials, except reuse for energy purposes, and reprocessing into materials that are intended for use as fuel or for landfill covering (Art. 5, point 27).

483. The obligations of other entities are also regulated: Obligations of Waste Carrier (Art. 28), Obligations of the Broker and Dealer (Art. 28a), Obligations of the Operator in the Waste Management Facility (Art. 29), Obligations of Waste Disposal Site Operator (Art. 30) and Qualified Person Responsible for Professional Activities (Art. 31).

484. *Waste collector* is a physical person or legal entity who collects the waste (Art. 5, point 29); *Waste collection* is the collection of waste, including preliminary sorting and preliminary storage of waste for the purposes of transportation to waste management facilities (Art. 5, point 28).

447. Waste treatment is performed applying the best-available techniques and technologies in accordance with this Law (Article 37, paragraph 1). Facility and equipment for waste treatment can be stationary or mobile (Article 37, paragraph 2). The treatment of waste in stationary or mobile facility shall be in accordance with a permit for treatment issued on the basis of this Law (Article 37, paragraph 3).

448. The competent authority for waste management takes necessary measures to ensure that the operations of waste reuse are carried out in accordance with Articles 3 and 6 of this Law (Article 38, paragraph 1). The Minister shall prescribe the conditions and manner of collection, transport, storage and treatment and recycling of wastes used as secondary raw materials or for energy production (Article 38, paragraph 10).

D. Management of Special Waste Streams

449. It is prohibited to transport batteries and accumulators containing more than 0.0005% mercury by weight, unless otherwise stipulated by this Law (Article 47, paragraph 1). It is prohibited to transport portable batteries and accumulators, including those that are built into devices, which contain more than 0.002% cadmium by weight, except those used in security and alarm systems, medical equipment or cordless electric tools, unless otherwise stipulated by this Law (Article 47, paragraph 3). The owner of waste batteries and accumulators, excluding household is obliged to hand them over for treatment to a person who has permission to do so (Article 47, paragraph 7). The Minister is in charge to prescribe the content and appearance of markings on the batteries, button cells and accumulators according to the content of hazardous substances, manner and procedure for managing waste batteries and accumulators, as well as devices with built-in batteries and accumulators (Article 47, paragraph 9).

450. Where waste oil is concerned, the Law prohibits: (1) discharge or spill of waste oil into or onto land, surface and underground water and sewage system; (2) disposal of waste oils and uncontrolled discharge of residues from the waste oil processing; (3) mixing of waste oil during collection and storage with Polychlorinated Biphenyl (PCB) and usage of PCB or halogenated substances and with substances that are not waste oil, or mixing with hazardous waste; (4) every kind of waste oil processing, which pollutes air in concentrations above the prescribed limits (Article 48, paragraph 2).[485]

451. The entity that collects, transports, treats or disposes of waste tires shall hold appropriate permit, maintain and keep records on quantities of collected and treated waste tires and shall submit such data to the Agency.[486]

452. The waste originating from electrical and electronic products is not to be mixed with other types of waste. It is prohibited to dispose electrical and electronic

485. Waste oil, for the purpose of this Law, are all mineral or synthetic oils or lubricants, which are useless for the purpose they were originally intended, such as hydraulic oils, engine oils, turbine oils or other lubricants, marine oil, oils or liquids for insulating or heat transfer, other mineral or synthetic oil, including oily residues from tanks, oil – water mixtures and emulsions (Art. 48, para. 1).

486. Waste tires, according to Art. 49, para. 1, are tires of motor vehicles (cars, buses, trucks, motorcycles, etc.), agricultural and construction machinery, trailers, towing machines, etc. after the end of their life cycle.

products' waste[487] without previous treatment (Article 50, paragraph 2). The components of electrical and electronic products waste that contain RSV must be separated and properly disposed (Article 50, paragraph 4). The producer or importer of electrical or electronic products is required to identify there cyclable components of these products (Article 50, paragraph 5). When placed on the market, the use of new electrical and electronic equipment containing lead, mercury, cadmium, hexavalentchromium, polibromovanebiphenyls (PBB) and polibromovanediphenylethers (PBDE) maybe prohibited or restricted (Article 50, paragraph 9).

453. Waste fluorescent tubes containing mercury are collected separately (Article 51, paragraph 1). It is prohibited to dispose such tubes without prior treatment (Article 51, paragraph 2). Also, the owner of waste fluorescent tubes containing mercury is obliged to hand them over for treatment to a person having permission to do so (Article 51, paragraph 3).

454. Waste containing PCB is to be collected separately (Article 52, paragraph 1). According to Article 52, points 1–6, it is prohibited to: (1) refill transformers with PCBs; (2) reuse PCB waste; (3) get PCB from PCB waste by recycling; (4) temporarily store PCBs, PCB waste and equipment containing PCB[488] for more than twenty-four months before securing their disposal or decontamination;[489] (5) incinerate PCB or PCB waste on ships; and (6) use equipment containing PCB in case they are not in working order or if they are leaking. An owner and/or other holder of equipment containing more than 5 dm^3 of PCB shall be obliged to report to the Ministry on such equipment, submit a replacement plan, i.e., equipment disposal and decontamination plan, ensure its disposal, i.e., decontamination, and inform the Ministry about all the changes in data pertaining to the equipment, within three months from the date of an occurred change (Article 52,paragraph 5).[490]

Disposal or decontamination of equipment referred to in Article 52, paragraph 5 of the Law on Waste Management (OJ RS, Nos 36/09 and 88/10) containing PCBs

487. Electrical and electronic products waste cannot be mixed with other types of waste (Art. 50, para. 1). Waste liquids originating from electrical and electronic products must be separated and treated in an appropriate way (Art. 50, para. 3).

488. All equipment containing PCBs, as well as rooms or facilities in which they are located, including decontaminated equipment, must be marked (Art. 52, para. 10).

489. *Decontamination* includes all operations that enable reuse, recycling, or safe disposal of the equipment, objects or materials contaminated by hazardous materials, and may include the removal or replacement of hazardous materials by suitable less harmful material (Art. 5, point 4).

490. Entities that conduct PCB disposal shall be obliged to deliver to holders used PCBs, and issue a confirmation in which they shall specify PCB properties and quantities. An owner and/or other holder of equipment containing PCBs shall be obliged to deliver PCB, PCB waste and/or equipment containing PCB to an entity that holds a permit in accordance with this Law, and take all the precaution measures in order to avoid a risk of fire, including keeping them away from flammable products. Equipment containing less than 5 dm^3 of PCBs which are integral parts of other equipment should be removed and separately collected, recycled or disposed, upon the termination of the use of the equipment of which they are integral parts (Art. 52,paras 6–8).

and disposal of PCB from such equipment shall be made no later than 31 December 2019 (Article 55 of the 2016 Amendments).[491]

455. The owner of Persistent Organic Pollutants (POPs) waste[492] is obliged to report to the ministry the type and quantity of POPs waste. The person performing treatment or disposal of POPs waste shall ensure that the remains after the treatment do not have characteristics of POPs substances (Article 53, paragraph 3).

456. The waste containing asbestos is separately collected, packed, stored and disposed of in a landfill in a visible marked place designated for the disposal of waste containing asbestos (Article 54, paragraph 1). The producer or owner of waste containing asbestos is required to implement measures to prevent dispersion of asbestos fibres and dust in the environment (Article 54, paragraph 2). The owner of scrap cars (if known) is obliged to hand over the vehicle to the person who has permission for their collection or treatment (Article 54, paragraph 4).[493] A local government regulates the procedure of collection and delivery vehicles and is entitled to charge the costs if the owner of scraped car is subsequently determined (Article 54, paragraph 6).

457. Producer of medical waste who produces more than 100 tons of non-hazardous medical waste and/or 200 kg of hazardous medical waste is obliged to prepare a medical waste management plan (Article 56, paragraph 1).

Ministry responsible for public health with prior opinion of the Institute for Public Health, established for the territory of the Republic of Serbia, in cooperation with Ministry gives consent on the plan for medical waste management plan from health institutions, from other forms of health services (hereinafter, private practice), other legal entities, i.e., Institutions that provide health care for people in accordance with the Law, as well as related medical, educational and scientific research activities that produce more than 500 kg of hazardous medical waste per year (Article 56, paragraph 2). Producer of medical waste provides, when possible, the reduction of quantities and/or hazardous characteristics of medical waste at the place of origin, as well as the reuse of waste (Article 56, paragraph 4). Producer of medical waste collects all waste at the place of origin and classify a hazardous from non-hazardous waste, i.e., different types of hazardous medical waste and dispose it in a suitable packaging adapted to its properties, quantity, to the way of temporary disposal method, transport and treatment (Article 56, paragraph 5).[494]

---

491. Notwithstanding para. 1 of this Article, the owner and/or holder of equipment containing PCB between 0.05%and0.005% by weight shall provide for disposal or decontamination of such device after termination of its use. A plan for replacement or disposal and decontamination of equipment containing PCB shall be developed by its owner and/or holder by 31 Dec. 2017 (paras 2 and 3).
492. *POPs waste*, in accordance with this Law, is waste consisting of, containing or contaminated with Persistent Organic Pollutants (POPs) substances (Art. 53, para. 1).
493. If the owner of scraped vehicle is unknown, local government unit shall provide collection and delivery vehicles to a person who has permission for treatment (Art. 54, para. 5).
494. Amendments to the law (2016) introduced, also, new provisions related to the management of pharmaceutical waste (Art. 56a and 56b).

458. Operations for disposal of titaniumdioxide waste[495] cannot be made without permission of the Ministry[496] or the competent authorities of the AP.

459. The material used for packaging must be manufactured and designed in a way that during their life cycle are eligible for environmental protection, safety and human health, the health safety of packaged products, as well as conditions for product transportation and waste management (Article 58, paragraph 1).[497]

E. Permits

460. To perform one or more activities in the field of waste management, permits[498] shall be obtained as follows: (1) permits for waste collection; (2) permits for waste transport; and (3) permits for waste treatment, specifically: – Storage permit; – Recovery permit; – Disposal permit (Article 59, paragraph 1). To perform more activities it may be issued only one integral permit for one operator. Permission for collection and transport of hazardous waste shall be issued in accordance with this Law and other regulations (Article 59, paragraphs 2 and 3).[499]

461. Permits for collection, transport, storage, treatment and disposal of hazardous waste, permits for the treatment of non-hazardous and inert waste by incineration and

495. Waste from titaniumdioxide, according to this Law, are all types of waste originating from titaniumdioxide production, which the manufacturer is obliged to store in compliance with this Law, as well as the residual generated during the treatment of these type of wastes (Art. 57, para. 1).

496. The producer and owner of waste is obliged to have a license, to keep and maintain records of quantities of this type of waste that is collected, stored, treated or disposed and shall submit information about that to the Agency (Art. 57, para. 3). The producer and owner of titaniumdioxide and waste from titaniumdioxide is obliged to implement measures for supervision of operations of the disposal, as well as controlling of land, water and air at the site where the waste from the titaniumdioxide has been used, stored or disposed of (Art. 57, para. 4).

497. Packaging and packaging of waste is managed in accordance with the special law (Art. 58, para. 2).

498. *Permit* is a decision of the competent authority to the legal entity or entrepreneur approving the collection, transport, import, export and transit, storage, treatment, and reuse or disposal of waste and sets out the conditions of waste management in a way that provides the lowest risk to human health and the environment (Art. 5, point 6).

499. The permits referred to in paras 1 and 2 of this Article shall be issued for business activities in the field of waste management other than those for which, according to the IPPC-related regulations, the integrated permit is issued. By way of an exception, the permit referred to in paras 1 and 2 of this Article shall also be issued for new and existing waste management plants which are subject to the issue of the integrated permit, including the duration of the trial period, but no longer than 240 days from the completion of the trial period, as a temporary permit pending the issue of the integrated permit. An operator may lodge a complaint against a decision which serves as a basis for the issuance of the permit referred to in para. 4 of this Article, within fifteen days from the day of reception of the decision (paras 4–6).

permits for waste treatment in mobile facility[500] are issued by the Ministry (Article 60, paragraph 1).

462. Permits for the storage, treatment and disposal of inert and non-hazardous waste for more than one local government are issued by the Ministry, while at the territory of AP[501] the competent body of the AP is in charge (Article 60, paragraph 2).

463. It is prescribed in Article 62 which documents are to be submitted in request for issuance of permits, as well as content of request for issuing of the permits (Article 62). Permit sets out the conditions for conducting activities of operator at the facility for treatment, i.e., storage, reuse and disposal of waste (Article 64, paragraph 1). Article 64 prescribes permit content.[502]

464. Permits for waste, treatment i.e., storage, reuse and disposal are issued for a period of ten years (Article 66, paragraph 1). The license may be renewed at the request submitted 120 days before the expiration of the license to ensure continuity of the license (Article 66, paragraph 3).

465. Permission to collect and/or transport waste shall be issued to a person registered for performing activities of collecting, or to a carrier in accordance with the laws governing the transportation in public transport, that is, to the domestic carrier, in accordance with the laws governing international public transport (Article 70, paragraph 1). Mandatory measures during collecting, transportation of inert, non-hazardous and hazardous waste, in accordance with the provisions of this Law and other regulations are prescribed in the permission. The permit shall be issued for a period of five years and may be renewed (Article 70).

500. *Mobile facility* for *waste* management is facility for collecting, preparation for reuse, reutilization and other operation of waste treatment from the R and D lists (R2–R13, D8 and D9), which is of such structure that is not connected to surface or object and can be moved from location to location, including a mobile facility that is used for remediation of contaminated sites, as a rule, on a site where waste is generated, i.e., at the location of the waste producer, or at another location of the waste owner for which the plant operator has a license for waste storage (Art. 5, point 14).

501. *AP* is in charge to issue permits for collection, transportation, storage, treatment and disposal of waste for all activities on the territory of the AP, as well as for each facility for which a permit for construction is issued by the competent authority of AP (Art. 60, para. 3). 'City, i.e.,*municipality*, entrusted with issuing permits for the collection, transport, treatment, i.e., storage, reuse and disposal of inert and non-hazardous waste on their territory' (Art. 60, para. 5). *The City* of Belgrade is entrusted with issuing permits for the collection, transport, treatment, i.e., storage, reuse and disposal of waste for all activities on the territory of city of Belgrade and for all plants possessing the construction license issued by the competent authority of the City of Belgrade (Art. 60, para. 4).

502. The permit for the mobile facility for waste treatment contains operator's obligation to notify the Ministry about any change of location, i.e., the competent authority of the AP and submit approval for location (Art. 64, para. 5).

F. *Reporting and Supervision*

466. Report on Waste Management in the territory of the Republic of Serbia is an integral part of the Report on the state of the environment and shall be submitted annually to the National Assembly (Article 74, paragraph 1).[503]

467. A producer, owner and/or other holder of waste, except households, shall maintain and keep daily records on waste and submit regular annual report to the Agency (Article 75, paragraph 1). Legal entities i.e., entrepreneurs that participate in the trade of waste shall be obliged to submit to the Agency data on the type and quantity of waste, including secondary raw materials that are placed on the market, in the prescribed manner (Article 75, paragraph 2).

468. The Ministry shall supervise the work of the Agency, AP, local governments, as well as authorized legal entities in performing of delegated tasks (Article 83).

G. *Financing of Waste Management*

469. Waste management costs are determined by the quantity and characteristics of waste in accordance with 'polluter pays' principle and include: (1) the cost of separate collection of waste;[504] (2) the cost of transportation of waste; (3) other costs of measures for waste management that are not covered by income generated by turnover of waste; (4) the costs for removal of waste which is left by an unknown person outside of the landfill;[505]and (5) costs for design and construction of facilities for storage, treatment and disposal of waste, facility costs, closing costs, its subsequent maintenance after termination of the work (Article 77, paragraph 1).

470. Households shall bear costs for waste management in compliance with regulations pertaining to utilities (Article 78, paragraph 3).[506]

471. Legal entity or entrepreneur performing the activity of collection, transport, treatment, and/or storage, recovery and disposal of waste shall charge for its services according to the price determined in compliance with the Law (Article 79, paragraph

503. The producer owner and/or other waste holder, except households, is obliged to keep and maintain daily records on waste and submit regular annual report to the Agency (Art. 75, para. 1).

504. Waste generator or owner shall bear costs for collection, transport, storage, treatment and disposal of waste, in compliance with this Law (Art. 78, para. 1). Legal entity or entrepreneur performing the activity of collection, transport, storage, treatment, reuse and disposal of waste shall charge for such services according to the price determined in compliance with law (Art. 79, para. 1).

505. Costs for removal of waste disposed of outside the landfill, origins of which cannot be established, i.e., its connection to the generator or to the person who disposed it cannot be established, shall be borne by LSG unit.

506. The price for the service of waste management, with pre-treatment included shall be determined depending upon the type, quantity, waste characteristics and frequency of services provided, as well as on length and conditions for transport of waste and other circumstances that affect price for organization of waste management (Art. 79, para. 2).

1).[507] Manufacturer or importer of products which become special waste streams upon the use of such products, shall pay the charge (Article 79, paragraph 4).[508]

472. Operator shall bear costs for administrative fees, determined compliant with special regulations, for the following: (1) applying for permit in compliance with this Law; (2) issuance of permit in compliance with this Law; (3) applying for exemption from permitting obligation in compliance with this Law; and (4) issuance of ruling on exemption from permitting obligation in compliance with this Law (Article 82).

473. Funds for the financing of waste management in the Republic of Serbia are provided from: (1) The budget of the Republic of Serbia; (2) The budget of the AP and Local Self-Governments; (3) EU funds and other international funds; (4) donations, gifts, contributions, assistance and similar sources for waste management; (5) loans from international financial institutions; and (6) other sources in accordance with the Law. The funds referred to in paragraph 1 of this Article may be used only for the purpose of in the manner prescribed by this Law and on the way prescribed by the Law governing environmental protection (Article 80, paragraphs 1 and 2).

IV. The Law on Packaging and Packaging Waste

474. The legal Act that regulates packaging and packaging waste in the Republic of Serbia is the Law on Packaging and Packaging Waste (OJ RS, No. 36/2009). It has the following nine parts: Part I – General Provisions (Articles 1–6), Part II – Environmental conditions that packing must fulfil to be placed on the market (Articles 7–15), Part III – Management of packaging and packaging waste (Articles 16–37), Part IV – Reporting on packaging and packaging waste (Articles 38–42), Part V – Economic instruments (Articles 43–45), Part VI – Supervision (Articles 46–49), Part VII – Jurisdiction on complaint resolution (Article 50), Part VIII – Penal provisions (Articles 51–53) and Part IX – Transitional and final provisions (Articles 54–57).

507. Price of waste landfilling service shall cover all costs of establishment and operation of the landfill, including financial guarantees or other equivalent instruments and estimated costs for closure and after-care for a period of at least 30 years, for all kinds of waste at the site (para. 3).

508. The funds collected from charges referred to in para. 4 of this Article shall be revenues of the Republic of Serbia budget and shall be used through Green Fund of the Republic of Serbia(Art. 79, para. 6).

475. This Law regulates the requirements for environmental protection that packaging[509] has to meet to be placed on the market, management of packaging and packaging waste,[510] reporting on packaging and packaging waste, economic instruments, as well as other issues important for the management of packaging and packaging waste (Article 1, paragraph 1).

476. Provisions of this Law shall apply[511] on imported packaging, packaging that is produced or placed on the market, and all packaging waste resulting from business activities on territory of the Republic of Serbia,[512] regardless of its origin, use and used packaging material (Article 1, paragraph 2).

477. The aim of this Law is, in accordance with the principle of sustainable development, to provide (Article 3, paragraph 1): (1) conservation of natural resources; (2) protection of environmental and human health; (3) development of modern technologies for packaging production; (4) establishment of optimal system for management of packaging and packaging waste management in accordance with principle of shared responsibility; (5) functioning of the market in the Republic of Serbia;and (6) preventing of trade barriers creation, avoidance of disturbance and restrictions in the competition.

478. The basic principles for management of packaging and packaging waste are (Article 4, paragraph 1): (1) sharing responsibility of all business entities in accordance with 'polluter pays' principle during the product life cycle; (2) preventing or reducing the generation of packaging and packaging waste, as well as their harmfulness

509. *Packaging* is a product made from materials with different properties, which is used for placing, storing, handling, delivery, presenting of the goods and the protection of its content. It includes items used as a supporting means for packaging, wrapping, binding, non-permeable closure, and preparing for shipment and labelling of goods. Packaging can be – *primary packaging* as the smallest packaging unit in which the product is sold to the final customer; *secondary packaging* as a packaging unit which includes multiple products in primary packaging intended that on point of sale enable grouping of certain number of units for sale, whether it is sold to the end user or it is used for supply at their tail stores. This package can be removed from the product without affecting its characteristics; *tertiary (transport) packaging* designed for safe transport and handling of products in the primary or secondary packaging. This package does not include containers for road, rail, water or air transport (Art. 5, point 1).
510. *Packaging waste* is any container or packaging material which cannot be used for its original purpose, except for residues resulting in the production process (Art. 5, point 5). *Packaging waste management* is planning and organizing activities related to the collection, transport, storage, treatment and disposal of packaging waste, supervision of these activities and taking care of facilities for waste management after closure (Art. 5, point 8).
511. The provisions of this Law shall not apply to containers and big facilities for packaging – IBC used for road, rail, water or air international transport (Art. 2, para. 1).
512. *Subjects for management of packaging and packaging waste* are (Art. 5, point 21): producer; importer, packer/filler; supplier; collector, the end user, the end supplier, carrier, operator of packaging waste management system (hereinafter, referred to as operator).

to the environment; (3) reuse[513] of packaging, recycling[514] and other forms of reutilization and reduce the final disposal of packaging waste; and (4) voluntary agreement on the management of packaging waste.

A. Packaging and Environment Protection

479. The packaging is compliant with the essential requirements for placing on the market if it complies with all specific requirements relating to (Article 8, paragraph 1): (1) packaging production,[515] (2) composition of packaging,[516] (3) reuse of packaging,[517] (4) packaging that is reusable by recycling[518] of materials, (5) packaging that is reusable by composting and biodegradation, and (6) packaging that is reusable in the form of energy.[519]

480. The producer and importer of packaging is required when placing packaging on the market or during its use to issue or provide a declaration on compliance of packaging with the requirements for placing on market in accordance with the Law[520] (Article 8, paragraph 5).

481. Packaging should be produced so that the total level of concentrations of lead, cadmium, mercury and hexavalentchromium in packaging or in its components

513. *Reuse* means any operation by which the packaging, planned and designed in the way to perform a minimum number of charging and discharging during usage (repeated use), and recharge or use for the same purpose for which it is planned, with or without supporting means presented in the market which enables recharging of packaging. Reused packaging becomes waste if it is not reused after a long time (Art. 5, point 10).
514. *Recycling of packaging waste* is the reprocessing of packaging waste in the production process for the original purpose or for other purposes, including organic recycling, but excluding utilization for energy purposes (Art. 5, point 17).
515. The requirements are applied on the entire packaging system (Art. 8, para. 2).
516. The requirements are applied on the component of packaging (Art. 8, para. 3).
517. Requirements for points 3–6 of this Article shall apply on the functional unit of packaging (Art. 8, para. 4).
518. The Minister in charge of environmental protection (hereinafter, Minister) provides criteria for determining what can be the packaging, with examples for the application of criteria and determine a list of Serbian standards related to the basic requirements (hereinafter, referred to as Serbian standards) (Art. 7, para. 2).
519. *Packaging waste utilization for energy purposes* is the use of packaging waste in direct incineration with or without the presence of other types of waste, with the primary goal of utilization of heat (Art. 5, point 18).
520. The packaging is compliant with certain specific request if it is made in accordance with the Serbian standard from the list of standards specified in Art. 7, para. 2 of this Law which applies to that specific request (Art. 8, para. 6). If the packaging is not produced in accordance with the Serbian standard, compliance of packaging with certain specific requirements may be proved with other appropriate means (technical specifications, technical documentation, with reports on examination, etc.) (Art. 8, para. 7).

does not exceed the prescribed limit values[521] (Article 10, paragraph 1). Packaging should be manufactured so that concentrations of hazardous substances in emissions, ash and leachate is minimized (Article 10, paragraph 3).[522]

482. Physical and other characteristics of the packaging must ensure adequate quality of packaging and allow its reuse for the same purpose so that: (1) package design enables recharging or reloading, as well as certain number of charging or discharging cycles; (2) packaging may be enabled for reuse, taking into account the health and safety requirements; and (3) there is an available system on the market to achieve reuse (the collection of returnable packaging,[523] refilling or shipping)[524] (Article 11, paragraph 1).

483. Packaging that cannot be reused, or that cannot be reused through recycling,[525] biodegradation or controlled incineration, becomes packaging waste intended for disposal[526] in accordance with the Law (Article 11, paragraph 3).

484. Packaging that is reusable by composting,[527] must be produced in the way that when it becomes packaging waste, that waste processed for composting purposes has such a natural biodegradable performance that does not prevent the separate process of collecting, composting or activity that has begun with this process (Article 13, paragraph 1).

485. Packaging reusable for biodegradation must be manufactured so that when it becomes packaging waste, the waste should have such natural properties that can be subjected to physical, chemical, thermal or biological decomposition, and that most

---

521. Determination of concentration of heavy metals, depending upon the packaging material or its components is done according to the methodology prescribed by the Serbian standard (Art. 10, para. 2). The Minister prescribes limit of total level concentration of lead, cadmium, mercury and hexavalentchromium in packaging or in its components, with the exception of application and deadline for limit values application (Art. 10, para. 6).
522. Identification of the presence of hazardous materials in the package or in its components and the possibility of their presence in emissions, ash and leachate from landfills is done in accordance with the Serbian standard (Art. 10, para. 4). If hazardous materials are identified in the package or in its components that can be released into the environment, packaging has to meet requirement for their minimization in the way determined by Serbian standards (Art. 10, para. 5).
523. *Returnable packaging* is packaging that, after returning from the consumer, is reusable for the same purpose (Art. 5, point 3).
524. Identifying the most appropriate reuse system for a particular type of packaging, taking into account the specific circumstances of its intended use is done according to the Serbian standard (Art. 11, para. 2).
525. The main criteria for packaging suitable for recycling, identified by Serbian standards, relate to: (1) design control, packaging composition and preparation process; (2) the existence of available recycling technologies; and (3) release to the environment as a result of the recycling process (Art. 12, para. 2).
526. *Disposal of packaging waste* is any process or method of handling the packaging waste when there are no possibilities for regeneration, recycling, processing, direct reuse or use as alternative energy sources, in accordance with the regulations governing waste management (Art. 5, point 20).
527. Packaging consisting of different components is considered suitable for composting or biodegradation if the components suitable for composting can be easily separated from components that are not suitable for composting or if all packaging materials are suitable for composting (Art. 13, para. 3).

of the finished compost are at the end decomposed into carbon dioxide, biomass and water (Article 13, paragraph 2). Packaging should be designed and manufactured in the way to meet thermodynamic requirements for allowed controlled burning of packaging waste with energy utilization (Article 14, paragraph 1).

B. Management of Packaging and Packaging Waste

486. National objectives for management of packaging and packaging waste are established by Plan for reduction of packaging waste[528] (hereinafter, referred to as Plan) (Article 16, paragraph 1). The Plan contains national objectives related to the collection of packaging and packaging waste, reuse[529] and recycling of packaging waste (Article 16, paragraph 1).

487. The producer, importer, packer/filler and the supplier are obliged to take over the secondary or tertiary packaging waste, free of charge on the request of the end user[530] (Article 18, paragraph 1). It is also required to provide a space for taking over, collecting, sorting and temporary storage of packaging waste, that is, in accordance with Article 18 of this Law, taken or created during their activities, if the annual quantity of packaging waste exceeds the prescribed quantity[531] (Article 19, paragraph 1).

488. The end user is required to collect, store, put off or forward the communal packaging waste,[532] in accordance with the Law governing waste management and the Law governing communal activities (Article 20, paragraph 1). The end user must ensure that packaging and packaging waste which is not communal waste,[533] that is, forwarded or returned, is not contaminated with hazardous or other substances that are not contained in packed goods, which make the reuse or recycling impossible, or which make it feasible only at a disproportionately higher cost (Article 21, paragraph 2).

489. Producer, importer, packer/filler and supplier that provides its own packaging waste management is required to (Article 26, paragraph 1): (1) ensure that packaging

528. The Government adopts Plan on the proposal of ministry responsible for environmental protection (hereinafter, the ministry) for a period of five years (Art. 16, para. 4).
529. *Reuse* is any procedure or method of utilization in terms of regulations governing the management of waste (Art. 5, point 16).
530. Manufacturer, importer, packer/filler and the supplier is obliged, at the request of the end user, to take free of charge packaging waste that is not communal waste, and that comes from the primary packaging, if a specific way of taking over and collecting of such packaging is not prescribed (Art. 18, para. 4).
531. Minister prescribes the annual amount of packaging waste by the type of waste for which space for downloading, collecting, sorting and temporary storage is provided (Art. 19, para. 3).
532. *Communal packaging waste* is waste from primary and secondary packaging generated as waste in households (household waste) or in industry, craft activities, services or other activities (commercial waste), which is similar to waste from households in terms of its nature or composition and that is collected from a certain territorial unit, in accordance with the Law (Art. 5, point 6).
533. *Packaging waste which is not communal waste* is waste from primary, secondary or tertiary packaging generated as waste during production, retail, service and other activities that has not been collected through the collection system organized by a public utility company or other legal entity or entrepreneur (hereinafter, referred to as utility) (Art. 5, point 7).

waste taken or collected in any calendar year to be reused, recycled or disposed to the end of that calendar year, in order to achieve the national objectives; (2) bear the cost of reutilization, recycling or disposal of packaging waste which, despite the established collection system, appears in the collection system implemented by the operator; and (3) inform end users, by notice on the packaging placed on the market, about the possibility to leave packaging waste at place of purchase, or to return it later for free to the end supplier at designated place.

490. The operator cannot manage packaging waste without a permit from the Ministry (Article 31, paragraph 1). The permit is issued to the operator who is (Article 31, paragraph 2): (1) registered for performing activities of collecting, taking away, reuse, recycling or disposal in accordance with the Law governing the classification of activities; (2) alone or whose subcontractor has equipment, facilities and units that provide management of packaging waste in accordance with the Law; and (3) alone or whose subcontractor provides conditions for reuse, recycling or disposal of packaging waste in accordance with the Law.

491. The operator is obliged to organize one or more centres for collection, sorting and temporary storage of collected packaging waste (Article 35, paragraph 1). The operator is obliged to arrange spaces for collection of packaging waste that is not communal waste, where the end user will bring the waste, if the taking over is not provided directly from the end user or from the end suppliers (Article 35, paragraph 2).

492. Reuse, recycling and disposal of packaging waste can be carried out in plants having permit for prescribed treatment and/or disposal, in accordance with the conditions stipulated by the Law governing waste management and by other regulations (Article 37, paragraph 1).

C. Economic Instruments

493. The supplier who packages or puts on the market a packaged product in the territory of the Republic of Serbia, shall pay a fee (Article 43, paragraph 1).[534] Funds generated from the fee under paragraph 1 of this Article contribute to the budget of the Republic of Serbia and are used specifically for waste management through the Fund for the Environment, in accordance with the Law (Article 43, paragraph 3).

494. The Government[535] may establish a deposit system for a disposable package when it is necessary to achieve the national objectives (Article 44, paragraph 1). The final supplier who places on the market the product packed in disposable packaging, charges from the end user's deposit per unit of sales of packaging to establish a return system of used disposable packaging (Article 44, paragraph 2).

534. The fee referred to in para. 1 of this Article shall be determined depending upon the type, quantity, composition and purpose of packaging, on material from which the packaging is made, as well as in relation to national objectives (Art. 43, para. 2). The Government prescribes criteria for the calculation of fees and exemption from payment of fees, taxpayers, the amount of fee, as well as the method for calculation and payments of fee (Art. 43, para. 4).

535. The Government provides types of disposable packaging for which the deposit system is established, the mode of operation of the system and deposit amount and method of its collection (Art. 44, para. 7).

495. The producer or importer of a product packaged in returnable packaging shall establish a refund system (Article 44, paragraph 3). The final supplier[536] who puts on the market a product packaged in returnable packaging is required to collect a bail for this type of packaging from the end user (Article 44, paragraph 4). The producer or importer[537] of certain chemicals is required to determine the amount of bail that consumer pays for a single packaging used for storing of chemicals (Article 45, paragraph 1).

D. Reporting and Monitoring

496. The operator is obliged to inform the public and end users about the purpose, objectives, manner and place for packaging collection, as well as about possibilities for reuse and recycling of packaging waste (Article 38, paragraph 1).[538]

497. The Ministry establishes and maintains a Register of permits issued[539] in accordance with this Law (Article 42, paragraph 1). Agency draws up and publishes an annual report on the quantity of produced, imported and exported packaging and management of waste packaging in the Republic of Serbia and submits it to the Ministry (Article 42, paragraph 3).

498. The Ministry supervises the work of the Agency, an AP, local government units, as well as authorized legal entity in performing delegated tasks, in accordance with the Law on Waste Management and with this Law (Article 46, paragraph 1). The inspection supervision on implementation of provisions of this Law and regulations adopted for its implementation shall be performed by the Ministry, unless otherwise is prescribed by the Law on Waste Management and by this Law (Article 47, paragraph 1).

499. In accordance with Article 101 of the Law on Waste Management, the Recycling Agency ceases its operation on the thirtieth day from the enactment of this Law.

V. Transboundary Movement of Waste

500. Transboundary transport of waste is regulated by the Basel Convention on the Control of Transboundary Movements of Hazardous Wastes and their Disposal (1989). The treaty was ratified by FR Yugoslavia in 1998 (OJ FRY – IT, No. 24/98).

---

536. The end supplier is obliged to accept from the end user disposable packaging and returnable packaging (Art. 44, para. 5). After return of packaging, the end supplier is obliged to return the charged deposit, i.e., the bail to the end user (Art. 44, para. 6).
537. The Minister prescribes (Art. 45, para. 5): (1) for which chemical producer or importer is obliged to establish a bail for a single package used for storing of that chemical and (2) the amount of bail for certain types of packaging depending upon the type of packaging or chemical packed in.
538. The operator shall inform public of the city, city of Belgrade, i.e., municipality on the territory of which point of collection is located, through public media or internet, i.e., in usual local manner (Art. 38, para. 2).
539. The Minister prescribes the content and method for keeping records of issued permits, as well as the form of the report from Arts 39and 40 of this Law (Art. 42, para. 4).

501. EPL prescribes general provisions on the import, export and transit of waste and its control. Import of hazardous waste to Serbia is prohibited by Article 57 of the EPL.[540]

502. Transboundary waste shipments are regulated by the Law on Waste Management. This Law regulates transboundary shipments of waste, specifically: terms and mode of transboundary waste shipments, import, export and transit of waste and prohibition of transboundary waste shipments, as the basis for implementing legislation that defines in more detail the mode and procedure for transboundary waste shipments.

503. Non-hazardous waste can be imported for the purpose of treatment. The import of waste for disposal and energy recovery purposes is prohibited. The import of hazardous waste is prohibited. Exceptionally, certain types of hazardous waste that are required as secondary raw materials for the processing industry in the Republic of Serbia, can be imported based on a permit issued by the Ministry. The import of hazardous waste can be permitted, provided that there is a facility for the treatment thereof, licensed to operate in accordance with the law.[541]

504. The by-laws regulating in more detail the area of transboundary waste shipments are, *inter alia*, the following:

- Rulebook on the content of documentation submitted in support of the application for the permit for import, export and transit of waste (OJ RS, Nos 60/09 and 101/10).
- Regulation on the lists of waste for cross-border movement, content and appearance of documents accompanying cross-border movement of waste with the filling in instructions (OJ RS, No. 60/09).
- Regulation on designating the types of hazardous wastes that may be imported as secondary raw materials (OJ RS, No. 60/09).
- Regulation on the list of non-hazardous waste not requiring a permit, with the documentation accompanying cross-border movement (OJ RS, No. 102/10).[542]

505. The total annual damage caused by inadequate waste management in Serbia (including air emissions and leakages from landfills, emissions from backyard burning of waste, damage caused by inadequate disposal of hazardous waste, fly ash, etc.) is estimated from EUR 98 to 276 million, equalling 0.4%–1.1% of GDP.[543]

540. License for import, export or transit of waste shall be issued by the Ministry in accordance with law and other regulations. When applying for permit for import, export and transit the applicant shall submit the documentation whose contents is prescribed by the Ministry. The Minister shall prescribe the conditions that must be fulfilled by expert organizations for waste testing.
541. Waste for which there are no environmentally sound and efficient treatment facilities and technical possibilities in the Republic of Serbia is exported.
542. Legislative provisions and implementing legislation related to the transboundary movement of waste regulate the documentation on shipments from the point of departure to the final destination, based on national and international standards and European regulations related to transboundary shipments of waste.
543. NEPP, 48.

VI. Other Relevant Waste Management Legislation

506. Besides the mentioned, the following legal Acts, *inter alia*, are also relevant when waste is concerned:

- Regulation on disposal of waste in landfills (OJ RS, No. 92/10).
- Regulation on programme of systematic monitoring of soil quality with indicators for assessment of soil degradation risk and methodology for creation of remediation programmes (OJ RS, No. 88/10).
- Regulation on types of waste which undergo thermal treatment, the terms and criteria for the choice of location, technical and technological requirements for project planning, construction, equipping and operation of the installation for thermal treatment of waste, manner of handling the remaining waste after incineration (OJ RS, Nos 102/10 and 50/12).
- Regulation on criteria for calculation deposit for packaging or packaged products and exemption from deposit payment, payment bonds, deposit amount, as well as method for calculating and payment of the deposit (OJ RS, Nos 8/10 and 22/16).
- Regulation on determining packaging waste reduction plan for the period 2015–2019 (OJ RS, No. 144/14).
- Regulation on type of pollution, criteria for calculation of cost recovery for environmental pollution, amount and the manner of calculation of fees (OJ RS, Nos 113/05, 6/07, 8/10, 102/10, 15/12 and 91/12).
- Regulation on parameters and criteria for recovery, exemption from or reduction of charges for environmental pollution (OJ RS, Nos 113/05 and 24/10).
- Regulation on products that after use become specific waste streams, form of daily records on the type and quantity of manufactured and imported products and the annual report, the methods and timeframe for submission of annual reports, taxpayers, criteria for the calculation, the amount and method of calculation and payment of fee (OJ RS, Nos 54/10, 86/11, 15/12 and 03/14).
- Rulebook on the list of electrical and electronic products, measures of prohibition and restrictions on the use of electrical and electronic equipment containing hazardous substances (OJ RS, No. 99/10).
- Rulebook on chemicals for which the producers or importers is obligated to establish a deposit for an individual packaging contained chemicals (OJ RS, No. 99/10).
- Rulebook on the procedure for end-of-life vehicle management (OJ RS, No. 98/10).
- Rulebook on conditions and manner of collection, transport, storage and treatment of waste that is used as a secondary raw material or for energy production (OJ RS, No. 98/10).
- Rulebook on the procedure for the management of waste fluorescent tubes containing mercury (OJ RS, No. 97/10).
- Rulebook on the contents, manner and appearance of the Register of issued permits for waste management (OJ RS, No.95/10).

- Rulebook on the forms of daily records and annual reports on waste with instructions to complete it (OJ RS, Nos 95/10 and 88/15).
- Rulebook on the manner of storage, packaging and labelling of hazardous waste (OJ RS, No.92/10).
- Rulebook on the procedure for management of waste batteries and accumulators (OJ RS, No.86/10).
- Rulebook on medical waste management (OJ RS, No.78/10).
- Rulebook on the manner and procedure of waste tires management (OJ RS, Nos 104/9 and 81/10).
- Rulebook on disposal of waste containing asbestos (OJ RS, No. 75/10).
- Rulebook on conditions, the methods and procedure of waste oil management (OJ RS, No. 72/10).
- Rulebook on the content of the certificate of exemption from the obligation of obtaining a permit to store of inert and non-hazardous waste (OJ RS, No. 73/10).
- Rulebook on categories, testing and classification of waste (OJ RS, No.56/10).
- Rulebook on the list of classified chemicals (OJ RS, No. 48/14).
- Rulebook on contents of accident prevention policy and the content and methodology of the report on the safety and accident protection plan (OJ RS, No.41/10).
- Rulebook on the content and design of the permit for storage, treatment and disposal of waste (OJ RS, No. 96/09).
- Rulebook on form of the report on packaging management and packaging waste (OJ RS, Nos 21/10 and 10/13).
- Rulebook on the contents and methods for keeping the Register of licenses issued for packaging waste management (OJ RS, No. 76/09).
- Rulebook on the criteria for determining whether something is package, with examples for the application of criteria and the list of Serbian standards regarding basic conditions which a package must fulfil to be placed on the market (OJ RS, No. 70/09).
- Rulebook on the annual quantity of packaging waste according to types which must be provided space for the takeover, collection, classification and temporary storage (OJ RS, No. 70/09).
- Rulebook on the manner of numbering, the abbreviations and symbols on which the system of identification and marking of packaging materials is based (OJ RS, No. 70/09).
- Rulebook on the type and annual quantity of packaging used for the packaged product placed on the market, for which the producer, importer, packer/filler and the supplier is not obliged to ensure packaging waste management (OJ RS, No. 70/09).
- Rulebook on the types of durable packaging (OJ RS, No. 70/09).
- Rulebook on the limit value of the total level of concentration of lead, cadmium, mercury and 6 valent chromium in the package or its components, exemptions from application and the deadline for limit value application (OJ RS, No. 70/09).
- Rulebook on the form of document on the movement of waste with the filling instructions (OJ RS, No. 114/13).
- Rulebook on the form of document on the movement of hazardous waste with the filling instructions (OJ RS, No. 114/13).

- Rulebook on the content of the permit for storage, treatment and disposal of waste (OJ RS, No. 96/09).
- Rulebook on permitted amounts of hazardous and harmful substances in soil and water for irrigation and methods of their testing (OJ RS, No. 23/94).

VII. Harmonization with EU Legislation

507. 'Regarding waste management, there is a good level of alignment with the EU's principal waste directives, with recent progress made regarding the waste framework, landfill and industrial emissions directives. Implementation remains at an early stage, with some progress noted in increased rates of municipal waste collection and sanitary landfilling.'[544] Serbia plans to achieve full implementation of the Directive 1999/31/EC on landfill of waste by the end of 2032, 'subject to revision after the preparation of a Directive Specific Implementation Plan envisaged for 2016'.[545]

The national waste management strategy and municipal waste management plans need to be updated to reflect the new legal provisions on e.g., waste minimization and waste separation at source, and to include quantitative targets for waste recovery and recycling. Increased efforts are needed to close Serbia's non-compliant landfills more quickly and invest in waste separation and recycling. A national integrated waste management plan and additional economic instruments for special waste streams need to be developed.[546]

544. CR, 76.
545. SRS, Ch. 27. 6. The full implementation of the Waste Framework Directive 2008/98/EC is envisaged by 2034, and the Directive 94/62/EC on packaging and packaging waste by 2020. *Ibid.*, 5.
546. *Ibid.* 76.

Chapter 5. Soil Pollution

§1. The State of Soil Pollution

508. Soil degradation in Serbia has been caused, generally speaking, by the following factors: open coal[547] and metal ore mining, uncontrolled and inadequate dumping of waste, waste water, heavy metals, radioactive materials, chemicals which cause salinization and acidification of the soil, etc. About 30% of the total degraded soil are open excavation sites, 20% are hydro-accumulations, 15% are dumping grounds with different waste, 10% are cities and other settlements, etc.

Destruction of agricultural land is one of the most dangerous forms of soil degradation. One of the main causes is erosion. It is estimated that it affects up to 80% of agricultural soil in Serbia. Large areas of agricultural soil in the vicinity of industrial complexes (Bor, Pancevo, Smederevo, Belgrade, etc.) and along highways are contaminated with various pollutants from industrial facilities and from road vehicles.[548]

Another cause of soil degradation is chemicals, especially pesticides, as well as the use of fertilizers containing some polluting substances (cadmium, nitrogen, etc.). Finally, soil degradation was caused, on some sites, by armed conflicts and especially by the 1999 NATO bombing.[549] The latest data from the Statistical Office states that 89.36% of the total land area is eroded. This figure was given for the whole review period from 2007 to 2013 and is based on the available data from the last version of the erosion map of 1983.[550]

509. There is no national programme on soil monitoring. However, some local governments adopt annual soil monitoring programmes in accordance with the relevant legislation.[551]

510. Several ministries and other bodies share competence concerning soil protection – the MEAP, including EPA, the Ministry of Mining and Energy, the Ministry

547. This is specially the case in Kostolac and Kolubara, coal basins where lignite is openly mined.
548. B. Karadžic (ed.), *Environment in Serbia – An Indicator-Based Review*, *supra* , 18.
549. According to NATO data, 112 locations in Kosovo and Metohija Province were contaminated with DU. The NATO claims that 31,000 30mm projectiles were used (equivalent to 10 tonnes of DU), but according to Serbian military data at least 50,000 projectiles were fired, equivalent to 15 tonnes of DU. Outside Kosovo, 3,000–5,000 projectiles were fired too, mostly in southern Serbia, *ibid.*, 117.
550. EPR (2015), 6. From a total of 398 identified potentially contaminated and contaminated sites, 200 belong to industrial sites. Within the industry the largest share belongs to the oil industry (47.5%), the chemical industry (16%) and the metal industry (14%). Analysis shows that the public municipal landfills contributes pollution with 45.48%, industrial waste landfills with 12.31% and industrial and commercial sites with 33.92%. Izveštaj o stanju životne sredine u Republici Srbiji za 2014. godinu [Report on the state of the environment in Serbia for 2014]. Ministarstvo poljoprivrede i zaštite životne sredine, Agencija za zaštitu životne sredine [Ministry of Agriculture and Environmental Protection, Environmental Protection Agency]. Beograd, 2015, p. 165.
551. EPR (2015), 93.

of Construction, Transport and Infrastructure, etc. The Statistical Office of the Republic of Serbia also plays an important role. It collects statistical data on the land area, by types of use, areas used and types of crops and areas for other cropped land, fallow land, etc.

§2. Legislation

511. Article 88 of the Constitution of Serbia prescribes that utilization and management of agricultural land, forestland and municipal building land on private assets shall be permitted.[552] Terms of utilization and management could be prescribed by Law, in order to eliminate the danger to environment or prevent violation of rights and legally based interests of other persons. The municipality shall, through its bodies, and in accordance with the Law, *inter alia*, regulate protection, improvement and use of agricultural land (Article 190).

512. It is prescribed, by Article 22 of EPL (OJ RS, Nos 135/04, 36/09 and 36/09 – other law, 72/09 – other law, 43/11 CC and 14/16), that:

> Protection of land area (land) and its sustainable use shall be achieved through the measures of systematic monitoring of land quality, monitoring of indicators for the assessment of risk of land degradation, as well as through the implementation of remediation programs for removing consequences of land contamination and degradation, regardless if they occur naturally or are caused by human activities. Upon change of the holder of the right to utilize land, the land user whose right to utilization ends, and whose activity has affected or could have affected or impeded natural functions of land, shall be obliged to prepare a report on the state of land.[553] Program of systematic monitoring of land quality, indicators for assessment of risk of land degradation and methodology for preparation of remediation programs referred to in paragraph 1 of this Article shall be prescribed by the Government.

Article 34, paragraph 2 of the same Law prescribes that the conditions for measures, for environmental protection in spatial and urban plans, 'shall be issued by the Ministry,

552. In accordance with Art. 86 private, cooperative and public ownership are guaranteed. Public property is State-owned property of the Republic of Serbia, the property owned by the AP, and property of the units of local government. All forms of ownership have equal legal protection, while public property is turned into private or State-owned property under the conditions, in a manner and within time limits prescribed by the Law. Subject of privatization may be the land entered in a relevant real estate rights registry as social, mixed or property of the subject to be privatized. The subject of privatization may not be natural resources, goods in general use, goods of general interest, as well as cultural assets under public ownership entered in the register of cultural heritage, which shall be conducted in accordance with the law governing cultural property (Art. 5. paras 2 and 3, Law on Privatisation, OJ of RS, Nos 83/14, 46/15, 112/15 and 20/16). However, only domestic legal or natural person may be the buyer of agricultural land (Art. 121, para 1).

553. The Minister shall prescribe the content and methodology for preparation of report on the state of land (Art. 22, para. 4).

AP body or self-governance units at request of the authority in charge of plan preparation and its passing in, and on the basis of conditions and measures of competent authorities'.

I. The Law on Soil Protection

513. The basic legal Act regulating Soil protection in the Republic of Serbia is the Law on Soil Protection (OJ RS, No. 112/15). It has the following nine parts: Part I – General Provisions (Articles 1–7), Part II – Preventive measures of soil protection (Articles 8–11); Part III – Soil Protection (Articles 12–27), Part IV –Programme of systematic monitoring of soil state and quality (Articles 28–34), Part V – Access to the information (Articles 35), Part VI – Financing of soil protection (Articles 36 and 37), Part VII – Supervision (Articles 38–42), Part VIII – Penalties (Articles 43–47), and Part IX – Transitional and final provisions (Articles 48–54).

According to Article 1, The Law on Soil Protection regulates the protection of soil, systematic monitoring of the soil quality, measures of sanation, remediation, reclamation, inspection and other issues of importance for the protection and preservation of soil as a natural resource of national importance.[554]

514. The purpose of this Law is to preserve areas and functions of the soil as a natural resource and to prevent or eliminate harmful changes in the soil that can occur as a result of: (1) erosion;[555](2) reducing the content of organic matters in the soil; (3) inappropriate agricultural and forest production (inadequate and uncontrolled agro-technical measures and meliorative, deforestation, etc.); (4) uncontrolled change of use, management and use of soil; (5) unplanned urbanization, construction and development of infrastructure; (6) acidic (acidification), salinity (salinization) and alkalization; (7) the soil compaction, landslides and avalanches; (8) fires and chemical accidents; (9) contamination[556] (resulting from waste management, the discharge of waste water, emissions from point and diffuse sources, chemical contamination, etc.); (10) exploitation of mineral and organic materials; (11) exploitation of gravel, sand and rock; and (12) illegal archaeological excavations and research, etc. (Article 3, paragraph 1).

515. The principles of soil protection

The following principles of soil protection are in use in the Republic of Serbia: Preserving of natural values of soil principle, Integrity in soil protection principle, Polluter pays principle, User pay principle, Principle of subsidiary responsibility, Information of public and public participation and Protecting the right to preserve the natural values of the soil (Article 5).

516. Subjects of the soil protection

554. The provisions of this Law shall apply to all types of soil in the Republic of Serbia as a natural resource, regardless of the form of ownership, its purpose and use (Art. 2).

555. *Erosion* –is the process of destruction and removal of the soil, caused by occurrence of natural and anthropogenic factors (Art. 4, para. 1, point 7).

556. *Soil pollution* is a process of disposal and the introduction of hazardous and harmful substances on the surface of the soil and in the soil caused by human activities or natural processes (Art. 4, para. 1, point 8).

Soil protection within their responsibilities and duties is provided by the Republic, AP, local self-government, legal entities, entrepreneurs and owners and users of soil that in carrying out activities threaten, degrade or pollute the soil (Article 6, paragraph 1).

517. Soil protection

Soil protection is provided and makes the implementation of strategic, planning and documentation for soil protection. Soil protection is achieved implementation of measures and activities in the process of planning, management, use, monitoring and protection from pollution, and soil degradation in order to preserve its natural characteristics and functions (Article 12, paragraphs 1–2).[557]

518. Financing of the soil protection and supervision

Financing of protection and improvement of soil quality is ensured from: (1) the budget of the Republic, the APs and local self-government units budget; (2) revenues from charges in accordance with Law; (3) proceeds in accordance with international cooperation programmes and projects; (4) the donation of domestic and foreign legal and natural persons; and (5) other sources in accordance to the Law (Article 36).[558]

II. Law on Planning and Construction

519. Land in Serbia is divided into three categories: construction land, agricultural land and forestland.

Construction land is the land on which structures have been built, as well as the land that serves for regular use of these structures, or the land designated by the urban plan for construction and regular use of structures. Construction land is divided into urban construction land and construction land outside the perimeter of urban construction land (Article 84 of the Law on Planning and Construction (OJ RS, Nos 72/2009 and 81/2009 – corr., 64/2010 CC, 24/2011, 121/12 and 42/13 – CC, 50/13 CC, 98/13 CC, 132/14 and 145/14).

III. Law on Agricultural Land

520. The key legal instrument for the protection of agricultural land is The Law on Agricultural Land (OJ RS, Nos 62/06, 41/09 and 112/2015). The Law has the following chapters: Basic Provisions (Articles 1–4); Planning of Protection, Organization and Utilization of Agricultural Land (Articles 5–14); Protection of Agricultural Land (Articles 15–29); Organization of the Agricultural Land (Articles 30–58); Utilization of Agricultural Land (Articles 59–75); Information System of Agricultural Land

557. In order to protect soil on the territory of the Republic, the following documents for soil protection are adopted: (1) Soil Protection Plan; (2) The Annual Program of soil protection and (3) Soil Program Monitoring (Art. 14, para. 1).

558. The Ministry supervises the work of the competent authority of the AP, the competent authority of local governments and Agencies in the performance of duties in accordance to this Law, as well as the work of authorized legal persons in performing of soil monitoring (Art. 38, para. 1).

(Articles 76 and 77); Administration for Agricultural Land (Articles 77a and 77b);[559] Authorization for Adoption Sub-legal Acts (Article 80), Supervision (Articles 81–84), Penal provisions (Articles 85–87), and Transitional provisions (Articles 88–96).

521. The Law defines agricultural land soil used for agricultural production (fields, gardens, orchards, vineyards, meadows, pastures, fish ponds and wet lands) and the land planned to be used for agricultural production (Article 2, point 1). It regulates planning, protection, management and utilization of agricultural land, supervision and other issues relevant for protection and utilization of agricultural land as good of general interest (Article 1). The Law stipulates that a foreign natural person or a corporation cannot own agricultural land (Article 1, paragraph 4).

522. A special part (Articles 15–29) of the Law is devoted to the protection of the agricultural land (Articles 15–29). These provisions include the following:

- ban of emission and dumping of dangerous and harmful substances, finding the existence of dangerous and harmful substances in agricultural land and in irrigation water;
- measures against erosion;
- control of fertility of agricultural cultivable land and the quantity of used mineral fertilizers and pesticides;
- ban of use of agricultural cultivable land for non-agricultural purposes;
- permission for change of use of agricultural cultivable land; and
- protection of agricultural land against frost, hail, fire, etc.

IV. Law on Forest

523. The Law on Forest (OJ RS, Nos 30/10, 93/12 and 89/15) prescribes that forestland mean the land on which a forest is cultivated, the land on which, because of its natural characteristics, it is more rational to grow forest, as well as the land covered with the features intended for forest and game management and for multiple forest functions, and which cannot be used for other purposes, except in cases and under the conditions laid down by this Law (Article 5, paragraph 5). Pursuant to Article 7 of the Forest Law, forest owner, that is, forest user has to implement the measures of forest protection, to protect forests and forestlands against degradation and erosion, to execute forest management plans, and to perform other measures stipulated by this Law and regulations passed based on the Law.[560]

524. Forest owner and forest user have to monitor the effects of biotic and abiotic factors on forest health and undertake timely measures for the protection of

559. Administration for agricultural land has been established in accordance with Art. 77a. It performs different activities including managing agricultural land owned by the State, carrying inspections and other activities in the field of agricultural land, establishing an information system, etc.

560. Change in land-use form of forestlands (and forest) can be carried out only in compliance with provisions of Art. 10 of the Law. Legal person shall be fined RSD 300,000–3,000,000 for the following economic offences, *inter alia*, land-use change of forestlands (and forest) contrary to Art. 10, para. 1 of this Law (Art. 111, para. 1 point 7). A physical person shall be fined in accordance with provisions of the Art. 113, paras 1 and 2.

forests and forestlands. The user or owner of forest that manages forest in accordance with the base is required to monitor the impact of biotic and abiotic factors on the health of forests and timely take measures for the protection of forests and forestlands (Article 42, paragraph 1).[561]

525. It shall be forbidden to dispose garbage, toxic substances and other dangerous waste in the forest and on forestland at a distance less than 200 m from the forest boundary, and to construct the improvements for the storage, conversion or destruction of garbage, toxic substances and other dangerous waste (Article 49, paragraph 1).[562] Forest owner, that is, forest user shall prevent the disposal of garbage, toxic substances and other dangerous waste and without delay notify the Ministry, and on the territory of the AP, the competent organ of the AP (Article 49, paragraph 2).

526. The compensation for the utilization of forestlands (and forest) shall be paid by the forest user, that is, owner (Article 85, paragraph 1).[563]

527. Forestlands (as well as State forest) shall not be alienated, except in cases of redistribution and consolidation, and in the cases stipulated by this Law (Article 98, paragraph 1).[564] However, a part of a State forestland (or State forest), in which rational management cannot be organized can be sold by forest user, with the Government's approval, under market conditions, or exchanged for a private forest or forestland if such forests are isolated, that is, if they are enclaves or semi-enclaves in the complexes of State forests (Article 98, paragraph 2).[565]

561. If a forest owner or forest user does not act in accordance with the provision under para. 1 of this Article, the Ministry, and on the territory of the AP, the competent organ of the AP, shall ensure the execution of the obligation at the expense of the forest owner, i.e., user (Art. 42, para. 2). Legal person shall be fined RSD 300,000–3,000,000 for the following economic offences, *inter alia*, failing to monitor the effects of biotic and abiotic factors on forest health and undertake timely measures for the protection of forests and forestlands (Art. 111, para. 1, point24).
562. Forest owner, i.e., forest user shall prevent the activities under para. 1 of this Article, remove the garbage, toxic substances and other dangerous waste, and undertake all measures to restore the damaged forest (Art. 49, para. 3). Legal person shall be fined RSD 100,000–1,000,000 for the following offences, *inter alia*, disposing garbage, toxic substances and other waste, and constructing the improvements for their storage, conversion or destruction, in the forest and on forestland at a distance less than 200 m from the forest (Art. 112, para. 1, point14). A physical person shall be fined in accordance with provisions of Art. 113, paras 1 and 2.
563. The basis for the calculation of the compensation consists of the total annual income of the forest user realized by forest management (Art. 85, para. 2).
564. State-owned forestlands can be leased prior to the reinstatement determined by forest management plans. The purpose of this land cannot be changed for the duration of the lease (Art. 99, paras 2 and 3).
565. The funds realized by virtue of para. 2 of this Article are the revenue of the Budget of the Republic of Serbia, i.e., Budget of the AP, and shall be used for special purposes through the Budget Funds under Arts 81 and 83 of this Law, primarily for the procurement of forests or forestlands, in the aim of enlargement and consolidation of holdings in State ownership (Art. 98, para. 3).

V. Law on Waters

528. Pursuant to Article 8, water land is the land on which water is permanently or intermittently present and thus creates special hydrological, geomorphological and biological interactions that reflect on aquatic and riparian ecosystems (paragraph 1).[566] Riparian land, as contemplated herein, is the belt of land adjacent to the major channel of a water course, which serves to maintain protective constructions, and the major channel, and which is used for other activities pertaining to water management (Article 9, paragraph 1). Water land is managed by a public water management company established for carrying out water activities in a given territory (Article 9a, paragraph 2).

529. The boundaries of water land, with respect to first order waters, shall be designated by the Ministry, and the competent authority of the AP within the territory of the AP (Article 11, paragraph 1).[567]

530. Water land is intended for the maintenance and improvement of the water regime in accordance with this Law and the acts based on this law, and in particular for:

(1) construction, reconstruction and rehabilitation of water facilities;
(2) maintenance of watercourses and water facilities; and
(3) Implementation of measures related to water management and protection against harmful effects of water, water management and water management and protection. In addition, water land may be, in accordance with this Law and the acts based on this law, used for the following:
(4) construction and maintenance of line infrastructure facilities;
(5) construction and maintenance of facilities intended for state defence;
(6) construction and maintenance of shipyards, as well as ports, docks, waterways and other facilities in accordance with the law regulating navigation;
(7) construction and maintenance of facilities for the use of natural baths and for the implementation of protective measures on natural baths;
(8) construction and maintenance of facilities for electricity generation; and
(9) performing economic activity, etc. (Article 10).

---

566. Water land holding flowing waters includes the major channel and the riparian land (para. 2); water land holding standing waters includes the channel and the belt of land adjacent to the standing-water channel, up to the highest water level on record (para. 3). Water land also includes any abandoned channel, sandbar or point bar, which water intermittently, inundates, and land flooded by water due to interventions works (damming of flowing water, extraction of mineral raw materials and the like) (para. 4).

567. The water land referred to in para. 1 of this Article shall be entered into public records of real estate and the rights conferred thereon (Art. 11, para. 2). The Minister shall stipulate the method to be used for the designation of water land boundaries (Art. 11, para. 4). Publicly owned waters and water lands are public water assets (Art. 5, para. 2). A public water asset is unalienable (Art. 5, para. 3). Public water assets shall be used in a manner that does not result in any adverse effects on water or the riparian ecosystem and that does not restrict the rights of others (Art. 5, para. 4). The right to use a public water asset may be acquired under the conditions set forth in this Law and a special law. On water land,public ownership may be acquired right to lease (Art. 5, para. 5).

531. Prohibitions, restrictions on rights and obligations of owner, and users of water land and water constructions are prescribed in Articles 133–139 (Chapter VI).[568]

VI. Other Legislation

532. Following legal Acts deserve attention:

- Law on Planning and Construction (OJ RS, Nos 72/09, 81/09, 64/10, 24/11, 121/12, 42/13 CC, 50/13 CC, 98/13 CC, 132/14 and 145/14).[569]
- Law on the Spatial Plan of the Republic of Serbia (OJ RS, No. 88/10).
- Law on Mining and Geological Explorations (OJ RS, No. 101/15).[570]
- Law on Public-Private Partnership and Concession (OJ RS, Nos 88/11, 15/16 and 104/16).[571]
- Law on the Basis of Property Relations (OJ SFRY, Nos 6/80 and 36/90, OJ FRY, No. 29/96, OJ RS, No. 115/05).[572]
- Law on Privatization (OJ RS, Nos 83/14, 46/15, 112/15 and 20/16).

568. In order to conserve and maintain surface water bodies, bodies of groundwater, protective water constructions and other water constructions, to prevent any deterioration of the water regime, to ensure the conveyance of high flows and the implementation of flood defence, and to protect the environment, the following shall be prohibited on water land: (i) to erect any constructions which reduce the conveyance capacity of a channel; (ii) to dispose of solid waste, hazardous material or harmful material; (iii) to store wood or other solid material in such a way that it interferes with the conveyance of high flows; (iv) to plant trees on any flood control dike, within the floodplain belt which is at least 10 m wide from the unprotected bottom of the dike on the water side, or in the protected zone contrary to the issued-water criteria; (v) to wash cars and other machines; (vi) to undertake other actions, except in the event of: (1) construction of public infrastructures pursuant to this Law or a special law; (2) implementation of any measures for the conservation, enhancement or presentation of natural treasures; (3) erection of any constructions for water use, watercourse development, assurance of navigation or implementation of protection measures in natural bathing areas, pursuant to this Law; (4) erection of any constructions for water protection from pollution; (5) erection of any constructions dedicated to national defence; (6) creation of any temporary sand or gravel dumpsites, such that they do not interfere with the conveyance of high flows, at a distance which shall not be less than 30 m from the unprotected bottom of the dike; (7) undertaking of any action aimed at protecting people, animals and/or property; and (8) extraction of any mineral raw materials pursuant to this Law and special law.
569. For more information, *see* chapter on zoning and land using.
570. For more information, *see* chapter on subsoil.
571. The law regulates, *inter alia*, the scope of concessions, protection of the rights of parties participating in the procedure, the authorities and parties in charge of the concession approval procedure, the termination of concessions, the conditions and manner for preparing, proposing and approving project proposals for public-private partnership, public bodies and parties in charge of proposing and implementing public-private partnership projects, the rights and obligations of public and private partners, public-private partnership contracts with or without concession elements, the establishment and the competences of the Commission, and other relevant issues.
572. This Law is still applied in Serbia for regulation property relations. It, however, does not specify quantitative limitations in property rights concerning the agricultural land.

533. Following legal and sub-legal Acts are also relevant for soil use and protection in Serbia:

- Law on Plant Protection Products (OJ FRY, No 41/09).
- Law on Chemicals (OJ RS, Nos 36/09, 88/2010, 92/2011, 93/2012 and 25/2015).
- Law on Biocidal Production (OJ RS, Nos 36/09, 88/2010, 92/2011 and 25/2015).
- Law on Organic Production (OJ RS, No. 30/10).[573]

534. Efficiency of implementation of legal regulation concerning the use and protection of soil should be viewed within the entire context of all environmental problems. Serbia adopted the Law on soil protection, but the enforcement of the law requires changes in the system and a certain period of time.

573. For the list of by-laws in the field of organic agriculture, chemicals, biocide products, etc. *see* the relevant parts of the book.

Chapter 6. Noise and Vibrations

535. Causes of environmental noise are all types of transport (road, railway and air), as well as operation of industrial facilities. Various local sources cause noise, such as catering services and craft workshops, and similar facilities.[574]

Generally, communal noise in big cities still exceeds prescribed levels, although some progress is done. Situation in Belgrade, capital of Serbia, can be mentioned as an example, where results of noise monitoring in 2006 were more favourable than in 2005. Relevant levels during the day reached 75 dB and during the night 70 dB.[575]

For the time being, there is no permanent monitoring of noise around airports in accordance with International Civil Aviation Organization (ICAO) Standards and Recommended Practice. Progressive programmes for reduction of noise and air pollution caused by aircraft are not applied.[576]

536. Noise protection in Serbia is in competence of the MAEP, the EPA, and the Ministry of Construction, Transport and Infrastructure, and the Civil Aviation Directorate. The Agency's responsibility is monitoring and registering environmental noise. The noise monitoring data management falls within the general scope of environmental protection informational system (various polluters, cadastre, etc.). The Ministry of Infrastructure is responsible for outdoor equipment, such as lawn mowers, and other outdoor machinery-produced noise. The Traffic Safety Department takes care of vehicle noise. The Civil Aviation Directorate is responsible for compliance with the rules and standards for using air space, including issuing certificates on aircraft noise levels.

It should be added that certain environmental responsibilities were, in 2002, delegated to the AP, including protection from noise and LSG.[577]

574. NEPP, 56.

575. Environment in the City of Belgrade (Belgrade: The Regional Environmental Centre for Central and Eastern Europe, Country Office Serbia: Institute of Public Health: Secretariat for Environmental Protection, 2007), 32.

576. AECQ, Ch. 14 (Transport Policy), Government of the Republic of Serbia, Belgrade, 2011, 75.

577. According to the Law on Noise Protection (OJ RS, Nos 36/09 and 88/10), the Republic of Serbia entrusts to the AP and/or LSG the following tasks: establish measures and conditions of protection against noise, i.e., sound protection in plans, programs and projects, including those for which approval is in the process of strategic impact assessment, EIA, i.e., in procedure for issuing integrated permits for installations and activities; perform acoustic zoning in their area, determine restriction measures and limitations in accordance with this Law; provide the development of strategic maps for noise within the competence of AP/LSG; adopt an action plan for agglomerations in the territory of AP/LSG as well as for facilities and activities for which integrated permit is issued by the competent authority of the AP/LSG for protection against noise in the environment, and provide conditions and take care of its implementation; provide and finance noise monitoring in the environment in the territory of AP/LSG. AP and LSG are obliged to provide to SEPA strategic noise maps, within one month from the date of their creation; supervise and control the implementation of measures for noise protection in the environment.

§1. Legislation

537. Two basic legal Acts concerning protection from the noise are the Law on Protection from the Noise in the Environment (OJ RS, Nos 36/09 and 88/10) and the EPL (OJ RS, Nos 135/04, 36/09, 72/09, 43/11 CC and 14/16).

I. The Law on Protection from Noise in the Environment

538. The Law on Protection from Noise in the Environment is divided into following nine chapters: Basic provisions (Articles 1–3); Subjects of protection from noise in the environment (Articles 4–10), Measures and conditions of protection from noise in the environment (Articles 11–22), Measuring noise in the environment (Articles 23–28), Access to information on noise (Articles 27 and 28),[578] Monitoring (Articles 29–32), Competence for solving complaints (Article 33); Penal provisions (Articles 34–36), and transitional and final provisions (Articles 37–41).

539. Protection from noise, within the scope of their competences, is provided by the Republic of Serbia, AP, unit of LSG, enterprises, county, city, and city of Belgrade (in following text, unit of LSG), business societies, legal persons and entrepreneurs (who while doing commercial activities emit noise), scientific and professional organizations and other public services, associations, citizens and other legal and physical persons (Articles 4–8).[579]

II. Measures and Conditions for Protection from Noise in the Environment

540. Preventive measures for protection from noise are related primarily to planning and construction. Projects, plans and programmes, to which is applied the Law on Procedure of Evaluation of Impact of Projects on the Environment, or procedure of strategic evaluation of the impact on the environment, must contain evaluation levels of noise and measures for protection from noise in the environment (Articles 11–13).

541. Indicators of noise are used for assessment of levels of noise in the environment, evaluation and forecast of noise levels and their impact, creation of strategic noise maps and planning protection measures from the noise. Value of noise indicators in the environment is set by methods of evaluation, as prescribed by this

578. State organs, organs of unit of local self-government, licensed and other organizations are obliged to provide the public with information and data from strategic maps of noise in the environment from action plans, including local action plans in accordance with this Law and the Law on Protection of the Environment (Arts 27 and 28).

579. Responsibility is prescribed for subjects, for any activity disturbing the environment with noise above prescribed values (Art. 9). Especially stressed obligation of all subjects of integral noise management in the environment to cooperate among themselves, to practice coordination and harmonization in adoption and in conveying of measures and decisions, as prescribed by this Law and the Law on Protection of the Environment (Art. 10).

Law (Article 14). Limit values are measured by indicators of noise as prescribed by this Law. Indicators of noise, limit values, methods of evaluation of indicators of noise, disturbance and harmful effects of noise in the environment to human health, as well as kinds and methods of data collection needed for their evaluation is prescribed by the Government (Article 15).[580] Article 16 of the Law on Environmental Noise Protection prescribes *that machines, equipment and means of transport* manufactured in Serbia or imported to the territory of the Republic of Serbia, must be in compliance with technical regulations related to limit noise level under certain conditions of use, and that products must be labelled in regard to noise generated during the use of the product.

542. Article 20, paragraph 1 of the Law prescribes obligation of strategic noise mapping for agglomerations having a population in excess of 100,000 persons, for major roads which have more than 3,000,000 vehicle passages a year, for major railways which have more than 30,000 train passages per year and for major airports. The Law and by-laws lay down that the strategic noise maps are made in two phases (2015 and 2020). Action plans are adopted, i.e., revised for a period of five years (Article 21, paragraph 5).[581]

543. Action plan of protection from noise in the environment for road, air and railroad transport, for agglomerations, for facilities and activities for which the Ministry issues integrated permit, as well as for areas near State border is prescribed by the Government. The action plan for agglomerations on the territory of AP, as well as for the facilities and activities for which integrated permit is issued by the competent organ of the AP, is produced by the competent organ of AP. The action plan for agglomerations on territory of unit of LSG, as well as for facilities and activities for which integrated permit is issued by the unit of local self-government, is produced by the unit of LSG. Two or more units of LSG adopt joint local action plans, if it is necessary for efficient and coordinated application of measures of protection from noise in the environment on the territory they cover.[582]

III. Measurement of Noise in the Environment

544. The Republic of Serbia, AP, or unit of LSG within the scope of their competence prescribed by this Law, provide evaluation, monitoring and control of levels the noise in the environment in accordance with this Law and the EPL. A legal or physical person who is the owner or user of the source of noise is obliged, in accordance with this Law, to organize measurement of noise, production of a report

580. Protection of noise from specific sources (engines, transport, gadgets and equipments, etc.) is regulated by Arts 16–18).

581. The Minister and the Minister competent for transport regulate in detail obligatory contents and methods of production of maps of noise in the environment, as well as the procedure of their presentation to the public (Art. 20).

582. The Minister prescribes methodology for production of action plans for protection from noise in the environment (Arts 21 and 22).

on measurement of noise and bear expenses of measurement of noise in the area of, in accordance with this Law.[583]

545. Measurement of noise in the environment can be done by a licensed professional organization if it fulfils prescribed conditions for the measurement of noise in accordance with this Law.[584]

546. Strategic noise maps are part of a unified information system environment in accordance with the Law governing the protection of the environment (Article 26).

IV. Supervision and Penal Provisions

547. The Ministry supervises the work of the Agency, AP, unit of LSG, as well as licensed legal persons, in doing their assigned activities. The AP does its inspectional supervision, over activities prescribed by this Law, via environmental inspectors. The unit of LSG does its inspectional supervision, over activities prescribed by this Law, via environmental inspectors (Articles 29 and 30).

548. By penal provisions (Articles 34–36) are prescribed sanctions for violations of this Law committed by enterprises and other domestic and foreign legal persons, as well as for responsible persons in organ of administration, LSG, or organization licensed to perform activity of public importance. Besides the fine for violation, enterprises and other domestic and foreign legal persons can be sentenced to be deprived of objects used or intended to be used for committing violation or which were created as a result of violation.

V. Law on Environmental Protection

549. The EPL (OJ RS, Nos 135/04, 36/09, 72/09, 43/11 CC and 14/16) contains some general provisions about noise. Besides the provisions of Article 3, point 9 (definitions),[585] the Law prescribes the following in Article 31: 'The user of a noise source may place on the market and may use noise sources according to regulated conditions and by applying regulated measures of protection by which noise emissions, that is, the use of facilities, devices, machines, transport means and gadgets that produce noise shall be abated'.

583. The Minister prescribes methods of measurement of noise, contents and volume of the report on measurement of noise (Arts 23 and 24).

584. The Minister prescribes in detail conditions that a professional organization must fulfil for measurement of noise, as well as documentation needed to be submitted with application for obtaining the license for measurement of noise (Art. 25). The Ministry will be issuing permits for environmental noise measurements. So far, thirty-seven organizations have been authorized to measure environmental noise. EPR (2015), 49.

585. Article 3 (point 9) prescribes that 'activity affecting the environment…is any action (permanent or temporary) which changes or may change the status and conditions in the environment and relates to: utilization of resources and natural goods; production and circulation processes; distribution and use of materials; emissions of pollution into water, air or soil; waste and wastewater management; chemicals and harmful substances management; noise and vibrations; ionizing and non-ionizing radiation; accidents'.

550. Vibrations have not yet been regulated and there are no regulations adopted within environmental protection area which regulate this area.[586] Protection from vibrations shall be enforced by undertaking measures by which threat towards the environment from effects of mechanical, periodical and individual vibrations caused by human activity shall be prevented and eliminated. Article 39, point 2 of the EPL defines obligation to establish integral norms 'in order to: control the quality of air, water and soil, procedures with waste and chemicals, wastewater treatment, industrial pollution and risk management, level of noise and vibrations, etc'. Article 65 of the same Law prescribes obligations regarding adoption of action plans: 'Action plans shell be made for, among other things, '... '12) protection from noise and vibrations'... and, finally, Article 70 prescribes that 'State monitoring shall be carried out by systematic measurement, examination and rating of indicators of the status and pollution of environment', including the noise.'

VI. Other Legislation

551. Another legal Act containing provisions on noise is the Air Transport Law (OJ RS, Nos 73/2010, 57/11, 93/12, 45/15 and 66/15). Articles 200–203 (Chapter IX) of the Law on Air Transportation (OJ RS, No. 73/2010) regulate issues related to protection against noise and exhaust gas emissions. The Law lays down that aviation entities shall be obliged to take measures for protection of environment against the aircraft noise and other noise related external factors that result from the operation or provision of services in civil aviation (Article 200 of the Law). An aerodrome operator shall be obliged to ensure the implementation of environment protection measures when airport is in use, in accordance with the Air Transport Law and the regulations that govern the environment protection (Article 201 of the Law).

552. Article 202 of the Law prescribes that noise and gas emission at airports and in the vicinity of the airports shall not be higher than prescribed limit values.[587] Aircraft operators shall pay the charge for environment protection against aircraft noise and aircraft gas emissions (Article 202, paragraph 3).[588]

553. Pursuant to Article 203 of the mentioned Law, the operators of general purpose airports and airports used for commercial air transport that, during the previous year, had more than 50,000 take-offs and landings, as well as the operator of the combined airport open for operations of military and jet aircraft, shall provide continual measuring of noise generated at airport and its vicinity as a result of aircraft take-offs and landings. The results received by noise measuring are used for development of strategic noise maps and action plans for environmental protection against noise and

586. NEPP, 57.

587. The Minister competent for transport affairs, with the consent of the Minister competent for environment protection affairs, prescribes allowed noise levels at airports, allowed gas emission levels at airports, methods of emission monitoring and operative restrictions at certain airport points, as well as the measures for the reduction of aircraft emission.

588. The Minister competent for transport affairs, with the consent of the Minister competent for environment protection affairs, prescribes the amount of the charge for the environmental protection against aircraft noise and gas emission.

vibrations in air transport and for designation of noise protected areas where aircraft noise exceeds allowed level.[589]

554. Pursuant to Article 14(2) of the *Law on Railway* (OJ RS, Nos 45/13 and 91/15) the manager of public railway infrastructure is obligated to, when performing his/her duties, take care of environment protection in accordance with Law and other regulations.

555. In the field of *road vehicles*, in the Republic of Serbia, international UN/ECE – Agreement Concerning the Adoption of Uniform Technical Prescriptions for Wheeled Vehicles, Equipment and Parts which can be fitted and/or be used on Wheeled Vehicles and Conditions for Reciprocal Recognition of Approvals Granted on the Basic of these Prescriptions is applied. The Road Traffic Safety Agency is responsible for implementation of the 1958 Agreement and for the relevant UN/ECE Regulations.[590]

556. During 2010 one regulation and five rulebooks were adopted. These are following:

- Regulation on noise indicators, limit values, methods for assessing indicators of noise, disturbance and harmful effects of noise to the environment and public health, as well as types and manner for collecting data necessary for their assessment (OJ RS No. 75/10).
- Rulebook on conditions which must be met by professional organization for noise measurement, as well as documents submitted together with application for authorization for noise measurement (OJ RS No. 72/10).
- Rulebook on methodology for drafting action plans (OJ RS No. 72/10).
- Rulebook on methodology for determining acoustic zones (OJ RS No. 72/10).
- Rulebook on measuring methods for noise, content and scope of the report on noise measurements (OJ RS No. 72/10).
- Rulebook on content and methods for drafting strategic noise maps in the environment and manner of their publication (OJ RS No. 80/10).

589. The Minister competent for traffic affairs, with the consent of the Minister competent for environment protection affairs, prescribes the method of noise measuring at airports.

590. Uniform provisions concerning the approval of category L2, L4 and L5 vehicles with regard to noise) (UN/ECE R. 9) (OJ SFRJ – IT, No. 16/72,) (corresponding to the EU Directive/Regulation with relevant amendments and modifications: 97/24); Uniform provisions concerning the approval of motor cycles with regard to noise (UN/ECE R.41) (OJ SFRJ, No. 60/86) (corresponding to the EU Directive/Regulation with relevant amendments and modifications: 97/24); Uniform provisions concerning the approval of motor vehicles having at least four wheels with regard to their noise emissions (UN/ECE R. 51) (OJ SFRJ, Nos 48/84 and 1/87) (corresponding to the EU Directive/Regulation with relevant amendments and modifications:70/157); Uniform provisions concerning the approval of replacement silencing systems (UN/ECE R. 59) (OJ SFRJ, No. 43/92) (corresponding to the EU Directive/Regulation with relevant amendments and modifications: 70/157 and 81/334); Uniform provisions concerning the approval of two-wheeled mopeds with regard to noise (UN/ECE R. 63) (OJ SFRJ, No. 73/87) (corresponding to the EU Directive/Regulation with relevant amendments and modifications: 97/24).

557. Serbia has achieved a good level of alignment but implementation is at an early stage. Serbia needs to build administrative capacity for drafting strategic noise maps and action plans.[591]

591. CR, 77.

Chapter 7. Radiation

§1. Levels of Radioactivity in Serbia

558. Generally speaking, levels of radioactivity in Serbia are within the permitted values. The overall results of radioactivity measuring, using the methodology of vertical analysis of the samples from the territory of Serbia in 2000, showed that the activity, both natural radionuclides and long-living radionuclides of artificial origin (mostly from the Chernobyl 1986 catastrophe), in different types of samples (air, precipitation, soil, river and drinking water, vegetation, food products, etc.), was within low limits.[592]

559. Presently, the Republic of Serbia has a system of eight stations for measuring radioactivity, which fall under the purview of Serbian Radiation Protection and Nuclear Safety Agency (SRPNA). Pursuant to Article 9 of the Law on Ionizing Radiation Protection and Nuclear Safety, the systematic examination of radioactivity in the environment/monitoring of radioactivity is performed in accordance with the Programme for Systematic Examination of Environmental Radioactivity, which was adopted by SRPNA with the approval of the Government of the Republic of Serbia.[593]

560. During the NATO intervention in 1999 ammunition with DU was used polluting a number of sites in Kosovo-Metohija, southern Serbia and Montenegro. There are four sites in Serbia (excluding Kosovo- and Metohija) which were contaminated by DU during the NATO air-raids in 1999. The contaminated soil was collected during the remediation process and stored temporarily in the Institute of Nuclear Sciences 'Vinca'. The storage of radioactive waste in Vinca does not meet legal requirements and because of that it is one of the main environmental problems in Serbia.[594]

Potential danger for Serbia is nuclear installations functioning in the region. There are, namely, thirty-nine reactors (mainly used for the production of electricity) in neighbouring countries, some of which are already relatively old.

561. Most of radioactive waste has been deposited in, as already mentioned, the Institute of Nuclear Sciences 'Vinca' situated in Vinca, a village near Belgrade. The main sources of the waste are research reactors in the Vinca Nuclear Institute (which contributed to about 4% of the total radioactive waste), remnants of isotopes used in medicine, industry, etc. radioactive materials used in medicine, radioactive waste from the industry of fertilizers especially phosphates, radioactive lightning rods, etc. A project of nuclear fuel transportation from Vinca to the Russian Federation has been started, with collaboration of the International Atomic Energy Agency (IAEA). The contract on repacking and transportation to the Russian Federation, where it will

592. Report on the State of the Environment in 2000 and Priorities in 2001 for Serbia (Belgrade: Ministry for Protection of Natural Resources and Environment, 2002), 172; *see also*, *Radioaktivnost životne sredine u Republici Srbiji u 2002* [*Radioactivity of Environment in the Republic of Serbia*] (Belgrade: Ministarstvo za zastitu prirodnih bogatstava i životne sredine, 2002).

593. AECQ, Ch. 15 (Energy), 77.

594. NES, 33.

be reprocessed, was signed between the IAEA, the Institute of Nuclear Sciences 'Vinca' and consortium of three Russian companies.[595]

It should be added that in Serbia about 1,800 sources of ionizing radiation from radioactive lightning protection rods remain to be removed. The five-year deadline for the removal of radioactive lightning rods expired on 23 May 2014.[596]

562. Protection from ionized radiation and of nuclear safety is in the competence of the MAEP, Ministry of Mining and Energy, the Ministry of Education, Science and Technological Development, according to the provisions of the Law on Ministries.[597]

Systematic monitoring of ionizing radiation, as prescribed by the decision on systematic testing of content of radionuclides in the environment, is performed in the Institute for Professional Medicine and Radiological Protection 'Dr Dragomir Karajovic' of the Clinical Centre of Serbia.[598]

Border control of radioactivity (dozimetric control and gamma-spectrometric measurement) of imported and exported goods, as well as the goods in transit, is performed since 2003, as prescribed in the Book of Regulations on Maximum Levels of Radioactive Contamination of the Environment and Decontamination Procedures.[599]

In accordance with the Law on Ionizing Radiation Protection and Nuclear Safety, the Serbian Agency for Ionizing Radiation Protection and Nuclear Safety[600] was established towards the end of 2009, as an independent regulatory body in compliance

595. IAEA – Annual Report 2007, 28, https://www.iaea.org/publications/reports/annual-report-2007; *see also*, NPI, 403.
596. *See* : http://www.srbatom.gov.rs/srbatom/#vest01 (18 Jun. 2017).
597. One of the problems relates to coordination within different ministries and other organizations (science, environment, health, defence, interior affairs, etc.).
598. OJ FRY, No. 45/97.
599. OJ FRY, No. 9/99.
600. At http://srbatom.gov.rs/cir/.

with the Law on Public Agencies (OJ RS, Nos 18/05 and 81/05 – corr. of 4 March 2005).[601]

§2. Legislation

563. The EPL contains only general provisions concerning radiation. In Article 32 it prescribes that protection from radiation shall be enforced by implementing measures, by which threat towards the environment and human health from the effects of radiation from ionizing and non-ionizing sources shall be prevented, and by which the consequences of emissions from those sources shall be prevented. Legal and natural persons may produce, circulate or use sources of ionizing and non-ionizing radiation according to existing legal regulation. Using the resources of the Green Fund of the Republic of Serbia shall be done in accordance with the Law, the NEPP and strategic documents, as well as a list of priority infrastructure projects in the field of environment,

601. Article 6 of the Law on Ionizing Radiation Protection and Nuclear Safety stipulates the following competences of the Agency:(1) to adopt by-laws for the implementation of this Law; (2) to adopt the Programme for Environmental Radioactivity Monitoring; (3) to adopt the Programme of additional training and qualification of occupationally exposed persons and persons in charge of ionizing radiation protection; (4) to adopt the Programme for early warning of emergencies; (5) to draw up proposals of Programmes referred to in Article 4 herein; (6) to draw up an Emergency Plan proposal; (7) to prepare guidance and procedures for the implementation of radiation and nuclear safety and security measures; (8) to issue, renew and revoke licenses for performing radiation practice and nuclear activity; (9) to issue and revoke permits for transferring radioactive and nuclear materials; (10) to issue, renew and revoke decisions to legal persons or entrepreneurs for performing ionizing radiation protection activities, radiation practice or nuclear activities; (11) to issue receipts on the registration of ionizing radiation sources; (12) to issue certificates to persons responsible for radiation protection; (13) to prescribe the amount of fees for the issuance of licenses, permits, decisions, registration receipts and certificates; (14) to administer a Register of applications and issued licenses, permits, decisions, registration receipts and certificates; (15) to establish and maintain a database (central Register) of radioactive sources and users of such sources, occupationally exposed persons and other information relevant to radiation protection and radiation and nuclear safety and security; (16) to administer central Register of nuclear facilities, nuclear materials and radioactive waste and to control the records kept by users; (17) to monitor the scope and change of radioactivity level and to assess its impact on the population and the environment, and, in that respect, to order and supervise the implementation of necessary measures; (18) to publish the annual reports about the level of exposure of the population in the Republic of Serbia to ionizing radiation; (19) to control the fulfilment of requirements for issuing licenses, permits and decisions, referred to under points (8), (9) and (10) herein; (20) to ensure transparency in the implementation of this Law and in the procedure of adopting by-laws; (21) to provide media, competent State authorities and the IAEA with the information relevant to radiation and nuclear safety and security; (22) to cooperate with competent State bodies within its purview; (23) to establish cooperation, independently or in cooperation with relevant State bodies, with the IAEA and other international bodies and competent authorities of other countries, in relation to the implementation of this Law; (24) to give its opinion, upon the request of competent State bodies, about the adherence to international conventions and other agreements in the field of radiation and nuclear safety and security; (25) to perform other tasks determined by law.

inter alia: the removal of sources of ionizing radiation from radioactive lightning rods and disposal of abandoned sources of ionizing radiation of unknown owners or users; the improvement and construction of infrastructure for protection from ionizing and non-ionizing radiation (Article 90c, paragraph 1, points 17 and 18).

I. Law on Ionizing Radiation Protection and Nuclear Safety

564. The legal Act that regulates ionizing radiation protection[602] and nuclear safety[603] in the Republic of Serbia is Law on Ionizing Radiation Protection and Nuclear Safety (OJ RS, Nos 36/2009 and 93/12). It has the following twelve parts: Part I – General Provisions (Articles 1–3); Part II – Radiation, nuclear safety and security programmes and radioactive waste[604] management programme (Article 4); Part III – Agency for ionizing radiation protection and nuclear safety of Serbia (Articles 5 and 6); Part IV – Ionizing radiation Protection (Articles 7–45); Part V – Nuclear safety and security (Articles 46–61); Part VI – Accident response (Article 62); Part VII – Radioactive waste management[605] (Articles 63 and 64); Part VIII – Traffic of ionizing radiation sources, radioactive and nuclear materials (Articles 65–71); Part IX – Liability for nuclear damages (Articles 72–75); Part X – Monitoring (Articles 76–83); Part XI – Penalty provisions (Articles 84–87); and Part XII – Transitional and final provisions (Articles 88–94).

565. This Law[606] prescribes measures for protection of human lives, public health and environment[607] against detrimental effects of the ionizing radiation, as well as nuclear safety measures in all procedures relevant to nuclear activities. It also prescribes conditions for carrying out nuclear activities[608] with respect to sources of

602. *Ionizing radiation protection* is a set of measures to prevent harmful effects of the exposure to ionizing radiation (Art. 3, point 8); *Ionizing radiation* is electromagnetic or particle radiation capable of producing ions which may cause harmful effects to human life, public health and to the environment (Art. 3, point 14).
603. *Nuclear safety* is a set of measures providing conditions for operation of nuclear facilities, prevention of nuclear accidents and mitigation of consequences thereof or reduction of the radiation risk to the prescribed level (Art. 3, point 23).
604. *Radioactive waste* is a radioactive material for which no further use is anticipated (Art. 3, point 43).
605. *Radioactive waste management* is a set of administrative and operational procedures involved with the activity of treatment, conditioning, storage, transport (only within certain location) and waste disposal, as well as release of effluents (Art. 3, point 51).
606. The provisions of this Law shall not apply to the natural level of ionizing radiation of cosmic, Earth's crust or human origin, when such radiation is not modified by the human activity (Art. 1, para. 2). The provisions of this Law shall not apply to the nuclear facilities that are forbidden for construction by a special law (Art. 1, para. 3).
607. *Environment* is a set of natural and created values whose mutual relations make surroundings, space and conditions for life (Art. 3, point 6).
608. *Nuclear activities* are import, export, use and transport of nuclear materials, exploitation of the ores containing nuclear material, locating, designing, constructing, probation, commissioning, usage, and permanent cessation and decommissioning of nuclear facilities and remediation of such sites, as well as radioactive waste management (Art. 3, point 24).

ionizing radiation and nuclear materials, as well as radioactive waste management (Article 1, paragraph 1).

Any activity[609] involving ionizing radiation sources and nuclear materials shall be prohibited, unless it has been previously authorized by the Agency for Radiation and Nuclear Safety of the Republic of Serbia (Article 2, paragraph 1).

566. The import of radioactive waste and used nuclear fuel of foreign origin shall be prohibited on the territory of the Republic of Serbia (Article 2, paragraph 3). The installation of radioactive lightning rods is prohibited on the territory of the Republic of Serbia (Article 2, paragraph 4). The installation of ionizing smoke detectors with gaseous radioactive source or with products in gaseous state shall be prohibited (Article 2, paragraph 5).[610]

A. Radioactive Waste Management, Nuclear Safety and Security Programmes

567. For the purpose of providing conditions for implementation of policy in the field of radiation and nuclear safety and security policy, and the radioactive waste management, the Government of the Republic of Serbia (Government), at the proposal of the Agency for Radiation and Nuclear Safety of the Republic of Serbia shall adopt the following: Programme on Radiation Safety and Security, Nuclear Safety and Security Programme, and Radioactive Waste Management Programme, in compliance with the regulation on the EIA Strategy (Article 4, paragraph 1).

568. The Agency for Radiation and Nuclear Safety shall submit the annual report on the implementation of Programmes referred to in paragraph 1 of Article 4, to the Government, Ministry competent for carrying out public administration activities related to nuclear safety, radioactive waste management issues and the authorities in charge for national security (Article 4, paragraph 3).

B. Agency for Ionizing Radiation Protection and Nuclear Safety[611]

569. For the purpose of providing quality and efficient implementation of radiation protection and nuclear safety measures, while carrying out radiation practice and nuclear activities, the Government shall establish the Agency for Ionizing Radiation Protection and Nuclear Safety of the Republic of Serbia (hereinafter, Agency), as an independent regulatory body, performing public competencies in accordance to this Law (Article 5, paragraph 1).

The fundamental principles applied to radiation practice, nuclear activities and radioactive waste management are the following: (1) *validity of usage* – requirements and authorization to carry out current and future practice, nuclear activities and radioactive waste management activities shall be determined and considered by taking

609. It shall be prohibited to undertake any type of research for the purpose of development, production and use of nuclear weapons, as well as to use nuclear materials for the production of nuclear weapons or other explosive devices (Art. 2, para. 2).

610. Sources of ionizing radiation from Art. 2, paras 4 and 5 of this Law must be removed within five years of entering into force of this Law (Art. 90, para. 2).

611. At http://srbatom.gov.rs/cir/.

into account economic, social and other benefits to the society compared to the radiation risks[612] which may occur while carrying out those activities and having in mind the most relevant and available records regarding either their efficiency or the consequences; (2) *optimization of radiation protection* – any activity must be executed in a way that exposure[613] to ionizing radiation is as low as it is possible to achieve, taking into account economic and social factors; (3) *individual exposure limit* – radiation activity[614] must be planned in a way that the exposure of individuals is always below prescribed limits (Article 7, paragraph 1).

C. *Radioactivity Protection, Monitoring and Reporting*

570. Protection measures carried out in order to protect human lives, health and environment from harmful effects of ionizing radiations are as follows: (1) environmental radioactivity[615] monitoring; (2) determination of conditions for production, trade and usage of ionizing radiation sources; (3) providing and using the equipment and devices for protection from ionizing radiation and efficiency control of such protection; (4) radioactivity monitoring, limitation or prohibition of production, trade and use of ionizing radiation sources; (5) inventory of ionizing radiation sources; (6) inventory of materials and raw materials which, in the course of technical-technological process, lead to increased concentration of natural radionuclide,[616] above the prescribed limits; (7) keeping record on occupational, medical and population exposure;[617] (8) determination of working conditions and implementation of measures for radiation protection at work; (9) health surveillance of occupationally exposed persons; (10) staff education and vocational training in the area of radiation protection; (11) personal and collective

612. *Radiation risk* shall designate endangering health hazard effect while being exposed to the sources of ionizing radiation, also having in mind the possibility of being exposed to such radiation, any safety risk related to ecosystems in the environment which may occur as a consequence to being exposed to the radiation, presence of the radioactive materials, including radioactive waste, or their emission in the environment, loss of control over nuclear reactor core, over nuclear chain reaction, over radioactive source or any other ionizing radiation source (Art. 3, point 41).
613. *Exposure to ionizing radiation* is the action or condition in which human body is exposed to ionizing radiation (Art. 3, point 11).
614. *Radiation activity* is any activity (act) involving sources of ionizing radiation which may cause increasing level of exposure to ionizing radiation occupationally exposed individuals and population (Art. 3, point 37).
615. *Radioactivity* shall designate a natural phenomenon of spontaneous disintegration of atoms accompanied by emission of one or more types of radiation, such as alpha, beta, neutron and gamma radiation (Art. 3, point 44).
616. *Radionuclide* is a nuclide, a type of atom specified by its atomic number, atomic mass and energy state that is radioactive (Art. 3, point 45).
617. *Population exposure* is exposure due to an accident and exposure due to approved application of ionizing radiation, except medical and professional exposure and exposure to normal level of radiation from the nature (Art. 3, point 10); *Medical exposure* is any exposure of patients and persons that help the patients while applying sources of ionizing radiation as a part of their medical treatment, other than those occupationally exposed, as well as persons voluntarily included in medical research programs involving sources of ionizing radiation (Art. 3, point 18).

public protection against ionizing radiation; (12) emergency plan implementation measures; (13) radioactive waste collecting, storage and treatment; (14) establishment of quality management system of radiation protection; (15) radioactivity control of goods during import, export and transit; (16) prevention of the illicit trafficking of radioactive and nuclear material;[618] and (17) decontamination[619] of persons, working area and the environment (Article 8, paragraph 1).

571. Systematic investigation of radioactivity in the environment (hereinafter, referred to as the monitoring of radioactivity)[620] is performed to determine the presence of radionuclide in the environment and estimation of exposure level of population to ionizing radiation in normal conditions, in case of suspicion of an accident, as well as during the accident (Article 9, paragraph 1).

572. Monitoring[621] of radioactivity, or particular issues within it, are to be performed by the legal entity,[622] provided that it: (1) has employed a person with acquired degree in academic studies in natural sciences or technological studies, with three years of working experience in radiation measurement in samples from the environment; (2) is equipped with proper laboratory for processing, measuring and keeping samples; (3) has standard laboratory equipment for sample preparation; (4) has specific measuring equipment fulfilling metrological conditions; (5) possesses appropriate computer and software equipment; and (6) is accredited with national or international Certification Agency (Article 10, paragraph 1).

573. The legal entity performing monitoring is obliged to submit to the Agency report on environmental radioactivity monitoring the latest by 31 January of the current

---

618. *Illicit trafficking of nuclear and radioactive materials* is any receipt, possession, delivery, use, transfer or disposal of nuclear and radioactive materials on the territory of the Republic of Serbia or when crossing of its borders, without previously obtained authorization of the Agency (Art. 3, point 20); *Authorization* is a set of actions and activities undertaken by the Agency within prescribed procedure and based on the relevant application submitted by a legal entity or entrepreneur in order to issue a license, permit, receipt or decision regarding fulfilment of the requirements and conditions to carry out a practice or any other activity described in this Law (Art. 3, point 28).
619. *Decontamination* is the process of removing or reducing level of contamination, including measures for the removal of immediate threat of potential contamination, measures for control of further spread of contamination, measures for the isolation and safe removal of sources of contamination, as well as activities related to the assessment and risk analysis of potential contamination and activities related to the assessment and analysis of damage to the environment due to contamination (Art. 3, point 4).
620. *Monitoring of radioactivity* is a set of measurements, processing and interpretation of radiation measurement results and other parameters related to the assessment and control of public exposure levels (Art. 3, point 19).
621. Monitoring as defined in para. 1 of this Article shall be carried out in compliance with the Program on environmental radioactivity monitoring, adopted by the Agency (Art. 9, para. 2). The programme referred to in para. 2 of this Article determines the locations, time intervals, types and methods of systematic radioactivity testing in the environment (Art. 9, para. 3). The Government shall authorize the programme referred to in para. 2 of this Article (Art. 9, para. 4).
622. The Agency prescribes the requirements to be met by a legal entity performing activities referred to in para. 1 of this Article (Art. 10, para. 2).

year for the preceding year, or immediately on Agency's request (Article 11, paragraph 1).

Based on the radioactivity monitoring results, the Agency monitors population exposure to ionizing radiation,[623] orders emergency measures in case of increasing level of radioactivity and performs assessment of received doses by population (Article 11, paragraph 3).

574. A legal entity or entrepreneur whose technical-technological process of production leads to increased concentrations of natural radionuclide above the limits prescribed for the contamination of the environment is required to keep records[624] about it and submit it to the Agency (Article 14, paragraph 1). On the basis of received records, the Agency shall evaluate the level of risk to the human health and environment and order implementation of protection measures against ionizing radiation (Article 14, paragraph 3).

D. Exposure to Ionizing Radiation

575. Drinking water, foodstuff, fodder, medicinal products, goods of general use, building materials and other products cannot be put in traffic if it contains radionuclide above the prescribed limits (Article 12, paragraph 1). The Agency shall prescribe radionuclide content limits for such products[625] (Article 12, paragraph 2).

576. For the purpose of early detection of emergencies threatening or potentially threatening territory of the Republic of Serbia, an early warning system shall be established providing continuous measurement level of ambient equivalent dose on the basis of the Programme[626] adopted by the Agency (Article 15, paragraph 1). The measurements intended for early warning in case of emergency shall be performed by the legal entity[627] (Article 16, paragraph 1).

623. The Agency shall publish the annual report on population exposure levels to ionizing radiation in a special technical publication (Art. 11, para. 4).

624. The Agency shall prescribe content and deadlines for submission of records referred to in para. 1 of this Article and determine the list of legal entities and entrepreneurs where elevation of the concentration of natural radionuclides shall occur within their technical-technological production process, above prescribed limits for the contamination of the environment (Art. 14, para. 2); *Natural radionuclides* are the nuclides occurred in the nature, not originating from human activity (uranium, radium, thorium and others) (Art. 3, point 34).

625. Measurements of radionuclides content in products referred to in para. 1 of Art. 12 of this Law can be performed by the legal entity (Art. 13, para. 1).

626. The Government shall approve such Program (Art. 15, para. 2).

627. The conditions to be fulfilled by legal entity performing measurement activities intended for early warning in case of emergency shall be prescribed by the Agency (Art. 16, para. 2).

577. Project for designing radiation safety and security measures[628] shall be an integral component of the technical documentation applied to the facilities in which sources of ionizing radiation are being or will be used, implementation of the project for designing radiation safety and security measures shall ensure that such facilities meet prescribed protection levels of occupationally exposed persons, population and environment against ionizing radiation (Article 17, paragraph 1).

578. For the purpose of assessing exposure level of occupationally exposed persons, patients and the population,[629] specific measurements shall be undertaken in accordance with this Law (Article 19, paragraph 1).

579. For the purpose of training and professional upgrading in the field of radiation protection, the Agency shall adopt the Programme for additional training and qualification of occupationally exposed persons[630] and persons in charge for protection against ionizing radiation,[631] and it shall be published in the 'Official Journal of the Republic of Serbia' (Article 21, paragraph 1) and approved by the Government (Article 21, paragraph 2).

580. Measurements for quality control management system can be performed by legal entity fulfilling requirements stipulated in Article 23, paragraph 1, while other conditions that need to be fulfilled by the legal entity performing such operations are to be prescribed by the Agency (paragraph 2).

581. Decontamination of the working area and the environment can be performed by the legal entity fulfilling the requirements prescribed in Article 24, paragraph 1. The Agency shall prescribe other conditions that need to be met by the legal entity in conducting decontamination of the working area and the environment (Article 24, paragraph 2).

---

628. The Agency shall approve the Project for designing radiation safety and security measures (Art. 17, para. 3), also the Agency shall prescribe the content of such project, for each specific radiation practice (Art. 17, para. 2). *Radiation safety* is a set of prescribed organizational and technical-technological measures ensuring optimum planned exposure to radiation and risk deriving from the use of sources of ionizing radiation, including radiation protection measures, measures for preventing the accidents, as well as measures for diminishing the consequences of accidents, if it occurs (Art. 3, point 39).
629. The Agency shall prescribe the type, method and time intervals of measuring for the purpose of assessing the level of exposure of occupationally exposed persons, patients and the population (Art. 19, para. 2). Measurements for the purpose of assessing level of exposure of occupationally exposed persons, patients and the population can be performed by legal entity fulfilling the requirements prescribed in Art. 19, para. 3 of this Law. Also, the legal entity is obliged to keep records on conducted measurements for the assessment of exposure levels of occupationally exposed persons, patients and the population to ionizing radiation and to submit a report to the Agency on performed measurements (Art. 20, para. 1).
630. *Occupationally exposed persons* are the persons operating with sources of ionizing radiation or who are in the field of ionizing radiation during work process (Art. 3, point 36).
631. Additional training and qualification of occupationally exposed persons and persons in charge for protection of ionizing radiation, in line with the programme from Art. 21 of this Law, can be conducted and organized by the legal entity fulfilling the requirements prescribed in Art. 22, para. 1. The Agency shall prescribe other conditions that need to be met by the legal entity (Art. 22, para. 2).

Decontamination of persons (hereinafter, human decontamination) can be performed by legal entity fulfilling the requirements prescribed in Article 25, paragraph 1 of this Law.[632]

E. Authorization for Performing Operations of Radiation Protection

582. On the basis of fulfilling prescribed conditions, the Agency shall issue decision[633] to a legal entity[634] authorizing it to perform operations from clauses 10, 13, 16, 18, 19, 20, 22, 23, 24, 25 and 70 of this Law (Article 26, paragraph 1) within thirty days from the date when the application was submitted (Article 26, paragraph 2). The decision shall be issued[635] for a validity period of five years and it shall not be transferable (Article 26, paragraph 3).

583. The authorized legal entity from Article 26, paragraph 1 of this Law is obliged to maintain records of work performed in the field of radiation protection and to submit to the Agency information from such record at the latest by 31 January of the current year for the preceding year (Article 28, paragraph 1). The Agency shall prescribe the form and content of the records (Article 28, paragraph 1).

584. Radiation practice can be performed by the legal entity or entrepreneur, if they fulfil the requirements prescribed in Article 29, paragraph 1, while the Agency shall prescribe other conditions that need to be met by the legal entity or entrepreneur for performing radiation practice (Article 29, paragraph 2). Based on fulfilment of the requirements prescribed in Article 29 of this Law, the Agency shall issue a license[636] to a legal entity or entrepreneur for performing radiation practice (Article 30, paragraph 1).

585. The license for performing radiation practice shall be issued in the form of a decision, within thirty days of the date when the application was submitted, enclosing prescribed documents, as evidence of the fulfilment of the prescribed conditions to perform radiation practice (Article 30, paragraph 3). The license for performing radiation practice shall be issued for a validity period of five years (Article 30, paragraph 4). The legal entity or entrepreneur holding a license to carry out radiation

---

632. The Agency shall prescribe other conditions that need to be met by the legal entity in conducting decontamination of persons (Art. 25, para. 2).
633. *Decision* is a written document issued by the Agency to a legal entity fulfilling the requirements for the activities in radiation protection, radiation practice or nuclear activity, or to the entrepreneur fulfilling requirements to carry out radiation activities, in accordance with this Law (Art. 3, point 46).
634. The list of authorized legal entities, performing operations referred to in para. 1 of this Article, shall be published in the 'Official Journal of the Republic of Serbia' (Art. 26, para. 10). The Agency shall maintain Register of all issued decisions (Art. 26, para. 11).
635. The conditions under which the Agency shall suspend the decision from legal entity, before its expiration are prescribed (Art. 27, para. 1).
636. *License* is a written authorization issued by the Agency to a legal entity or entrepreneur, as a proof that specific requirements and conditions for carrying out radiation practice or nuclear activity are fulfilled (Art. 3, point 17).

practice shall be obliged to appoint a person responsible for radiation protection[637] (Article 31, paragraph 1).

586. The legal entity or entrepreneur performing low radiation risk practice, or using ionizing radiation sources of low activity is not obliged to obtain license for such activity, but it is obliged to obtain certificate on registration of such sources[638] from the Agency (Article 32, paragraph 1).

F. *Obligations of the License Owner Towards Occupationally Exposed Persons*

587. The license owner for performance of radiation practice, or the license owner for performing nuclear activity,[639] is obliged to provide personal dosimeter control of occupationally exposed persons, to equip them with means for individual protection, to provide the control of adequate functioning of such means and their adequate use, to send occupationally exposed persons to regular medical examinations, and training and periodical additional retraining in compliance with the Programme referred to in Article 21, paragraph 1 of this Law. It is also obliged, depending on the type of radiation activity, that is, nuclear activity, to keep the radioactive waste resulting from its work, in the prescribed manner in its own storage[640] for a period of maximum one year, and the latest before expiration of that time, to hand it over to the license owner for radioactive waste storage[641] management (Article 35, paragraph 1).

588. The license owners for performing radiation activity, or performing nuclear activity, are obliged to keep and submit to the Agency, prescribed data on sources of ionizing radiation, on occupationally exposed persons and on radioactive waste[642] (Article 36, paragraph 1). They are also obliged to establish and implement a quality management system for ionizing radiation protection (Article 37, paragraph 1), as well as to carry out and to finance decontamination[643] of population, working area and the environment, contaminated by their radiation practice and/or nuclear activity, as well

637. On the basis of fulfilling the requirements, the Agency shall issue a certificate to the person responsible for radiation protection (Art. 31, para. 5).

638. The Agency shall determine the sources of ionizing radiation for which usage, a legal entity, i.e., entrepreneur is obliged to obtain a certificate on registration, as well as sources of ionizing radiation for which usage, it is not required to obtain a certificate on registration (Art. 32, para. 2).

639. The license owner referred to in para. 1 of this Article is obliged, depending upon the type of radiation practice or nuclear activity, to implement prescribed measurements from the Art. 19, paras 1 and 2 of this Law, for the purpose of evaluation of exposure levels of occupationally exposed persons (Art. 34, para. 2).

640. The Agency shall prescribe the manner of radioactive waste storage (Art. 35, para. 2).

641. *Radioactive waste storage* means storage of radioactive waste at place which is under supervision of an authorized legal entity (Art. 3, point 47).

642. The Agency shall keep the central Register on sources of ionizing radiation, on the license owners, on occupationally exposed persons and on radioactive waste (Art. 36, para. 4).

643. The license owner referred to in para. 1 of this Article, responsible for contamination and the authorized legal entity performing decontamination are obliged to submit report on those matters to the Agency, without delay (Art. 38, para. 4).

as to finance administrative costs for determination of immediate danger of contamination[644] and/or origin of the contamination[645] (Article 38, paragraph 1).

589. The license owner for performing radiation practice, or the license owner for performing nuclear activity is liable[646] for damage caused by radiation practice or nuclear activity, in accordance with the principle of objective responsibility (Article 39, paragraph 1).

590. Occupationally exposed persons must have the prescribed degree of qualification and must be qualified to work and implement measures of protection from ionizing radiation (Article 40, paragraph 1).

591. Operating with sources of ionizing radiation is forbidden to: (1) persons under the age of 18; (2) women during pregnancy; (3) women during infant breast-feeding, if operating with open sources of ionizing radiation (Article 41, paragraph 1).[647]

592. Occupationally exposed persons, persons undergoing training and the general population must not be exposed to ionizing radiation above the prescribed limits[648] (Article 42, paragraph 1).

593. Radiation practice and nuclear activities can be used in medicine in the prescribed manner if the medical doctor of relevant specialization shall assess the medical justification of such use and shall approve the diagnostic and therapeutic procedure with the implementation of principles and protection measures against ionizing radiation (Article 43, paragraph 1).

594. Systematic X-ray survey of the population shall be prohibited, except in exceptional cases, when the Ministry in charge of health care prescribes such measure, with the approval of the Agency on the fulfilment of protection measures concerning systematic x-ray survey of the population (Article 45, paragraph 1).

---

644. *Contamination* means an unintended and undesirable presence of radioactive substance, as well as the process resulting in its presence on surfaces or inside the solid, liquid or gaseous materials (including human body), above prescribed limits (Art. 3, point 15).
645. The Agency shall inform the occupationally exposed persons and general public on potential harmful effects of the exposure to ionizing radiation (Art. 38, para. 5).
646. In cases when it cannot be determined which license owner is responsible for contamination, the costs of decontamination and the respective damage, if it is necessary to be financed immediately, shall be borne by the Republic of Serbia (Art. 32, para. 2). The owner of the license determined to be responsible for contamination is obliged to pay in decontamination expenses to the budget of the Republic of Serbia (Art. 32, para. 3).
647. The persons under age 18, except persons over age 16 during the prescribed training activities during regular school for work with sources of ionizing radiation, shall be forbidden to be occupationally exposed. The owner of the license for performance of radiation practice, or the owner of the license performing nuclear activity, shall be obliged to undertake appropriate measures to prevent exposure above public exposure limits for:(1) working women during pregnancy;(2) working women during infant breastfeeding, if operating with open sources of ionizing radiation (Art. 41, paras 2 and 3).
648. The Agency prescribes the exposure limits for occupationally exposed persons, persons undergoing training and for general population (Art. 42, para. 2).

G. *Nuclear Safety and Facility*

595. Measures of nuclear safety and security implemented in all activities relevant to nuclear facilities, nuclear materials and radioactive waste, as well as in the case of an accident, shall be: (1) ensuring conditions for siting, design, construction, test running, commissioning, utilization, permanent shut down and decommissioning of the nuclear facility; (2) fulfilment of criteria for safety assessment of nuclear facility; (3) ensuring conditions for marketing and use of nuclear material; (4) ensuring and implementation of the protection measures against ionizing radiation in the nuclear facility and its vicinity; (5) establishing conditions to be fulfilled by persons employed in a nuclear facility; (6) providing conditions for collection, keeping records on, processing, storing and disposing of radioactive waste; (7) physical protection of the nuclear facility, (8) prevention of the illicit trafficking of nuclear materials; and (9) emergency planning and response (Article 46).

596. A nuclear facility can be constructed only within the location for which spatial and urban plans have been adopted, in accordance with programme from Article 4 of this Law, with regulations on planning and facility construction and with regulations regarding EIA (Article 48).

597. In accordance with Article 48a of the Law on Ionizing Radiation Protection and Nuclear Safety, in July 2009 the Public Enterprise 'Nuclear Facilities Serbia' was founded for the purpose of managing nuclear facilities in the Republic of Serbia.[649] The public enterprise has been managing the research reactors RA and RB, the storage of nuclear waste consisting of hangars H0, H1 and H2, and the closed mine and hydrometallurgic plant for the processing of uranium in Gabrovnica near Kalna.[650]

598. The operation of nuclear facility must be in accordance with operating and other technical instructions relevant to all modes of operation, handling of nuclear materials and transport thereof, maintenance and supervision of technical systems, internal controls and procedures in case of an accident (Article 52, paragraph 1).

599. A nuclear facility can be located, designed, constructed, commissioned, operated, permanently closed and decommissioned only with previously received license issued by the Agency (Article 49, paragraph 1).

600. The license referred to in paragraphs 1 and 2 of this Article may be issued only after determination that all measures of nuclear safety have been fulfilled in line with the prescribed nuclear safety report[651] and other documents prescribed by the Agency for each nuclear facility separately (Article 49, paragraph 5).

601. The license, referred to in paragraph 1 of this Article, shall be issued for a validity period of three years (Article 49, paragraph 7). The decision for issuing a license is to be published in the 'Official Journal of the Republic of Serbia' (Article 49, paragraph 9).

649. *See* http://www.nuklearniobjekti.rs.

650. AECQ, Ch. 15 (Energy), Government of the Republic of Serbia, Belgrade, 2011. 70.

651. The report content is prescribed in Art. 50, para. 1. The report on nuclear safety shall be amended in compliance with changes that occur during the construction, trial run, commissioning, operation and permanent closing of the nuclear facility, so that the report shall always refer to the existing status of the nuclear facility (Art. 50, para. 2).

602. The owner of the license of a nuclear facility shall submit to the Agency the following reports concerning: (1) any intended and implemented change of procedure referred to in Article 52, paragraph 2, clause 1 of this Law, change of equipment and operating modes, which are subject to prescribed conditions and operating limitations; (2) any failure of equipment and accidents in the nuclear facility and measures taken to remedy the consequences of accidents; (3) any personnel errors in operating the nuclear facility; (4) any excess above prescribed quantities and activities regarding the discharge of gaseous or liquid radioactive waste materials or deviation from prescribed conditions under which they may be discharged; and (5) any other circumstances of significance for the safety and security of nuclear facility (Article 53, paragraph 1).[652]

603. The owner of the nuclear facility is obliged to ensure physical protection[653] and other security measures of the nuclear facility, nuclear material[654] and radioactive waste, including security measures during transport of the nuclear material (Article 61, paragraph 1).

604. Measures for nuclear safety and security implemented in all activities relevant to nuclear facilities, nuclear materials and radioactive waste, as well as in case of an accident,[655] are the following: (1) ensuring conditions for sitting, design, construction, test running, commissioning, utilization, permanent shut down and decommissioning of the nuclear facility;[656] (2) fulfilment of criteria for safety assessment of nuclear facility; (3) ensuring conditions for marketing and use of nuclear material; (4) ensuring and implementation of the protection measures against ionizing radiation in the nuclear facility and its vicinity; (5) establishing conditions to be fulfilled by persons employed in a nuclear facility; (6) providing conditions for collection, keeping records on, processing, storing and disposing of radioactive waste; (7) physical protection of the nuclear facility; (8) prevention of the illicit trafficking of nuclear materials; and (9) emergency planning and response (Article 46, paragraph 1).

---

652. The license owner shall be obliged to submit to the Agency regular reports about the operation of the nuclear facility in timely intervals and in a manner required by the Agency (Art. 53, para. 2). The owner of the license shall be obliged, at the request of the Agency, to provide any information on nuclear safety measures and all other activities relevant to the implementation of this Law (Art. 53, para. 3).
653. The Government shall prescribe measures for physical protection of nuclear facility, nuclear materials, and supervise their implementation in compliance with the programmes on radiation, nuclear safety and security (Art. 61, para. 3).
654. *Nuclear material* is plutonium, except the one with isotopic concentration exceeding 80% in plutonium 238, uranium 233, uranium enriched in the isotope U-235 or U-233, uranium containing the mixture of isotopes as occurring in the nature, with concentration higher than one occurring in ores or in reprocessing remains, as well as the mixture of the foregoing materials (Art. 3, point 25).
655. *Accident* is an unintended event, human mistake, equipment failures or other irregularities, which consequences or potential consequences, are not negligible from the point of view of ionizing radiation protection, nuclear, i.e., radiation security or safety (Art. 3, point. 2).
656. *Nuclear facility* is a facility where nuclear materials are placed or used, including radioactive waste facilities for storage, treatment and disposal (Art. 3, point 26).

H. Permanent Closing and Decommissioning of Nuclear Facility

605. In case of permanent closing and decommissioning of a nuclear facility, the license owner is obliged, within time frame stated by the Agency, to implement adequate remediation measures on the site, in the facility and in its vicinity (Article 54).

606. The license owner for performing nuclear activity is obliged to organize radiation protection service (Article 55, paragraph 1). Also, it is obliged, in the prescribed manner and under the prescribed conditions, to carry out systematic testing of radioactivity in the environment, as well as in the vicinity of the nuclear facility[657] (Article 56, paragraph 1). Nuclear materials shall be handled only by persons who meet the prescribed conditions for handling such materials (Article 57, paragraph 1).

607. The license[658] owner for producing, processing, using or storing of nuclear materials is obliged to keep records[659] on those materials in line with ratified international agreements, and to submit relevant data from the record to the Agency (Article 58, paragraph 1). The license owner is obliged to adopt and implement the quality control system[660] (Article 60, paragraph 1).

608. The license owner for performing nuclear activity is obliged to ensure, to the representatives of the IAEA, in compliance with the international agreements, to perform supervision and inspection over nuclear materials from Article 58 of this Law (Article 59, paragraph 1).

---

657. The Agency shall prescribe the method and conditions for systematic testing of radioactivity in the environment in the vicinity of the nuclear facility (Art. 56, para. 2).
658. The Agency shall keep the central Register on nuclear materials and supervise the record keeping performed by the license owner (Art. 58, para. 3).
659. The Agency shall prescribe the manner of record keeping on nuclear materials (Art. 58, para. 2).
660. The license owner referred to in para. 1 of this Article is obliged to put in place a planned and systematic implementation of quality control measures, necessary to provide that all technical, structural, organizational and personnel factors are kept under control, also including the identification of safety requirements and implementation thereof (Art. 60, para. 2). The Agency shall prescribe the manner, types and time intervals in which quality control measures, referred to in para. 2 of this Article, shall be performed (Art. 60, para. 3).

I. Accident Response

609. In case of a nuclear accident, for the purpose of protection of lives, human health and environmental protection,[661] the Government shall adopt the Emergency response plan[662] (Article 62, paragraph 1).

The protection of lives, human health and the environment from ionizing radiation resulting from a nuclear accident or in case of emergency shall be carried out on the basis of prescribed measures for the prevention and remediation of effects that such an event may cause (Article 62, paragraph 4). Accident response plan shall be in compliance with the Convention on Early Notification of a Nuclear Accident and the Convention on the Assistance in the Case of a Nuclear Accident or a Radiological Emergency (Article 62, paragraph 6).

J. Radioactive Waste Management

610. The license owner for performing radiation practice, or license owner for performing nuclear activity, is obliged to collect, keep records and store radioactive waste in the prescribed manner and under prescribed conditions. The license owner is obliged to: (1) ensure that facilities and premises where radioactive waste is collected, kept, recorded and stored fully correspond to the technical, safety and other prescribed requirements providing human and environmental protection against ionizing radiation; (2) implementation of measures preventing radioactive waste to cause contamination of the environment; and (3) secure stored radioactive or nuclear material (Article 63, paragraph 1).

611. The Agency shall prescribe the method and conditions under which radioactive waste is to be collected, kept, recorded, stored, processed and disposed of (Article 63, paragraph 1). Temporary radioactive waste storage and final disposal shall be in the custody of the Republic of Serbia (Article 64, paragraph 1). Until providing conditions for final radioactive waste disposal, radioactive waste shall be temporary stored within legal entity licensed[663] for managing temporary radioactive waste storage (Article 64, paragraph 2).

---

661. *Environmental protection* is a set of measures for prevention of any potential harmful effects of ionizing radiation in the environment and mitigate the effects of such radiation (Art. 3, point 7).
662. The Plan referred to in para. 1 of this Article shall determine intervention levels and derive intervention levels of exposure to ionizing radiation and measures to be taken for the purpose of protecting humans and the environment from harmful effects of ionizing radiation, the method of informing public, and the programme of a periodic check up of adequacy of the Plan or parts thereof (Art. 62, para. 2); *Intervention levels* are levels of expected dose that may occur as a consequence of the accident or chronic exposure to ionizing radiation, when a specific protective measures or remedial action is taken (Art. 3, point 11).
663. The license owner for managing the temporary radioactive waste storage shall be obliged to maintain records of radioactive waste and to provide data from such records to the Agency within times and in a method specified by the Agency (Art. 64, para. 3).

K. *Traffic of Sources of Ionizing Radiation, Radioactive and Nuclear Materials*

612. Traffic of sources of ionizing radiation, radioactive and nuclear material shall be carried out by the legal entity or entrepreneur that fulfils requirements from Article 29 of this Law and license owner for carrying out traffic of sources of ionizing radiation, radioactive and nuclear material (Article 65, paragraph 1). Such activity is to be carried out only with previously obtained permit,[664] issued by the Agency[665] (Article 66, paragraph 1).

613. The Agency shall issue a license to the legal entity or entrepreneur who shall carry out import, export or transit of one or more sources of ionizing radiation, radioactive and nuclear material[666] if appropriate measures have been taken in order to ensure that such a transfer is carried out in compliance with ratified international conventions (Article 67, paragraph 1).

614. Import, export and transit of sources and nuclear materials shall be carried out only through the border crossing points with organized inspection services (Article 67, paragraph 4). The importer of one or more sources of ionizing radiation, and radioactive or nuclear materials, shall be obliged to inform, in due time frame, the competent inspector of the Agency about the shipment, at least sixty days in advance (Article 67, paragraph 5). In order to detect and prevent illicit trafficking of radioactive and nuclear materials across the borders of the Republic of Serbia,[667] radiation monitors shall be installed at border crossing points by the Government (Article 71, paragraph 1).

615. Transport of sources of ionizing radiation, radioactive and nuclear material, on the territory of the Republic of Serbia shall be carried out in compliance with the regulations for the safe transport of hazardous material, as well as in compliance with international conventions on transport of hazardous materials (Article 68, paragraph 1).

616. For the purpose of implementing radiation protection measures, it shall not be allowed to import foodstuffs, drinking water, fodder, fertilizers, and medicinal products, general purpose goods, building materials, ores, metal products, mineral raw materials, secondary raw materials and other goods if they contain radionuclide above

664. *Permit* is a written document issued by the Agency for the transport of one or several sources of ionizing radiation, as well as radioactive and nuclear materials (Art. 3, point 5).
665. The Agency shall issue permit for traffic of sources of ionizing radiation, radioactive and nuclear material only if such traffic is in accordance with the Law on Ratification of the Vienna Convention for Civil Liability for Nuclear Damage (Art. 66, para. 2).
666. The Agency shall issue a license to such entity or entrepreneur only with the prior notification and consent of the State of destination (Art. 67, para. 1).
667. The Agency shall prescribe procedure for installation of monitors, their application and intervention in the case of illicit trafficking of radioactive and nuclear materials, over the border of the Republic of Serbia (Art. 71, para. 2). *Interventions* are systematic and anticipated measures intended to reduce existing level of the exposure or the likelihood of exposure which are a consequence of an accident (Art. 3, point 13).

the prescribed limits (Article 69, paragraph 1).[668] The Agency shall prescribe the methods and the manner for carrying out control of radioactivity of goods referred to in Article 69, paragraph 1 of this Law (Article 70, paragraph 1).

L. *Liability for Nuclear Damages, Monitoring, Transitional and Final Provisions*

617. The license owner for performing nuclear activity shall be liable for nuclear damage caused by a nuclear accident, in compliance to Law on ratification of the Vienna Convention for Civil Liability for Nuclear Damage and in compliance to this Law (Article 72, paragraph 1). The right to compensation for nuclear damages[669] shall cease after the expiration of ten years of the date when the nuclear accident occurred (Article 74, paragraph 1).

618. Monitoring implementation of measures for protection from ionizing radiation shall be carried out only by the Minister competent for radiation protection through its inspectors for radiation protection (Article 76, paragraph 1). Monitoring implementation of nuclear safety measures shall be carried out only by the Minister competent for nuclear safety and radioactive waste management through its inspectors for nuclear safety and radioactive waste management (Article 76, paragraph 2).

II. Law on Prohibiting Construction of Nuclear Power Plants

619. Another law that should be mentioned is the Law on Prohibiting Construction of Nuclear Power Plants in FRY (OJ FRY, No. 12/95, OJ RS, No. 85/05) now in Serbia. It is a very concise legal Act containing only five Articles, which forbids construction of nuclear power plants, installations for production of nuclear fuel and installations for treatment of used nuclear fuel (Article 1). It does not forbid scientific and research activities, mining and geological research, and geological seismic research and educational activities (Article 2).

668. It shall not be allowed to export secondary raw materials, if they contain radionuclides above the limits prescribed by the Agency (Art. 69, para. 2). Also, transit over the territory of the Republic of Serbia shall be prohibited for secondary raw materials and metal products if they contain radionuclides above the prescribed limit (Art. 69, para. 3).

669. Claims for compensation for nuclear damages can be submitted within a period of three years from the time when the legal or physical persons who suffered damage learnt or should reasonably have learnt about the nuclear damage and about the user who is liable for it, provided that the time frames set out in Art. 74 of this Law shall not be exceeded (Art. 75, para. 1). If the nuclear damage was caused during transport of nuclear materials, decisions shall be in the jurisdiction of the court in the territory where the nuclear accident happened (Art. 75, para. 3).

III. Other Relevant Legislation

620. In line with Law on Ionized Radiation Protection and Nuclear Safety the Rulebook on the Programme for Systematic Examination of Radioactivity in Environment (OJ RS, No. 100/2010 of 28 December 2010) has been adopted.

621. Following by-laws are adopted on the base of the Law on Ionized Radiation Protection and on Nuclear Safety (OJ of RS, Nos 36/09 and 93/12):

- Regulation on determining the Programme of Nuclear Safety and Security (OJ of RS, No. 39/14).
- Regulation on the security measures of nuclear facilities and nuclear materials (OJ of RS, No. 39/14).
- Rulebook on Records on Performed Activities in the Field of Radiation Protection (OJ of RS, No. 17/11).
- Rulebook on Notification and Registration of Radiation Sources (OJ of RS, No. 25/11).
- Rulebook on procedure of keeping records of nuclear materials (OJ of RS, No. 27/11).
- Rulebook for Establishing Programme of Additional Training and Specialized Education of Occupationally Exposed Persons and Persons Responsible for Implementation of Radiation Protection Measures (OJ of RS, No. 31/11).
- Rulebook on the performance of nuclear activities (OJ of RS, No. 37/11).
- Rulebook on conditions for obtaining licence to perform nuclear activity (OJ of RS, No. 37/11).
- Rulebook on Limits of Radioactive Contamination of People, Working and Living Environment and Ways of Performing Decontamination (OJ of RS, No. 38/11).
- Rulebook on Limits of Exposure to Ionizing Radiation and Measurements for Assessment of the Exposure Levels (OJ of RS, No. 86/11).
- Rulebook on Radioactivity Control of Goods During the Import, Export and Transit (OJ of RS, No. 44/11).
- Rulebook on radioactive water management (OJ of RS, No. 60/11).
- Rulebook on Conditions for Obtaining Licence to Perform Radiation Practices (OJ of RS, No. 61/11 and 101/16).
- Rulebook for Establishing Programme for Early Warning of Emergency (OJ of RS, No. 70/11).
- Rulebook on Limits of Radionuclides Content in Drinking Water, Foodstuffs, Feeding Stuffs, Medicines, Products for General Use, Construction Materials and Other Goods That are Put on Market (OJ of RS, No. 86/11 and 97/13).
- Rulebook on the Records of Radiation Sources, Professionally Exposed Persons, Patients Exposure to Ionizing Radiation and Radioactive Waste (OJ of RS, No. 97/11).
- Rulebook on Radioactivity Monitoring (OJ of RS, No. 97/11).
- Rulebook on Application of the Radiation Sources in Medicine (OJ of RS, No. 1/12).
- Rulebook on Conditions for Obtaining Decisions to Perform Activities in the Field of Radiation Protection (OJ of RS, No. 101/16).

IV. International Conventions

622. Serbia is a contracting party to the following international conventions in the field of nuclear safety:

- Vienna Convention on Civil Liability for Nuclear Damage (1963) (OJ SFRY – IT, No. 5/77).
- Convention on the Physical Protection of Nuclear Material (1979) (OJ SFRY – IT, Nos 9/85 and 4/2016).
- Convention on Early Notification of a Nuclear Accident (1986) (OJSFRY – IT, No. 15/89).
- Treaty on the Non-Proliferation of Nuclear Weapons, Law on Ratification (OJ SFRY, No. 10/70).
- Statute of the IAEA (OJ SFRY, No. 01/58).
- Convention on Assistance in the Case of a Nuclear Accident or Radiological Emergency, Law on Ratification (OJ SFRY – IT, No. 04/91).
- Law on Ratification of the Law on Comprehensive Nuclear Test Ban with Protocol CTBT (OJ SM – IT, No. 4/04).
- Agreement between the Government of the Republic of Serbia and the Government of the Russian Federation Concerning Cooperation on the Import of Irradiated Nuclear Fuel from a Research Reactor into the Russian Federation (OJ RS – IT, No. 105/09).
- Agreement between the Government of Hungary and the Government of the Republic of Serbia for the Early Exchange of Information in the Event of Radiological Emergency (OJ of RS IT, No. 19/15).

In preparation for ratification are the following: Convention on Nuclear Safety, Joint Convention on the Safety of Spent Fuel Management and on the Safety of Radioactive Waste Management, and Protocol Additional to the Agreement for the Application of Safeguards in connection with the Treaty on the Non-Proliferation of Nuclear Weapons.[670]

623. 'On nuclear energy, nuclear security and radiation protection, Serbia's legislation is partially in line with the acquis. Further alignment is needed on radioactive waste management, radiation protection, spent fuel, nuclear safety and security. Serbia is a signatory of a number of key conventions, treaties and agreements including on non-proliferation, protection of nuclear material and notification of nuclear accidents.'[671]

670. *See* : http://www.srbatom.gov.rs/srbatom/medjunarodni-ugovori.htm (1Jun. 2017).

671. The Radiation Protection and Nuclear Safety Agency is insufficiently staffed to perform its duties. In December 2015, the number of permanent staff posts was reduced from thirty-five to twenty-four. Inspection functions have not yet been transferred to the Agency. The Agency's budget is insufficient to ensure its proper functioning and operational independence. CR, 47.

V. Non-ionizing Radiation

A. *The Law on Protection from Non-ionizing Radiation*

624. The Law on Protection from Non-ionizing Radiation (OJ RS, No. 36/09) contains twenty-three Articles divided into the following parts: Basic Provisions (Articles 1 and 2), Principles (Article 3), Measures of Protection from Non-ionizing Radiation[672] (Articles 4–13), Supervision (Articles 14–16), Competence for Complaints Resolving (Article 17), Penal Provisions (Articles 18–20), and Transitional and Final Provisions (Articles 21–23). The Law regulates conditions and measures of protection of human health and the environment from harmful impact of non-ionizing radiation. Protection from professional exposition to sources of non-ionizing radiation is not regulated by this Law (Article 1).[673]

B. *Principles*

625. Non-ionizing radiation protection is based on the following fundamental principles:

(1) *principle of prohibition* – exposition to non-ionizing radiation above prescribed limit and every unnecessary exposition are not allowed;
(2) *principle of proportionality* – conditions and permissibility of use of sources of non-ionizing radiation of special interest are determined and rated according to the benefit their use represents for the society, in relation to potential risks of harmful impact caused by their use, and taking into account the level and duration of exposition of population in each specific case, age and state of health of exposed population, method, time and place of use of such source, presence of other

672. *Non-ionizing radiations are* electromagnetic radiation that have photon energy below 12.4 eV. They include: ultraviolet radiation (wavelength 100–400 nm), visible radiation (wavelength 400–780 nm), infrared radiation (wavelength 780nm–1 mm), radiofrequency radiation (frequency 10 kHz–300 GHz), electromagnetic fields of low frequencies (frequency 0–10 kHz) and laser radiation. Non-ionizing radiation also includes ultrasound and sound that has frequency higher than 20 kHz (Art. 2, point 1).

673. Based on the Law on Protection from Non-ionizing Radiation several by-laws have been adopted. These are following: Regulation on determining the programme of systematic examination of the levels of non-ionizing radiation for the period 2017–2018 (OJ RS, No. 02/17), Rulebook on condition to be fulfilled by legal entities performing tasks of systematic examination of the levels of non-ionizing radiation, and the manner and methods of systematic examination in the environment (OJ RS, No. 104/09), Rulebook on the sources of non/ionizing radiation of special interest, types, sources, manner and period of their examination (OJ RS, No. 104/09), Rulebook on the contents of records of the sources of non-ionizing radiation of special interest (OJ RS, No. 104/09), Rulebook on the limits of exposure to non-ionizing radiation (OJ RS, No. 104/09), Rulebook on the content and appearance of the form of the report on systematic examination of the levels of non-ionizing radiation in the environment (OJ RS, No. 104/09), and Rulebook on the conditions to be fulfilled by legal entities performing tasks of examination of the levels of sources of non-ionizing radiation in the environment (OJ RS, No. 104/09).

sources with different frequencies, as well as other relevant circumstances of each specific case;
(3) *principle of publicity* – data on non-ionizing radiation are accessible to the public (Article 3).

C. *Measures of Protection from Non-ionizing Radiation*

626. During the process of protection from non-ionizing radiation the following measures are undertaken:

(1) regulation of limits of exposition to non-ionizing radiation;
(2) detection and measurement of levels of exposition to non-ionizing radiation;
(3) determination of conditions for use of sources of non-ionizing radiation of special interest;
(4) realization of organizational, technical, financial and other conditions for implementation of protection from non-ionizing radiation;
(5) keeping evidence of sources of non-ionizing radiation of special interest;
(6) labelling sources of non-ionizing radiation of special interest and zones of dangerous radiation in the prescribed way;
(7) implementation of control and assurance of quality of sources of non-ionizing radiation of special interest in the prescribed way;
(8) application of means and equipment for protection from non-ionizing radiation;
(9) control of levels of exposition to non-ionizing radiation in the environment and control of undertaken measures of protection from non-ionizing radiation;
(10) providing material, technical and other conditions for systematic testing and monitoring of levels of non-ionizing radiation in the environment;
(11) education and professional training of staff in the field of protection from non-ionizing radiation in the environment;
(12) informing population about impact on health of exposition to non-ionizing radiation and measures of protection and informing on level of exposition to non-ionizing radiation in the environment (Article 4).

627. Systematic testing of levels of non-ionizing radiation in the environment is performed, aimed at detecting presence, detecting danger, informing and undertaking measures of protection from non-ionizing radiation (Article 5).[674]

628. Systematic testing of levels of non-ionizing radiation in the environment can be performed by commercial society, enterprise and other legal person if they fulfil conditions regarding staff, equipment and space.

Persons who perform systematic testing of levels of non-ionizing radiation in the environment, are obliged to submit to the Ministry (and for territory of AP to the competent organ of AP) annual report on results of testing, at the latest till 31 March

674. The Government adopts the Programme systematic testing of levels of non-ionizing radiation in the environment for a period of two years (Art. 5, para. 2).

of the current year for previous year, and in the case of exceptional event immediately (Article 5).[675]

629. Commercial society, enterprise, other legal person and entrepreneur can use sources of non-ionizing radiation of special interest if they fulfil the following conditions: (1) if they have for the sources of non-ionizing radiation an estimate of their impact on the environment, in accordance with this Law; (2) if the level of exposition of the population does not exceed prescribed limits (Article 6, paragraph 1).[676] The entities referred to in paragraph 1 of this Article must not start the use of non-ionizing radiation source of the special interest before they receive the Act on compliance with all the conditions for their use.[677]

630. Also, commercial entity, enterprise or other legal entity can execute detection of the level of non-ionizing radiation sources of special interest in the environment if they comply with the conditions regarding personnel, equipment and space (Article 10). Compliance with paragraph 1 of this Article shall be determined by the Minister by issuing the decision, and for the territory of the AP the competent authority of the AP.[678]

D. *Obligations of Commercial Society, Enterprise, Other Legal Person and Entrepreneur Who Use Sources of Non-ionizing Radiation of Special Interest*[679]

631. Commercial society, enterprise, other legal person and entrepreneur, who use sources of non-ionizing radiation of special interest, are obliged to do the following:

675. The Minister prescribes in detail conditions that must be fulfilled by persons who perform systematic testing of levels of non-ionizing radiation, as well as ways and methods of systematic testing of levels of non-ionizing radiation in the environment (Art. 5, para. 8).
676. Compliance with the conditions of para. 1 of this Article shall be authorized by the Minister by issuing the decision, and for the territory of the AP the competent authority of the AP (Art. 2, para. 2). However, it should be mentioned that provisions of Art. 6 of this Law do not apply to sources of non-ionizing radiation of special interest registered by the Ministry competent for defence and the Ministry of Internal Affairs. Exceptionally, provisions of Art. 6 of this Law do not apply to: (1) sources of non-ionizing radiation that are transported by railway, motor vehicles, airplane or by water transport, if they are technically secured so that they cannot be used nor they can generate non-ionizing radiation and (2)sources of non-ionizing radiation that are stored or that are used for selling or in other purposes in such a state that they are not possible to be put in working function or used in a way which could represent potential danger (Art. 7).
677. The Minister prescribes: (1) limits of exposition to non-ionizing radiation and (2) sources that are regarded as sources of non-ionizing radiation of special interest, as well as the method of their testing (Art. 6, para. 6).
678. The Minister shall determine other conditions that entities referred to in para. 1 of this Article shall have to comply with. The Minister, or the competent authority of the AP, shall detract the license for detection of non-ionizing radiation sources referred to in para. 2 of this Article, if it is subsequently determined that the commercial entity, enterprise or other legal entity does not comply with the formal conditions or if it is determined that the decision is issued based on untrue or inaccurate data (Art. 10, paras 4 and 5).
679. Commercial entity, enterprise, other legal entity or entrepreneur that use the non-ionizing radiation sources are obligated to coordinate their operations with the provisions of this Law within three years of its coming into force (Art. 22).

- to keep record on these sources and to designate a person responsible for protection from non-ionizing radiation (Article 8, paragraph 1);[680]
- to organize testing of levels of their radiation in the environment (Article 9, paragraph 1);[681]
- to organize first testing of radiation of sources from paragraph 1 of this Article, before the commencement of their use, in case of increase of their number, or in case of change of conditions of their use, or in case of reconstruction of objects with sources of non-ionizing radiation.

632. Periodically, the detection of the level of the non-ionizing radiation source referred to in paragraph 1 of this Article shall be executed in the specified period of time (Article 9, paragraph 3).[682]

633. In addition to the above-mentioned commercial society, enterprise, other legal person and entrepreneur who use sources of non-ionizing radiation of special interest are obliged to keep evidence and documentation on testing of sources of non-ionizing radiation (Article 11).[683]

634. Commercial society, enterprise, other legal person and entrepreneur, that is, operator or manager, is obliged immediately, and at the latest in hours, to inform the Ministry about the extraordinary event, and for the territory of AP competent organ of AP, or organ of the unit of LSG competent for activities concerning protection of the environment (Article 12).[684]

E. Supervision

635. Supervision over application of provisions of this Law and regulations adopted on the basis of this Law is performed by the Ministry. The AP performs inspectoral supervision over sources of non-ionizing radiation on the territory of AP, in accordance with this Law. The unit of local self-government performs inspectoral supervision over sources of non-ionizing radiation for which the permit for construction and commencement of work has been issued by the competent organ of the unit of local self-government (Article 14). [685]

---

680. The Minister shall determine in detail the contents of the record (Art. 8, para. 3).
681. Costs of the detection of the sources referred to in para. 1 of this Article shall be beared by the user of the source.
682. The Minister shall determine the types of non-ionizing radiation sources of special interest for which the detection of the level of non-ionizing radiation is obligatory, as well as the period of time for their detection (Art. 9, para. 5).
683. Public has the right to access information in accordance with this Law (Art. 11, para. 2).
684. The notice referred to in para. 1 of this Article shall contain particularly information on circumstances of the emergency, place, time, direct danger for human health and the short description of undertaken measures (Art. 12, para. 2).
685. SEPA maintains records and prepares a database of sources of non-ionizing radiation of particular interest, which is envisaged to become a part of the National Register of Pollution Sources. EPR (2015), 19.

Chapter 8. Other Sectors

§1. Noxious Substances

636. Use and production of potentially dangerous chemicals in Serbia is one of the main hazards for the environment. The lack of financial means for renewal of technology and for environmental protection, obsolete technologies and other reasons have made some installations in this sector of industry sources of pollution. It should be added that the situation became especially bad during the UN sanctions and the 1999 NATO intervention. A number of potentially dangerous installations were bombed (especially Pancevo and Novi Sad refineries) and heavy pollution was caused, impact of which is still felt.

In 2008, 761 companies were engaged in the manufacture of chemicals and chemical products in the Republic of Serbia, which is 0.9% of total number of companies of non-financial business economy. The number of persons employed in this field was 24,849, which is 2.3% of persons employed in non-financial business economy. Turnover in manufacture of chemicals and chemical products in 2008 was RSD 1,77,124 million (EUR 1,999 million), which is 3.0% turnover in non-financial business economy.[686]

637. In order to identify locations which present highest potential chemical risks, a Preliminary List of Seveso II Establishments was developed in 2008, including first and second-tier establishments, containing 132 companies which are obligated to develop Safety Report and Contingency Plan, that is, that are obligated to develop accident prevention policy.[687]

---

686. AECQ, Chs 27, 235. 'Export of chemicals and chemical products from the Republic of Serbia into European Union in 2008 amounted to 396.1 million Euros, in 2009 163.1 million Euros, and in the first ten months of 2010 253.9 million Euros. Export of chemicals and chemical products from the Republic of Serbia into EFTA in 2008 amounted to 1.5 million Euros, in 2009 1.2 million Euros, and in the first ten months of 2010 2.8 million Euros. Number of products (at the level 10 digit of Serbia's custom tariff) exported to European Union countries in 2009 was 389, and into EFTA countries 38'. *Ibid.*, 236.

687. These are the companies which perform different industrial activities and which may have certain types of dangerous substances in their locations in quantities that exceed the prescribed ones. Some of them are: NIS a.d. Novi Sad, organizational parts Oil Refinery in Pancevo and Oil Refinery in Novi Sad, HIP Azotara – artificial fertilizers, HIP Petrohemija – petrochemical products- Bor (Mining and Smelter Complex Bor), Sabac (HI Zorka – artificial fertilizers, PVC, pesticides), Sremska Mitrovica ('Matroz' – pulp and paper production), Belgrade (Prva iskra Baric – basic chemicals, TPP 'Nikola Tesla' A and B), Subotica (Zorka Holding – artificial fertilizers, inorganic acids; Azotara –nitrogen and complex fertilizers), Loznica (production of pulp, synthetic fibres and plastic materials), NEPP, 54. 'Over the past five years, twelve people dies in chemical accidents, while even more were injured and intoxicated. Material damage was also made in those accidents. However, the environment was not significantly endangered in any of the cases.' *Ibid.*, 55.

638. In accordance with Article 5 of the Law on Chemicals (2009) the Government established the Chemical Agency, 'as an independent, developing, professional and regulatory organization performing public competences in compliance with the Law, in order to ensure administrative conditions for quality, efficient and sound chemicals and biocidal products management'.[688] However, Agency stopped to work by the adoption of Amendments of the Law on Chemicals, 25 September 2012. (OJ RS, No. 93/12). The rights and obligations of the Chemicals Agency, established by the Decision on the Establishment of the Chemicals Agency (OJ RS, No. 78/09), as well as employees, objects, equipment, archives, and registries, has been transferred to the Ministry of Energy, Development and Environmental Protection (Article 17).[689]

---

688. Pursuant to Art. 6 of the Law on Chemicals (2009) the Chemical Agency shall be responsible for: (1) enacting of sub-legal Acts for the implementation of the Law on Chemicals and Law on Biocidal Products; (2) adopting of a list of classified substances; (3) issuing of a ruling on entry of a chemical into the Chemicals Registry and keeping that Registry; (4) keeping the integrated Chemicals Registry; (5) publishing the list of substances of very high concern; (6) conducting of notification procedure and the prior informed consent procedure for import and export of certain hazardous chemicals; (7) issuing of permits for distribution and use of particularly hazardous chemicals; (8) issuing of an approval for use of surfactants in detergents; (9) preparation and implementation of the projects for monitoring if chemicals are placed on the market and used in such a way that they do not have adverse effects on human health, environment and property; (10) publishing of the lists of active substances in biocidal products; (11) issuing of ruling on the entry of biocidal product in temporary list for delivery of Technical Dossier; (12) issuing of the authorization for placing the biocidal product on the market; (13) assessment of Technical Dossier for the biocidal product; (14) preparation of annual declarations on production, processing and use of chemicals from the lists given by the law which regulates the prohibition of the development, production, stockpiling and use of chemical weapons and their destruction, as well as annual declarations on production of discreet organic substances and conducts other tasks pursuant to that Law; (15) providing professional and administrative – technical assistance for the Joint Body for the Integrated Chemicals Management; (16) Providing information and professional instructions to the economic operators, LSG units and inspectors, for the purpose of implementation of this Law and other laws under the competence of the Agency, as well as to provide professional assessment on properties and intended use of certain chemicals; (17) carrying out cooperation with the European Chemicals Agency, other countries Agencies and Secretariats of International Conventions which regulate chemical management and other international organizations dealing with different aspects of chemicals management; (18) carrying out activities of awareness raising on the effects of chemicals on human health and environment, risk reduction measures and sound use of chemicals; and (19) carrying out other activities set out in this Law, Law on Biocidal products and other laws.

689. Dismantling of the functional Chemicals Agency (and of the Green Fund), … remain issues of concern, especially in relation to the overall capacity of these institutions to ensure effective implementation and enforcement of the *acquis*. SRS, Chs 27, 18.

I. Legal Regulation

639. EPL contains general provisions concerning dangerous substances.[690] Article 10 of the Law prescribes that 'sustainable management of natural values as well as the protection of the environment shall be governed by this Law, special laws and other regulations, governing', *inter alia*, 'chemicals management'.[691] Management of dangerous substances shall be carried out under the conditions and in the manner that ensures reduction of risk from their properties dangerous to the environment and human health in the process of production, storage, utilization and disposal (Article 29). Legal or natural persons managing dangerous substances is obliged to plan, organize and undertake all the necessary preventive, protective, safety and rehabilitation measures by which the risk towards the environment and human health shall be reduced to the least possible level.

640. There are a number of other provisions of the EPL that are relevant to dangerous substances issue. These provisions relate to the following: Accident Risk Management and Obligation of Natural and Legal Entities (Article 38); Conditions for Facilities' Work and Activities (Article 40); Ecological Label (Article 53); Protection from the Chemical Accident – Obligations of Operators (Article 58);[692] Content of the Policy for Accident Prevention (Article 58a); Obligation to Submit Notification (Article 59); Content of the Report of the Safety and Plan on Protection from Accident (Article 60); Submitting the Report on Safety and Plan on Protection from Accident (Article 60a); Submitting Information from the Plan on Protection from Accident (Article 60b); Public Availability, Presentation and Public Debate on the Report on Safety (Article 60c); Evidence in the Report on Safety (Article 60d); Evidence in the Plan on Protection from Accident (Article 60e);Consent on the Report on Safety and the Plan on Protection from Accident (Article 60f); Decision Prohibiting Operation or Start-Up of Seveso Installation (Article 60g); Appointment of the Special Working Group (Article 60h); Obligation of Keeping Records (Article 60i); Register of Installations and Register of Reported Accidents (Article 60j); Informing of the Accident (Article 60k);Obligations of Responsible Authorities (Article 61); Notification on Operators or Seveso Installations or Establishments the Activities of Which May Cause Chemical Accident with Transboundary Effects (Article 61a); Obligation to Submit Notification of the Responsible Authority of Other Country (Article 61b); Exceptions (Article 61c);Proclamation of the State of Endangerment (Article 62); Rehabilitation Measures and Subsidiary

690. Dangerous substances are 'chemicals or other substances with harmful or hazardous intrinsic properties' (Art. 3, point 21). The definition is closely linked to the definition of 'accident'. *See* Part I (Ch. 1 General Law IV – Integrated Pollution Prevention and Control and Risk Management).

691. Similarly, like in case of Art. 65 which stipulate that Action plans shall be made for, *inter alia*, chemicals management.

692. Legal or natural person producing, transporting, placing on the market, use, processing, storing or disposing dangerous substances is obliged to: (1) make the plan for accident prevention and update or review the same every three years, at least, in compliance with the changes in the operations of the plant, applying technology or operations, including the check up readiness for its implementation; (2) implement preventive and other measures management of risk from accident from the plan of accident prevention; and (3) make the report on safety state which shall be available to public and, at least once in five years, like in case of changes in operation and activities of a plant, to review the report on safety state (Art. 58, para. 2).

Liability (Article 63); Rehabilitation Plan (Article 66); and Rights and Duties of the Inspector (Article 110) and Commercial Offences (Article 116).

II. Specific Legislation

A. Law on Chemicals

641. The Law on Chemicals (*Off. Jour. of RS*, Nos 36/2009, 88/2010, 92/2011, 93/2012 and 25/2015) is the basic legal Act regulating the use of chemicals as products.

It contains 108 Articles grouped in following groups: basic provisions (Articles 1–4); competencies of the Ministry responsible for environmental protection(Articles 5 and 6); integrated management of chemicals (Articles 7 and 8); classification, packing, labelling and storage of chemicals (Articles 9–33); counsellor for chemicals (Articles 34–37); integrated Register of chemicals (Articles 38–48); limits and prohibitions of production, marketing and use of chemicals (Articles 49 and 50); import and export of certain dangerous chemicals (Articles 51–62); permits for marketing and use of extra dangerous chemicals (Articles 63–72); detergents (Articles 73–81); taxes (Article 81a);systematic detection of chemicals (Articles 82 and 83); availability of data (Articles 84 and 85); supervision (Articles 86–96); penal provisions (Articles 97–101); and transitional and final provisions (Articles 102–108).

642. By this Law is regulated integrated management of chemicals[693] classification, packing, and labelling of chemicals, integrated Register of chemicals and Register of chemicals on the market, limits and prohibitions of production, marketing and use of chemicals, import and export of certain dangerous chemicals, permits for marketing and use of extra dangerous chemicals, marketing of detergents, systematic detection of chemicals, availability of data, supervision and other issues of importance for

693. *'Chemical'* means a substance and mixture (Art. 3, point 20).

management of chemicals (Article 1).[694] The Law is based on the principle of prevention and principle that the producer, importer or further user, produces, puts in the market and uses chemicals in such a way to avoid harmful consequences to human health and the environment (Article 2).

1. Competencies of the Ministry Responsible for Environmental Protection

643. The Ministry responsible for environmental protection provides conditions for quality, efficient, and safe management of chemicals and biocidal products (Article 5).

Some of the responsibilities of the Ministry responsible for the environmental protection are the following: (1) adopt the by-laws for implementation of the Law on Chemicals and Law on Biocidal Products; (2) adopt the list of classified substances; (3) issues a decision on registration of chemicals in the Register of chemicals and water that register; (4) keeps integrated register of chemicals; (5) publish the list of substances of very high concern; (6) issues permits for performing activities of transport particularly hazardous chemicals; (7) issues licenses for the use of surfactants in detergents; (8) develops and implements projects to monitor whether chemicals are placed on the market and used in such a way that they have no harmful effect on human health, the environment and property; (9) announces the list of the active substances in the biocide product; (10) adopt the decision on inclusion of the biocidal product into the Temporary List for the submission of the technical dossier; and (11) issue approvals for placing on the market of biocidal products, etc. (Article 6, paragraph 1).

694. Provisions of the Law do not apply to: (1) radioactive chemicals; (2) chemicals in transit; (3) transport of dangerous chemicals (Art. 4, para. 1) and the following:(1) chemicals that are regarded as waste according to provisions of the Law that regulate waste management and (2) chemicals that are under duty supervision in the duty storage or in free zones with intent to be exported again or sent into transit, if they are not prefabricated on the spot (Art. 4, para. 2). Provisions of the Law that regulate recording of chemicals in the Register of Chemicals and recording of substances that arise worry in the Register of Chemicals, do not apply to chemicals which are put on the market in their final form as: (1) biocide products; (2) means for plant protection; (3) medicines and medical supplies used in human and veterinary medicine; (4) cosmetic products; (5) food, food additives and aromas; (6) animal food and animal food additives (Art. 4, para. 2). Provisions of the Law that regulate classification, packing and labelling of chemicals, do not apply to chemicals:(1) that are used for scientific research and development and which are not on the market and which are kept under controlled conditions and low exposition and (2) which are put on the market in their final form as medicines and medical supplies used in human and veterinary medicine; cosmetic products; food, food additives and aromas; animal food and animal food additives (Art. 4, para. 3). Provisions of the Law from Ch. VIII (that regulate import and export of certain dangerous chemicals) do not apply to: (1) chemical weapons and precursors for chemical weapons; (2) precursors of narcotics and psychotropic substances; (3) food and food additives; (4) animal food and additives for that food; (5) medicines and medical supplies used in human and veterinary medicine; (6) chemicals used for scientific research and development in quantity which does not have harmful impact on human health and environment, and does not exceed 10 kg for each chemical in one import (Art. 4, para. 5).

2. Integrated Management of Chemicals

644. With intention to realize principles of strategic approach to the management of chemicals, to apply adequate management of chemicals in all stages of life cycle of chemicals, from production to import and dumping, as well as to contribute to sustainable development of the Republic of Serbia, the minister competent for the environment (minister), in accordance with regulations concerning State administration, with his/her decision establishes the joint body for integrated management of chemicals (Joint body) (Article 7, paragraph 1).[695]

645. Task of the Joint body is to prepare the integrated programme of management of chemicals and action plans for implementation of that programme, as well as implementation of programmes and action plans and coordination of activities in connection with secure management of chemicals(Article 7, paragraph 4).[696]

3. Classification, Packing, Labelling and Storage of Chemicals

646. Producer, importer or final user that puts chemicals and certain products on the market is obliged to classify them, and supplier of chemicals to label and pack them in accordance with this Law and regulations adopted on basis of it (Article 9, paragraph 1).[697]

647. Classification of chemicals and certain products is done on the basis of evaluation of their physical and chemical characteristics, characteristics that influence human life and health, characteristics that have an impact on the environment, as well as the established criteria of classification of different classes of danger (Article 10, paragraph 1).[698] Dangerous chemicals can be further classified in different ways depending on the impact they have on people or on the environment or on the base of the nature of the chemical effects (Article 10, paragraph 3).[699]

648. Supplier is obliged to keep evidence (record) about chemicals, especially concerning data of their identity, distributors, final users and quantity of distributed chemicals, as well as of total quantity of chemicals distributed to users during a calendar

695. The Joint body is composed of representatives of State organs, in the field of the chemical management, industry, scientific research organizations and NGOs (Art. 7, para. 2).
696. The integrated programme of management of chemicals is adopted by the Government (Art. 7, para. 5).
697. Exporter is obliged to label and pack chemicals in accordance with this Law and regulations adopted on basis of it, except in case when it is needed to label and pack chemicals in a different way, in accordance with international standards, and if the importing country wants so (Art. 9, para. 2).
698. A dangerous chemical is a chemical that belongs to at least one class of danger (Art. 10, para. 2).
699. The Ministry responsible for the environment regulates in detail the method of classification of chemicals and certain products (Art. 10, para. 4); the list of classified substances (Art. 11, para. 3); methods of testing dangerous characteristics of chemicals (Art. 15); method of packing and labelling of chemicals and certain products (Art. 16); method of advertising chemicals (Art. 17), etc.

year (Article 19).[700] Apart from this, supplier is obliged to produce a safety data sheet when he/she puts on the market a dangerous chemical, chemical which contains substances identified as persistent – bio cumulative – toxic (PBT) or very persistent – very bio cumulative (vPvB) and other chemicals having characteristics described in Article 43, paragraph 3 of this Law, or to any other distributor or final user in the supply chain without charge, in Serbian language in printed or electronic form (Article 20, paragraph 1). Exporter of chemicals is obliged to present to the importer a safety data sheet, and if possible the safety data sheet should be in the language of the importing country (Article 20, paragraph 2).[701] If the report on security of chemicals and scenario of exposition are prepared, information in safety data sheet must correspond to information from the report on security of chemicals, and scenario of exposition must be enclosed in the annex of the safety data sheet (Article 20, paragraph 4).

4. Chemicals Adviser

649. Supplier of dangerous chemicals is obliged to provide a person whose duty is to take care of correct management of chemicals (chemicals adviser) (Article 34, paragraph 1). Exceptionally, certain suppliers of dangerous chemicals are not obliged to provide a chemical adviser (Article 34, paragraph 2).[702] Chemicals adviser must have appropriate professional qualification and to have passed the examination for chemical adviser. Knowledge of the chemical adviser shall be tested every six years (Article 35, paragraphs 1–2).[703]

5. Integrated Register of Chemicals

650. Integrated Register of chemicals on the market of Republic of Serbia includes the Register of chemicals and the Register of biocide products, as well as of data concerning means for herbal protection (Article 38, paragraph 1).[704]

700. The Ministry responsible for the environment prescribes method of evidence (record) keeping (Art. 19, para. 5).
701. Safety data sheet contains identification of chemicals, data of their characteristics, method of use, preventive measures, and measures for lessening of risk and data about the supplier of chemicals (Art. 20, para. 3). The Ministry responsible for the environment prescribes criteria for identification of substances as PBT or vPvB, as well as precise contents of the safety data sheet (Art. 20, para. 5).
702. The Ministry responsible for the environment prescribes kind, sector and field of supplier's activity (Art. 34, para. 3).
703. The Ministry responsible for the environment shall lay down the professional qualification, the training programme and the type of examination for the chemicals adviser (Art. 35, para. 3).
704. For the purpose of data exchange and integrated chemicals management, the Ministry responsible for the environment shall keep the Integrated Chemicals Registry as an electronic database (Art. 38, para. 4). Any chemical manufactured or imported on the market of the Republic of Serbia shall be entered into the Chemicals Registry (Art. 39, para. 1).

651. In order to ensure risk control and replacement of certain substance with suitable safer alternative substance, the Ministry responsible for the environment shall publish the list of substances of very high concern (Article 43, paragraph 1).[705]

6. Bans and Restrictions of the Manufacturing, Placing on the Market and Use of the Chemicals

652. The Ministry responsible for the environment prescribes, for chemicals that represent unacceptable risk for human health and the environment, limitations and prohibitions of their production, marketing and use (limitations and prohibitions) (Article 49, paragraph 1).[706]

7. Import and Export of Certain Dangerous Chemicals

653. With an intent of improving, sharing of responsibility and cooperation in international trade of dangerous chemicals, in accordance with the Rotterdam Convention, concerning the procedure of giving consent on the basis of preliminary information for certain dangerous chemicals and pesticides in international trade (Rotterdam Convention) for import and export of certain substances for which were introduced limitations and prohibitions of production, marketing and use, as well as certain combination of products that contain this substance, applied is procedure of preliminary information that is, procedure of giving consent on the basis of preliminary information (PIC procedure) (Article 51, paragraph 1). Procedure of preliminary information is applied to chemicals from the list of chemicals for procedure of preliminary information, and PIC procedure is applied to chemicals from the list of chemicals for PIC procedure (Article 51, paragraph 3).[707]

654. Procedure of preliminary information for export is applied by the Ministry responsible for the environment. It sends to the competent organ of the country of import information on export of chemicals from the list of chemicals for procedure of preliminary information, that is, chemical that contains a substance from this list in

705. The list of substances of very high concern shall consist of substances which meet the criteria for classification as carcinogenic categories 1 and 2, mutagenic categories 1 and 2, reproductive toxic categories 1 and 2, as well as of substances identified as PBT or vPvB (Art. 43, para. 2). The list of substances of very high concern shall also consist of substances which may lead to disturbance of endocrine system or have the PBT or vPvB properties, but do not meet the criteria for identification as PBT or vPvB, and it is scientifically proved that they cause significant damage to human health and to the environment (Art. 43, para. 3).

706. Regulation referred to in para. 1 of this Article shall consist of banned, i.e., allowed uses, as well as other conditions for manufacturing, placing on the market and use of substance, mixture and Article (Art. 49, para. 2).

707. The list of chemicals for procedure of preliminary information especially contains names of chemicals, identification numbers of chemicals, tariff number and subcategory of chemicals. The list of chemicals for PIC procedure especially contains names of chemicals, identification numbers of chemicals, tariff number and category of chemicals. The list of chemicals for procedure of preliminary information contains certain chemicals from the list of chemicals for PIC procedure. The list of chemicals for PIC procedure contains chemicals from the list of Rotterdam convention (Art. 51, paras 4–7).

such concentration that it could be, according to this Law, regarded as dangerous, as well as information on export of products which contain chemicals from the list of chemicals for PIC procedure (Article 53, paragraph 1). Exporter of chemicals and products is obliged, before the export, to lodge an application to the Ministry responsible for the environment for undertaking procedure of preliminary information, and with the application to supply information containing especially identity of chemicals, data about exporter and importer of chemicals or products, as well as data on characteristics of chemicals and on measures for minimizing of risk (Article 53, paragraph 2).

655. On the basis of information from the application of exporter of chemicals, the Ministry responsible for the environment prepares information for importing country and applies the procedure of preliminary information. The Ministry responsible for the environment is obliged to issue to the exporter a certificate that the procedure of preliminary information has been undertaken (Article 53, paragraph 4).[708]

656. Procedure of preliminary information for import has to be undertaken for chemicals for which production, marketing and use are prohibited or limited by regulations of the country of export. The Ministry responsible for the environment, after receiving information on export from the competent organ of the country of export, is obliged to inform that organ that it received the information (Article 54).

8. PIC Procedure

657. PIC procedure has to be undertaken for import or export of chemicals from the list of chemicals for PIC procedure or chemical that contains substance from this list in such concentration that, according to this Law, it should be labelled as dangerous (Article 55, paragraph 1). The Ministry responsible for the environment is obliged to send to the Secretariat of Rotterdam Convention information concerning every chemical from the list of Rotterdam Convention. Apart from that, the Ministry responsible for the environment is obliged to take action concerning the import of chemicals that are not on the list of Rotterdam Convention, by asking the competent organ of the country of export, if the country prescribes preliminary concord according to the PIC procedure (Article 55, paragraphs 2–3).[709]

The exporter shall, for the chemical from the list of chemicals subject to PIC procedure that is, for chemical containing the substance from this list in such concentration

708. The Ministry responsible for the environment prescribes procedure and time limits for procedure of preliminary information, cases when procedure of preliminary information is not needed, contents of information on export, as well as documents needed for the procedure (Art. 53, para. 5).

709. Response from paras 2 and 3 of this Article may be consent, consent under certain conditions or no consent, and shall be made based on the bans and restrictions set out in Art. 49 of this Law or pursuant to the Act which allows placing on the market of the chemical in accordance with the legislation regulating plant protection products or biocidal products (Art. 55, para. 4). The response referred to in paras 2 and 3 of this Article, for plant protection products, shall be made by the Ministry responsible for the environment in cooperation with the competent authority in charge of plant protection, and for chemicals with pesticide effect with the authority in charge of those chemicals (Art. 55, para. 5).

that is labelled as hazardous pursuant to this Law, submit request to conduct the PIC procedure to the Ministry responsible for the environment (Article 56).[710]

The Ministry responsible for the environment shall lay down detailed conditions and deadlines regarding PIC procedure, and content of the request for conducting of the PIC procedure (Article 57).

9. Other Provisions Regarding Export and Import of Chemicals

658. Exporter of chemicals from the list of chemicals for procedure of preliminary information, or for chemicals containing substances from that list, as well as for chemicals from the list of Chemicals for PIC procedure, or for chemicals containing substances from that list, is obliged to inform the Ministry responsible for the environment by 31 March of the current year, on quantities of exported chemicals or products during the previous year, as well as on data of the importer and on the country of import (Article 58, paragraph 1).

Importer of chemicals from the list of chemicals for procedure of preliminary information, or for chemicals containing substances from that list, as well as for chemicals from the list of chemicals for PIC procedure, or for chemicals containing substances from that list, is obliged to inform the Ministry responsible for the environment by 31 March of the current year, on data for previous year as prescribed in Article 42, p. 1 of this Law, as well as data about the country of export (Article 58, paragraph 2). Importer of products containing chemicals from the list of chemicals for PIC procedure is obliged to inform the Ministry responsible for the environment till 31 March of the current year, on data for previous year about the imported quantities, as well as data about the country of export.[711]

659. Exporter is obliged to inform the Ministry responsible for the environment about the request by the competent organ of a country member of the Rotterdam Convention, for transit of chemicals from the list of Rotterdam Convention, via the territory of that country at least thirty days before the first transit occurs or eight days prior any following transit (Article 59, paragraph 1).[712]

660. Certain dangerous chemicals and products are prohibited for use and cannot be exported. The Ministry responsible for the environment prescribes the list of

710. By the way of derogation from para. 1 of this Article, the exporter is not obliged to submit the request for conduction of the PIC procedure for the chemicals from Rotterdam Convention List, where the Party of the Rotterdam Convention delivered its response related to that chemical to the Secretariat of that Convention (Art. 56, para. 2).

711. The Ministry responsible for the environment on the basis of data from paras 1, 2 and 3 of Art. 58, keeps evidence, in the form of electronic data basis, of imported and exported chemicals or products according to the procedure of preliminary information and PIC procedure (Art. 58, para. 4).

712. The Ministry responsible for the environment shall forward the information on transit of the chemical to designated national authority of the Party to the Rotterdam Convention referred to in para. 1 of this Article no later than fifteen days before the first transit or prior to any subsequent transit (Art. 59, para. 2). The Ministry responsible for the environment shall lay down the list of parties to the Rotterdam Convention requiring information concerning transit movements of chemicals and the content of this information (Art. 59, para. 3).

dangerous chemicals and products that are prohibited for export (Article 60, paragraphs 1 and 4).[713]

661. Customs authority shall examine whether the notification procedure and/or PIC procedure has been conducted (Article 62).

10. Permits for Activities Concerning Marketing of Chemicals and for Use of Very Dangerous Chemicals

662. Marketing of certain dangerous chemicals (very dangerous chemicals) can be done only by legal persons or entrepreneurs who have permit for marketing such chemicals (Article 63, paragraph 1). Permit for marketing of very dangerous chemicals is issued to legal persons or entrepreneurs who have provided such storage of very dangerous chemicals in such a way as not to be attainable to persons who could use them in illegal purposes, and who have undertaken preventive measures for secure keeping and storage of very dangerous chemicals (Article 63, paragraph 2).[714]

663. Physical persons who use very dangerous chemicals must have permit for their use (Article 64, paragraph 1).[715]

664. Permit for marketing of very dangerous chemicals to importer, producer or final user is issued by the Ministry responsible for the environment (Article 67, paragraph 1).[716]

665. The Ministry responsible for the environment, or the organ of a self-government unit, can withdraw permit if correct data were not given during the procedure of issuance or if other conditions for permit issuance were not fulfilled. Against the decision can be lodged a complaint to the Minister. However, the Minister's decision is final and against it is possible to start an administrative court procedure (Article 70, paragraphs 1–3).

---

713. The Ministry responsible for the environment shall lay down the list of hazardous chemicals and articles subject to export ban (Art. 60, para. 4).

714. The Ministry responsible for the environment prescribes for which very dangerous chemicals are needed permits, and for which very dangerous chemicals they are not needed (Art. 63, para. 3).

715. Permit for use of very dangerous chemicals is issued to physical person who uses them in artistic, scientific and other specific purposes, if instead of these chemicals other alternative chemicals cannot be used, if they are used and kept in a secure way, and if the person has not been sentenced to jail longer than six months (Art. 64, para. 2).

716. Permit for marketing of very dangerous chemicals to distributor who is not importer, producer or final user, is issued by the competent organ of the self-government unit (Art. 67, para. 2). Scientific research institutions, persons engaged in cultural activities, organs of State administration, public agencies and organs of self-government units which need very dangerous chemicals for their work, as well as legal and physical persons who have permit for production and marketing of medicines in accordance with the law which regulates medicines, do not need permit for marketing of very dangerous chemicals (Art. 71).

11. Detergents

666. Producer of detergents[717] can put detergent on the market if surfactant contained in the detergent fulfils criteria of complete aerobic biodegrading and if chemicals and surfactants contained in the detergent fulfil other conditions prescribed by this Law (Article 73, paragraph 1). Exceptionally, detergent that contains surfactant which does not fulfil criteria of complete aerobic biodegrading can be put on the market if the Ministry responsible for the environment has issued permit for the use of that surfactant in detergent or if use of the surfactant in detergents is allowed in EU (Article 73, paragraph 3). In this case producer of detergent is obliged to send to the Ministry responsible for the environment officially certified copy of the EU regulation legalizing the use of surfactant.[718]

667. The list of surfactants for which permits have been issued or for which there exists an EU regulation allowing use of the surfactant in detergent, as well as the list of surfactants for which permits were refused or which are forbidden in the EU, are published in 'Official Journal of the Republic of Serbia' (Article 79).

668. Laboratory testing biodegrading surfactant must be accredited for adequate method of testing or its work must be harmonized with principles of good laboratory practice (Article 80).

669. Producer of detergent is obliged to keep results of testing, which prove that criterion of complete aerobic biodegrading of surfactants is fulfilled, and to send the data to the Ministry responsible for the environment if it demands so (Article 81, paragraph 1). Besides the obligations from this Law regarding classification, packing and labelling, producer of detergent is obliged to label detergent in accordance with regulations on labelling adopted on the basis of this Law. Producer of detergent intended for general use is obliged to make list of ingredients of the detergent and to keep the list for five years, as well as to make accessible to the public on his/her internet site certain data from the list (Article 81, paragraphs 2–3).[719]

12. Systematic Monitoring of Chemicals

670. The Ministry responsible for the environment prepares and implements projects for monitoring of placing on the market and use of chemicals, monitoring of their metabolites and pathway of chemicals in the environment and living organisms in order to monitor risk that those chemicals pose on human health and environment, that is, control the intended use of the substances of very high concern and enforces

717. Producer of detergents is a legal person or entrepreneur who puts detergent or surfactant on the market, and who imports these products, labels and packs them (Art. 73, para. 2).

718. The Ministry responsible for the environment prescribes criteria and method of testing biodegrading surfactant (Art. 73, para. 5).

719. The Ministry responsible for the environment prescribes specific method of labelling detergents, contents of the list of ingredients of the detergent, as well as data from that list which must be made accessible to the public (Art. 81, para. 4).

the bans and restrictions of the manufacturing, placing on the market and use of chemicals (Article 82).[720]

671. The Poison Control Centre shall provide the Ministry responsible for the environment with data obtained in accordance with the Law regulating health protection (Article 83, paragraph 1). The Ministry responsible for the environment provides the Poison Control Centre information on chemicals and properties of chemicals it possesses, and which are necessary for work of that Centre (Article 83, paragraph 3).[721] The Poison Control Centre and other medical workers and/or associates may use obtained information for medical purposes only, that is, for the purpose of preventive and medical treatment measures, especially in emergency situations and may not be used for any other purposes (Article 83, paragraph 5).

13. Data Availability

672. Data submitted to the Ministry responsible for the environment in the process of entering of chemicals into the Chemicals Registry, as well as other data placed at the Ministry responsible for the environment disposal, shall be made available to public and, in particular, as follows: (1) chemical name according to the IUPAC nomenclature of hazardous substance contained in the chemical; (2) trade name of the chemical; (3) classification and labelling of the chemical; (4) data on physical and chemical properties of the chemical; (5) data concerning the pathways of the substance and its environmental fate; (6) the results of toxicological and eco-toxicological studies; (7) no-effect level; (8) the guidance on safe handling; and (9) analytical methods for identification of a hazardous substance when released into the environment and for determination of the direct exposure of humans (Article 84, paragraph 1).[722] In emergency cases, where necessary for the purpose of safety and protection of human health and environment, the Ministry responsible for the environment may make available data referred to in paragraph 3 of this Article (Article 84, paragraph 4).

673. Any person may submit the request to access to data at the Ministry responsible for the environment disposal (Article 85, paragraph 2).[723]

---

720. For the implementation of the projects referred to in para. 1 of this Article, the Ministry responsible for the environment may engage scientific research institutions (Art. 82, para. 3).
721. The Ministry responsible for the environment may use data referred to in para. 1 of this Article only for control of risk which some chemicals pose to human health and the environment (Art. 83, para. 2).
722. Besides the data referred to in para. 1 of this Article, data from notification referred to in Art. 53 of this Law shall also be available to public (Art. 84, para. 2). The Ministry responsible for the environment shall consider the following data as professional secrecy and shall not be available to public: (1) data on full composition of mixture; (2) precise intended use and application of the substance; (3) relations between the manufacturer, importer and downstream user in the supply chain; (4) precise quantity of the chemicals manufactured or placed on the market (Art. 84,para. 3).
723. The Ministry responsible for the environment shall deny access to data considered as confidential to the person referred to in para. 2 of this Article, if it assesses that it is necessary to restrict the access to this data in accordance with this Law and the law regulating free access to information of public importance, and shall issue Ruling on this deny (Art. 85, para. 3).

B. The Law on Biocidal Products

674. The legal Act that regulates biocidal products[724] in the Republic of Serbia is the Law on Biocidal Products (OJ RS, Nos 36/2009, 88/2010, 92/2011 and 25/2015). It has the following seventeen parts: Part I – General provisions (Articles 1–3); Part II – List of active substances (Article 4); Part III – Procedures for adoption of acts for putting on the market of biocidal products (Articles 5–32); Part IV – Limitations and prohibitions of putting on the market and use of biocidal products (Article 33); Part V –Register of biocidal products (Article 34); Part VI – Research and development of biocidal products (Articles 35 and 36); Part VII – Classification, packaging, labelling, advertising and safety data sheet of biocidal product (Article 37); Part VIII – Import of biocidal products (Article 38); Part IX –Safe use of biocidal products and retail (Articles 39–43); Part X –Commission on biocidal products (Article 44); Part XI – Technical assistance to the Ministry (Article 45); Part XII – Availability of data (Articles 46 and 47); Part XIII – Responsibility for damage (Article 48); Part XIV – Taxes (Article 49), Part XV – Supervision (Articles 50–58); Part XVI – Penalties (Articles 59–63); and Part XVII – Transitional and final provisions (Articles 64–66).

675. This Law regulates[725] the list of active substances,[726] procedures for issuing of the Acts on the basis of which the biocidal products are placed on the market, bans and restrictions for placing on the market[727] and use of biocidal products; research and development of the biocidal products; classification, packaging, labelling, advertising and safety data sheet of the biocidal products; Registry of biocidal products; safe use of the biocidal products; and supervision and other important issues related to safe placing on the market and use of biocidal products (Article 1).

724. *Biocidal products* means active substances or mixture containing one or more active substances, prepared in the form and supplied to the users, intended to destroy, distract, make harmless, prevent the influence or to control undesirable organisms by chemical or biological means (Art. 2, point 2).

725. Provisions of this Law shall not apply to: (1) medicines and medical devices used in human and veterinary medicine; (2) foodstuffs, food additives, flavourings and raw materials used for their production, materials and product being in contact with food; (3) animal feed and its additives or feeding stuff; (4) detergents without biocidal effect to which the Law on Chemicals is applied; (5) cosmetic products; and (6) plant protection products (Art. 3).

726. *Active substance* means substance or microorganism including a virus or a fungus having general or specific effects on undesirable organisms (Art. 2, point 1).

727. *Placing on the market* means supplying or making available active substances and biocidal products to third parties, on the territory of the Republic of Serbia, either charged or free of charge, wherein the import is deemed as placing on the market (Art. 2, point 13).

1. Lists of Active Substances

676. Active substances are included in: List I[728] – List of active substances; List Ia – List of active substance contained in low-risk biocidal product[729] and List Ib – List of basic substances;[730] which are published in the OJ of the EU[731] (Article 4, paragraph 1).

2. Procedures for Issuing of the Acts on the Basis of Which the Biocidal Products Are Placed on the Market

677. Biocidal products shall be classified into product types[732] based on their intended use, target organism they control, area where they are used and item, that is, treated surface (Article 5, paragraph 1).

678. According to Article 6, paragraph 1, biocidal product shall be placed on the market if: (1) manufacturer or importer obtains the authorization for placing it on the market; and (2) it is classified, packed and labelled and has safety data sheet, pursuant to this Law. Manufacturer or importer may place biocidal product on the market prior to obtaining the authorization for placing it on the market, when the

---

728. *Program for inclusion into the List I – List of active substances, List Ia – List of active substances contained in the low-risk biocidal product or List Ib – List of basic substances* means the EU programme (Review programme) which contains a list of active substances placed on EU market before EU legislation on biocidal products came into force and which contains the time period for submission of the Technical Dossier for inclusion of active substances in those lists (Art. 2, point 10).
729. *Low-risk biocidal product* means biocidal product containing one or more active substances listed in the List Ia – List of active substances contained in the low-risk biocidal product and other substances which are not substances of concern, used under conditions of having low risk to human, animals and to the environment (Art. 2, point 3). *Substance of concern* means any substance, other than the active substance, which has an inherent capacity to cause adverse effects on humans, animals and the environment, contained in a biocidal product in sufficient concentration to create such an effect. Such a substance, unless there are other grounds for concern, would be a substance classified as hazardous and present in the biocidal product in a concentration that is hazardous (Art. 2, point 14).
730. Basic substance shall be placed on the market and used for biocidal purposes if included in the List Ib – List of basic substances (Art. 4, para. 4). *Basic substance* is a substance listed in the List Ib (List of basic substances), which is generally not used as a pesticide, but which has some minor use as biocidal product, either directly or in a product consisting of that substance, and which is due to that not a substance of concern and which is not directly put on the market as a biocidal product, e.g., carbon dioxide, nitrogen, ethanol, 2-propanol, acetic acid, diatomaceous (infusorial) soil (Art. 2, point 8).
731. The lists shall in particularly determine: name of the active substance, the minimum purity of the active substance in the biocidal product, product type in which the substance may be used and conditions under which the Act for placing on the market and use of the biocidal product may be issued in regard to risk that active substance has on humans, animals and environment (Art. 4, para. 2).
732. Minister responsible for environmental protection established by separate Law (the Agency) shall lay down the biocidal products types (Art. 5, para. 2).

decision on inclusion of that biocidal product into the Temporary List[733] for delivery of Technical Dossier[734] was issued pursuant to this Law (Article 7, paragraph 1).

679. For the purpose of obtaining the decision on inclusion of the biocidal product into the Temporary List, manufacturer or importer of the biocidal product shall submit the application to the Ministry responsible for the environmental protection issues[735] (the applicant for inclusion into the Temporary List) (Article 9, paragraph 1). Application referred to in paragraph 1 of this Article may be submitted by more importers together (Article 9, paragraph 2). Upon the request of the Ministry, the applicant for inclusion into the Temporary List shall submit samples of the biocidal product and its components (Article 9, paragraph 5).

680. For the purpose of obtaining the authorization for placing of the biocidal product on the market (the authorization), manufacturer or importer of the biocidal product shall submit the application to the Ministry (the applicant for authorization)[736] (Article 12, paragraph 1). Application may be submitted by more importers together (Article 12, paragraph 2).

681. Test methods laid down in the Law on Chemicals shall be applied for obtaining of the data on physical, chemical, toxicological and eco-toxicological properties of the active substance and biocidal product necessary for the Technical Dossier (Article 14, paragraph 1). New testing of the active substance and biocidal product shall be carried out in the laboratory whose work is harmonized with the

733. Biocidal product shall be included into the Temporary List if it is placed on the market in the Republic of Serbia before this Law has entered into force or if active substance contained in that biocidal product is included in List I – List of active substances, List Ia – List of active substance contained in low-risk biocidal product or into the Programme, unless there is a reasonable doubt that such biocidal product poses unacceptable risk on humans, animals and environment (Art. 8).

734. Temporary List for delivery of Technical Dossier (Temporary List) contains data on biocidal products as well as deadlines for delivery of Technical Dossier for that biocidal product (Art. 7, para. 2). Ministry shall set up deadlines given in the Temporary List on the basis of whether the active substance contained in the biocidal product is included in the lists referred to in Art. 4 of this Law or into the Programme for inclusion into the List I – List of active substances, List Ia – List of active substance contained in low-risk biocidal product and List Ib – List of basic substances (the Programme), or on the basis of quantities of the biocidal product placed on the market, properties of the biocidal product that affect humans, animals and environment or lack of those data, biocidal product type and availability of data on assessment of active or any other substance contained in the biocidal product in compliance with other regulations (Art. 7, para. 3).

735. The Ministry shall, within thirty days at the latest from the day of submitting of the application from Art. 9 of this Law and the complete basic data, issue the decision on inclusion of the biocidal product into the Temporary List (Art. 11, para. 1). Where necessary, the decision may set out the conditions for placing on the market and use of the biocidal product, for the purpose of protection of human and animal health and the environment (Art. 11, para. 3).

736. Technical Dossier shall be presented along with application for authorization (Art. 13, para. 1). The Ministry shall lay down the scope and the content of the Technical Dossier for the biocidal product i.e., low-risk biocidal product (Art. 13, para. 9).

principles of Good Laboratory Practice[737] (Article 14, paragraph 4). Testing[738] of the efficacy of the active substance and biocidal product shall be carried out in the laboratory with quality control and quality insurance (Article 14, paragraph 5).

682. The Ministry shall, within one year from the day of submitting of the application for authorization and complete Technical Dossier, that is, sixty days for low-risk biocidal product and for biocidal product within the established frame formulation,[739] issue the authorization (Article 18, paragraph 1). The authorization[740] shall contain data on the applicant; trade name of the biocidal product; name and content of the active substances and other substances contained in the biocidal product whose concentration does not affect the efficacy and classification of the biocidal product; biocidal product type and conditions for placing it on the market and use; and period of validity of the authorization as well as other data (Article 18, paragraph 2).

683. Persons with the intention to carry out experiments involving vertebrates for the purpose of preparation of the Technical Dossier for the biocidal product shall require from the Ministry permit whether the experiments on vertebrates have already been carried out for the same active substance, or for the same or similar biocidal product (Article 19, paragraph 1).

684. The applicant for the authorization may submit the request to the Ministry for establishing a frame formulation for the biocidal product[741] (Article 21, paragraph 1).

685. Conditions for placing on the market and use, given in the authorization, shall be the same for all biocidal products within the established frame formulation (Article 22, paragraph 1).

---

737. *Good laboratory practice* means laboratory practice conducted in accordance with principles (directives) set out in the Law regulating medicines and medical devices (Art. 2, point 4).
738. The Ministry shall lay down test methods for the efficacy of the active substance and biocidal product (Art. 14, para. 6). On the basis of the Technical Dossier, the Ministry carries out the assessment of the biocidal product to determine its effects on humans and animals and the environment, possible unacceptable effects on target organisms as well as its efficacy and risk within the intended uses (Art. 16, para. 1).
739. *Frame formulation* means specification for the group of biocidal products having the same use and user type and which contains identical active substances. Variations in the composition of the biocidal products with the determined frame formulation, may be, for example, reduction in the percentage of the active substance in the biocidal product, alternation in the percentage of other substances in the biocidal product or replacement of pigments, dyes, perfumes by others presenting the same or a lower risk, and which do not decrease its efficacy (Art. 2, point 7).
740. The authorization shall be issued for a period of ten years or for a period for which active substance contained in that biocidal product is included in the List I – List of active substances and List Ia – List of active substance contained in low-risk biocidal product (Art. 18, para. 4).
741. The Ministry may even without the application establish a frame formulation when it has complete Technical Dossier for biocidal product (Art. 21, para. 3).

686. The Ministry[742] may issue authorization[743] for a biocidal product containing active substance included in the List I – List of active substances or List Ia – List of active substance contained in low-risk biocidal product, on the basis of an Act by which the competent authority of the EU Member State authorizes placing on the market of the biocidal product (Article 23, paragraph 1).

3. Temporary Permit

687. In the case of unforeseen danger which cannot be suppressed by other means or by biocidal products for which the decision on inclusion of the biocidal product into the Temporary List or authorization was issued, temporary permit may be issued for placing of the biocidal product on the market (temporary permit) (Article 30, paragraph 1). Temporary permit may also be issued for the new manner and conditions of use of the biocidal product for which the decision on inclusion of the biocidal product into the Temporary List or the authorization was issued (Article 30, paragraph 2). Manufacturer or importer of the biocidal product shall submit to the Ministry the application for the temporary permit[744] (the applicant for the temporary permit) (Article 30, paragraph 3).

688. The Ministry shall, on the basis of the evaluation of the data, issue the temporary permit within thirty days from the day of submitting of the complete application (Article 31, paragraph 2). Period of validity of the temporary permit shall not exceed 120 days (Article 31, paragraph 4) and it may be extended only in the case when, even after the expiry of 120 days, harmful organisms[745] were not sufficiently suppressed (Article 31, paragraph 5).

689. Holder of the temporary permit shall, after the completion of use of the biocidal products or the latest after validity of the temporary permit expires, submit to the Ministry report on used and unused quantities of the biocidal product and on the results of the systematic monitoring of use of such biocidal products (Article 32, paragraph 3).

742. The Ministry shall issue the authorization if it determines that placing on the market and use of the biocidal product, under the same conditions as in the Member State where biocidal product was authorized, presents acceptable risk to humans, animals and the environment (Art. 23, para. 4).
743. The Ministry shall issue the authorization from para. 1 of this Article within 120 days for the biocidal product, i.e., sixty days for the low-risk biocidal product, from the day when complete application was submitted (Art. 23, para. 5).
744. Along with the application for the temporary permit, the applicant shall be required to submit evidence on: unpredicted presence of harmful organism, justification of unavailability of biocidal product on the market which can suppress harmful organism, efficacy data of the biocidal product, quantities needed, and persons that will use biocidal product as well as proposal for systematic monitoring usage of biocidal product (Art. 31, para. 1).
745. *Harmful organism* means any organism which has an unwanted presence or detrimental effect on humans, their activities or the products they use or produce, on animals or on the environment (Art. 2, point 6).

4. Bans and Restrictions, Register of Biocidal Products

690. The Agency shall, in the case of reasonable doubt that active substance or biocidal product represents unacceptable risk on humans, animals and environment, lay down ban on placing on the market and use of the biocidal products or restriction on placing on the market or use of the biocidal product or active substance, in accordance with legislation regulating chemicals (Article 33, paragraph 1).

691. The Agency shall keep the Register of the biocidal products as an integral part of the Integrated Chemicals Registry established by the separate chemical law (Article 34, paragraph 1).[746]

5. Research and Development, Classification, Import and Safe Use of the Biocidal Product

692. Biocidal product, for which the decision on inclusion into the Temporary List or the authorization was not issued, may be placed on the market only for the purposes of scientific research and development or process-orientated research and development (Article 35 paragraph 1).[747] If, while using the biocidal product for scientific research and development,[748] or for process-orientated research and development, the release of that biocidal product into the environment may occur, the Ministry shall issue the permit for such research (Article 36, paragraph 1). The Ministry may specify conditions (e.g., quantity, treated area) in the permit under which the experiments are conducted (Article 36, paragraph 4).

693. Classification of biocidal product, content and delivery of safety data sheet for biocidal product shall be in compliance with legislation regulating chemicals, and packaging, labelling and advertising of biocidal product shall be in accordance with such legislation and specific requirements for the biocidal product (Article 37, paragraph 1).[749]

---

746. The Ministry shall, annually, publish in the 'Official Journal of the Republic of Serbia' following data from the Register of Biocidal Product: name and address of the holder of the decision on inclusion of the biocidal product into the Temporary List or holder of the authorization; trade name of biocidal product; and number, date of issue and period of validity of such Acts (Art. 34, para. 3).
747. The Ministry shall issue the certificate for placing on the market of the biocidal product used for process-orientated research and development (Art. 35, para. 2).
748. *Scientific research and development* means any scientific experiment, analysis or research of the active substance, i.e., biocidal product conducted under controlled conditions (Art. 2, point 5).
749. The Ministry shall lay down specific requirements for packaging, labelling and advertising of the biocidal product (Art. 37, para. 3).

6. Import of Biocidal Products

694. The customs authority shall allow the import of biocidal product for which the decision on inclusion into the Temporary List, authorization or temporary permit, or certificate was issued (Article 38, paragraph 1).[750]

7. Safe Use of Biocidal Products and Retail

695. Biocidal product shall be used[751] in a way that while handling it, it does not cause harmful effects on human and animal health and environment, taking care of the rational application of combination of physical, biological, chemical and other appropriate measures against target organisms as well as limiting its use to the minimum (Article 39, paragraph 1). Certain hazardous biocidal products[752] are not to be placed on the market for general use (Article 40, paragraph 1).

696. Systematic monitoring, placing on the market and use of the biocidal product, maximum residue limit[753] of the biocidal product, as well as their metabolites, shall be carried out pursuant to the legislation regulating chemicals and other specific legislation (Article 43, paragraph 1).

8. Commission for Biocidal Products

697. For the purpose of providing expert assistance in the most complicated tasks, the Minister shall establish the Commission for Biocidal products (the Commission) (Article 44, paragraph 1). The Commission shall give the opinion regarding issuing of the acts for placing on the market of biocidal products; make the proposal regarding bans and restrictions for placing on the market of biocidal product; give the opinion on the application for establishing the frame formulation (Article 44, paragraph 2).[754]

---

750. The customs authority shall submit to the Ministry by 31 March of the current year the report on import of biocidal products made in the previous year (Art. 38, para. 2).
751. The user of the biocidal product shall comply with all precautions for safety of humans and animals and environment, in accordance with the instruction for use and information from the safety data sheet (Art. 39, para. 2). Keeping hazardous biocidal products in the sales area and the way of marking of that area is carried out in accordance with the regulations governing chemicals (Art. 39, para. 3).
752. The Minister shall lay down such biocidal products (Art. 40, para. 2).
753. Maximum residues limit of the biocidal product in/on treated objects, premises, articles, organisms or other places, prescribed by this law and other specific laws, shall not be exceeded (Art. 43, para. 2). The Minister shall lay down the maximum residues limit of the biocidal product and the manner of determining whether the quantities have been exceeded (Art. 43, para. 3).*Residues of biocidal product* means one or more substances present in a biocidal product, which remain as a result of its use, including the metabolites of such substances and products that are a result of their degradation or reaction (Art. 2, point 9).
754. The members of the Commission shall be experts in toxicology, eco-toxicology, pharmacy, veterinary medicine, chemistry, medicine and other relevant natural sciences as well as representatives from the other authorities responsible for certain issues related to placing of the biocidal product on the market (Art. 44, para. 3).

9. Data Availability

698. The data held by the Ministry shall be available to anyone upon request (Article 46 paragraph 3). The Ministry shall not allow the access to the data which are indicated as confidential if it assesses that access to such data needs to be restricted pursuant to this Law and Law on Free Access to Information of Public Importance, and shall issue a decision on that (Article 46 paragraph 4).[755]

10. Liability for the Damage

699. Holder of the decision on inclusion of the biocidal product into the Temporary List, holder of the authorization and holder of the temporary permit shall be liable for the damage occurred on the territory of the Republic of Serbia in relation to the biocidal product due to failure to comply with the provisions of this Law and due to certain properties of the biocidal product on which such person might have the influence (Article 48).

11. Supervision

700. Supervision implementation provisions of this Law and relevant secondary legislation shall be conducted by the Ministry in charge of environmental protection (the Ministry) (Article 50, paragraph 1). The Ministry[756] through environmental inspectors shall conduct inspection supervision (Article 50, paragraph 2).

701. 'The inspector for environmental protection, sanitary and veterinary inspector may perform sampling of biocidal product to determine whether the conditions for the placing on the market or use of biocidal products are fulfilled.'[757] (Article 51, paragraph 1). If the inspector, while carrying out the supervision, finds out that other laws and regulations are violated, which may have impacts on human and animal health, environment and safety at work, he/she shall immediately inform the competent authority and jointly conduct supervision and take appropriate measures (Article 57, paragraph 1).

755. The applicant for inclusion into the Temporary List, applicant for authorization or temporarily permit may indicate certain data as confidential, with the written justification that disclosure of such data might harm his/her business activity (Art. 46, para. 1). Information regarded as relevant to safety of human and animal health, safety of the property and environmental protection cannot be indicated as confidential (Art. 47).

756. Supervision on classification, labelling, packing of the biocidal products, bans and restrictions for placing on the market and use of the biocidal products as well as supervision of the conditions of sale of the biocidal products for general use and their storage, in the retail shall be conducted by the ministry in charge of trade and trade inspectors (Art. 50, para. 3).

757. The costs of sampling and testing of a biocidal product shall be borne by the legal entity or natural person or entrepreneur from whom the sample was taken, if in the final procedure that does not comply with the terms of the marketing or use of biocidal products. If the sample matches the prescribed conditions for placing on the market or use of a biocidal product costs of sampling and testing of a biocidal product shall be borne by the funds envisaged by the budget of the Republic of Serbia (Art. 51, para. 3).

702. Transport of dangerous goods by road, railway, waterway and air is regulated by the Law on Transport of Dangerous Goods (OJ RS, Nos 88/10 and 104/16). Amendments adopted on 22 December 2016, but entered into force on 1 January 2017, except Article 6, paragraph 12, Article 46, paragraphs 13 and 14 and Article 75, paragraph 2 of this Law which will be effective from the day of Republic of Serbia accession to the EU, while Article 17, paragraphs 3, 4 and 5, Article 27, paragraph 1, item 18) and Article 44, paragraph 1, item 4) are effective as of 1 June 2019. By the day of the Republic of Serbia accession to the EU shall cease to apply paragraph 6 of Article 6 of this Law. By this Law the Administration for Transport of Dangerous Goods is established, being a body that is a constituent part of the ministry responsible for transport affairs, which is a central law enforcement authority.

703. The Authority responsible for the transport issues in the Republic of Serbia is the Ministry of Construction, Transport and Infrastructure. Functioning of each Transport Sectors is regulated by separate Laws: Law on Transport in Road Traffic (OJ RS, No. 68/15), Law on Transport in International Road Traffic (OJ RS, Nos 101/05, 18/10 and 68/15), Law on Railway (OJ RS, Nos 45/13 and 91/15), Law on Contracts on Transport in Railway Traffic (OJ RS, No. 38/15), Law on Air Transport (OJ RS, Nos 73/10, 57/11, 93/12, 45/15 and 66/15), Law on Navigation and Ports in Inland Waters (OJ RS, Nos 73/10, 121/12, 18/15, 96/15 and 92/16), and Law on Maritime Navigation (OJ RS, Nos 87/11, 104/13 and 18/15).

Some of the by-laws enacted in accordance with the Law on Transport of Dangerous Substances are in force, as follows: Rulebook concerning the Methods of Carriage of Dangerous Substances by Road (OJ RS, No. 125/14); Rulebook on the transport of the Dangerous Substances in road transport (OJ RS, No. 125/14); Rulebook on the way of the transport of the dangerous Substances through protected zones (OJ RS, No. 75/15); Rulebook on the mode of transport of dangerous substances in water transport and obligations of participants in the transport of dangerous substances in emergencies (OJ RS, No. 125/14), Rulebook on the content of the vocational training of the employees working on the transport of the dangerous substances in air transport (OJ RS, No. 91/15); Regulation on conditions for granting approval for the transport of dangerous goods by air carrier to whom the certificate of qualification issued by the competent authority of another Member (OJ RS, No. 75/15, of 31 August 2015); and Rules on compulsory mode of transport and operational monitoring of dangerous goods by rail, as well as the obligations of the participants in the transport of dangerous substances by rail and in emergencies (OJ RS, No. 81/2015, dated 24 September 2015), etc.

704. The following ratified international agreements on transport of dangerous goods are implemented:

(1) European Agreement concerning the International Carriage of Dangerous Goods by Road (ADR) (OJ RS – IT, No. 2/10).
(2) Agreement on Acceptance of Uniformed Conditions for Homologation and Mutual Recognition of Equipment and Motor Vehicle Parts Homologation (OJ FPRY – IT, No. 5/62).

(3) Annex C to the Convention on International Convention concerning Carriage by Rail (COTIF) – Regulations concerning the International Carriage of Dangerous Goods (RID).
(4) Annex 18 to the Convention on ICAO – the Safe Transport of Dangerous Goods by Air and ICAO Doc. 9284 AN/905 – Technical Instructions for the Safe Transport of Dangerous Goods by Air.
(5) European Agreement concerning the International Carriage of Dangerous Goods by Inland Waterways (ADN) (OJ RS – IT, No. 3/10).
(6) Convention on the Physical Protection of Nuclear Material (OJ SFRY – IT, No. 9/85), etc.

705. Other legal and sub-legal Acts to be mentioned are following:

- Law on Medicines and Medical Devices (OJ RS, Nos 30/2010 and 107/13).
- Law on the Prohibition of the Development, Production, Stockpiling and Use of Chemical Weapons and on their Destruction (OJ RS, No. 36/09).
- List of poisons whose production, marketing and use is forbidden (OJ RS, No. 72/2006).
- List of active substances in biocidal products (OJ RS, Nos 72/14 and 94/16).
- List of surfactants for which approval was issued or an Act adopted approving the use of surfactants in detergent in the EU (OJ RS, No. 94/10).
- List of surfactants for which application for approval was denied and surfactants which are prohibited in EU (OJ RS, No. 94/10).
- List of substances of concern (OJ RS, Nos 31/11 and 101/16).
- List of substances candidates for the List of substances of concern (OJ RS, No. 58/16).
- List of biocidal products registered in the Register of Biocidal Products in 2012, 2013 and 2014 (OJ RS, No. 60/2015).
- Rulebook on Chemicals Registry (OJ RS, No. 16/16).
- Rulebook on the method of keeping of the Register on biocidal products (OJ RS, No. 28/11).
- Rulebook on Advisor for Chemicals (OJ RS, Nos 13/11, 28/11 and 47/12).
- Rulebook on the List of Classified Substances (OJ RS, No. 48/14).
- Rulebook on permits for the performance of traffic activities or permits for the use of particularly hazardous chemicals (OJ RS, No. 6/17).
- Rulebook on criteria for identification on substances such as PBT and vPvB (OJ RS, No. 23/2010).
- Rulebook on content on basic information on biocidal products (OJ RS, Nos 23/2010 and 28/11).
- Rulebook on certain dangerous biocidal products that cannot be placed on the market for general use (OJ RS, No. 37/11).
- Rulebook on types of biocidal products (OJ RS, No. 23/2010).
- Rulebook on detergents (OJ RS, No. 25/15).
- Rulebook on specific requirements for packaging, labelling and advertising of biocidal products (OJ RS, Nos 59/2010 and 26/11).

- Rulebook on classification, packaging, labelling and advertising of chemicals and certain products (OJ RS, Nos 59/2010, 25/11 and 5/12).
- Rulebook on classification, packaging, labelling and advertising of chemical and certain article in accordance with UN Globally Harmonized System for Classification and Labeling (OJ RS, Nos 64/10, 26/11 and 105/13).
- Rulebook on volume and content of the technical dossier for biocidal product, that is, low-risk biocidal product (OJ RS, No. 97/10).
- Rulebook on content of safety data sheets (OJ RS, No.81/10).
- Rulebook on import and export of certain hazardous chemicals (OJ RS, Nos 89/10, 15/13 and 114/14).
- Rulebook on restrictions and bans on the manufacture, placing on the market and use of hazardous chemicals which represent unacceptable risk on human health and environment (OJRS, Nos 89/10, 25/15 and 2/16).
- Rulebook on guidelines for assessing biocidal products on the basis of technical dossier (OJ RS, No.28/11).
- Decree on the amount of tax, the payers, as well as the manner of payment of tax for assessment and verification of data on biocidal products (OJ RS, No. 90/15).

III. International Treaties and Harmonization with EU Legislation

706. Serbia has ratified the Rotterdam Convention on the prior informed consent procedure for certain hazardous chemicals and pesticides in the international trade (OJ RS-Int. treaties, No. 38/09) and Stockholm Convention on Persistent Organic Pollutants (OJ RS-Int. treaties, No. 42/09).

707. The 2009 Laws on chemicals and on biocidal products (amended in 2010), adhere to the principal concepts of the corresponding EU legislation, notably the EC Regulation on Registration, Evaluation, Authorization and Restriction of Chemicals Regulation (REACH) and the Regulation on classification, labelling and packaging of substances and mixtures and the Directive concerning the placing of biocidal products on the market.[758] Serbia has achieved a high level of alignment with the acquis on chemicals; it has an implementation and control structure in place. Additional work is required regarding REACH and CLP and alignment is pending for the legislation on animal experiments, asbestos and biocides. Serbia needs to enhance administrative capacity for implementation in these areas and ensure proper monitoring of POPs.[759]

758. 'By adoption of Law on Chemicals (O. Gazette of RS, Nos 36/09 and 88/10), a foundation for preparation of implementation of Regulation (EC) No. 1907/2006 on the List on Registration, Evaluation, Authorization and Restriction of Chemicals –REACH was created, as this Law is harmonized with REACH in the part that was possible to transpose into the national legislation. The provisions of REACH related to centralised procedures implemented in ECHA are not transposed, but approximated with the aim of better preparation of domestic industry for implementation of REACH.' AECQ, Chs 27, 235.

759. CR, 77.

§2. Rational Use of Energy

708. Potential to reduce energy consumption in Serbian households is estimated in more than 50%. The energy efficiency of industry is very low, three times lower than in Organisation for Economic Co-operation and Development (OECD) countries. That means that industry in Serbia could achieve annual savings exceeding EUR 70 million, only by increasing energy efficiency by 10%.[760]

During 1990–2005 period energy consumption was reduced by 6%. Another characteristic of this period was predominant use of fossil fuels (coal, oil and gas), mostly imported. There was a slow reduction of fossil fuel use, from 97.9% to 93.6% and increase of the energy consumption from renewable resources (mainly hydroelectric power plants) from 4.7% to 6.9%, what contributed to reduction of the impact of energy industry on the environment.[761]

709. Serbia has insufficient non-renewable energy resources. It is expected to exhaust its coal reserves within the next fifty-five years and oil and gas within next twenty years. Current hydroelectric power capacity is 10,200 GWh per year. Total potential hydroelectric capacity is estimated at 14,200 GWh per annum.[762]

The potential of renewable energy resources (biomass, small hydroelectric power plants, geothermal, wind and solar energy) is, however, significant and exceeds 3.8 Mtoe. A considerable percentage of energy production in Serbia is from renewable sources, and hydropower is the most important source of this kind of energy. The share of renewable energy resources in energy consumption in the period 1990–2005 increased to 2.2%. Energy consumption from hydroelectric power sources has risen from 32% in 1990 to 34.2% in 2005. According to these data, Serbia has already exceeded the goal, set by the EU, that renewable energy resources in the overall electricity consumption should be 21%.[763]

710. Main institutions competent for rational use of energy are: Ministry of Mining and Energy, MAEP; the Energy Efficiency Agency has ceased to exist on 25 September 2012 with the adoption of the Law on Amendments to the Law on Energy (OJ RS, No. 93/12). Rights, obligations, objects, equipment, archives, employees and appointed officials in the Energy Efficiency Agency, as at the date of entry into force of this law, takes over the Ministry of Energy, Development and Environmental Protection (Article 19 of the Law).

760. Supposing that the price of energy is set at EUR 7 cents per 1 kWh, NSDS, 100.
761. *Ibid.*, 17–18.
762. B. Karadžic (ed.), *Environment in Serbia – An Indicator-Based Review*, *supra* , 16.
763. *Ibid.*, 19. Pursuant to the Energy Balance for 2011, the share of RES in gross final energy consumption (GFEC) amounted to 21.2%. 'Until 2020, the Republic of Serbia should increase the share of RES to 27.0%. In compliance with the envisaged GFEC, the quantity of RES should amount to 2563.6 ktoe in 2020, meaning that in the period from 2009 to 2020 the increase of RES amounting to 621.0 ktoe should be achieved. Having in mind the available unused potential of RES, the Republic of Serbia can achieve the target set for 2020 from the domestic sources, except regarding the binding share of biofuels of 10% in the transport sector in 2020.' National Renewable Energy Action Plan of the Republic of Serbia (in accordance with the template foreseen in the Directive 2008/29/EC- Decision 2009/548/EC), Ministry of Energy, Development and Environmental Protection, Belgrade, 2013, 17.

I. Legal Regulation

A. National Regulations

711. When legal regulation of the energy sector in Serbia is concerned, first deserve to be mentioned are programmatic Acts:

- Energy Sector Development Strategy of the Republic of Serbia until 2015 (Official Journal of RS, No. 44/2005), defining long-term objectives in the energy sector.
- Energy Development Strategy of the Republic of Serbia until 2025, with projection until 2030 (OJ RS, No. 111/15)[764]
- Regulation on the Establishment of the Program for the Realization of the Energy Sector Development Strategy of the Republic of Serbia until 2015 for the period 2007–2012 (Official Journal of RS, Nos 17/2007 and 73/2007), defining conditions, manner and dynamics of Strategy implementation in the energy sector.
- Regulation on approval of the Programme for financing of activities and measures for the improvement of energy efficiency in 2016 (OJ RS, No. 13/16).
- National Renewable Energy Action Plan (OJ RS, No. 53/2013)

1. Environmental Protection Law

712. There are several provisions of the EPL concerning the energy and energy sector. Most of them have general character but some are very relevant and have practical implication for energy sector (Spatial and urban planning, Article 34, point 3; SEA, Article 35; EIA, Article 36; Limit values, Article 39; Requirements for operating the plant and performing the activities, Article 40; Ecological sign, Article 53, Registers of sources of environmental pollution, Article 75, Types of incentive measures, Article 101, etc.).

713. Funds of the Green Fund of the Republic of Serbia shall be carried out in accordance with the law, the national environmental protection programme and the strategic documents as well as the list of priority infrastructure projects in the field of environment, for, *inter alia*, Encouraging the use of renewable resources; 11) Encouraging sustainable development, apart from energy efficiency improvement projects, etc. (Article 90v).

714. Technologies and more environmentally friendly products than others due to the use of renewable energy sources (energy of the Sun, wind parks, biogas, etc.) plant and equipment directly protecting the environment, may have taxation, customs and other relief or exemption provided under the terms and conditions of special Law (Article 101).

715. While performing their activity, legal and natural persons shall be obliged to ensure environmental protection by, *inter alia*, sustainable use of natural resources, goods and energy by introducing energy efficient technologies and use of renewable natural resources (Article 102).

---

764. Proposal of the Regulation establishing a Programme for implementation of Energy Strategy of the Republic of Serbia in 2025, with projections to 2030, for the period 2017–2023 has been prepared.

2. Energy Law

716. Basic legal act regulating the field of energy in the Republic of Serbia is the Energy Law (hereinafter: The Law)(OJ of RS, No. 145/14), adopted in 2014. It has the following fourteen parts: Part I – General Provisions (Articles 1 and 2); Part II – Energy policy and energy development planning (Articles 3–15); Part III – Energy activities, licenses and energy permits (Articles 16–37); Part IV – Energy agency of The Republic of Serbia (AERS) (Articles 38–64); Part V – Renewable energy sources (Articles 65–87); Part VI – Prices of Energy, energy commodities and services (Articles 88–93); Part VII – Electricity (Articles 94–219); Part VIII – Natural gas (Articles 220–323); Part IX – Oil and oil derivatives (Articles 324–344); Part X – Energy reserves (Articles 345–353); Part XI – Heat energy (Articles 354–366); Part XII – Supervision (Articles 367–388); Part XIII – Penalties (Articles 389–391); and Part XIV – Transitory and final provisions (Articles 392–434).

717. The Law regulates the following: energy policy objectives and methods of their implementation; conditions for reliable, secure and quality energy[765] and energy commodities delivery; conditions for safe supply to the customers; protection of consumers of energy and energy commodities; conditions and manner for performing energy-related activities; conditions for constructing new energy facilities; rights and duties of governmental bodies and AERS (hereinafter: Agency); usage of renewable energy sources, incentives and guaranty of origin; manner of organizing and functioning of the electricity, natural gas and oil and oil derivatives market; rights and obligations of market participants; establishment of ownership of networks of operators of the system, as well as supervision over the implementation of this Law. This Law regulates the production, distribution and supply of heat energy as well as energy-related activities (Article 1).

718. The energy policy of the Republic of Serbia shall include measures and activities taken to achieve following long-term objectives: (1) reliable, safe and quality supply of energy and energy sources;[766](2) creating conditions for safe and reliable energy systems operation and sustainable development; (3) energy market competition based on the principles of non-discrimination, publicity and transparency; (4) providing conditions for promoting energy efficiency in carrying out energy activities and energy consumption; (5) creating economic, commercial and financial conditions for generating energy from renewable energy sources and combined heat and electricity generation;[767](6) creating regulatory, economic and commercial conditions for the improvement of efficiency in power system management, particularly having in mind the development of distributed electricity generation, development of distributed electricity storage capacities, introduction of a consumption management system, and introduction of the advanced network concept; (7) creating conditions for the use of new energy sources; (8) *improvement of environmental protection in all energy-related areas*; (9)

765. *Energy* means electricity and heat energy (Art. 2, point 24).

766. *Energy sources* are coal, natural gas, oil, oil derivatives, oil shale, renewable and other energy sources (Art. 2, point 20).

767. *Electricity generation* means production in hydropower plants, thermal power plants, CHP plants and other plants using renewable energy sources (hereinafter, power plants) (Art. 94, para. 1).

creating conditions for investments into the energy sector; (10) protection of energy and energy sources' customers; (11) connecting the energy system of the Republic of Serbia with the energy systems of other countries; and (12) electricity and natural gas market development and their relation with the regional and internal market of the EU (Article 3, paragraph 1).

719. Energy activity can be carried out by a public company, a company, and/or other legal entity or an entrepreneur, possessing license for carrying out energy activity, unless otherwise prescribed by this Law (Article 17, paragraph 1). [768] Energy entity can begin performing energy activity on the basis of a license issued by the Agency, unless otherwise regulated by this Law (Article 20, paragraph 1).

a. Energy Agency of the Republic of Serbia

720. The Agency is a regulatory body for energy sector established to improve and direct electricity and natural gas market development on the basis of principles of non-discrimination and efficient competition, by creating a stable regulatory framework, as well as for performing other activities defined by this Law (Article 38, paragraph 1).[769]

In performing regulatory operations stipulated by this Law, the Agency shall take measures to achieve or contribute to the achievement of the following objectives: (1) ensuring safe supply of energy to the customers through efficient functioning and sustainable development of energy systems, in accordance with the energy policy of the Republic of Serbia, including environmental protection and development of

768. According to Art. 16 the Law energy-related activities include the following: (1) electricity generation;(2) combined generation of electricity and thermal energy; (3) electricity transmission and electricity transmission system management; (4) electricity distribution and electricity distribution system management; (5) electricity distribution and closed distribution system management; (6) electricity supply; (7) wholesale electricity supply; (8) organized electricity market management; (9) natural gas transport and natural gas transport system management; (10) natural gas storage and natural gas storage facility management; (11) natural gas distribution and natural gas distribution system management; (12) natural gas supply; (13) public natural gas supply; (14) production of oil derivatives; (15) oil transport via oil pipelines; (16) oil derivatives transport via oil derivatives pipelines; (17) transport of oil, oil derivatives and biofuels by other transport modes; (18) oil, oil derivatives and biofuel storage; (19) trade in oil, oil derivatives, biofuels and compressed natural gas; (20) trade in fuels outside supply stations for vehicles; (21) filling of containers for liquid petroleum gas, compressed and liquefied natural gas; (22) trade in motor and other fuels at supply stations for vehicles; (23) trade in vessel fuels; (24) thermal energy generation; (25) thermal energy distribution; (26) thermal energy supply; (27) biofuel production; (28) bioliquid production; (29) blending of biofuels with fuels of oil origin. Energy-related activities under para. 1, items 1), 2), 6), 7), 8), 12), 14), 17), 18), 19), 20), 21), 22), 23), 27) and 29) of this Article shall be performed in accordance with market principles. Energy-related activities under para. 1, items 3), 4), 9), 10), 11), 13), 15), 16), 24), 25) and и 26) of this Article are activities of general interest, pursuant to a separate law. Energy-related activity under para. 1, item 5 of this Article shall be performed in accordance with the provisions of this Law.

769. The Agency is an autonomous legal entity and functionally independent from executive authority in carrying out its activities, as well as from other state authorities and organizations, legal entities and individuals engaged in energy activities (Art. 38, para. 2).

renewable energy sources; (2) development of the electricity market in the Republic of Serbia and its integration into the regional and Pan-European electricity market; (3) ensuring a stable, transparent and non-discriminatory regulatory framework for energy customers, system users and investors; (4) stimulating efficient functioning of energy systems; and (5) ensuring high standards of service in electricity and natural gas supply with the protection of energy vulnerable customers (Article 48).[770]

721. The Agency shall be financed by means of fees paid for licences for performing energy activities, a part of the price for system access determined by the methodologies referred to in Article 50, paragraph 1, items 1, 2, 6, 7, 8 and 10 of this Law, as well as other revenues made in performing operations within its competency in accordance with the Law (Article 62, paragraph 1).[771]

b. Energy from Renewable Energy Sources

722. The use of energy from renewable sources is in the interest of the Republic of Serbia. At the Ministry's proposal, the Government shall adopt the National Action Plan for renewable energy sources usage (hereinafter, National action plan)[772] which ensures that the share of renewable energy sources will be in line with confirmed international agreements (Article 65, paragraphs 1 and 2).[773]The Ministry shall monitor implementation of the National Action Plan and submit every second year report[774]on its implementation to the Government (Article 66, paragraph 1).

723. A guarantee of origin[775]is issued by the transmission system operator at the request of producers of electricity from renewable energy sources and is responsible for its accuracy, reliability and protection from abuse (Article 82, paragraph 1). A guarantee of origin is valid for a period of one year, starting from the last day of production period that is issued for (Article 82, paragraph 7).[776]

---

770. The Agency shall issue licenses for performing energy-related activities and adopt an act of license withdrawal, under conditions stipulated hereof, and shall keep registries of issued and withdrawn licenses (Art. 49).
771. The Agency may be funded by donations, except from donations of energy entities or entities related in any way to those entities (Art. 62, para. 2).
772. Content of the National Action Plan is prescribed in Art. 65, para. 4.
773. The objectives of the National Action Plan shall be established based on energy needs, economic potential and obligations of the Republic of Serbia undertaken by ratified international agreements (Art. 65, para. 3). National Action Plan must be harmonized with regulations governing energy efficiency and reduction emission of gases causing greenhouse effect (Art. 65, para. 5).
774. Content of the Report is prescribed in Art. 66, para. 2.
775. *Guarantee of origin* is an electronic document with a sole function of proving to the final customer that a given share or quantity of energy was produced from renewable energy sources, as well as from combined electricity and heat production with high energy conversion efficiency (Art. 2, point 12).
776. The procedure for issuing, transfer, utilization and termination of the guarantee of origin shall be based on the principles of objectivity, transparency and non-discrimination (para. 12).

c. Privileged Electricity and Heat Producers

724. Energy entities may, in accordance with this Law, acquire the status of a privileged producer of electricity (hereinafter, privileged producer) for power plant, i.e., part of power plant upon meeting the following conditions: (1) using renewable energy sources in the process of electricity generation and meets the requirements in terms of installed capacity: in hydroelectric power plant up to 30 MW, hydropower plant on the existing infrastructure up to 30 MW, biomass power plant, the biogas, wind, power plant on solar energy, geothermal and waste power plant and in other power plant in accordance with the act from Article 74 of this Law; (2) was built and fit for use in accordance with the law governing construction of buildings; (3) has a special measuring, separated from the measurement in other technological processes, in which measures are taken and handed over electricity, i.e., thermal energy in the system; (4) produces electricity in newly constructed or reconstructed facilities in which the unused equipment is installed; (5) is licensed to conduct activities in accordance with this Law; (6) use the wind and solar energy, and has installed capacity less than the free capacity determined by the act from Article 74 of this Law; (7) fulfil other conditions in accordance with the act from Article 74 of this Law (Article 70, paragraph 1).

Energy entity may acquire the status of a privileged producer of electricity also for power plant, i.e., power plant that produce energy from high combined production of electricity and heat energy (conditions are prescribed in Article 70, paragraph 2). Energy entity may acquire status of producer of electricity for renewable energy sources under conditions prescribed in Article 70, paragraph 3.[777]

725. The status of privileged producer, temporary privileged producer and producer from renewable sources, the Ministry shall establish in a period of thirty days of the request (Article 72, paragraph 1).[778]

---

777. The status of privileged producer, temporary status of privileged producers and status of producer from renewable sources can acquire a physical person generating electricity from renewable sources only for one power plant installed power of 30 kW under the conditions set out in paras 1–3 of this Article. The energy entity and physical person referred to in para. 5 of this Article may not at the same time have the status of energy producer from renewable sources and the status of privileged producer for the same power plant (Art. 70, para. 4–5). The energy entity or physical person referred to in Art. 70, para. 5 of this Law may, before acquiring the status of privileged producer, acquired a temporary status of privileged power producers for a period of three years (hereinafter, referred to as temporary privileged producer) under the conditions stipulated in Art. 71, para. 1.

778. The request for obtaining the status under para. 1 of this Article shall be submitted in a form of contents which shall be determined in accordance with the act under Art. 74 hereof. Enclosed with the request, the applicant shall submit the evidence of the fulfilment of conditions under Art. 70 hereof, as well as other evidence pursuant to this Law and regulations passed on the basis hereof. The decision under para. 1 of this Article may be appealed to the Government within fifteen days as of the decision receipt date.

d. Incentive Measures

726. Incentive measures, in accordance with this Law, shall include: (1) the obligation to purchase electricity from a privileged producer,(2) prices of the energy,(3) the period of validity of the obligation to purchase electric energy,(4)taking over balance liability, and (5) other incentive measures prescribed by the act (Article 76, paragraph 1).[779]

727. A temporary privileged producer shall be entitled to incentive measures by the conclusion of an agreement on electricity purchase with a guaranteed supplier, under suspensive condition to acquire the status of a privileged producer pursuant to this law and regulations passed on the basis hereof (Article 77, paragraph 1).[780]

728. Privileged heat energy producers are the producers using renewable energy sources in the process of heat energy production and fulfilling the conditions in terms of energy efficiency (Article 365).[781]

The local self-government unit shall keep the registry of privileged heat energy producers, which shall particularly comprise data on thermal energy production plants, their location, installed power of the heating plant, the time envisaged for exploitation, conditions of construction and exploitation for that plant, the type of primary source used, and entities performing the energy-related activity of heat energy production in those facilities (Article 366,paragraph 1).

729. Upon a proposal of the Ministry, the Government shall prescribe in more detail the share of biofuels in the market, reporting entities of the system for placing biofuels on the market and their obligations, incentives, measures and manner of placing biofuels on the market, reporting in the system for placing biofuels on the market, registry of reporting entities of the system for placing biofuels on the market

779. Privileged energy entity shall be entitled to use incentive purchase price (Art. 76, para. 2).

780. Upon a request of a temporary privileged producer, the guaranteed supplier shall conclude an agreement on electricity purchase within thirty days as of the request submission date (para. 2). A temporary privileged producer that has acquired the status of a privileged producer pursuant to this Law shall be entitled only to incentive measures applicable on the date of submission of the request for obtaining the status of a temporary privileged producer (para. 3). The Government shall prescribe in more details the categories of privileged electricity producers, incentive measures for electricity generation from renewable sources and from highly efficient combined generation of electricity and thermal energy, the conditions for their acquisition, the method for determining and the duration of the incentive period, rights and obligations arising from such measures of privileged electricity producers and other energy entities, and other matters in accordance with the law.

781. The local self-government unit shall prescribe incentive measures and conditions for acquiring the status of a privileged thermal energy producer and the criteria for the fulfilment of those conditions, and shall determine the manner and procedure for acquiring such status.

and their reports, as well as other elements of the system for placing biofuels on the market (Article 340, paragraph 1).[782]

3. Law on Efficient Use of Energy

730. The basic legal act regulating the field of efficient use of energy in the Republic of Serbia is the Law on Efficient Use of Energy (OJ RS, No. 25/2013), adopted in 2013. It has the following nine parts: Part I – General Provisions (Articles 1–5); Part II – Policy of efficient energy usage (Articles 6–12); Part III – The Energy Management System (Articles 13–36); Part IV – Labelling of energy efficiency (Articles 37–44); Part V – Minimum requirements of energy efficiency in production, transmission and distribution of electricity and heat energy, in transport and distribution of natural gas (Articles 45–56); Part VI – Financing, incentives and other measures of efficient energy usage (Articles 57–63); Part VII – Supervision (Articles 74–82); Part VIII – Penalties (Articles 83–91);and Part IX – Transitory and final provisions (Articles 92–96).

731. This Law regulates the conditions and method for efficient use of energy and energents (hereinafter referred to as energy) in the sector of production, transmission, distribution and energy consumption; policy of efficient energy use;[783] energy management system; labelling of energy efficiency level of products that affects energy consumption; minimum requirements of energy efficiency in the generation, transmission and distribution of electricity and heat energy and natural gas delivery; financing, incentives and other measures in this field, as well as other issues of importance to the rights and obligations of physical persons and legal entities in relation to the efficient energy use (Article 1, paragraph 1).

732. Efficient use of energy has to achieve the following objectives: (1) increasing the security of energy supply and its efficient use; (2) increasing the competitiveness of the economy; (3) reducing the negative impact of the energy sector on the environment; and (4) encouraging responsible behaviour towards energy, on the basis of the implementation of policies for efficient use of energy and energy efficiency measures in sectors of generation, transmission, distribution and consumption of energy (Article 2, paragraph 1).[784]

---

782. Upon a proposal of the Ministry, the Government shall prescribe in more detail the payers of biofuel fee. The funds which are used as an incentive for the system for placing biofuels on the market shall be provided from the budget of the Republic of Serbia, in an amount to be determined for each year by the Budget Law of the Republic of Serbia within the Ministry's compartments in accordance with the defined limits in the fiscal strategy for the current year, with projections for the following two years (Art. 341, paras 1 and 2).

783. *Efficient use of energy* is the use of energy for quality performing of relevant activities and providing services in a manner that achieves minimal power consumption, within technical capabilities of modern facilities, equipment and devices (Art. 5, para. 1, point 3).

784. The basic principles of the efficient use of energy are the following: (1) Energy security; (2) The competitiveness of products and services; (3) Sustainability of energy use; (4) Organized energy management – power management;(5) Economic viability of energy efficiency measures; and (6) Minimum energy efficiency requirements (Art. 3, para. 1, points 1–6).

a. Policy of Efficient Energy Use

733. The basic acts determining policies for efficient use of energy are: (1) Strategy of energy development of the Republic of Serbia regulating the energy sector (Strategy), prepared and adopted in the manner stipulated by the Law; (2) the programme of implementation of Strategy for Energy Development in the Republic of Serbia (Strategy Implementation Programme), which was prepared and adopted in a way regulated by the Law governing the energy sector; (3) Action Plan for Energy Efficiency in the Republic of Serbia;[785](4) programme and the energy efficiency plan, adopted by the local government; and (5) programme and the energy efficiency plan, adopted by other payers of energy management system (Article 6, paragraph 1).

b. Energy Management System

734. Subjects of the energy management system are: the Government, the Ministry, payers of energy management systems, energy managers and authorized Energy advisors (Article 13, paragraph 1). The Government as the subject of energy management, on a proposal from the Ministry, adopts rules in the field of efficient energy use in accordance with the provisions of this Law (Article 14, paragraph 1). The Ministry organizes, implements and monitors functioning of the system and implementation of the objectives of the energy management system (Article 15, paragraph 1).

c. The Objectives of Energy Savings and Limit Values of Spending

735. At the proposal of the Ministry, Government shall establish annual targets of planned energy savings for payers of the system, in accordance with the Action Plan, the limit value of energy consumption to determine which companies are payers of the system, as well as the application form on the realized energy consumption (Article 17, paragraph 1).

736. Energy Manager is a natural person appointed by the payers of the system, who is liable in particular to: (1) collect and analyse data on the ways of use of energy of the payers of the system; (2) the preparation of programmes and plans referred to in Article 6, paragraph 1, items(4) and (5) of this Law; (3) propose measures which contribute to the efficient energy use and participates in their realization; (4) ensure the preparation of the annual report referred to in Article 18, paragraph 1, item 6) of

785. '… the measures planned in the First Energy Efficiency Action Plan for the period 2010–2012 were either not implemented at all or only partly implemented because of delays in the adoption of the Law on Efficient Use of Energy and the accompanying by-laws, as well as lack of funding.' EPR 2015, xxviii. *See also*: The Second Action Plan for Energy Efficiency of the Republic of Serbia for the Period 2013–2015 (OJ RS, No. 98/13), and The Third Action Plan for Energy Efficiency of the Republic of Serbia for the Period by 2018 (OJ RS, No. 1/17). *See also*: Regulation on Establishing a Program for Financing Activities and Measures to Improve Energy Efficiency in 2016 (OJ RS, No. 13/16).

this Law; (5) undertake other activities and measure prescribed by the Law (Article 19, paragraph 1).[786]

737. The Certified Energy Adviser performs energy review and energy audit. The certified energy adviser is a natural person or legal entity registered in the register of certified energy advisors, kept by the Ministry. The authorized energy adviser shall upon the completion of energy review,[787]submit the audit report to the Ministry data on the survey or energy auditing in the manner and form determined by the Ministry (Article 20, paragraphs 1–3).

738. Certificate of passed exam to conduct activities of energy manager and certified energy advisor shall be issued to a person who has passed the exam for energy managers (Article 30, paragraph 1). Licenses for conducting activities of energy manager, according to the type of the taxpayer of the system, are issued by the Minister. The license is issued by Decision, within thirty days from the date of application, if the conditions are met prescribed by the Law and the regulations adopted on the base on it (Article 33, paragraphs 1–2).

License for conducting activities of certified energy advisor is issued by the Minister. The license is issued by Decision, within thirty days from the date of application, if the conditions are met prescribed by the law and the regulations adopted on the base on it (Article 35, paragraphs 1–2).[788]

d. Financing of Efficient Use of Energy

739. Jobs in the field of efficient use of energy, which are financed or co-financed in accordance with this Law, are jobs related to producing projects and programmes, as well as the implementation of activities, in particular for: (1) the application of technical measures aimed at efficient use of energy in the sectors of generation, transmission, distribution and consumption of energy; (2) encouraging the development of energy management systems for entities that are not payers of the system; (3) promotion and implementation of energy audits of buildings, manufacturing processes and services; (4) construction of the system for combined heat and electricity production, if energy requirements are met in terms of energy efficiency of the facilities, prescribed in accordance with the Law governing the field of energy, and the investor heat and electricity use exclusively for its own use; (5) encouraging the development of energy services at the market of the Republic of Serbia; (6) encouraging the use of renewable energy sources for electricity and heat energy production for its own needs; and (7) other activities aimed at more efficient use of energy (Article 57, paragraph 1).

786. The tasks of the energy manager may be performed by a person who is licensed to conducting energy manager tasks (Art. 19, para. 2).
787. Content of energy review is prescribed in Art. 24, para. 1.
788. The Ministry keeps the register of the certified energy managers and energy advisors. (Art. 35, para. 8).

Funds for financing the activities referred to in Article 57 of this Law shall be provided from: (1) The budget of the Republic of Serbia;[789](2) The budget of the AP and local self-government; (3) EU funds and other international funds; (4) donations, gifts, contributions, assistance, etc. to increase the capacity for implementation of the Law;(5) loans from international financial institutions; and (6) other sources in accordance with the Law (Article 58, paragraph 1).

740. Budgetary fund for the promotion of energy efficiency of the Republic of Serbia (Budget Fund) shall be established for recording the funds intended for the financing of operations for efficient use of energy which are funded in accordance to this Law and regulations adopted on the base of this Law. Budget Fund is established for an indefinite period, in accordance with the Law regulating the budget system. Budgetary fund is managed by the Ministry (Article 59, paragraph 1).[790]

741. The competent authority of the AP or local self-government by its act may establish specific financial and other incentives, establishment of budget funds and the use of funds from existing own funds for projects of other activities for energy efficiency in their territories, in accordance with the law (Article 63 paragraph 1).[791]

4. Other Legal Regulation

742. The Law on Mining Geological Exploration (OJ RS, No. 101/15) regulates geological exploration, exploitation of mineral raw materials, revenue generation by the State, establishment of the Mining Agency, as well as other relevant matters.[792]

743. The Law on Excises (OJ RS, Nos 22/2001, 73/2001, 80/2002, 43/2003, 72/2003, 43/2004, 55/2004, 135/2004, 46/2005, 101/2005,61/2007, 5/09, 31/09, 101/10, 43/11, 101/11, 6/12, 43/12, 76/12, 93/12, 119/12, 8/13, 47/13, 4/14, 68/14, 142/14, 4/15, 55/15, 103/15, 5/16 and 108/16) proscribes, *inter alia*, excises for oil derivatives.

744. The following sub-legal Acts have been adopted:

- Decree on the conditions of electricity delivery (OJ RS, No. 63/13).
- Decree on the conditions for natural gas delivery (OJ RS, No. 47/2006, 3/10, 48/10).
- Decree on conditions and procedure of acquiring the status of privileged producer of electricity, temporary privileged producer and producer of electricity from renewable energy sources (OJ RS, No. 56/16).
- Decree on incentive measures for privileged power producers (OJ RS, No. 8/13).

789. According to the Decision on the opening of a budget fund for the improvement of energy efficiency (OJ RS, No. 92/13) and the Programme for Financing of Activities and Measures for the Improvement of Energy Efficiency in 2014 (OJ RS, Nos 4/14 and 27/14) the budget fund began to operate from January 2014.

790. Funds for financing the Budget Fund shall be provided: (1) from the appropriation in the budget of the Republic of Serbia for the current year and(2) from grants and loans (Art. 60, para. 1).

791. About their activities in terms of para. 1 of this Article, the competent authority of the AP and local self-government is obliged to inform the Ministry (para. 2).

792. For more details *see* , chapter devoted to subsoil and minerals.

- Decree on incentives measures for production of electricity from renewable sources and from high-efficiency combined production of electricity and heat energy (OJ RS, No. 56/16).
- Decree on the contract on purchase of electricity (OJ RS, No. 56/16).
- Decree on fee for incentive of privileged power producers (OJ RS, No. 12/16).
- Decree on energetic-endangered customer (OJ RS, No. 113/15).
- Rulebook on guarantee of origin of electricity produced from renewable energy sources (OJ RS, No. 24/14).
- Rulebook on energy permit (OJRS, No. 15/15).[793]
- Rulebook on licenses for carrying out energy activities and certification (OJ RS, No. 87/15).
- Rulebook on energy efficiency in buildings (OJ RS, No. 61/11).
- Rulebook on energy efficiency labelling of air conditioning (OJ RS, No. 25/14).
- Decision on the opening of a budget fund for the improvement of energy efficiency (OJ RS, No. 92/13).

745. Law on Pipeline Transportation of Gaseous and Liquid Hydrocarbons and Distribution of Gaseous Hydrocarbons (OJ RS, No. 104/09) regulates the requirements for safe and undisturbed pipeline transport of gaseous and liquid hydrocarbons and distribution of gaseous hydrocarbons, design, construction and maintenance and use of pipelines, and indoor gas installations (Article 1).[794]

746. Following by-laws, *inter alia*, regulate oil and oil derivatives market:

- Regulation on technical conditions for unhindered and safe transportation of oil (OJ RS, No. 37/13).
- Regulation on labelling (marking) of petroleum products (OJ RS, No. 51/15).
- Regulation on monitoring the quality of oil derivatives and biofuels (OJ RS, No. 97/15).
- Regulation on the amount, method of calculation, payment and charge for establishing mandatory reserves of oil and oil derivatives (OJ RS, No. 108/14).[795]

747. The main authority in the energy field in Serbia is the Ministry of Mining and Energy performs the activities concerning mining and energy. The other body is the AERS established in 2005, which is competent for protection of customers, as well

793. For the list and text of legislation, *see* on the site: http://www.mre.gov.rs/dokumenta-efikasnost-izvori.php (10 May 2017).

794. 'Pipeline transport' – transport of gaseous and liquid hydrocarbons via oil pipelines, oil product pipelines and gas pipelines having operating pressure greater than sixteen bar; 'Distribution' – transfer of gaseous hydrocarbons from transport gas pipeline to customer via gas pipelines having operating pressure sixteen bar or lower (Arts 2, 1 and 2).

795. For more information about legislation *see* http://www.mre.gov.rs/http://www.aers.rs/Index.asp?l=2&a=92, http://www.seea.gov.rs/English/Prezentacija1.htm. http://www.mre.gov.rs/dokumenta-nafta-i-gas.php.

as improvement and guide of energy market development (price regulation, issuing licenses for energy activities, etc.)[796] and implementation of international treaties.

B. International Legal Regulation and Harmonization with EU Legislation

748. Serbia has ratified the Treaty establishing the Energy Community between the European Community and the Republic of Albania, Republic of Bulgaria, Bosnia and Herzegovina, the Republic of Croatia, former Yugoslav Republic of Macedonia, the Republic of Montenegro, Romania, the Republic of Serbia and United Nations Interim Administration Mission in Kosovo, according to the Security Council Regulation 1244 (OJ RS, No. 62/2006). The Treaty established the legal and institutional framework for electricity and natural gas trade in South-Eastern Europe. It is completely harmonized with the relevant EU regulations, including regulation concerning the environmental protection.

In 2007 Serbia also ratified the Kyoto Protocol, a Non-Annex 1 country. That means that Serbia has the opportunity to use the CDM for financing the projects in the energy efficiency and renewable energy sources fields.[797]

749. The Republic of Serbia signed the following agreements/conventions in the field of energy with non-Member States of the EU:

(1) Agreement Between the Federal Government of the FRY and the Government of the Russian Federation on Cooperation on the construction of the Gas Pipeline on the Territory of FRY (OJ FRY – IT, No.4/96).
(2) Agreement Between the Serbian Government and the Government of the Russian Federation on Cooperation in the Oil and Gas Sector (OJ RS – IT, No. 83/08).
(3) Agreement on Economic and Technical Cooperation in the Field of Infrastructure Between the Government of the Republic of Serbia and the Government of the People's Republic of China (OJ RS – IT, No. 90/09).
(4) Agreement Between the Government of the Republic of Serbia and the Government of the Swiss Confederation Concerning of the Granting of the Financial Assistance for the Project 'Modernization Of The Monitoring And Control System Of NikolaTesla Thermal Power Plant B' of 6 May 2009.
(5) Statute of the IRENA (OJ RS – IT, No. 105/09).
Agreement between the Government of the Republic of Serbia and the Government of the Republic of Italy on cooperation in the field of energy, signed in Rome on 25 October 2011 (OJ RS – IT, No. 7/12).

796. The AERS has, among other things, elaborated tariff systems. http://www.aers.rs/Index.asp?l=2&a=92. However, The Energy Agency 'has no jurisdiction in the field of energy efficiency'. According to the Law on Rational Use of Energy (OJ RS, No. 25/13) the jurisdiction in this area lies with the Government, ministry in charge of energy issues and local self-government. *See* : http://www.aers.rs/Index.asp?l=2&a=127 (10 May 2017).

797. The World Bank has completed study on 'Analysis of Policies to Promote Low Carbon Energy Alternatives' which recommends important policy actions to support new renewable energy projects in Serbia. *Environmental Protection in Serbia, Progress since Kiev 2003 and Challenges Ahead*, World Bank, October 2007, 22.

Agreement Between the Government of the Republic of Serbia and the Government of Japan on the Project of construction of the desulphurization facility for the thermo-power plant 'Nikola Tesla' (OJ RS – IT, No. 1/12).
Agreement Between the Government of the Republic of Serbia and the Government of Russian Federation on Natural Gas Supply from Russian Federation to the Republic of Serbia (OJ RS – IT, No. 3/13).

750. It could be concluded that the development and promotion of the use of renewable energy sources, with the aim to reduce the consumption of fossil fuels, reduce import dependency and produce electrical and heat energy with reduced adverse environmental effects, remains an important goal to be attained by Serbia. Despite the adoption of the strategic documents and relevant parts of legislations, and the fact that great efforts have been made to improve the situation, the energy sector remains the key for investment in environmental improvements and one of the main goals towards sustainable development.[798] 'There are no major investment projects in the renewable energy sector; large scale investment has so far been hampered by difficulties in obtaining bankable power purchase agreements. In June 2016, Serbia adopted a new model for power purchase agreements to address the issue, together with a new feed-in tariff system valid until 2018 and legislation on the procedure for acquiring privileged producer status and on incentives for renewable energy production.'[799]

751. 'Serbia is moderately prepared in the field of energy. Some progress was made in the internal energy market and security of supply. No progress has been made in addressing most of last year's recommendations.'[800] Serbia should therefore in particular: fully implement the connectivity reform measures in the energy sector as agreed; improve alignment with the *acquis*, strengthen capacity and promote investment in energy efficiency and renewable energy as well as achieve cost-reflective electricity tariffs. Regarding efficient use of energy, the current law on efficient use of energy and legislation on the energy performance of buildings are partly in line with the energy efficiency and energy performance of buildings Directives. Serbia continued to implement the energy efficiency *acquis*. Capacity needs to be considerably strengthened.[801]

798. NSDS, 101.
799. CR, 47.
800. CR, 46. Serbia's law on energy is in line with the renewable energy Directive but further by-laws need to be passed to allow full implementation. *Ibid.*, 47.
801. An energy efficiency fund has been set up as a Ministry budget line; its current endowment of around EUR 1.2 million for 2016 is seriously insufficient to meet demands. CR, 47.

Part II. Nature Conservation and Management

752. In accordance with Article 87 of the Constitution of Serbia 'natural resources, goods which are stipulated by the Law as goods of public interest and assets used by the bodies of the Republic of Serbia shall be the State assets. State assets shall include other things and rights, according to the Law'. Natural resources shall be utilized under the terms and in a manner stipulated by the Law. Natural and legal entities may obtain particular rights on particular goods in public use, under the terms and in a manner stipulated by the Law.

753. Provisions directly relevant for nature conservation and management are contained in the EPL (2004). Complete Part II of the 2004 EPL is devoted to the 'management of natural values' (Articles 11–32).[802] This part of the EPL is divided in two chapters: (1) Planning and Utilization of Natural Values (Articles 11–20) and (2) Protection of Natural Values (Articles 21–32).

754. The Law prescribes in general that sustainable management of natural values and environmental protection shall be realized in accordance 'with this Law' (Article 2, paragraph 2). The system of environmental protection shall comprise measures, conditions and instruments for, *inter alia*, sustainable management, preservation of nature balance, integrity, diversity and quality of natural values and conditions for survival of all living beings. General interest is basic element of the notion 'protected natural good'.[803] However, EPL also defined notion 'public natural good'.[804]

755. The Law on Nature Protection (OJ RS, Nos 36/2009, 88/2010 and 91/2010 – corr and 14/2016) regulates the protection and conservation of nature, as well as biological, geological and landscape diversity as part of the environment. According to this Law and to special laws, nature as a resource of common interest to the Republic of Serbia shall enjoy special protection (Article 1).

756. The Law on Nature Protection consists of XVII chapters. Basic provisions of the Law are given in Chapter I consisting of six Articles (Articles 1–6). Provisions for Nature Protection are given in Chapter II (Articles 7–26) which is divided into two subchapters – Subchapter 1– Planning, regulation and space usage, natural resources,

802. Notion of 'natural value' is defined very widely. It is 'natural wealth which comprises air, water, soil, forests, geological resources, plants and animal life' (Art. 3, point 3).

803. 'Protected natural good' is a preserved part of nature with special values and characteristics (geodiversity, biodiversity, scenery, landscape, etc.), due to which they have permanent ecological, scientific, cultural, educational, health recreational, tourist and other significance and therefore as a public good it enjoys special protection (Art. 3, point 4).

804. Public natural good is defined as a cultivated or uncultivated part of natural wealth (i.e., air, water goods, water-fronts, underground goods, forests, sceneries or landscapes equally accessible to all) (Art. 3, point 5).

protected areas and ecological network (Articles 8–13) and Subchapter 2 – Subjects of protection (Articles 14–26). Chapter III – Protected natural goods (Articles 27–40) consists of following three Subchapters: 1. Protected areas (Articles 28–35); Subchapter 2. Protected species (Article 36) and Subchapter 3. Mobile protected natural documents (Articles 37–40). Procedure for declaration of protected natural goods is given in Chapter IV (Articles 41–50). Chapter IV also consists of 3 subchapters: (1) Categorization of protected areas (Articles 41–47);(2) Strictly protected and protected wild spaces (Article 48) and(3) Mobile protected natural documents (Articles 49 and 50). Provisions for management and use of protected area are given in Chapter V (Articles 51–70). Regulations about protection and conservation of wild species are given in Chapter VI (Articles 71–96). Chapter VII prescribes measures for protection of mobile protected natural documents (Articles 97–100). Organization of nature protection is prescribed in Chapter VIII (Articles 101–104). Chapter IX – Nature protection sign consists of two Articles 105 and 106, as well as Chapter XI – Guarding of protected areas (Articles 109 and 110). Nature protection documents are prescribed in Chapter XII (Articles 111–114), while access to information and public participation are prescribed in Chapter XIII (Articles 115–117). Supervision is regulated by Chapter XIV (Articles 118–123). Chapter XV – Competence for settlement of complaints consists of only one Article (Article 124). Penalty provisions are prescribed in Chapter XVI (Articles 125–129), while the final Chapter XVII prescribes transitional and final provisions (Articles 130–135).[805]

805. Nature protection is also regulated, *inter alia*, by the Law on Forests (OJ RS, Nos 30/10, 93/12 and 89/15), the Law on Game and Hunting (OJ RS, No. 18/10), and relevant implementing legislation adopted based on these laws, as well as Spatial Plan for the period 2010–2020 (OJ RS, No. 88/10).

Chapter 1. Monuments and Landscapes

757. In Serbian legislation protection and conservation of monuments and landscapes could be divided into two closely related subgroups of regulation (monuments and landscapes), with less attention paid to the landscapes.

§1. Monuments

758. Due to the geographical position and the fact that various cultures and religions have through the history been here intermixing with each other, the territory of Serbia is exceptionally rich in cultural monuments from various historical periods. Some of the most valuable have been put on the UNESCO list of the World Cultural Heritage (the Medieval Serbian capitol Ras, Sopocani Monastery, Studenica Monastery, etc.).

There are several categories of cultural monuments in Serbia. They include the following types (census 1994): archaeological finds (197); area and architectural wholes (eighty-one); residential architecture (508); public architecture (230); religious architecture (721); military architecture (sixty-five); economic purposes' architecture (204); memorial architecture (341), etc.[806]

759. State of the monuments differs. It is estimated that less than two-thirds of them are preserved. The most important factors that contribute to their degradation are inadequate location of industrial plants, tourist activities, transport, electric energy production, uncontrolled growth of cities and other settlements, etc. The 1999 NATO intervention, as well as attacks of ethnic Albanians against Serbs and Serbian cultural monuments in March 2004 in Kosovo-Metohija,[807] caused destruction and serious damage to many monuments in Serbia.

760. In accordance with the Law on Ministries (OJ RS, Nos 44/14, 14/15, 54/15 and 96/15), the Ministry of Culture and Information[808] performs public administrative tasks which relates to, *inter alia*, the development and promotion of culture and artistic creativity; protection of cultural property; endowments, foundations and funds; cooperation in the field of cultural heritage protection, etc. The Sector for Heritage Protection does work related to the: monitoring and analysis of the heritage protection situation and recommendation of measures for their improvement; monitoring of proceedings in the area of protection of monuments and artefacts, etc.

Article 61 of the Law on the Cultural Property (OJ RS, Nos 71/94, 52/11 and 99/11) prescribes, *inter alia*, that the Institute for the protection of cultural monuments

806. *Statistical Yearbook*, 2007, 379.

807. *See* , Cultural Heritage in South-East Europe, Kosovo Protection and Conservation, A Multi-ethnic Heritage in Danger, Mission Report 26–30 Apr. 2004, http://unesdoc.unesco.org/images/0013/ 001389/138966eb.pdf, 10 Oct. 2008; Cultural properties at Risk in Kosovo and Metohija http://www.media.srbija.gov.rs/medsrp/dokumenti/sudbina_kulturne_bastine.pdf, 10 Jul. 2008.

808. *See* , http://www.kultura.gov.rs/en/; *see also*, Institute for protection of monuments of culture, http://www.heritage.gov.rs/latinica/index.php.

of the Republic of Serbia, National Museum in Belgrade, the Serbian Archive, National Library of Serbia and the Yugoslav Film Archive are responsible for keeping the Register of cultural property (National Inventory).

§2. Legal Regulation

761. There are numerous legal and sub-legal Acts relevant for protection of monuments. Article 89 of the Serbian Constitution (protection of heritage) prescribes that 'everyone shall be obliged to protect natural rarities and scientific, cultural and historical heritage, as well as goods of public interest in accordance with the Law. The Republic of Serbia, APs and LSG units shall be held particularly accountable for the protection of heritage'.

762. According to the Spatial Plan of Serbia (OJ RS, No. 88/10) 'the basic goal' in the field of protection and sustainable use of cultural heritage is 'to articulate cultural heritage as a development resource, protect, develop and use it in a manner which will contribute to the establishment of regional and local identity in accordance with European standards of protection'.[809]

I. Law on Environmental Protection

763. The EPL (OJ RS, Nos 135/04, 36/09, 72/09, 43/11CC and 14/16) contains several basic provisions relevant to the protection of monuments linking them to protection of the environment. The notion of 'protected natural good' is defined in such a way that it is linked to nature. Article 3, point 4 prescribes that 'preserved part of nature with special values and characteristics (geodiversity,[810] biodiversity,[811] scenery, landscape, etc.), due to which they have permanent ecological, scientific, cultural, educational, health recreational, tourist and other significance and therefore as a public good it enjoys special protection'.

764. General obligations have been stipulated in Article 17 of the Law. According to the Article, natural goods are to be used and developed in the manner that enables their permanent preservation and advancement in accordance with the Law on Nature Protection. The 'activities which threaten environmental capacity, natural balance, biodiversity, hydrographic, geomorphologic, geological, cultural and landscape values,

809. *Spatial Plan of the Republic of Serbia 2010–2014–2020*, Abridged Version, Ministry of Environment and Spatial Planning, Belgrade, November 2010, 24.

810. Article 3, point 6 of the EPL defines 'geodiversity (geological diversity)' as a presence or dispersion of different elements and features of geological texture, geological structure and processes, geochronological units, rocks and minerals of different composition and genesis types and different paleoecosystems which have been changed in space under influence of internal or external geodynamic components in the course of geological time.

811. Article 3, point 6 of the EPL defines 'biodiversity (biological diversity)' as a diversity of organisms within specie, among the species and ecosystems and it covers full genetic diversity, species and ecosystems diversity at local, national, regional and global level.

or which in any way degrade the quality and properties of the natural good shall not be allowed within a protected natural good'.

765. Cultural goods have been included in Strategic EIA (Article 35) and EIA (Article 36). The strategic EIA shall be made for certain plans, programmes and principles in the domain of, *inter alia*, protection of natural and culture goods, flora and fauna and their habitats, etc. and shall be an integral part of the plan, programme or principle. On the same way, EIA shall cover 'all the projects planned on the protected natural goods and in the protected environment of non-movable culture good' as well as projects in industry, mining, energy, traffic, tourism, agriculture, forestry, water management and communal activities.

766. The environmental protection organization may decide to place a temporary prohibition on the on-going activity.[812] If the Act, by which a natural resource is placed under protection, is not adopted, the temporary ban concerning the execution of work is lifted. A complaint on the decision does not suspend its implementation.

II. Law on Planning and Construction

767. 'Culture' and 'cultural asset and values' are part of the provisions of the Law on Planning and Construction (OJ RS, Nos 72/2009, 81/2009 –corr, 64/2010 –CC, 24/2011, 121/2012, 42/2013 –CC, 50/2013 –CC, 98/2013 –CC, 132/2014 and 145/2014), because culture and cultural asset and values must be taken into account in space planning.

768. The development and use of space is, *inter alia,* based on the following principles: sustainable development; the encouragement of even regional development; reconciliation of social development, economic and energy efficiency and the protection and revitalization of the environment and building heritage, *natural, cultural and historic values*, etc. (Article 3 paragraph 1).[813]

769. According to Article 15, the Spatial Plan of the Republic of Serbia[814] particularly includes the following, *inter alia*: goals and principles of spatial planning; principles and proposals for the protection, landscaping and development of nature and natural systems; measures of protection, landscaping and improving natural and cultural property; and measures of environmental protection (Article 15 points 9 and 10).

---

812. A decision concerning a temporary prohibition concerning the execution of work is submitted to the investor, the contractor and to the competent body which issued the building permit or the permit to carry out other type of work and to the body competent for placing the natural within a three-month period.

813. The principles also include the instruments for implementation (Art. 3, para. 5).

814. The Spatial Plan of the Republic of Serbia is passed for the territory of the Republic of Serbia and constitutes the basic planning document of spatial planning and development in the Republic. Other planning documents must comply with the Spatial Plan. It has a strategic-developmental and general regulatory function and it is adopted for a period of at least ten years, and a maximum of twenty-five years. However, it can be changed even before the expiration of the deadline for which it was drawn up (Art. 14).

770. The General Regulation Plan[815] particularly includes the following: (8) rules of landscaping and rules of construction by zones and wholes; (9) zones for which the drawing up of a Detailed Regulation Plan is mandatory; (10) locations for which an Urban Design Project is in progress; (11) deadlines for the production of detailed regulation with mandatory prohibition of building new facilities and reconstruction[816] of existing facilities (construction of facilities or execution of works which alter the state in the space), until the adoption of the Plan; (12) measures of protection of *cultural and historic monuments, and protected natural wholes*; (13) engineering and geological conditions; (14) measures of energy efficiency in construction, etc. (Article 26).

771. A Detailed Regulation Plan is drawn up for undeveloped parts of a populated locality, bringing in order informal settlements, zones of urban renewal, infrastructural corridors and facilities, construction of facilities or populated localities on build able land outside of populated localities, as well as in protected surroundings of *immobile cultural property* (Article 27).[817]

772. In accordance with Article 117, the general project contains particularly the data about the macro location of the facility, general disposition of the facility, technical and technological concept of the facility, the method of providing the infrastructure, the possible options for the spatial and technical solutions, from the point of fitting into the space, the natural conditions, the effect on the environment, geological engineering and technical characteristics of the land from the aspect of determining the general concept and justifiability of construction of the facility, investigation work made for the preparation of the preliminary project, and *the protection of natural and immovable cultural property*, the functionality and rationality of the project.

773. The preliminary project contains the situational solution and the data about the micro location of the facility, the functional, construction and representational properties of the facility, the technical and technological and exploitation characteristics of the facility, the geological engineering and technical properties of the terrain and soil with preliminary calculations of stability and safety of the facility, the decision about the founding of the facility, the technical, technological and organizational

---

815. The General Regulation Plan is mandatory for a populated settlement which is the seat of a unit of local administration, and can also be drawn up for other populated settlements in the territory of a municipality, i.e., the City of Belgrade, when this is provided for in the spatial plan of the unit of local administration. It is mandatory for units of local administration for which a General Urban Plan is being drawn up following this Law, that the General Regulation Plans are drawn up for the whole buildable area of the inhabited settlement, by parts of the inhabited settlement (Art. 25).

816. '*Reconstruction*' is the execution of construction and other works on an existing facility, by which the stability and safety of the facility are affected; structural elements are replaced or the technological process changed; the exterior elevation of the facility is altered; the number of functional units is increased; influence is exerted on the safety of adjacent facilities, traffic fire fighting and environmental protection; the regime of waters is changed; and *the protection of natural or immobile cultural property* is affected, along with its protected surroundings (Art. 2, point 32).

817. A Detailed Regulation Plan particularly includes, *inter alia*: (5) rules of landscaping and rules of construction by wholes and zones (Art. 28).

elements of construction of the facility, the measures for the prevention or reduction of negative influences on the environment, the preliminary project of the infrastructure, comparative analysis of alternative technical solutions in view of the properties of the soil, functionality, stability, and estimate of the influence on the environment, *natural and immovable cultural property*, rationality of the construction, costs of construction, transport, maintenance, energy provision and other costs (Article 118).

774. Technical documentation necessary for taking measures of technical protection on *immoveable cultural property* can be prepared by the organization which performs the activity of protection of cultural property (Article 127 paragraph 4).[818]

775. Article 133 prescribes that the building permit for the construction of a facility is issued by the ministry authorized for the tasks in construction (Ministry), if it is not otherwise determined by this Law.[819] The Ministry issues the building permit for following facilities: *cultural property of exceptional importance* and their protected surroundings with clearly determined borders of land registry lot; cultural property entered in the World list of cultural and natural heritage and facilities in protected areas in accordance with the Act on protection of cultural property (except the transformation of common premises into a flat, or business premise in the protected surroundings of cultural property of exceptional importance and cultural property entered into the World list of cultural heritage) as well as facilities within national parks and facilities within a protected natural property of exceptional importance (except residential facilities, agricultural and economic facilities and infrastructure facilities which are important for them and which are built-in villages), in accordance with the Law.

---

818. The technical documentation for the construction of a facility can be prepared by a company or other legal entity, or a contractor which are entered into the appropriate Register for the preparation of technical documentation (Art. 126, para. 1). The person employed in a company, other legal entity or contractor firm who is authorized to determine any of the conditions on the basis of which the technical documentation is prepared cannot participate in the preparation of the technical documentation (Art. 127, para. 1). The person who carries out the supervision over the application of the provisions of this Law cannot participate in the preparation in the technical documentation (Art. 127, para. 2). The legal entity performing communal activities or activities of general interest can prepare the technical documentation for the construction of facilities which it will use for the performance of its activity under the conditions prescribed by this Law (Art. 127, para. 3).

819. The issue of the building permit is entrusted to the AP for the construction of facilities determined by Art. 133 of this Law, which is completely built on the territory of the AP. The issue of the building permit is entrusted to the local government units for the construction of facilities which are not determined in Art. 133 of this Law (Art. 134).

776. According to Article 145, the construction of facilities referred to in Article 2, paragraph 1, items 24[820] and 25[821] of this Law, execution of works on capital maintenance of facilities and removal of obstruction for persons with invalidity, adaptation, repair and change of the purpose of facilities, are made based on the decision which approves execution of this work, or change of purpose of these facilities, which is issued by the agency authorized for issuing building permits (paragraph 1).

777. For the works mentioned in paragraph 1 of Article 145 on *facilities of cultural and historic importance* and facilities for which before renewal (restoration, conservation, revitalization)[822] or adaptation must be issued conservation conditions, the agreement of the agency or organization authorized for tasks of *protection of cultural property* about the preliminary or main project must be submitted (Article 145 paragraph 3).[823]

778. Removal of a facility, or part thereof, except in the case of execution of a decision by the inspection, can be carried out only based on the permission for the removal of the facility or part thereof (Article 168 paragraph 1). Together with the request for permission for the removal of the facility, or part thereof, it is also necessary to submit, *inter alia*, special conditions, in case of a facility whose removal would

820. 'An auxiliary facility' is a facility which is linked to the primary facility, and is built on the same lot as the primary residential, business, or facility of public use (garage parking, storage, septic tank, wells, cisterns, etc.).

821. 'A special type of facility for which building permits are not issued' are anti-hail facilities; type encasements of basic stations on appropriate supports, aerial supports with antennas, except parabolic antennas of radio stations whose diameter is not larger than 2.5m (except aerial systems of ground antenna stations), containers holding telecommunication equipment and devices, typical lockers for interior and exterior fitting for holding telecommunication equipment, micro-ditches for optical and other cables, etc. single electric power distribution on transmission poles, part of the low voltage grid which includes a 10 kV or 20 kV line, typical 10/04 kV or 20/04 kV transformer stations and the part of the electric power distribution grid from the 10/04 kV or 20/04 kV transformer station to the connection point on the facility of the client (1 kV); connections to a completed gas distribution grid; typical hot water connections; fitting of interior installations (gas, electric power, water, heating, etc.) in an existing facility.

822. 'Restoration, conservation and revitalization works on cultural property' are works carried out on *immobile cultural property* and their protected surrounding, in compliance with this and special laws (Art. 2, point 37).

823. Exceptionally, in reference to the provisions of para. 1 of this Article, requests for the issue of decisions for approval of execution of works on construction, or execution of works on construction of facilities mentioned in Art. 2, item 24 of this Law, as well as for the adaptation and repair of facilities within boundaries of national parks and facilities within boundaries of *protection of cultural property of exceptional importance*, as well as for execution of work on capital maintenance, adaptation and repair in the protected *surroundings of cultural property of exceptional importance* entered in the World list of cultural heritage, are solved by the authorized agency of the local government unit on whose territory are the subject facilities (Art. 145, para. 4).

endanger the public interest (protection of existing and other infrastructure, *protection of cultural goods, protection of the environment*, etc.) (Article 168 paragraph 2).[824]

779. The construction permit cannot be issued later for facilities which are constructed, or reconstructed, or enlarged, without construction permit, if the facility has been constructed, or reconstructed, in the *zone of protection of natural and cultural goods* (Article 187, point 4).[825]

III. Specific Legislation

780. Besides the mentioned general legislation, following specific legal instruments in the field of culture and protection of monuments are in force:

- Law on Cultural Properties (OJ RS, Nos 71/94, 52/11 and 99/11).
- Law on Culture (OJ RS, Nos 72/09, 13/16 and 30/16 – corr).
- Law on Library and Information Sector (OJ RS, No. 52/11).
- Law on Old and Rare Library Materials (OJ RS, No. 52/11).
- Law on Deposit of Publication (OJ RS, Nos 52/11 and 13/16).
- Copyright Law (OJ RS, Nos 104/09, 99/11, 119/12 and 29/16 CC).
- Law on reconstruction of cultural and historical heritage and development support of Sremski Karlovci (OJ RS, Nos 37/91, 53/93 –other law, 67/93 – other law, 48/94 –other law and 101/2005 – other law).
- Law on Endowments and Foundations (OJ RS, Nos 88/10 and 99/11 – other law).
- Law on Establishment of the Museum of Genocide Victims (OJ RS, Nos 49/92, 53/93- other law, 67/93 – other law, 48/94 – other law and 101/2005 – other law).
- Law on Matica Srpska (OJ RS, No. 49/92).
- Law on Cinematography (OJ RS, Nos 99/11, 2/12 – corr and 46/14 CC).
- Publishing Law (OJ RS, Nos 37/91, 53/93 – other law, 67/93 – other law, 48/94 – other law, 135/2004 and 101/2005 – other law).
- Law on the Serbian Literary Cooperative (OJ RS, No. 20/97), etc.

781. The Law on Cultural Property (OJ RS, Nos 71/94, 52/11 and 99/11) is the basic document in the field of protection and use of cultural properties. The Law is divided into twelve chapters that concern the following:

(1) General Regulations – among others, these regulations define the category of cultural properties.

---

824. The permission for the removal of the facility, or part thereof, is issued within fifteen days from submission of adequate documentation. An appeal can be submitted against the resolution referred to in para. 3 of this Article within fifteen days from delivery of the resolution (Art. 168, paras 3 and 4).

825. Legalization, according to this Law, is the later date issue of construction and usage licenses for a facility, or parts of a facility, which is constructed, or reconstructed without the construction permit. The construction permit, referred to in para. 1 of this Article, will be issued for all constructed, reconstructed or enlarged facilities without construction permit up to the date when this Law became effective (Art. 185, paras 1 and 2).

(2) The Types of Cultural Property.
(3) The Rights, Obligations and Responsibilities of the Owners of Cultural Properties.
(4) Establishment of Cultural Properties.
(5) Inscription in the Register of Cultural Properties.
(6) Cultural Property Protection Activity and Institutions for the Protection of Cultural Properties.
(7) Protection Measures and Other Works on Cultural Properties.
(8) Trade and Expropriation of Cultural Properties.
(9) Guarantees for Foreign Exhibitions.
(10) Supervision over the Implementation of the Law.
(11) Violation Regulations.
(12) Transitional and Final Regulations.

782. Article 19 of the Law on Cultural Property defines that a cultural monument is a building – architectural structure of special cultural and historical significance, including its architectural complex, a structure of national architecture, other immovable object, part of the object or part of the complex characteristic for certain area, a work of monumental and decorative art, sculpture, applied arts and technical culture, as well as other movable object of special cultural and historical significance located inside it.

783. Besides the definition of the 'cultural monument', the Law defines the following notions:

– A spatial cultural-historical ensemble is an urban or rural settlement, or parts of such settlements, that is, an area comprising several immovable cultural properties of special cultural and historical significance (Article 20).
– An archaeological site is a part of land or part of area under water containing remains of structures and other immovable objects, grave finds and other finds, as well as movable objects from previous historical periods, which are of special cultural and historical significance (Article 21).
– A historic site is an area associated with an event of special historical significance, an area with pronounced elements of natural and man-made values which represent a unique whole, as well as memorial graves or graveyards and other memorials built for the purpose of permanent preservation of memory of significant events, personalities and places from the national history (memorials), of special cultural and historical significance (Article 22).

The Law prescribes possible restrictions of ownership rights when it is necessary to implement measures for the protection or preservation of cultural properties (Articles 30–46).

784. Part IV of the Law (Articles 47–58) defines establishment of cultural properties, and prescribes methods and procedures of establishing immovable and movable cultural properties, methods of establishing protection, as well as establishment of cultural properties of great or exceptional significance. Institute for Protection of Cultural Monuments of Serbia has several obligations and duties in the process of proposal preparation for establishment of immovable cultural properties (Article 48).

The Serbian Government is competent for preparing World Heritage nominations. The Ministry of Culture, in collaboration with the Institute for the Protection of Cultural Monuments of Serbia, submits nominations for cultural properties. The methods of the inscription of cultural properties in the Register of cultural properties and the competent institutions responsible for keeping the Register of immovable and movable cultural properties are prescribed by Articles 59–64.

785. The Law on Protection of Freedoms and Rights of National Minorities (OJ FRY, No. 11/2002, OJ S&M, No. 1/2003, OJ RS, No. 72/2009 – other law, 79/13 CC) prescribes, in its Article 12, that in order to preserve and develop national and ethnic particularities, members of national minorities have the rights to establish special cultural, artistic and scientific institutions, societies and associations. The State is obliged to participate in financing of those societies and associations, in accordance with its possibilities. The museums, archives and institutions for protection of the cultural monuments, which are founded by the State, are obliged to ensure presentation and protection of the cultural and historical heritage of the national minorities on its territory.

786. The following sub-legal Acts regulating the protection of cultural goods are also relevant:

- Regulation on special award for contribution to the development of culture (OJ RS, No. 91/10).
- Regulation on detailed conditions and manner of awarding recognition for outstanding contribution to national culture and culture of national minorities (OJ RS, Nos 36/10 and 146/14).
- Rulebook on the content and the way of keeping of records of the public cultural institutions located on the territory of the Republic of Serbia (OJ RS, No. 38/10).
- Rulebook on keeping records of persons who perform independent artistic or other activity in the field of culture (OJ RS, No. 41/10).
- Rulebook on determining composition and operation of the Commission determining representativeness of the associations and the termination of the status of representative associations in culture (OJ RS, Nos 57/10 and 21/13).
- Rulebook on detailed conditions for the start of work of institutions for protection of cultural property (OJ RS, No. 21/95).
- Rulebook on the procedure of keeping the evidence of the immovable areas which are under prior protection (OJ RS, No. 19/95).
- Rulebook on labelling the immovable cultural goods (OJ RS, No. 51/96).
- Rulebook on the data which are to be entered into the Register, procedure of keeping the Register and the Central Register of the immovable cultural goods and on the documentation concerning the cultural goods (OJ RS, No. 30/95 and 37/95).
- Rulebook on the registers of archival material (OJ RS, No. 24/97).
- Rulebook on the registers of film material (OJ RS, No. 47/96).
- Rulebook on registers of artistic-historical works (OJ RS, No. 35/96).
- Rulebook on forms for documentation carried on archaeological excavations and research (OJ RS, Nos 19/95 and 102/06), etc.

787. Serbia is a contracting party to the following international treaties regulating the protection of cultural heritage:

- European Convention on the Protection of Archaeological Heritage (1969) (OJ SFRY – IT, No. 9/90).
- Convention on Protection of Cultural Goods in Case of Armed Disputes (1954) (OJ FPRY – IT, No. 4/56).
- Convention on Measures for Banning and Preventing Illegal Import, Export and Transfer of Properties of Cultural Goods (1970) (OJ SFRY – IT, No. 50/73).
- Convention Concerning the Protection of the World Cultural and Natural Heritage (1972) (OJ SFRY – IT, No. 56/74).
- Convention for the Protection of the European Architectural Heritage (1985) (OJ SFRY – IN, No. 4/91).
- Convention on the Archaeological Heritage (Revised) (1992) (OJ RS – IT, No. 42/09).
- European Convention on Cinematographic Coproduction (1992) (OJ SM – IT, No. 204).
- Council of Europe Framework Convention on the Value of Cultural Heritage of Society (2005) (OJ RS – IT, No. 1/10).
- Convention on Protection and Promotion of Diversity of Cultural Expressions (UNESCO, 2005) (OJ RS – IT, No. 42/09).
- Convention for the Safeguarding of the Intangible Cultural Heritage (OJ RS – IT, No. 1/10).
- European Convention for the Protection of the Audiovisual Heritage (OJ RS – IT, No. 7/14), etc.

§3. Landscapes

788. According to the Law on Nature Protection (OJ RS, Nos 36/09, 88/10, 91/10 – corr., and 14/16) areas of exceptional geological, biological, ecosystem and/or landscape diversity can be declared as protected areas of general interest (Article 28). List of protected area in the Republic of Serbia includes sixteen landscapes of extraordinary characteristics (Klisura Reke Gradac, Dolina Pčinje, Ovčarsko-Kablarska klisura, Miruša, Lepterija-Sokograd, Subotičak pešćara, Veliko ratno ostrvo, Kosmaj, Vlasina, Vršačke planine, Avala).[826]

§4. Legal Regulation

789. The basic legal Acts regulating protection of landscapes in Serbia are:

- *EPL* (OJ RS, Nos 135/04, 36/09, 36/09 – other law, 72/09 –other law, 43/11 CC and 14/16).

826. I. Radović & M. Kozomora (eds), *Biodivesity Strategy of The Republic of Serbia for the period 2011–2018* 116–117 (Ministry of Environment and Spatial Planning 2011).

- Law on Nature Protection (OJ RS, Nos 36/09, 88/2010 and 91/2010 – corr., and 14/16).
- Law on National Parks (OJ RS, No. 84/15).
- Law on Spatial Plan of the Republic of Serbia (OJ RS, No. 88/10, etc.).

790. Protection of natural landscapes is mentioned in the EPL. In Article 3, point 4 of the Law, it is stated that protected natural good 'is a preserved part of nature with special values and characteristics (geodiversity, biodiversity, scenery, landscape, etc.), due to which they have permanent ecological, scientific, cultural, educational, health recreational, tourist and other significance and therefore as a public good it enjoys special protection'. In the same Article of the mentioned Law, there is a provision that public natural good is 'a cultivated or uncultivated part of natural wealth, that is, air, water goods, water-fronts, underground goods, forests, sceneries or landscapes equally accessible to all' (Article 3, point 5).

791. The EPL also prescribes that public natural goods 'shall be used in a way and under conditions which shall enable development and permanency of their natural, physical, health or aesthetic values in accordance with the regulations' (Article 18). Finally, the same Law prescribes that an action plan shall be made for 'Advancement of Spatial Planning and Landscaping' (Article 65, point 1).

792. According to Article 26 of the Law on Nature Protection of landscapes shall imply planning and implementation of measures which prevent unwanted changes, disturbances or destruction of significant landscape characteristics, their diversity, uniqueness and aesthetical values and enable the traditional way of using the landscape.[827] Conservation of significant and characteristic features of the landscape must be provided for when planning and organizing space and when planning and using natural resources.[828]

I. Landscape of Exceptional Characteristics

793. The activities and operations which disturb primary natural and created values and landscape character shall be prohibited within the landscape of exceptional characteristics (Article 33, paragraph 5).Landscape of exceptional characteristics shall be an area of recognizable appearance with significant natural, biological-ecological, aesthetic and cultural-historical values, which developed in time as a result of interaction between the nature, natural potentials of the area and the traditional way of life of the local population. Landscape of exceptional characteristics can be a natural landscape

827. Landscape is a certain territory whose character represents a specific joint of natural and created values characteristic for the given region (Art. 4, point 56).
828. According to their natural and created characteristics, landscapes shall be divided into landscape types which express the diversity of natural and cultural heritage (Art. 26, para. 1).

of exceptional characteristics[829] and a cultural landscape of exceptional characteristics[830] (Article 33, paragraphs 1 and 2). Protection measures, the mode for carrying out economic and traditional activities and use of natural and created values within the landscape of exceptional characteristics shall be closely established in the formal decision on proclamation of protected area (Article 33, paragraph 6).

794. Serbia ratified the European Landscape Convention (Florence, 2000) (OJ RS – IT, No. 4/11). Serbia is, since 2002, a member of the Joint Secretariat of the Pan-European Biological and Landscape Diversity Strategy (PEBLD).

829. Natural landscape of exceptional characteristics shall be an area of significant biological-ecological and aesthetic value, in which the traditional way of life of the local population has not significantly disturbed the nature and natural ecosystems (Art. 33, para. 3).
830. Cultural landscape of exceptional characteristics shall be an area of significant landscape, aesthetic and cultural-historical value, which developed in time as a result of interaction between the nature, natural potentials of the area and the traditional way of life of the local population (Art. 33, para. 4).

Chapter 2. Parks and Reserves

§1. Physical Context

795. Total surface of protected natural resources is around 578,500 ha, which makes around 6.5% of the territory of the Republic of Serbia.[831]

The surface coverage of existing protected areas: 5 national parks (158,986 ha); 16 nature parks (213,303 ha); 16 landscapes of outstanding features (45,656 ha); 67 nature reserves (88,868 ha); 42 cultural and historical areas (2,507 ha); and 315 natural monuments (8,598 ha).[832]

796. The preliminary list of proposals for UNESCO world heritage contains five protected areas: National Parks Đerdap, Tara and Sar Mountain; Monument of Nature Đavolja varos and Special Nature Reserve Deliblato Sands. Within the UNESCO 'Man and Biosphere' programme, Nature Park 'Golija' joined the biosphere reserve network in 2001 when it was named 'Golija-Studenica'. Another nine natural areas have been nominated for biosphere reserve status. Based on the Ramsar Convention on Wetlands of International Importance, nine areas have gained Ramsar Area status, of which eight are protected. These include: Special Nature Reserves 'Obedska bara' 'Carska bara', 'Ludasko jezero', 'Slano kopovo' 'Labudovo okno' (part of the Deliblato Sands Special Nature Reserve), 'GornjePodunavlje' and 'Zasavica', Landscape of Exceptional Characteristics 'Vlasinsko jezero' and 'Karajukica bunari' in Pester field, covering an area of 55,627 ha.[833]

§2. Legal Regulation

797. Legal protection of national parks and other specially protected zones has a relatively long tradition in Serbia (Yugoslavia). A decree regulating protection of national parks was, for example, enacted already in 1938. It should be stressed that legal regulation concerning parks and reserves is closely related not only to other fields, in the first place with wildlife protection, but also with other fields as, for example, water, forestry, fishing, hunting, mining, spatial planning, traffic, tourism,

---

831. *Biodiversity indicators in the Republic of Serbia for 2015*, MAEP, EPA, 2015, 1. The spatial plan of the RS (OJ RS, No. 88/10), envisages that by the year 2015 around 10% of the Serbian surface would be protected, and that by the year 2021 around 12% of the territory of the RS would be under a form of protection.

832. The surface coverage of protected areas planned for protection by 2015, stand at around 10% and by 2021 around 12%. AECQ, Chs 27, 192. *See also*, *Prostorni plan Republike Srbije od 2010. do 2020. godine (Spatial plan of the Republic of Serbia from 2010 to 2020)*, OJ RS, No. 88/2010); *See also*, I. Radović & M. Kozomora (ed.), *Biodivesity Strategy of The Republic of Serbia: for the period 2011–2018*29 (Ministry of Environment and Spatial Planning 2011). The list and map of protected areas are provided in Annexes 1 and 2.

833. I. Radović & M. Kozomora, *supra* , 29. Detailed lists of Important Bird Area (IBA), Important Plane Area (IPA) and Prime Butterfly Areas (PBA) are provided in Annex 3.

etc. So, in many cases the same legal or sub-legal Act is relevant for two or more of the above-mentioned domains.

798. Presently, there are several basic legal Acts regulating protection of parks and reserves:

- The Law on Nature Protection (OJ RS, Nos 36/09, 88/2010 and 91/2010 – corr., and 14/2016).
- The Law on National Parks (OJ RS, No. 84/2015).
- The Law on Forests (OJ RS, Nos 30/10, 93/12 and 89/15).
- The Law on Protection and Sustainable Use of Fish Resources (OJ RS, No. 128/14).
- The Law on Wildlife and Hunting (OJ RS, No. 18/10).

I. The Law on Nature Protection

799. The definition of 'protected area' is given in Article 28 of the Law on Nature Protection. It says that areas which have strong geological, biological, ecosystem and/or landscape diversity and which are important as habitats of birds and other migratory species, that are important in accordance to the international regulations, can be declared as protected areas of general interest.[834] Protected areas can be associated with the transboundary protected areas of the neighbouring countries.[835]

A. Strict and Special Natural Reserves

800. Article 29 gives definitions of strict and special natural reserve, as well as it prescribes which operations and activities are prohibited within strict and special natural reserve. Strict natural reserve is an area of unchanged natural characteristics with representative natural ecosystems, intended solely to preserve the original nature, gene fund, ecologic equilibrium, monitoring of natural phenomena and processes, scientific research that does not affect the natural characteristics, values, phenomena and processes.[836] Special natural reserve is an area of unchanged or with slightly changed nature, of particular importance due to its uniqueness, rareness or representativeness,

834. There are three protection regimes prescribed to be established in protected area: (1) First degree – strict protection; (2) Second degree – active protection and (3) Third degree – proactive protection (Art. 35).

835. The management plan and measures for protection of a protected area which has been connected in transboundary manner with a protected area in the neighbouring country shall be established by mutual consent with the competent authorities of that country, with consent of the Ministry.

836. Within the strict and the special natural reserve it shall be prohibited to carry out operations and activities and perform actions which can impair the features due to which they have been declared as protected natural asset (picking and destroying of plants, disturbing, catching and killing of animals, introducing new biological species, melioration works, various forms of economical and other usage, etc.) (Art. 29, para. 4). All economic and other activities shall be prohibited in the strict natural reserve (Art. 29, para. 8). Measures for protection of strict and special natural reserve shall be closely determined by the decision on the proclamation of protected area (Art. 29, para. 6).

which includes a habitat of endangered wild species of plants, animals and fungi, without settlements or with scarce settlements in which people live in harmony with the nature, and which are intended for conservation of the existing natural features, gene fund, ecological equilibrium, natural phenomena and processes, scientific research and education, controlled visits and preservation of traditional ways of life.

B. National Park

801. Article 30 contains definition of national park. It says that national park is an area with a large number of diverse natural ecosystems of national importance, with distinguished landscape characteristics and cultural heritage in which people live in harmony with the nature, intended for conservation of the existing natural values and resources, with overall landscape, geological and biological diversity, as well as for meeting of scientific, educational, spiritual, aesthetical, cultural, touristic, health and recreational needs and other activities in accordance with the principles of nature protection and sustainable development.[837] Activities and operations that do not disturb the original state of nature shall be allowed in the national park, as well as carrying out activities that have the function within education, health and recreational and touristic needs, continuation of the traditional way of life of local communities, and in the way that does not jeopardize the survival of species of the natural ecosystems and landscapes, in accordance with this Law and the management plan adopted by the manager (Article 30 paragraph 2).[838]

C. Natural Monument

802. It is prescribed in Article 31 that natural monument is a less unchanged or partially changed natural spatial entity, object or phenomenon, physically clearly distinguished, recognizable and/or unique, with representative geomorphological, geological, hydrographical, botanical and/or other characteristics, as well as by human labour created value of botanical, aesthetic, cultural or educational significance. Any actions or activities on the natural monument that endanger its characteristics and values shall be prohibited.[839]

D. Protected Habitat

803. Article 32 prescribes that protected habitat is an area which includes one or more types of natural habitats important for conservation of one or more populations of wild species and their communities. Also, Article 32 prescribes objectives of habitat

837. The measures for protection of the national park and the manner of its use shall be determined in detail by a special Law (Art. 30, para. 6).
838. The activities referred to in para. 2 of this Article can be limited with purpose of preserving the original state of nature in the national park (Art. 30, para. 3).
839. Measures to protect the natural monument and the mode for its use shall be defined in detail by the Act on proclamation of protected area (Art. 31, para. 4).

at protection (paragraph 2). The activities and operations which endanger or damage one or more habitat types shall be prohibited within the protected habitats.[840]

E. *Landscape of Exceptional Characteristics*

804. Landscape of exceptional feature is an area of recognizable appearance with significant natural, biological-ecological, aesthetic and cultural-historical values that is developed over time as a result of interaction between the nature, natural potentials of the area and the traditional way of life of the local population. Landscape of exceptional features can be a natural landscape[841] and a cultural landscape of exceptional features[842] (Article 33). The activities and operations which disturb primary natural and created values and landscape character shall be prohibited within the landscape of exceptional characteristics (Article 33 paragraph 5).[843]

F. *Natural Park*

805. Natural park is an area of well-preserved natural values with mostly preserved natural ecosystems and picturesque landscapes, intended for conservation of the overall geological, biological and landscape diversity, as well as meeting of scientific, educational, spiritual, aesthetic, cultural, touristic, health-recreational needs and other activities harmonized with the traditional way of life and principles of sustainable development. Within the natural park, economic or other activities which threaten its substantial characteristics and values are not allowed (Article 34).[844]

II. Law on National Parks

806. The basic legal act regulating the field of national parks in the Republic of Serbia is the Law on National Parks (OJ RS, No. 84/2015), adopted in 2015. It has the following six parts: Part I – General Provisions (Article 1); Part II – The Objective of the Law (Article 2); Part III – Values, size, boundaries and protection regimes (Articles 3–10); Part IV – Management and sustainable usage of national park (Articles

840. The importance, purpose and protection measures are determined in Act on proclamation of protected habitat (Art. 32, para. 4).
841. Natural landscape of exceptional characteristics shall be an area of significant biological-ecological and aesthetic value, in which the traditional way of life of the local population has not significantly disturbed the nature and natural ecosystems (Art. 33, para. 3).
842. Cultural landscape of exceptional characteristics shall be an area of significant landscape, aesthetic and cultural-historical value, which developed in time as a result of interaction between the nature, natural potentials of the area and the traditional way of life of the local population (Art. 33, para. 4).
843. Protection measures, the mode for carrying out economic and traditional activities and use of natural and created values within the landscape of exceptional characteristics shall be closely established in the formal decision on proclamation of protected area (Art. 33, para. 6).
844. Protection measures, the mode for carrying out economic activities and use of natural values within the natural park shall be closely established in the formal decision on proclamation of protected area (Art. 34, para. 3).

11–24); Part V – Supervision (Article 25) and Part VI – Transitory and final provisions (Articles 26–29).

This Law regulates the goals, values, size, boundaries and protection regimes, management and sustainable use of the National Park 'Fruška Gora' National Park 'Đerdap' National Park 'Tara' National Park 'Kopaonik' and the National Park 'Šar planina' (hereinafter, the National park) (Article 1, paragraph 1).

807. The objectives to be achieved by this Law are: (1) the preservation and improvement of the value of biodiversity, geodiversity as well as cultural and historical value; (2) the preservation and improvement of ecologically important areas and diversity of landscapes; (3) preservation of geological heritage facilities;(4) preservation and improvement of habitats, types of habitats and wild flora and fauna; (5) preservation and improvement of adequate quality of life in the National Park through the development of social, cultural and economic activity; (6) preservation of cultural and historical heritage; (7) preservation of traditional ways of life; (8) Preservation of natural processes and the balance between natural processes and human activities, i.e., sustainable development of the national park; and (9) formidable nature experience for visitors, education, research, sport and recreation (Article 2, paragraph 1).

808. Protection and sustainable use of the National Park is conducted in accordancewith the National Park Management Plan for a period of ten years and other acts adopted on the basis of this Law, regulating the protection of nature. At the area of the National Park shall be established regimes of protection of I, II and III grade, on which are applied prohibitions and restrictions on works and activities, identified in the Management Plan and regulations governing the nature protection. The Management Plan and spatial plan of the special purpose areas must not be contrary (Article 10, paragraphs 1–3). The management plan includes measures, prohibitions and restrictions on works and activities in accordance with prescribed protection regimes (Article 12, paragraph 1–2).

In the area of the National Park, the construction of buildings, which is contrary with the spatial plan for special purpose areas, is prohibited (Article 10, paragraph 4).

809. The Government gives approval on the Management Plan, after previously obtained opinion of the competent ministries. The Management plan is implemented by an annual National Park Management Programme (hereinafter, Programme Management)(Article 12, paragraphs 4–5).

The spatial plan of the special purpose area for the area of the National Park will be developed with the protection regimes I, II and III, prescribed by this Law. Urban development plans at the area of the National Park shall be adopted with prior approval of the Ministry(Article 19, paragraph 1–2).

810. The Professional Council of the National Park is a professional and consultative body that monitors and analyses the programmes and projects in the field of nature conservation and sustainable use of natural resources, in particular: (1) National Park Management Plan; (2) The National Park Management Programme; (3) Programmes and projects to implement the measures and activities for protection and development of the National Park; and (4) Consider other activities of the Manager relating to operations of protection and development of National park (Article 22, paragraph 1).

The Ministry shall supervise over the implementation of the provisions of this Law (Article 25, paragraph 1).

811. It should be added that the regime of protection of specific locations is regulated by sub-legal Acts adopted for each individual protected area, as for example:

- Regulation on protection of a special nature reserve 'Stari Begej-Carska Bara Swamp' (OJ RS, No. 56/94).
- Regulation on protection of special reserve 'Ludasko Lake' (OJ RS, No. 56/94).
- Regulation on protection of special nature reserve 'Obedska swamp' (OJ RS, No. 56/94).
- Regulation on protection of general nature reserve 'Vitanovaca' (OJ RS, No. 9/95).
- Regulations on protection of special nature reserve 'Jelasnicka klisure gorge' (OJ RS, No. 9/95).
- Regulation on protection of natural monument 'Homoljska Potajnica' (OJ RS, No. 9/95).
- Regulation on protection of natural monument 'Risovaca' (OJ RS, No. 9/95).
- Regulation on protection of natural monument 'Vrelo Mlave' (OJ RS, No. 9/95).
- Regulation on protection of natural monument 'Resavska cave' (OJ RS, No. 9/95).
- Regulation on protection of natural monument 'Krupajsko vrelo' (OJ RS, No. 9/95).
- Regulation on protection of natural monument 'Lisine' (OJ RS, No. 9/95).
- Regulation on protection of natural monument 'Đavolja Varos' (OJ RS, No. 9/95).[845]
- Rulebook on the form of national park supervisor official ID (OJ RS, Nos 117/14 and 97/15).

812. Serbia is a contracting party of the following international treaties related to the nature protection:

- International Plant Protection Convention (1951) (OJ FPRY –IT, No. 7/55).
- Ramsar Convention on Wetlands of International – Importance Especially as Waterfowl Habitat (1971) (OJ SFRY – IT, No. 9/77).
- International Convention for the Protection of Birds (OJ SFRY – IT, No. 6/73).
- Convention on International Trade in Endangered Species of Wild Fauna and Flora (1979) (CITES) (OJ SFRY – IT, No. 11/01).

845. *See also* following regulations regarding:(1) natural monuments: 'Prerasti – Vratne' (OJ RS, No. 99/14), 'Promuklica' (OJ RS, No. 101/14); (2) special nature reserve: 'Goč – Gvozdac' (OJ RS, No. 99/14), 'Klisura reke Maleševke' (OJ RS, No. 104/14), 'Mala jasenova glava' (OJ RS, No. 116/14), 'Ritovi donjeg Potisja' (OJ RS, No. 121/14), 'Suva planina' (OJ RS, No. 72/15), 'Iznad Tatalije' (OJ RS, No. 72/15), 'Tesne Jaruge' (OJ RS, No. 72/15), 'Zelenika' (OJ RS, No. 72/15) and 'Peštersko polje' (OJ RS, No. 114/15); and (3) strict nature reserves 'Mustava' (OJ RS, No. 99/14, 'Kukavica' (OJ RS, No. 107/14), 'Felješana' (OJ RS, No. 107/14), 'Dolina potoka Bigar' (OJ RS, No. 72/15); landscape of exceptional properties: 'Kamena gora' (OJ RS, No. 99/14), 'Ozren – Jadovnik' (OJ RS, No. 107/14).

- Convention on Biological Diversity (OJ SFRY – IT, No. 11/01) and Cartagena Protocol on Biosafety (OJ SM – IT, No.16/05).
- Convention on Conservation of Migratory Species of Wild Animals Bonn Convention (OJ RS –IT, No. 102/07).
- Regulation on labelling (marking) of petroleum products (OJ RS, No. 51/15). Convention on the Conservation of European Wildlife and Natural Habitats – Bern Convention (OJ RS – IT, No. 102/07).
- Regulation on labelling (marking) of petroleum products (OJ RS, No. 51/15). Convention on the Protection and Sustainable Development of the Carpathians – Carpathian Convention (OJ RS – IT, No. 102/07).[846]
- United Nations Convention to Combat Desertification in Countries Experiencing Serious Drought and/or Desertification, Particularly in Africa (OJ RS – IT, No. 102 /07).
- European Landscape Convention (OJ RS – IT, No. 4/2011).

Serbia is, since 2002, a member of the Joint Secretariat of the Pan-European Biological and Landscape Diversity Strategy (PEBLDS).

813. 'In the area of nature protection, Serbia is partially aligned with the *acquis*. The Implementation of the acquis remains at an early stage.'[847]

846. Serbia also ratified the following protocols: Protocol on Conservation and Sustainable Use of Biological and Landscape Diversity to the Framework Convention on the Protection and Sustainable Development of the Carpathians (OJ RS – IT, No. 1/13); Protocol on Sustainable Forest Management to the Framework Convention on the Protection and Sustainable Development of the Carpathians (OJ RS – IT, No. 5/15); and Protocol on Sustainable Tourism to the Framework Convention on the Protection and Sustainable Development of the Carpathians (OJ RS – IT, No. 5/15).
847. SRS, Chs 27, 22. Special attention needs to be paid for the development of a strong inspection network capable of enforcing the provisions of all nature protection legislation. *Ibid.*, 23. 'Systematic assessment and collection of data for the designation of future Natura 2,000 sites has started. The institutional framework for Natura 2,000 needs to be streamlined and adequately resourced.' CR, 77.

Chapter 3. Wildlife Protection

§1. Introduction

814. The Republic of Serbia is characterized by high genetic, species and ecosystem diversity. The highland and mountainous regions of the Republic of Serbia, as a part of Balkan Peninsula, are one of the six European biodiversity centres. Moreover, in terms of the wealth of its flora, the Republic of Serbia is potentially one of the global centres of plant diversity. Although the Republic of Serbia's 88,361 km^2 represent only 2.1% of European territory, biodiversity of different groups of organisms remains high. The Republic of Serbia hosts: 39% of European vascular flora, 51% of European fish fauna, 49% of European reptile and amphibian fauna, 74% of European bird fauna and 67% of European mammal fauna.[848] In the territory of the RS 2,628 species are protected, out of which 1,760 are strictly protected.[849]

815. Generally speaking, the MAEP and the Nature Protection Institute are main institutions competent in the field. Besides them, certain competences are also, as in the case of parks and reserves, given to the EPA (data collection and reporting on the status of biodiversity) and to the Secretariat for Environmental Protection and Sustainable Development of the APV.

§2. Legal Regulation

816. Wildlife protection is presently in Serbia regulated by numerous legal and sub-legal Acts.[850] They are often the same as those regulating parks and reserves and mentioned in the previous chapter. As already mentioned Article 89 of the Constitution prescribes that everyone shall be obliged to protect natural rarities (scientific, cultural and historical heritage), as well as goods of public interest in accordance with the Law (The Republic of Serbia, APs and LSG units shall be held particularly accountable for the protection of heritage).

817. The following could be regarded as the most important legal regulations:

(1) *EPL* (OJ RS, Nos 135/04, 36/09, 72/09, 43/11CC and 14/16).
(2) Law on Nature Protection (OJ RS, Nos 36/09, 88/2010 and 91/2010 – corr, and 14/16).

848. I. Radović & M. Kozomora, *supra* , 18. *See also*, NEPP, 34–37.
849. *Biodiversity indicators in the Republic of Serbia for 2015*, MAEP, EPA, 2015, 3.
850. For a more detailed commentary, *see* , G. Petković, *Legislative Concept of the Biodiversity Protection, Pravni život, No. 9/2006*, 533–579. D. Todić, Biodiverzitet i genetički resursi u svetlu principa međunarodnog prava životne sredine [*Biodiversity and Genetic Resources in Principles of International Environmental Law*], Arhiv za poljoprivredne nauke [*Archive for Agricultural Sciences*], br. 2005/5 (Belgrade: Savez poljoprivrednih inzenjra i tehnicara Srbije i Crne Gore), 201–208.

(3) Law on National Parks (OJ RS, No. 84/15).[851]
(4) Regulation on the control of use and trade of wild flora and fauna (OJ RS, Nos 31/05, 45/05, 22/07, 38/08, 9/10 and 69/11).
(5) Rulebook on transboundary movement and trade in protected species (OJ RS, Nos 99/09 and 6/14).[852]

I. Law on Environmental Protection

818. The EPL (OJ RS, Nos 135/04, 36/09, 72/09, 43/11CC and 14/16) has several provisions concerning biodiversity, which is defined as 'a diversity of organisms within a specie, among the species and ecosystems and it covers full genetic diversity, species and ecosystems diversity at local, national, regional and global level' (Article 3, point 7).

---

851. Several other laws could be relevant too. These are: Law on Game and Hunting (OJ RS, No. 18/10); Law on the Protection and Sustainable Use of Fish Stocks (OJ RS, No. 128/14); Law on the Welfare of Animals (OJ RS, No. 41/09); Law on Forests (OJ RS, Nos 30/10, 93/12 and 89/15); Law on Agriculture and Rural Development (OJ RS, Nos 41/09, 10/13 and 101/16); Law on the Spatial Plan of the Republic of Serbia from 2010 until 2020 (OJ RS, No. 88/10); Law on Food Security (OJ RS, No. 41/09); Law on Animal Husbandry (OJ RS, Nos 41/09, 93/12 and 14/16); Law on the Protection of Rights of Breeders of Plant Varieties (OJ RS, No. 41/09); Law on GMOs (OJ RS, No. 41/09); Law on Tourism (OJ RS, Nos 36/09, 88/10, 99/11, 93/12 and 84/15), etc.

852. A part from that, list of relevant by-laws include, *inter alia*, the following: Regulation on the ecological network (OJ RS, No. 102/10); Rulebook on contents and operational methods of the protected areas' register (OJ RS, No. 81/10); Rulebook on conditions to be fulfilled by protected area managers (OJ RS, No. 85/09); Rulebook on protected area rangers' identity cards (OJ RS, No. 84/09); Rulebook on the appearance (look) of the nature protection logo and procedure and conditions for its use (OJ RS, No. 84/09); Rulebook on proclamation and protection of strictly protected and protected species of wild plants, animals and fungi (OJ RS, Nos 5/10, 47/11, 32/16 and 98/16); Rulebook on distinguishing criteria of habitat types, habitat types, sensitive, threatened, rare and priority habitats for protection, as well as protection measures for the conservation of habitat types (OJ RS, No. 35/10); Rulebook on compensation tariffs for determining compensation levels for damage caused through an unauthorized act in relation to strictly protected and protected wild species (OJ RS, No. 37/10); Rulebook on methods, tools and resources for commercial fishing, as well as methods, tools and resources for recreational fishing (OJ of RS, No. 42/16); Regulation on the method of determining costs and their amount for damage caused to fish stock (OJ of RS, No. 3/16); Rulebook on conditions, programme and methods for fishing guard examinations and professional examinations for fishermen (OJ RS, Nos 60/15 and 96/16); Rulebook on categorization of fishing waters (OJ of RS, No. 10/12); Rulebook on conditions and methods for organizing fishing guards, legitimization form for fishing guards and appearance (look) of the fishing guards badge (OJ of RS, No. 07/10); Rulebook on entering into the production of GMOs and products of GMOs (OJ FRY, No. 62/02, and OJ RS, No. 29/09), Regulation on regimes of protection (OJ RS, No. 31/12), Regulation on compensatory measures (OJ the RS, No. 20/10), Regulation on evaluation criteria and procedure for classification of protected areas (Official Journal of RS, No. 97/15), Rulebook on fish warden uniforms, appearance of the warden badge and fish warden official ID form (OJ RS, No. 39/16).

819. As already mentioned, the whole second part of the Law is devoted to 'management of natural values' (Articles 11–32). On the basis of the Law, a ten-year Strategy for the Sustainable Use of Natural Resources has been adopted (OJ RS, No. 33/12). It will be followed by specific plans for APs and LSGs. The nature protection law improves nature management.[853] Article 26 of the EPL prescribes that:

> biodiversity protection, use of biological resources, genetically modified organism and biotechnology shall be executed on the basis of this Law and obligations taken through international agreements. Biodiversity and biological resources shall be protected and used in a way that shall enable their survival, diversity, renewal and improvement in case of misbalance.

820. Concrete measures to be taken in connection with protection and use of flora and fauna and trade with endangered and protected species of wild flora and fauna are indicated in Articles 27 and 28.

In order to protect biodiversity and biological resources, the Ministry and other competent bodies and organizations have obligations to control import and growth of plant and animal species of foreign origin (Article 27).[854]

II. The Law on Nature Protection

821. The Law on Nature Protection (OJ RS, Nos 36/2009, 88/2010 and 91/2010 – corr., and 14/16) prescribes in Article 36 that wild species that are threatened or may become endangered, which have special significance from the genetic, ecological, ecosystem, scientific, health, economical and other aspects, shall be protected as strictly

853. It is prescribed by the Art. 17 of the EPL, that the activities which threaten the environment, natural balance, biodiversity, hydrographic, geomorphologic, geological, cultural and landscape values, or which in any way degrade the quality and properties of the natural good, are not be allowed within a protected natural good (para. 2).

854. It is prohibited to harass, abuse, hurt and destroy wild fauna and to demolish their habitats. Apart from that, it is also prohibited to destroy, tear or in any other way to desertification of wild flora or to destroy and demolish its habitats (Art. 27, paras 2 and 3).

protected wild species or protected wild species (Article 36 paragraph 1).[855] It is prescribed which wild species can be declared as strictly protected[856] or protected.[857]

822. Protected species, within the meaning of this Law, are determined on the basis of national and international red lists or red books, expert findings and scientific knowledge (Article 36 paragraph 3).[858] The ecological network is established as a functionally and spatially connected entity in order to conserve habitat types of particular importance for the protection, renewal and/or improvement of degraded habitats, and for the conservation of habitats of wild species of flora and fauna (Article 38).[859]

823. On the basis of the estimate of endangerment for certain wild species, and the obligations from the approved international agreements, as well as on the basis of the national and international red lists and/or red books and/or other professional documentation, the Minister shall, by mutual consent with the Minister competent for the agriculture, forestry and water management, and at the proposal of the Institute, and/or other authorized scientific or expert organizations, declare the wild species as strictly protected wildlife species or protected wildlife species (Article 48, paragraph 1).[860] The Institute shall take care about the species, as well as holders of such species,

---

855. Wild species are all types of animals, plants and fungi that are naturally evolved, including hybrids and all specimens reproduced in captivity or under artificial conditions, with the exception of domesticated races on whose evolutionary process has affected the man for its own purposes (Art. 4, para. 13).
856. The following wild species can be declared as strictly protected: (1) species extinct in the Republic of Serbia and return through a reintroduction programme; (2) extremely endangered wild species; (3) endangered wild species; (4) relict species; (5) local endemite; (6) stenoendemite; (7) wild species subject to a ratified international agreement; and (8) a species requiring strict protection for other reasons (Art. 36, para. 2).
857. The following wild species can be declared as protected: (1) vulnerable wild species; (2) endemic species; (3) indicator, key and umbrella species; (4) relict species; (5) wild species subject to a ratified international agreement; (6) wild species not endangered, but, due to its appearance, can be easily confused with an endangered wild species; and(7) wild species of economic importance which can be endangered by uncontrolled exploitation or destruction of the habitat (Art. 36, para. 3).
858. Strictly protected and protected wild species in terms of this Law, are determined on the basis of national and international red lists or red books, ratified international treaties, expert findings and/or scientific knowledge. Red List and Red Book of endangered wild species with places where they are located, population abundance and the level of vulnerability, are determined by the Ministry, at the proposal of the institution (Art. 36, para. 4 and 5).
859. The ecological network shall be made up of important ecological areas and ecological corridors. Important ecological areas are: (1) areas of national importance which by their bio-geographic presence and representativeness contribute to the conservation of biological diversity in the Republic of Serbia; and (2) areas of international importance which by their bio-geographic presence and representativeness contribute to the conservation of habitat types and habitats of species including birds in accordance with ratified international agreements and common rules of international Law. The ecological network of the Republic of Serbia is established by the Government (Art. 38, paras 2, 3 and 4).
860. *See* , Rulebook on declaring and protection of the strictly protected and protected wild plants, animals and fungi (OJ RS, Nos 5/2010, 47/11, 36/16 and 98/16). There are a total of 1,760 strictly protected wild species of algae, plants, animals and fungi. *See* , I. Radović & M. Kozomora, *supra* , 32.

protected areas managers, public enterprises for forest management, users of hunting areas and fishery areas who are obligated to plan and implement measures and activities of monitoring and management of strictly protected species and protected wild species populations within the management programmes and plans, in compliance with this and special laws (Article 48, paragraph 2).

824. Article 64 of the Law prescribes responsibility for damage caused by wild species. Namely, this Article defines that the Republic of Serbia is not responsible for damage caused by wild species, except in the cases laid down by this Law and other regulations. A legal entity, entrepreneur or private entity to whom strictly protected or protected wild species may cause economic or any other damage shall be obliged to duly and at his/her on expense undertake all authorized actions and activities in order to prevent the occurrence of damage (Article 64 paragraph 2).[861] However, the injured party has the right to reimbursement in the amount of the real damage induced by strictly protected and protected species if the injured party implemented prescribed measures and activities.[862]

A. Protection and Conservation of Wild Species

825. Prevention of all activities that contribute to disturbance of favourable state of wild species populations, destruction or damage to their habitats, nests, litters or disruption of their life cycle and/or favourable state[863] shall be deemed as protection and conservation of wild species (Article 71). During the execution of work and activities in nature and use of natural values in the wild species habitats, measures, methods and technical means that contribute to the conservation of favourable state of species and/or do not endanger wild species and/or disturb the habitats of their populations shall be applied, or these works and activities may be restricted in the period overlapping with significant stages of the life cycle of the species (Article 72).

B. Strictly Protected Wild Species

826. Strictly protected wild species can be protected in the entire territory of the Republic of Serbia or in individual parts thereof (Article 73, paragraph 1).[864]

---

861. Under the action or activity in terms of para. 2 of this Article the following shall be understood: fencing, safeguarding of goods and chasing out of strictly protected animal species, from the place wherein directly threaten the goods and in the manner not threatening for the survival of species.

862. The amount of reimbursement for damage (in line with criteria for the estimation of damage prescribed by the Minister) is fixed in agreement between the Ministry, i.e., competent body of the AP and the injured party, while the court shall fix the amount of damage in the case of dispute (Art. 65, para. 5).

863. The favourable state of wild species shall be provided by the protection of their habitats and protection measures for particular species in compliance with this Law (Art. 71, para. 2).

864. If an area is the temporary habitat of a strictly protected wild species and its protection cannot be provided in some other way, the Ministry can, by a special decision, with prior opinion of the Ministry responsible for agriculture and forestry, declare that area or the part thereof is temporarily protected as long as the need for protection exists (Art. 73, para. 2).

827. It shall be prohibited to use, destroy, and execute other activities that could endanger strictly protected wild plant, animal including birds and fungi species and their habitats (Article 74, paragraph 1).[865] The following shall be prohibited: (1) to destroy specimens of plant and fungi species and the development forms thereof by picking, collecting, cutting, or uprooting or digging in all stages of the biological cycle, and to endanger or destroy their habitats; (2) to keep and trade in strictly protected plant and fungi species growing in the wild and the development forms thereof; (3) capture, keep and/or kill strictly protected wild animal species in all stages of the biological cycle, damage or destroy the development forms thereof, eggs, nests and litters, as well as the area of their breeding sites and resting places and to endanger or destroy their habitats; (4) to significantly disturb these species, particularly during the period of breeding, rearing, hibernation and migration; (5) to cut off migratory routes; (6) to hide, keep, breed, trade in, export, transport and offer for sale or exchange or in any other way acquire or publicly expose animal species including all their derivatives and development forms (Article 74, paragraph 2).[866]

C. *Protected Wild Species*

828. Protected wild species can be protected in the entire territory of the Republic of Serbia or in individual parts thereof (Article 76, paragraph 1).[867] Protected wild species of fungi, lichens, plants, animals or their parts, can be collected for the purpose of processing, trading, cross-boundary commerce, as well as cultivation and rearing, on the basis of a permit issued by the Ministry in accordance with law (paragraph 3).[868]

---

865. Notwithstanding the provisions of Art. 74 of this Law, when there is no other satisfactory solution and the exemption is not damaging the survival of populations of strictly protected wild species at a favourable conservation status in their natural habitat, i.e., when there is no other satisfactory solution for wild bird species, the Ministry may allow activities that aim at: (1) research and education, recolonization (repopulation), reintroduction and breeding operations in in-situ and ex-situ conditions; (2) prevention of serious damage to crops, livestock, forests, fishponds and water and other forms of property; (3) protection of public health and public safety and in case of birds the air safety as well, or for other reasons of predominant public interest, including reasons of social and economic nature and beneficial consequences of primary importance for the environment; (4) protection of wild plant and animal species and conservation of wild habitats; (5) allowing, under strictly controlled conditions and under limited scope, taking or keeping of certain specimens in limited quantity (Art. 75, para. 1). A permit for the situation referred to in para. 1 of this Article shall be issued by the Ministry upon previously obtained opinion of the Institute.
866. Fine ranging between RSD 500,000 and 2,000,000 shall be imposed to legal entity for the offence if such legal entity undertakes actions which may endanger strictly protected species of plants, animals, fungi and their habitats (Art. 126, point 11).
867. The management of populations of protected wild species that is not regulated by rules concerning hunting and fisheries shall be implemented on the basis of a permit issued by the Ministry in accordance with law (Art. 76, para. 2).
868. The detailed conditions and protection measures for protected wild species and measures for the protection of their habitats shall be specified by the decision referred to in Art. 48 of this Law (para. 4).

D. *The Use and Collecting of Protected Wild Species*

829. Pursuant to Article 77 the use and collecting of protected wild species shall be allowed exclusively in the way that does not endanger favourable status of the population.[869] The Institute for Nature Protection shall register the manner and scope of usage of protected wild species for the purpose of determination and follow-up of population status including wild species whose usage is regulated by the Law on Hunting and the Law on Fishery.

E. *Permit to Research Strictly Protected and Protected Wild Species*

830. The Ministry shall issue the permit for scientific research and educational purposes for the researches of strictly protected and protected wild species that is performed by methods that could endanger the species (such as capturing, collecting, marking, sampling, etc.), with previously obtained opinion from the Institute (Article 78, paragraph 1).[870] The research reports referred to in paragraph 1 of this Article shall be submitted to the Ministry, the Institute and the Manager of the protected area by the end of the calendar year (Article 78, paragraph 3). Taking out of specimens of strictly protected and protected wild species and/or their parts and derivatives referred to in paragraph 1 of this Article for scientific and research purposes shall be carried out on the basis of a permit issued by the Ministry, pursuant to Article 94 of this Law (Article 78, paragraph 4).

F. *Wild Animals*

831. The use of certain means for capturing and killing of wild animals, that endanger or disturb their populations and/or habitats, affect their welfare, and that can cause their local disappearance shall be prohibited. The prohibited means are prescribed in Article 79. The prohibited means shall be considered the following in particular: (1) traps; (2) adhesives; (3) chemical means like attractants; (4) live animals used as decoys in hunting of birds and game; (5) crossbows, bows, arrows and/or other weapon with strings, that can fling an arrow or other projectile by pulling the string or some other elastic; (6) bird hunting with nets; (7) lethal or stunning electrical devices; (8) luminous devices; (9) mirrors and other dazzling devices;(10) sound transmitters (tape recorders, cassette recorders, audio recorders and players, etc.) that emit sound of calling, crying or responding; (11) devices for illuminating targets; (12) sighting devices for night shooting comprising an electronic image magnifier or image converter; (13) explosives; (14) poisons or anaesthetic baits;(15) automatic weapons; (16) aircrafts;

869. The Minister shall prescribe in more detail the conditions and measures for the protection of protected wild species including the following: (1) prohibition of use in terms of time; (2) quantitative and qualitative restrictions in their use; (3) prohibition of use in terms of space aiming at recovery of population to a satisfactory level (Art. 77, para. 2). Should it be established that due to usage a protected wild species is endangered, the Minister can prohibit or restrict the use of that species, previously acquiring the opinion of the Institute (Art. 77, para. 4).

870. No complaint against the decision referred to in para. 1 shall be allowed, but administrative dispute may be instituted against it (Art. 78, para. 5).

(17) motor-driven vehicles in motion used to hunt animals; and (18) other devices specified by other law and ratified international agreements (Article 79, paragraph 2).[871]

G. *Migratory Species*

832. Public roads and other traffic routes, telecommunication and electric systems, waterworks and other buildings whose construction cuts off usual corridors for daily and seasonal migration of wild animals, causes habitat fragmentation or in some other way disturbs their normal life cycle, shall be constructed so as to reduce negative impacts with the application of special construction and technical solutions on the buildings and around them, during the periods of both construction and exploitation (Article 80, paragraph 1).[872] Special technological solutions enabling free and secure communication of wild animals shall be prescribed by the Minister (Article 80, paragraph 2).

H. *Allochthonous Species*

833. Introduction of allochthonous wild species and hybrids thereof into the wild on the territory of the Republic of Serbia shall be prohibited.[873] (Article 82, paragraph 1).[874] Exceptionally, introduction referred to in paragraph 1 of the present Article shall be permitted if scientifically and professionally proven and acceptable from the aspect of nature protection and sustainable management, that is, if such introduction does not endanger populations or natural habitat of autochthonous wild species (Article 83, paragraph 2). In case of unintentional introduction of allochthonous wild species and hybrids thereof into the free nature on the territory of the Republic of Serbia, or if there is a reasonable doubt that such introduction will occur, the Minister shall stipulate actions to exterminate or prevent further spread of introduced allochthonous wild species and hybrids thereof (Article 83).

871. Certain means referred to in para. 2 of this Article can be used exceptionally and restrictively for scientific and research purposes. The permit to use the means referred to in para. 3 of this Article shall be issued by the Ministry by a ruling, with prior opinion of other competent authorities (Art. 79, para. 3). No complaint against the decision shall be allowed but administrative dispute may be instituted against it (Art. 79, para. 4).

872. Towers and technical components of medium and high voltage ducts shall be so executed as to protect birds and bats against the electric shock and mechanical injury. Locations of wind powered generators (windmills) shall be so determined as to avoid important habitats and migration routes thereof (Art. 81, paras 1 and 2). Usage of strong light sources (advertising rotating reflectors, lasers and the like) pointed towards the sky shall not be allowed, unless when used for safety and air traffic control purposes (Art. 81, para. 5).

873. An allochthonous species is a species that came into ecosystems on the territory of the Republic of Serbia by intentional or accidental introduction (Art. 4, para. 2).

874. Fine ranging between RSD 500,000 and 2,000,000 shall be imposed to legal entity for the offence if such legal entity introduces allochthonous wild species and their hybrids into free nature contrary to Art. 82 of this Law (Art. 126, point 17).

I. Relocation of Specimens of Autochthonous Species

834. Relocation of live specimens of autochthonous wild species in free nature on the territory of the Republic of Serbia can be carried out based on research and planning documents, in accordance with the present and other laws. Relocation referred to in the preceding paragraph can be carried out provided that research findings show that such action would not endanger in any way the favourable status of species population, that is, the animal welfare, and in case of accidental occurrences (floods, fires, droughts, etc.) (Article 84, paragraphs 1 and 2).[875]

J. Reintroduction of Wild Species

835. Reintroduction of wild species into the free nature on the territory of the Republic of Serbia can be carried out based on research, reintroduction programme and permit.[876] Reintroduction of wild species can be carried out provided that research findings show that such action contributes to the favourable status of the species.[877]

K. Wild Animal Species

836. Live specimens of wild animal species may be kept in captivity only if they are provided with living conditions in accordance with the law, well-suited for the type, breed, gender, age, physical and biological specificities and ethological needs of the species (Article 86, paragraph 1).[878] The Minister shall prescribe conditions that must be fulfilled by zoos and other facilities and/or spaces for keeping animals in the sense of paragraph 1 of this Article, the conditions for keeping, prohibition or restriction on keeping certain species, training and educational programmes and the manner of marking and recording specimens of wild animal species referred to in paragraph 1 of this Article (paragraph 4). Amendments to the Law (2016) introduced, *inter alia*, new provisions related to the zoo (Article 86a).

875. Relocation of live specimens of autochthonous wild species in free nature shall be approved by the Ministry upon obtaining the opinion of the Institute (Art. 84, para. 3).
876. The permit referred to in para. 1 of the present Article shall be issued by the Ministry through the Resolution (Art. 85, para. 5).
877. Feasibility Study and EIA Study should be done prior to any reintroduction (Art. 85, para. 2).
878. Legal persons, entrepreneurs and natural persons keeping specimens of strictly protected and protected wild species shall keep evidence confirming that these are: (1) lawfully imported specimens; (2) lawfully acquired specimens before the species was protected by the Law; (3) specimens originating from breeding in accordance with this Law; (4) specimens or their offspring, that were in accordance with this Law reported to the Ministry by 1 June 2011 (Art. 87, para. 1). The permits and certificates issued in accordance with this Law, the regulations adopted based on this Law or in accordance with the Law on the Ratification of the CITES (OJ FRY – IT, No. 11/01 – hereinafter, CITES Convention), as well as other substantiated evidence based on which the Ministry can determine the lawful acquisition of specimens, including the results of laboratory and other technical analysis carried out by institutions designated by the Ministry for determining the origin of specimens, shall be deemed proof of origin referred to in paragraph 1 of this Article (para. 2).

837. A legal person, entrepreneur or natural person keeping a specimen of strictly protected or protected wild species in captivity shall submit an application to the Ministry for a certificate, in accordance with the regulation governing transboundary movement and trade in wild flora and fauna species, except in cases when for the concerned species there is already a valid certificate issued by the ministry or when an exemption has been stipulated (Article 88, paragraph 1). The certificate referred to in paragraph 1 of this Article shall be issued if the applicant proves that the conditions imposed by this Law and the regulation on transboundary movement and trade in wild flora and fauna species have been met (Article 88, paragraph 2).[879]

838. A legal person, entrepreneur or natural person who intends to breed or artificially propagate specimens of strictly protected or protected wild species shall obtain a licence in accordance with this Law (Article 89, paragraph 1).[880] If, during the validity of the license referred to in paragraph 1 of this Article, an inspection procedure in accordance with this Law determines that breeding or artificial propagation are performed contrary to conditions based on which the license was issued, the Ministry shall revoke the license (Article 89, paragraph 3).[881]

L. Trade in Wild Animals

839. A legal person, entrepreneur or natural person engaged in trade in specimens of strictly protected, i.e., protected wild animal species shall keep live animals in accordance with Article 86 of this Law, shall treat specimens in accordance with Article 87 of this Law and shall conduct trade in accordance with regulation governing transboundary movement and trade in specimens of wild species (Article 90, paragraph 1).[882] When performing trade in specimens of strictly protected or protected wild animal species, the seller, i.e., owner shall provide the new owner with the proof of origin in accordance with Article 87 of this Law (paragraph 3).[883]

840. For the purpose of temporary and/or permanent care of live specimens of wild animal species, the Ministry shall establish rescue centres, zoos or other legal or natural persons (Article 91, paragraph 1). The Minister, in consent with the minister

879. The Ministry shall keep a register of specimens of strictly protected and protected wild animal species for which the certificates referred to in para. 1 of this Article have been issued (Art. 88, para. 3).
880. The owner of specimens of strictly protected or protected wild animal species referred to in para. 1 of this Article shall ensure that those specimens do not escape into the wild and shall be responsible for damages caused by those animals if they escape (Art. 89, para.4).
881. Breeding places of specimens of strictly protected or protected wild species, in accordance with the CITES convention, can apply for permits for transboundary trade of these specimens for commercial purposes, only if the breeding place was registered with the CITES Secretariat (para. 5).
882. The trade referred to in para. 1 of this Article shall cover the sale and purchase, acquisition for commercial purposes, presentation to the public for profit, use with the aim of acquiring profit, keeping for sale, offering for sale, requesting for purchase or transport for sale, rent, exchange or any other form of change in ownership (Art. 90, para. 2).
883. Certificates and other documents issued on the basis of this Law for the purpose of trade in strictly protected or protected wild animal species shall be used only for the specimens to which they relate (Art. 90, para. 4).

responsible for veterinary activities, shall stipulate conditions to be met by the rescue centres referred to in paragraph 1 of the present Article (paragraph 2).[884]

841. Specimens of strictly protected, protected and allochthonous wild species that are handled contrary to provisions of this Law shall be confiscated in accordance with this Law and a notice of confiscation containing data on the confiscated specimens shall be issued (Article 92, paragraph 1).[885]

842. A person who finds a specimen of a strictly protected or protected wild animal species shall immediately notify the Ministry and the Institute of: (1) dead specimens found and (2) live specimens that are sick, injured or unable to survive in the wild by themselves (Article 93, paragraph 1).[886]

III. Permit for Collection and Place on Market

843. In accordance with Article 27, paragraph 4 of the EPL some protected species of wild flora and fauna, their developing forms and parts, may be collected and placed on the market only in the way and under conditions determined in the permit issued by the Ministry. Such a permit is issued after the Ministry obtains positive opinion by the organization in charge of nature protection.

844. Legal or natural person that carries out the trade with wild flora and fauna is obliged to pay a charge.[887]

According to Article 76 of the Law on Nature Protection protected wild species of fungi, lichens, plants, animals or their parts can be collected for the purpose of processing, trading and cross-boundary commerce, as well as cultivation and rearing, on the basis of a permit issued by the Ministry in accordance with Law (paragraph 3). The detailed conditions and protection measures for protected wild species and measures for the protection of their habitats shall be specified by the decision referred to in

884. The rescue centre referred to in this Article shall be obliged to obtain an operating licence issued by the Ministry by virtue of a decision (Art. 91, para. 3).
885. The Ministry shall decide how the temporarily kept, temporarily confiscated, permanently confiscated and abandoned specimens of strictly protected, protected and allochthonous wild species are handled, in accordance with the regulation on transboundary movement and trade in wild flora and fauna species (para. 2).
886. The Ministry may establish a special team of experts – natural and/or legal persons for cases requiring intervention on living specimens of wild animals in the wilderness or in captivity. Mutual rights and obligations shall be regulated by an agreement concluded between the Ministry and the persons referred to in para. 2 of this Article (Art. 93, paras 2 and 3).
887. The amount of the charge form para. 5 of this Article shall be determined by the Act for putting under control the usage and trade of wild flora and fauna which shall be enacted by the Government (Art. 27, para. 6).

Article 48 of this Law (paragraph 4).[888] The management of protected wild species population, which is not governed by the regulations from the field of hunting and fishing, is done on the basis of permits issued by the Ministry in accordance with the Law, on the base of previously obtained decision of the Institution (paragraphs 2 and 5).

845. The Regulation on the control of use and marketing of wild flora and fauna (OJ RS, Nos 31/05,45/05, 22/07, 38/07 and 9/10) prescribes protection of endangered wild species of flora, fauna and fungi, their gathering from natural habitats, utilization, breeding and trade, and determines compensation for their exploitation (Article 1). In three Annexes are listed the species protected by this Regulation, and sanctions are defined in Articles 21 and 23.[889]

IV. Import and Export of Endangered and Protected Species

846. Export and import or transit of protected wild plant and animal species, their parts and derivatives are carried out in accordance with the Law on Ratification of the Convention on International Trade in Endangered Species of Wild Fauna and Flora (OJ FRY – IT, No. 11/01), EPL, Law on Nature Protection (OJ RS, No. 36/09), and regulation on putting under control the use and trade of wild flora and fauna Rulebook on the Transboundary Movement and Trade in Protected Species (OJ RS, Nos 99/2009 and 6/2014).[890]

General provisions concerning import and export of endangered and protected species of wild flora and fauna are contained in Article 28 of the EPL. These activities must be carried in such a way that 'the exported quantity or the number of specimens of the endangered and protected species of wild flora and fauna shall not be detrimental to the survival of the species concerned in the Republic, as well as under other conditions regulated by law, on the basis of the permit issued by the Ministry'.

888. On the basis of the estimate of certain endangered species, and the obligations from the approved international agreements, as well as on the basis of the national and international red lists and/or red books and/or other professional documentation, the Minister shall, by mutual consent with the Minister competent for the agriculture, forestry and water management, and at the proposal of the Institute, declare wild species as strictly protected wildlife species or protected wildlife species. The decision referred to in para. 1 of this Article shall establish the protection measures for the strictly protected and protected wild plant, animal and fungi species, as well as the measures for protecting their habitats. The decision shall be published in the 'Official Journal of the Republic of Serbia' (Art. 48).

889. The first control (State monitoring) started in 1993 through the by-law (Ordinance on collection of wild plant and animal species). Today, the Regulation covers 105 protected species, particularly: seventy-eight plant species, three lichen species, fifteen fungus species and nine animal species.

890. *See also*, Art. 14(1) and (3) of the Law on Foreign Trade (OJ RS, Nos 36/09 and 36/11 – other law, 88/11 and 89/15) and the Decision on determining goods subject to issuance of specific documents on importation, exportation and transit (OJ RS, No. 32/15).

847. An import/export permit is needed for endangered and protected species of wild flora and fauna, as well as their different lifecycle forms and parts. An application for such a permit must be submitted[891] with:

(1) the opinion of a scientific and professional organization that exports of the endangered or protected species of wild flora and fauna in the requested quantity or number of specimens shall not be detrimental to their survival;
(2) statement by the importer, and/or exporter, concerning the intended use of the specimen; and
(3) any other prescribed documentation.[892]

848. On the base of opinion of the authorized scientific or professional organizations, the Ministry issues licenses and other documents (certificates, opinions, information, etc.) approving the import, export, entry and carry out specimens of wild species, their parts and derivatives, protected under the Law and confirmed international treaties, as well as for the import of live specimens of allochthonous wild species that are not protected (Article 94).[893] In the course of import, export, carrying in and out, or transit, living animals must be transported and kept in the way to avoid any injury or harm to their health and to avoid inhuman treatment, in line with the special regulations (Article 94, paragraph 9).

849. Transboundary transport of strictly protected and protected species, their parts and derivatives, as well as import or export or live spaces of allochthonous wild spaces must be reported to customs service, in accordance with the provisions of the present Law and other regulations (Article 95, paragraph 1).[894]Veterinary medical and phytosanitary inspection of consignments referred to in paragraph 1 of Article 95 which have jurisdiction over the border phytosanitary and veterinary inspection is carried out in accordance with special regulations. Minister sets the border crossings where import, export, carrying in and out and transit of strictly protected and protected wild species, their parts and derivatives can be performed, as well as the requirements in terms of their equipment and competence to carry out these tasks (Article 95, paragraph 3 and 4).

850. The custom authority shall carry out checks of the import, export, carrying in and out, re-export and transit of specimens in terms of this Law, within its authority (Article 96, paragraph 1). For spaces from Article 95, paragraph 1 of this Law, the customs authority do special checks whether valid licenses, certificates or other

---

891. The competent Minister closely prescribes documentation that is to be submitted, contents and design of the permit and keeps the Register of issued permits. He/she also designates scientific and professional organizations authorized to give opinion concerning the export of wild.
892. Ministry is obliged to keep the Register of issued permits (Art. 28, para. 6).
893. The permit referred to in para. 1 of the present Article shall be issued provided that: (1) the right to dispose of unit of wild animal, fungus and plant species is lawfully obtained; (2) the animals or consignment are duly marked; and (3) all measures for animal welfare in the course of transport are taken (Art. 94, para. 2).
894. The customs service shall, in the course of import, export, carrying in and out, or transit of species examine the corresponding permits and verify crossing of the border in the dedicated column of the permit form (Art. 95, para. 3).

documents, issued in accordance with the regulation referred to in Article 94 of this Law, are submitted, and/or other prescribed licenses of the other state issued in accordance with the CITES (Article 96, paragraph 2). The customs authority with the permits and certificates referred to in paragraph 2 of this Article shall act in a manner prescribed by regulation on the transboundary movement of protected wildlife in Article 94 of this Law (Article 96, paragraph 3).

851. Rulebook on transboundary movement and trade in protected species (OJ RS, Nos 99/09 and 6/2014) prescribes the following: conditions for import, export, introduction, taking out or transit, trade and breeding of endangered and protected plant and animal species (hereinafter, referred to as protected species), parts and derivatives thereof; issuance of permits and other documents (verifications, certificates and opinions); documents that are submitted with permit application, contents and layout of the permit; list of species, parts and derivatives thereof, whose import or export is strictly forbidden, restricted or halted; exemptions from permitting obligations; methods of marking animals or deliveries; and implementation of inspection activities, maintenance of records and reporting.

852. It should be added that Serbia implements CITES.[895]

853. However, in the course of 2007 the Republic inspectors temporary seized the following protected species on the lists of CITES: 748 forest turtle; three iguana; one python; four imperial scorpions; one falcon; ninety-eight butterflies, etc. Temporary seized species were given to the Palic Zoo and Natural Museum in Belgrade. Proposals for criminal prosecutions were issued.[896]

'The implementation of CITES and the relevant national wildlife-trade-related legislation has improved in recent years, with a steady increase in the number of seizures, confiscations and convictions made regarding illegal transboundary and internal trade in protected species.'[897] The EC Report (2016) explains the progress made in CITES more precisely. Implementation of the CITES 'improved as responsibilities of competent bodies in the area of wildlife trade control were clarified'.[898]

V. Harmonization of National Legislation with EU Legislation

854. Serbia needs to fully transpose the Habitats and Birds Directives into national legislation. There are still significant gaps in transposition, for example by allowing hunting of non-huntable species of birds or lacking clear provisions on the derogation system under the directives. Also, legislation will have to be aligned with the Directive on wild animals in zoos. Regarding Nagoya Protocol Serbia will need

895. *See* , Republic of Serbia – CITES Biennial Report 2007/2008, https://cites.org/sites/default/files/reports/07-08Serbia.pdf.
896. Izveštajo stanju životne sredine u Republic Srbiju u 2007. godlni (Report on the state of the environment in Serbia for 2007), Ministanstro životne sredine i prostooneg planiranja (Ministry for Environment and Spatial Planning), Beograd, 2008, 226.
897. The most frequent seizures are live reptiles and birds. In addition, seizures of other taxonomic groups were also recorded, as well as seizures of parts, derivatives and products of protected species. EPR (2015), 101.
898. CR, 77.

to designate competent authorities and set up a system of penalties for infringement of the Regulation 511/2014.[899]

899. SRS, Chs 27, 2. Legislation implementing the CITES has been updated. Important seizures of illegally traded endangered species were made. However, the capacity of the CITES unit and that of the enforcement agencies need to be enhanced.

Chapter 4. Agricultural Resources

§1. Conditions for Agricultural Production

855. Generally speaking, conditions for agricultural production (natural characteristics of soil, climate and water resources, etc.) are favourable in Serbia, not only in the Northern Province of Vojvodina, but also in many other parts.

One of the basic components of Serbian economic development is agriculture. Besides the economic importance, it has an exceptional social and ecological one. In comparison with EU countries, Serbian agriculture represents a relatively high percentage (15.3%), while the industrial production participates with around 24.4% in gross domestic product in 2005, which is somewhat higher than the EU average.[900]

856. More than 10% of labour force works in agriculture, contributing to the total export from Serbia with 26%. The structure of farms is very unsatisfactory with average size of only 3 ha, and with only 5.5% farmers, out of the total number of 778,891, with estates over 10 ha.[901]

There are 5,734,000 ha of agricultural land or 0.56 ha per capita (4,867,000 ha arable, 1,006,473 ha pastures and 37,504 ha fish ponds). Farmland covers 70% of the total surface area of Serbia, while about 30% are forests. Irrigation system covers 180,000 ha. One of the main problems in Serbian agriculture is, however, the fact that only 30,000 ha are actually irrigated. Production of livestock is focused predominately on cattle breeding.

857. One of the sectoral objectives in agriculture is 'increase areas under organic farming and other environmentally friendly farming production systems'.[902]The total area with the organic production in 2014 amounted to 9,446.58 ha, which is 1,218.57 ha more than in 2013. These include surfaces which are in the process of conversion and the surface that have an organic status. The share of agricultural land under organic agriculture in relation to the utilized agricultural area in 2014 is 0.27%.[903]

858. The main institution in Serbia dealing with agricultural policy is the MAEP. Plant protection products and residues are regulated by following three ministries:

---

900. Nacionalna strategija privrednog razvoja Republike Srbije od 2006. do 2012. godine [*National Strategy on Economic Development of the Republic of Serbia from 2006 to 2012*], 5.
901. Strategija razvoja poljoprivredne Srbije [*Strategy of Agricultural Development of Serbia*], 9. *See also*, Sustainable Development Strategy, 101–103. However, a tendency of concentration and centralization of farms according to the size can be noted. According to the 2012 agriculture census, 3.1% of the total number of farms are over 20 ha, and this group of farmers use 44% of the total used farmland. On the other hand, agricultural farms using up to 5 ha make up 77.7% of the total number of registered farms, which makes 25.2% of the used agricultural land. Strategija poljoprivrede i ruralnog razvoja RS za period 2014–2024 [Strategy for Agriculture and Rural Development for the period 2014–2024], (OJ RS, No. 85/14), http://uap.gov.rs/wp-content/uploads/2016/05/STRATEGIJA-2014-2020-.pdf, 10.
902. NSDS, 103.
903. *Poljoprivreda i životna sredina u Republici Srbiji - indikatorski prikaz [Agriculture and the Environment in Serbia]*, MAEP, EPA, Beograd, 2015, 61.

MAEP – Phytosanitary Directorate, Forest Directorate, Veterinary Directorate, Agricultural Land Directorate, Directorate for Agrarian Payments, etc. Ministry of Mining and Energy, Ministry of Construction, Transport and Infrastructure, and Ministry of Health. The MAEP is competent for fertilizers.[904]

§2. Legislation

859. Due to the fact that the agriculture is given high importance in Serbia, legal Acts regulating it are numerous.

The Constitution of Serbia prescribes in Article 88 that utilization and management of agricultural land, forestland and municipal building land on private assets shall be permitted. The Law may restrict the models of utilization and management, by prescribing terms of utilization and management, in order to eliminate the danger for the environment, and in order to prevent violation of rights and legally based interests of other persons.

The Constitution prescribes that APs shall, in accordance with the Law, regulate following matters of provincial interest: agriculture, water economy, forestry, hunting, fishery, tourism, catering, spas and health resorts, environmental protection, industry and craftsmanship, road, river and railway transport and road repairs, organizing fairs and other economic events (Article 183, point 2). Municipalities are responsible for protection, improvement and use of agricultural land (Article 190, point 7).

I. General Legislation

860. The current basic framework of agricultural policy is contained in several documents, including the following: Agriculture and Rural Development Strategy of the Republic of Serbia for the period 2014–2024 (OJ RS, No. 85/14); EPL (OJ RS, Nos 135/04, 36/09, 72/09, 43/11CC and 14/16); Law on Agriculture and Rural Development (OJRS, Nos 41/09, 10/13 and 101/16); Law on Agricultural Land (OJ RS, Nos 62/06, 41/09 and 112/15); Law on Soil Protection (OJ RS, No. 112/15);[905] Law on Public Health (OJRS, No. 15/16); Law on Plant Protection Products (OJRS, No. 41/09), Law on Plant Nutrition Products and Soil Enhancers (OJRS, No. 41/09), Law on Privatization OJ 2014 (OJ RS, Nos 83/14, 46/15, 112/15 and 20/16); Law on Food Safety (OJRS, No. 41/09); Law on Organic Production (OJRS, No. 30/10); Law

904. Agricultural Inspection Sector as an administrative body within the MAEP, conducts supervision of the implementation of the relevant laws including, *inter alia*, Law on Agricultural Land (OJ RS, Nos 62/06, 65/08 – other law, 41/09 and 112/15) Law on Plant Health (OJ RS, No. 41/09), Law on Food Safety (OJ RS, No. 41/09), Law on Plant Protection Products (OJ RS, No. 41/09), Law on Plant Nutrition Products and Soil Enhancers (OJ RS, No. 41/09), Law on GMOs (OJ RS, No. 41/09), Law on Organic Production (OJ RS, No. 30/10), Law on Wine (OJ RS, Nos 41/09 and 93/12), Law on Agriculture and Rural Development (OJ RS, Nos 41/09 and 10/13 – other law, 101/16), and regulations adopted under these laws.

905. For more details *see* , chapter devoted to soil pollution.

on Livestock (OJ RS, Nos 41/09 and 93/12); Law on Wine (OJRS, Nos 41/09 and 93/12), etc.

861. The existing strategic document is the Agriculture and Rural Development Strategy of the Republic of Serbia(OJ RS, No. 85/14), in which one of the strategic goals, among other issues (the production growth and stability of the producers' income, competitiveness improvement with adjustments to requirements of the domestic and international markets and with technological and technical improvement of the sector, sustainable resources management, improvement of the quality of life in rural areas and poverty reduction, efficient public policy management and institutional framework improvement for agricultural and rural areas development), is environment protection. According to the Sustainable Development Strategy, the main objective of the Agricultural policy is development of sustainable, cost-effective and environment friendly agriculture, as the basis for rural development and competitiveness needed for access to the EU market.[906]

862. EPL contains the following provisions relevant for agriculture: Article 22 (Protection of Land and Soil), Article 33 (Planning and Construction); Article 34 (Spatial and Urban Planning),;Article 35 (Strategic Environmental Assessment); Article 36 (EIA) and Article 124 (Transitional and Final Provisions).

863. The Law on Agriculture and Rural Development (OJ RS, Nos 41/09, 10/13 and 101/16) regulates the following: objectives of agricultural policy and manner of achieving thereof; types of incentives in agriculture; conditions for exercising rights to incentives; incentive beneficiaries; Register of agricultural households, record keeping and reporting in agriculture; integrated agricultural information system and supervision over implementation of this Law (Article 1).[907]

864. Agricultural policy and rural development policy of the Republic of Serbia shall include measures and activities undertaken by competent authorities with the objectives of, *inter alia*, protecting the environment from adverse effects of agricultural production (Article 3, point 5).

865. The Law lays down the duty to adopt a Strategy for Agriculture (Article 4) as well as two national programmes – for agriculture and for rural development (Articles 5 and 6).

866. Pursuant to Article 12 (Forms of Structural Incentives) rural development measures shall be the type of incentives which support improvement of competitiveness in agriculture and forestry (investment in agriculture and forestry and introduction of new standards in production and circulation of agricultural products), improvement of environmental protection programmes, preservation of biodiversity and programme for rural economy diversification and upgradation of life quality in rural areas (paragraph 2).

867. Article 18 prescribes that incentive beneficiary shall be obliged to observe regulations governing environmental quality standards, public health protection, animal

906. NSDS, 103.

907. This Law shall establish Administration for Agricultural Payments, as an administration authority within the ministry in charge of agriculture and shall govern its competences (Art. 1, para. 2).

and plant health protection, protection of animal welfare and protection of agricultural land.[908]

868. Law on Agricultural Land (OJ RS, Nos 62/06, 65/08, 41/09 and 112/15) regulates planning, protection and use of agricultural land. This Law stipulates that the State agricultural land can be leased on the basis of market principles, or provides equal right to lease to all natural and legal persons.[909] This Law establishes the Agricultural Land Administration as the administrative bodies within the ministry responsible for agriculture affairs and regulates its scope (Article 1,paragraph 3, and Article 77a, 77b).

869. Law on Food Safety (OJ RS, No. 41/09) governs general conditions for safety of food and feed, duties and responsibilities of food and feed business operators, rapid alert system, emergency measures and crisis management, food and feed hygiene and quality (Article 1).[910] The objective of this Law is to ensure a high level of protection of human life and health and protection of consumer interests, including the principle of honesty and good faith in the food trade, taking into account protection of animal health and welfare and plant health and environmental protection, where appropriate (Article 3). The Law is based on the principle of risk analysis, precaution, protection of consumer interests and the principle of transparency in the procedures in selection of the appropriate measures in the field of food and feed safety (Articles 6–10).

II. Phytosanitary Policy

870. Legal framework in the field of phytosanitary policy is established on the basis of the following laws: The Law on Plant Health (OJRS, No. 41/09), The Law on Plant Protection Products (OJRS, No. 41/09), The Law on Plant Nutrition Products and Soil Enhancers (OJRS, No. 41/09), The Law on Seed (OJRS, Nos 45/05 and 30/10), The Law on Planting Material of Fruit Trees, Vine and Hops (OJRS, No. 18/05), The Law on Seed and Planting Material (OJRS, Nos 54/93, 67/93, 35/94 and 43/94 –corr., 135/2004, 18/2005, 45/2005 and 101/2005), The Law on Protection of Plant Breeders Rights (OJRS, No. 41/09), The Law on Plant Varieties Registration (OJRS, No. 30/10), The Law on Genetically Modified Organisms (OJRS, No.41/09), The Law on Forest Reproductive Material (OJ RS), Nos 135/04,8/05 and 41/09), The Law on Forestry (OJRS, Nos 30/10, 93/12 and 89/15).

908. Under the conditions specified in this Law, right to incentives shall be given to agricultural households and family agricultural households that are entered in the Register of Agricultural Households, LSG units, as well as other persons and organizations (incentive beneficiaries) (Art. 15).

909. The Law defines that the agricultural land cannot be alienated and that the owner of agricultural land cannot be a foreign natural or legal person, unless registered in the Republic of Serbia (Art. 1). However, Serbia agreed that it will adjust its legislation (by 1 Sep. 2017), so as to enable EU nationals to acquire real estate in Serbia – under the same conditions as Serbian nationals. This includes, also, legislation governing the sale of agricultural land (Art. 63. of SAA).

910. The provisions of this Law shall not apply to primary food production and preparation, handling and storage of food for private domestic use, as well as feed for non-food-producing animals (Art. 2).

871. The Law on Plant Health regulate the protection and promotion of plant health; measures for preventing introduction of harmful organisms, for detecting them, preventing their spread and suppressing them; phytosanitary control; requirements for the production, processing, finishing, importation, storage and circulation of plants,[911] plant products[912] and regulated objects, as well as requirements for providing services in the sphere of the protection of plant health (Article 1).

872. According to Article 107 of the Law on Plant Health, the Law on the Protection of Plants (OJ FRY, Nos 24/98 and 26/98 and OJ RS, No. 101/05) and other law shall cease to apply from the effective date of this Law, except for provisions referred to pesticides and fertilizers, while Articles 26 and 32 of that Law shall cease to apply from 1 January 2011.[913]

873. The Law on Plant Protection Products governs the registration, control, circulation, importation, and application of plant protection products in agriculture and forestry, the tasks of public interest in the area of plant protection products, and other issues relevant for plant protection products[914] (Article 1). This Law governs the establishment of maximum residue levels of plant protection products and their control in food and feed.

874. The Law on Plant Nutrition Products and Soil Enhancers governs classification, quality, labelling, phytosanitary control, sampling in the circulation, importation and use of plant nutrition products and soil enhancers and testing of plant nutrition products and soil enhancers, as well as other issues of significance for plant

---

911. 'Plants' means living plants and live plant segments, including seeds (Art. 4, point 2).
912. 'Plant products' shall mean all products of plant origin, unprocessed or subjected to simple processing methods, on account of which they can no longer be regarded as plants, as well as wood, if it retains fully or partially its naturally rounded surface, with or without bark, or if it is in the form of chipboard, sawdust, small fragments or wood waste or if it is used in the form of sawn timber, packaging, laths, pallets and packing materials in the transportation of consignments, and may be a risk for the plant health (Art. 4, point 3).
913. Law on the Protection of Plants from Diseases and Pests (OJ SRS, Nos 14/84 and 6/89 – other law, OJ RS, Nos 53/93, 67/93, 48/94 and 101/05) also shall cease to apply from the effective date of the Law on Plant Health.
914. Plant protection products, for the purpose of this Law, shall be: (1) plant protection products; (2) products of general use for plant protection; (3) ancillary plant protection products; (4) other plant protection products which contain one or more basic substances (hereinafter, other products). Plant protection products, for the purpose of this Law, shall be deemed to be also plant protection products which are used in organic production and the plant protection products which contain or are composed of GMOs, or which are obtained from them, provided that the intentional introduction into the environment, placement into circulation or transit of such organisms is allowed based on the assessment of risk to the environment and human health, in accordance with the law governing GMOs (Art. 2).

nutrition products and soil enhancers (Article 1).[915] Plant nutrition products and soil enhancers which also contain the plant protection products, namely the chemicals, may be produced, placed into circulation, and used in the territory of the Republic of Serbia if they are classified, packaged and labelled in accordance with this Law and the regulations adopted based on this Law and the regulations governing the plant protection products, namely the chemicals (Article 3).

875. Pursuant to *the Law on Plant Protection* pesticides and fertilizers could be placed on market only, as prescribed by Article 47, on the basis of permit given by competent authority. The Law stipulates conditions for getting permanent and temporary permits for pesticides (Article 48) and permanent permit for fertilizer (Article 49).[916]

Articles 64–68 regulate import of the pesticides and fertilizers.[917] Permit for import of already prepared pesticides and fertilizers is issued by the competent authority only when this kind of pesticides and fertilizers is not possible to produce in country, or if the existing quantity is not enough to satisfy domestic needs.[918] Article 67 prescribes conditions for import for scientific purposes and temporary import or import of elements for domestic production.[919]

---

915. On the day this Law comes into force, the provisions of the Law on Plant Protection (OJ FRY, Nos 24/98 and 26/98 – correction, and OJ RS, No. 101/05 – other law) shall cease to apply in the part governing fertilizers (Art. 51). According to the Art. 50, the regulations adopted based on the authorizations from this Law shall be adopted within one year from the date this Law comes into force. Until the adoption of regulations referred to in para. 1 of this Article, the regulations adopted based on the Law on Plant Protection (OJ FRY, Nos 24/98 and 26/98 – corr., and OJRS, No. 101/05 – other law) shall apply, except for provisions of such regulations that are not in compliance with this Law.
916. Articles 51–54 of the Law regulate procedure for testing of the pesticides and fertilizers and procedure for registration of pesticides and fertilizers is regulated by Arts 55–59.
917. Besides, it should be mentioned that several other laws are also relevant for foreign trade issues, like the Law on Foreign Trade (OJ RS, Nos 36/09 and 36/11 – other law, 88/11, 89/15 – other law), the Law on Customs Tariff (OJ RS, Nos 62/05,61/2007 and 5/2009), Customs Law (OJ RS, Nos 18/10, 111/12, 29/15), etc.
918. The Rulebook on Trade, Imports and Sampling of Pesticides (OJ FRY, No. 59/01 and OJ RS, No. 104/05), regulate trade, import and sampling of pesticides. Import permits for plant protection products must be obtained from the Serbian Ministry of Agriculture, Phytosanitary Departments. *See also*, Decision on the amount of reimbursement for the conducted phytosanitary examination of plants and the control of pesticides and fertilizers in trade over the State border (OJ RS, No. 113/13).
919. There is a specific ordinance, when the food safety is concerned, on residue limits for pesticides and other contaminants (e.g., hormones, antibiotics and mycotoxins) which can be found in food. The Rulebook on quantities of pesticides, metals and metalloids and other toxic substances, chemotherapeutics, anabolics and other substances that may be found in foodstuffs (OJ FRY, Nos 5/92 and 11/92 – corr. 32/02 and OJ RS, No. 25/10 – other rulebook, and 28/11 – other rulebook). *See also*, The Rulebook concerning the maximum residue limits on plant protection agents in food and feed and also concerning the food and feed to be checked for maximum residue limits on plant protection agents (OJ RS, Nos 29/14 and 37/14 – corr, 39/14, 72/14, 80/15, 84/15, 35/16 and 81/16), Rulebook on health safety of dietetic products (OJ RS, Nos 45/2010, 27/11, 50/12, 21/15 and 75/15), and Rulebook on pesticide testing methods (OJ FRY, Nos 63/2001 and 65/2001, OJ RS, No. 93/2005).

876. Plant Variety Protection (plant breeders' rights) in the Republic of Serbia is regulated by the *Law on Protection of Plant Breeders' Rights.*[920] In March 2010 Serbia ratified International Convention for the Protection of New Varieties of Plants (OJRS – IT, No.19/10).

III. Veterinary Legislation

877. The Laws on Veterinary Medicine (OJRS, Nos 91/05, 30/10 and 93/12), Law on Animal Welfare (OJRS, No. 41/09), Law on Livestock Production (OJ RS, Nos 41/09, 93/12 and 14/16), Law on Food Safety (OJRS, No. 41/09) and Law on Drugs and Medical Products (OJRS, Nos 30/10 and 107/12) have established a legal framework in the field.

Law on Veterinary Medicine regulates the protection and promotion of animal health and welfare, determines the infectious animal diseases and measures to prevent the occurrence, detection, prevention of spreading, suppression and eradication of infectious animal diseases and diseases that can be transmitted from animals to humans, veterinary and sanitary control and conditions for production and trade of animals, animal products, feed of animal origin, animal feed, and the requirements for performing veterinary practice.

878. Law on Animal Welfare regulates the welfare, rights, obligations and responsibilities of natural and legal persons, that is, entrepreneurs in animal welfare, treatment of animals and protection of animals from torture, protection of animal welfare at killing, during keeping, breeding, trade, transport, slaughtering and conducting experiments on animals, as well as other issues of importance for the protection of animal welfare.[921]

879. Law on Livestock Production establishes objectives in livestock production; livestock entities and their organizational forms; breeding objectives and implementation of breeding programmes, control of productivity and preservation of characteristics of domestic animals; breeding of domestic animals, bee keeping, aquaculture, game raising, preservation of genetic reserves of domestic animals biodiversity in livestock production; production and trade of food of plant origin for domestic animals and

920. So far three following regulations have been adopted based on the Law on Protection of Plant Breeders' Rights: Rulebook on content and manner of keeping the Register of applications for granting plant breeders' rights, Register of granted breeders' rights, Register of transferred rights and Register of license agreement (OJRS, No. 70/09); Rulebook on form and content of the application for granting plant breeders' right, the required documentation, the amount and manner of delivery of reproductive material samples (OJRS, No. 82/2009) and Rulebook on the list of species of agricultural plants to which are related exceptions to the breeder's right and the elements for establishing small farmers (OJRS, No. 38/10), etc.

921. The general requirements for keeping and handling of animals are prescribed by the Law on Animal Welfare, and one of the basic principles of this Law is the principle of responsibility referring to all owners and keepers of animals, regardless of business operations they perform in connection with animals and different animal species. The Law prescribes that all legal and natural persons are entitled to keep and breed animals if they meet the requirements for keeping and breeding the animals. For more information, *see* , AECQ, Ch. 12 (Food safety, veterinary and phytosanitary policy), Government of the Republic of Serbia, Belgrade, 2011, 197–202.

products of animal origin; and trade in breeding material and other issues of importance for animal husbandry.[922]

IV. Organic Agriculture

880. The area of organic farming increased from around 1,000 ha in 2009 to 7,000 ha of arable land in 2013. The main products are cereals, fruits, fodder plants and industrial plants. Organic animal production is limited to around 5,000 animals (of which ≈ 70% in the phase of conversion). Organic sheep (50%) and poultry (35%) production prevails. In 2012 there were 1,061 operators registered as organic, including group production.[923]

881. Organic production is regulated by the Law on Organic Production (OJ RS No. 30/10), which has been in force since 1 January 2011.[924] The Law regulates in detail the organic production of agricultural and other products; organic production aims and principles (Articles 1–6); subjects of organic production (Articles 7–9); control organizations (Articles 9–16); organic production methods (Articles 14–16); control and certification in organic production (Articles 17–25); processing, labelling, transportation, placing on the market, imports and exports of organic products (Articles 26–32); supervision of the performance of delegated tasks (Articles 33–39); and other matters relevant to organic production (Articles 40–51).

882. The 2013 Law on Incentives in Agriculture and Rural Development (OJ RS, Nos 10/13, 142/2014, 103/2015, 101/2016) provides incentives for the implementation of agro-environmental measures, incentives for organic production and incentives, etc. (Articles 37 and 38). In February 2013, the Government adopted the Rulebook on Payment of Agriculture Subsides (OJ RS, No. 20/13). The law envisions the following four groups of government incentives: (1) Direct payments (i.e., production subsidies, compensation for agriculture inputs, credit support) (Articles 14–3); (2) Rural development payments (i.e., incentives to improve agricultural competitiveness and investments in sustainable rural development) (Articles 34–40); (3) Specific incentives (i.e., funds to develop a market-information system in agriculture, provide extension services and support science-based projects in agriculture) (Articles 41 and 42); and (4) credit support (Article 42a).

883. On the basis of Law on Organic Agriculture and Organic Products (OJRS No. 30/10), following sub-legal Acts have been adopted, *inter alia*:

922. Provisions of this Law relate to breeding of cattle, buffalo, sheep, goats, horses, donkeys, pigs, poultry, fur animals, rabbits, bees, raising game, fish and other aquatic animals and other farmed animals.
923. Screening report Serbia Ch. 11 – Agriculture and Rural Development, WP Enlargement + Countries Negotiating Accession to EU MD 29/15 24.02.15, p. 15. However, according to CR, the area under organic production is increased and stands at present at 15,000 ha equivalent to 0.4% of the utilized agricultural area. CR, 43.
924. Before the implementation of this Law commenced, the provisions of the Law on Organic Agriculture and Organic Products (OJ RS No. 62/06) were applicable; the pertinent rulebooks, which still apply, were developed on the basis of this Law.

- Rulebook on control and certification in organic farming and organic production methods (OJ RS, No. 48/2011 i 40/2012).
- Rulebook on documents submitted to the authorized control organizations for the purpose of issuing certificates, and the terms and conditions of sales of organic products (OJ RS, No. 88/16).
- The list of authorized inspection agency for controlling and certification of organic production for 2017 (OJ RS, No. 96/16).
- Rulebook on the use of incentives for organic production (OJ RS, Nos 52/14, 62/15 and 33/16).
- Rulebook on the use of subsidies in organic livestock production per hive of bees (OJ RS, No. 15/16).
- Rulebook on the use of subsidies in organic livestock production for suckler cows (OJ RS, No. 42/14).

V. Harmonization with EU Legislation and International Treaties

884. Serbia's policy on rural development is partly aligned with that of the EU. This approach will need to be further strengthened and consolidated in line with EU requirements. [925] 'Progress has been noted on adoption of implementing legislation, for example on maximum residue levels of plant protection products in food and on plant-breeders' rights. However, the procedure for registration of new plant protection products is not harmonized with the EU *acquis* and an official pesticide residues monitoring programme meeting EU requirements has yet to be put in place. The Phytosanitary Strategy for introduction of a plant passport system has not been formally adopted and the plant passport system has not yet been implemented. The capacity of both the national reference laboratory and the regional laboratories for control of seed and seed material and for pesticide residue analysis requires further strengthening to meet EU requirements'.[926] The legislative framework in the veterinary sector has been established. However, official controls of implementation of the animal identification and registration system (including control of cattle markets) need to be improved. As regards quality policy, Serbia has legislation in place which regulates protection of designations of origin, geographical indications and traditional names. This legislation needs to be amended and updated to bring it fully in line with the EU *acquis*.[927] Serbia's legislation on organic farming is broadly aligned with the acquis. Further alignment is required and the control system needs to be further strengthened.[928]

885. Serbia is a contracting party to the following international treaties: European Convention for the Protection of Animals for Slaughter (CETS No.: 102); European Convention for the Protection of Animals kept for Farming Purposes (CETS No.: 087); European Convention for the Protection of Vertebrate Animals used for Experimental and other Scientific Purposes (CETS No.: 123) and European Convention for the

925. Screening report Serbia Ch. 11 – Agriculture and Rural Development, *op. cit*, p. 18.
926. *Ibid.*, 78–79.
927. *Ibid.*, 76.
928. Screening report Serbia Ch. 11 – Agriculture and Rural Development, *op. cit*, p. 19.

Protection of Pet Animals (CETS No.: 125).[929] Serbia is not a contracting party to the European Convention for the Protection of Animals during International Transport (CETS No.: 065); Serbia ratified the Convention on the Prior Informed Consent Procedure for Certain Hazardous Chemicals and Pesticides in International Trade (Rotterdam Convention) and the Convention on POPs (Stockholm Convention).

929. At http://conventions.coe.int/Treaty/Commun/ListeTraites.asp?PO=SAM&MA=999&SI=2&DF=&CM=3&CL=ENG.

Chapter 5. Biotechnology

886. Biotechnology is still not sufficiently developed activity in Serbia. Eight institutions for bio-safety currently work with GMOs or are involved in their detection. Five of them are research institutes, one university faculty and two laboratories for GMO detection. Two institutes conduct field tests with GMO maize. A GMO product (soybean meal) has been approved for placing on the market:[930]

> Growing evidence suggests that genetically modified organisms (GMOs) may present threats to autochthonous biodiversity when deliberately or accidentally released into an environment. In some cases, such as endangered species, such threats could be significant. Risks are centred on possibilities of gene flow and hybridization between GMOs and autochthonous species, as well as impacts that GMOs may have on ecosystem food webs and human health. These impacts could in turn result in further chain reactions and negative overall impacts to conservation and the sustainable use of biological diversity.[931]

887. Biotechnology is in competence of the MAEP. In the MAEP activities related to GMOs are carried out by Plant Protection Directorate,[932] General Inspectorate

930. Development of National Biosafety Framework for Serbia and Montenegro, Belgrade and Novi Sad, UNEP, GEF, 2006, 6, http://unep.ch/biosafety/old_site/development/Countryreports/YUNBFrep.pdf.
931. Radović, I, Kozomora, M., *supra* , 60.
932. Plant Protection Directorate, as an authority within the Ministry, in the field of GMO is in charge of receiving and reviewing applications for approval to work with GMOs in closed systems and the deliberate release of GMOs into the environment (field trials with GMOs) or for all expert and technical tasks related to biological protection in the use of GMOs. In accordance with Art. 61 of the Law on Food Safety, MAEP is responsible for issuing permits for first placing of GMO foods and GMO feeds on the market, and on the basis of a prior opinion of the Expert Council for risk assessment in the field of Security of food, and in accordance with the regulation concerning the conditions of placing of GMOs on the market.

and Veterinary Directorate.[933] Besides the Ministry, in the activities in the field of GMOs participate Expert Council for Biosafety,[934] and accredited laboratories.[935]

§1. Legal Regulation

888. The Agriculture and Rural Development Strategy of the Republic of Serbia for the period 2014–2024 (OJ RS, No. 85/14) does not define specific targets for GMOs.

889. EPL prescribes that 'biodiversity protection, use of biological resources, genetically modified organism and biotechnology shall be executed on the basis of this Law and obligations taken through international agreements' (Article 26, paragraph 3).

890. The matter of GMO in the Republic of Serbia is regulated by the Law on Genetically Modified Organisms (OJRS, No. 41/09) and the Law on Food Safety (OJRS, No. 41/09).

891. The Republic of Serbia ratified the Cartagena Protocol on Biosafety to the Convention on Biological Diversity, with annexes (OJ SMN – IT, No. 16/05), and became a member of the Cartagena Protocol on Biosafety.

892. The basic legal Act regulating biotechnology in Serbia is the Law on Genetically Modified Organisms (Law on GMO) (OJ RS, No. 41/09). It prescribes the general framework for handling and use of GMOs, and detailed conditions are defined in sub-legal Acts. The Law comprises fifty-three Articles in eight following parts: I Basic Provisions (Articles 1–8); II Permitting Procedure (Articles 9–18); III Requirements for use in close systems and for deliberate release into the environment of the GMOs (Articles 19–27); IV Handling, packaging and transport of GMO and GMO products (Articles 28–31); V Register of GMO and GMO products and license Register (Articles 32–36); VI Supervision (Articles 37–44); VII Penal provisions (Articles 45–49); VII Transitional and final provisions (Article 50–53).

893. The Law on GMO prescribes the procedure for issuing approvals for use in closed systems, for deliberate release into the environment, for placing on the market

933. General Inspectorate and the Veterinary Directorate (organizations within the Ministry), are responsible for the supervision and control of experimental work with GMOs. Pursuant to the Art. 12 of The Law on Food Safety Veterinary Directorate controls GMO feed all stages of production, processing and placing on the market. General Inspectorate, control GMO food through all stages of food production, processing and transport of GMOs.

934. According to the Art. 6 of the Law on GMO, for the considerations of expert issues and providing expert opinion related to GMOs, Expert Council for Biosafety has been established, consisting of eighteen members chosen among outstanding scientists and experts in the fields that are relevant for biosafety (biologists, geneticists, entomologists, ecologists, veterinarians, agronomists, nutritionists, toxicologists, allergists and other professions).

935. Testing of GMOs and GMO products for the purpose of identification and quantification of genetic modification is carried out by laboratory accredited by the Ministry. At this point, the four laboratories are accredited for GMO analyses. These are the following: SP Laboratory, Novi Bečej; Institute of Molecular Genetics and Genetic Engineering – Laboratory of Molecular Biology, Belgrade; Institute of Field and Vegetable Crops, Novi Sad; A Bio Tech Lab, Sremska Kamenica. NPAA, revision II, 647. *See also*, EPR (2015), 15.

or for transit of GMOs[936] and products containing GMOs, conditions for use in closed systems and for deliberate release into the environment of GMOs, handling, packaging and transport of GMOs and products containing GMOs, as well as other issues of importance for GMOs and products containing GMOs (Article 1).[937]

894. No GMOs or product containing GMOs can be traded or grown for commercial use in the territory of the Republic of Serbia (Article 2).[938]

895. The Law on Food Safety (OJ RS, No. 41/09) stipulates the first marketing of GMO foods and genetically modified feed (GMO animal feed), the method of issuing permits for the first placement on the market of GMO food and GMO feed records of licenses issued, traceability and labelling of GMOs in particular GMO food and feed, and inspections in these fields. For the first placement on the market of genetically modified food and genetically modified feed in the Republic of Serbia, business operator that is distributing food or feed must be licensed.[939]

896. The following by-laws are applied:

Rulebook on the content and the application form for use of genetically modified organisms in closed systems, manner of protection confidential data from the application, as well as on the content of the application for renewal of approval for use in closed systems (OJ RS, No. 69/12)

Rulebook on limited usage of genetically modified organisms (OJ of FRY, No. 62/02, Ceased to be valid: OJ RS, No. 69/12), except the several provisions.

---

936. Genetic material shall mean part of a plant, animal, fungus, microorganism, virus or viroid containing hereditary information (Art. 4, point 1). Pursuant to the Art. 3 of the Law agriculture products of non-animal origin are not considered GMOs if they contain up to 0.9% threshold of GMOs and impurities of GMOs. Apart from that, seed and reproductive material are not considered GMOs if they contain up to 0.1% threshold of GMOs and impurities of GMOs.

937. The provisions of this Law shall not apply to the product containing GMO product which is not a living modified organism (LMO) and is not used as food, feed, medicine or auxiliary medicine. The provisions of this Law shall not apply to GMOs and to GMO products which are not LMOs, if they are intended for medical use and if their use is governed entirely by other regulations (Art. 5).

938. The person that, contrary to the provisions of this Law, commences the use of GMOs and GMO products in closed systems, deliberate release into the environment, placing on the market or transit, or disposes of them into the environment and thus causes harmful consequences for human health and the environment, shall be punished for a criminal offence by imprisonment of up to three years. The GMOs and GMO products referred to in para. 1 of this Article shall be confiscated and destroyed at the expense of the person having committed the criminal offence (Art. 45).

939. Permit is issued by the Minister, based on the prior opinion of the expert scientific advice, in accordance with the regulation concerning the conditions for the marketing of genetically modified food and genetically modified feed.

897. It was planned to develop and adopt a set of regulations, by-laws that are necessary to implement legislation in the field of biological safety when working with GMOs.[940]

898. The Serbian GMO Law prohibits the placing on the market of GMOs and products of GMOs, as well as commercial growing of GMOs. 'Given that the ban on the placing on the market of GMOs and products of GMOs, and the ban on the commercial growing of GMOs is not in compliance with EU legislation in this area, Serbia has to amend the Law by weakening its national legislation.'[941] 'There was no progress on aligning the law on genetically modified organisms with the acquis, which is a prerequisite for Serbia's accession to the World Trade Organisation (WTO).'[942] In addition, Serbia has not ratified the GMO amendment to the Aarhus Convention (Almaty 2005):

> It is evident that an issue of the use of genetically modified food and genetically modified feed needs to be further regulated so that the existing discrepancy could be resolved: on the one hand the Law on Genetically Modified Organisms prohibits commercial growing and marketing of GMOs and GMO products, including GM food and GM feed, and on the other hand The Law on Food Safety, prescribes procedures for issuing permits for trade in GM food and GM feed.[943]

---

940. Rules will be harmonized with relevant EU legislation in the field of work with GMOs. AECQ, Ch. 12 (Food safety, veterinary and phytosanitary policy), *supra* , 309. However, the deadline for adopting new GMO regulations has not yet been established. NPAA, II revision, 648–650.
941. EPR (2015), 102.
942. CR, 43.
943. AECQ, Ch. 12 (Food safety, veterinary and phytosanitary policy), *supra* , 312.

Chapter 6. Forests

899. The situation with the exploitation of forests in Serbia is generally speaking positive (wood volume is increasing faster than the annual cut), but the forests are endangered by different causes and especially by illicit cutting, other damage caused by man including pollution, damage caused by insects, damage by natural catastrophes and storms, damage caused by plant diseases, damage by fire, etc.[944] The forested area in the RS (without the territory of the AP of Kosovo-Metohija) was 2,373,740 ha (2012, CORINE Land Cover) which makes up to 30% of the territory. Forested surface increased (2012) by over 1,200,000 hectares, which is about 100% increase in comparison with 1953.[945]

Forestry traditionally plays an important role in economic development of Serbia and it also has a long tradition of legal regulation.[946] Forests are both State and privately owned. State-owned forests are mostly managed by State-founded public enterprise 'Srbijašume' (85%) and in the APV by the enterprise 'Vojvodinašume' (7.5%), national parks (6.5%), and educational and research institutions (1%).[947]

900. The MAEP is the main institution competent in the field of forestry. Its Forestry Department is responsible for all activities concerning forests, including the inspection. State forests are managed by public companies whose founder is the State – 'Srbijasume' (Serbia Forests) and 'Vojvodinasume' (Vojvodina Forests) while five public enterprises are managed by national parks. Scientific institutions also play important role and especially, Forestry Institute in Belgrade, and Research and Development Institute for lowland forestry and the environment in Novi Sad.[948] The Statistical Office makes a survey on areas under forests, once in three years, and annual surveys on planting, growing and exploitation of forests, forest damages and surveys on forest roads, transportation and mechanization. Surveys on the production and sale of forest products are done on monthly basis, and surveys on hunting biannually.

944. For general data, *see* , National Report to the Fifth Session of the United Nations Forum on Forests, FRY (Serbia and Montenegro), December 2004, http://www.un.org/esa/forests/pdf/national_reports/unff5/serbiamontenegro.pdf; *see also*, B. Glavonjić, et al., Forest and Forest Products Country Profile: Serbia and Montenegro, Geneva Timber and Forest Discussion Paper 40, UNECE/FAO, Geneva, 2005.

945. *Biodiversity indicators in the Republic of Serbia for 2015*, MAEP, EPA, 2015, 9.

946. For example, Duke Milos's decree on prohibition of uncontrolled wood cutting from 1821. *See* , Strategija razvoja šumarstva Republike Srbije [*Forestry Development Strategy of the Republic of Serbia*], Ministry of Agriculture Forestry and Water Management, Belgrade, 2004, 4; *see also*, N. Veličković, Razvoj zakonodavstva o šumarstvu od 1836 do 1990 [*Development of Forest Legislation from 1836 to 1990*], Peščanik I [*Sandglass I*], Istorijski arhiv grada Niša, Niš, 2003.

947. B. Karadžić (ed.), Environment in Serbia – An Indicator-Based Review, *supra* , 41.

948. They are, *inter alia*, engaged in the International Co-operative Programme on Assessment and Monitoring of Air Pollution Effects on Forests (*ICP Forest*), operating under the UNECE CLRTAP. One of their projects was Bio indicator Points Network Revitalization in 2003, originally instituted in 1986.

901. Forestry Development Strategy of the Republic of Serbia was, adopted in 2006,[949] defines current conditions in forestry and developmental goals. The Strategy is guided by the principle of sustainable use of forests and their protection, according to obligations stemming from the acceptance of the Ministerial Conference on the Protection of Forests in Europe (MCPFE). Prior to developing the National Action Plan for Forests, which is being drafted, a complete inventory of the forests in the Republic was conducted between 2004 and 2007.

§1. Legal Regulation

902. The Serbian Constitution contains provisions, in its Article 88, relevant for forests, and by Article 183 prescribes that competence is given to APs too, 'in accordance with the Law', for regulating matters of provincial interest in different fields, including the forestry.

903. Provisions concerning forest policy, and the framework for specific legal regulation, are also contained in the Law on Spatial Plan of the Republic of Serbia (OJ RS, No. 88/10).

904. EPL (OJRS, Nos 135/04, 36/09, 43/2011 and 14/2016) also contains some basic provisions concerning protection of forests. Article 25, for example, prescribes that:

> In order to preserve and enhance forest ecosystems, forests shall be managed in a way that shall ensure rational forest management, genetic fund preservation, enhancement of the structure and realization of forests priority function. State authorities, forests owners and users are obliged to undertake necessary measures for preservation and sustainable use of forests, measures of renewal, afforest ration and improvement, as well as control and protection of forests in case of transboundary pollution.

905. The Law on Forests (OJ RS, 30/2010, 93/2012 and 89/2015) is the main legal Act concerning protection of forests in Serbia.

It has the following fourteen parts: Part I – General Provisions (Articles 1–8), Part II – Forest conservation (Articles 9–16), Part III – Planning (Articles 17–38), Part IV – Forest Management (Articles 39–66), Part V – Forest inventory and forest information system (Articles 67 and 68), Part VI – Organization of forest management (Articles 69–75), Part VII – Financing (Articles 76–89), Part VIII – Forest value (Article 90), Part IX – The Chamber of forestry engineers (Articles 91–96), Part X – Performing the activities in forestry (Article 97), Part XI – Property rights (Articles 98–103), Part XII – Supervision (Articles 104–110), Part XIII – Penalty provisions (Articles 111–113) and Part XIV – Transitional and final provisions (Articles 114–121).

949. *See also*, A. Mihajlov & A. Vasiljević, *The Forests in EU Strategies for Sustainable use of Natural Resources and Sustainable Development*, F.Schmithusen, P. Herbst, et al., *Legal Aspects of European Forest Sustainable Development*57–64(Swiss Federal Institute of Technology 2006), ISBN 1420-1143.

Also, inventory of forests and forestlands of forest areas is attached to this Law making its integral part.

906. This Law regulates conservation, protection, planning, cultivation and usage of forests, management of forests[950] and forestland,[951] monitoring implementation of this Law and other issues relevant to the forests and forestland (Article 1). Provisions of this Law relate to forests and forestland in all forms of property (Article 2).

907. The Law provides conditions for sustainable forest management[952] and forestland as a resource of common interest, in the manner and to the extent to which they permanently maintain and enhance their productive capacity, biological diversity, as well as the capacity of renewal and vitality. Also, it enhances their potential to mitigate climate change, as well as their economic, ecological and social functions, and it does not harm the surrounding ecosystems (Article 3).

908. Conservation, protection and improvement of forest conditions, the use of forest resources and their functions and planting of new forests in order to achieve optimal forest cover, spatial distribution and structure of forest fund in the Republic of Serbia, are the activities of common interest (Article 4, paragraph 1).[953] Protection of public interest from paragraph 1 of this Article is provided by (Article 4, paragraph 2): (1) permanent prohibition of forest areas reduction; (2) increasing of total forest fund, as well as the share of State ownership of forests in the Republic of Serbia, especially in forests with special purpose; (3) funding of the conservation, protection and improvement state of the existing and the establishment of new forests, preparation of plans and programmes of forest management through the Forest Budget Fund of the Republic of Serbia (hereinafter, Budget Fund), that is, funding of the conservation, protection and state improvement of the existing and building of new forest, development plans and programmes of forest management through the Forest Budget Fund of the AP (hereinafter, referred to as the Provincial Budget Fund); (4) adoption of the programme for development of forestry, forest management plans and their implementation; (5) setting up of legal entities for the management of State-owned forests; (6) establishment, maintenance and usage of national information system in forestry; (7) providing financial, technical and advisory support to the owners of forests; (8)

950. *Forest*, in terms of this Law, means a land area covered by forest trees, a minimum area of 5 acres, the minimum coverage area of the crowns of the trees 30%. Under forest are considered forest nurseries in complex of forest and seed plantations, as well as protective belts of trees larger than 5 acres. Under forest are not considered, parks in urban areas, as well as trees under power lines and in corridor of transmission lines, regardless of the surface (Art. 5, paras 1–4).

951. *Forestland* is land on which forest is grown, land on which is, due to its natural characteristics, more rational to grow forest, land on which facilities for forest and wild life management are built, as well as realization of forest functions and which cannot be used for other purposes except in cases and under conditions specified by this Law (Art. 5, para. 4).

952. *Forest management* is a set of agreed professionally-scientific, technical and technological, economic, organizational and social activities undertaken in a certain period in the forest for its protection, maintenance, improvement and usage (Art. 8, point 7).

953. Activities of common interest referred to in Art. 4 of this Law shall be financed from: (1) funds for the renovation-reproduction of forests; (2) Budget of the Republic of Serbia or AP; (3) Budget Fund or Budget Provincial Fund. Activities of public interest referred to in Art. 4 of this Law may be financed from the budget of local government units, in accordance with this Law (Art. 76, paras 1 and 2).

prohibition of alienation of State-owned forests, except in cases stipulated by this Law; (9) preservation and protection of forests as environmental factors; and (10) performing other tasks in accordance with this Law and regulations adopted pursuant to the Law.

I. Forest Conservation, Monitoring and Sanation

909. In order to preserve forests, except when otherwise provided by this Law, following is prohibited: (1) devastation[954] and deforestation;[955] (2) total deforestation[956] which is not planned as a regular form of reforestation; (3) cutting, which is inconsistent with the forest management plans; (4) felling of protected trees and strictly protected species;(5) whitening of trees; (6) pasture, cattle browsing and acorning in the woods; (7) the collection of other forest products (mushrooms, fruits, herbs, snails and others); (8) cutting of seed stands and seed trees which is not prescribed by forest management plans; (9) use of stone, gravel, sand, humus, soil and peat, except for the construction of infrastructure facilities for forest management; (10) arbitrary seizure of forests, destruction or damage of forest plantations, marking and boundary signs, as well as construction of buildings that are not intended for forest management; (11) disposal of waste, harmful substances and hazardous materials and waste, as well as noise pollution in any way; and (12) taking other actions which might yield weak forests or that might endanger forest functions (Article 9, paragraph 1).

910. Change of purpose of forests and forestland can be made: (1) when it is determined by the development plan of the forest area; (2) if it is required by public interest established by Law or special Act of the Government; (3) for construction of buildings for protection of people and property from natural disasters and for national defence; (4) in the process of regrouping and consolidation of agricultural land and forests; (5) for the construction of economic and residential buildings of forest owners on an area of up to 10 acres; (6) for the purpose of construction of facilities for the use of other renewable energy sources of small capacity (small power stations and other similar facilities, in terms of regulations governing the energy sector) and the exploitation of mineral resources, if the area of forests and forestlands for these purposes is less than 15 hectares (Article 10, paragraph 1).[957]

911. It is prohibited that cutting of trees, destruction of young trees and collecting of seeds strictly protected and protected forest tree species identified by a special regulation governing the protection of nature, unless they are source of infection from diseases and pests, that is, if they threaten people and facilities (Article 13, paragraph

954. *Forest devastations* are illegal operations which endanger or prevent the durability of forest production or cultivation of forests on the land and threaten the survival of forests and their socially useful functions (large-scale felling similar to total cutting, any action that may cause taking roots, rinsing and removal of soil by wind or water, etc.) (Art. 8, point 15).
955. *Forest clearing* involves the removal of forest tree species in a particular area for conversion of forestland (Art. 8, point 8).
956. *Total deforestation* is the removal of all or nearly all trees in a particular area (Art. 8, point 2).
957. Change of purpose of forests in para. 1, items (4)–(6) of this Article shall be made with the consent of the Ministry (Art. 10, para. 2).

1).[958] In order to preserve and use genetic resources species directed in paragraph 1 of this Article, forest management plans include measures for the protection, use and expanding of area of these species (Article 13, paragraph 3).

912. Monitoring the impact of transboundary air pollution is a system of continuous monitoring and analysis of the overall situation of forest ecosystems caused by the impact of transboundary air pollution, in accordance with internationally accepted methodology. These activities are performed by the Ministry or by the organization appointed by the Ministry and financed from the Republic of Serbia budget (Article 15, paragraphs 1–4).

913. The owner, that is, user of forest[959] is required to carry out sanation, as follows: bare surface effect resulting from natural disasters (fire, wind, snow, etc.), the surface on which the rejuvenation and afforestation has failed; areas where the devastation was committed – illegal total cutting or deforestation or illegal cutting of trees of rare species (Article 16, paragraph 1).

II. Forests, Forestland and Forest Planning

914. The forest areas are established with the aim to provide conditions for balanced and sustainable development of forests, the rational implementation of forest management measures and other forest resources in a particular territory (Article 17, paragraph 1).[960] Forests and forestland included in forest areas and national parks are determined in the inventory of forests and forestlands of forest areas, which is attached to this Law making its integral part (Article 17, paragraph 4).

915. Management units,[961] as the basic unit of planning, are established by the development plan of the forest area, according to the needs of the organization of forest management and according to criteria for the division of forest areas (Article 18, paragraph 1).

916. Forestry Development Programme in the Republic of Serbia is the strategic planning documents by which are set out the directions of development of forests and forestry with an action plan for their implementation.[962]

958. The species referred to in para. 1 of this Article may be used with the consent of the Ministry, but at the territory of AP with the consent of the competent authorities of the AP (Art. 13, para. 2).
959. *Forest user* is a legal entity that manages the State-owned forests in accordance with this Law and other regulations (Art. 8, point 9).
960. The forest area is planned geographic and natural entity that includes forests and forestland of forest area and of national parks (Art. 17, para. 2). Forest area covers forests in all forms of ownership and for all purposes, other than forest in national parks (Art. 17, para. 5).
961. Management Unit, as a rule makes territorial integrity of forests and forestlands, except forest owner – a natural person, and includes the entire complex or just part of it (Art. 18, para. 2). Management unit includes forests and forestland of the same type of ownership, in the forest area of 5,000 acres (Art. 18, para. 3).
962. Forestry Development Programme on territory of the Republic of Serbia adopts the Government for a period of ten years (Art. 19, para. 3).

917. Forest management plans are: (1) forest area development plan, that is, forest area development plan in a national park; (2) the basis for forest management and (3) programme for forest management (Article 20, paragraph 1).

918. National Forest Inventory is carried out to determine the condition of forests for the purpose of strategic planning, other State agencies, other branches of economy, defence, scientific research, as a rule every ten years (Article 38, paragraph 1).[963]

III. Forest Protection and Management

919. Protection of forests from unlawful appropriation, usage, destruction and other illegal activities (disposal of waste and toxic pollutants, forest pollution, destruction of border signs and labels, etc.) is provided by the user, that is, owner of the forest[964] (Article 39, paragraph 1).

920. The owner and beneficiary of forest is required to monitor the impact of biotic and abiotic factors on the health of forests and promptly take measures to protect forests and forestlands[965] (Article 42, paragraph 1).

921. In cases of significant disturbance of biological balance and serious damage of forest ecosystems caused by the effect of natural disasters, the Ministry shall determine the measures for protection and rehabilitation of forests carried out by owners, that is, users of forests and provide financial resources (Article 45, paragraph 1).

922. Forest user is obliged to issue a plan for forest protection from fire in the forest area for all forests regardless of the ownership, for a period of five years (Article 46, paragraph 1). Ignition of open fire is forbidden in the forest and on land proximity to the forest, at a distance less than 200m from the woods edge (Article 47, paragraph 1).[966]

923. Natural and legal persons which caused the damage are obliged to compensate for the damage to the owner, that is, to the forest user (Article 48).

924. Waste disposal is forbidden in the forest, on forestland at a distance less than 200m from the edge of the forest, of toxic substances and other hazardous wastes, as well as construction of facilities for storage, processing or destruction of waste, toxic substances and other hazardous waste (Article 49, paragraph 1).[967]

---

963. National Forest Inventory is to be performed by the Ministry or it can be delegated by the advertisement published in the OJ of the Republic of Serbia (Art. 38, paras 2 and 3).
964. Forest owner is a natural or legal persons (company, cooperatives, churches and religious communities, association), owning the forests (Art. 8, point 18).
965. If owner, i.e., user of the forest does not act in accordance with para. 1 this Article, the Ministry, i.e., the competent authority of the AP at the territory of AP, shall ensure the enforcement of these obligations at the expense of owners, i.e., users of the forest (Art. 42, para. 2).
966. Notwithstanding to para. 1 this Article, the fire can be stoked in the forest and on forestland, at a place specified just for that purpose, settled up and clearly marked, implementing of measures stipulated in Art. 61 of this Law (Art. 47, para. 2).
967. The owner, i.e., the user of forest is required to prevent the actions specified in para. 1this Article, remove garbage, toxic substances and other hazardous waste, as well as to undertake all measures for rehabilitation of damaged forests (Art. 49, para. 3).

925. The owner, that is, user of forest is required to prevent dumping of waste, toxic substances and other hazardous waste, as well as that without delay notify the Ministry, at the territory of AP the competent authority of AP (Article 49, paragraph 2).

926. It is forbidden to drain and to perform work which change water regime in the forest so that it threatens the survival and vitality of the forest (Article 50, paragraph 1).[968]

927. The following are forbidden in the forest without agreement of owners, that is, user of forest: (1) setting up of temporary buildings, tents and camping establishment; (2) organizing a mass meeting which might be detrimental to the forest; (3) setting up the board and signs which damage the tree; (4) setting up the fences; (5) movement of motor vehicles off roads intended for that purpose, except for official purposes; (6) the movement in a closed and restricted areas, roads, fenced hunting grounds, experimental and business buildings; (7) moving in the areas where the following works are carried out – forest works and afforestation, logging, building construction, hunting, etc. (Article 51, paragraph 1).

928. The citizens have free access to the forest for the purpose of enjoyment, relaxation and recreation, on their own responsibility for their safety and with obligation not to harm the forest (Article 51, paragraph 2). Free access can be restricted in protected forest areas or in forest areas where people's security might be threatened (Article 51, paragraph 3).[969]

929. Pasture, browsing or acornation in the forest can be done only with the permission of owners that is, user of the forest, which can issue the license only if pasture, browsing or acornation are allowed in forest management plans, and if forest is not in process of renewing (Article 52, paragraph 1).[970]

930. Legal entities entrusted to manage the game, in accordance with the regulations governing wildlife and hunting, are obliged to number the types of game and maintain at a level that does not disrupt the biological balance of forest ecosystems and does not prevent the implementation of forest management objectives (Article 53, paragraph 1).

IV. Forest Management Organization and Inventory of Forests and Forestland

931. Management of forests as a natural resource is under the jurisdiction of the Republic of Serbia (Article 69, paragraph 1). The Ministry is in charge for forest

968. The elaboration and implementation of the projects of headwater management in forest ecosystems, enacted in accordance with special regulations, shall ensure a sufficient quantity of free water (the biological minimum) to meet the needs of plants and animals in the forest (Art. 50, para. 2).
969. The owner, i.e., user of the forest is required to mark with visible warning signs part of the forest where access is forbidden (Art. 51, para. 4).
970. Pasture is allowed on forestland until its afforestation (Art. 52, para. 2). Live stockholders can use the forest for pasture, browse or acornation, only under the supervision of shepherd (Art. 52, para. 3).

management at the Republic of Serbia level, and at the territory of AP competent authorities of the AP are in charge. Also, the forest management is performed through State-owned legal entities for forest management and through legal entities for management of forest owners (Article 69, paragraph 2).

932. State-owned forests in the area covered by forest, that is, national park area are managed by a public company or a company founded by the Republic of Serbia or AP, which meets the requirements established by this Law and by special regulations (Article 70, paragraph 1).

933. Forest users managing forest and forestland shall keep and maintain records of these items (the Forests Cadastre) (Article 67, paragraph 1).[971] The authority responsible for keeping records of real estate is required to enable to the Ministry free of charge usage of data on forests and forestland for production of forest management plans (Article 67, paragraph 3).[972]

934. The Ministry establishes and maintains a single information system for forests and forestry of the Republic of Serbia (Article 68, paragraph 1).

935. The following legal and sub-legal Acts are also important:

- Law on Wild Game and Hunting (OJ RS, No. 18/10).
- Rulebook on forest reproductive materials (OJ RS, No. 46/11).
- Rulebook on the contents of medium-term plan for the protection of forests against plant diseases and pests (OJ RS, No. 35/11).
- Law on public property (OJ RS, Nos 72/11, 88/13 and 105/14).

The *EPL* (OJ RS, Nos 135/04, 36/09 and 14/2016).

936. Serbia (FR Yugoslavia) has ratified Protocol to the CLRTAP on Financing of the Cooperative Programme for Monitoring and Evaluation of the Long-Range Transmission of Air Pollutants in Europe (EMEP) in 1986, which is of importance for forest protection. Serbia has also ratified the United Nations Convention to Combat Desertification in Countries Experiencing Serious Drought and/or Desertification, particularly in Africa (1994).

971. Forest users are obliged to apply to the State agency responsible for keeping records of real estate to record changes made in the previous year, not later than 31 March of current year (Art. 67, para. 2).

972. The Minister shall prescribe the content and manner of forest cadastre (Art. 67, para. 4).

Chapter 7. Hunting and Fishery

937. Hunting and Fishery in Serbia are not too important from the economic point of view, although both activities contribute to a certain extent to overall food production and to the tourist industry.

Total hunting area in Serbia is 8,828,588 ha (73.6% hunting grounds and 26.4% non-hunting grounds). There are 323 hunting sites: 199 in Central Serbia, ninety-one in the APV and thirty-three in Kosovo and Metohija out of ninety-four registered mammal species only twenty-two have the status of hunting wildlife and of the 360 registered bird species, only twenty-four are hunting species.[973] Because of their decline, populations of some species of game and fishes are under protection.

938. When diversity of fishing species in fishing waters is concerned, situation in Serbia is more or less similar to the situation in other countries in the region, but in spite of favourable natural potential, number of registered fishermen and the productivity in fish production are among the lowest in Europe,[974] due to the fact that until recently the sector of fishery has not been given adequate priority. Ichthyofauna of Serbian waters includes about a hundred fish species, which somewhat exceeds 50% of overall European ichthyofauna. The richest ichthyofauna is the one found in the Danube watershed, but according to the importance and conservation status, ichthyofauna of the Adriatic and Aegean Sea basins are also very significant. Out of seven endemic fish species of the Danube basin, five live in the Republic of Serbia.[975] Since 2003 a mild growth of catch has been generally recorded for all fish species of ecosystem of inland waters that are target catch of recreational and commercial fishing, while the increase in catch recorded for carp, catfish, pikeperch and somewhat pike has been markedly high due to the increase in demand of these species on Serbian market.[976]

939. MAEP – Forestry Department (Hunting) have certain competencies and responsibilities. The affairs in fishing are conducted by the MAEP (Veterinary Directorate).

MAEP is competent for managing fishing resources in fishing waters, which entails preservation and protection, catch and use of fish and farming all species and age categories of fish. Fishing resource management is done in accordance with the principle of sustainable use, which contributes to preservation of ichtiofaunistic diversity

973. NEPP, 82. So far 110 species and sub-species of lampreys and *Clupeidae* were identified (inland water of RS) –twenty-three types of which are aliant species (23.5%) and twelve of them may be considered as invasive. Out of the entire number of species, fifty-three fish species (54.1%), including ten aliant species are subject to commercial and sports hunting. From the point of view of commercial hunting, twenty-nine species are important for the economy and twelve of them are a target group for fishing activities. *Biodiversity indicators in the Republic of Serbia for 2015*, MAEP, EPA, 2015, 18.

974. NSDS, 104.

975. NEPP, 83.

976. Since 2005 a mild increase in export in the field of fisheries has been recorded and import has been increased by approximately 40%. The import significantly surpasses the export, both in terms of quantity and value. AECQ, Ch. 13 (Fisheries), Government of the Republic of Serbia, Belgrade, 2011, 11. *See* : http://www.seio.gov.rs/eng/documents/national-documents/answer-to-the-european-commision-s-questionnaire (17 Jun. 2017).

and ecological integrity of water ecosystems. Fish farming covers production of spawn, young fish and fish in fisheries, in confined parts of fishing waters and fishing water cages.

§1. Legal Regulation

I. General Regulations

940. The Constitution of Serbia explicitly mentions 'hunting and fishery' only once in Article 183, that prescribes that APs shall, in accordance with the Law, regulate the matters of provincial interest in various fields, including hunting and fishery.

941. EPL (OJ RS, Nos 135/04, 36/09 and 36/09 – other law, 72/09 – other law, 43/11CC and 14/16) contains provisions on hunting and fishing in Article 33 (Planning and Construction) and in Article 35 (Strategic EIA).

942. The Law on Strategic Environmental Assessment (OJ RS, Nos 135/04 and 88/10) prescribes in Article 5 that strategic assessment shall be carried out for all plans, programmes bases and strategies (hereinafter, referred to as plans and programmes) in the areas of spatial and urban planning or land-use planning, agriculture, forestry, fishery, *hunting,* energy, industry, transport, waste management, water management, telecommunications, tourism, conservation of natural habitats and wild flora and fauna, that set the frameworks for granting the approval for future development projects defined by the EIA related regulations.

II. Law on Wild Game and Hunting

943. The Law on Wild Game and Hunting (OJ RS, No. 18/10) is the main legal Act regulating protection of wild game and hunting in Serbia. It consists of 115 Articles divided into eleven parts as follows: I. Basic Provisions (Articles 1–4); II. Organization of the Hunting (Articles 5–8); III. Chamber of Hunting (Articles 9–19); IV. Protection of Wild Game (Articles 20–30); V. The Hunting Grounds and Hunting Area (Articles 31–37); VI. Management of the Hunting Ground and Wild Game (Articles 38–77); VII. Financing (Articles 78–86); VIII. Damages and Compensation of Damages (Articles 87–91); IX. Monitoring (Articles 92–101); X. Penal Provisions (Articles 102–105); and XI. Transitional and Final Provisions (Articles 106–115).

944. The basic aim of the Law is described in first three Articles. It is stated that wild game is a natural resource of Serbia (Article 1) and that protection, breeding, hunting and usage of wild game are activities of public interest (Article 3). It should be also added that Article 4 contains precise definitions of some notions used in the Law. Organization of the hunting is mainly regulated by Articles 5–8. Article 5, paragraph 1 prescribes that the competent organ for hunting in the Republic of Serbia is the Ministry for hunting (the Ministry). According to paragraph 2 of the same Article, AP regulates the hunting in matters of provincial interest on its territory. The matters are enumerated in Article 6.

945. The Law also prescribes certain managerial responsibilities to public enterprises, business associations and Serbian Hunting Association (Articles 7 and 8) which are obliged to cooperate with each other in matters concerning hunting and to exchange relevant information (Article 8, paragraph 4).[977]

946. Articles 9–19 of the Law regulate establishment, composition, activities, structure, statute, financing, issuance of licenses, evaluation of professional work and some other issues, of the Chamber of Hunting. The institution has been established with the task of 'realization and protection of rights and interests of persons engaged in activities concerning hunting, as well as improvement of hunting in accordance with management of population of wild game, public interest and universally accepted international standards…'(Article 9).

947. The Law prescribes protection of wild game by dividing it into two categories (1) game species protected by a permanent hunting ban and (2) species of game that are prohibited from hunting during a certain period (Article 20). Procedure of declaring seasonal hunting periods is regulated by Article 21, according to the game species, obligations of hunters concerning animal welfare, and hunting grounds management. A number of prohibitions are prescribed by Article 22 (e.g., to catch protected game; to keep it in closed or fenced spaces, to destruct wild game lairs, nests and eggs; to collect eggs of protected birds, etc.), as well as exceptional cases when these prohibitions do not apply (Article 23). It does not apply to the organized catching of injured game or game which is endangered by natural catastrophes, or for implementing measures regarding their breeding and populating. The Law also regulates introduction of new wild game into existing hunting grounds (Articles 24 and 25), measures of wild game health protection (Article 26), measures regarding their breeding and populating (Article 27), measures regarding protection of wild game outside hunting grounds (Article 28), protection of wild game from stray dogs and cats (Article 29) and entrance to the hunting grounds which is allowed only to 'persons armed with hunting rifles and other means prescribed for hunting, if they have hunting card and hunting license' (Article 30).

948. Establishment of hunting territory and hunting grounds is regulated by Articles 31–37. While the whole territory of Serbia is regarded as one hunting territory (Article 31) hunting grounds are divided into open and fenced ones (Article 32). Rules of establishment hunting grounds are regulated in detail (Articles 33–35 and 37) and definition of non-hunting grounds is given (Article 36).

949. A large part of the Law contains provisions dealing with management of the hunting ground and wild game (Articles 38–77). It is prescribed in detail how a legal person obtains the right to use a hunting ground, how long the contract lasts, what are the exceptions, etc. (Articles 38–43). The Minister prescribes, besides other matters, procedure for establishment of hunting areas and hunting grounds, conditions for hunting management, public procedure for obtaining the right to use a hunting

977. According to Art. 7, public enterprises and business associations are responsible for protection, breeding, hunting and sustainable usage of wild game as a natural resource, for hunting grounds management, distribution of hunting maps, etc. Pursuant to Art. 8, Serbian Hunting Association is the institution responsible for establishing various commissions (for evaluation of wild game trophies, for exhibition of the trophies, for passing hunting examination, etc.) issuance of hunting licenses, publishing activities, etc.

ground, contents of the contract and the amount of guarantee to be given by the legal person who wants to obtain the right for hunting management (Article 44).

950. Several Articles of the Law are devoted to planning documents. The basic document is Strategy of Developing Hunting in the Republic of Serbia adopted by the Government for a period of fifteen years (Article 45). Another planning document prescribed by the Law is the Programme of development of a hunting area (Article 46). There must also be prepared the so-called hunting basics for every hunting ground –a document which regulates protection, breeding, hunting and usage of wild game and hunting grounds management (Article 47). The user of a hunting ground is also obliged to prepare an annual plan for management of his/her ground based on the above-mentioned hunting basics (Article 48).[978]

951. Articles 54–58 of the Law regulate position and duties of game wardens and management of the hunting grounds. Articles 59–77 regulate various aspects of hunting (hunting examination, hunting card, prescribe hunting periods seasonally, according to the game species, the right to hunting, license to hunt big game, use of hunting dogs, battle against poachers, hunting tourism, exception when it is possible to hunt protected game, etc.) game trophies, export of game, and other use of hunted game.[979]

952. Other legal Acts relevant to hunting in Serbia are, *inter alia*, following:

- Law on Forests (OJ RS, Nos 30/10, 93/12 and 89/15).
- Law on Animal Welfare (OJ RS, No. 41/09).
- Law on Veterinary Medicine (OJ RS, Nos 91/05, 30/10 and 93/12).
- *EPL* (OJ RS, Nos 135/04, 36/09, 72/09, 43/11 CC and 14/16).
- Law on National Parks (OJ RS, No. 84/15).
- Law on Tourism (OJ RS, Nos 36/09, 88/10, 99/11, 93/12 and 84/15).
- Law on Weapons and Ammunition (OJ RS No. 20/15).
- Law on Associations (OJ RS, Nos 51/10 and 99/11).
- Rulebook on the establishment of hunting areas in the Republic of Serbia (OJ RS, No. 5/11).
- Rulebook on cadastre of hunting ground and central database (OJ RS, No. 40/12).
- Rulebook on measures for preventing damages from wild animals and damage to wildlife and the procedure and method of determining damages (OJ RS, No. 2/12).
- Rulebook on the format and content of the official identity card and official badge of hunting inspector, as well as the manner of use of protective equipment (OJ RS, No. 60/11).

978. Articles 50–52 regulate rights and duties of users of neighbouring hunting grounds, users and owners of land, waters and forests, and users (i.e., managers) of protected natural resources. Article 53 deals with the Cadastre of hunting grounds and Central basis of data, kept by the Ministry.

979. Financing is regulated by Arts 78–86. Damages and Compensation of Damages by Arts 87–91. Monitoring is regulated by Part IX of the Law (Arts 92–101), while penal provisions are contained in Part X (Arts 102–105). Transitional and final provisions are contained in Arts 106–115.

- Rulebook on professional examination for obtaining a license to perform certain hunting activities (OJ RS, No. 65/11).
- Rulebook on the manner of marking and labelling of boundaries and hunting-technical facilities in the hunting areas (OJ RS, No. 76/11).
- Rulebook on the security measures in the hunting areas (OJ RS, No. 76/11).
- Rulebook on hunting dogs (OJ RS, No. 80/11).
- Rulebook on the game warden service (OJ RS, Nos 84/11 and 56/15).
- Order on game closed season (OJ RS, 55/06).
- Rulebook on proclamation of closed season for protected wild species (OJ RS, Nos 9/12, 31/13, 55/15 and 67/15 and 75/16).

III. Law on Conservation and Sustainable Use of Fish Resources

953. Law on Conservation and Sustainable Use of Fish Resources (OJ RS, No. 128/14) contains following eight chapters: Basic provisions (Articles 1 and 2); fishing areas (Articles 3–21); conservation and protection of the fish stock (Articles 22–31); fishing (Articles 32–49); turnover of fishes (Articles 50 and 51); supervision (Articles 53–57); penal provisions (Articles 58–63);and transitional and final provisions (Articles 64–68).[980]

954. The Law regulates management of the fish stock in fishing waters that includes protection and sustainable use of the fish stock as public interest. Management of fish resources shall be done according to the principle of sustainable use that contributes to the protection of ichthyofauna diversity and ecological integrity of aquatic ecosystems (Article 1).[981]

A. Fishing Areas

955. Fishing areas are established for the purpose of sustainable use of fish resources[982] in fishing waters. Fishing area is established by the Minister responsible for the fishing stock issues (Minister) (Article 3 paragraph 1).[983] Fishing area in the protected area is declared and used by controller of the protected area, with prior approval of the Minister and the controller is user of the fishing area (Article 3 paragraph 2).

980. On the date of enactment of this Law, the Law on Fishery (OJ RS, Nos 36/09 and 32/13 CC) shall cease to be effective (Art. 67). The secondary legislation to be adopted on the base of this Law shall be issued within one year from the date of entry into force of this Law. Until issuing the regulations referred to in para. 1 of Art. 66, the Decision on the determination of fishing areas (OJ RS, Nos 115/07, 49/10 and 60/12) and regulations adopted pursuant to the Law on the protection and sustainable use of fish stocks (OJ RS, Nos 36/09 and 32/13 – US), except for provisions of these regulations that are not in accordance with the Law (Art. 66, paras 1–2).

981. The fish resources in fishing waters are owned by the State (Art. 1, para. 4).

982. The fish resources include all kinds of fish, mollusks, crabs and other aquatic organisms which are protected and sustainable used (Art. 2, point 25).

983. The Act referred to in paras 2 and 3 of this Article regulates boundaries and purpose of the fishing area with regard to the type of fishing performed therein (commercial and/or recreational) (Art. 3, para. 4).

956. The fishing waters that are at the same time the state border, border fishing areas are determined according to the state border. Water fishing in fishing areas, and the prescribed measures Protection and Sustainable Use of fish resources are entered in the fishing water cadastre kept by the Ministry responsible for environmental protection and sustainable utilization of the fish stock (hereinafter, referred to as the Ministry) (Article 3 paragraph 5–6).

The fishing area may be conceded for use to a commercial entity or public enterprise (hereinafter, referred to as user) satisfying the following requirements: (1) it is registered by the competent authority and entered in the appropriate register; (2) they shall be technically and professionally equipped for performing the activity, that is, they have an employee in continuous employment with minimum university degree of the second grade (masteracademic studies, specialized academic studies and specialized professional studies), or on the basic studies of at least four years, biological, environmental, veterinary, or livestock (zoo technical) orientation, with attended, and passed the course(s) from the field of fishery or ichthyology (hereinafter, referred to a specialist); (3) that, within two years prior to announcement of the competition for concession of the fishing area for use, they were not sanctioned for corporate offences or corporate minor offences, etc. (Article 6, paragraph 1, points 1–3).

957. The Law defines that fishing area may be granted for use to a company or public company or user fulfilling certain conditions and that fishing area shall be granted for use for certain charge (Article 7).[984]

The contract on the use of fishing area is negotiated by the Minister, or the competent organ of the province, with the user of fishing area (Article 8). It is prescribed that the user is obliged to organize protection of the fishing area (Article 11).

958. Fish watchman license is issued by the competent ministry to the person who has passed professional exam for a fish watchman, his/her authority as an official person has been prescribed by the Law (Articles 13 and 14).

Legal person, entrepreneur or physical person who is by practicing fishing braking provisions of this Law, or in some other way causes harm to fish resources, is obliged to recompense the damage to the user of fishing area (Article 16, paragraph 1).[985]

959. The user is obliged to have the programme of management of fishing area and to obtain approval for it (Article 17, paragraph 1).[986]Manager of the protected areas is required to harmonize programme management fishing area with management plans (Article 20, paragraph 1). For fishing waters for which consent for declaration

984. Charges for the use of fishing area are revenue in the budget of the Republic of Serbia, while charges for the use of fishing area in the territory of AP are revenue in the budget of the AP. Amount of charges that are revenue for Republic of Serbia budget shall be 15% from fees paid for license issuance for commercial fishing and 10% from fees paid for license issuance for recreational fishing (annual, daily, for more days) (Art. 7, paras 2–4).

985. The Minister prescribes the Regulation on the amount of charges for damage done to fish resources and Regulation on categorization of fishing waters (Art. 16, para. 4).

986. In accordance with the fishing area management programme, the user shall enact the annual fishing area management programme at the latest by the end of the current year for the following year (Art. 17, para. 2).

of fishing area is not given, controller prescribes protective measures and usage of fish stock in Protected area Management plan (Article 20, paragraph 3).[987]

B. Preservation and Protection of Fish Resources

960. Actions forbidden in the fishing area are prescribed in Article 22, paragraph 1. To preserve and protect fish stocks a closed season is established for all or certain types of fish in the fishing area, as well as the prohibition of hunting fish that do not have the required size. The Minister shall prescribe measures for the conservation and protection of fish stocks (Article 23, paragraphs 1–2).

961. It is not allowed to introduce allochthonous (non-native) types of fish into fishing waters (Article 30). Apart from that, it is not allowed to introduce fish species from regionally remote geographic areas, as well as species that originate from geographically close but mutually isolated basins.

C. Fishing

962. Commercial fishing in a fishing area can be done by a commercial society or an entrepreneur who fulfils conditions prescribed by this Law (Article 32, paragraph 1).[988] Commercial fishing is practiced by entrepreneur and commercial society in accordance with the contract with the user of fishing area and the annual permit for commercial fishing, according to the programme of management of fishing area and the annual programme of management of fishing area, as well as the temporary programme of management of fishing area and categorization of fishing waters (Article 32, paragraph 4).[989]

963. Register of commercial fishers is kept by the Ministry (Article 34).[990]

---

987. The user of the fishing area is required to prepare an annual report on the use of fishing area and submit it to the competent ministry or the provincial authority and the Agency for Environmental Protection, not later than 1 March of the current year for the previous year (Art. 21).

988. Commercial society can practice commercial fishing provided that it has only employed persons with VII degree of professional education (or master studies), in biology, ecology or cattle breeding; they should be enlisted in the Register of commercial fishers (Art. 30, para. 2). An entrepreneur can practice commercial fishing if he is entered in the Register of Commercial Fishermen (Art. 32, para. 3).

989. 'Commercial fishing is carried out on the Danube, the Sava and the Tisa rivers. Although these are the largest rivers flowing through Serbia, their geographic contribution in relation to the entire territory is reduced to one-third of the country's territory. In accordance with the Regional Strategy for Conservation and Sustainable Management of Sturgeon Population of the North-West Black Sea and Lower Danube River in accordance with CITES, November 26 2003, Tulcea, Romania, the fishing on the Danube River from 863 km to 860 km (Hydroelectric Power Plant "Đerdap II") is prohibited.' AECQ, Ch. 13 (Fisheries), *supra* , 14.

990. The Minister shall prescribe in detail the contents and method of keeping the Register of commercial fishers (Art. 34, para. 2).

964. Annual permit for commercial fishing is issued by the user of fishing area on request by commercial society or an entrepreneur (Article 35).[991] The user of the fishing area, for the purpose of preservation of fish resource as a natural resource, shall issue the number of annual commercial fishing permits specified by the fishing area management programme and categorization of fishing waters (Article 35). A commercial entity and entrepreneur shall perform commercial fishing by means of fishing hooks, fishing nets and traps not jeopardizing the juvenile fish species and animals eaten by the fish (Article 37).[992] The commercial entity or entrepreneur performing commercial fishing shall be obliged to keep daily records on fish catching, to prepare a monthly and annual report and submit them to the user of the fishing area at the end of current month, that is, year (Article 39 paragraph 1).[993]

965. Recreative and sport fishing can be done by persons with the permit for recreative fishing.[994]

966. Fishing for scientific research purposes shall be performed in the presence of the inspector in charge of activities of protection and sustainable use of fish resources based on permit issued by the Minister and on the territory of the AP the competent provincial body (Article 47 paragraph 1).[995]

Fishing for scientific research purposes may be performed by means of any fishing hooks, fishing nets and traps and electro fishing device, to the extent and scope which does not disturb the composition of ichthyofauna or significantly reduce the existing fish resources (Article 48, paragraph 1).[996]

967. Electro fishing is done with the permit issued by the Minister, i.e., competent body of the AP and supervised by an inspector. In exceptional case, electro fishing can be done in cases of fish stocking and in cases of saving fish in a flooded area with the permit issued by the Minister (Article 49).

---

991. For issuing of the annual permit referred to in para. 1 of this Article, the commercial entity or entrepreneur shall pay the costs of permit issuance established by the user (Art. 33, para. 2).
992. The user of the fishing area intended for commercial fishing may, through the fishing area management programme, restrict or ban use of certain tools used for commercial fishing. For the purpose of protection of fish resources, the user of the fishing area may, with the consent of the Minister, i.e., competent provincial authority, temporarily and maximum for a period of one year, ban commercial fishing in a certain part of the fishing area (Art. 38, paras 1 and 2).
993. The user may not issue a commercial fishing permit in the current year to the commercial entity or entrepreneur which failed to submit the annual report for the previous year (Art. 39, para. 2).
994. Persons younger than 14 years can practice recreative fishing without the permit with one fishing rod if they are in company of persons with the permit for recreative fishing (Art. 40, para. 2).
995. The holder of the permit shall be obliged to notify the user and the Ministry, i.e., competent body of the AP of the time when fishing for scientific research purposes is to be performed and to prepare a report on performed fishing and submit it to the Ministry (Art. 47, para. 3).
996. Fishing for scientific research purposes may be performed by organizations registered for expert and scientific research from the field of fishing fishery, ichthyology, fish biology or ecology of continental waters (Art. 48, para. 2).

D. *Trade in Fish*

968. Trade in fish can be done by legal persons and entrepreneurs registered for fish trade, as well as companies and entrepreneurs engaged in commercial fishing, in accordance with special regulations (Article 50, paragraph 1).[997]

It shall be prohibited to place on the market the fish under the prescribed size or fish caught during the closed season (Article 51 paragraph 1).[998] Apart from that, it is prohibited to place on the market prepared trophy fish or their parts without consent of the Ministry (Article 51, paragraph 4). Fish caught in fishing waters before closed fishing season cannot be put in the market after twenty-four hours from commencement of closed fishing season (Article 51, paragraph 2).

E. *Supervision*

969. The inspection of enforcement of provisions of this Law and regulations enacted on the basis of this Law shall be performed by the Ministry through competent inspector (Article 54, paragraph 1). The Ministry, in supervising the work of the relevant Provincial authority, users and managers of protected area, may require the submission of reports, information on the performance of delegated tasks, to give the required instructions and warns of failure to perform the delegated tasks in accordance with the Law (Article 53, paragraphs 2–3).[999]

970. The law on animal husbandry (OJ RS, Nos 41/2009, 93/2012 and 14/2016) regulates the goals in animal husbandry; agents in livestock production and their organizational forms; breeding objectives and the implementation of breeding programmes; control of productivity and maintenance of properties of domestic animals; breeding of domestic animals; beekeeping; aquaculture; breeding of wild animals; conservation of genetic reserves of domestic animals and biological diversity in livestock; fishery products; primary production of food for domestic animals and animal products; transport breeding material, as well as other issues of importance to animal husbandry (Article 1). Conditions for conducting aquaculture are regulated by Articles 65 and 66 of the Act. The law also regulates the import, export and transit of fishery products (Article 66b).

971. Besides the Law on Fishing and the Law on animal husbandry a number of specific by-laws regulate protection of fish.[1000] They are, *inter alia* following:

- Rulebook on the form, content and scope of final report on the use of fishing area (OJ RS, No. 70/10).

997. Associations, recreative fishing and other persons cannot put in the market caught fish (Art. 50, para. 3).
998. When are traded during the time of closed seasons or traded in fishes which do not have prescribed size, the legal person and the entrepreneur must have documentation to prove the origin of the fish, the species and the quantity of fish (Art. 51, para. 4).
999. The Ministry shall perform supervision over the work of the competent authority of the AP in performing the entrusted activities (Art. 50, para. 2).
1000. On this subject, *see also*, S. Nojković, Zakonodavstvo u oblasti ribarstva [*Legislation in Field of Fishery*], *Pravni život*, No. 9/2005.

- Rulebook on the categorization of fishing waters (OJ RS, No.10/12).
- Rulebook on conditions and manner of organizing fish warden service, warden ID forms and appearance of the warden badge (OJ RS, No.07/10).
- Rulebook on the content of the recreational fishing permit form (OJ RS, No. 73/10).
- Rulebook on the amount of costs for the issuance of annual recreational fishing permits (OJ RS, No.87/12).
- Rulebook on the manner of determining and the amount of compensation of damage caused to fish resources (OJ RS, No.03/2016).
- Rulebook on the monitoring programme for monitoring the status of fish resources in fishing waters (OJ RS, No.71/10).
- Rulebook on the content of the annual commercial fishing permit form (OJ RS, No.56/2015).
- Rulebook on the appearance and content of the form of records of fishermen catch, and the manner of keeping records of fish catch (OJ RS, No.34/15).
- Rulebook on the appearance and content of the form of records of commercial fishermen catch and the manner of keeping records of fish catch (OJ RS, No.37/15).
- Rulebook on conditions, programmed and manner of going for an examination for fish warden and professional fisherman examination (OJ RS, No.60/15).
- Rulebook on the content of form of one-day, multi-day and annual permit for recreational fishing, and one-day, multi-day and annual permit for recreational fishing in protected area (OJ RS, No.15/15).
- Rulebook on conditions to be fulfilled by ranching materials (OJ RS, No.86/15).
- Rulebook on conditions and procedure for the issuance and withdrawal of fish warden licenses and the manner of keeping the register of issued fish warden licenses (OJ RS, No.02/16).
- Rulebook on the content and manner of keeping the fishing water cadastre (OJ RS, No.03/2016).
- Rulebook on conditions and manner of organizing fish warden service and the form of keeping records of daily activities of fish warden service (OJ RS, No.03/2016).
- Rulebook on the scope and content of the recreational fishermen educational programme (OJ RS, No.03/2016).
- Rulebook on fish warden uniforms, appearance of the warden badge and fish warden official ID form (OJ RS, No.39/2016).
- Rulebook on the manner, tools and means for commercial fishing, and the manner, tools, equipment and means for recreational fishing (OJ RS, No.42/16).
- Rulebook on the value of one-day, multi-day and annual permit for recreational fishing for 2017 (OJ RS, No.96/2016).
- Rulebook amending rulebook on conditions, programme and manner of going for a professional fish warden examination and professional fisherman examination (OJ RS, No.96/2016).

IV. International Treaties and Harmonization with EU Legislation

972. The Republic of Serbia is a party to the following agreements:

- Agreement on fisheries in the Danube River waters (Bucharest 1958) between the Government of the Federative People's Republic of Yugoslavia, People's Republic of Bulgaria, the People's Republic of Romania and the Union of Soviet Socialist Republics.
- Agreement on fisheries in border waters (Timisoara, 1961) signed between the Government of the Federative People's Republic of Yugoslavia and the People's Republic of Romania governing fishing and fisheries in boundary waters.
- Agreement on boundary waters fishing (Belgrade, 1961) signed between the Government of the Federative People's Republic of Yugoslavia and the People's Republic of Bulgaria, governing fishing and fisheries in boundary waters.
- Regional Strategy for Conservation and Sustainable Management of Sturgeon Population of the North-West Black Sea and Lower Danube River in accordance with CITES, 26 November 2003, Tulcea, Romania.

973. Serious steps have been undertaken towards improvement of legal regulation in the fields of hunting and fishery.[1001]

The Serbian fishing industry is very small and consists of inland fishing, which is not covered by the EU *acquis*. The administrative body for the fisheries sector needs to be adapted to the needs of the CFP, while the capacity of the administration dealing with management and control of fishing activities needs to be enhanced and brought into line with CFP obligations. Overall, Serbia should be able to align with the EU *acquis* in the fisheries chapter and to implement it effectively in the medium term.[1002] According to the last EC report, Serbia is moderately prepared in the area of fisheries. Some progress was made through adoption of changes to the law on animal husbandry, establishing the legal base for a national catch certification scheme. In the coming period, Serbia should in particular establish an operational national catch certification scheme and a system for collecting market data.[1003]

1001. Problems in illegal hunting and fishing have increased in the recent years. Illegal export of birds in particular has increased. EPR (2003), 120.
1002. CO, 80.
1003. CR, 2016, 44.

Chapter 8. Subsoil and Minerals

§1. Mineral Resources in Serbia

974. Serbia has diversified mineral resources. Energy mineral resources have a significant place (coal, oil and gas). There are also metallic mineral resources (copper, lead, zinc, antimony, nickel, and also gold, silver, bismuth, cadmium, platinum, selenium, molybdenum, titanium, radium, palladium, etc.). There are non-metallic mineral resources too (zeolite, etc.).

Almost 90% of energy mineral resources of Serbia are lignite of low quality and oil and gas account for less than 10%. Reserves of coal are insufficient what may be a limiting factor to the development of the energy sector.

Deposits of metallic mineral resources are not very rich. Copper is the most important mineral resource with significant economic potential.[1004]

There are numerous sources (more than 1,000) of mineral, thermal and thermal-mineral water. Their total yields more than 1,000 l/s.[1005]

975. The Ministry of Mining and Energy is competent for the activities concerning mining. Another institution, established as an independent regulatory body, is the AERS. There are plans for establishment of the Mining Agency as a separate organization which will participate in the mining activities, such as the supervision and forecast of production trends, price of mineral raw materials, in the country and abroad, and the participation in the draft of balance sheets of all mineral raw materials reserves.[1006]

§2. Legislation

976. Article 87 of the Constitution of Serbia prescribes that 'Natural resources shall be utilized under the terms and in a manner stipulated by the Law'. Natural and legal persons may obtain particular rights on particular goods in public use, under the terms and in a manner stipulated by Law. Article 22 prescribes that protection, utilization and arrangement of land, agricultural and forest soil and goods of general interest shall comprise preservation of productivity, structure, layers, rocks and mineral formation, as well as their natural and transitive shapes and processes. Throughout project realization as well as before its execution (constructing, mineral raw material exploiting, etc.), the protection of land and soil shall be ensured.

1004. NSDS, 84–89. *See also*, EPR (2007), 7. For more details *see* : Strategija upravljanja mineralnim resursima Republike Srbije do 2030. [Mineral Resources Management Strategy of the Republic of Serbia until 2030] http://www.zzps.rs/novo/kontent/stranicy/propisi_strategije/s_mineralni_resursi.pdf (3 Apr. 2015), 4–11. *See also*, National Natural resources and Assets Sustainable Use Strategy(OJ RS, No. 33/2012), http://www.zzps.rs/novo/kontent/stranicy/propisi_strategije/S_prirodnih%20resursa.pdf (23 Apr. 2015).

1005. EPR (2007), 81.

1006. NPI, 392.

977. According to Article 34, spatial and urban plans shall ensure measures and conditions of environmental protection and in particular, to determine special regimes for preservation and use of the areas of protected natural goods, water springs, thermal and mineral springs, forests, agricultural land, public green areas, recreation areas and spas.

978. The main laws regulating geological exploration and exploitation of mineral raw materials are:

- Law on Mining and Geological Exploration (OJ RS, No. 101/15).
- Law on Public-Private Partnership and Concessions (OJ RS, Nos 88/11, 15/16 and 104/16).[1007]

979. The Law on Mining and Geological Exploration regulates regulate measures and activities of the mineral policy and the manner of implementation thereof, conditions and manner of execution of geological explorations of mineral and other geological resources, researching of geological environment, as well as geological explorations for the purpose of spatial and urban planning, designing, construction of buildings and remediation of site, manner of classification of resources and reserves of mineral raw materials and ground waters, exploitations of reserves of mineral raw materials and geothermal resources, construction, use and maintenance of mining facilities, plants, machines and equipment, execution of mining works, mining waste management, remediation and recultivation of abandoned mining facilities, as well as inspection over the implementation of the present Law (Article1). The legal act is divided in the following chapters: Basic Provisions (Articles 1–10); Mineral policy and development plan of geological explorations and mining industry of the Republic of Serbia (Articles 11–13); Geological institute of the Republic of Serbia (Articles 14 and 15); Geological explorations (Articles 16–82); Investment-Technical documentation for conducting the mining works (Articles 83–125); Licenses for performing the specific activities in geological explorations and exploitations (Articles 126–128); Protective measures (Articles 129–143); Other provisions on exploitations (Articles 144–156); Royalties for geological explorations of mineral resources and geothermal resources (Articles 157–160); Cadastre and information system in the field of geological explorations and mining (Articles 161–167); Inspection supervision (Articles 168–176); Penalty provisions (Articles 177–186); and Transitional and final provisions (Articles 187–195).

980. According to Article 3 geological explorations shall be a complex process and a set of activities comprising the application of adequate methods and technical means, which are performed in order to look into the development, composition and structure of the Earth's crust, to find, test and assess the mineral and other geological resources in geological-economic terms, to prospect and determine the reserves of mineral raw materials and the possibility of their mining, to determine and assess the geological, engineering-geological and hydrogeological properties of the site being explored, particularly from the standpoint of spatial and town planning, design and construction of facilities, and to identify and eliminate the harmful impacts of geological

1007. Energy Law (OJ RS, No. 145/14) also deserves mentioning. For more details *see* chapter devoted to 'rational use of energy'.

and technogenic processes on geological and living environment, and cultural assets and assets enjoying prior protection (point 12).

981. Geological explorations can be conducted by the foreign legal entities under conditions and in the manner prescribed by this Law and the law which establishes the rights of foreign persons in respect of the use of assets of the public interest and in accordance with the laws governing the area of defence and the confidentiality of data (Article 22, paragraph 5).

982. Mineral resources, ground water resources, geothermal resources as well as the other geological resources shall be the natural assets in the ownership of the Republic of Serbia, which may be used under the conditions and in the manner set forth by this Law. Mineral resources or mineral raw materials of strategic importance for the Republic of Serbia are: (1) Oil and natural gas; (2) Coal; (3) Copper and gold ore; (4) Lead and zinc ore; (5) Boron and lithium ore; (6) Oil slates (oil shales or shales); and (7) Other mineral resources, as determined by a separate Act of the Serbian Government on a proposal of the Ministry responsible for geological explorations and/ or mining (Article 4, paragraphs 1 and 2).

Mineral policy and development plan of geological explorations and mining is pursued through the implementation strategy for managing the mineral resources and other geological resources of the Republic of Serbia (Article 11, paragraph 3). The Strategy shall be enacted by the National Assembly at the proposal of the Government, for a period of minimum ten years (Article 12, paragraph 3).

983. The Government shall at the proposal of the Ministry enact a Plan and Programme for implementation of the Strategy (Article 13, paragraph 1). A competent authority of the AP shall propose a part of the programme on its territory in accordance with the development plan of the Autonomous Province and the Republic of Serbia (Article 13, paragraph 6).

984. For the purposes of this Law, geological explorations are basic and applied (Article 16). The basic geological explorations shall be performed by the Institute according to the Long-term Basic Geological Prospecting Development Programme (the Long-Term Programme) and the Annual Basic Geological Explorations Programme (the Annual Programme) (Article 19). The applied geological explorations of mineral and other geological resources are carried out on the basis of Decision on approval for geological explorations issued by the Ministry, at the request of the company, or other legal entities and entrepreneurs. The applied engineering-geological-geotechnical explorations for the needs of construction the infrastructure facilities (high dams, hydropower plants, thermal power plants, regional roads and railways, oil pipelines, gas pipelines, airports, etc.) of strategic importance for the Republic of Serbia, as well as the engineering-geological-geotechnical explorations for the needs of construction and rehabilitation of the facilities of mining infrastructure shall be performed on the basis of the Decision on approval of geological explorations issued by the Ministry, at the request of a company or other legal entity (Article 30).

985. The holder of exploration shall be entitled to use and dispose the results of the applied geological explorations and documents which contain the geological exploration results. Three years after termination of the applied geological explorations, the Republic of Serbia can use the results of the same explorations in a way that does not jeopardize the interests of the data owner, taking into account the rules governing the protection of data, and only in the case of: defence of the country and raising the level of general security of the population, rehabilitation of the results of geological hazards (earthquakes, floods, landslides, rockslides, etc.), development of the strategic study research for the purpose of determining and evaluating the overall mineral potentials of geological environment or other geological resources, as well as the needs of spatial planning and other long-term strategic documents of general interest (Article 49).

986. The approval for exploration of hydrocarbons in liquid and gaseous state (oil and gas) and other natural gases shall be given to a company or other legal entity or entrepreneur, selected on the basis of conducting a public tender procedure (Article 54). Decision on conducting a public tender for the exploration of hydrocarbons in liquid and gaseous state (oil and gas) and other natural gases shall be made by the Ministry or the competent provincial authority if the raw material is on the territory of the AP, if it assesses that there is a need for establishing the same mineral raw materials in a certain area or on the basis of a proposal by a company or another legal entity and entrepreneur registered for the exploration of mineral raw materials.

987. Holder of explorations or a company i.e., another legal entity and entrepreneur that a holder of explorations assigned the right of usage of the results of exploration, or the certificate on reserves and resources, shall obtain a decision on approval for exploitation and/or exploitation field, in accordance with this Law. Mining of mineral raw material reserves may also be performed by the foreign legal entities under the conditions and in the manner prescribed by this Law and the law setting the rights of foreign persons with respect to utilization of the assets of public interest (Article 65).[1008]

988. Exploitation of the reserves of mineral resources and exploitation of non-metallic mineral resources for obtaining the construction materials (hereinafter, exploitation) is done on the basis of the decision, which shall issue: (1) approval for exploitation field or approval for exploitation; (2) approval for the construction of mining facilities and/or conducting the mining operations; and (3) approval for the use of mining facilities (Article 68).

Manual washing of precious metals from alluvial sediments and collecting other minerals from the earth surface may be granted to a natural person. The holder of approval shall offer the washed quantities of metal to the National Bank of Serbia at market prices, to submit the report for washed precious metals and to collect other minerals to the Ministry on quantities and place where they are washed or collected (Article 75).

989. Exploitation of the non-metallic mineral raw materials for obtaining the construction materials and exploitation of mineral resources for obtaining the natural construction materials is carried out on the basis of the decision on approval for exploitation issued by the Ministry, i.e., the competent authority of AP if the exploitation is carried out on the territory of the AP (Article 77).

1008. Exploitation of the reserves of mineral resources and exploitation of non-metallic mineral resources for obtaining the construction of materials (hereinafter, exploitation) is done on the basis of the decision, which shall issue: (1) approval for exploitation of the field or approval for exploitation; (2) approval for the construction of mining facilities and/or conducting the mining operations; and (3) approval for the use of mining facilities (Art. 68).

990. The exploitation of reserves and resources of mineral resources is carried out according to the investment-technical documentation for construction of the mining facilities and/or conducting the mining works, exploitation of the non-metallic resources for obtaining the construction materials and exploitation of the mineral resources for obtaining the natural construction materials (Article 83). For the purposes of this Law, the investment-technical documentation shall mean: (1) pre-feasibility study; (2) feasibility study of mining the deposits of mineral raw materials; (3) long-term mining programme; (4) mining projects; and(5) annual operating plan (Article 84).

Technical control shall be performed for mining projects from Article 84, paragraph 2, points (1)–(5) of this Law (Article 97, paragraph 1). The Minister shall prescribe more specifically the conditions and manner for performing the control of mining projects (paragraph 4).

991. In order to protect water and the environment, the company shall have to: (1) plan measures that prevent endangering the water regime and environment, or remediation and rehabilitation measures, and ensure implementation of the prescribed measures; (2) keep data on types and quantities of dangerous and harmful matters used in performing its activities, or keep data on types and quantities of dangerous, harmful and waste matters emitted or disposed in the environment; and (3) implement the measures and conditions which prevent endangering the water regimes and environment, contained in the analysis of the activity impact on the environment and water regime in accordance to the special Law (Article 130).

992. The Minister shall prescribe special measures and the manner of controlling the application of measures for protection against fire and explosions in the mining facilities for underground mining. In other mining facilities, the regulations in force shall be applied in the area of protection against fire and explosion. The Minister shall prescribe the special measures and the manner of controlling the occupational safety and health measures in performing the works of geological explorations and exploitation of mineral resources. In terms of measure for occupational safety and health, environment protection against fire and explosions and other measures of protection relating to performing the mining works that are not regulated by this Law, the provisions of special regulations shall be applied governing such measures of protection (Article 143).

993. The holder of exploitation shall in the course and upon finalization of exploitation works no later than one year from the date of finalization of works in the areas where mining works were completed, carry out a reclamation of the land fully in accordance with the technical project of technical and biological reclamation, that is a constituent part of the main or supplementary mining design. The Ministry or competent authority of AP and the Ministry responsible for agriculture and water management or the ministry responsible for environmental protection shall be notified on measures referred to in paragraph 1 of this Article (Article 153, paragraphs 1 and 2).

994. For the use of data and documentation relating to the basic geological explorations that are financed from the budget of the Republic of Serbia as the activities of public interest, as well as for the use of data and documentation of geological explorations that have become the public property-state property on the basis of concession contracts, the royalty shall be paid in the amount of up to 5% of the real value of the performed explorations on a specific exploration area (Article 157).[1009] The holder of exploitation that has been granted for conducting the mining works shall pay the royalty for the use of mineral raw materials and geothermal resources in accordance with this Law (Article 159). Assets realized in accordance with Article 159 of this Law from the royalty for the use of mineral raw materials and geothermal resources, in the amount of 60% shall be the revenue of the budget of the Republic of Serbia and in the amount of 40% shall be the revenue of the local government unit on the territory of exploitation (Article 160).

995. The Geological Institute of Serbia (hereinafter, the Institute) shall perform the basic geological explorations pursuant to Articles 17 and 18 of this Law and other geological explorations included in the annual programme referred to in Article 20 of this Law, as well as the activities of applied geological explorations of importance for the Republic of Serbia, on the basis of a special decision by the Government on the proposal of Ministry. The Institute shall also perform other activities of interest for the Republic of Serbia, such as: elaboration and printing of geological maps at a scale of 1:25,000 and more detailed; and elaboration of specialized and thematic geological maps (metallogenetic or mineralgenetic, geomagnetic, gravimetric, radiogravimetric, geochemical, hydrogeological, engineering-geological, structural-tectonic, seismic, geoecologic, etc.) (Article 14).

996. Inspection supervision over the application of provisions and regulations adopted for implementation thereof shall be performed by the Ministry through geological and mining inspectors (Article 168). In the case of conducting geological explorations and exploitation on the basis of decisions issued by the competent provincial authority on the basis of conducting delegated activities, the inspection supervision over implementation of the provisions of this Law and the regulations adopted for its implementation shall be performed by the competent authority of the AP (Article 168, paragraph 3).

997. Articles 177–186 prescribe three kinds of penalty: criminal offences, corporate (commercial) offences and offences.

998. The Law on Public-Private Partnership and Concessions (OF RS, Nos 88/11, 15/16 and 104/16) regulates granting concessions for utilizing natural resources (Article 11).[1010]

999. Following sub-legal Acts, *inter alia*, have also been adopted:

1009. The holder of explorations shall pay a royalty for the applied geological explorations of mineral and other geological resources, and a royalty for retention the exploration area in accordance with this Law (Art. 158).

1010. The Law regulates, *inter alia*, conditions and method of concession awarding, subject matter of concession, entities competent, i.e., authorized to conduct concession award procedure, termination of concession, protection of rights of the participants in public contract award procedures, form and content of contracts on public-private partnership with or without elements of concession (the public contract) and legal protection in public contract award procedures, conditions and method of drawing up, proposing and approval of public-private partnership projects, specify the entities competent, i.e., authorized to propose and realize the public-private partnership projects, rights and obligations of public and private partners, etc.

(1) Rulebook on the criteria for determination of potentiality of areas concerning mineral raw materials occurrences (OJ RS, No. 51/1996).
(2) Rulebook on the method for mining measures performance (OJ RS, No. 40/1997).
(3) Rulebook on the content of the long-term programme for exploitation of mineral raw materials deposits and annual plans for mining works (OJ RS, No. 27/1997).
(4) Rulebook on the criteria for the award of geological exploration works and of associated funds (OJ RS, No. 51/1996).
(5) Rulebook on the content of the feasibility study for the exploitation of mineral raw materials deposits (OJ RS, No. 108/2006).
(6) Rulebook on the classification and categorization replenish solid mineral resources and maintenance of records about them (OJ RS, No. 53/79).
(7) Rulebook on the classification and categorization of groundwater and maintenance of records about them (OJ SFRJ, No. 34/79).
(8) Rulebook on the contents of geological research projects and studies on the results of geological exploration (OJ RS, No. 51/96).
(9) Rulebook on the contents of mining projects (OJ RS, No. 27/97).
(10) Rulebook on conditions performing certain professional tasks on exploitation mineral (OJ RS, Nos 40/97 and 32/98).
(11) Rulebook on conditions and manner of conducting technical review of mining facilities (OJ RS, No. 40/97).
(12) Regulation on fees for the use of non-metallic raw material for obtaining construction materials for 2017 (OJ RS, No. 98/16).
(13) Rulebook on Establishing the Annual Programme of Basic Geological Surveys for 2016 (OJ RS, No. 20/16).

1000. Priorities for further development in various domains, including the mining sector, are defined in several strategic documents – Energy Development Strategy of the Republic of Serbia until 2025, with projection until 2030, National Strategy for Sustainable Use of Natural Resources and Goods, Mineral Resources Management Strategy of the Republic of Serbia until 2030, Waste Management Strategy for 2010–2019, National Plan for the Adoption of Acquis for the period 2014–2018, etc.

Part III. Zoning and Land-Use Planning

§1. Introduction

1001. Serbia has a relatively long tradition in legal regulation concerning zoning and land-use planning. Already in the first part of nineteenth century there were enacted some Acts regulating this field, for instance, the 1837 Decree on village street planning.

1002. The process of urbanization in Serbia has been quite fast. According to the population census of 1948, percentage of urban population was 20.7% and in 2002 it reached 56.4%, and is still growing.[1011] The urbanization has caused, among other things, environmental problems, especially in large cities, and to depopulation of rural areas. The increase of inhabitants has not been followed by adequate measures, in different sectors including the environment (air pollution, sewerage, waste management, illegal construction,[1012] etc.) what contributed to the violation of spatial plans and threatened rational use of space.

§2. General Environmental Legislations

1003. The Serbian Constitution regulates spatial planning and land use in several provisions. It prescribes that the National Assembly shall adopt development plan and spatial plan (Article 99, paragraph 1, point 10). In accordance to Article 183 'autonomous provinces shall, in accordance with the Law, regulate the matters of provincial interest in..., *inter alia*, urban planning and development...'.

1004. Article 88 prescribes that:

> Utilisation and management of agricultural land, forest land and municipal building land on private assets shall be permitted. The Law may restrict the models of utilisation and management that is stipulate terms of utilisation and

1011. Sustainable development strategy, 69.

1012. 'There has been enormous illegal construction which started in the late 1960s, and culminated in the 1990s, under the circumstances of a widespread societal anomie.... Responsible authorities were estimating that the total number of illegal building in Serbia surpassed one million. However, more reliable are estimates pitching at the interval between 400,000 and 500,000 illegal constructions'. M. Vujošević & N. Spasić, *The Transition Changes and Their Impact on Sustainable Spatial, Urban and Rural Development of Serbia*, in *Sustainable Spatial Development on Towns and Cities* 14 (M. Vujošević, International Scientific Conference, Conference Proceedings, Book I, Institute of Architecture and Civil Engineering in Belgrade 2007).

management, in order to eliminate the danger of causing damage to environment or prevent violation of rights and legally based interests of other persons.

According to Article 190,point 7 the municipality shall, through its bodies, and in accordance with the Law provide for the protection, improvement and use of agricultural land. Besides that, the Municipal Assembly shall pass general acts within its competences, *inter alia*, and adopt the development plan and the municipal spatial plan (Article 191).

1005. According to Article 20 of the Law on Ministries, the Ministry of Environment, Mining and Spatial Planning is the focal point for activities in the field of spatial planning. Several other ministries and other institutions have also some competence in this field (Ministry of Infrastructure, Ministry of Agriculture, Trade, Forestry and Water Management (MATFW), Ministry of Economy and Regional Development, Ministry of Mining and Energy, Republic's Geodesy Institute, Environment Protection Agency, Nature Protection Institute, etc.).

1006. The Spatial Planning Agency has been established for the purpose of more efficient implementation and promotion of the spatial planning and design policy.[1013] Its competence is defined by Article 8 of the Law on Spatial Planning and Building and it covers the following:

(1) preparing and proposing the Space Development Strategy for the Republic of Serbia,[1014] coordinating and following up on its elaboration, and overseeing implementation;
(2) participating in the elaboration of space development schemes and coordinating the work of pertinent ministries in the preparation of space development schemes;
(3) preparing and proposing the space plan for the special purpose areas, coordinating and following up on its elaboration, in cooperation with pertinent ministries and other offices and organizations;
(4) performing the duties of expert supervision over the space plan for the special purpose areas and for the regional space plan, unless specified otherwise by law;
(5) international cooperation in the area of space planning;
(6) providing expert assistance in the plans' elaboration;
(7) development of a unified and comprehensive space information system;
(8) keeping the registry of planning documents for the territory of the Republic of Serbia;
(9) preparing and implementing educational programmes for the purposes of planning documents preparation; and
(10) performing other activities in accordance with the Law and the Statute.

1013. *See* , http://www.rapp.gov.rs/en-GB/content/cid310/spatial-plan-for-the-republic-of-serbia (20 May 2017).

1014. According to Art. 17, the Space Development Strategy determines the long-term objectives of space planning and development in accordance with total economic, social, ecological, cultural and historical development. The Strategy especially defines the issues, fields and modalities of transborder and international cooperation in the area of space planning and development. The Strategy is adopted by the National Assembly of the Republic of Serbia upon the proposal by the Government of the Republic of Serbia.

1007. The EPL has a number of provisions concerning spatial planning. Besides the definition provisions, the following Articles should be mentioned: 12, 19, 20, 33–36, 64–66, 68, 74, 81, 105, 120 (p. 4) and 124 (p. 2).

1008. The following provisions deserve special attention: (1) according to Article 12, sustainable use and protection of natural values shall be provided by, *inter alia*, the Strategy for spatial development of the Republic, besides the National Strategy of Sustainable Use of Natural Resources and Goods. In the same subchapter (devoted to 'planning and utilization of natural values'), Article 19 prescribes that the developing and spatial plan shall determine the construction zones depending on the environmental capacity, the degree of load and objectives of the construction.[1015]

1009. The 'planning and construction' and 'spatial and urban planning' are regulated by Articles 33 and 34. Article 33 prescribes that:

> spatial planning, use of natural resources and goods established by spatial and urban plans and other plans (plans of spatial arranging and agricultural land basis, forests, water-system, hunting basis and programs of enhancement of fishery in fishing areas as well as other plans) must be regulated by the obligation to (1) preserve and enhance natural resources and goods at greatest possible extent, and if they are not renewable, to use them rationally; (2) ensure protection and smooth realization of functions of protected natural values with their protected environment and to preserve wild plant and animal species habitats and communities at greatest possible extent; (3) ensure preservation of built-up areas; (4) ensure conditions for human relaxation and leisure; (5) establish measures of environmental protection; (6) show existent status following the elements from points 1-4 of this Article and planned status with measures needed for the fulfilment of those plans.[1016]

1010. Article 34 of the EPL prescribes second important authorization for the competent authorities in the environmental. According to this article, 'spatial and urban plans must ensure measures and conditions of environmental protection'[1017] and conditions for this measure will be issued by the Ministry, AP body or self-governance

1015. In certain zones, in which protected distance or area have been established, it shall be allowed to carry out the activities in a way determined by special regulations in accordance with natural load of the environment.

1016. The Ministry, competent authority of the AP or local self-governance unit participates in the procedure of preparation and planning in a way established by law.

1017. These measures and conditions of environmental protection relate, 'in particular: (1) to determination of special regimes for preservation and use of the areas of protected natural goods, water springs, thermal and mineral springs, forests, agricultural land, public green areas, recreation areas and spas; (2) to determination of areas of threatened parts of the environment (polluted areas, areas endangered with erosion and torrents, exploitation of mineral raw materials, flooded areas and so on) and determination of measures for these areas rehabilitation; (3) to determination of measures and conditions of environmental protection according to which space intended to be exploited for minerals shall be utilized, or according to which industrial and energetic plants shall be constructed, as well as facilities for waste treatment and disposal, infrastructure and other facilities whose construction or utilization may threaten the environment'.

units at request of the authority in charge of plan preparation and its passing in, and on the basis of conditions and measures of competent authorities.

1011. Article 65 of the EPL prescribes adoption of the action plan for advancement of spatial planning and landscaping as an obligation.[1018]

1012. The Law on Strategic Environmental Assessment prescribes that strategic assessment shall be carried out for all plans, programmes and sectoral master-plans in the following fields: town planning, land use, agriculture planning, forestry, fishing industry, hunting, energy, industry, transport, waste management, water management, telecommunications, tourism, preservation of natural habitats and wildlife (flora and fauna). It means that all national plans and programmes, as well as municipal spatial and land-use plans, should undergo the assessment.[1019]

§3. Legislation on Spatial Organization and Construction

1013. Two legal Acts are relevant for spatial organization and construction in Serbia:

- Law on Spatial Plan of the Republic of Serbia (OJ RS, No. 88/10).
- Law on Planning and Construction (OJ RS, Nos 72/09, 81/09, 64/10, 24/11, 121/12, 42/13-CC, 50/13-CC, 98/13-CC, 132/14 and 145/14).

1014. The Law on Spatial Plan of the Republic of Serbia from 2010 to 2020 (OJ RS, No. 88/10) was adopted by the Serbian Parliament at the meeting held on 23 November 2010. The spatial plan set the long-term basis of organization, development, protection and use of space in Serbia, in order to coordinate economic and social development of natural, ecological and cultural resources and restrictions on the territory of the Republic of Serbia.[1020] In the field of protection and improvement of the quality of environment, strategic priorities until 2014 are continuation and further

1018. Action and rehabilitation plans are prepared by the Ministry in cooperation with other ministries in charge of certain areas (Art. 67, para. 2). The AP and local self-governance units are in charge to adopt local action and rehabilitation plans for their territory and in accordance with the National Programme and plans (Art. 68).

1019. The SEA reports have mostly been issued for spatial and urban plans. In 2005 and 2006, the Directorate for Environmental Protection issued eleven opinions on decisions to develop SEA at the national level, two consents on SEA reports, and 137 opinions on draft decisions to implement SEA at the local level. The Secretariat for environmental protection of the City of Belgrade has issued eighty-three SEA opinions on draft decisions on SEA and four consents on SEA reports. EPR (2007), 25.

1020. 'Based on experiences of previous Spatial Plan of the Republic from 1996 as well as learning from processes in spatial development of Serbia in the period of its implementation until 2009, this Spatial Plan analyses the perspective of long-term spatial development, taking into account the difficulties, both internal (financial and economic crisis, missing legislations) and external (international relations, status of Kosovo). For those reasons, the Spatial Plan determines the future spatial development framework oriented towards two time horizons.' *Spatial Plan of the Republic of Serbia 2010–2014–2020*, Abridged Version, Ministry of Environment and Spatial Planning, Belgrade, November 2010,14.

systematic development of the campaign 'Cleaning Serbia', along with the engagement of all actors and LSGs; rehabilitation of all polluted industrial and mining-energy sites; reduction of air pollution which originates from energy production and other industries; improvement of the quality of surface and underground water; prevention of further deprivation of land and preserving and improving its quality; reducing the level of noise along roads and industries that endanger housing; harmonizing national regulations in the field of environmental protection with EU legislature, along with strengthening institutional capacity; establishing and extending monitoring and further development of an integrated cadastre of polluters; improving public access to information on the quality of environment and developing public awareness; promoting rational use of natural resources and maximum use of secondary raw materials; and reducing emission of polluted materials and introducing cleaner production technologies.[1021]

I. The Law on Planning and Construction

1015. The Law consists of the following chapters: I Basic provisions (Articles 1–9); II Spatial and urban planning (Articles 10–70); III Spatial Planning Agency of the Republic (Articles 71–81); IV Buildable land (Articles 82–109); V Construction of facilities (Articles 110–132); VI Building permit (Articles 133–147); VII Construction (Articles 148–153); VIII Usage permit (Articles 154–160); IX Professional exam and licenses for the responsible planner, the urban planner, the designer and contractor (Articles 161 and 162); X Engineering Chamber of Serbia (Articles 163–166); XI Removal of facilities (Articles 167–171); XII Supervision (Articles 172–184); XIII Legalization of facilities (Articles 185–200); XIV Authorization for introducing by-laws (Article 201); XV Penalty provisions (Articles 202–212); and XVI Transitional and final provisions (Articles 213–223).

1016. The Law regulates the conditions and modalities of spatial planning and development; the development and use of buildable land and the construction of facilities; carrying out supervision over the application of this Law and supervisory inspections; other issues of significance in the development of space, landscaping and use of buildable land, and the construction of facilities (Article 1, paragraph 1).[1022]

II. Principles of Development and Use of Space

1017. Pursuant to Article 3 of the Law the development and use of space is based on several principles including the following: (1) sustainable development through an integrated approach to the planning; (2) balanced territorial development; (3) rational use of soil encouraging measures urban and rural renovation and reconstruction; (4) rational and sustainable utilization of non-renewable resources and the optimal use

1021. *Ibid.*, 20–21.

1022. The provisions of this Law do not apply to the construction of facilities which, in terms of the Law governing affairs of defence, are considered military facilities, as well as the construction of facilities which in terms of the Law governing mining are considered as mining facilities, plants and equipment (Art. 1, para. 2).

of the renewable resources; (5) protection and sustainable use of natural resources and immovable cultural assets; (6) Prevention of technical and technological accidents, fire and explosion protection from the elements, eliminating the causes for climate changes; (7) planning and development of space for defence purposes; (8) compliance with European regulations and standards in the field of spatial planning; (9) improvement and use of information technologies that contribute to better efficiency and effectiveness of public administration in the construction business; (10) public participation; (11) preservation of customs and traditions; (12) the preservation of specificity of the compartment; and (13) horizontal and vertical coordination.[1023]

III. Energy Properties of Facilities

1018. In accordance with Article 4, improving energy efficiency means reduction of consumption of all types of energy, energy savings and ensuring sustainable construction by applying technical measures, standards, and requirements planning, design, construction and use of buildings and spaces.[1024]The building in which the functioning involves consumption of energy must be designed, built, used and maintained in a manner that provides the prescribed energy performance of buildings (Article 4, paragraphs 1–2).

1023. It should be noticed that the Law does not contain explanations of the meaning of these principles. Therefore, it is not quite clear what elements they comprise and what are their real consequences.

1024. Energy properties of facilities are consumed or calculated amount of energy to meet the different needs related to the standardized use relate in particular to energy for heating, hot water, cooling, ventilation and lighting. Energy properties certificates shall be determined by the release of the Energy Properties of Facility issued by an authorized organization that meets the requirements for certification of energy performance of buildings. The fulfilment of the conditions shall be determined by special decision of the Minister in charge for construction affairs (Art. 4, paras 3–4 and 6).

IV. Documents of Spatial and Urban Planning

1019. Documents of spatial and urban planning are as follows: (1) Planning Documents;[1025] (2) Documents for the Implementation of Spatial Plans;[1026]and (3) Urban Technical Plans[1027] (Article 10).

1020. Documents of spatial and urban planning must be reconciled, so that documents of a smaller region are in compliance with documents of wider region (Article 33, paragraph 1).[1028]

V. Content of the Planning Documents

1021. Relevant Planning documents have to contain environmental protection measures. The Law prescribes that strategic EIA is an integral part of following planning documents: the Spatial Plan of the Republic of Serbia (Article 15, paragraph 1, point 10[1029] and paragraph 2); the Regional Spatial Plan (Article 18, paragraph 1, point 12 and paragraph 2); the Spatial Plan of LSG units (Article 20, paragraph 2) and the Spatial Plan for a Special Purpose Area (Article 22, paragraph 1, point 13 and paragraph 2). Integral parts of the spatial plan for special purpose, spatial plan of the Local self-government unit and urban plans are: (1) the rules of organization; (2) the rules of construction; and (3) the graphical part (Article 29).

1025. Planning documents are Spatial and Urban Plans. Spatial plans are as follows: (1) Spatial Plan of the Republic of Serbia; (2) Regional Spatial Plan; (3) Spatial Plan of the unit of local administration; and (4) Spatial Plan of the region of special use. Urban plans are as follows: (1) General Urban Plan; (2) General Regulation Plan; and (3) Detailed Regulation Plan (Art. 11).

1026. Implementation programs of spatial plans are as follows: (1) Implementation programme for the Spatial Plan of the Republic of Serbia and (2) Implementation programme for the Regional Spatial Plan (Art. 12).

1027. Urban and technical documents for the implementation of planning documents are as follows: (1) urban design project; (2) design project of reallotment and allotment; and (3) design project of correction of borders of adjoining lots and merge two adjacent allotments of the same owner (Art. 13).

1028. Planning documents must be in compliance with the Spatial Plan of the Republic of Serbia. Urban plans must be in compliance with spatial plans (Art. 33, para. 2).

1029. Apart from the following: (1) starting points for the production of the plan; (2) assessment of the existing situation; (3) goals and principles of spatial planning; (4) principles and proposals for the protection, landscaping and development of nature and natural systems; (5) spatial development and distribution of the population; (6) networks of settlements and public services; (7) spatial development of traffic and infrastructural systems of significance for the Republic of Serbia; (8) concept and proposals for spatial development of industry; (9) measures of protection, landscaping and improving natural and cultural property; (10) Measures for environmental protection;(11) definition of inter-regional and intraregional functional networks; (12) planned entities of common spatial and developmental characteristics, for which spatial plans of a lower order will be drawn up; (13) measures for the implementation of Spatial Plan; and (14) long-term developmental strategies of the Republic of Serbia. Report on strategic EIA is an integral part of the documentation basis of the planning document (Art. 15).

1022. Planning rules contained in the land-use plan of special purpose, spatial plan of the Local government and urban plans include, in particular: conditions and measures for the protection of natural resources and immovable cultural property and the protection of natural and cultural heritage, the environment and human life and the health; and building energy efficiency measures (Article 30, paragraph 1, points 4 and 7).[1030]

1023. The graphic part[1031] of the Spatial Plan shows solutions in accordance with the contents of the plan.

VI. Procedure for Adoption of Planning Documents

1024. According to Article 46, the decision[1032] on drawing up a planning document is brought by the organ authorized to pass it, upon prior securing of the opinion of the organ responsible for professional control, that is, the committee for plans. Competencies for drawing up planning documents are regulated by Article 35.

1025. The presentation of the planning document for public insight is made after the professional verification is completed. The presentation of the planning document for public insight is announced in daily and local newspapers, and lasts thirty days from the date of announcement (Article 50, paragraph 1).[1033] The presentation of the planning document for public insight is overseen by the Ministry responsible

1030. Reconstruction is the execution of construction and other works on an existing facility, by which the stability, safety of the facility and fire protection are affected; structural elements are replaced or the technological process to be changed; the exterior elevation of the facility is altered; the number of functional units is increased; and the replacement devices, plant, equipment and installations with a capacity increase (Art. 2, point 32).

1031. Graphic part of the Spatial plan is made on topographic maps (Art. 32, para. 2).

1032. Prior to deciding on the development of the planning document, the bearer of the plan development will obtain from the authority responsible for environmental protection opinion on the draft decision on preparation or not preparation of strategic impact assessment. Before deciding on the development of the planning document, the bearer of the Plan shall obtain the opinion of the competent authority for environmental protection on the need for strategic EIA preparation (paras 7–8). The decision to go forward is announced in the appropriate official newspaper. Agencies, organizations and public companies which are licensed to determine special conditions for the protection and regulation of space and the construction of facilities in the stage of drawing up or modifying planning documents are obliged, depending upon the request from the bearer of the of the plan production, to submit all requested data within thirty days, without compensation (paras 3 and 4).

1033. Planning documents with their supplements must be accessible to the public at the premises of the entity which passed them, except a specific annex referring to special preparatory measures of territory for defence purposes (Art. 41).

for spatial planning affairs, that is, the organ of the unit of local administration with jurisdiction over affairs of spatial and urban planning (Article 50, paragraph 1).[1034]

VII. Location Permit

1026. Articles 53a–57 regulate location permit's relevant issues. Pursuant to Article 53a location permits are issued for facilities for which building permits are issued by this Law, as well as for the objects that are connected to the utility and other infrastructure, and which fulfil all the conditions and data required for preparing the technical documents, in compliance with the valid planning document.[1035] The location permit for facilities from Article 133 of this Law is issued by the Ministry with

1034. The responsible organ, i.e., the committee for plans, writes a report on the completed public insight into the planning document, which includes data on the completed public insight, with all remarks and decisions for each remark. The report from para. 3 of this Article is submitted to the bearer of the preparation of the planning document, who is obliged to act on the decisions included in para. 3 of this Article within thirty days from the day of delivery of the report (Art. 50, paras 3 and 4).

1035. A location permit can also anticipate building in stages (Art. 53a, para. 7).

jurisdiction over affairs of urbanism, that is, by the AP (Article 53a, paragraph 4).[1036] The location permit for facilities not determined in Article 133 of this Law is issued by the authorized organ of the unit of local administration (Article 53a, paragraph 5).

1036. In accordance with Art. 133 of the Law the building permit for the construction of a facility is issued by the ministry authorized for the tasks in construction (Ministry), unless otherwise determined by this Law. The Ministry issues the building permit for facilities as follows: (1) high dams and accumulations filled with water, waste and ashes for which is prescribed technical surveillance; (2) nuclear and other facilities which are used for the production of nuclear power, radio isotopes, radiation, storage of radioactive waste materials for scientific research purposes; (3) facilities for processing crude oil and gas, international and pole delivery lines, gas and crude oil pipelines for transport, gas pipelines of nominal working pressure of over sixteen bar, if they cross over at least two municipalities, storage of crude oil, gas and crude oil derivatives with capacity over 500 tonnes; (4) facilities for the basic chemical and manufacturing industries, black and non-ferrous metallurgy, facilities for the treatment of rubber, facilities for the production of cellulose and paper, and facilities for the processing of non-metal mineral raw materials, except facilities for the primary processing of decorative and precious stones; (5) stadiums for 20,000 or more viewers, facilities of construction range of 50 m or more, facilities of height of 50 m or more, silos with capacity over 20,000 m^3, facilities of penal and correctional institutions, etc. (6) thermoelectric power stations of power 10 and more MW and thermoelectric power stations and heating stations of power 10 and more MW and power lines and transformer stations of 110 and more kV; (7) inter-regional and regional facilities for water supply and sewage, drinking water production plants of capacity over 200 l/s and plants for the purification of waste water capacity over 200 l/s; (8) regulation jobs for the protection of city and rural areas greater than 300 ha from floods; (9) facilities within the boundaries of immovable cultural property of exceptional importance and cultural property registered at the UNESCO list of World Cultural and Natural Heritage, facilities in the protected surroundings of cultural property of great importance to certain borders of land plots and buildings in the protected surroundings of cultural assets registered in the UNESCO list of World Cultural and Natural Heritage, facilities in the protected areas in accordance with the act on the protection of cultural property (except the transformation of common premises into a flat or business premises in the protected surroundings of cultural property of outstanding significance and cultural assets registered in the world heritage list), as well as facilities within national parks and facilities within the boundaries of protected natural goods of great importance (except for family houses, agricultural and economic facilities and their infrastructure facilities that are being built in the villages), in accordance with the Law; (10) plants for the treatment of non-dangerous waste by incineration or chemical treatment, capacity of more than 70 tons per day;(11) Plant for the treatment of hazardous waste by incineration, thermal and/or physical, physicochemical and chemical treatments, as well as the central storage and/or landfill for hazardous waste disposal; (12) airports; (13) passenger ports, harbours, landing places and marines; (14) State-owned roads of the first and second class, travelling facilities and traffic connections to these roads and border crossings; (15) public railroad infrastructure with connections and the underground railway; (16) telecommunication facilities and network, systems or resources which are of international or trunk importance and those which are being constructed on the territory of two or more municipalities; (17) hydroconstruction facilities on waterways; (18) waterway canals and ship locks which are not part of the hydro-energy system; (19) regional dumps, and dumps for the storage of non-dangerous waste for zones with over 200,000 inhabitants; and (20) facilities for the production of energy out of renewable sources with power of 10 or more MW.

1027. Before submitting a request for issuing of a location permit, a buildable lot is formed, in compliance with this Law, except in cases anticipated in Article 69, paragraphs 1, 3, 5 and 6 of this Law (Article 54, paragraph 10).[1037]

1028. Location permit for facilities referred to in Article 133 of this Law is issued by the Ministry in charge for urban planning, or a competent authority of the AP of the facilities referred to in Article 134 of this Law.[1038] Location permit for facilities that are not specified in Articles 133 and 134 of this Law will be issued by the competent authority of the Local self-government unit. Together with a Request for the issuance of Location permit shall be submitted the conceptual design of the future building or part thereof (sketch, drawing, graphic, etc.) (Article 53a, paragraphs 4–6).If a planning document, or separate document, do not contain possibilities, limitations and conditions for the construction of buildings, and all the conditions for accession to the utility, transport and other infrastructure, the competent authority that conditions shall obtain ex officio, at the expense of the applicant in amount of actual costs of issuance. Holders of public authority shall make such requirements at the

---

1037. Article 69 relates to the 'separate cases of construction lot formation'. For construction or building of electro-energy and telecommunication facilities or appliances a construction lot of area with different size or location than the one prescribed by the planning document for this zone can be formed on condition that there is access to the facility or appliances for the purpose of maintenance and removal of defects or damage (para. 1). When provisions about formation of construction lots prescribed by this Law do not apply for construction of pole transformer stations 10/04 kV and 20/04 kV (para. 2). If the overhead line infrastructural facility covers the territory of two or more cadastral municipalities, prior to issuing the occupancy permit, forming one or more building lots, so that a building plot represents the sum of the parts of individual cadastral parcels within the cadastral boundaries of municipalities, except in the case as evidence of resolved property-legal relations in the process of issuing building permits filed an objection about the right, in accordance with this Law (para. 5). If the overland line infrastructural facility covers the territories before issue of the usage permit one or more construction lots are formed so that one construction lot represents the sum of parts of separate land registry lots within the borders of the land registry municipality, except in the case when as proof of resolved ownership and legal relations during the procedure of issue of location and building permits was used, the contract about the right of usage, in accordance with this Law (para. 6).

1038. The building permit is issued to the investor. Together with the request for issuing of a building permit must be submitted the project for building permit. The investor must have the appropriate rights to the land or premises, and it needs to submit the evidence required by Law that regulates the specific content and method of issuing the building permit and paid the corresponding administrative fees. An integral part of the application is a copy of the project for issuing of the building permit signed and stamped with personal license stamp by the chief designer (Art. 135, para. 1). For the construction of line infrastructural facilities, proof of appropriate Law serves as the legally binding or final decision about expropriation concluding a contract on the right of easement in accordance with this Law and concluding a lease agreement on the land in private ownership, as well as other evidence set forth in Art. 69 of this Law. For the construction or performance of work on construction land or facility owned by more than one person, as proof of proper Law, it is also necessary to enclose the certified agreement of these persons, while if or of adding floors to a residential building, it is also necessary to enclose the contract concluded in accordance with a separate Law. For the construction of energy facilities, prior to the issuance of the construction permit, it is also necessary to enclose the energy permit in accordance with a separate Law (Art. 135, paras 4, 6 and 9).

request of the competent authority within a period of fifteen days from the date of receipt of the Request (Article 54, paragraph 1).

1029. Location Conditions contain all the urban, technical and other conditions and data necessary for the preparation of idea project, and project for a building permit and the project for execution (Article 55). The competent authority shall issue the location conditions within five working days of obtaining all necessary conditions and other data from the holder of public authority (Article 56, paragraph 1).

1030. The location permit is issued on the basis of the spatial plan of an area of special purposes, and the spatial plan of a unit of local administration, for parts of the territory within the catchment area of the plan for which no preparation of an urban plan is anticipated; on the basis of the general regulation plan, for parts of the territory within the catchment area of the plan for which no preparation of a detailed regulation plan is anticipated; and on the basis of the detailed regulation plan (Article 57,paragraphs 1–3).[1039]

VIII. Buildable Land

1031. Buildable land can be held in all forms of ownership (Article 84, paragraph 1).[1040] Buildable land is marketable. The right of ownership of buildable land in public ownership[1041] can be held by the Republic of Serbia, the AP, that is, a unit of local administration (Article 84, paragraph 2).

1032. Pursuant to Article 87, buildable land can be: (1) developed and undeveloped (built and unbuilt); and (2) arranged and unarranged.

IX. Construction of Facilities

1033. In the part related to the construction of facilities[1042] the Law in Article 112 prescribes that previous work, depending on the type and characteristics of the facility, comprises conditions for fire protection and the protection of the environment as well as the investigation and preparation of analyses and projects, and other expert material; procurement of information which analyse and elaborate geological engineering,

1039. If the planning documents anticipate the preparation of an urban plan or the urban project is made at request of the investor, the location permit is issued on the basis of that planning document and the urban design project (Art. 57, para. 4).

1040. Buildable land is a land designated by Law and planning documents for the construction and use of buildings, as well as land on which buildings are constructed in accordance to the Law (Art. 82).

1041. Buildable land in public ownership is marketable, under conditions set forth in this and other Laws (Art. 85, paras 1 and 2).

1042. 'Construction of the facility' is the sum of operations which include the following: preliminary works, the production and control of the technical documents, preparatory works for construction, the construction of the facility and professional supervision during the construction of facility (Art. 2, point 30). The construction of facilities is carried out based on the building permit and technical documentation, under the conditions and in the way which is determined by this Law (Art. 110).

technical, hydrological, meteorological, urban, technical, technological, economic, energy, seismic, water supply and traffic conditions; and other conditions which affect the construction and use of a certain facility.

X. Previous Feasibility Study

1034. The previous feasibility study enables the determination especially of the spatial, *ecological,* social financial, market and economic justification of the investment for various solutions defined by the general project, based on which the planning document is prepared, and the decision made on the feasibility of investing into previous work for the preliminary design and feasibility study (Article 113, paragraph 1). The previous feasibility study contains the general project referred to in Article 117 of this Law (Article 113, paragraph 2).

XI. Feasibility Study

1035. The feasibility study particularly determines the spatial, *ecological,* social, financial, market and economic justification of the investment into the chosen solution, elaborated by the preliminary design, based on which the feasibility of the investment is decided (Article 114, paragraph 1). The feasibility study contains the preliminary design referred to in Article 118 of this Law (Article 114, paragraph 2).

XII. The General Project

1036. The general project contains particularly the data about the macro location of the facility, general disposition of the facility, technical and technological concept of the facility, the method of providing the infrastructure, the possible options for the spatial and technical solutions, from the point of fitting into the space, the natural conditions, the EIA, geological engineering and technical characteristics of the land from the aspect of determining the general concept and justifiability construction of the facility, investigation work made for the preparation of preliminary project, the protection of natural and immovable cultural property, and the functionality and rationality of the project (Article 117).

XIII. The Preliminary Project and Preliminary Design

1037. The preliminary design is made for the purpose of obtaining location requirements, and can be part of the urban project for the needs of urban-architectural elaboration of location (Article 117a). The preliminary project is made for the construction of facilities and performing works from Article 145 of this Law, as well as for facilities referred to in Article 133 of this Law, when subject to professional scrutiny by the review committee (Article 118).[1043]

XIV. Technical Inspection

1038. The technical inspection of the main project can be performed by a company, other legal entity or contractor which fulfils the conditions for the preparation of technical documentation prescribed by the Law and determined by the investor (Article 129, paragraph 2).[1044]

1039. The technical inspection of the main project specially comprises the control of compatibility with all the conditions and regulations contained in the location permit, with the Law and other regulations, with the technical norms, standards and quality norms, as well as with all parts of the technical documentation; compatibility of the project with the results of the previous studies; assessment of the appropriate soil for founding of the facility; check the validity and accuracy of the technical and technological solutions and the construction solution of the facility; stability and safety; rationality of the project materials; effect on the *environment* and adjacent facilities (Article 129, paragraph 4).

XV. Review of the Project

1040. The general project and the preliminary project, the previous feasibility study and the feasibility study for facilities referred to in Article 133 of this Law is subject to review (professional inspection) by a commission formed by the minister authorized for tasks in construction (review commission) (Article 131,paragraph 1).[1045]

1043. The project for the building permit is made for the purpose of obtaining the decision on the building permit (Art. 118a, para. 1). The project for execution is to be prepared for the purpose of execution of the works on the building (Art. 123, para. 1). The project of built facility is prepared for the purposes of obtaining of use permit, use and maintenance of the facility. The project of the built facility is to be prepared for all objects for which building permit is to be obtained, according to the provisions of this Law (Art. 124, paras 1 and 2).

1044. The technical inspection of the main project cannot be performed by the authorized designer who prepared the project, or who is employed in the company which prepared the project, or in the company which is the investor (Art. 129, para. 3).

1045. The professional inspection is concerned with the concept of the facility, particularly from the aspect of adequacy of the location in view of the type and use of the facility; the conditions for construction of the facility in view of the application of measures for the protection of the *environment*; the seismic, geological and technical, traffic and other conditions; the provision of energy conditions in comparison with the type of planned energy sources; the technical and technological properties of the facility; the technical, technological and organizational solutions for construction of the facility; updatedness of the technical solutions and compatibility with the development programs in this field, as well as other prescribed conditions for the construction of the facility (Art. 132, para. 1).

XVI. Building Permit

1041. According to Article 133 the building permit for the construction of a facility is issued by the ministry authorized for the tasks in construction (Ministry), if it is not otherwise determined by this Law.[1046] The issue of the building permit is entrusted to the AP for the construction of facilities determined by Article 133 of this Law, which is completely built on the territory of AP. The issue of the building permit is entrusted to the local government units for the construction of facilities which are not determined in Article 133 of this Law (Article 134).[1047] The building permit shall lapse if the construction of the facility, or execution of the work, is not started within two years from the validity date of the decision by which the building permit was issued (Article 140).

XVII. Construction of Facilities and Execution of Work for Which the Building Permit Is Not Issued

1042. It is not necessary to provide building permit for performing works on the regular maintenance of building or apartment, installation of wire or wooden fences, anti-hail construction of facilities and construction of simple facilities. Simple facilities which are built on the same land registry lot on which the main facility is constructed which are performed in a way that do not interfere regular use of adjacent buildings (garden shadows with base up to 15 m^2, paths, terraces, garden pools and fish ponds up to 12m^2 and depth up to 1m, shelters with base up to 10m^2, children playfields, courtyard fireplaces of area up to 2m and height up to 3m, car accesses to facilities of width 2.5–3m, solar collectors that are not connected to the electricity grid, etc.), cattle pits up to 20m^2 in base; graves and monuments on the cemetery; pedestrian paths, information boards up to 6m^2 and other equipment in protected natural property (in accordance with the decision of public companies which manage these properties); telecommunication devices which are placed or installed on telecommunication cables and networks, antenna pillars on existing buildings, roads, rooms, telecommunication infrastructure and containers, standard base station cabinets on appropriate beams, containers for the storage of telecommunication equipment and devices, standard cabinets for internal and external installation for the storage of telecommunication equipment, etc. pillars for cathode protection of steel pipelines and cathode protection stations, mileage tags, turning marks and protection pipes on crossings with roads and railroads on line infrastructural facilities like gas pipelines, crude oil pipelines and

1046. *See* explanations for 'location permit' (Arts 53a–57).

1047. Appeals on the decision about the building permit issued by the LSG unit are solved by the ministry authorized for tasks in construction. The AP is entrusted with the solution of appeals against the first-degree decision about the building permit issued by the LSG unit, made for the construction of facilities which are built on the territory of the AP. The City of Belgrade is entrusted with the solution of appeals against the first-degree decision for the building permit issued for construction or reconstruction of facilities up to 800m^2 of gross developed construction area and the first instance decision on the approval of the works referred to in Art. 145 of this Law, on the territory of the City of Belgrade (Art. 139, paras 1–3).

product pipelines that are considered as special type of facilities or works for which is not necessary to obtain an act of the competent authority for construction or for performing work (Article 144).

1043. The construction of facilities referred to in Article 2, paragraph 1, items 24[1048] and 24a of this Law, execution of works on capital maintenance of facilities and removal of obstruction for persons with disabilities, adaptation,[1049] repair and change of the purpose of facilities, etc. are made based on the decision which approves execution of this work, or change of purpose of these facilities, which is issued by the organ authorized for issuing building permits (Article 145, paragraph 1).[1050] For the works mentioned in paragraph 1 of this Article on facilities of cultural and historic importance and facilities for which before renewal (restoration, conservation, revitalization) or adaptation, conservation conditions must be issued, the agreement of the organ or organization authorized for tasks of protection of cultural property about the preliminary or main project must be submitted (Article 145, paragraph 3).[1051]

XVIII. Temporary Building Permit

1044. The temporary building permit is issued for the construction of: asphalt plants, aggregate separators, concrete factories; independent anchored meteorological anemometric poles as well as poles for other purposes; temporary roads and connectors, connectors to the utility network for the needs of the construction or operation of facilities; temporary roads, as well as for performance of exploration work on the location, for the purpose of determining special conditions for the preparation of the main project and for the removal of existing installations (Article 147, paragraph 1).

1048. 'An auxiliary facility' is a facility which is linked to the primary facility, and is built on the same lot as the primary residential, business, or facility of public use (garage parking, storage, septic tank, wells, cisterns, etc.).

1049. 'Adaptation' is the execution of construction and other works on an existing facility, by which the change of organization of space is carried out, the replacement of appliances, plant, equipment, and installations of the same capacity, but which do not affect the stability and safety of the facility, do not involve the replacement of structural elements, the alteration of the exterior elevation, and does not affect the safety of adjoining facilities, transport, fire and *environmental* protection (Art. 2, para. 1, point 34).

1050. Exceptionally, in reference to the provisions of para. 1 of this Article, requests for the issue of decisions for approval of execution of works on construction, or execution of works on construction of facilities mentioned in Art. 2, item 24 and 24a of this Law, as well as for the reconstruction, adaptation and repair of facilities within boundaries of national parks and facilities within boundaries of protection of cultural property of exceptional importance, as well as for execution of work on capital maintenance, adaptation and repair in the protected surroundings of cultural property of exceptional importance entered in the World list of cultural heritage are solved by the authorized organ of the LSG unit on whose territory are the subject facilities (Art. 145, para.3).

1051. The setting up and removal of smaller temporary pre-fabricated facilities on public purpose areas (booths, summer and winter gardens, stalls and other moveable furnitures), bubble halls for sport, shelters for people in public transport, facilities for depositing and separation of river aggregates and floating plants on wetlands, is provided by and managed by the local government unit (Art. 146, para. 1).

1045. Depending on the type of facility and works, the temporary building permit is issued for the precisely determined period in which the facility can be used, or the works carried out, and it cannot be longer than three years from the date of the decision about the temporary building permit (Article 147, paragraph 5).[1052]

XIX. Usage Permit

1046. The suitability of the building for use is determined by the technical inspection (Article 154, paragraph 1).[1053] In performing the technical inspection, for facilities for which a study was made about the effect on the *environment*, a person who is an expert in the field which is the subject of the study, and who has acquired the academic diploma of master in the appropriate profession, on the second degree studies, on the specialized academic studies, or on the basic studies for the duration of at least five years must participate (Article 156, paragraph 2).[1054]

1047. The facility can be used after previously obtaining the usage permit (Article 158, paragraph 1).[1055] The organ authorized for issuing the building permit issues, by decision will issue, the usage permit, within five days from the date of submission of the application for issuance of usage permits (Article 158, paragraph 2).[1056] The usage permit is issued for the whole facility, or part of a facility which

1052. In case the investor himself does not remove the temporary facility in the determined term, the authority which made the decision about the temporary building permit, will ex officio, submit a request to the construction inspection for the removal. The appeal to the decision of the construction inspector does not delay execution of the decision (Art. 147, paras 6 and 7).

1053. Technical inspection of the facility shall be made upon completion of the facility, or part thereof, which represents a technical-technological unity and can as such be used independently, in accordance to this Law. Technical inspection may be conducted in parallel with the execution of the works (Art. 154, paras 2 and3).

1054. In performing the technical inspection persons who cannot participate are those who are employed in the company or other legal entity who has prepared the technical documentation, or was the contractor with the investor, persons who have participated in the preparation of the technical documentation and the study about the effect on the environment, or in execution of the work with the investor, persons who performed the professional supervision, persons who are performing inspection supervision, as well as persons who work on the job of issuing building permits in the agency authorized for issuing building permits (Art. 156, para. 3).

1055. The usage permit is issued when it is determined that the facility, or part of it, is suitable for use. The usage permit contains the warranty period for the facility and certain types of work determined by special regulation (Art. 158, paras 4 and 5).

1056. The authority responsible for issuing the building permit shall issue a permit for use within five working days from the date of submission of the application for the issuance of the use permit (Art. 158, Para. 2). An appeal can be made to the decision mentioned in para. 2 of this Article within eight days from the date of delivery. When the decision is made by the ministry authorized for tasks in construction, or the agency of the AP, then appeal cannot be made to the decision mentioned in para. 2 of this Article, but it is possible to start a lawsuit within thirty days from the delivery date (Art. 158, paras 8 and 9).

represents a technical and technological unity and can, as such, be used independently (Article 158, paragraph 4).[1057]

1048. If, for the purpose of determining the suitability of the facility for use, it is necessary to carry out previous examinations and inspection of the installations, appliances, plants, stability and safety of the facility, appliances and plants for the protection of the *environment*, appliances for protection against fire, or other examinations, or if it is prescribed by the technical documentation, the commission for the technical examination, a company or other legal entity which is entrusted to carry out the technical examination can propose to the authorized organ to allow the trial operation of the facility, if they determine that conditions are fulfilled for it and shall immediately inform the competent authority on it (Article 157, paragraph 1).[1058]

XX. Permit for the Removal of Facility

1049. Removal of a facility or part thereof, except in the case of execution of a decision by the inspection, can be carried out only based on the permission for the removal of the facility or part thereof (Article 168, paragraph 1).[1059] Together with the request for permission for the removal of the facility, or part thereof, it is also necessary to submit: (1) the main project for the removal with technical inspection; (2) proof of ownership of the facility; (3) special conditions, in case of a facility whose removal would endanger the public interest (protection of existing and other infrastructure, protection of cultural goods, protection of *the environment*, etc.) (Article 168, paragraph 2).

1050. The permission for the removal of the facility, or part thereof, is issued within eight days from submission of adequate documentation (Article 168, paragraph 3).[1060]

1057. The owner of the facility for which is issued the usage permit enables execution of work on capital and current maintenance of the facility, as well as the regular, exceptional and specialized examinations of the facility, in accordance with separate regulations (Art. 159).

1058. Trial operation cannot last more than one year. It is the responsibility of investors to monitor the results of the trial operation (Art. 157, para. 2), (Art. 157, para. 2).

1059. A body of the local government unit responsible for construction will approve, by decision, ex officio, or upon request by an interested party, the removal of a facility, or a part thereof, when it is determined that its stability is endangered due to deterioration or major damage and that it represents imminent threat to the life and health of people, nearby facilities and safety in traffic (Art. 167, para. 1).

1060. An appeal can be submitted against the resolution referred to in para. 3 of this Article within fifteen days from delivery of the resolution. When the resolution is issued by the ministry responsible for construction, or the appropriate body of the AP, an appeal cannot be submitted, but an administrative dispute can be started by filing a lawsuit within thirty days from the delivery of the resolution (Art. 168, paras 4 and 5).

XXI. Rights and Duties of the Building Inspector

1051. Pursuant to Article 175 the building inspector has the right and duty to check, *inter alia*, 'whether the contractor has undertaken the necessary measures for the safety of the facility, the surrounding facilities, traffic and the *environment*;' (Article 175, paragraph 1, point 7).[1061]

1052. It is the duty of the building inspector to provide expert assistance in fulfilling the entrusted jobs in the field of inspection and to give expert explanations and opinions, as well as to participate in the inspection when necessary. When the building inspector during inspection determines that during construction, measures were not taken for the safety of the facility, the traffic, the surroundings and for the protection of the *environment,* he/she will order the investor, or contractor to remove noted deficiencies, set the term for compliance, as well as suspend further work until these measures are performed, under threat of forced execution which will be charged to the investor, or contractor (Article 177, paragraph 1, point 1). If the building inspector during inspection determines that use of the facility represents a threat for the life and health of people, the safety of neighbouring facilities, or to the surroundings, or is a threat to the environment, he/she will order that necessary work is done, or he/she will forbid the use of the facility, or part thereof (Article 178, paragraph 1, point 5).

1053. Many other legal and sub-legal Acts are relevant for spatial organization and construction in Serbia, as for example the following:

- Law on State Survey and Cadastre (OJ RS, Nos 72/09, 18/10, 65/13, 15/15 CC and 96/15).
- Law on Social Housing (OJ RS, No. 72/09).
- Law on Public Property (OJ RS, Nos 72/11, 88/13, 105/14, 104/16 and 108/16).
- Law on Expropriation (OJ RS, Nos 53/95, 16/01, 23/01, 20/09, 55/13 CC and 106/16).
- Law on Legalization of Buildings (OJ RS, No. 96/2015).
- Law on Conversion of the Right of Use to the Right of Ownership over Construction Land for a Fee (OJ RS, No. 64/2015).
- Law on Returning of Seized Property and Indemnification (OJ RS, No. 55/2013).
- Law on Transfer of Real Property (OJ RS, Nos 93/14, 121/14 and 6/15).
- Mortgage Law (OJ RS, Nos 115/05, 60/15, 63/15 CC and 83/15).
- Law on Agriculture Land (OJ RS, Nos 62/06, 65/08, 41/09 and 112/15).
- Law on Housing and Building Maintenance (OJ RS, No. 104/16).
- Regulation on Location Conditions (OJ RS, No. 35/2015 and 114/2015).
- Regulation on conditions, criteria and manner of exercising the right to convert the rights of use to the rights of ownership with compensation, as well as the manner for determining the market value of buildable land and the amount of fees on conversion of the rights of use to the rights of ownership with compensation (OJ RS, Nos 67/11, 20/12 and 109/13).

1061. The building inspector is authorized to supervise the use of the facility and to take action if he/she determines that use of the facility endangers the life and health of people, the safety of the surroundings, *the environment*, and if inappropriately used affects the stability and safety of the facility (Art. 175, para. 2).

- Regulation on conditions, manner and procedure under which buildable land in public ownership can alienate or lease for less than the market price, or rent, or free of charge, and the conditions, manner and procedure of the property exchange (OJ RS, No. 61/15).
- Rulebook on the classification of buildings (OJ RS, No. 22/2015).
- Rulebook on general rules for the parcelling, regulation and construction (OJ RS, No. 22/2015).
- Rulebook of procedure for implementation of a unified procedure electronically (OJ RS, Nos 113/15 and 96/16).
- Rulebook on manners of closure and labelling of closed construction site (OJ RS, No. 22/15).
- Rulebook on the Content, Method and Procedure for Drafting Physical and Urban Planning Documents (OJ RS, No. 64/15).
- Rulebook on an identity card and type of equipment of urban planning and construction inspector (OJ RS, Nos 30/15 and 81/15).
- Rulebook on taking professional exam in the field of spatial and urban planning, technical documentation preparation, construction and energy efficiency and on licensing and on issuance and revocation of licenses for responsible urban planners, designers, contractors and responsible planner (OJ RS, No. 27/15).
- Rulebook on the content, manner and procedure of preparation of spatial and urban planning documents (OJ RS, No. 64/15).
- Rulebook on the criteria for determining fee in procedures of legalization (OJ RS, Nos 89/90 and 5/10).
- Rulebook on the content and manner for conducting of professional supervision (OJ RS, No. 7/10).
- Rulebook on the content of information on the location and content of location permit (OJ RS, No. 3/10).
- Rulebook on the content and manner of issuing building permits (OJ RS, Nos 4/10 and 26/10).
- Rulebook on energy efficiency of buildings (OJ RS, No. 61/11).
- Rulebook on the conditions, content and method of issuance of certificate on energy performance of buildings (OJ RS, No. 69/12).
- Rulebook on general rules of parcelling out, regulation and building (OJ RS, No. 22/15).

Part IV. Liability Questions

1054. Liability for the environmental damage is doubtlessly one of the most complex and most important problems of the contemporary environmental law. The fact that the definition of environment is steadily being widened and that there is still not enough legal practice in applying the existing legal regulation on liability, makes things even more complex.[1062]

There are grounds in Serbian law for liability for actions contrary to the prescribed environmental standards, in civil law, criminal law and administrative law.[1063]

1055. Serbia has not ratified yet the Convention on Civil Liability for Damage resulting from Activities Dangerous to the Environment (CETS No.: 150), nor the Convention on the Protection of Environment through Criminal Law (CETS No.: 172). According to the available information, those conventions are still not on the priority list for ratification.

1062. On this subject, *see also*, D. Todić, *Odgovornost za stete u životnoj sredini u pravu životne sredine* [Environmental liability with regard to the prevention and remedying of environmental damage in the EU law], *Evropsko zakonodavstvo* [EU Legislation] (Belgrade: Institut za međunarodnu politiku i privredu), No. 13/2005, 51–54.

1063. The total number of inspections carried out by the Republic (7,614) and the Provincial (1,816) environmental inspectorate during 2014 is 9,430. Observed during the period 2010–2014, it can be concluded that the number of inspections varies slightly in the last three years in the APV, while in the other part of the Republic of Serbia it is declining. The number of applications for economic offences and criminal charges in 2014 was higher in relation to the previous year. Izveštaj o stanju životne sredine u Republici Srbiji za 2014. godinu, [*Report on the state of the environment in Serbia for 2014*]. Ministarstvo poljoprivrede i zaštite životne sredine, Agencija za zaštitu životne sredine [Ministry of Agriculture and Environmental Protection, Environmental Protection Agency]. Beograd, 2015, 152.

Chapter 1. Civil Liability

1056. Civil law protection of the environment is essentially based on principles of prevention and restitution or on combination of these two principles. Important is also the regulating principle. The application in civil law of the principle of prevention, which is one of the most important principles in environmental law, means, besides other things, that the court can prohibit some activity which could endanger the environment above the permitted levels of pollution.

§1. Law on Environmental Protection

1057. EPL regulates environmental liability in a rather general way. Article 5 prescribes that subjects of liabilities are 'the Republic, Autonomous Province, and local self-governance body, legal and natural entities'. All of them are responsible for every activity by which environmental status and conditions could be changed. The following formulation in paragraph 2 of the mentioned Article has a special importance:

> In performing their activities, legal and natural entities are obliged to provide: rational use of natural resources, calculation of environmental protection expenditures in their investment and running costs, implement regulations, namely take environmental protection measures in compliance with the law.

1058. Article 9, paragraph 5 of the same Law also deserves mentioning. It prescribes that 'Any legal or natural entity who shall be involved in environmental pollution by its illegal or improper activities shall be liable in compliance with the law.' In the case of liquidation or bankruptcy of a company or other legal person, the polluter is liable for environmental pollution. The polluter, or its legal successor, is also obliged to eliminate the cause of pollution and the consequences of direct or indirect environmental pollution.

1059. One of the basic principles of environmental protection is, according to the Law, the principle of subsidiary liability. It is defined by Article 9, paragraph 8 which prescribes that 'state authorities, within their financial abilities, shall eliminate the consequences of environmental pollution and reduce damages when the polluter is unknown, and when pollution originates from the sources outside the territory of the Republic'.

1060. Chapter VII (Articles 102–108) of the EPL is devoted to questions of responsibility for environmental pollution.

1061. Article 102 of the Law prescribes general measures and activities that are obligatory for legal and private entities. These are: (1) applying and implementing regulations on environmental protection; (2) sustainable use of natural resources, goods and energy; (3) introducing energy efficient technologies and use of renewable natural resources; (4) using products, processes, technologies and practice less harmful to the environment; (5) undertaking preventive measures or eliminating the consequences of threat and damage to the environment; (6) keeping records in a prescribed way on raw materials and energy consumption, polluting matters and energy release, classification, characteristics and quantities of waste, as well as on other data and their submission to competent authorities; (7) controlling the activities and operation of plants that may represent risk or that may cause danger towards human health and environment; and (8) other measures in compliance with law. 'Legal and private entity shall implement measures of environmental protection from paragraph 1 of this Article on their own or via authorized organization.'

1062. Principle of objective responsibility, as a basic for polluter responsibilities, has been formulated in Article 103.

1063. Polluters have obligation to undertake measures determined by rehabilitation and plan of protection from accident,[1064] namely to undertake necessary measures in order to reduce damage in the environment or eliminate further risks, hazard or rehabilitation of the damage in the environment. If the damage made to the environment cannot be rehabilitated through adequate measures, the person who has caused it shall be responsible to pay a charge equivalent to the value of the destroyed good (Article 104).[1065]

1064. The polluter is liable for the damage made to the environment. He/she is obliged to cover expenditures for the evaluation of damage and elimination of it. In particular, it includes: (1) costs of urgent interventions undertaken at the moment of the damage occurrence which are necessary for organizing and preventing the effects of damage towards the environment, space and human health; (2) direct and indirect costs of rehabilitation, establishment of new or recovery of the previous environmental and spatial status, as well as monitoring of rehabilitation and environmental damage effects; (3) costs for prevention of the occurrence of the same or similar damage towards the environment and space; and (4) charge costs which are to be paid to persons directly threatened by environmental and spatial damage. The polluter is obliged to ensure financial or other warranties in order to ensure the payment of the charge from paragraph 1 of this Article, during and after performance of the activity. The Government

1064. Article 63 (Rehabilitation Measures and Subsidiary Liability) prescribes, when 'handling with dangerous substances' is concerned, that 'to prevent further spread of pollution caused by an accident, legal and natural entity shall immediately take rehabilitation measures planned for protection at its own cost'. If the polluter responsible for the accident is found subsequently, the authority that paid the cost of elimination of the consequences of environmental pollution shall claim the reimbursement.

1065. Generally speaking, the rehabilitation plan shall be made whenever pollution in the given area exceeds the effects of the measures taken, namely when the capacity of the environment is at risk or there is a risk of permanent degradation of the quality or damage in the environment. The Government is, according to the Art. 66, responsible for rehabilitation plans in following cases: (1) when the level and the scope of degradation of the environment exceeds the rehabilitation possibilities of the AP, namely local self-governance unit; (2) when the responsible polluter is unknown and the environmental pollution causes harmful consequences across the borders of the Republic; (3) when the responsible polluter is beyond the jurisdiction of the Republic, and the environmental pollution causes harmful effects in its territory; (4) when the environmental pollution endangers an area of extraordinary relevance for the Republic or causes harmful effects; and (5) when it is necessary to take urgent and intervention measures in emergency cases.

shall prescribe types of warranty from paragraph 2 of this Article, the amount of the means and validity period of the warranty supplied by the polluters (Article 105).

1065. Every person affected by damage shall have right to reimbursement. The request for reimbursement may be submitted directly to the polluter or insurer (financial guarantee)[1066] of the polluter, if such insurer of financial guarantee exists.

1066. If several polluters are responsible for the environmental damage, and if it is not possible to determine share of certain polluters, the costs shall be borne jointly and individually.

1067. The procedure for reimbursement shall be out-of-date in three years from the date when the damaged party found out about the damage and the damage maker. However, this claim shall be out-of-date in twenty years after the occurrence of the damage. Court procedure for reimbursement shall be urgent. The Republic shall keep the right to reimburse the means if there are no other persons with such right (Article 107).

1068. Article 108 of the EPL prescribes that 'to the issues regarding liability for damage to the environment which have not been particularly regulated by this Law, general rules of the Law on Obligations shall be applied'.

§2. Law on Obligation Relations

1069. Liability for causing the danger of damage is prescribed by the Law on Obligation Relations (OJs of SFRY, Nos 29/78, 39/85, 45/89, 57/89 and of the SRY, Nos 31/93, 22/99, 23/99, 35/99, 44/99 and OJ of SCG, No. 1/2003). That means that in some cases a person could be responsible even when actual damage is not done, for instance for activities that are potentially dangerous for the environment. One who causes such a danger is always the potential polluter, his/her responsibility is objective and his/her guilt is not necessary to prove. The potential victim is the person (or persons) who are in danger to suffer damage if the pollution occurs.

1070. There are different forms of the court actions in cases of environmental damage. The court can decide on:

- compensation for the damage (pecuniary or non-pecuniary);
- prohibition of activities which cause or can cause the damage;
- socially justified measures for removing the danger for the environment.

1071. When it comes to compensation, there are two situations. If the damage is result of activities licensed as activities of public importance, then the polluter pays only for the damage above the permitted level of pollution. In another situation, when the polluter is not licensed, he/she is obliged to compensate (in kind or pecuniary, depending on the courts' decision) the whole damage. The court can also prohibit further activity that endangers the environment. Such a prohibition can be the only sanction or it may be combined with compensation.

1066. It is prescribed by Art. 106 of the Law that polluter, whose installation or activity represent threat towards human health and environment is obliged to insure him against liability for possible damage caused to third party in an accident.

Socially justified measures for removing the cause of the environmental danger can also be ordered by the court, especially in cases in which a larger number of people is in potential danger of serious pollution.

1072. Socially justified measures for removing the cause of the environmental danger (pollution of air, water, soil, etc.) are usually based, in Serbian judicial practice, upon Article 156 of the Law of Obligations (*actio popularis*).[1067]

1073. The mentioned Article establishes the so-called ecological claim prescribing the right to demand removal of the danger from damage or disturbance:

(1) Everybody can claim from other persons to remove the source of danger which could cause more considerable damage to the claimant or indefinite number of other persons, as well as to abstinence from activities which causes disturbance or danger from damage, if the disturbance or damage cannot be prevented by adequate measures.
(2) The court, reacting to the claim of interested person, will order undertaking adequate measures for preventing the damage or disturbance, or to remove the source of danger. This will be done on the expense of the owner of the source of danger, if he/she himself does not do it.
(3) If the damage is caused in the course of activity which has general interest which is authorized by competent authority, only compensation for damage which overpasses normal thresholds could be demanded.
(4) But, even in that case it is possible to demand undertaking of socially acceptable measures for prevention of the damage or its minimizing.

§3. Law on Basic Proprietary Relations

1074. The Law on Basic Proprietary Relations (OJs of SFRY, Nos 6/80 and 36/90 and of SRY, No. 29/96, OJ of RS, No. 115/2005) is another important legal Act to be mentioned. Article 5[1068] of the Law prescribes two elements of key importance:

(1) It is the duty of the owner of the real estate to, while using his/her real estate, avoid activities:

- by which usage of other real estate is made harder (transmission of smoke, unpleasant smelt, heat, soot, vibrations, noise, outlet of wastewater, etc.) above the measure which is usual (common) regarding to the nature and purpose of real estate as well as local circumstance; or
- by which more considerable damage is caused.

1067. On this subject, *see* , V. Rakić-Vodinelić, Ekološka tužba, *Pravni život*, No. 4-5/89; N. Petrušić, Zaštita od imisija u građanskom sudskom postupku (Protection from imissionin court procedure), *Pravni život*, Belgrade, No. 12/2003.

1068. Everybody is obliged to restrain from infringing the ownership rights of others (Art. 3, para. 2).

(2) Duty of the owner of the real estate to remove causes which originated from his/her real estate and – by which usage of other real estate is made harder (transmission of smoke, unpleasant smelt, heat, soot, vibrations, noise, outlet of wastewater, etc.) above the measure which is usual (common) regarding to the nature and purpose of real estate as well as local circumstance, or by which is caused more considerable damage.

§4. Law on Privatization

1075. The Law on Privatization[1069](OJ RS, Nos 83/14, 46/15, 112/15 and 20/16) comprises the following eighteen Chapters: I Basic provisions (Articles 1–17); II Preparation for privatization (Articles 18–22); III Methods of privatization (Articles 23–35); IV Sale of Capital (Articles 36–47);. V Sale of Property (Articles 48–56); VI Control Procedure and method of performance of obligations from sale contract of capital or property (Article 57),;VII Sale of shares and stakes (Articles 58–60); VIII Transfer of capital free of charge (Articles 61–65); IX Strategic Partnership (Articles 66–74); X Measures for preparation and discharge of privatization subjects' obligations (Articles 75–78),;XI Privatization of state capital from succession (Article 79); XII Pronouncing bankruptcy to end the privatization (Article 80);XIII Privatization of privatization subjects with minority capital (Article 81); XIV Special Provisions (Articles 82 and 83); XV Supervision over implementation of the Law (Article 84); XVI Criminal act (Article 85); XVII Appropriate application of the Laws and suspension of proceedings (Articles 86 and 87); and XVIII Transitional and final provisions (Articles 88–95).

The Law on Privatization regulates the conditions and procedure for change of ownership of social and public capital[1070] and property (Article 1, paragraph 1).

1076. In the process of privatization property or part of the property, the subject to privatization can be sold. The sale of property is organized and conducted by the Ministry in charge for economic affairs (Article 48, paragraphs 1 and2). The Programme for sell of property is issued by the competent authority of the privatization entity (Article 49, paragraph 1). The Programme includes in particular: data about the business entity to be privatized, property values, social programme, i.e., obligations to employees, a programme of environmental protection, as well as other data of importance for the sale of property of the privatization entity (Article 50, paragraph 1).

1077. The funds[1071] for repairing the damage which is the subject of privatization caused to the environment prior to the conclusion of the sales contract, i.e., a contract on the recapitalization provided to the budget of the Republic of Serbia (Article 83, paragraph 1).

1069. *Privatization,* in terms of this of Law, means changing of capital and property ownership of legal entities that operate with social and public capital (Art. 2, para. 1, point 1).

1070. *Public capital is* the capital of the Republic of Serbia, APs and local self-government (Art. 2, para. 1, point 2).

1071. The Government shall prescribe the manner and conditions of use of the funds (Art. 83, para. 2).

Chapter 2. Criminal Liability

1078. Most of criminal acts concerning the environment are prescribed by the Criminal Code, but several other laws also contain provision on criminal responsibilities.[1072]

§1. Criminal Code

1079. The Criminal Code (OJ RS, Nos 85/05, 88/05, 107/05, 72/09, 111/09, 121/12 and 104/13) contains a separate chapter (Chapter XXIV) devoted to criminal acts against the environment and besides that several other provisions of the Code are related to the environment. The Code contains following eighteen criminal acts against the environment:[1073]

(1) Environmental pollution (Article 260).
(2) Omission to apply measures of environmental protection (Article 261).
(3) Illegal building and use of objects and installations which pollute environment (Article 262).
(4) Damage of objects and installations for environmental protection (Article 263).
(5) Impairment of environment (Article 264).
(6) Destroying, damaging and taking abroad a protected natural asset (Article 265).
(7) Bringing dangerous substances into Serbia and unlawful processing, depositing and stockpiling of dangerous substances (Article 266).
(8) Illegal construction of nuclear plants (Article 267).
(9) Endangerment of right to information on the state of the environment (Article 268).
(10) Killing and wanton cruelty to animals (Article 269).
(11) Transmitting of contagious animal and plant diseases (Article 270).
(12) Malpractice in Veterinary Services (Article 271).
(13) Producing harmful products for treating animals (Article 272).
(14) Pollution of livestock fodder and water (Article 273).
(15) Devastation of forests (Article 274).
(16) Forest theft (Article 275).
(17) Poaching game (Article 276).
(18) Poaching fish (Article 277).

1080. Article 260 deserves a special attention. It prescribes that:

1072. 'The most frequently committed environmental crimes are devastation of forests, illegal logging, poaching game, illegal fishing, and killing and cruelty to animals, while the number of charges filed for the criminal offences related to environmental pollution, failure to undertake environmental protection measures or damaging the environment is much smaller.' EPR (2015), 56.

1073. For judicial practice based on the old Criminal Code, *see* , V. Joldžic, *Ekološki kriminalitet u pravu i stvarnosti* [Ecological Crime in Law and Reality] (Beograd: *Ecologica*, 1995); On this subject, *see also*, D. Jovašević, *Zaštita životne sredine* [Environmental Protection] (Belgrade: Sluzbeni list SRJ, 2005).

(1) persons who by breaking rules on protection, conservation and improvement of environment, pollute air, water or soil in considerable measure or in wider space shall be punished by imprisonment up to three years;
(2) if the act from paragraph 1 of this Article is done by negligence the perpetrator will be fined or punished by prison up to one year;
(3) if the act from paragraph 1 of this Article caused destruction or damage of the animal or plant life to a greater extent or to environmental pollution which is so intensive that for its rehabilitation are needed longer time and considerable expenditure the perpetrator will be punished in prison from one to eight years;
(4) if the act from paragraph 2 of this Article caused destruction or damage of the animal or plant life to a greater extent or to environmental pollution which is so intensive that for its rehabilitation are needed longer time and considerable expenditure the perpetrator will be punished by prison from six months to five years;
(5) if the conditional verdict for acts from paragraphs from 1 to 4 of this Article is decided, the court could prescribe the obligation for the perpetrator to undertake certain measures aimed at protection, conservation and improvement the environment.

1081. Article 268 deals with endangerment of right to environmental information on the state of the environment. It prescribes that 'whoever contrary to regulations withholds information or gives false information on the state of the environment and events that is required for evaluation of environmental hazard and undertaking measures for protection of human life and health, shall be punished by fine or imprisonment up to one year'.[1074]

§2. Law on the Liability of Legal Persons for Criminal Offences

1082. Liability of legal persons for criminal acts, as well as the sanctions of legal persons for criminal acts, is regulated by the Law on the Liability of Legal Persons for Criminal Acts (OJ RS, No. 97/08). The Law regulates conditions governing the liability of legal entities for criminal offences, penal sanctions that may be imposed on legal entities as well as procedural rules when ruling on the liability of legal entities,[1075] on imposing penal sanctions, passing a decision on rehabilitation, termination

1074. Previous EPL (OJ RS, No. 66/91) contained provisions concerning the right to information to a certain extent different from those in the new EPL 'Whosoever proclaims as confidential information essential for assessing dangers to the human environment and for taking up action and measures aimed at protecting the life and health of person shall be fined and punished by imprisonment of up to five years for a criminal offence committed. An attempt that is made to this effect shall be punished' (Art. 109).

1075. A legal person is a national or a foreign entity considered as a legal person under positive legislation of the Republic. A liable person is a natural person legally or de facto entrusted with certain duties within a legal entity, as well as a person authorized, that is, a person who may reasonably be considered as authorized to act on behalf of a legal entity. (Art. 5).

of security measures or legal consequences of the conviction, and on enforcement of court decisions (Article 1).

1083. This Law shall be applicable to the following: to national and foreign legal persons held accountable for a criminal offence committed in the territory of the Republic; to foreign legal entities held accountable for criminal offences committed abroad to the detriment of the Republic, nationals thereof or national legal persons; and to national legal entities held accountable for criminal offences committed abroad (Article 4, paragraphs 1–3).[1076]

1084. A legal entity may be liable for criminal offences constituted under a special part of the Criminal Code and under other laws if the conditions governing the liability of legal entities provided for by this Law are satisfied (Article 2).[1077]

1085. Conditions for establishing liability of legal entities for criminal offences are prescribed in the general part of the Law (Second part: Articles 6–11 with sanctions in Articles 12–26). Elements of the criminal proceedings are defined in the second part of the Law (Articles 35–54)[1078] as well as enforcement of court decision in Articles 55–71.

§3. Other Sources of Law

1086. The four basic laws on environmental protection (EPL, Law on Environmental Impact Assessment, Law on Strategic Environmental Impact Assessment, Law on Integrated Prevention and Pollution Control) do not contain provisions on criminal responsibility.

1087. Several other laws contain provisions against environmental crimes such as the Law on Water (OJ RS, Nos 30/2010, 93/12 and 101/16), the Law on Prohibition to Build Nuclear Power Plants (OJ FRY, No. 12/1995), the Law on Mining and Geological Explorations (OJ RS, No. 101/15), and others, etc.

1088. The Law on Water has provisions on the following criminal acts:

- Unauthorized charging or use of a reservoir (Article 209).[1079]

1076. In cases referred to in paras 2 and 3 of this Article, this Law shall not apply if special conditions governing criminal prosecution referred to in Art. 10, para. 1 of the Criminal Code are fulfilled (Art. 4, para. 4).

1077. The Republic of Serbia (the Republic), the AP and the local self-government unit, that is, government authorities and authorities of the AP and LSG unit cannot be liable for criminal offences. Other legal entities vested with public powers by virtue of law cannot be liable for criminal offences committed when exercising such public powers (Art. 3).

1078. Unless otherwise stipulated by this Law, the provisions of the Criminal Procedural Code shall be applicable by analogy in the criminal proceedings conducted against an accused legal entity (Art. 54).

1079. Any person who has charged a reservoir or used water from a reservoir, and thereby caused a threat to human life or health or property, shall be charged with a criminal offence and sentenced to a prison term of six months to five years.

– Damage during extraction of river deposits (Article 2010).[1080]

1089. Law on Prohibition on Building Nuclear Plants in FRY in Article 3 sanctions as a criminal act 'preparation, permitting of building or commencement of building of nuclear power plants, installations of production of nuclear fuel or installations for processing of used nuclear fuel' in the territory of FRY.

1080. Any person who has damaged a channel, bank, or control construction as a result of extraction of river deposits from the channel of watercourse, shall be charged with a criminal offence and sentenced to a prison term of six months to five years, or assessed a fine. In addition to the penalty for a criminal offence per para. 1 of this Article, any object used in committing the criminal offence shall be confiscated from the perpetrator.

Chapter 3. Other Forms of Liability

§1. Law on Economic Offences

1090. According to the definition taken from the Law on Economic Offences (OJs of SFRY, Nos 4/1977, 36/1977, 14/1985, 74/1987, 57/1989 and 3/1990, and FRY, Nos 27/1992, 24/1994, 28/1996 and 64/2001), an economic offence is a socially harmful violation of regulations on economic or financial business which causes or may cause serious consequences, and which is qualified as a commercial offence by the competent authority (Article 2).

1091. Responsible for an offence can be a legal person (and responsible person in legal person), an entrepreneur and a physical person. State authorities and authorities of local governments cannot be responsible for offences but responsible persons in these authorities can be. Enterprises and other legal entities can be held responsible for a criminal act.

1092. Each of the environmental laws in force provide a penalty for economic (commercial) offences (the EPL, the Law on Environment Protection Fund, the Law on Environmental Impact Assessment, the Law on Integrated Pollution Prevention and Control, the Law on Strategic Environmental Assessment, the Law on Waste Management, the Law on Packaging and Packaging Waste, the Law on Biocidal Products, the Law on Chemicals, the Law on Nature Protection, the Law on National Parks, the Law on Prohibition of Development, Production, Storage and Use of Chemical Weapons and its Destruction, the Law on Protection and Sustainable Use of Fishing Resources, the Law on Environmental Noise, the Law on Ionizing Radiation Protection and Nuclear Safety, the Law on Non-ionizing Radiation Protection, the Law on Air Protection, the Law on Waters).

§2. Law on Offences

1093. Offences are illegal acts, defined in Article 2 of the Law on Offences (OJ RS, Nos 65/13, 13/16 and 98/16CC). They may be prescribed by laws, decrees of the Government and of municipal, city or AP's authorities (Article 4). They cover activities of enterprises or other legal entities, entrepreneurs and natural persons, as defined by the Law.

1094. Sanctions for offences have been prescribed by all environmental laws, for example:

- *EPL* prescribes offences of the legal entity, responsible person within legal entity, natural entity and responsible person within competent authority or organization carrying out public authorizations (Articles 117–121).
- Law on Environmental Impact Assessment (Articles 42 and 43).
- Law on Strategic Environmental Assessment (Article 25).

– Law on Integrated Environmental Pollution, Prevention and Control (Articles 30–32).[1081]

1095. It could be added, as a concluding remark, that there are many systematic problems concerning the environmental liability in Serbia. Provisions related to competencies and to instruments for implementation in some basic sources of Serbian environmental law, are still not sufficiently harmonized. Enforcement of environmental legislation in Serbia is not always efficient enough and suffers from serious drawbacks, and especially because of weak monitoring system, lack of certain environmental standards, insufficient coordination between environmental laws and other laws defining other responsibilities of institutions at the national and sub-national levels, the insufficient capacity of municipal-level environmental inspection bodies, charges and sanctions envisaged by legal provisions are not properly enforced and are not high enough to be real deterrents, the generally low awareness of and compliance with the law, etc.

1096. Serbian judiciary system is still not efficient enough, when imposing sanctions for environmental offences is concerned. It usually takes time for a court proceeding to result in a court order and an adequate sanction, which are sometimes inadequate or are largely symbolic. Judges need more training in environmental law, as well as prosecutors and police bodies. Due to the fact that there are no sufficient data regarding the relation between lawsuits (both administrative and criminal) and the sanctions imposed, it is presently not possible to assess the effectiveness of enforcement.[1082]

1097. Sector for control and surveillance (Ministry of Environment, Mining and Spatial Planning) organized trainings for judges and public prosecutors (2008) and for magistrates and environmental protection inspectors (2009) in cooperation with Organization for Security and Co-operation in Europe (OSCE) and the Ministry of Justice. The aim of these trainings was to increase penalties in the field of environmental protection, to speed up processing of inspector complaints and to help inspectors to learn how to compile claims for instituting infringement procedures.[1083] However, there are needs for additional trainings of judges and public prosecutors.[1084]

1081. Besides the above-mentioned and in relation with 'administrative responsibility', it should be mentioned that there are several relevant sources of law. Law on Civil Servants (OJ RS, Nos 79/05, 81/05 – corr., 83/05 – corr., 64/07, 67707 – corr., 116/08, 104/09 and 99/14) contains several provisions of general character in Ch. IX (civil servants liability) and Arts 121–126 deal with 'liability for damage'.

1082. EPR (2007), 27–32.

1083. AECQ, Chs 27, 70.

1084. D. Todić, *Review of Serbian Implementation and Enforcement Procedures in the Environment Sector*, *supra* , 73. For the overview of submitted applications 2007–2009, for commercial offences, for instigating misdemeanour proceedings and for criminal charges *see* , *ibid.,* 43.

Part V. Juridical Actions of Individuals

§1. Introduction: Constitution of Serbia

1098. Articles 22 and 36 of the Constitution of Serbia (OJ RS, No. 83/06) guarantee the right to an effective legal remedy. Article 22 prescribes that 'judicial protection when any of their human or minority rights guaranteed by the Constitution have been violated or denied. They also have the right to elimination of consequences arising from the violation. The citizens have the right to address international institutions in order to protect their freedoms and rights guaranteed by the Constitution'.

1099. In Article 36 it is stated that 'Equal protection of rights before courts and other State bodies, entities exercising public powers and bodies of the AP or LSG shall be guaranteed. Everyone shall have the right to an appeal or other legal remedy against any decision on his/her rights, obligations or lawful interests.'

1100. Article 97, p. 2 of the Constitution prescribes that the Republic of Serbia shall organize and provide for:

> exercise and protection of freedoms and rights of citizens; constitutionality and legality; proceedings before courts and other state bodies; liabilities and sanctions for violation of freedoms and rights of citizens stipulated by the Constitution and for violation of laws, other regulations and general acts; amnesty and pardon for criminal offences.

1101. The CC has been established by Article 168. According to the mentioned Article, the Court is competent to decide, *inter alia*, on compliance of laws and other general acts with the Constitution, generally accepted rules of the international law and ratified international treaties, compliance of ratified international treaties with the Constitution, compliance of other general acts with the Law, compliance of the Statute and general acts of APs and LSG units with the Constitution and the Law, etc.

1102. The basis for 'constitutional appeal' has been established by Article 170 of the Constitution. The appeal may be lodged against individual general acts or actions performed by State bodies or organizations exercising delegated public powers which violate or deny human or minority rights and freedoms guaranteed by the Constitution, if other legal remedies for their protection have already been applied or not specified.

1103. Individuals can realize constitutional right to healthy environment (Article 74 of the Constitution)[1085] and above-mentioned rights in different procedures: administrative and juridical (civil, criminal, etc.). Which procedure will be started depends on rights that are violated, on the way by which they were violated and on

1085. *See* , title 'constitutional provisions', Introduction (Ch. 2).

the choice of the individual who lodges the appeal. Administrative and judicial procedures can be started parallel and independently, if legally prescribed conditions are fulfilled.[1086]

1086. For three Serbian cases, *see* , *Handbook on Access to Justice under the Aarhus Convention* 185–190(S. Stec, The Regional Environmental Centre for Central and Eastern Europe, 2003); *See also*, D. Todić & M. Durać, *Demokratizacija politike životne sredine (Democratization of environmental policy)* (REC, 2003), 73–88.

Chapter 1. Administrative Remedies

1104. There are many questions in the field of environment that could be involved in administrative procedure (for instance, issuing of various permits, asking for opinion, decisions of inspection, etc.). The Law on Administrative Procedure is the basic source of Law, although several other laws and by-laws are also relevant to a certain extent.

§1. Law on Administrative Procedure

1105. It is prescribed by Article 113 of the Law on Administrative Procedure (OJ FRY, Nos 33/97 and 31/01, OJ RS, No. 30/10) that the competent authority shall institute a procedure either ex officio or at the request of a party. 'A party' is a person at whose request a procedure has been instituted or against whom a procedure is conducted or who is entitled to participate in a procedure for the purpose of protection of his/her rights or legal interests (Article 39). The procedure can be started by physical or legal persons and in exceptional cases even by interest groups that do not have the status of a legal person.

1106. According to Article 12, one of the basic principles of the Law is 'Principle of Two Instances (Right to Appeal)' Part III of the Law is devoted to the 'legal remedies' (Articles 213–238). General time limit for lodging an appeal is fifteen days (Article 220) and the competent authority must decide about it in two months (Article 237), if the Law does not prescribe a shorter period.

1107. The general principle is that 'a party has the right to appeal against first instance decisions' (Article 213). The first instance decision adopted by a ministry or other autonomous administrative authority or administrative organization, can be appealed, only in the cases specified by the law and in administrative matters in which an administrative dispute proceeding may not be initiated. No appeal may be filed against a decision adopted by the National Assembly and the Government (Article 214).

1108. According to Article 239, the decision against which there is no regular legal remedy (final decision) can be reopened if, *inter alia*, new facts have become known which could have resulted in a different decision had such facts or evidence been presented or used in the earlier procedure; the decision was based on false documents or testimony; at the party's request or ex officio by the authority that adopted the decision concluding the procedure.

1109. Extraordinary legal remedies are:

- Deciding on reopening of procedure (Article 245).
- Amendment and annulment of decisions related to administrative disputes (Article 251).
- Request for protection of legality (Article 252).
- Annulment and cancellation upon official control (Article 253).
- Cancellation and amendment of final decisions upon consent or request of parties (Article 255).

- Extraordinary cancellation of decisions (Article 256).
- Declaring decisions null and void (Article 257).

§2. Law on State Administration

1110. According to the Law on State Administration (OJ RS, Nos 79/05, 101/07, 95/10 and 99/14) natural and legal persons have several rights. Article 80 of this Law prescribes that State administration authorities are obliged to, upon the request, give opinions on interpretation of provision of laws and other general acts in the time limit of thirty days. The authorities are also obliged to enable everyone adequate ways for the submission of complaints about their work and about improper conduct of employees. In the case of a submitted complaint, the authorities have to respond in fifteen days from the date the complaint was filed (Article 81).

§3. Law on Environmental Protection

1111. The EPL (OJ RS, Nos 135/04, 36/09 and 14/16) regulates, among other things, administrative procedure in cases of appeals lodged against administrative decisions in the field of environmental protection (i.e., competence issues).

Pursuant to Article 81a the interested public, in the process of exercising right to a healthy environment, shall have the right to as a party to initiate the decision-review procedure before the responsible authority or court, in accordance with the law.

1112. According to Article 114 of the Law, the Minister shall decide on the appeal against the first instance decision of the responsible municipal and/or city authority or authority of the city of Belgrade that was adopted in the course of performing delegated tasks (paragraph 1). The responsible authority of the AP shall decide on the appeal against first instance decision of the responsible municipal, namely city authority from the territory of the AP, adopted in the course of performing delegated tasks (paragraph 2). The Minister shall decide on the appeal against the first instance decision of the regional unit of the Ministry and on the appeal against the first instance decision of the responsible authority of the AP (paragraphs 3 and 4).

1113. The appeal against first-degree ruling of the Ministry shall be decided by the Government (paragraph 5).

§4. Law on Environmental Impact Assessment

1114. According to Article 11 of the Law on Environmental Impact Assessment, the project developer[1087] and the public concerned[1088] are entitled to file a complaint against the decision of the competent authority concerning the application for a decision on the need for an impact assessment. The complaint referred to in paragraph 1 of this Article 'shall be submitted to the competent authority of the second instance in accordance with the law regulating environmental protection. The competent authority of the second instance shall decide on the complaint within twenty days from the date of receipt of the complaint'.

1115. The right to appeal against the decision made on the application for a decision on the scope and content of the EIA Study is established by Article 15 of the Law. Public concerned and the project developer are entitled to file a complaint against the decision of the competent authority on the application for a decision on the scope and content of the EIA Study.[1089]

1116. The complaint against the decision of the inspector, referred to in Article 37, paragraph 1, points 1–5, may be submitted to the Minister within fifteen days from the date of receipt of the decision. The same period is prescribed for the complaint against the decision of the inspector of the AP and the LSG unit (Article 39, paragraph 2).[1090]

§5. Law on Integrated Environmental Pollution Prevention and Control

1117. Article 15 of the Law on Integrated Environmental Pollution Prevention and Control prescribes, when the decision on permit[1091] granting is concerned, that 'no

1087. 'Project developer' means the applicant for a permit or an approval for construction or reconstruction of structures or for other interventions in nature and the environment (Arts 2, 3).

1088. Public concerned includes the public affected by or likely to be affected by the project, including NGOs that promote environmental protection and are registered with the competent authority (Arts 2 and 7).

1089. The complaint shall be submitted to the competent authority of the second instance in accordance with the law regulating environmental protection. The competent authority of the second instance shall decide on the complaint within twenty days from the date of receipt of the complaint.

1090. The AP and the LSG unit are entrusted with the inspection supervision tasks relating to the enforcement of the provisions of this Law for projects that are under the responsibility of the competent authority of the AP and of the LSG with respect to the impact assessment procedure.

1091. Integrated permit means the decision of the competent authority adopted in the written form, approving the start-up of the whole or a part of installation, or the execution of the activity, the integral part of which is the documentation containing the set conditions which guarantee that such installation or activity is in compliance with the requirements prescribed by this Law (Arts 2 and 10).

complaints can be filed against the decision of the competent authority[1092] ... while administrative court proceeding can be instigated'.

1118. It is prescribed by Article 22 of the Law that the competent authority shall adopt conclusion initiating the permit, revoke procedure and inform the operator within five days from the date of procedure initiating and submitting evidence for initiating it. The operator is entitled to file the complaint against the conclusion within eight days from its receipt.

Complaint against the inspector's decision can be submitted to the Minister within fifteen days from the date of its receipt (Article 28).[1093]

1092. The competent authority can issue the decision on permit granting or refuse the permit granting application.

1093. The complaint does not postpone the execution of the decision and Minister's decisions are final.

Chapter 2. Judicial Remedies

1119. Judicial system is regulated by the relevant provisions of the Constitution of the Republic of Serbia (Articles 142–152) and by following laws:

- Law on Organization of Courts (OJ RS, Nos 116/08, 104/09, 101/10 and 101/13).
- Law on Constitutional Court (OJ RS, Nos 109/07, 97/2011 and 18/13 CC).
- Law on the Seats and Territories of Courts and Public Prosecutions (OJ RS, Nos 116/08 and 101/13).
- Law on Public Prosecution (OJ RS, Nos 63/2001, 42/2002, 39/2003,44/2004, 61/2005, 46/06, 106/2006 CC, 116/08, 101/2011, 38/2012 CC, 121/12, 101/13, 111/14 – CC and 117/14).
- Law on High Judicial Council (OJ RS, Nos 116/2008, 101/2010 and 88/2011).
- Law on Judges (OJ RS, Nos116/08, 58/09CC, 104/09, 101/10, 8/12CC, 121/12, 124/12CC, 101/13, 111/14CC and 117/14).
- Law on Training of Judges, Public Prosecutors, Deputy Public Prosecutors and Judicial and Prosecutorial Assistants (OJ RS, No. 46/2006).

1120. In 2006 two important documents were adopted – the National Judicial Reform Strategy (OJ RS, No. 44/2006) and the Action Plan for Strategy Implementation. According to the Strategy, effective judiciary relies on four basic principles: independence, transparency, accountability and efficiency.[1094]

On 1 July 2013, the National Assembly of the Republic of Serbia adopted the National Strategy of Judicial Reform for the period 2013–2018.[1095]

1121. The kind of judicial remedy depends on the character of the procedure. In principle, there are regular and irregular judicial remedies. The regular ones are used in cases of decisions that have not come to force yet and the second ones in cases of decisions which have come to force.

Most common judicial remedy in all three procedures (criminal, civil and administrative) is appeal. As a rule, the upper court decides about the appeal and the procedure, both in criminal and civil procedures, postpones implementation of the

1094. A number of laws were adopted as part of the National Judicial Reform leading to the establishment of a new organization of the judiciary and the prosecution, namely, the Law on High Judicial Council, Law on State Prosecutorial Council, Law on Judges, Law on Public Prosecution, Law on Organization of Courts and Law on the Seats and Territorial Jurisdiction of Courts and Public Prosecutor's Office. These pieces of legislation regulating the judiciary introduced new institutions, such as High Judicial Council, State Prosecutorial Council and Administrative Court that guarantee the independence of judges and prosecutors. The establishment of the Judicial Academy, carrying out initial and continuous training of members of the judiciary is also very important. The new organization of courts, introduced by the above-mentioned laws, became operational on 1 Jan. 2010. The new organization of the judiciary meant the distribution of cases according to specialties, which allowed a more efficient and objective processing of cases and facilitated public access to justice. Aarhus Convention Implementation Report, Republic of Serbia, 2010. http://www.unece.org/fileadmin/DAM/env/pp/reporting/NIRs%202011/Serbia_NIR_2011_e.pdf, 63.

1095. At http://www.mpravde.gov.rs/tekst/2959/nacionalna-strategija-reforme-pravosudja.php.

contested decision of the lower court. The right to lodge appeals have the parties, attorneys, and prosecutor and, of course, those persons who suffered damage which depends on concrete case.

§1. Criminal Procedure

1122. According to the Criminal Procedure Code (OJ RS, 72/11, 101/11, 121/12, 32/13, 32/13, 45/13 and 55/14), 'prosecutor' is a public prosecutor, private prosecutor and subsidiary prosecutor (Article2, p. 5). The public prosecutor is the authorized prosecutor for criminal offences which are prosecuted ex officio, and the private prosecutor is the authorized prosecutor for criminal offences prosecutable by private prosecution (Article 5).[1096]

1123. In accordance with Article 280 State and other bodies, legal and natural persons report criminal offences which are prosecutable ex officio about which they were informed or they learn in other manner, under the conditions stipulated by law or other regulation (paragraph 1).[1097]

1124. The motion for criminal prosecution is submitted within three months of the date when the injured party learnt about the criminal offence and the suspect (Article 53, paragraph 2).[1098] Private lawsuit is filed within three months of the date the injured party learnt about the criminal offence and the suspect (Article 65).

1125. A motion for prosecuting criminal offences which are prosecuted on the basis of a motion by an injured party is submitted to the competent public prosecutor (Article 53, paragraph 1). Private lawsuit is filed with the competent court (Article 65, paragraph 1). [1099]

1096. Criminal prosecution is initiated: (1) by the first action of the public prosecutor, or authorized police personnel based on a request of a public prosecutor, undertaken in accordance with this Code for the purpose of investigating the grounds for suspicion that a criminal offence has been committed or a certain person has committed a criminal offence; and(2) by the submission of private prosecution where a public prosecutor declares that he is abandoning prosecution (Art. 52),or he may be replaced by a subsidiary prosecutor, under the conditions prescribed by this Code (Art. 5, paras 2 and 3).

1097. The cases in which failure to report a criminal offence represents a criminal offence are prescribed by the Criminal Code (Art. 280, para. 2).

1098. An injured party as a subsidiary prosecutor is entitled to: (1) represent the prosecution in accordance with the provisions of this Code; (2) submit a motion and evidence for realizing a restitution claim and a motion for interim measures to secure it; (3) retain a proxy from among attorneys; (4) request the appointment of a proxy; (5) perform other actions provided for by this Code. Besides the rights referred to in para. 1 of this Article, a subsidiary prosecutor also exercises the rights of the public prosecutor, except those that the public prosecutor has in his capacity as a public authority (Art. 58).

1099. Private prosecutors are entitled to: (1) bring and represent a private lawsuit; (2) submit a motion and evidence for realizing a restitution claim and a motion for interim measures to secure it; (3) retain a proxy from among attorneys; and (4) perform other actions provided for by this Code (Art. 64).

1126. Regular legal remedies are: appeals against first-instance court judgments (Articles 432–462);[1100] appeals against judgments of courts of second instance (Articles 463 and 464)[1101] and appeals against rulings (Articles 465–469).[1102]

1127. Extraordinary legal remedies are reopening for criminal proceedings (Articles 470–481)[1103] and motions for the Protection of Legality (Articles 482–494).[1104]

1128. Serbia is a contracting party of following conventions of the Council of Europe relating to the legal cooperation in criminal matters:

- European Convention on Extradition (ETS 24).
- European Convention on Mutual Assistance in Criminal Matters (ETS 30).
- European Convention on the Supervision of Conditionally Sentenced or Conditionally Released Offenders (ETS 51).
- European Convention on the International Validity of Criminal Judgments (ETS 70).
- European Convention on the Transfer of Proceedings in Criminal Matters (ETS 73).

1100. Authorized persons may file an appeal against a judgment issued in the first instance within fifteen days of the date of delivery of a copy of the judgment. Especially in complex cases, the parties and the defence counsel may immediately after the judgment is proclaimed request an extension of the time limit for filing an appeal. A timely and admissible appeal against a judgment stays execution of the judgment (Art. 432, paras 1, 2 and 4). The parties, the defence counsel and the injured party may file an appeal (Art. 433, para. 1).

1101. An appeal may only be filed against a judgment by which the court of second instance reversed a first-instance judgment, which acquitted the defendant of the charges, and pronounced a judgment finding of the defendant guilty (Art. 463). An appellate court adjudicates an appeal against a judgment of a court of second instance pursuant to the provisions of this Code applicable to second-instance proceedings. The provisions of Art. 454 of this Code will also be applied to a co-defendant who was not entitled to file an appeal against a second-instance judgment (Art. 464).

1102. The parties and persons whose rights are violated may appeal against rulings of the investigating judge and other rulings issued by courts in the first instance at all times, except where explicitly specified in this Code on which no appeal is permitted (Art. 465, para. 1). A ruling of the panel issued during the investigation and the indicting procedure is not appealable, unless otherwise specified by this Code. Rulings issued for the purpose of preparing and conducting the trial may only be challenged in the appeal against the judgment. Rulings of the second instance court are not appealable, unless otherwise specified by this Code. Rulings of the Supreme Court of Cassation are not appealable (Art. 465, paras 2–5).

1103. Criminal proceedings concluded by a final ruling or a final judgment may at the request of an authorized person be reopened in the cases and under the conditions prescribed by this Code (Art. 470).

1104. A request for the protection of legality may be submitted by the Republic Public Prosecutor, the defendant and his defence counsel (Art. 483). An authorized person may submit in accordance with conditions prescribed in this Code a request for the protection of legality against a final decision of the public prosecutor or the court or for violation of provisions of the procedure which preceded its issuance. A request for the protection of legality is not allowed against a decision on the protection of legality or violation of provisions of the procedure before the Supreme Court of Cassation which preceded its issuance (Art. 482).

- European Convention on the Non-Applicability of Statutory Limitation to Crimes against Humanity and War Crimes (ETS 82).
- Additional Protocol to the European Convention on Extradition (ETS 86).
- European Convention on the International Effects of Deprivation of the Right to Drive Motor Vehicles (ETS 88).
- European Convention on the Suppression of Terrorism (ETS 90).
- Additional Protocol to the European Convention on Information on Foreign Law (ETS 97).
- Second Additional Protocol to the European Convention on Extradition (ETS 98).
- Additional Protocol to the European Convention on Mutual Assistance in Criminal Matters (ETS 99).
- Convention on the Transfer of Sentenced Persons (ETS 112).
- European Convention on the Compensation of Victims of Violent Crimes (ETS 116).
- Convention on Laundering, Search, Seizure and Confiscation of the Proceeds from Crime (ETS 141).
- Additional Protocol to the Convention on the Transfer of Sentenced Persons (ETS 167).
- Criminal Law Convention on Corruption (CETS No.: 173).
- Second Additional Protocol to the European Convention on Mutual Assistance in Criminal Matters 182).
- Convention on Cybercrime (ETS 185).
- Additional Protocol to the Convention on Cybercrime, concerning the criminalization of acts of a racist and xenophobic nature committed through computer systems (ETS 189).
- Protocol amending the European Convention on the Suppression of Terrorism (ETS 190).
- Additional Protocol to the Criminal Law Convention on Corruption (ETS 191).
- Council of Europe Convention on the Prevention of Terrorism (ETS 196).
- Council of Europe Convention on Action against Trafficking in Human Beings (ETS 197).
- Council of Europe Convention on Laundering, Search, Seizure and Confiscation of the Proceeds from Crime and on the Financing of Terrorism (ETS 198).
- Third Additional Protocol to the European Convention on Extradition (ETS 209).
- Fourth Additional Protocol to the European Convention on Extradition (ETS 212).
- Convention of Europe Convention on the Manipulation of Sports Competitions (ETS 215).[1105]

1105. *See* : http://www.coe.int/en/web/conventions/search-on-states/-/conventions/treaty/search/states_coe (5 May 2017).

§2. Civil Procedure

1129. Article 191 of the Civil Procedure Code (OJ RS, Nos 72/11, 48/13 CC, 74/13 CC and 55/14) prescribes that a civil action is initiated by filing a complaint.

1130. Any natural or legal person may be a party to the proceedings (Article 74). Exceptionally, a litigation court may recognize attributes of a party to associations that do not have litigant competence in terms of provisions of this Article. In such a case they essentially fulfil the vital prerequisites for acquiring litigant competence, especially if they possess property on which enforcement may be conducted (Article 74, paragraph 4).

1131. Two kinds of legal remedies have been established by the Civil Procedure Code – ordinary legal remedies and extraordinary legal remedies.

I. Ordinary Legal Remedies

1132. Ordinary legal remedies are appeals against judgments and against decisions. Article 367 of the Civil Procedure Code prescribes that parties may file an appeal against the first instance judgment within fifteen days from the day when judgment transcript is delivered to them, unless otherwise regulated by this Law. Time limit to file an appeal is eight days in litigations concerning bills of exchange and checks.

A timely filed appeal prevents the judgment to become enforceable in the part challenged by the appeal (Article 367, paragraph 2).

1133. It is prescribed by Article 373 that a judgment may be challenged in the following cases: (1) in case of significant violation of civil procedure rules; (2) due to an incorrect or incomplete fact finding; and (3) due to incorrect application of material law.

1134. According to Article 377, the appeal is submitted to the court which rendered the first instance judgment, in sufficient number of copies for the court and for the other party. Article 399 prescribes that decision of the first instance court may be appealed unless otherwise provided in this Law. If this Law specifically provides that no special appeal is allowed, a decision of the first instance court can be challenged only in the appeal against the final decision (Article 399, paragraph 2).

II. The Extraordinary Legal Remedies

1135. The extraordinary legal remedies are:

- Revision (403–420).
- A request for review of a final judgment (Articles 421–425).
- Repeated trial (Articles 426–435).

1136. According to provisions of Article 389, parties may file an appeal against a first instance judgment, to the Supreme Court of Serbia within fifteen days of the delivery, if a party requests that the Supreme Court adjudicates the appeal and the other party agrees. This legal remedy may be invoked in civil actions, where review is allowed, only in case of an incorrect application of substantive law and a significant violation of civil procedure rules specified under Article 361, paragraph 2, item 5.[1106]

1137. According to Article 394, parties may file a request for review of a final second instance judgment, in all civil action proceedings within thirty days of the delivery of the judgment. Review is not allowed in litigations concerning property where the claim is related to pecuniary value or handing over of things or performance of another obligation, if the value of the subject of litigation, in regard to the challenged part of a final judgment, does not exceed RSD 500,000.

1138. Review is not allowed in property-related litigation where the claim is not related to pecuniary value or handing over of things or performance of another obligation, if the value of the subject of litigation does not exceed RSD 500,000. Exceptions are prescribed by this Article too.[1107]

1139. The Supreme Court of Serbia rules on a motion for review (Article 396).

1140. The Motion for the Protection of Legality is defined by Article 413. The public prosecutor may file a motion for the protection of legality against a final court decision or upon the proposal of a party within three months. The time limit for the Motion for the Protection of Legality starts to run:

- In case of a first instance decision which has not been appealed – as of the day when such decision may not be appealed any more.
- In case of a second instance decision against which a motion for review has not been filed – as of the day when such decision is delivered to the party who last received such decision.

1141. Article 422 prescribes that the trial completed by a final court decision may be repeated upon the request of a party in following cases:

(1) If a party did not have an opportunity to argue before the court due to an illegal action, and in particular due to the failure of the court to effect service.
(2) If a person who cannot be a party to the proceedings took part in the proceedings as the plaintiff or defendant.
(3) If a party who is a legal entity was not represented by an authorized person.
(4) If a party incompetent for litigation was not represented by a legal representative.

1106. A significant violation of civil procedure provisions exists if the court does not apply, or improperly applies certain provision of this Law in the course of the proceedings, which affected or might have affected rendering of a lawful and proper judgment. Significant violations of civil procedure provisions occur, *inter alia*, if contrary to the provisions of this Law, the Court made a decision on a claim that the parties could not dispose with (Art. 3, para. 3).

1107. Review of the final second instance court judgment that cannot be reviewed according to the provisions of Art. 394 is exceptionally allowed, if appellate court rules that it is necessary to interpret a legal issue of general interest or ensure uniform case law or when new interpretation of the law is necessary.

(5) If a legal representative or attorney of a party was not properly authorized to participate in the proceedings or as regards to certain actions in the proceedings, unless their participation in the proceedings or certain actions was later approved.
(6) If a decision of the court was founded on a false testimony of a witness or expert witness.
(7) If a decision of the court was based on a counterfeited document or document certifying false contents.
(8) If a decision of the court was made through a criminal offence of the judge, or lay judge, legal representative or attorney of a party, the other party or third party.
(9) If a party gains a possibility to use a final decision of the court made earlier between the same parties about the same claim.
(10) If a decision of the court is based on another decision of the court or another body, and such decisions are subsequently reversed, set aside or annulled.
(11) If an interlocutory issue (Article 12) was subsequently decided before the competent body and the decision was based on the decision about such issue.
(12) If a party learns about new facts or finds or obtains a possibility to use new evidence, which could have resulted in a more favourable decision for such party had it been used in the previous proceedings.
(13) If European Court for Human Rights, after final decision of the national court, passed a decision about the same or similar legal relation against Serbia and Montenegro.[1108]

§3. Administrative Dispute

1142. It is prescribed by Article 14 of the Law on Administrative Disputes (OJ RS, No. 111/09) that an administrative dispute[1109] can be initiated against an administrative Act which was passed in the second degree and against the first instance administrative Act against which no appeal is allowed in administrative procedure.[1110]

1108. Repeated procedure may not be requested due to reasons referred to in Art. 422, points 1–3 of this Law if such reasons were presented unsuccessfully in the course of previous proceedings. Trial may be repeated due to circumstances stipulated in Art. 422, points 1, 7, 8 and 9 of this Law only if a party was unable, through no fault of his/her own, to present such circumstances before the previous proceedings were finished by a final court decision (Art. 423).

1109. In an administrative dispute the court decides about the legality of final administrative Acts, except those for which another kind of judicial protection was prescribed. The court also decides about the legality of final individual acts dealing with right, obligation, or on the law-based interest, for which is not prescribed other kinds of judicial protection. The court also decides about the legality of other final individual Acts when it is prescribed by law. Provisions of this Law concerning the administrative Act are applied to other Acts against which an Administrative dispute could be initiated (Art. 3).

1110. Administrative disputes may be initiated when the competent authority on the application, or a party's appeal, has not brought an administrative Act, under the conditions stipulated by this law (Art. 15).

1143. Administrative dispute is initiated by a lawsuit (Article 17). The lawsuit shall be filed within thirty days of receipt of the administrative Act to the party that filed the lawsuit or by law required shorter period (Article 18, paragraph 1).[1111]

1144. Extraordinary legal remedies are request for review of court decisions (Articles 49–55) and repetition of the procedure (Articles 56–65). In accordance with Article 49 of the Law against a final decision of the Administrative Court, party and the competent public prosecutor may file a request for review of Court's decision to the Supreme Court of Cassation.[1112]

1145. Pursuant to Article 56 procedure completed by a final verdict or decision of the Court shall be reopened by the party's lawsuit in following cases: (1) if the party finds new facts, or finds and acquires the ability to use new evidences, which would resolve the dispute better if presented or used in earlier proceedings; (2) if the Court's decision has resulted from criminal acts of a judge or Court employee, or the decision was obtained by making fraudulent act of the agent or representative of a party, his/her opponent or the opponent's attorney or representative, and if such action constitutes a criminal offence; (3) if the Court's decision was based on the adopted verdict in criminal or civil matters, and such Act was later repealed by another final Court decision; (4) if the documents underlying the Court's decision were false or fraudulently altered, or if the witness, expert or party at the hearing before the court, gave false testimony, and the court decision was based on that testimony; (5) if the party finds or acquires the ability to use an earlier court decision made in the same dispute; (6) if an interested person was not allowed to participate in the administrative proceedings; and (7) if the subsequent attitude of the decision of the European Court of Human Rights, in the same case, affects the legality of validly completed court trial.

1111. The term referred to in para. 1 of this Article applies to the authority authorized to file an action if it is an administrative document (Art. 18, para. 2). If the authority authorized to file the lawsuit, or interested party, has not been submitted to an administrative Act, the authority or interested person may file a lawsuit, within sixty days from receipt of the administrative Act to the party (Art. 18, para. 3).

1112. The request may also be submitted in the following cases: (1) when the law approves it; (2) in cases where the court had the jurisdiction to decide in full; (3) in matters in which an administrative appeal procedure was excluded (Art. 49, para. 2). The request may be filed for violation of the Law, other regulation or general Act, or violation of rules of procedure that could have affected the decision (Art. 49, para. 3).

Chapter 3. Other Forms of Juridical Actions of Individuals

§1. The Protector of Citizens (Ombudsman)

1146. The Protector of Citizens (Ombudsman) is a public authority established in 2007 by the Law on the Protector of Citizens (OJ RS, Nos 79/2005 and 54/2007).[1113] The Protector of Citizens is established as an independent body that shall protect the rights of citizens and control the work of Government agencies. It is also authorized for legal protection of property rights and interests of the Republic of Serbia and other bodies and organizations, enterprises and institutions which have public authority (administrative authorities) (Article 1).

1147. The Protector of Citizens has the power to control respect of the rights of citizens, establish violations resulting from acts, actions or failure to act by administrative authorities, if they are violations of the laws, regulations and other general acts of the republic. Apart from that, the Protector of Citizens shall have the power to control the legality and regularity of the work of administrative authorities (Article 17, paragraphs 1 and 2).[1114]

1148. Pursuant to Article 24 the Protector of Citizens initiates proceedings following the complaint of a citizen or on his/her own initiative.[1115] In addition to the right to initiate and run proceedings, the Protector of Citizens has the right to act preventively by offering good services, negotiating and giving advice and opinions related to issues from his/her competency, with the view of improving the work of administrative authorities and protection of human rights and freedoms.[1116]

1113. The Provincial Ombudsman was established in 2002 by virtue of the decision of Provincial Assembly on Provincial Ombudsman (OJ AVP, Nos 23/02,5/04 and 16/05). *See also*, OJ AVP, No. 37/14. The Law on Local Self-government (OJ RS, Nos 129/07 and 83/14) envisages the institution of ombudsman at the local level.

1114. The Protector of Citizens is entitled to propose laws which fall within his/her mandate; to launch initiatives with the Government or National Assembly for the amendment of laws or other regulations or general acts, if he/she deems that violations of citizens' rights are a result of deficiencies of such regulations. He/she shall also have the power to launch initiatives for new laws, other regulations and general acts, if he/she considers it significant for exercising and protecting citizens' rights (Art. 18).

1115. The Protector of Citizens may act on his/her own initiative when on the basis of his/her own knowledge or information received from other sources, and only exceptionally on the basis of anonymous complaints, he/she estimates that an act, undertaking or inactivity of an administrative authority caused violation of human rights and freedoms (Art. 32, para. 1).

1116. In case the Protector of Citizens receives a complaint related to the violation of citizens' rights by an act, undertaking or inactivity of administrative authorities, not connected with the violation of the laws, other regulations and general acts of the Republic, but with the violation of regulations or general acts of an AP or LSG unit, the Protector of Citizens shall refer the complaint without delay to the Ombudsman of the AP i.e., civil defender (Ombudsman) of the LSG unit, if such is established (Art. 35, para. 1).

1149. Any physical or legal, local or foreign person who considers that their rights have been violated by an act, action or failure to act of an administrative authority may file a complaint with the Protector of Citizens (Article 25, paragraph 1). Prior to submitting a complaint, a citizen is required to endeavour to protect his/her rights in appropriate legal proceedings (Article 25, paragraph 3).[1117] Exceptionally, the Protector of Citizens may initiate proceedings even before all legal remedies have been exhausted if the complainant would sustain irreparable damage or if the complaint is related to violation of good governance principle, particularly incorrect attitude of administrative authorities towards the complainant or other violations of rules of ethical behaviours of administrative authority's employees (Article 25, paragraph 5).

1150. The Protector of Citizens shall not proceed on anonymous complaints (Article 25, paragraph 6).[1118]

1151. A complaint is filed in writing or orally on record and shall not require payment of any fees or other dues. A complaint may be filed not later than one year from the day the violation of the right of citizen occurred, and/or from the date of the last action undertaken by the administrative authority in respect of the violation (Article 26).[1119]

1152. The Protector of Citizens shall notify the complainant and the administrative authority involved about the beginning and end of a proceeding (Article 29, paragraph 1).[1120]

1153. Upon determination of all relevant facts and circumstances, the Protector of Citizens may inform the complainant that his/her complaint is unfounded or may find that irregularities existed in the work of the administrative authority (Article 31, paragraph 1). If the Protector of Citizens determines that irregularities existed in the work of the administrative authority, he/she shall deliver a recommendation to the

1117. The Protector of Citizens shall direct the complainant to instigate relevant legal proceedings when such proceedings are provided, and shall not instigate investigation until all legal remedies have been exhausted (Art. 25, para. 4).

1118. Exceptionally, if the Protector of Citizens considers that an anonymous complaint provides basis for his/her operation, he/she may initiate proceedings on his/her own initiative (Art. 25, para. 7).

1119. The Protector of Citizens shall act on each complaint except: (1) if the case is not within the competence of the Protector of Citizens; (2) if it is filed after the expiry of the statutory deadline; (3) if it is filed prior to exhausting all available legal remedies, and the requirements specified under para. 5 of Art. 25 are not fulfilled; (4) if a complaint is anonymous; (5) if it does not contain information required to proceed, and the complainant has neither corrected such deficiency even in the period determined for supplementing the complaint nor asked the Protector of Citizens' Secretariat to assist him in correcting such deficiencies. If for any of the reasons specified in para. 1 of this Article, there are no grounds for an action of the Protector of Citizens, he/she shall reject the complaint and notify the complainant, stating the reasons for rejecting the complaint (Art. 28).

1120. The administrative authority is required to respond to all requests of the Protector of Citizens and to provide all requested information and documents within a period set by the Protector of Citizens that may not be shorter than fifteen or longer than sixty days (Art. 29, para. 2).

administrative authority on steps to be undertaken in order to rectify the noted irregularity.[1121]

1154. If the administrative authority fails to proceed pursuant to the recommendation, the Protector of Citizens may so inform the public, the National Assembly and the Government, and may recommend proceedings to determine the accountability of the official in charge of the administrative authority.[1122]

§2. The Commissioner for the Information of Public Importance and the Protection of Personal Data

1155. The Commissioner for the Information of Public Importance and the Protection of Personal data was established by Article 1, paragraph 2 of Law on Free Access to the Information of Public Importance (OJ RS, Nos 120/04, 54/07, 104/09 and 36/10) as an autonomous and independent State authority.[1123]

1156. Pursuant to Article 16, if a public authority does not respond to a request within the specified deadline, an applicant may lodge a complaint with the Commissioner, except in cases where this Law provides otherwise (paragraph 4).

1157. An applicant may lodge a complaint with the Commissioner if:(1) a public authority rejects or denies an applicant's request, within fifteen days of service of the relevant decision or other document; (2)a public authority, in contravention of Article 16, paragraph 2 of this Law, failed to reply to a submitted request within the statutory time limit; (3) a public authority, in contravention of Article 17, paragraph 2 of this Law, made the issuance of a copy of a document containing the requested information

---

1121. The administrative authority is obliged to inform the Protector of Citizens at latest within sixty days of the day it received the recommendation whether it proceeded pursuant to the recommendation and eliminated the irregularity, or about reasons why it failed to proceed pursuant to the recommendation. Exceptionally, where there is danger that the rights of complainant might be permanently and seriously violated if irregularities are not corrected, the Protector of Citizens may, in his/her recommendation to the administrative authority, determine a shorter period for elimination of such irregularities, which shall not be shorter than fifteen days (Art. 31, paras 3 and 4).

1122. The Protector of Citizens shall submit a regular annual report to the Assembly that shall include information on activities in the preceding year, noted irregularities in the work of administrative authorities and recommendations to improve the status of citizens in relation to administrative authorities (Art. 33, para. 1). For the annual reports (2008–2015) *see* : http://www.ombudsman.org.rs/index.php?option=com_content&view=category&layout=blog&id=11&Itemid=13 (3 May 2017).

1123. For more information, *See* Part I: General Law, Access to Information and Public Participation in the Field of the Environment. 'Since 2011, when the process of amending the Law on Access to Information was initiated and then suspended in 2012, its amendments have not been passed and the timeframe for doing so has been extended year after year without proper reason. As a result, the obstacles that should be eliminated by amendments to the Law hamper the exercise of the freedom of information and impede the Commissioner's work.' *Report on the implementation of the Law on Free Access to Information of Public Importance and the Law on Personal Data Protection for 2016*, Republic of Serbia, Commissioner for the Information of Public Importance and Personal Data Protection, Belgrade, March 2017, 13. http://www.poverenik.org.rs/en/commissioners-report/2568-izvestaj-poverenika-za-2016-godinu.html (2 Apr. 2017).

conditional on the payment of a fee exceeding the necessary reproduction costs; (4) a public authority does not grant access to a document containing the requested information in the manner set forth in Article 18, paragraph 1 of this Law; (5) a public authority does not grant access to a document containing the requested information and/or does not issue a copy of the document in the manner set out in Article 18, paragraph 4 of this Law; or (6) a public authority otherwise obstructs or prevents an applicant from exercising his/her freedom of access to information of public importance, in contravention to the provisions of this Law (Article 22, paragraph 1). However, complaints shall be inadmissible if lodged against decisions of the National Assembly, the President of the Republic, the Government of the Republic of Serbia, the Supreme Court of Serbia, the CC and the Republic Public Prosecutor (Article 22, paragraph 2).[1124]

§3. The Commissioner for the Protection of Equality

1158. The Law on Prohibition of Discrimination (OJ RS, No. 22/09)[1125] established the Commissioner for the Protection of Equality appointed by the National Assembly (Article 28).

1159. According to Article 33 of the Law the Commissioner: (1) shall receive and review complaints pertaining to violations of provisions of this Law, provide opinions and recommendations in specific cases, and pass measures in accordance with the provisions of Article 40 of this Law; (2) shall provide information to the person lodging a complaint concerning his/her rights and the possibility of initiating court proceedings or some other proceedings for the purpose of protection, or recommend reconciliation; (3) shall file charges in accordance with Article 43 of this Law, pertaining to violations of rights guaranteed by this Law, in his/her own name, and with the agreement and on behalf of the person discriminated against, unless proceedings before a court of law have already been initiated or concluded by passing an enforceable decision; (4) shall submit misdemeanour notices on account of violations of rights guaranteed by this Law; (5) shall submit an annual report and special reports to the National Assembly about the situation concerning the protection of equality; (6) shall warn the public of the most frequent, typical and severe cases of discrimination; (7) shall monitor the implementation of laws and other regulations, initiate the passing or amending of regulations for the purpose of implementing and developing protection against discrimination, and provide opinions concerning the provisions of draft laws and other regulations pertaining to the prohibition of discrimination; (8) shall establish and maintain cooperation with organs authorized to ensure equality and the protection of human rights on the territory of an AP or a local government; and (9) shall recommend measures to public administration organs and other persons aimed at ensuring equality.

1124. An administrative dispute complaint may be lodged against the decision in para. 2 of this Article, in accordance with Law, which fact shall be notified to the Commissioner by the relevant court ex officio (Art. 22, para. 3).

1125. *See* http://www.ravnopravnost.gov.rs/engleski.php. For the information about activities of the Commissioner for the Protection of Equality (2010–2016) *see* : http://ravnopravnost.gov.rs/en/reports/ (3 May 2017).

1160. Pursuant to Article 17 discrimination in the provision of public services shall be considered to occur if a legal or physical entity, within the framework of its/his/her activities or profession, refuses to provide a service on the grounds of a personal characteristic of an individual or a group of persons, or if the said entity, in order to provide the service in question, requires the fulfilment of some condition that is not required of other individuals or group of persons, or if the said entity unwarrantedly gives priority to another individual or a group of persons when it comes to providing a service.[1126]

§4. Mediation

1161. In relation to judicial and administrative proceedings, mediation (conciliation) represents an alternative mechanism for settling of disputes.[1127]

1162. According to Article 1 of the Law on Mediation in Dispute Resolution (OJ RS, No. 55/14) this Law regulates the notion, principles, procedure and legal effect of mediation in dispute settlement, conditions for mediation, the rights and duties of intermediaries and the training programme of mediators.[1128] Mediation is applied in disputed relationships where the parties may freely dispose of their claims, unless another law prescribes exclusive jurisdiction of a court or another authority, regardless of whether mediation is carried out before or after the initiation of judicial or other proceedings (Article 3, paragraph 1). Mediation is possible especially in the following disputes: property-related disputes concerning the fulfilment of the obligation to act, in other property disputes, disputes relating to environmental protection issues, consumer disputes, in family, commercial disputes, administrative matters, and in all other contentious relations where mediation is appropriate to the nature of the contentious relations and can aid in their resolution (Article 3, paragraph 2). The Law shall also apply to mediation in criminal and misdemeanour proceedings with respect to property claims and claims for damages, as well as in labour disputes unless otherwise stipulated by a special law (Article 3, paragraph 2).[1129]

1126. Everyone shall have the right to equal access to objects in public use (objects where the head offices of public administration organs are located, objects used in the sphere of education, health care, social welfare, culture, sports, tourism, objects used for the purpose of *environmental protection*, protection against natural disasters and the like), as well as public spaces (parks, squares, streets, pedestrian crossings and other public transport routes and the like), in accordance with the Law (Art. 17, para. 2).

1127. Mediation is any procedure, notwithstanding its name, whereby the parties wish to settle their dispute through one or more mediators assisting the parties to reach an agreement (Art. 2).

1128. Key novelties of the Law includes, *inter alia*, following: introduction of a Registry of Mediators kept by the Ministry of Justice as a public central electronic database (Art. 42); licensing system for mediators (Ch. VII); power of an enforceable document if agreement on dispute resolution contains enforceability clause, or if the signatures of the parties and the mediator are certified by a court or a notary; establishing system of training for mediators (Ch. VIII); non-compulsory Tariff on Mediation Fees enacted by the Minister of Justice; possibility of court tax exemption incentive (Art. 31), etc.

1129. The provisions of this Act shall not apply to the settlement of disputes relating to the determination and collection of public revenues (Art.3, para. 4).

1163. The mediation process is initiated by the conclusion of an agreement on mediation (Article 18, paragraph 1), i.e., mediation procedure is initiated by submission of the mediation agreement to the court or other authority conducting the proceedings.[1130]

1164. Relationships between mediation and judicial or other proceedings are regulated by Chapter V (Articles 30–32).[1131]

1130. In this case, stay of judicial proceedings is no longer than sixty days (Art. 18, para. 3).

1131. Mediation procedure may be initiated before or after the judicial proceedings have been initiated, during the proceedings on legal remedies or in the course of enforcement proceedings.

Selected Bibliography

Aarhus Convention Implementation Report, Republic of Serbia, 2010. http://www.unece.org/fileadmin/DAM/env/pp/reporting/NIRs%202011/Serbia_NIR_2011_e.pdf.

Aarhus Convention Implementation Report, Republic of Serbia, 2014. https://www.unece.org/env/pp/reports_trc_implementation_2014.html (3.5.2017).

Answers to the European Commission's Questionnaire, Chapter 11 (Agriculture and rural development), Government of the Republic of Serbia, Belgrade, 2011. http://www.seio.gov.rs/eng/documents/national-documents/answer-to-the-european-commision-s-questionnaire

Answers to the European Commission's Questionnaire, Chapter 12 (Food safety, veterinary and phytosanitary policy), Government of the Republic of Serbia, Belgrade, 2011. http://www.seio.gov.rs/eng/documents/national-documents/answer-to-the-european-commision-s-questionnaire

Answers to the European Commission's Questionnaire, Chapter 13(Fisheries), Government of the Republic of Serbia, Belgrade, 2011. http://www.seio.gov.rs/eng/documents/national-documents/answer-to-the-european-commision-s-questionnaire

Answers to the European Commission's Questionnaire, Chapter 14 (Transport Policy), Government of the Republic of Serbia, Belgrade, 2011. http://www.seio.gov.rs/eng/documents/national-documents/answer-to-the-european-commision-s-questionnaire

Answers to the European Commission's Questionnaire, Chapter 15 (Energy), Government of the Republic of Serbia, Belgrade, 2011. http://www.seio.gov.rs/eng/documents/national-documents/answer-to-the-european-commision-s-questionnaire

Answers to the European Commission's Questionnaire, Chapter 27 (Environment), Government of the Republic of Serbia, Belgrade, 2011. http://www.seio.gov.rs/eng/documents/national-documents/answer-to-the-european-commision-s-questionnaire

Bobić M., Todić, D. Harmonisation of national regulations of the Republic of Serbia with EU regulations and public participation, in G.Marković (Ed). Collection of Papers, *Relationship between the EU Law and the Law in the Region*, Istočno Sarajevo: Pravni fakultet, 2015, 458–472.

Bogdanović, S. & M. Gucić. *Arhuska Konvencija u Republici Srbiji – vodic kroz propise o ucescu javnosti u donosenju odluka i pravu na zastitu u pitanjima zastite životne sredine* [*Arhus Convention in the Republic of Serbia – Guide Through Legislation on Public Participation and Access to Justice in the Environmental Maters*]. Beograd: Reginalni centrar za zivotnu sredinu za centralnu i istocnu Evropu, 2006.

Bogdanović, S. (ed.). *Zastita životne sredine Republike Srbije – između politike i prakse približivanja EU* [*Protection of the Environment of the Republic of Serbia – Between Policy and Practice of Association with the EU*]. Novi Sad: Jugoslovensko udruženje za vodno pravo, 2008.

Bogdanović, S. *Koriscenje voda u poljoprivredi Srbije-Propisi i institucije, stanje i trendovi* ['Use of Water in Agriculture of Serbia – Legislation and Institutions, Current State and Trends']. In Agrarna i ruralna politika Srbije – reforme u periodu tranzicije i predlog mera za 2008 [*Proceedings of the Society of Agrar Economists*]. Belgrade, 2007; 79–87.

Bogdanović, S. *The Sava River Basin – New Legal Frameworks for Shared Water Resources*. Novi Sad: YUAWL – Yugoslav Association for Water Law, 2004.

Bogdanović, S., S. Nojković & A. Vesić. *Vodič kroz postupak procene uticaja na životnu sredinu* [*Guide Through the Legislation on Environmenal Impact Assessment*]. Espoo: Ramboll – Finnconsult; Stockholm: Ramboll – Natura; Beograd: REC; Novi Sad: Ministarstvo za nauku i zastitu životne sredine Republike Srbije, 2005.

Brussels, 9.11.2016.

Čavoški, A. & Matić, M. '*Application of the EU Acquis in the field of environment*' in the Manual for petty offence judges, Serbian Association of Magistrates, Belgrade 2010, 8–36.

Čavoški, A. '*Environment in the Serbian and the EU legal System*'. in the Textbook for magistrates and public prosecutors 'Proceedings before the petty offence courts for environmental offences', OSCE and the Association of Public Prosecutors and Deputy Public Prosecutors of Serbia, Belgrade 2010, 115–129.

Čavoški, A. 'Environmental Protection Reform in the EU'. *Legal Records, Union University Law School Review* 1 (2011): 171–182.

Čavoški, A. 'Transposition of Acquis – Challenges and Difficulties Facing the Serbian Administration'. *European Review of Public Law* 22, no. 4 (winter 2010): 1179–1197.

City of Belgrade Development Strategy (Draft). Belgrade: Palgo Centar, 2008.

Čok, V. 'Međunarodnopravna zastita kulturnih dobara'. *Pravni život*, 12 (2004).

Čok, V. Legal Grounds of Environmental Protection in Yugoslavia. *Yugoslav Law*, No. 3/1998, 159–174, Belgrade: Institute of Comparative Law.

Selected Bibliography

Commission Opinion on Serbia's application for membership of the European Union, Communication from the Commission to the European Parliament and the Council, (COM (2011) 668), SEC (2011) 1208, European Commission, Brussels, 12 October 2011.

Commission Report – European Commission, Serbia 2016 Report, SWD(2016) 361 final.

Cultural Heritage in South-East Europe, Kosovo Protection and Conservation: A Multi-ethnic Heritage in Danger, Mission Report 26–30 April 2004. http://unesdoc.unesco.org/images/0013/001389/138966eb.pdf, 10 October 2008.

Cultural properties at Risk in Kosovo and Metohija. http://www.media.srbia.sr.gov.yu/medeng/documents/cult_properties_at_risk.pdf, 10 July 2008.

Dabić, Lj. Procena uticaja na životnu sredinu [Environmental Impact Assessment], *Pravni zivot*, No. 9/2004.

Depleted Uranium in Kosovo, Post-Conflict environmental assessment. UNEP, 2001.

Development of National Biosafety Framework for Serbia and Montenegro. Belgrade and Novi Sad: UNEP, GEF, 2006, 6. http://www.gmo-free-regions.org/fileadmin/files/gmo-free-regions/Montenegro/Development_of_National_Biosafety_Framework.pdf.

Environmental Performance Reviews, Republic of Serbia. Second Review, New York and Geneva: United Nations, 2007.

Environmental Performance Reviews, Serbia, Third Review, New York and Geneva: United Nations, 2015.

Environmental Performance Reviews, Yugoslavia. New York and Geneva: United Nations, 2003.

Environmental Protection in Serbia, Progress since Kiev 2003 and Challenges Ahead. World Bank, October 2007.

Failure to Protect: Anti-Minority Violence in Kosovo, March 2004. Human Right Watch, July 2004, Vol. 16 No. 6(D).

First Biennial Update Report of the Republic of Serbia under the United Nations Framework Convention on Climate Change, Ministry of Agriculture and Environmental Protection, Belgrade, February 2016, http://www.eko.minpolj.gov.rs/dokumenti/ (30.4.2017).

*First National Report of the Republic of Serbia to the United Nations Convention on Biological Diversity, Republic of Serbia, Ministry of Environment and Spatial Planning, July 2010.*http://www.cbd.int/doc/world/cs/cs-nr-01-en.pdf.

From Conflict to Sustainable Development – Assessment of Environmental Hot Spots – Serbia and Montenegro, UNEP, Ministry of Science and Environmental Protection of the Republic of Serbia, Ministry of Environmental Protection and Physical Planning of the Republic of Montenegro, 2004.

Gajić, D. Zastita nacionalnih parkova u Republici Srbiji [Protection of national parks in Republic of Serbia], *Pravni život*, No. 9/2006.

Glavonjić, B. et al. *Forest and Forest Products Country Profile: Serbia and Montenegro*. Geneva Timber and Forest Discussion Paper 40, Geneva: UNECE/FAO, 2005.

Grbić, A. & Todić, D. 'Javne politike i učešće javnosti u njihovom kreiranju (Public policies and public participation in their creation)'.*(Megatrend Review)* 8, no. 2 (2011): 379–407.

Grbić, V. & Todić, D. Ekonomski instrumenti za upravljanje otpadom u ruralnim regionima jugoistične Evrope (Economic instruments for waste management in rural regions of South East Europe), *Ekonomika poljoprivrede*, 2/2011, 55–61.

Ignjatić, M., Todić, D. Rezultati i problemi u sprovođenju IPA programa prekogranične saradnje od značaja za oblast životne sredine i Poglavlje 27. [Results and Problems in the Implementation of the IPA Cross Border Cooperation Program relevant for Environmental field and Chapter 27], Collection of Papers, A.Mihajlov (ur). *Poglavlje 27- Životna sredina i klimatske promene*, Beograd: Ambasadori održivog razvoja i životne sredine, 2014, str. 16–21.

Ignjatović, J. & S. Đorđević. *Prirucnik za predstavnike javne vlasti o pristupu informacijama od javnog znacaja u oblasti voda i životne sredine* [*Guide of Public Authorities on Access to Information of Publice Importance in the Field of Water and Environment*]. Beograd: Reginalni centrar za zivotnu sredinu za centralnu i istocnu Evropu [REC – Regional Environmental Centre for Central and East Europe], 2006.

Ilić-Popov, G. *Ekoloski porezi* [*Environmental taxes*]. Faculty of Law Beograd, 2000.

Ilić-Popov, G. Princip 'zagađivac placa' kod ekoloskog poreza – podsticaj ili kazna ['Polluter Pays' Principle and Environmental Tax – Incentive or Penalty]. *Pravni život*, No. 10-2001.

Informator o radu Ministarstva životne sredine, rudarstva i prostornog planiranja (Information booklet on work of the Ministry of Environment, Mining and Spatial Planning), Ministarstvo životne sredine, rudarstva i prostornog planiranja (Ministry of Environment, Mining and Spatial Planning), Beograd, 2011.

Initial Nacional Comunication of the Republic of Serbia under the United Nations Framework Convention on Climate Change, The Ministry of Environment and Spatial Planning, Belgrade, November 2010, *http://unfccc.int/resource/docs/natc/srbnc1.pdf*, *International Law and the Baia Mare Cyanide Spill.* Regional Environmental Centre for Central and Eastern Europe, with the support of the Government of the United Kingdom September 2001.

Izvestaj o stanju životne sredine u Republici Srbiji u 2007. godini [*Report on the state of the environment in Serbia for 2007*]. Ministarstvo životne sredine i prostornog planiranja [*Ministry for Environment and Spatial Planning*]. Beograd, 2008. http://www.sepa.gov.rs/download/Izvestaj_2007_Web.pdf.

Selected Bibliography

Izveštaj o stanju životne sredine u Republici Srbiji u 2010. godini [*Report on the state of the environment in Serbia for 2010*]. Ministarstvo životne sredine, rudarstva i prostornog planiranja, Agencija za zaštitu životne sredine [*Ministry of Environment, Mining and Spatial Planning, Serbian Environment Protection Agency*]. Beograd, 2011. http://www.sepa.gov.rs/download/Izvestaj_o_stanju_zivotne_sredine_za_2010_godinu.pdf.

Izveštaj o stanju životne sredine u Republici Srbiji za 2014. godinu, [*Report on the state of the environment in Serbia for 2014*]. Ministarstvo poljoprivrede i zaštite životne sredine, Agencija za zaštitu životne sredine [Ministry of Agriculture and Environmental Protection, Environmental Protection Agency]. Beograd, 2015.

Jerosimić, A. (ed.). *Human Rights in Serbia 2007: Legal Provisions and Practice Compared to International Human Rights Standards*. Belgrade: The Belgrade Centre for Human Rights, 2008.

Joldžić, V. & G. Milićević. *Životna sredina i međunarodni ugovori od značaja za Saveznu Republiku Jugoslaviju* [*Environment and International Treaties Relevant for FR Yugoslavia*]. Beograd: Savezno ministarstvo za razvoj, nauku i životnu sredinu, 1995.

Joldžić, V. *Ekološki kriminalitet u pravu i stvarnosti* [*Ecology Crime in Law and Reality*]. Beograd: Ecologica, 1995.

Joldžić, V. *Ekološko pravo – opšti i posebni deo* [*Ecology Law*]. Beograd: Savezni sekretarijat za rad, zdravstvo i socijalno staranje, 2002.

Jovašević, D. *Zašita životne sredine* [*Environmental Protection*]. Beograd: Službeni list, 2005.

Jovović, A. et al. 'Waste Management Engineering and Practice in Western Balkan Countries'. *Annual Journal of IIE (HK)* 26 (2006): 11–20.

Karadžić, B. (ed.). *Environment in Serbia: An Indicator-Based Review*. Beograd: Ministarstvo nauke i zastite životne sredine Republike Srbije (Ministry of Science and Environmental Protection of the Republic of Serbia), 2007.

Kavran, D. & G. Petković (ed.). *Pravo i životna sredina* [*Law and the Environment*]. Beograd: Udruženje pravnika Jugoslavije, 1997.

Kvalitet životne sredine grada Beograda u 2007. godini [*Quality of the Environment in Belgrade*]. Beograd: Sekretarijat za zastitu životne sredine, Gradski zavod za javno zdravlje, Regionalni centar za životnu sredinu za Centralnu i Istocnu Evropu, 2007.

Lilić, S. 'Environmental Inspection in the Legislation of Serbia and the European Union'. In *fifty Years of the European Union*, edited by Jovan Ciric. Belgrade, Institute of Comparative Law and the European Integration Office of the Serbian Government, 2007, 277–287.

Lilić, S. 'The Aarhus Convention and Access to Justice in the European Union and Serbia'. In *European Integration Studies*, edited by Kaunas. Lithuania: Institute of Europe, Kaunas University of Technology, 2007, 7–15.

Mihajlov, A. & A. Vasiljević. 'The Forests in EU Strategies for Sustainable use of Natural Resources and Sustainable Development'. In *Legal Aspects of European Forest Sustainable Development*, edited by U. Franz Schmithusen, Peter Herbst, Dragan Nonić, Dragan Jović & Mirjana Stanisić. Zurich: Swiss Federal Institute of Technology, 2006, 57–64.

Mihajlov, A. et al. *Integrated Waste Management Strategy for the Country in Transition as the Tool for Efficient Inclusion in International Trade*. The Twentieth International Conference on Solid Waste Technology and Management, Philadelphia, USA: Widener University, April 2005, 774–783.

Milenković, D. *Zbirka propisa u oblasti zaštite životne sredine* [*Collection of the Environmental Regulations*], Beograd: Službeni glasnik, 2006.

Millennium Development Goals. Belgrade: Government of the Republic of Serbia, 2006.

Nacionalna strategija za aproksimaciju u oblasti životne sredine (National Environmental Approximation Strategy for the Republic of Serbia), Vlada Republike Srbije (Government of the Republic of Serbia) 2011.

National Environmental Protection Programme, Government of the Republic of Serbia, Belgrade, 2010, Off. Jour of RS, No. 12/2010) (*Nacionalni program zaštite životne sredine.* Vlada Republike Srbije. Beograd, 2010) (OJ RS, No. 12/2010); http://www.ekoplan.gov.rs/src/7-Ostala-dokumenta-127-document.htm.

National implementation plan for implementation of the Stockholm convention, Ministry of Environment and Spatial Planning of the Republic of Serbia, January 2010; (Nacionalni implementacioni plan za sprovo đenje Stokholmske konvencije, Vlada Republike Srbije, Beograd, 2009.

National Natural resources and Assets Sustainable Use Strategy(OJ RS, No. 33/2012).

National Programme for Integration with European Union. Belgrade: The Republic of Serbia, The Government, May 2008.

National Programme for the adoption of the EU acquis, European Integration Office, Belgrade, July 2014.http://www.seio.gov.rs/upload/documents/nacionalna_dokumenta/npaa/npaa_eng__2014_2018.pdf (19.6.2017).

National Programme for the adoption of the EU acquis, Second Revision, European Integration Office, November 2016. http://www.seio.gov.rs/eng/news/348/192/335/details/the-second-revised-national-programme-for-the-adoption-of-the-eu-acquis-npaa-has-been-adopted/ (19.6.2017).

National Strategy for Incorporation of the Republic of Serbia into Clean Development Mechanism -Waste Management, Agriculture and Forestry Sector – Belgrade, 2010 (Nacionalna strategija za uključivanje Republike Srbije u mehanizam čistog razvoja Kjoto protokola za sektore upravljanja otpadom, poljoprivrede i šumarstva, Beograd, http://www.srbija.gov.rs/vesti/dokumenti_sekcija.php?id=45678.

Selected Bibliography

National sustainable development strategy, Government of the Republic of Serbia, Belgrade, 2008, Off. Jour. of RS, No. 57/2008) (*Nacionalna strategija održivog razvoja,* Vlada Republike Srbije. Beograd, 2008. (OJ RS, No. 57/2008).

Nojković, S. Zakonodavstvo u oblasti ribarstva [Legislation in Field of Fishery], *Pravni život*, No. 9/2005.

Palačković, D. Građansko-pravna ekoloska zastita [Environmental Protection in Civil Law], *Pravni život*, No. 9/95.

Petković, G. Novo zakonodavstvo u oblasti upravljanja zastitom životne sredine [New Legislation on Environmental Management], Pravni život, No. 9/2005, 551–572.

Petković, G. Pravni aspect integrisanog sprecavanja i kontrole zagađivanja životne sredine [Legal Aspect of Integrated Environmental Prevention and Pollution Control], *Pravni život*, No. 9/2003, 14.

Petković, G. Zakonodavno pravni koncept zastite biodiverziteta [Legislative Concept of the Biodiversity Protection], *Pravni život*, No. 9/2006, 533–579.

Petrović, D., D. Todić & Z. Isoski. 'EMAS u Srbiji – korak bliže Evropskoj uniji' (EMAS in Serbia – One Step Closer to the European Union), Proceedings, 'Ekoloska istina' ('Ekoist 07'), Sokobanja (Hotel Zdravljak), 27–30 May 2007, 444–449.

Petrušić, N. Zastita od imisija u građanskom sudskom postupku [Protection from Imission in Court Procedure], *Pravni život*, No. 12/2003.

Poverty Reduction in Serbia – The Role of Civil Society. Belgrade: UNDP, 2005, 162–180.

Prostorni plan Republike Srbije od 2010. do 2020. godine (Spatial plan of the Republic of Serbia from 2010 to 2020), OJ RS, No. 88/2010).

Radioaktivnost životne sredine u Republici Srbiji u 2002 [*Radioactivity of Environment in the Republic of Serbia*]. Beograd: Ministarstvo za zastitu prirodnih bogatstava i životne sredine, 2002.

Radović, I. & Kozomora, M. (ed.). *Biodivesity Strategy of The Republic of Serbia: for the Period 2011–2018*. Belgrade: Ministry of Environment and Spatial Planning, 2011.

Rakić-Vodinelić, V. Ekoloska tužba, *Pravni život*, No. 4–5/89.

Rakić-Vodinelić, V. Ekolosko pravo kao pravo coveka, *Pravni život*, No. 9/95.

Report of the Secretary-General on the United Nations Interim Administration Mission in Kosovo S/2004/348, 30 April 2004, paragraphs 2–17.

Report on Implementation of the Law on Free Access to Information of Public Importance in 2007. Belgrade: Commissioner for Information of Public Importance, 2008.

Salma, J. Nacela i sistem ekoloskog prava [Principles and System of Ecology Law], *Pravni život*, No. 9/95.

Salma, J. Prirodno pravo i kodifikacija građanskog prava [Natural Law and Codification of Civil Law], *Pravni život*, No. 10/2002.

Screening report Serbia, Chapter 27 – Environment, WP Enlargement + Countires Negotiating Accession to EU MD 114/16, 08.06.16. https://ec.europa.eu/neighbourhood-enlargement/sites/near/files/screening_report_serbia_-_chapter_27_-_environment.pdf (19.6.2017).

Second Progress Report on the Implementation of the Poverty Reduction Strategy in Serbia. Belgrade: Government of Serbia, 2007.

Serbia 2006 Progress Report. Brussels, Commission Staff Working Document, 8 November 2006, SEC (2006) 1389, 31.

Serbia 2007 Progress Report. Commission of the European Communities, Commission Staff Working Document, Brussels, 6 November 2007, SEC (2007)1435, 33–34.

Skulić, M. Krivicno-pravna zastita životne sredine [Environmental Protection in Criminal Law], *Pravni život*, No. 9-2001.

Šolak, Z. Pravo na zdravlje i ekonomska osnova njegovog ostvarenja [Right to Health and Economic Bases of Its Realization], *Pravni život*, godina LVI, br. 9/2007, 277–308.

Spatial Plan of the Republic of Serbia 2010-2014-2020, Abridged Version, Ministry of Environment and Spatial Planning, Belgrade, November 2010.

Statistical Yearbook of Serbia (2005, 2006, 2007). Belgrade: Statistical Office of the Republic of Serbia. http://www.stat.gov.rs/WebSite/Public/PageView.aspx?pKey=431&URL=http://pod2.stat.gov.rs/ElektronskaBiblioteka2/Pretraga.aspx?pubType=1%26areaId=26

Statistical Yearbook of the Republic of Serbia 2015, Belgrade: Statistical Office of the Republic of Serbia, http://webrzs.stat.gov.rs/WebSite/userFiles/file/Aktuelnosti/StatGod2015.pdf (16.4.2017).

Stec, S. (ed.). *Handbook on Access to Justice under the Aarhus Convention*. Szentendre, Hungary: The Regional Environmental Centre for Central and Eastern Europe, 2003. http://www.rec.org/REC/Programs/EnvironmentalLaw/PDF/accesstojustice.pdf.

Strategija poljoprivrede i ruralnog razvoja RS za period 2014-2024 [Strategy for Agriculture and Rural Development for the period 2014–2024], (OJ RS, No. 85/14).

Strategija razvoja energetike Republike Srbije do 2015 (Strategy on energetic development till 2015). Beograd: Government of the Republic of Serbia.

Strategija razvoja energetike Republike Srbije do 2015, godine sa projekcijama do 2030 (OJ RS, 101/15) [Energy Development Strategy of the Republic of Serbia until 2025, with projection until 2030].

Selected Bibliography

Strategija razvoja poljoprivredne Srbije (*Strategy of agricultural development of Serbia*). Beograd: Government of the Republic of Serbia, 2005. Government of the Republic of Serbia 2005, http://www.srbija.gov.rs/vesti/dokumenti_sekcija.php? id=45678.

Strategija razvoja šumarstva Republike Srbije (*Forestry Development Strategy of the Republic of Serbia*) Beograd: Ministry of Agriculture Forestry and Water Management, 2004. Ministry of Agriculture, Forestry and Water Management http://www.srbija.gov.rs/vesti/dokumenti_sekcija.php?id=45678.

Strategija upravljanja mineralnim resursima Republike Srbije do 2030. [Mineral Resources Management Strategy of the Republic of Serbia until 2030] http://www.zzps.rs/novo/kontent/stranicy/propisi_strategije/s_mineralni_resursi.pdf (3/4/2017)

Strategija upravljanja otpadom za period 2010-2019. godine [Waste management strategy 2010-2019] (OJ RS, No. 29/10)

Strategija upravljanja vodama na teritoriji Republike Srbije do 2034. (OJ RS, No. 3/17) [Water Management Strategy in the Republic of Serbia for the period up to 2034].

Strategija uvođenja čistije proizvodnje u Republici Srbiji [Strategy of introducing cleaner production in the Republic of Serbia] (OJ RS, No. 17/09)

The Consequences of NATO Bombing for the Environment in FR Yugoslavia. Belgrade: Federal Ministry for Development, science and the environment, February 2000.

Todić D. Grbić V., Strategija 'Evropa 2020', klimatske promene i Republika Srbija ['Europe 2020' Strategy, Climate Change and the Republic of Seriba], *Međunarodna politika*, 1157/januar – mart 2015, 48-59.

Todić D., Grbić V. Dunavska saradnja u oblasti klimatskih promena i pozicija Srbije u upravljanju vodnim resursima [Danube Cooperation in the field of climate change and position of the Republic of Serbia in the water resources management], *Megatrend revija*, 12, 3/2015, 231–246.

Todić, C.D., Todosijević, M., Grbić, A.V. Land protection and climate change in the Regulations of the Republic of Serbia (Harmonisation of the national legislation with EU legislation), In Zlatić M., Kostadinov, S. (Eds.), *Challenges: Sustainable Land Management – Climate Change, Advances in Geoecology*, 43, 2014, 211–221.

Todić, D. & G. Milićević. 'The Right to a Healthy Environment'. *Pravni život*, No. 9/1995, 281–289.

Todić, D. & V. Vukasović (ed.),*Pravo na dostupnost informacija, učešće javnosti u donošenju odluka i dostupnost pravosuđa prema Arhuskoj konvenciji i jugoslovenskim propisima*, [*Right to Access to Information, Public Participation and Access to Justice According to the Aarhus Convention and Yugoslav Regulations*]. Beograd: Reginalni centrar za životnu sredinu za centralnu i istocnu Evropu (REC – Regional Environmental Centre for Central and East Europe), 2006.

Todić, D. & V. Vukasović. *Ekološka kriza u svetu i odgovor međunarodne zajednice – izbor najznačajnijih međunarodnih dokumenata i jugoslovenskih propisa* [*Environmental Crises and Responses of International Community*]. Beograd: Savezni sekretarijat za rad, zdravstvo i socijalno staranje, Institut za međunarodnu politiku i privredu, 2002.

Todić, D. & V. Vukasović. *Zbirka propisa u oblasti životne sredine* [*Collection of the Environmental Regulations*]. Belgrade: Megatrend univerzitet, 2007.

Todić, D. 'Pravni okviri politike Evropske unije u oblasti organske poljoprivrede i životne sredine' ['Legal Framework of the EU Policy in the Field of Organic Agriculture and Environment']. *Ekonomika poljoprivrede* [*Economic of Agriculture*]. The Society of Agricultural Economists, Institute of Agricultural Economics Beograd, April–June 2006, 425–440.

Todić, D. 'Sistem upravljanja i kontrole zastite životne sredine (EMAS) u pravu Evropske unije' ['Environmental Management System – EMAS – in EU Law'], *Evropsko zakonodavstvo* [*European Law*], Beograd: Institut za međunarodnu politiku i privredu (Institute for International Policy and Economy), No. 11/05, 44–47.

Todić, D. 'Social and Environmental Issues Related to the Security in SEE Countries'. In *Environmental Security in South – Eastern Europe*, edited by Montini, M. & S. Bogdanović, Springer Science + Business Media B.V, 2011, 43–58.

Todić, D. 'Trgovina ugroženim vrstama divlje faune i flore u pravu Evropske unije' Trade in Endangered Species of Wild Fauna and Flora in EU Low, *Evropsko zakonadavstvo* [*European Law*], Beograd: Institut za međunarodnu politiku i privredu (Institute for international policy and economy), br. 9-10/2004, str. 50–53.

Todić, D. *Ekološki menadžment u uslovima globalizacije* [*Environmental Management and Globalization*]. Beograd: Megatrend Univerzitet, 2008.

Todić, D. Evropske integracije i nacionalni interesi [European integration and the 'national interests'], *Politička revija,* 44, 2/2015, 1–18

Todić, D. Harmonization of legislation of the Republic of Serbia with EU law: open issues and dilemmas, *Review of international affairs,* 1–2/2014, 96–109.

Todić, D. Klimatske promene i odgovornost u međunarodnom pravu i pravu EU (Climate change and responsibilities in international and EU law), *Pravni život*, No. 9/2011, 53–547.

Selected Bibliography

Todić, D. Komparativna politika i pravo klimatskih promena: Bosna i Herzegovina, Crna Gora, Hrvatska i Srbija - osnovni elementi [Comparative climate change policy and law: Bosnia and Herzegovina, Montenegro, Croatia – basic elements], *Strani pravni život*, 1/2014, 181–194.

Todić, D. *Međunarodne konvencije u oblasti životne sredine i SR Jugoslavija* [*International Conventions in the Field of Environment and FR Yugoslavia*]. Belgrade: REC, 2002.

Todić, D. *Međunarodnopravna zastita životne sredine za vreme oružanih sukoba* [International-Law Protection of the Environment in Time of Armed Conflicts]. Belgrade: Vojno delo, No. 2/98, 40–55.

Todić, D. Novi zakoni Republike Srbije u oblasti životne sredine i univerzalne vrednosti [New Environmental Laws of the Republic of Serbia and Universal Values], *Pravni život*, No. 9/2005, 573–586.

Todić, D. Održivi razvoj i principi politike i prava životne sredine [Sustainable Development and Principles of Environmental Policy and Law], *Pravni život*, br. 9/2007, Godina LVI, Knjiga 509, 429–443.

Todić, D. Pariski sporazum o klimi u sistemu međunarodnih ugovora od značaja za EU integracije Republike Srbije [Paris Agreement on Climate in the System of International Agreements relevant for the EU Integration of the Republic of Seriba], *Evropsko zakonodavstvo*, 58/2016, 111–129.

Todić, D. *Review of Serbian Implementation and Enforcement Procedures in the Environment Sector*, Country External Assessment Report – Serbia, Regional Environmental Network for Accession, Working Group 4, Activity 4.2. (July 2011), http://www.renanetwork.org/index.php?view=wgroup&groups=wgroups&id_group=4.

Todić, D. *Savremena politika i pravo životne sredine* [*Contemporary Environmental Policy and Law*]. Beograd: Megatrend Univerzitet, 2008.

Todić, D. Strateška procena uticaja na životnu sredinu u pravu Evropske unije [Strategic Environmental Assessment in the EU law], *Evropsko zakonodavstvo* [*European Law*], Beograd: Institut za međunarodnu politiku i privredu (Institute for international policy and economy), No. 7/2004, 57–60.

Todić, D. *Vodiči kroz EU politike – Životna sredina (Manuals trough EU policies - Environment)*, Beograd, Evropski pokret u Srbiji (European Movement in Serbia), 2011.

Todić, D., Dimitrijević, D., Priority goals in international co-operation of the Republic of Serbia in the field of environment and sustainable development, *International Environmental Agreements: Politics, Law and Economics*: 14, 2/2014, 163–179. DOI: 10.1007/s10784-013-9207-4.

Tomić, N. Odgovornost i efikasnost inspektora kao vršilaca upravnog nadzora u pravnom sistemu Srbije i Crne Gore [Responsibility and Efficiency of Inspectors as Administrative Supervisor in Legal System of Serbia and Montenegro], *Pravni život*, No. 9-2004.

UNMIK Regulations, http://www.un.org/peace/kosovo/regulations/regs.html.

Veličković, N. Razvoj zakonodavstva o šumarstvu od 1836 do 1990 [Development of Forest Legislation from 1836 to 1990], *Peščanik I (Sandglass I)*, Istorijski arhiv grada Niša, Niš, 2003.

Vujošević, M. & N. Spasić. 'The Transition Changes and Their Impact on Sustainable Spatial, Urban and Rural Development of Serbia'. In *Sustainable Spatial Development on Towns and Cities*. edited by M. Vujošević. Belgrade: International Scientific Conference, 25–26 January 2008. Conference Proceedings, Book I, Institute of Architecture and Civil Engineering in Belgrade, 2007, 1–45.

Vukasović, V. & D. Todić. *Monograph, Serbia and Montenegro, Environmental Law, International Encyclopaedia of Laws*, Supplement 37. The Hague, London, New York: Kluwer Law International, 2002.

Vukasović, V. Međunarodnopravno regulisanje zaštite i održivog korišćenja vodnih resursa sa posebnim osvrtom na sliv reke Save, *Međunarodni problemi*, br.1–2, 2006, 157–183.

Vukasović, V. Pravno regulisanje zaštite životne sredine u Srbiji sa posebnim osvrtom na primenu pravne regulative u praksi [Legal Environmental Regulation in Serbia with Special Regard to the Application of the Legal Regulation in Practice]. In *Zaštita životne sredine u Grčkoj i Srbiji* [*Environmental Protection in Greece and Serbia*], edited by Zbornik. Beograd: Beogradski centar za evropske integracije, 2005, 49–72.

Official Journals

Official Journal of the City of Belgrade (Službeni list grada Beograda)

Official Journal of the Federal Republic of Yugoslavia (Službeni list Savezne Republike Jugoslavije)

Official Journal of the Republic of Montenegro (Službeni list Republike Crne Gore)

Official Journal of the Republic of Serbia (Službeni glasnik Republike Srbije)

Official Journal of the Serbia and Montenegro (Službeni list Srbije i Crne Gore)

Official Journal of the Socialist Autonomous Province of Kosovo-Metohija (Službeni list Socijalističke autonomne pokrajine Kosova i Metohije)

Official Journal of the Socialist Autonomous Province of Vojvodina (Službeni list Socijalističke autonomne pokrajine Vojvodine)

Official Journal of the Socialist Federal Republic of Yugoslavia (Službeni list Socijalističke Federativne Republike Jugoslavije)

Official Journal of the Socialist Republic of Montenegro (Službeni list Socijalističke Republike Crne Gore)

Selected Bibliography

Official Journal of the Socialist Republic of Serbia (Službeni glasnik Socijalističke Republike Srbije)

Instead of a footnote: All the Republics and Provinces in the former Yugoslavia (Socialist Federal Republic of Yugoslavia) had in their name the attribute 'Socialist'. Due to that, all official journals had to change their titles after disintegration of the former Yugoslavia.

Selected Bibliography

Index

The numbers here refer to paragraph numbers.

Made in United States
Orlando, FL
04 November 2026

90201250R00238